Trade and Competition Law in the EU and Beyond

This book is dedicated to Jacques Bourgeois our dear friend and widely appreciated colleague, in honour of his 75 years of accumulated wisdom and 'savoir vivre'

Trade and Competition Law in the EU and Beyond

Edited by

Inge Govaere

Ghent University, Belgium

Reinhard Quick

Verband der Chemischen Industrie e. V., Germany

Marco Bronckers

University of Leiden, The Netherlands

Edward Elgar

Cheltenham, UK • Northampton, MA, USA

Published by
Edward Elgar Publishing Limited
The Lypiatts
15 Lansdown Road
Cheltenham
Glos GL50 2JA
UK

Edward Elgar Publishing, Inc.
William Pratt House
9 Dewey Court
Northampton
Massachusetts 01060
USA

A catalogue record for this book is available from the British Library

Library of Congress Control Number: 2011925765

MIX
Paper from responsible sources
FSC® C018575

ISBN 978 0 85793 566 3

Typeset by Columns Design XML Ltd, Reading, Berkshire
Printed and bound by MPG Books Group, UK

Contents

Enforcement and Litigation

Contributors

Stefan D. Amarasinha is currently Head of the Trade and Economic Section of the EU Office to Hong Kong and Macau. He previously worked for the Directorate-General for Trade of the European Commission dealing with various issues relating to the DDA, the institutional function of the WTO, the OECD, and WTO dispute settlement.

Leonardo Armati is an associate at the Brussels office of Bonelli Erede Pappalardo. He practises in the field of EU law and antitrust law, both in Italy and other EU countries. He has written on and gives lectures in the field of EU and competition law.

William Bishop, Vice President of Charles River Associates, London, has 26 years of experience as an advisor to companies on antitrust matters. He has held academic posts at the London School of Economics, Oxford University, and at universities in Canada, Australia, and the United States. He is currently professor of the economics of competition law at the College of Europe in Bruges. He is also a (non-practising) member of the English bar. He has appeared as an expert witness before the courts of several European countries, before the European Commission, the Monopolies and Mergers Commission, and the Ways and Means Committee of the US House of Representatives. He has conducted research and written economic analyses on more than 100 industries in the course of advising on litigation and on investigations by the OFT, the MMC, the European Commission, and national competition authorities. He has been an advisor to DGIV on its Market Definition Notice, on Quantitative Techniques and on Remedies, and to the DTI on the UK Competition Act.

Hendrik Bourgeois is General Counsel, Europe at General Electric Company (GE). Prior to that, he was serving as Senior Counsel, Competition, Regulation and Government Relations for Europe at GE, and before that he was GE's European Competition Counsel, serving all GE businesses on a wide variety of competition law matters involving mergers and acquisitions, distribution, R&D activities, and compliance issues. Previously, he was the European General Counsel of one of GE's business divisions, GE Industrial Systems. Prior to joining GE, he was a member of the Brussels and New York Bars, and an attorney with Jones Day, based in Washington DC and Brussels, where he practised mainly US antitrust, and respectively European competition law. He has an LLM degree from Harvard Law School and obtained his law degree at the Rijksuniversiteit Ghent, Belgium. He is a frequent speaker and writer on competition law issues.

Marco Bronckers is a professor of law at the University of Leiden, where he holds the chair of WTO and EU law. He received his legal education in the Netherlands (University of Amsterdam, JD 1979; PhD 1985) and the United States (University of Michigan, LLM 1980). He practised law in the United States and the Netherlands, following an internship with the European Commission's Legal Service. Since 1990 he has been based in Brussels. Having been a partner in leading Dutch and American law firms, he created his own firm with Vermulst Verhaeghe Graafsma & Bronckers in 2009. His legal specialties are European law, international trade law, and competition law. During his career as a practising lawyer, he has published and lectured widely. In addition, he is a regular lecturer at the World Trade Institute, University of Bern (MILE program), and the University of Barcelona (IELPO program). He is an associate editor of the *Journal of International Economic Law* (published by Oxford University Press), and on the advisory board of the *European Journal of Risk Regulation* (Lexxion) and *Legal Issues of Economic Integration* (Kluwer).

Thomas Cottier is a Managing Director of the World Trade Institute and the Institute of European and International Economic Law, a Professor of European and International Economic Law at the University of Bern. He is the managing director of the World Trade Institute and directs the national research programme on trade law and policy (NCCR Trade Regulation: From Fragmentation to Coherence) located at the WTI. He has a long-standing involvement in GATT/WTO activities. He served on the Swiss negotiating team of the Uruguay Round from 1986 to 1993, first as chief negotiator on dispute settlement and subsidies for Switzerland and subsequently as chief negotiator on TRIPs. He was the Deputy-Director General of the Swiss Intellectual Property Office and served as a member or chair of several GATT and WTO panels. He has written and publishes on a wide range of trade, European law and international law issues.

William J. Davey retired as the Guy Raymond Jones Chair in Law at the University of Illinois College of Law in August 2008. He had taught at the College since 1984 and continues to teach a course on international trade law. From 1995 to 1999, he was the Director of the Legal Affairs Division of the World Trade Organization. He is the author of *Legal Problems of International Economic Relations* (St Paul, MN, Thomson/West,5th edn, 2008, with Jackson & Sykes); *Enforcing World Trade Rules*

(London, Cameron May, 2006); *European Union Law* (St Paul, West, 3rd edn, 2011, with Bermann, Goebel & Fox); *Pine & Swine: Canada–United States Trade Dispute Settlement* (Ottawa, Centre for Trade Policy and Law, 1996); and *Handbook of WTO/GATT Dispute Settlement* (Ardsley-on-Hudson, NY, Transnational Juris Publications, Inc., 1991–2000, with Pescatore & Lowenfeld), and the editor (with Jackson) of *The Future of International Economic Law* (Oxford, Oxford University Press, 2008), as well as the author of many articles on various international trade law issues.

Philippe De Baere is a partner with the Brussels law firm of Van Bael & Bellis where he specializes in international trade and customs law. He has been involved in most major EU anti-dumping, anti-circumvention and anti-subsidy proceedings since 1990. In this field, he has represented numerous clients before the European Commission and the Court of Justice of the European Union. In the field of international trade law, he has assisted WTO members in various WTO dispute settlement proceedings, in particular involving anti-dumping issues.

Gérard Depayre is a consultant in international trade in Geneva. He worked for the European Commission from 1976 to 2005, serving as Deputy Head of the European Commission's Delegation in Washington, DC, from May 2001 to August 2005. During his 30-year career with the European Commission, he served as Deputy Director-General for EU Trade Policy and Relations with North America, Asia, Australia, New Zealand, the North American Free Trade Agreement (NAFTA), and the Asia-Pacific Economic Cooperation (APEC) (1996–99). In this position, he was the Commission's negotiator for China's accession to the World Trade Organization (WTO) and led the implementation of the Transatlantic Economic Partnership. He was Head of Unit from 1987 to 1994 and then Director of EU Trade Policy Instruments from 1994 to 1996, covering anti-dumping, safeguards, subsidies, and other instruments of external economic policy. He negotiated for the Commission the WTO Agreement on Subsidies and Countervailing Duties in the Uruguay Round. He served in the cabinet of former EU External Relations and Trade Commissioner Willy Declercq from 1985 to 1987 after two years (1983–85) as principal administrator handling industrial problems with non-EU countries, notably Japan.

Piet Eeckhout studied law (lic iur) and European law (lic Eur iur) at the University of Ghent, Belgium, where he also obtained his PhD degree. Before joining King's in 1998 he taught at the University of Ghent and at the University of Brussels (VUB). Between 1994 and 1998 he worked in the chambers of Advocate General Jacobs at the European Court of Justice. He is Director of the Centre of European Law, at King's (see www.kcl.ac.uk/cel). He is co-editor of the *Yearbook of European Law*, and also teaches at the College of Europe, Bruges. He is an associate academic member of Matrix Chambers, London. He is a leading authority EU law and international economic law. He is the author of *External Relations of the European Union* (Oxford, Oxford University Press, 2004).

Lothar Ehring currently is the Assistant to Mr. Péter Balás, Deputy Director-General at the Directorate-General for Trade of the European Commission, responsible for multilateral affairs, as well as trade defence instruments and bilateral trade relations with Eastern Europe and Central Asia. Until 2008, he served in the Unit of the European Commission's Directorate-General for Trade that is responsible for Legal Aspects of Trade Policy. He was the Coordinator for legal issues of multilateral trade, handled several WTO disputes and also represented the European Community in the negotiations on the reform of the WTO Dispute Settlement Understanding. He specializes on horizontal questions of dispute settlement, the law of non-discrimination, trade in agriculture and institutional questions of the WTO, topics on which he also lectures at universities and publishes in law reviews.

Simon J. Evenett is Professor of International Trade and Economic Development at the University of St Gallen, Switzerland, and Co-Director of the CEPR's Programme on International Trade and Regional Economics, Europe's most established group of international trade researchers. He is also the coordinator of the Global Trade Alert, the independent trade policy monitoring service.

Ian S. Forrester practises European law with lawyers from eight jurisdictions in the Brussels office of White & Case. He has practised as an advocate in Scotland and as a barrister before the English courts. He has participated in many cases before the European courts, the European Commission and national competition agencies. He represented the European Commission (with Jacques Bourgeois) before the European courts in the *Magill* case about refusals to license by dominant companies, and UEFA in the *Bosman* case about professional football. He specialises in the fields of competition, trade, sport, broadcasting and pharmaceutical regulation, having acted in contentious proceedings for Canon, Du Pont, GlaxoSmithKline, Microsoft, Pfizer, Toyota and other leading companies. He has lectured on EC legal and policy topics to academic and private bodies in many countries, and has published extensively on these themes. His numerous articles on competition law include an annual survey of EC competition law developments in the *Oxford Yearbook of European Law* (Oxford, Oxford University Press, 1981 to date). He was appointed Queen's Counsel in 1988, and Visiting Professor (1991) then Honorary Professor and Honorary Doctor of Laws (2009) at Glasgow University.

He has served as an arbitrator under the rules of the International Chamber of Commerce and the International Centre for Settlement of Investment Disputes. He is a Trustee of the European Union Baroque Orchestra, and an Elder of St Andrew's Church of Scotland in Brussels.

Damien Geradin is Partner at Covington & Burling and Professor of Competition Law and Economics at Tilburg University. His areas of research include antitrust, network industries (telecommunications, postal services, energy and transport), and economic regulation in general. He also held visiting professorships in a number of leading US universities including Columbia, Harvard, UCLA and Yale. He has published more than 50 legal and economic papers in a variety of academic journals, including the *Common Market Law Review*, the *European Law Review*, the *Journal of Competition Law and Economics*, the *Berkeley Technology Law Journal*, the *Columbia Journal of European Law*, the *Journal of World Trade*, the *Journal of International Economic Law*, the *European Foreign Affairs Review*, and the *Utilities Law Review*. His work has been quoted by the European Court of Justice, the US Court of Appeals (10th Circuit), as well as in numerous regulatory proceedings.

Inge Govaere is Professor of European Law at Ghent University and Director of the European Legal Studies Department at the College of Europe, Bruges. Law studies at Ghent University (1987) and PhD at the European University Institute (EUI) in Florence (Italy, 1994). Fulbright Scholar-in-Residence at Cornell University, NY (United States, 1998). Visiting Professor, guest-lectures and conferences in Belgium and abroad, a.o. European University Institute (EUI, Florence), Yale University (United States), Columbia University (NY, United States), Pittsburgh University (United States), Bond University (Queensland, Australia), Sao Paolo (Brazil), Lima (Peru), La Paz (Bolivia), Sofia (Bulgaria), Budapest (Hungary), Warsaw (Poland), Tunis (Tunisia), Ankara (Turkey). Publications include, *inter alia*, *The 1992 Challenge at National Level* (Nomos, Nomos Verlagsgesellschaft, 1990), *The Use and Abuse of Intellectual Property Rights in EC Law* (London, Sweet & Maxwell, 1996), entries in the second volume of T*he Oxford Encyclopaedia of EC Law* (Oxford, Oxford University Press, 2005), *European Legal Dynamics/Dynamiques Juridiques Européennes* (Bruxelles, PIE, 2007), *Intellectual Property, Public Policy and International Trade* (Brussels, PIE, 2007), *Intellectual Property, Market Power and the Public Interest* (Brussels, PIE, 2008), *La Fonction Publique Communautaire* (Bruxelles, Bruylant, 2008).

Barry E. Hawk is Director at Fordham Competition Law Institute and Professor at Fordham Law School; former partner and head of international antitrust practice group, Skadden, Arps, Slate, Meagher & Flom LLP. For many years he has conducted annual seminars on antitrust law and policy for officials of the Commission of the European Communities as well as officials and judges for antitrust authorities throughout the world. He also has served as a consultant to the Commission's Legal Service and to the OECD. He has authored many books and articles on European and US antitrust law and policy.

John H. Jackson is University Professor and Director at the Institute of International Economic Law, Princeton; University of Michigan. His most recent important honours include the Manley O. Hudson medal awarded him in April 2008 by the American Society of International Law, and an honorary doctorate award in October 2008 by the European Union Institute in Florence to honour the excellence of lifetime work of legal scholarship related to international economic relations and activity. He joined the Georgetown faculty after a distinguished career as Hessel E. Yntema Professor of Law at the University of Michigan. He has been a visiting faculty member at the University of Delhi in Delhi, India and the University of Brussels in Brussels, Belgium, a Consultant on Legal Education to the Ford Foundation, a Research Scholar at the headquarters of General Agreement on Tariffs and Trade (GATT) in Geneva, Switzerland, and a Rockefeller Foundation Fellow in Brussels, Belgium. He has served as General Counsel for the Office of the President's Special Representative for Trade in the US Executive Office of the President in Washington, DC (1973–74), and Associate Vice President for Academic Affairs at the University of Michigan (1988–89). Over the years, he has also advised the US and various foreign governments, international organizations, and in 2000, served as chairperson of a WTO panel for a trade dispute settlement procedure. Professor Jackson has served as a member of the board of editors for the *American Journal of International Law*, *Law and Policy in International Business*, *International Tax & Business Lawyer*, *Fordham International Law Journal*, and the *Maryland Journal of International Law & Trade*. He is a member of the editorial board for *The World Economy* and a past member of the editorial boards for the International Bar Association and the *Journal of World Trade Law*. He is the editor in chief and a founding editor of the *Journal of International Economic Law* (JIEL), published by Oxford University Press since 1998. In 1998, he was formally inaugurated to the position of University Professor at GULC. He is also Director of the Institute of International Economic Law at GULC.

James A. Keyte is Partner at Skadden where he handles a wide variety of antitrust litigation, transactional and advisory matters across numerous industries. In the transactional arena, he has represented numerous clients before the Department of Justice and the Federal Trade Commission. He also regularly appears before the antitrust agencies in a variety of investigational contexts. He is a frequent contributor of antitrust articles to the *Antitrust Law Journal* and *Antitrust Magazine* on a variety of topics, including merger analysis, market definition and conduct-related issues. He is a senior editor of the *Antitrust Law Journal* and a former editor of *Antitrust Magazine*. He has been repeatedly selected for inclusion in *Chambers USA: America's Leading Lawyers for Business*.

Pieter Jan Kuijper has been Professor of the Law of International (Economic) Organizations at the Faculty of Law of the University of Amsterdam (UvA), the Netherlands, since 2007. Prior to his appointment at the UvA, he was Principal Legal Advisor and Director of the External Relations and International Trade team of the Legal Service of the European Commission (2002–07). He is currently an editor of the *Common Market Law Review*, *Legal Issues of Economic Integration* and the *Journal of International Economic Law*. He also serves on the advisory board of the *International Organizations Law Review*, and is an active member of various learned societies.

Juan A. Marchetti is counsellor in the Trade in Services Division of the World Trade Organization (WTO), and is currently the secretary of the WTO Committee on Trade in Financial Services. He holds a university degree in economics, and specialises in the area of trade policy in services, particularly in the field of trade in financial services. Before joining the WTO Secretariat, his previous positions included the following: secretary of embassy at the permanent mission of Argentina to the WTO, where he was responsible for services negotiations, and economist at the technical division of the Buenos Aires Stock Exchange.

Marc Maresceau studied at Ghent University, The Johns Hopkins University, Bologna and the *Institut de hautes études internationales*, University of Geneva and was Leverhulme Fellow at the University of Edinburgh. At Ghent University, he teaches European Law and Institutions. He is director of the European Institute of Ghent University, holds a Jean Monnet Chair and is coordinator of the Ghent University Jean Monnet Centre of Excellence. Many of his publications concentrate on legal and political aspects of external relations of the EU and on EU enlargement. He had visiting chairs at various universities, including the Université de Bordeaux IV; Université de Rennes 1; Paris II (Panthéon-Assas); King's College, University of London; The Hebrew University, Jerusalem; College of Europe, Bruges and Warsaw; Università di Bologna; Scuola Sant'Anna, Università di Pisa; the University of Georgia (Athens, United States). He also taught at the Academy of International Law, The Hague, on 'Bilateral Agreements concluded by the European Community' and has many publications on his name.

Petros C. Mavroidis is Edwin B. Parker Professor of Law at Columbia Law School, and Professor of Law at the University of Neuchâtel. He is, along with Henrik Horn, chief reporter of the American Law Institute (ALI) project 'Principles of International Trade Law: the WTO'.

Massimo Merola is the managing partner responsible for the Brussels Office of Bonelli Erede Pappalardo and is the scientific director of the firm's European Law and Antitrust group. He oversees a broad regulatory practice specializing in EU law, European and Italian competition law, state aid law. He regularly appears before the European Commission and diverse national agencies and sanctioning bodies in various EU member states to represent leading corporate clients in sectors like telecommunications, energy and air transportation. In conjunction with his active legal practice, he has lectured since 1993 as a visiting professor at the College of Europe in Bruges and at other universities in Italy and Spain. He is a regular speaker at European conferences and seminars on competition and state aid and the author of several publications.

Frank Montag is a senior partner in Freshfields Bruckhaus Deringer's antitrust, competition and trade (ACT) group, based in the Brussels office. A member of the Brussels and Cologne Bars, his practice focuses on European, German and international competition and trade law. He has represented companies across a wide range of industries before national competition authorities and the European Commission, in particular in merger control filings, cartel investigations and proceedings under Regulation No. 1/2003. In addition, he has represented companies and public institutions in state aid proceedings as well as in trade cases and has also acted for companies, trade associations and governments in several dozen proceedings before the European Court of Justice and General Court, and the European Free Trade Association court. For many years, he has been recognized as a leader in his fields by the principal legal directories. He graduated from the United World College of the Atlantic, Wales (IB 1976) and the Universities of Bonn (Dr iur 1984) and Georgia, United States (LLM 1982). He speaks German, English and French.

Tetyana Payosova is a PhD student and a research fellow at the Institute of European and International Economic Law, University of Bern, Switzerland. She was educated at Odessa National Law Academy in Ukraine, as well as at the Law Faculty of the University of Bern, Switzerland. Her main research areas are trade and international law, energy law, European law and intellectual property law.

Ernst-Ulrich Petersmann is Professor at the European University Institute at Florence. He has published more than 25 books and more than 200 articles on international and European law. He practised international economic law for more than 30 years as representative of Germany in European and UN institutions, as legal advisor in GATT, as well as in the World Trade Organization, and as legal consultant for the EU Commission, the European Parliament, the OECD and UNCTAD. He served as legal secretary, member or chairman of numerous GATT and WTO dispute settlement panels and was proposed twice by Germany as official candidate for the WTO Appellate Body. He served as Head of the Law Department of the European University Institute (2006–09) and was a visiting professor at Michigan University Law School, Columbia University Law School and Yale Law School (United States), Stellenbosch University Law School (South Africa), the Academy of European Law (Florence), the Academy of International Trade Law (Macau), the Hague Academy of International Law (2000), and the Xiamen Academy of International Law in China (2006). He continues to serve as associate editor of the *Journal of International Economic Law* and as Chairman (since 2000) of the International Trade Law Committee of the International Law Association.

Nicolas Petit is Professor at the Law School of the University of Liege (ULg), Belgium, and Visiting Professor at the EDHEC Business School, Lille, France. He is the Director of the ULg LLM in European Competition and Intellectual Property Law, co-Director of the Institute for European Legal Studies and Director of the Global Competition Law Centre of the College of Europe. He was formerly an Associate at Howrey LLP, Brussels and served as a clerk at the Commercial Chamber of the French Supreme Court. He holds a PhD in law (2007), which was prized both by the review Concurrences and by the International League of Competition Law (LIDC). In 2009, he was appointed International Reporter of the LIDC. In 2005 he was selected to become a member of Harvard Law School's Visiting Researchers Programme.

Reinhard Quick received his legal education in Germany (Dr iur) and a Master of Laws (LLM) from the University in Michigan. During this period he was a stagiaire with the EC Commission in Brussels and the GATT Secretariat in Geneva. In 1984 he became a Trade Policy Adviser for the German Chemical Industries Association (VCI) in Frankfurt. In 1987 he was appointed Head of the Legal Service of the European Chemical Industry Council (CEFIC) based in Brussels. Since October 1993 he has been the director of the VCI Liaison Office in Brussels. In 2006 he was appointed honorary professor for international economic law at the University of Saarland in Saarbrücken where he teaches a course on trade and environment. He has published several articles on trade policy and European Community affairs.

Raimund Raith is Legal Adviser at the Legal Service of the European Commission. Previously he served as Minister-Counsellor/Legal Adviser at the EC Delegation in Geneva. He has extensive experience in all aspects of WTO activities, in particular dispute settlement. Prior to that he held various positions in the Commission's Directorate General for External Relations, including for seven years Head of the Intellectual Property and Investment Section which had responsibility for the Uruguay Round Negotiations on TRIPs and TRIMs. Previously he was case handler for anti-dumping in the Commercial Defence Division of this Directorate General.

Before joining the Commision he held the position of an assistant professor in the law department of the European University Institute in Florence.

He also holds a permanent appointment as professor for international economic law at the Saarland University and has lectured at numerous academic institutions including the Salzburg Seminar. He publishes regularly on topics of intellectual property law and international trade/economic law.

He has studied law and economics at the universities of Tubingen (PhD), Geneva (including HEI) and Ann Arbor, Michigan (LLM) and has been a member of the New York Bar since 1982.

José Rivas is Head of Bird & Bird's international EU & Competition Group. He has extensive litigation experience before the European Courts in Luxembourg – having represented clients in competition, trade and institutional EU law. He has represented clients under investigation by the European Commission and other national competition authorities, and has filed complaints with such authorities. He is editor of the *World Competition, Law and Economics Journal* (Kluwer) and has written extensively on competition law in both English and Spanish. He is a visiting Professor of Competition and State Aids Law at the College of Europe, Natolin Campus, and is a frequent speaker at conferences and seminars. He is also a member of the Working Groups on Competition and State Aids Law of the European Confederation of Business Associations (Business Europe). A member of the Madrid bar since 1986, he studied law at the Universities of Exeter and Zaragoza. He also holds a Master's degree in EU law from the College of Europe in Bruges.

Catherine Smits is Partner at Koan and Member of the Brussels Bar. After her studies at the Institute for European Studies, Department of European Law at the Free University of Brussels (ULB), she became Full-time Research & Teaching Assistant. She is also Member of the inter-university Centre of Research (*Pôle d'attraction interuniversitaire* PAI) on internal and external dimensions of EC Law, coordinated by the Institute for European Legal Studies of the University of Liège and in which the European Institute of Ghent and the Institute of Political Studies of Paris also took part. She has published several articles on European law and competition.

Jacques Steenbergen is Director General in the Belgian Competition Authority. He teaches competition law at the KU Leuven. Before joining the competition authority, he was partner in the Brussels office of Allen & Overy, and legal secretary to the President of the Court of Justice. He is also editor in chief of the *Dutch–Belgian European Law Review SEW*, Chairman of the Board of the Stichting van het Koninklijk Conservatorium of Brussels (the foundation of the royal academy for music of Brussels), and honorary member of the Bar of Brussels. He lectured or gave conferences and served as member of nomination committees or PhD examination committees in institutes and universities in Austria, Belgium, China, Germany, Hungary, Italy, the Netherlands, Poland, Spain, the United Kingdom, and the United States. He publishes regularly on EU and competition law. He obtained a PhD at the KU Leuven on legal remedies and ailing industries (1978). He holds a masters degree in law from the KU Leuven (1972), and bachelor degrees or equivalent certificates in law, philosophy and economics from the University of Antwerp (UFSIA) (1969).

John Temple Lang is a consultant based in the Brussels office of Cleary Gottlieb Steen and Hamilton LLP. His practice focuses primarily on all aspects of EU competition law. From 1995 to 2000, he was Director responsible for telecommunications and media in the Competition Directorate General of the European Commission. He was a Director there beginning in 1988, and from 1974 to 1988 he was in the Legal Service of the European Commission, dealing primarily with competition law issues. He has published a book on European Community law and more than 250 articles on a wide variety of legal and related subjects, mostly concerned with EU competition law. He has lectured widely in the United States, Canada and in many European countries. He joined the firm as counsel in 2000. He is an Irish lawyer, and graduated with first class honours from Trinity College, Dublin, obtaining his LLD in 1980. He is now Senior Visiting Research Fellow at the University of Oxford and a Visiting Professor at Trinity College, Dublin. He is a member of the Bar in Brussels and a solicitor in Ireland.

Denis Waelbroeck is a Professor in European Competition Law at the College of Europe in Bruges and in European Competition Law and Judicial Protection in the EU at the Free University of Brussels. He has published several books and articles on EU law. He is also partner at Ashurst LLP and has now practised EU law for 30 years.

Hannes Welge is Adviser in the Directorate for Trade Defence at DG Trade of the European Commission, responsible, inter alia, for the negotiations on Rules in the DDA. He is a lawyer and served at the EU Mission in Geneva, where he represented the EU in the area of trade remedies, trade and competition and general WTO matters. He served as panellist in WTO dispute settlement cases on lumber. In 1997, he was a Guest Scholar on International Trade at the Brookings Institution in Washington. Prior to joining the European Commission in 1989, he served as a judge in Germany in the areas of competition and intellectual property.

Preface

In the triple foreword by Paul Demaret, Koen Lenaerts and Carl Baudenbacher it is eloquently set out why Jacques Bourgeois fully merits a *Festschrift* from his friends and colleagues on the happy occasion of his 75th birthday. It is a tribute to a remarkable legal scholar, practitioner and personality.

That Jacques, of all people, merited a *Festschrift* was therefore an easy decision for us. Things became already a bit more complicated when trying to choose a subject for the book. Jacques Bourgeois is known to be a Renaissance man, and no single subject would do him justice. We therefore decided to settle on two themes that are not unrelated, although very few lawyers have been able to combine them as has Jacques: trade and competition law. Where matters became really difficult was in choosing contributors to the book. Jacques' network of professional acquaintances is legendary – he seems to know at least half the globe. With a heavy heart we assume the responsibility of having unwittingly omitted some of his friends who might have very much wanted to write a testimonial of their appreciation for Jacques as well. But the response we received of the people we did contact was overwhelming. As the reader will see, the result is an embarrassment of riches: a stellar cast of authors, delivering an overview of cutting edge issues arising in the areas of trade and competition law.

The quality of the contributions has been matched by the always enthusiastic and highly professional editorial support given to us by Valérie Hauspie, to whom we hereby extend a warm thanks. A special word of thanks goes also to the very helpful staff of our publisher, Edward Elgar, especially Jessica Westwood, Jean-Paul McDonald and Julian Roskams, who took on the publication and distribution of this book as a matter of priority.

We should end these introductory words on a technical note. Various contributions deal with EU law. A number of important terminological changes in EU law were introduced by the Lisbon Treaty, which finally entered into force in December 2009. As is still true elsewhere, different authors in this volume have integrated these recent terminological changes in various ways. As a consensus on the terminology for historical as opposed to current developments in European law has yet to emerge, we have made the editorial decision of letting these variations stand.

Inge Govaere
Marco Bronckers
Reinhard Quick

Foreword: Jacques Bourgeois, a European lawyers' lawyer

Paul Demaret*

When I first learned of the project to prepare a *Festschrift* for the 75th birthday of Jacques Bourgeois, I could not hide my surprise, since I could hardly believe that Jacques Bourgeois was about to turn 75, for none of us had observed any let up in his activities, neither as a practitioner nor as an academic. He is as busy as ever and he continues to display that rare combination of analytical sharpness, breadth of vision, freshness in outlook and enthusiasm, which is his hallmark.

However, his CV confirms that he was born in 1936. He obtained his law degree from the University of Ghent in 1959 and a Master degree in Comparative Law from the University of Michigan in 1960, and started his professional career in the early 1960s, soon after the Rome Treaty had entered into force. In other words, Jacques Bourgeois' career spans half a century of European integration.

I felt greatly honoured when my colleagues Marco Bronckers, Reinhard Quick and Inge Govaere invited me to write a foreword to this *Festschrift*, because of the particular reputation the name of Jacques Bourgeois carries with it. The list of contributors to this volume testifies eloquently to that.

At the same time, writing such a foreword is a challenge precisely because Jacques Bourgeois is so well known in European and international legal circles. It is also a challenge for another reason. Jacques and I have known each other and have been colleagues for more than 30 years and we have worked together on many different occasions. We even co-authored a paper, where we tried to measure the respective importance of the competition, industrial and commercial policies in the EC Treaty. Because of the lasting friendship that binds us, I might thus seem prejudiced. My only defence against that potential criticism would be that whoever meets Jacques Bourgeois, deals with him, collaborates with him, studies under him, reads his publications, listens to his presentations, ends up sharing the same prejudice.

* Rector, College of Europe; Former head of the European Law Department (1981–2003), College of Europe; Former Professor of Law, University of Liège.

Jacques Bourgeois is a fully accomplished European lawyer since he has dealt with European law from different perspectives: that of a European civil servant, that of a private practitioner and also that of a law professor.

After a brief stint with the Ghent bar, in 1962, he joined the Commission of the European Atomic Energy Community, before, in 1965, becoming member of the Commission legal team. In that latter capacity, his responsibilities related successively to institutional, agricultural and external trade matters. In 1983, he was appointed Head of the Trade Policy Instruments Division in DG Relex, being thus responsible for the implementation of antidumping and countervailing duties, safeguard measures and measures aimed at illicit commercial practices, while at the same time trying to make sure that these European trade measures would be in conformity with GATT law and other trade agreements concluded by the European Economic Community. In 1987, he went back to the Commission legal service and was promoted to the position of Principal Legal Advisor, where his main responsibilities concerned first trade protection and state aids, then competition policy.

In 1991, he left the Commission and returned to private practice, joining as a partner Baker and McKenzie and thereafter Akin Gump Strauss Hauer & Feld. Since 2007, he has worked as a counsel for WilmerHale, dealing more particularly with EU competition matters and international trade law.

Next to his career as a Commission official and then as a high-flyer attorney, Jacques Bourgeois pursued what amounts to a third career, that of a law professor. In 1976, he was invited as visiting professor by the University of Michigan Law School. In 1992–93, he held the Jean Monnet Chair at the University of Bonn. He is a guest professor at Ghent University and regularly teaches at the University of Sankt-Gallen. However, the academic institute that has most benefited from Jacques Bourgeois is certainly the College of Europe and its programme of European legal studies.

Between Jacques Bourgeois and the College of Europe, there is something like a long-standing love affair. He started teaching at the College back in 1972 and he is now responsible for the seminar on 'The Law of the EU Trade Policy'.

Jacques Bourgeois is a brilliant teacher, who puts to full use the vast experience he has accumulated in his career as a European civil servant and as an attorney. He is particularly good at stressing the interaction between European and international trade law. His knowledge of US federal law also helps him to portray European trade and competition law in a comparative perspective. He likes to set legal issues in their proper economic, political and cultural context. Admittedly, some students consider that, as a professor, he is quite demanding and rather parsimonious regarding marks. But this is how things should be at the College. Professors ought to be demanding and students need to work hard if they expect to receive high marks. Achieving quality entails a price.

Jacques Bourgeois' role at the College goes beyond that of a visiting professor. He has truly become a pillar of the Law department. He has taken an active part in the organization of several academic conferences covering international trade or competition law issues at the College. When he is not himself among the organizers of a conference, the latter eagerly seek his contribution, for he is a first-rate speaker, renowned for his clear and articulate presentations. He is an outstanding debater, who can engage in robust exchanges, but also in nimble footwork when this is needed.

The College of Europe is indebted to Jacques Bourgeois on two other counts. First, he is one of the representatives of the Law department in the Academic Council. Second, he is a founding and leading member of the Global Competition Law Centre of the College, which was set up in 2004 at the initiative of Damien Geradin. At the request of his colleagues, Jacques Bourgeois accepted to serve as President of the GCLC for a two-year period (2008–10).

Both in the Academic Council of the College and the GCLC, Jacques Bourgeois plays an active role and his contribution is highly valued, whether it consists in proposals, remarks or criticisms, knowing that Jacques Bourgeois' criticisms are always of a constructive nature and never meant to start polemics. At various times, his analytical rigour has helped clarify issues, that at first seemed complex, if not muddled, or identify the risks and pitfalls that had to be avoided if the planned objectives were to be secured.

In parallel with his careers as a European civil servant, private practitioner and law professor, Jacques Bourgeois has accumulated an impressive list of publications, which some full-time academics might envy. He has written on many topics, including the CAP. However, the bulk of his publications addresses topics related to the external trade relations of the EU, GATT and WTO law and EU competition matters.

All trade issues of some importance for the EU, GATT or the WTO, whether of a substantive or of a procedural nature, have received Jacques Bourgeois' careful attention. He is equally at ease dealing with the large picture as with individual cases.

If Jacques Bourgeois has led three different legal careers, his professional life demonstrates a great unity, since he has for a great many years pursued the same interests. This, his publications clearly reflect. They have made him a leading authority in the field of international trade law and many will regard him as the leading authority with respect to the interplay between EU trade policy and WTO law.

Many honours, awards and memberships have been bestowed on Jacques Bourgeois by his colleagues and peers in recognition of the special status he has achieved in his field. Among these, I would like to single out the fact that he was called on to serve as President of a GATT panel and later of a WTO panel. This indicates that Jacques Bourgeois is not only seen as an exceptionally able trade lawyer, but also as a diplomat. Indeed, by temperament, he is a conflict solver.

Jacques Bourgeois is also a true European, well served as it is, by his remarkable language skills. He is fully trilingual (Dutch, French, English) and he is at ease in German, Spanish and Italian. His mastery of languages, together with his other talents, has served him well in his professional career and also socially.

Jacques exudes warmth, armed with an infectious smile, he goes out of his way to meet others. This explains why he has made many lasting friendships. He will speak his mind, if always with great urbanity. He is endowed with a keen sense of humour. Actually, Jacques enjoys a good laugh as much as a great wine. All this makes him an ideal companion.

He likes to travel and he has travelled all over the world, but his roots are in Ghent, where he was born and where he lived until quite recently. Ghent is a part of Jacques as much as Jacques, for me, remains part of Ghent.

We are many to feel privileged for being Jacques' colleague and for being counted among his friends.

Long live Jacques, the colleague, the friend, the European lawyer.

Foreword

Koen Lenaerts*

It is a great privilege to write a foreword to this *Festschrift*, which is being offered to Jacques Bourgeois on the occasion of his 75th birthday.

When, last year, I was asked to contribute to the *Festschrift*, my first reaction was: 'Is he 65 already?' So it is even harder for me to believe that Jacques turns 75 this August. He doesn't seem to have aged in the slightest since we first met many years ago. The passing of time has certainly not affected his work, his energy or his enthusiasm for the law.

Jacques' career has been a rich one. To borrow the words of the EU motto, it is characterized by 'unity in diversity'. The practice of European and international law, and in particular of competition law and of trade law, is the unifying factor, while the different perspectives from which Jacques has practised the law provide the elements of diversity.

As a 30-year-old man, Jacques joined the European Commission, the institution that is the guardian of the European Treaties. As one would expect of the outstanding person we are honouring in this book, he rose rapidly through the ranks and served for several years as head of the Trade Policy Instruments Division in the Directorate General for External Relations. From 1987 to 1991, he was principal legal adviser to the Commission, first in respect of foreign trade policy and later of antitrust policy.

In 1991, his professional career underwent a big change when he moved to private practice. His charming personality, his extensive knowledge of every aspect of competition and trade law as well as of the internal 'cuisine' of the Commission proved to be the perfect combination and made Jacques one of the most successful attorneys at the Brussels bar.

Thus, in private practice, Jacques Bourgeois excelled once again. He was recognized in the 2009 list of the 'Best lawyers in Belgium' in the areas of competition and trade law.

Jacques is also an outstanding academic. He is a professor at the prestigious College of Europe in Bruges, a guest professor at the University of Ghent and was previously a visiting professor at the University of Michigan

* Judge of the Court of Justice of the European Union; Professor of European Law, Institute for European Law, KU Leuven.

Law School. He has written numerous articles on the subject of competition and trade law. In the library of the Court of Justice alone I counted about 80 of his contributions.

His work as an academic has been of great value not only to other scholars, attorneys and judges, but also to policy-makers. Indeed, in his articles he not only explains the law as it is but sheds light on any shortcomings in the existing rules and makes specific proposals as to how they might be improved. For example, in a recent article,[1] he demonstrates how the current public system for the enforcement of competition law in the EU might be harnessed to help provide compensation for consumers, otherwise than through the up to now largely theoretical possibility of their obtaining damages through private enforcement actions.

As a renowned scholar, Jacques Bourgeois is also a member of the board of editors of many law journals. To me personally, it is a real pleasure to see Jacques during the regular meetings of the board of editors of *Sociaal-Economische Wetgeving*. It is always an intellectually rewarding experience to discuss with him, on the occasion of such meetings, recent developments in the field of competition and trade law.

Above all, Jacques is a friend to all of us who have contributed to this book. Knowing Jacques' warm personality, it did not come as a surprise to learn that limiting the number of contributors has been the main challenge for the editors.

The *Festschrift* reflects two of the main areas of Jacques' professional interests, namely 'competition' and 'trade'. The first part of the book covers different aspects of competition law. Some contributions concern Article 101 TFEU; others examine abusive practices under Article 102 TFEU or merger control. The second part, which relates to trade law, offers the same diversity of topics ranging from WTO dispute settlement to the possibility of bringing actions before the General Court of the EU in the field of trade law. However, all of the contributions have in common the fact that they are all outstanding essays. I am sure that Jacques Bourgeois, as well as the readers of this book, will greatly appreciate them.

Last, but not least, a word about why we are offering Jacques this book now. I am conscious that a *Festschrift* is normally offered at the moment when the person concerned puts an end to his professional activities. Since the word 'retirement' does not figure in Jacques' lexicon, it was deemed appropriate to publish this book in honour of his 75th birthday.

Happy birthday Jacques and *ad multos annos*!

---

[1] Jacques H.J. Bourgeois and Stéphanie Strevie, 'EU Competition Remedies in Consumer Cases: Thinking Out of the Shopping Bag', *World Competition*, Vol. 33, No. 2, 2010, pp. 241–55.

Foreword

Carl Baudenbacher*

I am deeply honoured that the editors of this unusually rich book have invited me to write a foreword. Much has been said about Jacques Bourgeois' highly successful career as a Commission official, a GATT and WTO panellist, a professor at universities in several European countries and in the United States, and an attorney at law advising and representing clients in what turned out to be landmark cases. In fact, this whole *Festschrift* bears witness of that. I would like to add some rather personal remarks.

I met Jacques for the first time at a relatively late stage of our lives in his *Club de Warande* in Brussels. He had invited me to lunch and within an hour I had convinced him to teach in the University of St Gallen's Executive Master of Business Law programme. For a number of years he acted as a chairman of the programme's one-week WTO law module, which at the time was held in Geneva. I was impressed with his legal knowledge and his flair for economics, but also, and in particular, with his independent mind. He obviously did not care about whether his views were shared by the powerful or not, but went for what he thought was right. As examples, I may mention his position on anti-dumping or on international exhaustion of intellectual property rights. But I was equally struck by Jacques' humbleness, by the way he treated the students (all practitioners in their mid-30s) as interlocutors to be taken seriously, and by his fairness and generosity in grading exams. Jacques still serves as a member of the EMBL programme's Academic Advisory Board. St Gallen University owes him a great deal of thanks.

Several times I had the privilege of sitting on panels with the birthday boy where controversial subjects of WTO law and of European competition law were debated, e.g. in Vienna or in St Gallen. Jacques made his point with ease and his opponents had to wrap up warmly. But he did this with his friendly smile and at times with a *clin d'oeil*. He was very serious, but did not take himself too seriously. And he was and is always ready to

* President of the EFTA Court in Luxembourg and Professor of the Universities of St Gallen and of Iceland.

step in for others. I will never forget the following. Once one of Jacques' colleagues was a gifted young American professor of International Trade Law. When he heard that she had been denied tenure at her American university, essentially because she lacked international exposure, he spontaneously offered his help and saw to it that she could spend time as a visiting scholar at the WTO Secretariat in Geneva. On the second attempt she was awarded tenure.

I also discovered with joy that as far as European law is concerned, Jacques' interest does not stop at the borders of the European Union. From the beginning, he dealt with the challenges of the EEA Agreement, in particular with its competition law chapter. He explored, *inter alia*, the question of whether the one-stop-shop system underlying those provisions would leave room for the application of the *ne bis in idem* principle in the relationship between the EFTA Surveillance Authority and the European Commission, and he concluded that the principle should apply. In another article, Jacques Bourgeois suggested that should a consensus emerge in the WTO concerning negotiations on an agreement on competition, the respective provisions of the EEA Agreement would offer some interesting solutions.

But academic and professional success is not everything in life. What makes Jacques so special is his humaneness. I remember evenings after the conference work was done when the famous EU and WTO lawyer enjoyed a good meal and a good wine together with colleagues and friends laughing and talking about everything but business. Apart from that, my wife Doris and I have witnessed aspects of Jacques that remained hidden to most. We are fortunate that for years he has, together with Marie-Christine, been one of the best disguised guests at our annual costume party. Party secrets should remain secret. But I think I can reveal one thing: over time Jacques has proven to be a worthy opponent of the European judiciary and of the diplomatic corps in Luxembourg in our traditional cherry pit-spitting contest.

Thank you Jacques and warmest congratulations on your milestone birthday.

PART I

Trade and competition

1. Competition and trade policy and the challenge of globalization

Jacques Steenbergen

1.1 GLOBALIZATION: AN UNAVOIDABLE CHALLENGE[1]

The globalization of markets as we know it now as a globally interdependent economy, was a virtually unavoidable consequence of technological developments. We learned to produce services as well as industrial and agricultural products on a scale that does no longer correspond with the needs of national societies. The development of production both enabled and required the development of trade and it has resulted in a gradual shift from autarky to interdependence on an ever larger scale.[2] We grew accustomed to a standard of living and a pattern of consumption that is only sustainable if we make use of modern technology. Disposable income and cost of consumption are not only dependent on the ability to sell goods and services beyond the borders of our domestic markets but also on cheap imports. Globalization may mostly be perceived as a threat to employment by imports and dislocation, but access to markets abroad is also a condition for preserving our standard of living and employment in all sectors that can only justify present levels of activity by access to foreign markets.

As I concluded in the 1970s together with G. De Clercq and R. Foqué in a study that was published in English thanks to the support of Jacques

---

[1] Section 1.1 draws on Foqué, R. and Steenbergen, J., 'Regionalism: A constitutional framework for global challenges?', in M. Farrell, B. Hettne and L. Van Langenhove (eds), *Global Politics of Regionalism*, London, Pluto Press, pp. 54–68.

[2] See e.g. for a colourful description of these developments earlier in the past century on the life on rural estates: Gravin Dönhof, M., *Kinderjaren in een verloren land,* Amsterdam, Uitgeverij Contact, 1990, and esp. pp. 72–7.

Bourgeois,[3] we therefore face the choice between a protected market with a significant contraction of the economy, and the degree of free trade necessary for the preservation of export-dependent employment.[4] While parts of our societies find it increasingly difficult to handle the pressure of globalization, others may go elsewhere if they become convinced that they are fighting a lost battle at home. Brain drain is among the worst that can happen when a society needs to rethink itself.

But we cannot be blind for the challenges. Loss of employment is the most visible damage caused by globalization. Other types of damage caused by globalization can be even more significant than the loss of employment itself. The confrontation with successive rationalization and restructuring schemes in enterprises, repeated changes in management and management objectives, the fear for the unknown in multicultural societies, all mean that people loose their benchmarks. And when people loose the confidence that problems can be solved by rational interaction in existing frameworks, they risk loosing their ability to respond constructively to challenges, and to cope with change as well as loss.

1.2 GLOBALIZATION CAME IN WAVES: FROM TRADE VIA COLONIZATION AND PROTECTIONISM TO FREE TRADE

Global trade dates back, at least, to 400 BC when Phoenicians sailed not only the coasts of western as well as southern Europe but also of western and eastern Africa. It was well developed when Europe and Asia traded in various products and commodities such as silk and various spices in the Middle Ages. The massive import of Central American gold and silver by the Spanish in the sixteenth century caused a rampant inflation that is said to have impacted on economic developments in Europe for more than a century.[5] Economic interdependence was skilfully seen as an opportunity

---

[3] Steenbergen, J., De Clercq, G. en Foqué, R., *Change and adjustment: external relations and industrial policy of the EC*, Deventer, Kluwer Law & Taxation, 1983, p. 216 and in particular p. 177 *et seq*.

[4] See e.g. Laïdi, Z., *La Grande Perturbation*, Paris, Flammarion, 2004, p. 343. See for an example of the consequences of economic isolationism in a European environment e.g. the lessons from the economic history of Spain and in particular Franco's policy of autarky: see e.g. Preston, P., *Franco*, London, Harper Collins, 1993,pp. 344 *et seq*. Franco was the last who tried to impose such policy in western Europe.

[5] See for a succinct survey e.g. Green, S., *Good value: reflections on morals, money, morality and an uncertain world*, London, Allen Lane, 2009, p. 52 *et seq*.

by traders and bankers in Venice, Bruges, Antwerp, Amsterdam and other trading centres of medieval, renaissance and post-renaissance Europe, as well as by the infant multinationals such as the Verenigde Oost-Indische Compagnie and its less well-known competitors. China, which is now seen as one of the principal new drivers of globalization, is no newcomer to the group of economic powers. China is said to have had the highest per capita income in the world in the fifteenth century, and to have accounted for one-third of the world's GDP as recently as 1820 at a time that the United States only accounted for 2 per cent.[6]

Economic interdependence became a key factor of the political as well as of the economic tissue of our societies by the development of colonial empires. Colonization helps to explain that globalization only became a genuine challenge to the (European) nation states some hundred years after the industrial revolution. During colonial times, global economic interdependence was politically primarily a domestic issue within (not always peacefully) coexisting empires.

The existence of colonial empires and the illusion they may have given of self-sufficiency may also help to explain why politicians across the political spectrum gave in to protectionist pressures when the international economy collapsed in the aftermath of the World War I.[7]

Decolonization and the emergence of newly industrialized countries gradually redefined the balance of power. But established trade patterns did not change overnight and the need to trade remained.[8] However, while trade could be centrally managed if not imposed within colonial empires, economic interdependence became an interstate instead of a largely domestic issue after decolonization. Trade required global trade arrangements. Thanks to half a century of efforts in GATT (and now the WTO) to

---

[6] Green, *supra,* p. 39 referring to *The Economist*.

[7] Even the more convinced free traders turned towards protectionism. See e.g. on Lloyd George and the then UK government: Lord Home, *The Way the Wind Blows*, Glasgow, Fontana/Collins, 3rd imp., 1979, p. 56. As indicated above it has been estimated that the average tariff for level of France, Germany, the United Kingdom and the United States rose between 1913 and 1932 from approx. 15 per cent to 30 per cent (Green, *supra,* p. 83). Producers need an extremely convincing competitive advantage to overcome such barriers. And tariffs were only part of the armoury. Quota were often an even more formidable barrier.

[8] Colonies, and later the newly independent developing countries, could only satisfy their need for investment and consumer goods by imports from the industrializsed world. Trade restrictions and the limited convertibility of currencies tended to consolidate also in the post-colonial period traditional trade patterns with former colonial powers.

liberalize world markets,[9] the development of trade among the major trading partners and the emergence of new markets continued to benefit the old industrial powers after they lost the political power to impose their exports. But trade now increasingly had to be organized on the basis of reciprocity between sovereign partners.[10] This in turn implied that European countries could no longer hope to limit the impact of the

---

[9] It has been said that the Kennedy Round (1964–67) led to concessions covering 70 per cent of world trade volume, and that two-thirds of the concessions reduced tariffs by more than 50 per cent. The parties negotiated on the basis of linear reduction coefficient. See Dam, K.W., *The GATT, Law and International Organisation*, Chicago 1970, p. 56.

In the Tokyo Round (1974–79), the contracting parties aimed at a higher reduction of high tariffs than of low tariffs. The average tariff reduction was estimated at 25.5 per cent for the EC, 28.5 per cent for the United States, 25 per cent for Japan and 34 per cent for Canada. See Director General of the GATT, *The Multilateral Trade Negotiations of the Tokyo Round*, Geneva, 1979, p. 57 *et seq*. It should be added that as from the Tokyo Round the trade liberalization efforts in GATT were perhaps even more important in respect of non-tariff trade barriers. See e.g. Bourgeois, J.H.J., 'The Tokyo Round Agreements on Technical Barriers to Trade and on Government Procurement in International and in EEC Perspective', *Common Market Law Review*, 1982, p. 22.

See for an assessment of the results of the Uruguay Round: GATT, *Increases in Market Access Resulting from the Uruguay Round*, Genève, April 1994, p. 25; and *European Report*, 16 April 1994, V 5. It has been estimated that tariffs were reduced on average by 38 per cent, with a reduction of the average tariff between industrialized countries from 6.3 to 3.9 per cent. 43 per cent of trade between industrialized countries is no longer subject to tariffs, as compared to 20 per cent before the closing of the Uruguay Round. This means that after the implementation of the Uruguay Round, we could finally claim that trade was more free than it was before World War I. It has been estimated that the average tariff for level of France, Germany, the United Kingdom and the United States was approx. 15 per cent in 1913 (but increased to 30 per cent by 1932) (Green, *supra,* p. 83). See further Bourgeois, J.H.J., 'The Uruguay Round of the GATT: Some General Comments from an EC Standpoint', in N. Emiliou and D. O'Keeffe (eds), *The European Union and World Trade Law : After the GATT Uruguay Round,* Chichester, Wiley, 1996, pp. 81–90; and with Bourgeois, J.H.J., 'The Uruguay Round results from a European Lawyers' Perspective: An Introduction', in J.H.J. Bourgeois et al. (eds), *The Uruguay Round Results; a European Lawyers' Perpective,* Brussels, European Interuniversity Press, 1995, p. 19.

[10] See on the European perception of the reinterpretation of the concept of reciprocity in the Uruguay Round: Paemen, H. and Bensch, A., *Du GATT à l'OMC*, Leuven, 1995, p. 152. UNCTAD and later the Tokyo Round also provided for 'a reversed unilateral preference': the unilateral schemes of preferences to the benefit of developing countries that were 'multilateralized' (or legalized) in the Tokyo Round. See e.g. Balassa, B., 'The Tokyo Round and the Developing Countries', *Journal of World Trade Law*, Vol. 14, 1980, p. 93 *et seq*.

globalization of markets by import restrictions without losing export opportunities and causing a significant drop in the standard of living.[11]

It should be added that 'globalization' only gradually became global. Just as the US market can to a significant extent sustain the economic activity in the United States, the completion of the common market was for a long time all that was needed in Europe (with the possible exception of the United Kingdom). This holds true in particular for the many smaller and medium sized European economies.[12]

Although trade and investment policies (as the terms suggest) became an issue for states and other public institutions, trade remained in the first place an activity of private undertakings. Their impact on trade management is probably greater than ever before. It has been estimated that a third of all transactions are intra-group transactions within multinational groups, and that such groups are party to another third of all transactions.[13] Up to two-thirds of all trade flows may therefore be managed on the basis of make-or-buy decisions of multinational corporations. This means that a significant part of trade is more determined by investment decisions on the geographic spread of production units than by traditional trade considerations. Tax, labour market or environmental and other policies

---

[11] This logic convinced conservative politicians already in the early days that the United Kingodm could not afford to stay out of the EC. See e.g. Lord Home, *supra*, p. 174.

[12] In the early 1980s when the common market had already a significant impact and globalization did not yet figure as prominently on the agenda, this was particularly striking in the smaller member states. Exports represented in 1980 24 per cent of the GDP of the member states, but this figure was much higher in Belgium and Luxembourg (50.7 per cent) or the Netherlands (42.7 per cent). And while exports to third countries represented on average 46.4 per cent of total exports, that figure was significantly lower for Belgium and Luxembourg (28.2 per cent) or the Netherlands (27.8 per cent). Eurostat, *Basic statistics* (1981), table 101.

In 2008 the intra EU-27 trade of Belgium was still 2.3 more important than its extra EU-27 trade (€221.59 million as compared to €95.46 million) while the figure for the EU-27 was 1.6 times more important (€2623.34 million as compared to €1565.03 million (Eurostat, *Foreign trade*, Main tables).

See for an analysis of the development in the large economies Laïdi, *supra*, pp. 361–3. This analysis shows that they were on average in 1960 less dependent on foreign trade than in 1890 or in 1913, but that had started to change by 1980.

[13] Corcos, G., Irac, D., Mion, G. and Verdier, Th., 'The Determinants of Intra-Firm Trade', Centro Studi Luca d'Agliano Development Studies Working Paper No. 267, 1 November 2008. Available at SSRN: http://ssrn.com/abstract=1408182. See also Gilroy, B.M., *The Role of Intra-Firm Trade,* 1987, http://mpra.ub.uni-muenchen.de/18039/.

may thus have acquired a more direct impact on trade than they would otherwise have had.

We saw a similar development in the field of monetary policy and the management of money flows. Exchange rate policies were historically, together with tariffs and quota, a key instrument for the management of trade flows. But while exchange rates still have an impact on trade and the recent history of US–Chinese trade relations shows that trade imbalances still impact (or are expected to impact) on monetary policy and exchange rates, financial transactions have now had for some time a more important impact on monetary developments than trade flows.

1.3 THE MANAGEMENT OF GLOBALIZATION: COMPETITION AND TRADE POLICY

It follows that globalization has at the same time become more important and more difficult to manage. It is truly multi-polar as it involves both the community of states that has become increasingly multi-polar and the world of multinational enterprises. Its development is influenced by decisions and policies that are driven by considerations that do not take into account their potential impact on globalization. Trade policy and competition policy are two policy areas that can be expected to figure among the tools of all who attempt to manage globalization.

Competition and trade policy are two policy areas for which the European Commission has exclusive powers.[14] They are also two areas on which Jacques Bourgeois has focussed and where he figures prominently both within the domestic context of the European integration and of the multilateral as well as bilateral management of transatlantic relations.[15]

---

[14] See e.g. by Bourgeois, J.H.J. (among his many other contributions): 'Some Comments on the Practice', in C.W.A. Timmermans and E.L.M. Voelker (eds), *The Division of Powers between the EC and their Member-States in the Field of External Relations,* Kluwer, Deventer, 1981, p. 97.

[15] See e.g. among many other contributions on both instutional and substantive law aspects Bourgeois, J.H.J., 'De GATT Overeenkomst en het EEG Verdrag, *Sociaal-Economische Wetgeving*, 1974, p. 411; 'De GATT Overeenkomst en de EEG Landbouwregelingen', *Sociaal-Economische Wetgeving*, 1974, p. 579.

And see on both competition and trade law e.g. Bourgeois, J.H.J., 'Trade Measures, Competition Policy, and the Consumer', in P. Demaret, J. Bourgeois, and I. Van Bael (eds), *Trade Laws of the EC and the US in a Comparative Perspective*, Gent/Brugge, Story Scientia/College of Europe, 1992, p. 227; or Bourgeois, J.H.J. and Demaret, P., 'The Working of EC Policies on Competition, Industry and Trade: a Legal Analysis', in P. Buigues, A. Jacquemin, and A. Sapir

1.4 EUROPEAN INTEGRATION AND GLOBALIZATION: A DRIVER AS WELL AS A RESPONSE?[16]

European integration was in the 1950s, like the attempts to structure a world monetary system in the Bretton Woods agreements or to open markets for free trade in the GATT, partly a response to the conclusion that isolationism and protectionism had been inadequate responses to the economic crisis of the 1930s, and that they would equally impede post-war reconstruction. It was also a pragmatic response to the fact that the (impoverished) European nation states did no longer have the scale and means required to deal with the challenges of the post-war world,[17] as well as a more conceptual reaction to nationalism that was perceived by many as one of the main causes for the escalation of conflicts. The post-war promotion of the interdependence of economies by free trade must be seen in the context of the search for a sustainable peace. This also holds true, at least in part, for the efforts to dilute both state and private power by the combined promotion of free enterprise and open competition.[18]

European integration thus contributed to a more open and potentially globalized economy for a variety of sometimes conflicting reasons.

Western Europe's attitude towards an open economic system remained, however, quite ambiguous.[19] France for instance opted in the post-war years for a rigorously planned economy on a strictly national scale.[20] It

---

(eds), *European Policies on Competition, Trade and Industry*, Aldershot, Edward Elgar, 1995, pp. 71–2.

And in the context of trade relations between the EU and Nafta: Bourgeois, J.H.J., 'The European Court of Justice and the WTO: Problems and Challenges' in J.H.H. Weiler (ed.), *The EU, the WTO and the NAFTA: Towards a Common Law of Trade*, Oxford, Oxford University Press, 2000, pp. 71–123.

[16] This and the next paragraph are based on the opening paragraphs of Foqué, R. and Steenbergen, J., 'The Limits of the Law and the Development of the EU' in E. Claes, W. Devroe, and B. Keirsbilck (eds), *Facing the Limits of the Law*, Berlin/Heidelberg, Springer, 2009, pp. 205–36.

[17] See e.g. with reference to General de Gaulle van Middelaar, L., *De Passage naar Europa*, Brussel, Historische Uitgeverij, 2009, p. 192.

[18] See the introduction of competition law in Germany and Japan after World War II at the insistence of the United States as a guarantee against the re-emergence of the industrial conglomerates that had, in the opinion of the allies, greatly contributed to the war efforts of the axis powers.

[19] See Laïdi, *La Grande Perturbation*, *supra*, pp. 367–73.

[20] See e.g. Monnet, J., *Mémoires*, p. 275 *et seq*. The founding father of the 'common market' still refers to this period in his autobiography as '*La France se modernise*'.

would take the convictions of a new generation of intellectuals[21] and the end of the colonial period before France started to embrace the idea that it needed to think in terms of a more open world of which metropolitan France could not hope to be the uncontested centre.[22] Many especially more vulnerable members of society, not only in countries with a tradition of autarky such as France, have always continued to believe that protectionism was a necessary economic defence. And while Britain was more inclined to see the benefits of open markets, it was even more reluctant than France to acknowledge that post-war developments significantly eroded the substance of its sovereignty.[23]

1.5 GLOBALIZATION AS A CHALLENGE TO THE EU

Globalisation initially facilitated the acceptance of European integration, but it has increasingly turned into a challenge to the EU institutions and their political legitimacy.

First, more than 60 years after the last war in western Europe, the first western European generations for as long as we can remember that have not seen war in their country see no risk of an armed conflict between nation states in Europe. And Europeans in enlargement countries, with a more vivid memory of the threats of foreign armies, tend to see NATO (and the United States) as a more credible deterrent than the EU. EU citizens are therefore (rightly or wrongly) no longer motivated to accept any real or perceived price for the functioning of European institutions by their wish to preserve peace.[24]

---

21 See e.g. Servan Schreiber, J.J., *Le Défi Américain*, Paris, Denoël, 1967.

22 See however already Monnet, J., *Mémoires*, p. 321 *et seq.*

23 See e.g. Patten, C., *Not Quite the Diplomat*, London, Penguin Books, 2006, pp. 61 *et seq.*

24 See Verhofstadt, G., *De Verenigde Staten van Europa,* Antwerpen/Amsterdam, Houtekiet, 2005, pp. 53–5. See on Europe's ambiguous attitude to military power e.g. Laïdi, Z., *La Norme sans la Force,* Paris, Presses de Science Po, 2005, p. 21 *et seq.* and *La Grande Perturbation,* pp. 46 and 150 *et seq*. The ability of European politics to confuse is illustrated by the fact that this attitude should not be read as a wish for isolationism or a rejection of any type of interventionism. Europe, both in the EU and NATO, has in recent years, without apparent opposition in most countries, been more active outside its borders than ever since the end of the colonial period. See for a survey Wouters, J. and Naert, F., 'The EU and Conflict Prevention: A Brief Historic Overview' in V. Kronenberger and J. Wouters (eds), *The European Union and Conflict Prevention,* The Hague, T.M.C. Asser Press, 2004, pp. 33–66.

However, the lack of a perceived threat of armed conflicts in Europe does not imply that Europeans feel secure. But the perceived security risks are associated with terrorism, crime and immigration. These risks are seen as by-products of globalization. Any institution aiming at the free movement of persons and goods tends therefore to be perceived as a contributing factor to the perceived security risks rather than as an effective remedy. In the absence of rational solutions, reasonable people can be tempted by populism and by extremist views at either end of the political spectrum. Isolationism, protectionism and militant nationalism are logical defence strategies in societies who hope to restore or preserve what little control can be maintained over their cultural, socio-economic and political environment.

And while the European market may still be all that most European companies can be expected to explore, the pressure of imports and the risk of dislocation is now genuinely global. Enlargement has not only opened welcome new markets, it has also fuelled intra-European relocation. Enlargement has thus increased the tendency to see the European institutions as one of the driving forces of globalization, rather than as a European response.

1.6 TRADE POLICY AND THE RESPONSE TO GLOBALIZATION

The main lesson we learn from the crisis in the 1930s and from various experiences with protectionism[25] is that protectionism is rarely an effective response to an economic crisis. For the above-mentioned reasons protectionism is as much a threat to employment as an excessive pursuit of competitiveness by relentless rationalization. The WTO director general said (we may assume with some relief) that the economic crisis has had a negative impact on trade because of a reduced level of economic activity, but that we did not see a new wave of protectionist measures.[26] And the OECD could state that OECD countries have benefited through trade

[25] See e.g. on the lessons from the economic history of Spain and in particular Franco's policy of autarky: Preston, *supra*, p. 344 *et seq*. See also on China's 'retrenchment' policy started in the fifteenth century Green, *supra*, p. 34.

[26] See e.g. speech by WTO director general Lamy to the European Policy Centre in Brussels on 24 February 2010 in which he said that one year on from the onset of the financial crisis 'the multilateral trading system has proven its sturdiness as a bulwark against runaway protectionism' (at http://www.wto.org/english/news_e/sppl_e/sppl148_e.htm).

linkages from strong activity growth in the large emerging-market economies, including China, India and Brazil.[27] The OECD went further in stating that:

- a 10 per cent increase in trade is associated with a 4 per cent rise in per capita income;
- an 'open' foreign direct investment climate could be expected to yield a ¾ per cent increase in the OECD area GDP per capita;
- more efficient customs procedures could improve global welfare by US$100 billion;
- full tariff liberalization in agriculture and industrial goods could increase global welfare a further US$100 billion; and
- much higher gains would be expected if services trade was liberalized.[28]

Defensive trade policies are nevertheless often seen as the conceptually most obvious response to the pressures of globalization. In the aftermath (at least that is what we hope) of the financial crisis and given the loss of confidence in markets we cannot ignore such pressures without risking a dangerous backlash. We therefore need to continue to explore ways to address pre-conditions or consequences of globalization for which there can be a multilateral basis or support.[29]

Low cost and ease of transport are e.g. prerequisites for globalization. Environmental disasters caused by antiquated ships sailed by non-trained staff and transporting hazardous cargo,[30] massive road accidents bringing economies to a virtual halt that are caused by overloaded trucks driven by sleepy, underpaid truckers, decisions taken by management with a view to

---

[27] OECD website: Home: Economic Outlook > OECD Economic Outlook: interim assessment, April 2010.

[28] OECD website: Home: Trade > Trade policy response to the global economic crisis.

[29] The suggestions that follow on trade policy are taken from Foqué, R. and Steenbergen, J., 'Regionalism: A Constitutional Framework for Global Challenges?', in M. Farrell, B. Hettne and L. Van Langenhove (eds), *supra*, pp. 54–68. *OECD Insights: International Trade: Free, Fair and Open?* (OECD, Paris, 2009) also argues that prosperity has rarely, if ever, been achieved or sustained without trade but that trade alone is not enough. This study refers to policies targeting employment, education, health and other issues rather than more trade policy specific measures in order to promote well-being and tackle the challenges of a globalized economy.

[30] See e.g. Valatsos, V., 'Production Swaps: politique de l'environnement, politique de concurrence, politique des transports', PhD thesis, K.U.Leuven, 2000.

obtaining bonuses that are totally out of proportion of the merit of the decisions they take and the medium to long-term value they may either create or destroy, total reliance on the internet while its management and sustainability remain opaque, are all examples that globalization may partly be based on questionable premises. The elimination of unacceptable risks and a realistic costing of all necessary interfaces will not eliminate the threats of globalization, but they may reduce the pressure to more manageable proportions.

The same holds true for improved and better enforced international environmental and labour standards. Loss of employment by foreign competition is perceived as more threatening if a society is exposed to competition that is deemed to be unfair. It is increasingly held that competitive pressure should not be allowed to endanger our social model if the exporters derive their competitive advantage from a blatant disregard for minimal labour standards. There are therefore good reasons to complement existing product standards[31] increasingly by environmental[32] and/or labour standards relating to their production process. The ILO has worked for decades towards globally acceptable minimum labour standards.[33]

An approach based on multilaterally agreed labour or environmental standards addresses the problems of globalization at the roots because such standards have an impact on the conditions and cost of production in the countries of origin. They try to eliminate the 'unfairness' in competition as is illustrated by the use of terms such as 'fair trade' and 'social dumping'. But there lies also their major disadvantage or limitation: rules on domestic subsidies in international trade,[34] labour protection and environmental standards aim at regulating domestic policies of foreign countries. They

---

[31] See on product standards in the WTO e.g. Sacerdoti, G., 'Standards of treatment, harmonisation and mutual recognition: a comparison between regional areas and the global trading system', in P. Demaret, J-F. Bellis, and G.García Jiménez (eds), *Regionalism and Multilateralism after the Uruguay Round*, Brussels, European Interuniversity Press, 1997, p. 613 *et seq.*

[32] See on environmental standards and international trade law e.g. Esty, D.C. and Geradin, D., 'Environmental protection in regional trade agreements: the EC and NAFTA', in Demaret, Bellis and García Jiménez, *supra*, p. 579 *et seq.*

[33] See e.g. Hansenne, M., 'Trade and labour standards: can common rules be agreed', Wilton Park Conference, 6 March 1996 and Canela-Cacho, J.A., 'The social dimension of the liberalisation of world trade and trade labour standards: can common rules be agreed', in Demaret, Bellis and García Jiménez, *supra*, p. 519 *et seq.*

[34] See on the domestic policy dimension of state aids and its foreign policy consequences e.g. Paemen and Bensch, *supra,* p. 162 *et seq.*; or Steenbergen, J., 'Regulation of Subsidies in International Trade', in J.H.J. Bourgeois (ed.), *Subsidies and International Trade*, Deventer, Kluwer, Deventer, pp. 21–31.

can therefore not be imposed without those countries' agreement, if not active involvement.

1.7 COMPETITION POLICY AND THE RESPONSE TO GLOBALIZATION

Although one can discuss assessment methods and figures, an active enforcement of competition policy contributes to the sustainable development of economies[35] and may thus help to offset any negative consequences of globalization. When discussing the financial crisis, the OECD Competition Committee stressed more specifically with references to the experiences of Japan and Korea as well as to an impact study of the US 'New Deal' policies in the 1930s, that recoveries from past financial crises were delayed when competition enforcement was relaxed. The impact study indicated that policies that reduced competition resulted in a reduction of investments and consumption by approximately 15 per cent relative to competitive levels.[36]

---

[35] J. Konings, P. Van Cayseele, and F. Warzynski estimated the positive impact of effective competition law enforcement at minimum 0.1 per cent of GDP ('The dynamics of industrial mark-ups in two small open economies: does national competition policy matter?', *International Journal of Industrial Organisation*, Vol. 19, 2001, pp. 841–59). That equals approximately €250 million per year for Belgium and at that time approx. €8.8 billion for the EU15.

Based on a more conservative variation of the assessment method used by the European Commission, the Belgian Competition Authority has estimated its contributions for the years 2007, 2008, 2009 and 2010 respectively at approximately €2.5 million, €45,5 million, €60 million and €131 million (See *Annual Reports* of the Directorate General for Competition 2007, 2008, 2009 and 2010 at http://economie.fgov.be/en/entreprises/competition/Belgian_Competition_Authority/Annual_Reports/index.jsp).

The Dutch NMa estimated its contribution for the period 2002–04 at €900 million (*Jaarverslag 2004 NMa en DTe*, 61), and for the year 2008 already at €700 million (*NMa Jaarverslag 2008,* 4 en 46).

The European Commission estimated its contribution for 2008 at €11 billion (Directorate General for Competition, *Annual activity report 2008,* p. 7).

The OECD has estimated that 'lower regulatory barriers to competition could result in a 2–3 per cent increase in OECD area GDP per capita' (OECD website: Home: Trade > Trade policy response to the global economic crisis).

[36] See OECD, *Competition and financial markets, key findings*, OECD, Paris, 2009. See on the assessment of New Deal policies: Cole, H.L. and Ohanian, L.E., 'New Deal Policies and the Persistence of the Great Depression: a General Equilibrium', *Journal of Political Economy*, Vol. 112, pp. 779–816.

One of the main problems competition authorities have to face is that the contribution of competition policy to the management of globalization is inevitably less direct and more difficult to bring across than trade policy measures. In the aftermath of the financial crisis in which the confidence in market mechanisms suffered a severe blow, competition authorities need to focus at least as much as free trade advocates on the strengthening of the legitimacy of their policies by coherent advocacy that openly addresses criticism.

We may point out for instance that competition policy aims at promoting fair competition. Competition rules should not be confused with rules on unfair trade practices.[37] But that does not imply that competition authorities cannot contribute to the promotion of fair competition.[38]

Competition policy is moreover in the EU not developed in a vacuum as a self-sufficient goal. It is related to a more comprehensive set of socio-economic objectives. Article 9 TFEU states that 'in defining and implementing its policies and activities' (i.e. including its competition policy) 'the Union shall take into account requirements linked to the promotion of a high level of employment, the guarantee of adequate social protection, the fight against social exclusion, and a high level of education, training and protection of human health'. This provision is not new. It was introduced by the Treaty of Amsterdam as Article 127(2) EC[39] and should be read

---

[37] See e.g. Vandermeersch, D., *De Mededingingswet,* Mechelen, Kluwer, 2007, pp. 20–23; and also Faull, J. and Nickpay, A., *The EC Law of Competition,* Oxford, Oxford University Press, 2nd edn, 2007, para. 2.59.

[38] The Belgian Competition Authority provided e.g. associations with written advice, to be compared with comfort letters, in respect of several fair trade labels or arrangements e.g. in the margin of the milk crisis of 2009. See *Annual Report 2009* of the Directorate General for Competition. Not all so-called fair trading rules can however be accepted. See e.g. on IFTRA rules the Commission decisions of 15 May 1974 (OJ (1974) L 160/1) and 15 July 1975 (OJ (1975) L 228/3).

[39] See for an earlier applicaton of this approach Case C-67/96, *Albany* [1999] ECR I-5751.

Contrary to what has been suggested, competition was never mentioned as a goal of the EU or EC in the Treaties. Article 3(g) EC referred to competition as an instrument for the realization of the goals defined in Article 2 EC: 'to promote throughout the Community a harmonious, balanced and sustainable development of economic activities, a high level of employment and of social protection, equality between men and women, sustainable and non-inflationary growth, a high degree of competitiveness and convergence of economic performance, a high level of protection and improvement of the quality of the environment, the raising of the standard of living and quality of life, and economic and social cohesion and solidarity among Member States'. Only the non-ratified constitutional treaty referred to competition as a goal of the Union (Article I-1 (3)). See further Steenbergen, J., 'Het Mededingingsbeleid en het Verdrag van Lissabon', *Sociaal-Economische Wetgeving,*

together with Article 3(3) TEU[40] and Protocol No. 27 on the internal market and competition.[41]

When we look at the provisions concerning the specific goals of related policies such as the economic and industrial policy, we see that the economic policy should be 'conducted in accordance with the principle of an open market economy with free competition'.[42] And the industrial policy should according to Article 170(2) TFEU ensure that the conditions necessary for the competitiveness of the Union's industry exist and be pursued 'in accordance with a system of open and competitive markets'.

The Treaties do not clearly define a hierarchy of objectives. 'Taking into account' does not imply that other policies aiming at the goals listed in Article 9 TFEU have priority over competition policy. Especially the provisions in respect of economic and industrial policy suggest rather that the promotion of open competition is at least the 'default' policy that is assumed to serve the above-mentioned goals. But now that the confidence in market mechanisms has been eroded by the financial crisis and the pressures of globalization, it is prudent to defend the legitimacy of competition policy by explaining carefully how competition policy contributes to the achievement of the overall objectives. The increased references to consumer welfare in competition policy documents are

---

2008, pp. 136–43; later also published in van Ooik, R.H. en Wessel, R.A. (eds), *De Europese Unie na het Verdrag van Lissabon,* Deventer, Kluwer, 2009, pp. 123–37. See on the evolvement of the thinking on the goals of competition policy also Ottervanger, T.R., 'Maatschappelijk Verantwoord Concurreren: Mededingingsrecht in een Veranderende Wereld', oratie Universiteit Leiden, 19 maart 2010.

[40] Article 3(3) TEU 'The Union shall establish an internal market. It shall work for the sustainable development of Europe based on balanced economic growth and price stability, a highly competitive social market economy, aiming at full employment and social progress, and a high level of protection and improvement of the quality of the environment. It shall promote scientific and technological advance. It shall combat social exclusion and discrimination, and shall promote social justice and protection, equality between women and men, solidarity between generations and protection of the rights of the child. It shall promote economic, social and territorial cohesion, and solidarity among Member States. It shall respect its rich cultural and linguistic diversity, and shall ensure that Europe's cultural heritage is safeguarded and enhanced.'

[41] Protocol 27 states as follows: 'Considering that the internal market as set out in Article 3 of the Treaty on European Union includes a system ensuring that competition is not distorted, (…). To this end, the Union shall, if necessary, take action under the provisions of the Treaties, including under Article 352 of the Treaty on the Functioning of the European Union.' The protocols are part of the treaties and form an integral part thereof (Article 51 TEU).

[42] Article 119 and also Article 120 TFEU.

certainly an important step in that direction,[43] but the concept of 'social welfare' might from this perspective be more convincing.

1.8 CONCLUSION

For as long as I have had the pleasure and privilege of knowing Jacques Bourgeois, he has focussed and helped others to focus on policies and legal instruments that try to respond to some of the key concerns of our societies. This is a never finished business. I am therefore not only most grateful for all what Jacques already contributed but also relieved that we continue to benefit of his contributions.

---

43 See e.g. 'DG Competition staff paper on the application of article 82 of the Treaty to exclusionary abuses', December 2005, DG Comp website. See further e.g. Bishop, S. and Walker, M., *The Economics of EC Competition Law,* London, Sweet & Maxwell, 2nd edn, 2002, pp. 23–7; Motta, M., *Competition Policy, Theory and Practice*, Cambridge, Cambridge University Press, 2004, pp. 18–22.It is somewhat surprising that these publications do not refer in respect of these concepts to Article 127(2) EC and a possible link with employment policies.

2. Towards a WTO business-enabling compact

Stefan D. Amarasinha and Simon J. Evenett*

2.1 GLOBAL COMPANIES – PAST FAILURES

According to the *World Investment Report 2009* developing countries were hosts to the parent corporations of 21,245 multinationals and to 425,258 affiliates of foreign multinationals.[1] Brazil, India, and China (BICs) have approximately 4,500 multinationals operating overseas, with the number of Chinese multinationals exceeding that of the United States by 50 per cent.[2] Even during the recent global economic crisis outward FDI from the BICs exceeded US$90 billion in 2008.[3] However, going back just a decade or two, the picture was of course a very different one, largely dominated by western multinationals.[4]

The BICs are increasingly taking a vocal role in speaking up for their multinationals in connection with regulatory hurdles and discriminatory practices faced abroad. Examples include Arcelor/Mittal,[5] CNOOC/UNOCAL, and more recently the Chinese company Huawei – partnering with Bain – having to abandon its proposed acquisition of the US company

* The views expressed in this text are those of the author(s) and should not be seen or interpreted as an official position of the European Commission.

1 The comparable totals for 'developed countries' were 58,783 and 366,681, respectively. See Annex Table A.1.8. of *World Investment Report 2009: Transnational Corporations, Agricultural Production and Development*.

2 Although in terms of market capitalization, most US multinationals are still much larger.

3 See Annex Table B.1 of *World Investment Report 2009: Transnational Corporations, Agricultural Production and Development*.

4 For an insightful take on the rising importance and activity of emerging country multinationals and 'state capitalists', see Bremmer, I., 'The end of the Free Market', United States, Portfolio, 2010.

5 Although listed in the Netherlands, India batted for the company when seeking to acquire rival firm Arcelor.

3Com. Needless to say, the difficulties developing and emerging country multinationals occasionally face are not only in developed countries, such as the EU and the United States, but also just as importantly in other developing and emerging economies. Consequently, the BICs (and their multinationals) are likely to have a growing interest in a rules-agenda focussing on the establishment of certain global standards of treatment of foreign companies and investors, especially in the area of mergers and acquisitions and FDI more broadly.[6]

Similarly, EU and US companies face difficulties in the context of mergers and acquisitions and inward FDI in the BICs and in other countries, as illustrated by the difficulties the Carlyle Group encountered in China with the need for multiple (and competing) agencies' authorization of their various investments in Chinese companies; UK's TCI being forced to withdraw plans for a greater stake in Japan's J-Power due to stated security concerns; and the 2009 blockage by the Chinese competition authorities of Coca-Cola's bid for the Huiyuan Juice company.[7]

There are multiple, legitimate reasons why companies choose to invest abroad, including through mergers and acquisitions. As put by one economist:[8]

> (...) complementary geographic coverage can be very important, especially in international mergers. It can be less expensive to expand into a new market by simply buying someone who is there, someone who knows what's going on on the ground rather than having to do those investments yourself.

In addition to that, proximity to raw materials and other sources of input, infrastructure and tariff-jumping are other strong incentives for investment, including through mergers and acquisitions.

The *World Investment Report 2008*, published by UNCTAD, includes additional evidence as to the importance of cross-border mergers and

---

6 Prominent emerging country multinationals include Petronas, Cemex, Petrobras, CITIC Group, Taiwan Semiconductors, Hyundai and Tata.

7 See http://money.cnn.com/news/newsfeeds/articles/djf500/200903180615 DOWJONESDJONLINE000428_FORTUNE5.htm. One commentator noted: 'The issue will likely give other countries an excuse to reject China's investments overseas. Though it seems that the decision can protect the domestic industry in the short term, for Chinese companies looking for overseas expansion, they may lose the best timing and prices to acquire assets.' The Chinese authorities have responded to criticism of the decision in the following manner: 'The Ministry of Commerce's decision to block the acquisition was neither affected by disturbing external factors and nor was it protectionism' and 'The decision in the case has nothing to do with China's policies about foreign capital.'

8 Testimony of Dr James A. Langenfeld before the International Competition Policy Advisory Committee delivered on 3 November 1998.

acquisitions. The report shows that 2007, despite the current financial crisis, broke the record of year 2000 in terms of the value of cross-border mergers and acquisitions. The Report also shows that while the majority of legislative changes adopted globally were aimed at encouraging inward FDI, there has also been a clear increase in measures with the opposite aim and effect.[9] Finally, the Report notes that for the estimated 79,000 multinationals the ones in the area of services are becoming increasingly important.

2.1.1 Global Companies – New Solutions?

All the above considerations suggest broader support than might otherwise have been expected for better standards of treatment to the benefit of developed and emerging economy multinationals alike. Such standards could be contained in a 'Business Enabling Compact' (BEC). The BEC would not initially aim at investment liberalization *per se*, but this could be added (be it immediately or later) on a voluntary opt-in basis. The BEC would be a flexible instrument and would allow for exclusions and exemptions to the agreed standards and disciplines. The WTO could be the appropriate forum for the negotiation and development of such standards, where exclusions and exemptions could be subject to a notification/transparency requirement somewhat similar to GATT Article X. Ideally, the core of the BEC containing the more fundamental principles such as non-discrimination, transparency and procedural guarantees would be subject to WTO dispute settlement.

The remainder of this chapter is organized as follows. Section 2.2 below will address how a new approach to certain aspects of competition and inward FDI could be formulated, and proposes four categories of binding and non-binding elements of a so-called critical mass BEC. Section 2.3 will address how critical mass could be defined as regards these four categories and how best to organize and conduct the negotiations on the BEC. Sections 2.4 and 2.5 address the MFN issue and the free rider problem, as well as other relevant considerations.

2.2 WHAT NOW, AND HOW?

Needless to say, before launching any negotiations on investment and competition, one needs to be mindful of the lessons offered by the defunct

---

9 UNCTAD World Investment Report 2008 (Overview), p. 7.

OECD negotiations on the Multilateral Agreement on Investment, as well as the Singapore Issues of competition and investment that were eventually jettisoned from the DDA.

Rather than attempting to resurrect 'investment' and 'competition' as the issues were addressed as Singapore Issues (including in their separate and distinct WTO Working Groups), a BEC would take a rather different starting point: the BEC could start by establishing certain 'fundamental principles' such as non-discrimination, transparency and due process as they would apply in the context of mergers and acquisitions and inward FDI more broadly. The BEC approach recognizes the fact that the former are a significant – and in many years, the largest – component of the latter.

While many jurisdictions would claim to adhere to and provide for such fundamental principles (claims that may well be true in the vast majority of cases), locking them firmly into the core of the BEC would serve at least three important purposes:

- it would represent a binding, legally enforceable agreement between all BEC participants;
- it would make political interference in investment and competition matters more difficult;
- it could set the standard for non-BEC countries to follow.

While such principles would not necessarily guarantee companies the desired outcome in each and every competition law enforcement and investment policy matter, binding commitments regarding non-discrimination (including national treatment) and permitting reviews of administrative decisions would be constitute a major step forward. These principles would not – and should not – require complete harmonization of domestic competition and investment regimes, as all jurisdictions have different legal traditions and approaches. What matters is that the accepted principles would lay down rules from which only limited deviations would be allowed.

Moreover, borrowing from the established precedent of the WTO's Agreement on Government Procurement, and for that matter many provisions on government procurement in free trade agreements, the review of administrative decisions could be conducted by a domestic body that adhered to certain accepted legal standards. Again, what matters is not institutional uniformity but adherence to core principles. No accusations of 'one size fits all' could then be levelled at the BEC, if that accusation is meant to imply harmonization towards any one model, including the model of any proponent of the BEC.

By identifying such a core as the starting point, including through direct contacts with business and industry in all relevant countries, one would also avoid the false logic dogging the Singapore Issues where the EU was persistently seen as the main '*demandeur*' (i.e. the one somehow having to pay), and where business support gradually faded as ambitions were dampened.

Moreover, the very scale of cross-border business would ensure that enough WTO members had enough at stake ('skin in the game') as to be self-balancing. In principle, proposals for a BEC could be advanced independently of others at the WTO (including the DDA itself), avoiding any draw backs from issue-linkage. Or put differently: the negotiations would be about the BEC and only the BEC.

The above approach would ensure that the core is a shared priority desirable to all relevant WTO members (and their multinationals) and could further ensure that it would include no more elements than the 'traffic could bear' at that particular point in time. Indeed, it is possible to conceive of a BEC evolving over time or members within the BEC evolving at different speeds (so-called 'flexible geometry'). The trend towards the ever-greater globalization of business will reinforce the constituencies calling for greater ambition over time. The critical mass format, if properly implemented, allows for this will to manifest itself in a self-reinforcing upward spiral of multilateral trade disciplines.

2.2.1 The Core Elements of the BEC

With mergers and acquisitions as the initial focal point, one could envisage a BEC that would place – at its very core – 'fundamental principles' of common and shared interest to the BICs, the EU, the US and other main players such as Australia, Canada, Egypt, Indonesia, Japan, Malaysia and South Africa.[10]

It should also be noted that for mergers and acquisitions (as well as other competition issues) there are existing non-binding instruments from both the ICN[11] and the OECD[12] that could be adapted and locked into a BEC,

---

[10] Note that in the run-up to the 2003 WTO ministerial, the Confederation of Indian Industry (CII), along with its Dutch and German counterparts, issued a statement endorsing WTO negotiations on both investment and competition. That prompted a strong rebuke from the Indian government causing the CII to disown itself from the statement. See http://www.dailyexcelsior.com/web1/03sep13/busi.htm#3.

[11] For the multitude of ICBN Guidelines and Best Practices documents, see http://www.internationalcompetitionnetwork.org/index.php/en/library/doc-type/1.

just as one could look to BITs, the Energy Charter Treaty, and the MAI draft text for investment treatment standards and other elements of common interest. Such precedents could provide important inspiration for the development of a BEC. Indeed, the very fact that so many existing free trade agreements and BITs include provisions on core principles similar to those advocated here grounds proposals for BEC in contemporary reality, and not as the pipe dream of certain analysts with too much spare time on their hands.

2.2.2 'BEC Plus'

2.2.2.1 Additional substantive disciplines directly related to the core

With the 'fundamental principles' discussed above constituting the binding core of a BEC, one could then envisage further binding as well as non-binding elements to be added onto the core. Such disciplines would constitute 'BEC plus' commitments.

The BEC plus commitments could either be added to the core of the BEC up-front or at a later stage as voluntary opt-ins. For such BEC plus commitments one could envision e.g. additional rules relating to the competition area (including definitions and disciplines on certain types of subsidies not currently within the scope of the SCM Agreement), hard-core cartels, and investment (e.g. definitions of 'investor' and 'investment', commitments regarding inward FDI in specified sectors and protection against expropriation). BEC plus commitments could also include abuse of dominance, as well as state-owned and state-trading enterprises adding further to the limited disciplines of GATT Article XVII.

2.2.2.2 Regulatory and agency discretion

An additional area for possible BEC plus commitments is where relevant national agencies enjoy wide discretion, e.g. as regards 'national security' and other exceptions (e.g. the US CFIUS process and other investment screening mechanisms). For example, the implicit recognition that national telecommunications infrastructures are now part of the national security apparatus in an era of cyber terrorism and warfare has, during 2010, been at the centre of disputes between governments.

While such discretion is necessary and justified, it does hold the potential for discriminatory abuse, especially where the relevant standards are so

---

[12] The non-binding OECD National Treatment Instrument is one example and has already been referred to by arbitral panels in international investment disputes. See http://www.oecd.org/document/48/0,3343,en_2649_34887_1932976_1_1_1_1,00.html.

vague and elastic that they can mean just about anything in any given context. Similarly, vague and elastic standards may also inadvertently 'invite' interference from the political establishment as was seen in the Dubai Ports case in the United States.[13] Needless to say, one would need to be mindful of any unwarranted restrictions and on the ability to react and respond to unforeseen circumstances like the current financial crisis. Balancing competing and legitimate influences on government policymaking while discouraging illegitimate factors is something that the WTO has plenty of experience with (see, for example, the SPS and TBT agreements). Such ingenuity needs to be applied to investment and competition policy as a matter of urgency.[14]

A BEC could articulate certain 'guiding principles' for the exercise of such discretion, and could also make the relevant rules subject to general transparency obligations as well as due process guarantees to provide foreign companies with a better understanding of the likely exercise of the discretion and application of the exceptions, and to limit the risk of abuse of such discretion and exceptions.

2.2.2.3 Multinationals and their conduct abroad

The BEC could 'balance' its obligations on governments with those on multinational corporations. Certain core environmental, human rights and labour standards, as well as anti-bribery instruments could form part of a BEC-plus. Such minimum standards would not only help prevent a 'race to the bottom' among host countries that otherwise might engage in a lowering of environmental and labour standards in order to attract foreign investment, but also signal clearly to the public that the BEC is not a one-way street benefiting only multinationals and their shareholders.

It is worth noting that international law already reflects a clear trend towards greater recognition of the responsibility of non-state actors in the area of human rights,[15] and where states are willing to confer rights and

---

13 http://www.economist.com/node/6891387.

14 As regards legislation that is broad and subject to interpretation and gap-filling by agencies and courts such as the US Sherman Act and the relevant provisions of the EC Treaty, BEC participants should be obliged to make all implementing legislation, guidelines and decisions of general application publicly available.

15 See e.g. the 'Interim report of the Special Representative of the Secretary-General on the issue of human rights and transnational corporations and other business enterprises to the United Nations Economic and Social Council', E/CN.4/2006/97 of 22 February 2006 (hereinafter referred to as the Ruggie Report). The Special Representative, John Ruggie acknowledges (para. 61) that '[u]nder customary international law, emerging practice and expert opinion increasingly do

benefits on companies under international law, a logical corollary of that would be certain obligations and corporate responsibility.

Already at present, OECD instruments like the Guidelines for Multinationals and the Anti-Bribery Convention are directly aimed at regulating the conduct of multinationals abroad. The same goes for the US Foreign Corrupt Practices Act (FCPA). Although the OECD Convention requires implementation at domestic level, the ultimate addressees of the obligations under the Convention are multinationals, rather than states. The Model International Investment Agreement for Sustainable Development (IIADS) also contains an entire section on Foreign Investor Obligations and Duties and further inspiration may be found there.[16] One might also envision specific transparency obligations for sovereign wealth funds and other non-private entities or entities enjoying special relations with their national governments, according to which they would make the origin of their funding as well their overall investment objectives known.

Industries that are often singled out for particular criticism tend to be labour intensive ones, such as textiles and apparel, as well as the extractive industry.[17] Specifically for the extractive industry, this sector may warrant emphasis on further obligations upon multinationals, such as those correlated to the rights of indigenous peoples, the rights to food and health given the possible environmental impact of an investment, and a range of civil rights, e.g. the right to security of the person, given the occasional involvement of private military companies acting on their behalf in the protection of their investment.

If elements relating to environment, labour, and certain human rights were added as BEC plus elements, that could help address the frequent NGO criticism that investment rules tend to be all about one-sided protection of and benefits for multinationals. This might in turn allow NGOs to apply pressure on WTO members not adhering to the disciplines. The

---

suggest that corporations may be held liable for committing, or for complicity in, the most heinous human rights violations amounting to international crimes, including genocide, slavery, human trafficking, forced labour, torture and some crimes against humanity'.

16 See also De Schutter, O., 'Transnational Corporations as Instruments of Human Development' in Alston, P. and Robinson, M. (eds), *Human Rights and Development – Towards Multilateral Reinforcement*, Oxford, Oxford University Press, 2005, p. 403, as well as Salomon, M.E., 'Global Responsibility for Human Rights', Oxford, Oxford University Press, in particular p. 160 *et seq*.

17 For EU companies operating outside the EU, see study prepared for the European Union by the University of Edinburgh, available at http://ec.europa.eu/enterprise/policies/sustainable-business/files/business-human-rights/101025_ec_study_final_report_en.pdf.

elements would be upon the multinationals themselves, rather than the host countries that may not have the adequate capacity to monitor and discipline the behaviour of the multinationals. Monitoring and disciplining could be a joint responsibility shared by the host country and the country of domicile of the multinational, thereby also reducing the risk of the host country being overly vigilant, and the country of domicile being too complacent.

In addition, for companies that are already subject to CSR, OECD, and other instruments, by being subject to BEC plus disciplines such companies may become more competitive as an increasing middle-class (including in the BICs) may be expected to make more ethical and informed choices regarding the goods and services they consume and the corporate behaviour of the producers and service suppliers.

2.2.2.4 Critical mass

Critical mass for the core of a BEC could be objectively defined on the basis of a certain percentage of FDI flows, companies operating overseas, or the number of mergers and acquisitions for each member involving a foreign company. With countries such as the ones listed above one would be able reach such critical mass provided the elements for the core of the BEC are properly identified and defined in collaboration with industry in all relevant countries.

As regards the core of the BEC, the elements are not likely to be novel to the WTO members in question as most – if not all – currently provide for non-discriminatory treatment, procedural guarantees, and transparency in some shape or form. What would be new would be the actual binding of such elements, but as they have already been signed up to by most of the key countries in the context of recent FTAs, locking in such elements by way of the BEC would come at a minimal cost.

Critical mass would likely be less of an issue for the various 'BEC plus' disciplines as these would be on an opt-in basis (either at the conclusion of the initial negotiations or later) and would be additional elements absent which the core of the BEC could still operate and provide important benefits on its own. Still, difficulties may arise should one group of WTO members seek to go further than others; in particular since the DDA appears to have set the precedent that the latter must be 'paid off' to allow negotiations amongst others to proceed.

As already noted, with proper identification of the critical mass of WTO members and the issues of common and shared interest to form the core of a BEC, the launch of negotiations and later institutional anchoring of a critical mass agreement in the WTO should be less burdensome (while by no means an absolute certainty).

In order to avoid a situation where some WTO members might criticize the negotiating process for being non-inclusive and the outcome predetermined, it might be advisable to devise a formula whereby all interested WTO members could participate in the negotiations and make their views known regarding the likely BEC core as well as the BEC plus elements. That said, however, it would seem equally advisable to have an agreed cut-off point by which members must indicate whether they are 'in or out'. With the likely smaller circle resulting from such a cut-off mechanism, the level of ambition could eventually be adjusted further upwards, just as more elements could be made binding as part of the BEC core (without setting the bar so high as to deter future participants from signing up).

Following the conclusion of the agreement, and any necessary institutional and budgetary arrangements in support thereof, the agreement should be open to participation by all WTO members willing and able to meet the BEC core standards (and, ideally, some of the BEC plus elements).

2.2.2.5 MFN and free-rider implications

MFN-treatment could be extended to non-participants, at least as regards the core of the BEC, also as WTO members are not likely to want to apply different treatment standards, transparency policies and due process guarantees to different groups of WTO members.

However, as regards BEC plus commitments such as the scheduling of access for FDI and the like, these are elements that could be retained for the actual participants, rather than the full WTO membership, also to ensure a certain degree of symmetry in terms of market access commitments.

2.2.2.6 Other pertinent considerations

As will be clear from the above discussion of the elements and aim of the BEC, agencies such as competition authorities and inter-agency configurations such as CFIUS will be affected. That would suggest not only their involvement during the actual negotiations, but also adequate consultation beforehand.

While some competition authorities had misgivings about the previous attempt to include competition in the WTO as one of the four Singapore Issues (the main argument being that trade officials supposedly did not understand the finer points and purity of competition law and policy and that competition policy would be readily traded away in a mercantilist bazaar), the BECs suggested inclusion of standards and best practices as also developed by competition authorities themselves in the OECD and the ICN, would make it infinitely more difficult for them to make that argument anew. Likewise, certain competition authorities' argument that competition law and policy operates in a perfect vacuum free from political interference has been weakened significantly by the relaxation of the applicable rules as a result of the global financial crisis.

Table 2.1: Elements of a Business Enabling Compact

Nature of instrument	**Obligation**	**Application of WTO DS mechanism?**
Critical mass Binding core elements	Transparency and notification, procedural guarantees, and non-discrimination (subject to qualifications and exceptions – see below)	Yes, but not to individual decisions of relevant agencies
BEC plus Optional elements related to the binding core elements for which Members would opt in	Specific scheduling of access for FDI/new entrants, definition of investment and investor, and possible substantive obligations, e.g. on hard-core cartels and subsidies (beyond the SCM Agreement disciplines).	Ideally yes. Alternatively mediation mechanism and/or peer review mechanism
BEC plus Guidelines on exercise of discretion in areas such as 'national security' and other exceptions, coupled with general transparency and due process obligations (see above)	Guidelines and binding obligations	Peer review and possible mediation mechanism as regards the areas of exercise of discretion WTO dispute settlement as regards the *binding* obligations

Nature of instrument	Obligation	Application of WTO DS mechanism?
BEC plus Standards relating to the conduct abroad of multinationals	Core labour standards, basic human rights, anti-bribery instruments, polluter-pays-principle, and transparency on investment strategies of SWFs	Such obligations would relate directly to the conduct of companies, rather than governments and application of government-to-government WTO DS may not be appropriate. Peer review – and a possible mediation mechanism – could be applied. Also, one might consider some application of WTO DS if a WTO Member (be it the host country or the country of domicile) turns a blind eye to repeated violations of these provisions by its companies abroad.

PART II

Trade

Rules and rulemaking

3. Challenges in international monetary law

Thomas Cottier and Tetyana Payosova

3.1 INTRODUCTION

Jacques Bourgeois – as an EC Commission official and a practicing lawyer – has been accustomed all his professional life to dealing with current affairs and burning issues. At the same time – as an academic and a distinguished scholar and professor – he has had a keen interest in the long-term issues of the multilateral trading system and the European Union's role in it. He has always approached these issues with inspiring enthusiasm, enjoying the intricacies of a particular problem. It is therefore an appropriate homage to him, as a friend and colleague, to address a difficult challenge and issue that is both timely and long-term: the relationship between monetary and exchange rate policies currently being debated,[1] and the potential role of the World Trade Organization (WTO) in addressing the subsidizing impact of undervalued currencies within the Agreement on Subsidies and Countervailing Duties. The chapter briefly expounds the current role of the International Monetary Fund (IMF) in monetary affairs and points out existing shortcomings. They run the risk of imposing burdens upon the WTO for which the Organization is not designed. The rule-based system may attract disputes of a magnitude and impact that would need to be addressed within a multilateral monetary system. The chapter makes a number of proposals as to how the IMF should be reformed, learning from the experiences of the rule-based trading system. While litigation on exchange rates policies may be beyond the law, properly speaking, mechanisms of organized fact-finding, monitoring and obligations to consult may comprise important steps towards a greater role of law in this field in securing stable and peaceful international

[1] 'IMF Takes Up Arms in Exchange Rate Battle', *Financial Times*, 6 October 2010.

relations. We are confident that Jacques Bourgeois with his belief in the power of law will appreciate this endeavour by which we seek to pay him tribute for all his efforts in strengthening the rule of law in European and international law.

3.2 SETTING THE STAGE – INTERNATIONAL MONETARY LAW AND NATIONAL MONETARY POLICIES

The essential purpose of the international monetary system is to facilitate the exchange of goods, services and capital between countries.[2] It plays a crucial supporting role in the trading system and the real economy. The IMF is supposed to oversee the international monetary system. It provides technical assistance and loans, usually subject to conditionality requirements, to enable countries to meet their international payments, and should support, through its policies, adjustment to trade liberalization.[3] While giving loans is mostly in the hands of the IMF and depends on payments made by each country to the Fund, monitoring of the international and national system still has quite a recommendatory character and the organization itself does not have any real powers to influence, for example, countries' exchange rate policies. During the age of the gold standard and of the par value system countries' currencies were pegged to gold or later to the dollar, which itself had a fixed gold value.[4] Since the United States left the gold standard in 1971, industrialized countries have preferred to manage currency relations outside the IMF within informal clubs and groupings, and the organizations essentially focused, on a par with the World Bank, on supporting and disciplining developing countries that have found themselves in monetary and balance of payments difficulties. The de facto abandonment of the par value regime and the shift from the fixed to a floating exchange rate led to the need for the Second Amendment of the IMF Articles of Agreement (AoA). As of 1 April 1978, states were

---

[2] IMF, *Factsheet, IMF surveillance*, 28 September 2010, to be found at: www.imf.org/external/np/exr/facts/surv.htm (accessed on 5 October 2010).

[3] *The Ministerial Declaration on the Contribution of the WTO to Achieving Greater Coherence in Global Economic Policymaking*, to be found at: www.wto.org/english/docs_e/legal_e/32-dcohr.pdf (accessed on 5 October 2010).

[4] Lastra, R.M., *Legal Foundations of International Monetary Stability*, Oxford, Oxford University Press, 2006, p. 356; Lowenfeld, A.F., 'The International Monetary System: A Look Back over Seven Decades', *Journal of International Economic Law*, Vol. 13, No. 3, 2010, pp. 575–95.

basically granted freedom to choose exchange arrangements. Thus, members could determine the external value of the currency themselves. The new Article IV, section 2(b) provided that:

> ... exchange arrangements may include (i) the maintenance by a member of a value for its currency in terms of the special drawing right or another denominator, other than gold, selected by the member or (ii) cooperative arrangements by which members maintain the value of their currencies in relation to the value of the currency of other members or (iii) other exchange arrangements of a member's choice.

Thus, the Fund has basically lost its right to determine exchange rate policies.[5] The current system of exchange rates is marked by freedom to choose policies – floating or pegged, unlike before 1973 when all currencies were pegged first to gold and then through the US dollar to gold. The members are sovereign and can choose any type of exchange rate – they may leave it up to the market forces (flexible rates, floating currencies) or control it through national legislation (pegged currencies). In both cases exchange rates are unstable and are subject to fluctuations, which are, however, influenced by the market or by government intervention.[6]

Under such conditions, the IMF's lack of effective enforcement powers is becoming a more pressing problem, especially in situations where countries organize their internal monetary policies in a way that affects other countries in what amounts to a zero sum game and beggar-your-neighbour policies uncontained under current monetary law. Especially after the shift from the fixed to a floating exchange rate, such practices and incidences became more frequent. Following the crises of 2007–09 many countries have taken recourse to currency policies to improve the situation – among them Japan, Ukraine, Switzerland and China.[7] The current situation with Chinese currency has led to a wide discussion on the international level, foremost in the United States,[8] but also in Europe. At first, the Chinese currency (renminbi) RMB was pegged to the US dollar, and since 2005 – to a group of major currencies, which in turn has caused the appreciation of

---

5 *Idem*, p. 365.

6 *Idem*, p. 367.

7 'Países promovem "guerra de moedas" ', *Economía & Negocios*, to be found at: http://economia.estadao.com.br/noticias/economia,paises-promovem-guerra-de-moedas,35806,0.htm (accessed on 5 October 2010).

8 Morrison, W.M., and Labonte M., 'China's Currency: Economic Issues and Options for U.S. Trade Policy', in L.C. Hilbert, *Currency Interventions, Fluctuations and Economic Issues*, New York, Nova Science Publishers, 2007, pp. 1–49.

RMB against the US dollar. Notwithstanding these changes, the Chinese currency is still considered to be undervalued.[9]

However, neither the current situation with the Chinese RMB, nor with currency policies of other countries, is new. The problem has existed for a long time. In the 1930s and later in 1971, the United States, facing balance of payment problems and a trade deficit, not only made efforts to devaluate its currency, but also applied import surcharge tariffs as a retaliatory measure against other countries. The hallmark Smoot-Hawley Tariff Act of 1930 resulted in the adoption of comparable legislation in other countries, which led ultimately to trade wars. In 1982 the Swedish krona was devalued by 16 per cent and basically there was no formal decision or sanctions by the IMF.[10] In the early 1990s US authorities lowered US dollar interest rates several times.[11]

Today, the possibility of retaliatory measures is again being discussed in relation to the Chinese currency, and legislation to this effect has been introduced to Congress.[12] However, the current situation is different in many respects. With the advent of the WTO and binding dispute settlement, retaliatory measures (like surcharge import tariffs) have clear legal implications and thus will raise concerns and possibly disputes. While nations are sovereign in terms of monetary policy, members of the WTO are legally embedded in a multilateral rule-based system that limits their room for manoeuvre, reflecting experience in the past century that such measures do not tend to be efficient and can lead to trade wars rather than facilitating trade and to even deeper imbalances in the monetary system.

The active intervention in foreign exchange markets has caused and is still causing concern to all other countries, since such policies can (but do not necessarily) influence exports (which become cheaper) and imports (which become more expensive) and thus distort international trade.[13]

Such close interlinkages between international monetary policies and international trade are also partly reflected in the international trade

---

[9] Staiger, R.W. and Sykes, A.O., ' "Currency Manipulation" and World Trade', Working Paper 14600, National Bureau of Economic Research, 2008. To be found at: www.nber.org/papers/w14600, p. 2.

[10] Lastra, *supra*, p. 366; Lowenfeld, A.F., *International Economic Law*, Oxford, Oxford University Press, 2nd edn, 2008, pp. 635–6.

[11] Lowenfeld, *supra*, p. 637.

[12] See e.g. Evenett, S.J., 'Is the 1971 'import surcharge' a useful precedent?', in S. Evenett (ed.), *The US-Sino Currency Dispute: New Insights from Economics, Politics and Law*, Center for Economic Policy Research, April 2010, to be found at: www.voxeu.org/reports/currency_dispute.pdf (accessed 5 October 2010).

[13] See Zimmermann, C.D., *Currency Manipulation and the Paralysis of the Law*, to be found at: http://ssrn.com/abstract=1300542 (accessed 5 October 2010).

agreements. Thus, the balance of payments is addressed by Articles XII and XVIII:B of the General Agreement on Tariffs and Trade (GATT) and Article XII General Agreement on Trade in Services (GATS).[14] WTO members are allowed to restrict the quantity or value of imported merchandise in order to safeguard their external financial position. Article XV GATT addresses exchange arrangements and basically instructs countries to deal with all issues related to monetary reserves, balances of payments and foreign exchange arrangements through consultation with the IMF.[15] The WTO thus recognizes the IMF to be the appropriate institution to deal with these issues. It essentially relies upon the Fund's procedural arrangements for surveillance.

3.3 THE FUND'S SURVEILLANCE

The Fund's activity related to overseeing the international monetary system and monitoring the economic and financial policies of the member states is known as surveillance. The core question concerns the provisions of Article IV(1)(iii) of the IMF AoA. These provisions state that it is the general obligation of the members to avoid manipulating exchange rates or the international monetary system in order to prevent effective balance of payments adjustment or to gain an unfair competitive advantage over other members. However, the level of control powers granted to the IMF in the area of bilateral surveillance related to evaluation of and advice on national policies is minimal. The countries are obliged to comply with the

---

[14] See more on balance of payments (BoP) related trade measures under WTO law in Horlick G. and Dubeck, M.E., 'Balance of Payments Measures Understanding on the Balance-of-Payments Provisions of the General Agreement on Tariffs and Trade 1994' in R. Wolfrum, P.-T. Stoll and M. Koebele (eds), *WTO-Trade Remedies*, Leiden, Brill, 2008, pp. 941–9; Lal Das, B., *The WTO Agreements: Deficiencies, Imbalances and Required Changes*, New York, Zed Books, 1998, pp. 33–8; Macrory, P.F.J., Appleton, A.E., Plummer M.G. (eds), *The World Trade Organization: Legal, Economic and Political Analysis*, Vol. I, Berlin/Heidelberg/New York, Springer, 2005, p. 131 *et seq.*; Ahn, D., 'Linkages between International Financial and Trade Institutions: IMF, World Bank and WTO', *Journal of World Trade*, Vol. 34, No. 4, 2000, pp. 1–35.

[15] See e.g. Mitchell, A.D. and Sheargold, E., 'GATT Art. XV: Exchange Arrangements', in R. Wolfrum, P.-T. Stoll (eds), *Max Planck Commentaries on World Trade Law*, Leiden, Brill, 2009; Siegel, D.E., 'Legal Aspects of the IMF/WTO Relationship: The Fund's Articles of Agreement and the WTO Agreements', *American Journal of International Law*, Vol. 96, 2002, p. 561; see also Zimmermann, *supra*, p. 29 *et seq.*; Miranda, J., 'Currency undervaluation as a violation of GATT Article XV(4)', in Evenett, *supra*, p. 115 *et seq.*

IMF request to supply information and to enter into consultations concerning their exchange policies, but no more.[16] Even for the obligation to inform there are some limitations. For example, a member does not have to provide information 'in such detail that the affairs of individuals or corporations are disclosed'.[17] Thus, in practice, even if the country violates Article IV(3) of the IMF AoA there are no complaint procedures available for members comparable to those in the WTO system or any sanctions for such non-compliance. Lowenfeld mentions that in the early 1990s when the US authorities several times lowered US dollar interest rates, the only thing the IMF did (and which was made public) – was to criticize US exchange rate policies in its Annual Report.[18]

For the purpose of clarification of Article IV IMF AoA on Surveillance, the executive directors of the IMF adopted a Decision on Surveillance of 29 April 1977.[19] This Decision contains an illustrative list of state policies, which may indicate inconsistencies with Article IV. The overarching principle of the surveillance is that the IMF 'shall respect domestic social and political policies of members, and in applying these principles the Fund shall pay due regard to the circumstances of members'. Therefore, in the end it is up to the members to decide how they want to arrange their currency policies. As noted by Lastra, provisions of Article IV IMF AoA dealing with members' obligations as to their exchange rate are 'rather generic in their formulation'.[20] Even Article IV(1)(iii) prescribing that countries shall avoid exchange rate manipulation does not provide for an enforcement mechanism, giving countries complete freedom and depending on their good faith.

In 2007 the IMF, in its policy decision on surveillance, decided that 'a Member should avoid exchange rate policies *that result in external instability*' (italics added).[21] Furthermore this decision clarified what is meant by Article IV section 1 (iii) – behaviour inconsistent with this provision consists in 'moving or preventing from moving of exchange rate for the purpose of securing fundamental exchange rate misalignment in the form

---

[16] Article IV(3) of the IMF AoA.

[17] See IMF, *Strengthening the Effectiveness of Article VIII, Section 5* (Decision No. 13183-(04/10), adopted 30 January 2004, as amended).

[18] Lowenfeld, *supra*, p. 637.

[19] IMF, *Factsheet, supra*.

[20] Lastra, *supra*, p. 365. The IMF, on the contrary, defines the rules envisaged in Article IV(1)(iii) as being of 'hard nature' – see IMF, *The Fund's Mandate – The Legal Framework*, 22 February 2010, to be found at: www.imf.org/external/np/pp/eng/2010/022210.pdf (accessed on 5 October 2010), p. 6.

[21] IMF, *Decision on Bilateral Surveillance*, 2007, to be found at: www.imf.org/external/np/sec/pn/2007/pn0769.htm (accessed on 5 October 2010).

of an undervalued exchange rate to increase net exports'. Thus, such policies are ultimately targeted at increasing exports. However, in practice it seems to be difficult to demonstrate a violation of Article IV. The only mechanism available for fact-finding is the consultation procedure. Members are obliged to provide all the necessary information to the Fund in the course of regular annual consultation procedures, which are finalized and summarized in the conclusions of the IMF Executive Board within 65 days after the termination of discussions. If needed, there is also a possibility to conduct ad hoc and special consultations. So far there have been more than forty thousand consultations on bilateral surveillance according to Article IV since it was ratified; however, none of them resulted in a conclusion by the Executive Board that a country had not complied with the abovementioned provisions.[22]

Notwithstanding all these procedures the IMF does not have a mandate to compel a country to change its exchange rate policies. Through discussions and consultations it may try to influence the situation. But it has no enforcement powers. Even though the Third Amendment of the IMF as of 1992 provided for the possibility to suspend voting and other related rights of the members for their non-compliance with the AoA, this sanction has never been used. It seems that the efficiency of the IMF's influence on the national exchange rate policies depends largely on the political and economic strength of the country. It is without powers to address difficulties caused by major powers which, moreover, control the Fund. The IMF therefore is not in a position to offer a sound solution at this time.

After the current controversy over the Chinese currency emerged, it was suggested by some countries that a solution should be sought and found outside the IMF system – namely within the framework of the WTO. The WTO offers not only the material provisions, but also the procedural provisions for dispute settlement and enforcement if members violate their obligations under the WTO law. In contrast to the IMF, the WTO aims at reducing, and possibly eliminating, trade barriers and efficiently increasing trade flows. However, only trade measures related to balance-of-payments difficulties are explicitly mentioned in the WTO Agreements. It is thus not clear whether other types of currency-related disputes fall under WTO jurisdiction.

---

[22] Mussa, M., 'IMF Surveillance over China's Exchange Rate Policy', Peterson Institute of Economics, 19 October 2007, to be found at: http://www.iie.com/publications/papers/mussa1007.pdf (accessed 5 October 2010).

3.4 CURRENCY EXCHANGE RATE POLICIES IN WTO LAW

According to the IMF Decision of 2007, currency manipulation for gaining a competitive advantage over other members occurs only if the member in question is undervaluing the exchange rate of its currency *and* is doing so for the purpose of increasing net exports. Therefore, there is a direct link to the export performance of the country. Measures related to increasing exports are also addressed within the WTO framework – namely as export subsidies.

The WTO Agreement on Subsidies and Countervailing Measures provides in Article 1.1 that there is a subsidy, if there is a 'financial contribution by a government or a public body' or 'income or price support' and it confers a *benefit* – either to a recipient directly or to a beneficiary (as in the case of upstream or downstream subsidies).[23] Paragraph (a)(1) of the provision continues with an enumeration of the possible forms of the financial contribution – i.e. direct transfer of funds, government revenue otherwise due which is foregone or not collected, provision of goods and services by the government at conditions that are better than market ones, or any of those mentioned above performed by a private body entrusted to do so by a government.

Exchange rate policies most probably cannot fall under the definition of a financial contribution since they do not correspond to any of the forms listed in paragraph (a)(1) of Article 1.1 SCM Agreement. However, taking into consideration the effects of currency manipulations, especially currency undervaluation, it can be presumed that there may be some kind of price support since producers can export their goods at lower prices due to an undervalued currency exchange rate. The issue is not yet settled. Firstly, it is not clear from Article 1.1(a)(2) of the SCM Agreement itself whether 'income or price support' includes such a broad spectrum of measures. Rubini, analysing the scope of 'income and price support', explains that while in the early cases it was interpreted rather narrowly,[24] the textual

---

[23] Article 1 SCM Agreement. See Clarke, P.A. and Horlick, G.N., 'The Agreement on Subsidies and Countervailing Measures', in Macrory, Appleton, Plummer, *supra*, p. 679 *et seq*., Cottier, T. and Oesch, M., *International Trade Regulation. Law and Policy in the WTO, the European Union and Switzerland. Cases, Materials and Comments*, Staempfli/Cameron May, Bern/London, 2005, p. 990 *et seq*., Adamantopoulos, K., 'Article 1 SCMA', in Wolfrum, Stoll, Koebele, *supra*, p. 423 *et seq*.

[24] See Panel Report, *US-Exports Restraints*, para. 8.38, where it was concluded that price support through imposition of high import tariffs does not fall within the scope of Article 1 SCM.

interpretation and recent case law support 'a more expansive reading' of this provision.[25] Therefore, in principle, certain exchange rate policies, as complex regulatory measures, may fall within the scope of Article 1 SCM Agreement. Secondly, the concept of 'benefit' is not developed in the SCM Agreement. According to the Appellate Body Report, it means that the financial contribution makes a recipient or a beneficiary 'better off' than otherwise would have been possible.[26]

The SCM Agreement distinguishes two main categories of subsidies – prohibited and actionable. The former include the export contingent subsidies[27] and local content subsidies (import subsidies). The category of actionable subsidies is very broad and encompasses all other subsidies, which can be qualified as such under the SCM Agreement. Apart from the two criteria mentioned above, there is a specificity requirement to be met – meaning that subsidies are specific if they are limited to certain enterprises or to a certain region. However, according to Article 2.3 of the SCM Agreement, export and import subsidies are considered specific *per se* and, therefore, the third step in the 'subsidy-test' under the SCM Agreement can be omitted.

As was mentioned above, the first category of prohibited subsidies has to be contingent on exports. The de facto export contingency can be proved if a subsidy is tied to actual or anticipated exports or export earnings.[28] The Appellate Body in *Canada-Civil Aircraft I* noted that the anticipation of the resulting exports by a government granting the subsidy is not enough but shall be *contingent* upon export performance.[29] Further, in *EC-Aircraft* the panel specified that contingency means that the subsidy 'must be conditional or dependent upon actual or anticipated export performance; or …, a subsidy must be granted *because of* actual or anticipated export performance' and repeated that the 'mere anticipation of export performance on the part of a granting authority … is not enough' to show such contingency.[30] Thus, further study is required to determine whether currency

---

[25] Rubini, L., *The Definition of Subsidy and State Aid*, Oxford, Oxford University Press, 2009, pp. 123–5.

[26] Appellate Body Report, *Canada–Civil Aircraft I*, para. 157.

[27] See also special rules for developing countries in Annex VII SCM Agreement. See also on export subsidies Green, A., Trebilcock, M., Milat, V., 'The Enduring Problem of WTO Export Subsidies Rules', *American Law and Economics Association Annual Meetings*, Paper 9, 2007.

[28] Clarke, P.A. and Horlick, G.N., 'The Agreement on Subsidies and Countervailing Measures', in Macrory, Appleton, Plummer, *supra*, p. 696; Art. 3.1(a), n. 4 SCM Agreement.

[29] Appellate Body Report, *Canada-Civil Aircraft I*, para. 171.

[30] Panel Report, *EC-Aircraft*, para. 7.648.

manipulation can be qualified under the SCM provisions as being contingent on actual or anticipated export performance.

As a remedy against export subsidies any member can initiate negotiations under Article 4 of the SCM Agreement and if no agreement is reached within 30 days can refer the case to the Dispute Settlement Body. The duration of the whole dispute settlement procedure can amount to three years and therefore this may be not a suitable solution for disputes related to currency manipulation. The second avenue open to the affected WTO members is to impose countervailing duties in order to offset the negative impacts of such subsidization, pursuant to an investigation procedure and specific rules according to Part V of the SCM Agreement.[31]

Recourse to WTO law and possibly countervailing duties therefore entails legal insecurity. The imposition of countervailing duties inevitably leads to dispute settlement. As with other trade remedies, the measure will offer relief for some three years until a final and binding decision is made possibly by the Appellate Body. Since WTO law, as currently developed, has neither preliminary injunctions nor retroactive compensation, countries in distress may be tempted to use this route and implement legislation accordingly. They merely risk having to lift the measure if it is found unlawful.[32] Such policies could destroy the WTO. They are likely to cause unlawful retaliation and escalation of protectionist measures. The law is poorly equipped to handle cases of this magnitude. The SCM Agreement was not drawn up with a view to addressing currency manipulation and corresponding countervailing measures across all imports from a particular country.[33] The matter needs to be taken up elsewhere.

3.5 WAYS FORWARD

The IMF Decision of 2007 on Bilateral Surveillance stresses that 'dialogue and persuasion are key pillars of effective surveillance'. While this is true, it is also insufficient. The current crisis shows that more is required. Unfettered sovereignty in matters relating to the currency monopoly of states no longer matches the levels of economic interdependence and globalization

---

[31] Clarke and Horlick, *supra*, p. 707 *et seq*.

[32] See also Staiger, R.W. and Sykes A.O., ' "Currency Manipulation" and World Trade', *World Trade Review*, Vol. 9, No. 4, 2010, pp. 583–627.

[33] See e.g. Mattoo, A. and Subramanian, A., 'Currency Undervaluation and Sovereign Wealth Funds: A New Role for the World Trade Organization, Peterson Institute for International Economics', WP 08–2, January 2008, to be found at: www.iie.com/publications/wp/wp08–2.pdf (accessed on 5 October 2010).

reached. Much as the WTO limits sovereignty in terms of subsidization, the IMF needs to develop substantive and procedural disciplines limiting subsidization of exports by way of currency manipulation. The lack of disciplines within the IMF carries risks of overstressing the WTO and thus threatens a key pillar upon which the overall system of freely floating currencies relies.[34] It is therefore imperative to achieve an overall balance between the WTO and the IMF. The latter needs to develop a rule-based approach that would allow it to address currency disputes following well-structured procedures of consultation, fact-finding and decision-making.

A viable option might be to amend the current version of Article IV (1)(iii) of the IMF AoA.[35] Going beyond exiting consultation and examination, it would be possible to use the experience of the trade policy review mechanism in the WTO for the monetary policy review mechanism in the IMF and thus prepare the ground for enhanced systematic reviews of monetary policies of members. Moreover, obligations to consult and to negotiate in good faith should be introduced.[36] Members should no longer be able to block discussions on a topic of interest to the global economy by insisting on monetary sovereignty. They should be obliged to undergo all the comprehensive fact-finding and economic analysis undertaken by the IMF and the results should be introduced into the process of consultation and negotiations.

Finally, avenues through which to install proper dispute settlement in cases of failed consultations and negotiations should be studied. First this will entail legal research assessing to what extent monetary affairs are or are not suitable for determination on the basis of legal criteria – a matter neglected for far too long. All this amounts to a paradigm shift in achieving greater coherence between the IMF and the disciplines of the WTO. For obvious reasons, it will be difficult to achieve. Amendments to the AoA have to be approved by the Board of Governors and ratified by three-fifths of the members that have 85 per cent of the total voting power.[37] These barriers are formidable in a multipolar world. As a possible alternative it

---

34 See Baltensperger, E. and Cottier, T., 'The Role of International Law in Monetary Affairs', *Journal of International Economic Law*, Vol. 13, No. 3, 2010, pp. 911–37.

35 Sanford, J.E., 'Currency Manipulation: The IMF and WTO', in Hilbert, *supra*, pp. 129–37, see also Waibel, M., 'Retaliating against Exchange-Rate Manipulation under WTO Rules', in Evenett, *supra*, pp. 136–7.

36 See for some other suggestions on negotiations, however with an emphasis on the role of the WTO Mattoo and Subramanian, *supra*, pp. 20–22.

37 Article XXVIII IMF AoA. In this light the United States with its 16 per cent of voting power is able to block any decision which requires a qualified majority of 85 per cent.

has also been proposed to revise not the rules on surveillance themselves, but to draft new guidelines on surveillance,[38] thus avoiding the complex amendment procedures.

Perhaps the most promising avenues consist in learning by doing and further developing the mechanisms of consultation and negotiations in monetary diplomacy within the IMF, and to build these on reports and assessments made by the Fund. The recent internal policy reviews by the IMF show that the IMF is currently focusing on domestic policies, including those related to currency exchange rates, in light of their importance for external and systemic stability.[39] In the 2008 Triennial Surveillance Review the Executive Board outlined four main areas where improvements are required and expected: risk assessment, financial sector surveillance, analysis of exchange rate risks and external risks, and multilateral perspective.[40] Following these developments and discussions, the Executive Board recently decided that financial stability assessment under the Financial Sector Assessment Program (FSAP) shall be integrated into the system of bilateral surveillance under Article IV IMF AoA.[41] It will not create any new obligations for the members, since the financial stability assessment will be conducted as part of the normal procedure of bilateral surveillance on a mandatory triennial basis. Recently, the IMF has made a shift towards a risk-based approach, based on two main criteria of the financial sector of a country – namely, its size (measured by the volume of financial services) and interconnectedness with financial sectors in other countries (analysed on the basis of bank-based network).[42] These are all important steps into the right direction, and it will be interesting to follow implications of the risk-based approach for the traditional bilateral surveillance procedures

---

[38] Goldstein, M., 'Currency Manipulation and Enforcing the Rules of the International Monetary System' to be found at: www.piie.com/publications/chapters_preview/3870/05iie3870.pdf (accessed 5 October 2010), p. 154.

[39] IMF, *The Fund's Mandate, supra*, at 7; see also: IMF, *Modernizing the Surveillance Mandate and Modalities*, 26 March 2010, to be found at: www.imf.org/external/np/pp/eng/2010/032610.pdf (accessed 5 October 2010).

[40] IMF, *2008 Triennial Surveillance Review – Overview Paper*, 2 September 2008, to be found at: www.imf.org/external/np/pp/eng/2008/090208a.pdf (accessed 5 October 2010).

[41] IMF, *Public Information Note No. 10/135*, 27 September 2010, available at: www.imf.org/external/np/sec/pn/2010/pn10135.htm (accessed 5 October 2010). See also Hagan, S., 'Enhancing the IMF's Regulatory Authority', *Journal of International Economic Law*, Vol. 13, No. 3, 2010, pp 955–68.

[42] IMF, *Integrating Stability Assessments under the Financial Sector Assessment Program into Article IV Surveillance: Background Material*, 27 August 2010, to be found at: www.imf.org/external/np/pp/eng/2010/082710a.pdf (accessed 5 October 2010), pp. 3, 13–14.

related to exchange rates. These policies are able to bring about awareness and change attitudes towards global responsibility in monetary affairs. They may be able to build the groundwork for moving into a more rule-oriented system commensurate with the work of the generation of trade lawyers which Jacques Bourgeois so ably and nobly represents.

4. From reluctant participant to key player: EU and the negotiation of the GATS*

Juan A. Marchetti and Petros C. Mavroidis

The EU did not enthusiastically endorse the requests for a new trade round in the 1980s. Having decided that it did not want to dismantle its controversial Common Agricultural Policy (CAP), it feared that aggressive attitude in other areas would provoke requests to do so. Its original position underwent substantive change following pressure by, *inter alia*, its services lobby and the awareness of gains in various other fields of economic activity. It emerged as one of the key players in drafting the GATS and can legitimately claim property rights for many a GATS institution.

4.1 THE GATS: NO INSTANT HIT

The thesis that we advance could be summarized as follows:

- The services negotiation and the GATS architecture are very much the product of those Uruguay Round participants that had elaborate (or relatively speaking, the most elaborate) domestic regulations for

* We had to turn for help to a number of people when preparing this study. It is no exaggeration to state that our work would be highly incomplete (as it probably still is) without their help: Eyal Benvenisti, Americo Beviglia-Zampetti, Tomer Broude, Theofanis Christoforou, John Croome, Panayotis Delimatsis, Bart De Meester, Dorothy Dwoskin, Murray Gibbs, David Hartridge, Rob Howse, Doug Irwin, Felipe Jaramillo, Mario Kakabadse, Abdel-Hamid Mamdouh, Aaditya Mattoo, Andre Sapir, David Palmeter, Federico Ortino, John Richardson, Gary Sampson, Jonathan Scheele, Dick Self, Harsha Singh, Vassilis Tzevelekos, Jorge Vigano, David Walker, Bruce Wilson, and Rufus Yerxa shared their experience with us, and graciously responded to the many questions we had prepared, and to the many more that actually propped up during our meetings.

most service sectors, were aware of the potential of exporting services, *and* were actually interested in export markets. These are the United States and the EU.[1] The former was decisive in introducing the issue of 'services' in the negotiating agenda, and in initiating the negotiation, while the latter was certainly decisive in the drafting stage.[2]

- It took time but it was essential to persuade developing countries, who can be usefully divided into two groups: those that were flexible and saw opportunities in the negotiation of the agreement, and those that kept an inflexible stance until late in the game. They managed to influence only a few provisions of the agreement, notably the introduction of the fourth mode of supply (that is, movement of natural persons as suppliers of services), and the incorporation of developing-country-friendly provisions throughout the agreement aiming at moderating its liberalization impact. The fact that developing countries influenced provisions of the agreement does not mean that they actually drafted them.
- The GATT Secretariat played an active role throughout the negotiation, occasionally steering it, in the name of technical advice, towards conclusion.
- Within this context, the EU, after it managed to overcome its original diffidence, became a key player:
  - the EU services lobby played a key role in moving the EU position towards active participation. Political economy explanations are thus, the basis of this study;
  - the EU was, relatively speaking, in a better position than most participants with respect to services-related expertise, since it

[1] Throughout this document we refer to the European Union (EU) and use the term EC (European Communities) only when referring to documents carrying this title.

[2] Uruguay Round participants of smaller size, such as Sweden (not an EU member state when the Uruguay Round started), and Switzerland, also made significant contributions to the elaboration of the framework. And indeed, it is very much the case that these two countries (and others in more or less the same position) influenced the shaping of GATS. We will be referring to their positions when warranted since these countries did not advance a comprehensive position in the manner that the EU and the US dIdem We know from the testimony of direct participants in the negotiation, that on some occasions smaller countries had submitted proposals under their own name that reflected, nonetheless, the agreement of other, more important players (who preferred to stay on the sidelines in order to advance the process, fearing outright rejections of their proposals if submitted under their own name).

had been facing similar questions when dealing with its own integration process;

- although one might legitimately hypothesize that the distribution of competences was a hindrance towards achieving its goals, EU negotiators managed to avoid that this becomes a true issue and presented coherent (most of the time) proposals to the negotiating table. It was almost as if the EU was negotiating with one voice. It is probably expertise embedded in EU institutions and lacking at the member state-level (as far as most member states are concerned) that probably explains that;
- protection of its farm policy (CAP) was originally a hindrance but the EU negotiators managed to use it as an advantage: the EU defensive position on CAP placed it half way between the US gung-ho policies and the developing countries unwillingness to negotiate trade in services and ensured that the EU evolves into a useful mediator between the two approaches;
- EU negotiators had a heavy hand in drafting the key GATS institutions.

4.2 BEFORE THE NEGOTIATION (PRE-1986)

4.2.1 Regulation of Trade in Services

In February 1995, the Council for Trade in Services (CTS), the body overseeing the GATS held its first meeting.[3] For many it was a milestone, the day when they could celebrate the end of a road and the beginning of a new era. Moving from absence to presence of an international multilateral framework regulating trade in services was not an easy exercise. And here is why.

Trade in services, besides national legislation, was regulated in the years before the advent of the GATS through bilateral and regional schemes.[4]

---

[3] WTO Doc. S/C/W/1 of 15 February 1995.

[4] It took some time before we reached this stage. As Bhagwati mentions, in early economic analysis services were considered non-tradable, see Bhagwati, J., 'The Role of Services in Development', in *Services and Development, The Role of Foreign Direct Investment and Trade*, United Nations Centre on Transnational Corporations, UN Doc. ST/CTC/95, 1989, pp. 5–8. Norman and Strandenes rightly noted early on in the discussion that the same holds for some goods as well that are not tradable, see Norman, V.D. and Stradenes, S.P., 'International Trade in Services: A Comment', in O. Giarini (ed.), *The Emerging Services Economy*, New York, Pergamon Press, 1987, pp. 44–49. In the same line of thinking, van Holst notes that, the

The focus of each of these schemes was quite narrow. A comprehensive scheme regulating trade in services was missing.[5] It is not that trade in services is totally absent in the GATT agreements: following a US initiative, three Tokyo Round agreements (Codes) contained provisions that regulated, albeit in incidental manner, trade in services: the agreement on government procurement (GPA), the agreement on technical barriers (TBT), and the agreement on subsidies and countervailing measures (SCM).

The United States had had a comprehensive regulation of its own services market, and had concluded a number of treaties of Friendship, Commerce and Navigation (FCN) that regulated relations across countries with respect to specific services, such as, aviation, shipping and communications.[6] Besides that, the US had concluded two preferential trade agreements (PTAs):

- the US–Israel Free Trade Agreement, and
- the Canada–US Free Trade Agreement.[7]

The former was non-binding with respect to services trade, the parties undertaking however, the obligation to adhere to certain core principles. Section 1401 of the latter limited its applicability to specific sectors only. Canada and Israel are rather homogeneous (to the United States) trading partners. There was no North–South precedent in which the US had

---

merits of this discussion notwithstanding, services have been traded for centuries, see van Host, B., 'The Internationalization of Trade in Services', in D.I. Riddle (ed.), *Information Economy and Development*, Bonn, Friedrich-Ebert-Stiftung, 1988, pp. 59–66.

[5] Still, for a number of reasons, that we discuss *infra*, there was a growth in trade in services, although until the end of the eighties it did not surpass one quarter of the volume of international trade.

[6] Brock, W.E., 'A Simple Plan for Negotiating on Trade in Services', *The World Economy*, Vol. 5, 1982, pp. 229–40 at p. 236 *et seq*. The United States stopped negotiating FCNs already in the 1950s.

[7] See on this score, that is, the impact that this agreement had on the GATS negotiation, Nyahoho, E., 'Libéralisation multilateral dui commerce des services: enjeux et stratégie des négociations', *Etudes Internationales*, Vol. 21, 1990, pp. 55–80. Krommenacker mentions an agreement between Japan and the United States (implemented on 1 April 1987) concerning the possibility for lawyers from the two countries to work in each other's territory under strict conditions specified in the agreement, see Krommenacker, R.J., 'Multilateral Services Negotiations: From Interest-Lateralism to Reasoned Multilateralism in the Context of the Servicization of the Economy', in E.U. Petersmann and M. Hilf (eds), *The New GATT Round of Multilateral Trade Negotiations, Legal and Economic Problems*, Dewenter, Boston, Kluwer, 1987, pp. 455–63.

participated before the advent of the GATS. Moreover, because of the then relative newness of the two PTAs, an evaluation of their success was unavailable at the moment the GATS negotiation starts.[8]

On the other hand, the EU was the only entity with *substantial* experience in regional liberalization: its integration process included comprehensive obligations regarding liberalization of trade in services. The EU was imposing a requirement to liberalize trade in services on all countries that signed association agreements with a view to accession to the EU. Further, the EEA (European Economic Area), an association between the EU and Iceland, Liechtenstein, and Norway, also contains a chapter on services liberalization. But of course, the EU is an idiosyncratic integration process.[9] The same is true for the EEA.

There was also some industry-specific cooperation: the International Telecommunications Unions (ITU) allocates broadcasting frequencies; the Bank for International Settlements (BIS) discusses and sets standards on international banking regulation and supervision; the International Civil Aviation Organization (ICAO) administers agreements on civil aviation; the International Maritime Organization (IMO) is in charge of agreements on shipping. Within the OECD, the Code of Liberalisation of Current Invisible Operations, and the Code of Liberalisation of Capital Movements have contributed towards reducing restrictions on current invisible transactions and transfers, as well as abolishing some restrictions on cash flows.

The absence of a genuine multilateral scheme was no obstacle to the fast increase of the volume of services traded. There are a number of reasons for this:

- technology (e.g. the telecoms revolution). It made it possible to perform a wide variety of services at a distant geographical location thus opening up the road to trade opportunities: trade analysts in Washington D.C could, for example, have access to data maintained in various parts of the world;[10]

---

8 See Whitford, E.M., 'A Rainy Day for the GATT Umbrella: Trade Negotiations in Services', *North Carolina Journal of International Law and Commerce Regulation*, Vol. 14, 1989, pp. 121–33.

9 The EU aims at going beyond trade liberalization and at the time of the GATS negotiation it was still EC-10, that is, a relatively speaking group of homogeneous players across which instruments of integration, such as mutual recognition, were a viable option.

10 The term 'technology' needs some explanation: it is not only for example, through the advances in telecoms that services could by-pass national frontiers. It is also the service-product itself that benefitted from technological advances and incorporated elements un-bestowed to it previously.

- the increasing connection between goods and services, since many services were inputs to goods, and liberalization of trade in goods *ipso facto* amounted to liberalization of trade in services as well;[11]
- the shift in employment from manufacturing to services in most OECD countries;[12]
- the trend towards greater specialization in services and the ensuing gains in productivity.

The IMF data suggest that in the late 1970s, that is, before the discussion to liberalize started gaining pace, trade in services was in the vicinity of US$400 billion, or close to one-fifth of world trade in goods.[13] However, what is more noticeable is that trade in services (as recorded at that time) doubled between 1960 and 1970, and once again between 1970 and 1975, and this upward trend more or less continued after 1975 as well. The World Bank data suggest the following:

Table 4.1: Global Trade Flows, 1980 and 1992 (US$ billion and percentage)[14]

	1980	**1992**	**Average annual change**
Total trade in services	358	931	8.3
OECD (shares in parentheses)	283 (79%)	765 (82%)	8.6
Rest of world	75 (21%)	166 (18%)	6.8
Services as share of goods *and* services	17.0	22.0	2.2
OECD	18.8	22.7	1.6
Rest of world	12.7	19.2	3.5

[11] See Schott, J. and Mazza, J., 'Trade in Services and Developing Countries', *Journal of World Trade*, Vol. 20, 1986, pp. 253–73.

[12] Brock, *supra*, cites statistics to the effect that in the US in 1981, 72 per cent of the non-agricultural population was engaged in service activities (63 per cent in 1961). This was not just a US phenomenon: in Japan the corresponding numbers were 49 per cent and 37 per cent.

[13] *Balance of Payments Statistics*, IMF, Washington, Vol. XXXII, 1981, part 2. McCulloch, R., 'Services and the Uruguay Round', *The World Economy*, Vol. 13, 1990, pp. 329–48 at p. 331 mentions that in GATT's estimate, the value of world trade of services for 1988 rose up to US$ 600 billion.

[14] Source: World Bank, data pertain only to countries reporting to the IMF.

Table 4.2: Shares in Global Service Exports and Relative Specialization, 1980 and 1992[15]

Country group	Travel		Transport		All Other	
	1980	**1992**	**1980**	**1992**	**1980**	**1992**
Share in global trade:						
OECD members	71.6	77.9	78.4	81.8	80.2	84.6
Developing countries	21.8	17.3	16.5	12.5	15.3	11.7
Relative specialization:						
OECD members	1.01	0.96	1.10	1.02	1.13	1.06
Developing countries	0.93	1.12	0.65	0.82	0.65	0.74
Small LDCs (1 million people or fewer)	2.19	3.45	1.19	1.85	0.39	1.11

In the United States alone, the value of exports reached US$42 billion in 1981, an increase of about 300 per cent from its 1970 level.[16] Brock cites a number of studies that all suggest that these and similar numbers significantly understated the true value of exports: a named source estimated that the trade in services in 1980 was not US$35 billion, as *per* the Survey of Current Business prepared by the Bureau of Economic Analysis of the US Department of Commerce (DOC), but rather closer to US$60 billion.[17]

Others provide different numbers.[18] The numbers however, do not add up: the reason for the discrepancy in the estimation has to do with the inherent difficulties in measuring services (unlike the case of goods), and with the fact that very few governments had developed at that time reliable comprehensive data collection systems. As a result, recourse was often made to imperfect proxies, such as measuring the volume by reference to balance of payment (BoP) statistics kept by the IMF. The IMF data suffer from many deficiencies: they are not available on a sufficiently disaggregated level; BoP data report transactions in services between one country and the rest of the world, and not between exporter and importer; they are

15 *Ibid.*

16 *Survey of Current Business*, Bureau of Economic Analysis, United States Department of Commerce, Washington, June 1982.

17 *The International Operations of US Service Industries: Current Data Collection and Analysis*, Final Report prepared for the United States Departments of State and Commerce and the Office of the United States Trade Representative, Washington, Economic Consulting Services, 1981.

18 See Rivers, R.R., Slater, V.A., and Paolini, A.J., 'Putting Services on the Table: the New GATT Round', *Stanford Journal of International Law*, Vol. 23, 1987, pp. 13–30.

often inaccurate since they do not control for services incorporated in final goods.[19] The figures provided are, therefore, probably inaccurate. They all point nonetheless, to the same direction: the volume and value of services traded was increasing despite the absence of an international agreement.

If trade in services was growing in the absence of a comprehensive framework *à la* GATS, so why bother negotiating one? Brock speaks of a trend of *new protectionism*. In his words:[20]

> Restrictive measures under consideration in a number of countries in telecommunications, data processing and information services have already created much uncertainty in the business community about the future ability of firms to utilise communication and data-processing facilities; it has hurt investments and reduced trade opportunities. If the trend of increasing barriers to trade in services continues unchecked, trade opportunities could be markedly reduced and the international trading system could be seriously harmed.[21]

The sequence here probably holds the key to understand what in part at least motivated the GATS negotiation: technology opened foreign markets to some extent, by making long-standing barriers in some services markets (essentially financial and telecoms) increasingly obsolete. Technological developments (especially in telecoms) were making it possible for economic agents to circumvent existing barriers to entry. Some (developing) countries reacted by enacting (or threatening to enact) new barriers to ensure that their control over key services sectors would not be undermined by foreign

---

[19] Nayyar, D., 'Some Reflections on the Uruguay Round and Trade in Services', *Journal of World Trade*, Vol. 22, 1988, pp. 35 48 at p. 35 *et seq.*). Bhagwati distinguishes between embodied and disembodied services: the former are incorporated in the final good, whereas the latter could, for example, be sold over the telephone: see Bhagwati, J., 'Splintering and Disembodiment of Services and Developing Nations', *The World Economy*, Vol. 7, 1984, pp. 133–44. Statistical evidence provided by the EU supports this conclusion (Europeans call it the asymmetry discomfort). In their calculations, Europeans find that in the period between 1972–82, the trade between EU and the rest of the world grew substantially: export trade grew from 20 to 111.8 billion *ECU*s (the *European Currency Unit*, in a way the predecessor of the Euro), that is an increase of 16.6 per cent per annum, whereas import trade grew from 19.8 to 103.2 billion ECUs, that is an annual growth of 16.2 per cent. The main trading partners of the EU in that period were the US, Canada, Australia, and New Zealand, see GATT Doc. MTN.GNS/W/23 of 30 October 1987.

[20] Brock, *supra*, p. 234.

[21] The idea that the US world leadership on trade in services was gradually eroding due in part to other nations' protectionist measures gained ground in the early1980s in the US, see Eason, H., 'America's 'Invisible' Trade Surplus – Exporting of Services', *Nation's Business*, November 1984.

firms accessing what they considered strategic sectors of their economy; it is against this threat (or the actual imposition) of new barriers that Brock wants to rally his troops (or his troops want him to rally). Importantly, Brock wants all barriers notified to the multilateral institution to be negotiable and those not notified to be applied on a non-discriminatory basis across domestic and foreign suppliers.[22] That is, following his approach, new protectionism would either be negotiable or non-discriminatory.

4.2.2 American Express and the US Push for Negotiation

It is commonplace among commentators that it was the US financial services sectors that first argued systematically in favour of a trade round that would include a chapter on liberalization of trade in services.[23] And its voice did not fall on deaf ears: the United States was experiencing substantial trade deficits at that time (late 1970s, early 1980s), which were politically unsustainable. These deficits resulted from significant deficits in trade in goods, which were partially offset by surplus in trade in services. Indeed, shortly after the launching the Uruguay Round, Michael Smith, the Deputy USTR, revealed as much to the trading nations:[24]

> It will come as no surprise for you to hear that we face enormous domestic pressure on the trade front. In my country, the Administration must deal every day with substantial scepticism in the business community and the Congress over the utility of GATT negotiations. This is, in part, a reflection of the picture at home. While recent indicators are encouraging, we are still facing a trade deficit for 1986 of approximately $170 billion. Reflected in this deficit is a substantial decline in both our manufactures and our agricultural trade positions. In the current environment in the United States, the absence of – or prolonged delay in – decisive progress to strengthen the trading system, and to expand and liberalize market access, will lead to a diminished level of political attention and commitment to the negotiations, just further adding to the scepticism to which I just referred.

An agreement to liberalize trade in services would buy the US government precious political capital, indeed it would be killing two birds with one

[22] See on this score, Sapir, A., 'North-South Issues in Trade in Services', *The World Economy*, Vol. 8, 1985, pp. 27–42.

[23] Freeman, H., 'The Services Sector: Yesterday, Today, and Tomorrow', *Economic Perspectives*, Vol. 1, 1996, pp. 19–21 and Feketekuty, G., *International Trade in Services: an Overview and Blueprint for Negotiations*, Washington DC, American Enterprise Institute, 1988.

[24] GATT Doc. SR.42/ST/19 of 18 December 1986 at pp. 2–3.

stone: and lobbies would be pacified, and the wider public would be seeing a substantially reduced (if not eliminated altogether) trade deficit; since the United States had competitive advantage in many services sectors, reduction of its trade deficit was well in the cards. Let us see how the story unfolds.[25]

The US first introduced in their 1974 Trade Act legislation to protect its domestic interests in services trade.[26] The 1984 Trade and Tariff Act (that amended the 1974 Trade Act) explicitly identified the reduction of barriers to trade in services among the objectives included in section 302.[27] In between, the United States managed to insert, as we saw *supra*, services-related provisions in three Tokyo Round agreements. Freeman believes that the work done by the then USTR, Robert Strauss, during the Tokyo Round, laid the foundations for the subsequent work, which for US negotiators (and lobbyists) consisted in delineating a workable negotiating item that could be included in the future agenda of trade rounds.[28] During the negotiation of the Tokyo Round, a young official was hired by the USTR (Bruce Wilson) and was asked to examine the merits of an international agreement. The mention of services in three Tokyo Round agreements was only the beginning. Before Tokyo Round, Freeman states, only academics had been occupied with this issue.[29]

The inclusion of services-related provisions in three Tokyo Round agreements is evidence that the United States was from day one clear on one

---

[25] One should not quickly discard other explanations for the US stance on this score: Gibbs mentions a report from the US Congress, *Office of Technology Assessment*, where it was stated that the contribution of liberalization of trade in services was important to the US not so much as a source of employment or to correct the numbers in BoP statistics, but as a contributor to the strength of service firms and their strategic support to other sectors, particularly the manufacturing sector, see Gibbs, M., 'Means to Enhance the Competitive Position and Export Capacity of Service Industries of Developing Countries', in *Services and Development, The Role of Foreign Direct Investment and Trade*, United Nations Centre on Transnational Corporations, UN Doc. ST/CTC/95, 1989, pp. 104–7.

[26] Feketekuty, G., 'US Policy on 301 and Super 301', in J. Bhagwati and H.T. Patrick (eds), *Aggressive Unilateralism: America's 301 Trade Policy and the World Trading System*, The University of Michigan Press, Ann Arbor, Michigan, 1990, pp. 91–103 and for a legal analysis of these provisions, see Hudec, R.E., 'Thinking About the New Section 301: Beyond Good and Evil', in Bhagwati and Patrick, *supra*, pp. 113–59. The US initiatives are succinctly discussed in McCulloch, *supra*.

[27] The United States Trade Representative (USTR) established the Services Policy Advisory Committee (SPAC) and the US Department of Commerce, the Industry Sector Advisory Committee (ISAC) that helped, along with the US Census Bureau, the Bureau of Labor Statistics, and the Bureau of Economic Analysis, gather and process technical information about trade in services.

[28] Freeman, *supra*.

[29] Harry Freeman was with *American Express* at that time.

issue: it was the GATT that should be the forum for an (eventual) agreement on services, and it should be reformed accordingly. The US subsequent attitude confirmed this point.[30]

Domestic lobbies wanted the US government to go the extra mile and negotiate a comprehensive agreement on services: chief among them the Coalition of Service Industries (CSI),[31] which played an important role in sensitizing the US government about the importance of liberalizing trade in services for the US economy. The focus of CSI was on banking, insurance and the right of establishment (of banking and insurance) in foreign countries: the CSI was thus, originally at least, contemplating in terms of negotiating an agreement that would liberalize foreign direct investment rather than trade in services.[32]

The CSI developed its own strategy in an effort to sensitize first its government and then the world about the importance of negotiating a global agreement on international trade in services: as early as the 1970s, it started to gather data, organized conferences (in order to increase public awareness), engaged in extensive public lecturing, and heavily lobbied the US government to this effect. Prominent members of the services industry (like Shelp from AIG) provided testimony to the US Senate Finance Committee (SFC) arguing the case for a global agreement.[33]

---

[30] This was not the case as far as (many) developing countries were concerned and they voiced their willingness to see, if at all, an agreement outside the confines of the GATT during the Punta del Este meeting (1986), see *infra.* In academic discourse, there were voices which were not necessarily opposed to a negotiation of services among like-minded countries, that is, a sub-group of the GATT, see McCulloch, R., 'International Competition in Services', *NBER Working Paper Series,* Working Paper No. 2235, 1987.

[31] CSI is a coalition of US economic operators, established in 1982, and includes major international companies from the banking, insurance, telecommunications, information technology, express delivery, audiovisual energy services, and other service industries. It conducts business in all 50 US states and in over 100 countries around the world. The CSI membership is predominantly corporations engaging in trade of financial services. See Lang, J.M., 'The First Five Years of the WTO: General Agreement on Trade in Services', *Law and Policy in International Business*, Vol. 31, 1999, pp. 801–9, and the CSI website at www.uscsi.org.

[32] Feketekuty, *supra*, mentions that key members were Shelp (from AIG, and previously the US Department of Commerce; Shelp, R.K., 'Trade in Services', *Foreign Policy*, Vol. 65, 1987, pp. 64–84), Harry Freeman and Joan Spero (American Express). This perspective is not the same as an agreement to liberalize investment in services: see Hansen, P., 'Frameworks for Foreign Direct Investment', in *Services and Development, The Role of Foreign Direct Investment and Trade*, United Nations Centre on Transnational Corporations, UN Doc. ST/CTC/95, 1989, pp. 161–2.

[33] See the appendix in Feketekuty, *supra*.

The links between US lobbies and US government were not limited to providing testimonies: John Reed of Citibank is heading one of the advisory groups organized by the United States Trade Representative (USTR), the Services Policy Advisory Committee (SPAC), while James Robinson, the head of American Express, is heading the Advisory Committee on Trade Negotiations. Representatives from the financial services sector are omnipresent in the trade dialogue these days.[34] The USTR, through these links, had the privilege to receive priceless information regarding barriers to trade in services from the private sector: Cloney (1989), the then President of the International Insurance Council, as well as Cohen and Morante (1981), the former being Manager of Public Affairs for the American International Group (AIG) provide evidence to this effect.

The role of American Express in getting the multilateral negotiation on trade in services off the ground is pivotal and needs some further explanation. Yoffie is the author of the standard work in this context.[35] In his account, the company adopted a Vince Lombardi strategy, named after the famous college football coach and described in the following terms by Joan Spero, vice President for International Corporate Affairs:[36]

> The best defence was a good offense. The company did not want to be a passive observer of events. On the contrary the fundamental principle guiding American Express' actions was that 'if you don't like the environment, you should try to change it.

[34] Preeg quotes at p. 53 Brock stating: 'our business community will be able to accuse us with some justification that we fiddled while the trading system was breaking down around us': see Preeg, E.H., *Traders in a Brave New World: The Uruguay Round and the Future of the International Trading System*, Chicago, University of Chicago Press, Illinois, 1995. Ostry suggests that for the US new issues (such as services) was crucial in sustaining support for multilateralism in general. In her view, the support for the new round in the US was originally moderate. It is the inclusion of the 'new issues', such as services, that tilted the balance in favour of supporting the new round, see Ostry, S., 'Trade, Development, and the Doha Development Agenda', in D. Lee and R. Wilkinson (eds), *The WTO After Hong Kong*, London and New York, Routledge, 2007, pp. 26–33 at p. 27. See also Ostry, S., 'Convergence and Sovereignty: Policy Scope for Compromise?', in A. Prakash and J.A. Hart (eds), *Coping with Globalization*, Routledge, London and New York, 2000, pp. 52–76 at p. 55 *et seq*. and Ostry, S., *The Post-Cold War Trading System: Who's on First?*, Chicago, Illinois, University of Chicago Press, 1997, at p. 175 *et seq*.

[35] Yoffie, D.B., 'Trade in Services and American Express', in D.B. Yoffie, *International Trade and Competition: Cases and Notes in Strategy and Management*, New York, McGraw-Hill Publishing Company, 1990, pp. 367–86.

[36] Yoffie, *supra*, at p. 375.

And, indeed, change it attempted (and eventually, did). The strategy, in operational terms was consisting of:

- illumination: James Robinson, Harry Freeman, and Joan Spero gave hundreds of speeches and interviews to reputed magazines of wide circulation, such as the *Economist, Fortune, Business Week, The Washington Post, The New York Times,* etc.;[37]
- building up the domestic lobby: the CSI, mentioned above, was established in 1982 by American Express, along with Bechtel, Peat Marwick, Citibank and some other firms operating in the banking sector;
- building bridges between the CSI and services lobbies around the world;
- influencing the US government through direct links: besides participation in entities like SPAC mentioned above, in 1982, James Robinson was one of the six private sector members of the US delegation to the GATT meetings (that led all the way to the Ministerial Conference which we discuss *infra*).[38]

Why did American Express invest so much energy in this discussion? The company was specializing in travellers' cheques, charge cards, insurance, and investment services. This business depends on the rapid transmission of sophisticated computer and telecommunications networks to transfer large amounts of data across national borders. Trans-border data flows were threatened by protection, and so was data processing. This was of utmost importance to American Express, since trans-border data flows had become essential to international banking, and financial services. The rationale for protection varied across countries: privacy reasons, protection of strategic sectors, infant industry, safeguarding employment.[39] A new agreement regulating trade in services should aim at disciplining the rationale for protection opening up trade on a worldwide basis.[40]

The United States, quite aware of its services potential in the services sector, and having experienced itself the gains from deregulation of its

---

[37] Their involvement continued well into the Uruguay Round: see for example, Spero, J., 'Tear Down Barriers to Export of Services', *New York Times*, 30 July 1991.

[38] Yoffie, *supra*, pp. 367 and 375 *et seq.*

[39] Gibbs, *supra*, explains how import substitution policies in services could work for the benefit of developing countries.

[40] Yoffie (*supra*, p. 378) reports that the 1982 GATT *Ministerial Decision* to open up the door to services (see *infra*) was a triumph.

national services market, saw no reason why its own experience cannot be transplanted in the world scene: in dramatic fashion, in 1982, President Reagan, ordered the dismantlement of the national telecoms carrier, AT & T, which, following this act, was limited to international services leaving the US market to other firms. It is following this act that the various Baby Bells emerged in the US market. It would be unfair though, to credit President Reagan with the deregulation assault, a process that started earlier under the presidency of Jimmy Carter.[41] This is how the US delegate to the GATT described the motives behind deregulation:[42]

> The motive behind deregulation in a number of sectors in the United States had been the feeling that there was not enough competition, nor enough companies. As could be seen from the situation in coastal shipping, the degree of free competition needed was also an issue in his country. On the other hand, the dynamism that may have resulted from deregulation, say in telecommunications, could be attributed to management styles rather than to global trade trends, and of course some dominant firms remained in the market.

The US was the first, but not the only entity experiencing a sea-change in the supply of services. Up to the late 1970s, the prevailing orthodoxy (for the overwhelming majority of regulators but for many economists as well) was that services were natural monopolies and/or that they concerned strategic sectors of the national economy: the natural consequence of this thinking was that (many) services should be supplied by state-owned (monopolistic) entities since they could not be trusted to the private sector.[43] Both premises were put into question, timidly at first, with

---

41 The airlines (1978), trucking (1980), railroads (late 1970s and 1980), telecommunications (1977 and, as mentioned, 1982), cable television (late 1970s and 1984), brokerage (1975), banking (1980 and 1982), petroleum (1979) and natural gas industry (1978) were liberalized in that period, see Winston, C., 'Economic Deregulation: Days of Reckoning for Microeconomists', *Journal of Economic Literature*, Vol. 31, 1993, pp. 1263–89. On AT &T and its break-up, see Cowhey, P. and Richards, J., 'Dialing for Dollars: Institutional Designs for the Globalization of the Market for Basic Telecommunications Services', in A. Prakash and J.A. Hart (eds), *Coping with Globalization*, London and New York, Routledge, 2000, pp. 148–69. Some empirical work establishes a clear link between the globalization of form and capital and the restriction of state power, see Spar, D.L. and Yoffie, D.B., 'A Race to the Bottom or Governance from the Top?', in Prakash and Hart, *supra,* pp. 31–51 at p. 33 *et seq*.

42 GATT Doc. MDF/10 of 21 May 1985.

43 In simplistic terms one often refers to this discussion as 'deregulation vs. monopoly'. As Robinson (Robinson, P., 'An International Policy Framework for Trade in Services and Data Services: The Current Debate', in D.I. Riddle (ed.),

increased intensity soon: privatization of services at home provided the impetus for the discussion on their international tradability. The gains from privatization at home increased substantially the argument for a multilateral framework on trade in services. The road towards GATS starts probably in the corridors of the White House, but it is very much the outcome, the natural consequence indeed of the phenomenon described above.

The US made a negotiation on services the flagship of its national agenda for a new GATT multilateral round. In 1985, as the time for the launching of the new round was approaching, the then USTR, Clayton Yeutter, had even conditioned the participation of the US in the Uruguay Round upon the inclusion of a negotiation on trade in services in the agenda.[44]

4.2.3 Between the CAP and the Rest: Paris, Brussels

The EU was in a different position to the United States regarding its view on trade in services. To start with, although the EU contained detailed provisions regarding its internal liberalization of trade in services, it was far from being an integrated services market in the early 1980s. In fact, it still is some way towards achieving this objective and its services is substantially less integrated than its goods market. Its focus was more on integrating its own market rather than anything else.[45]

On the other hand, the EU did not have competence to speak with one voice on all services. Indeed, Opinion 1/94 (by the European Court of Justice (ECJ)), which was issued several years later (at the end of the Uruguay Round), clarified that only services supplied without any physical movement of either the supplier or the customer came under the exclusive competence of the EU.[46] During the negotiations, the EU was represented by the Commission, and, in theory at least, it could be the hostage of an intense dialogue between its member states that might not provide it with sufficient discretion. In practice, this was less of a concern than it might

---

Information Economy and Development, Bonn, Friedrich-Ebert-Stiftung, 1988, pp. 164–74 at p. 171) underscores however, the real issue is 'how to adapt national telecommunications policies to a growing competitive telecommunications environment internationally'.

[44] See 'Yeutter Cites Preconditions on Trade Talks', *Journal of Commerce*, 9 December 1985 at p. 3A.

[45] According to its own statistical evidence, the extra-EU services grew faster than its intra-EU counterpart in the period 1979–84, GATT Doc. MTN.GNS/W/23 of 30 October 1987.

[46] More recently, in its Opinion 1/08 (30 November 2009) the ECJ held that services is a shared competence between member states and the EU.

seem: the Chairman of Committee 113 was always included in the negotiations, and thus, the EU delegation was composed by the Commission as well as the member states' representative.[47]

But there is another, probably more persuasive, reason explaining why, while the United States adopted a gung-ho attitude pushing for a negotiation at all costs, the EU in general, adopted from early on a rather defensive stance (towards the negotiation of the GATS): Paemen and Bentsch[48] have argued that this is due to the fact that the EU wanted to avoid finger pointing against its own farm policy; being aggressive in the services context could have provoked (especially in developing countries) an aggressive attitude against the EU CAP, which the EU wanted, initially at least, to defend at any price.

Against this background, it should come as no surprise that the French President, François Mitterand, as late as January 1985, refused to agree to a precise date for the launching of the Uruguay Round.[49] The EU was not initially a *demandeur* for a round in general, never mind trade in services. However, once the original diffidence was overcome, the EU sided with those requesting liberalization of trade in services (in large part due to the fact that its own market had been quite liberalized, even though the integration process was still ongoing). The link between negotiations on farm trade and trade in services is evident in the Decision adopted by the Council of Ministers, adopted on 19 March 1985, to participate in the

---

[47] Committee 113 (later, Committee 133) is the EU Committee in charge of the EU Common Commercial Policy. It owes its name to the provision in the Treaty Establishing the European Community (EC Treaty) which provided for a common commercial policy. The chairman of this committee was a delegate of the member state assuming the presidency of the EU (which rotates every six months). See in this respect, the excellent analysis of Bourgeois in Bourgeois, J., 'The Uruguay Round of GATT: Some General Comments from an EC Standpoint', in N. Emiliou and D. O'Keeffe (eds), *The European Union and World Trade Law*, Chichester, Wiley, 1996, pp. 81–90 and Bourgeois, J., 'The EC's Trade Policy Powers After Nice: Painting Oneself in a Corner', in G. Vandersanden (ed.), *Mélanges Offerts à Jean-Victor Louis*, Brussels, Editions de l'Université de Bruxelles, 2003, pp. 29–38. In practice, this did not prove to be too much of an obstacle though.

[48] Paemen, H. and Bentsch, A., *From the GATT to the WTO, The European Community in the* Uruguay Round, Leuven, Leuven University Press, 1995, p. 32 *et seq*.

[49] Paemen and Bentsch, *supra*, at p. 46. See also Croome, J., *Reshaping the World Trading System*, Geneva, The World Trade Organization, 1995, at p. 16 *et seq*.

Uruguay Round that urged the European negotiators to safeguard the CAP while encouraging meaningful negotiations in services.[50]

What explained the change in the mood in the EU? There is probably no dominant explanation and some truth must lie in the following factors:

- The EU must have felt that it would have been awkward to incur the political cost of blocking altogether a round in the name of the protection of its internal farm market. This line of thinking would not argue in favour of enthusiastic support, but definitely in favour of no isolation.
- The emergence of its services sector and the establishment of non-negligible (from a political economy perspective) lobbies undeniably helped the EU bureaucracy realize the potential gains from opening up the services markets worldwide. A series of national studies that saw the light of day in the early to mid 1980s unveiled the importance of the services economy to EU bureaucrats. The EU Commissioner at the time, Willy De Clercq, is quoted as becoming sensitized to the importance of trade in services following this type of information.[51] And this is the kind of information that the services lobbies inside the EU commissioned and exploited in an effort to persuade the EU authorities to change their view on the necessity to negotiate a new round with services in its agenda. Inside the EU, the ECSG (European Community Services Group), which represented services exporters in the EU and the EFTA (the European Free Trade Association), was set up at the invitation of the European Commission in 1985, with the Uruguay Round of trade negotiations in prospect. It was composed mainly of national chambers of commerce, employers' federations, and services coalitions such as the Liberalisation of Trade in Services (LOTIS) committee[52] of the British Invisible Exports Council.[53] The Banking and Insurance Associations, and the Fédération des Experts Comptables Européens for the accountants

---

[50] Paemen and Bentsch, *supra*, at p. 45 *et seq*. Eventually, the EU would have to give in a bit in its objectives to safeguard its CAP in order to extract concessions in trade in services.

[51] Drake, W.J. and Nicolaidis, K., 'Ideas, Interests and Institutionalization: 'Trade in Services' and the Uruguay Round', *International Organization*, Vol. 46, 1992, pp. 37–100 at p. 57 *et seq*.

[52] LOTIS is a committee of British industries formed in order to brief the UK government on private sector's views on international trade issues (trade in services).

[53] This entity is a confederation of trade association representing the British services industries.

figure also among the important lobbies. UNICE, the Federation of European Employers, was providing meeting facilities. There is evidence of co-ordination between the EU and North American interests during the Uruguay Round: US Chamber of Commerce in Brussels, which represents US affiliates based in the EU, and the US and Canadian CSI had been the guests of the ECSG;[54]

- it should further come as no surprise that the EU bureaucracy was fully behind the negotiation of an agreement. For the EU Commission, trade was the only area where the EU could reaffirm its persona at the international plane, since the EU enjoyed no competence in any other field of international relations and trade was the area where it could speak with one voice. Granted, it was unclear whether the EU had competence on services. This would not, however, stop the EU Commission from pushing the agenda further: adding services in the trade agenda would augment its competences and its relative position towards the Council in the inter-agency game.[55]

Bhagwati mentions three other factors that contributed to this change of mood in Brussels:[56]

- besides services, the EU must have been well aware of gains in other areas especially in new areas such as TRIPs (trade-related intellectual property rights). The EU TRIPs lobbies were certainly pushing for participation in the new round;
- the need to put a stop to US regionalism also played a role. Paradoxically, it was the EU that was now reacting to what it had been practising for years: following the EU example, the US had already signed its preferential agreement with Canada and, at that moment, there was at least uncertainty as to the identity of those that would follow in signing similar agreements with the US. Moreover, there was uncertainty as to the commitment of the US to the multilateral trading system, some fearing that it might see preferential agreements not as *complement* but as *substitute* to the multilateral system. Indeed, President Reagan was in favour of a new round, under conditions though. His message to his team was 'if

---

[54] Arkell, J., *The Role of Services in Socio-economic Transformation and the Integration of Western and Eastern Europe*, Budapest, Institute for World Economics, 1990. See also, Woll, C., 'Trade Policy Lobbying in the European Union: Who Captures Whom?', Mimeo, 2007.

[55] The EU Parliament did not have decisive competences at that time, it does though now.

[56] Bhagwati, *supra*, pp. 1–48 at p. 33. On this last point, see also Waelbroeck, J., 1987. International Trade in Services: a Comment, pp. 54–7 in O. Giarini (ed.), *The Emerging Services Economy*, New York, Pergamon Press.

these negotiations are not initiated or if insignificant progress is made, I am instructing our trade negotiators to explore regional and bilateral agreements with other nations'.[57] Maybe President Reagan was bluffing, but was the EU prepared to call on his bluff;

- finally the US Congress was getting into a protectionist mood: although the *Jenkins Bill* on textiles was voted down, there was fear that similar initiatives would soon see the light of the day. In general, the EU felt that a multilateral initiative would remove the argument from those in the US Congress pushing for even more aggressive unilateralism and supporting additional Section 301 initiatives.

The EU gradually became more influential, especially after the Mid-Term Review of the Uruguay Round (Montreal), when it sided with a host of developing countries and produced a text to keep the negotiation alive, and later in the design of the various GATS instruments:[58] being itself an integration process, it was well aware of the limited usefulness of some instruments that its services regulation had 'borrowed' from its goods regulation. The GATS followed, as we will see in more detail *infra*, an integration process *à la* EU: first evaluate how much of the GATT can be meaningfully transposed and then negotiate adjustments, if warranted.

One last point: approximately at the same time, the EU was negotiating the completion of its own single market. Although the objectives of the EU single market and the new multilateral round were not the same (far from it), still the EU agent entrusted with the task to negotiate at the international plane (Commission) benefited from cross-fertilization in light of the similarity of the instruments used in the two processes.[59]

4.2.4 The Rest of the OECD is prepared to Follow

OECD (Organization for Economic Cooperation and Development) members were in favour of the negotiation, in general, without necessarily sharing the US enthusiasm. Capling's detailed account of the Australian

---

[57] Quoted in Preeg, *supra*, at p. 51.

[58] This is not to suggest that the United States did not influence the shaping of GATS instruments; to the contrary, although its position changed substantially as we detail *infra* (the United States had to accept that its investment model would not see the light of the day), the United States participated in the negotiation of each and every GATS instrument.

[59] Ehlermann, C.D. and Campogrande, G., 'Rules on Services in the EEC: A Model for Negotiating World-Wide Rules?' in E.U. Petersmann and M. Hilf (eds), *The New GATT Round of Multilateral Trade Negotiations, Legal and Economic Problems*, Dewenter, Boston, Kluwer, 1987, pp. 481–98.

participation in the Uruguay Round points to an attitude that resembles more that of the EU rather than that of the United States.[60]

In her account, the (original) Australian diffidence was due to various factors:

- the willingness to continue protecting Australian culture through local content requirements in broadcasting;
- the uncertainty as to the coverage of the eventual agreement (fearing that the United States could be excluding sectors of export interest to Australia);
- the suspicion that the United Stateswas diverting attention from the 'real issues', that is, the opening up of farm markets; and
- finally, because Australian lobbies were not *demandeurs* for such negotiation.

The change in attitude was due, in her view, to the fact that the government was eventually persuaded by the epistemic community that there were real advantages in the opening up of services markets (both at the national and the international level). Australia had its own services lobby: the Australian Coalition of Services Industries (ACSI), modelled after the European and the American associations was created in 1987. New Zealand followed a similar path: following deregulation of its national market, New Zealand sided with those requesting opening up trade in services, its main (export) interest being in various professional services. Canada was more or less on the same wavelength: well aware of its export potential in some services, but quite unwilling to open up others, like audio-visual, which meant a lot especially to its French-speaking community.[61] Japan was a net importer of services but very much interested in negotiating a multilateral framework to liberalize trade.[62]

---

[60] See Capling, A., *Australia and the Global Trade System: From Havana to Seattle*, Cambridge and New York, Cambridge University Press, 2001, p. 149 *et seq.*

[61] Hart, M., *A Trading Nation*, Vancouver, UBC Press, 2002, p. 398 *et seq.*

[62] See GATT Doc. MTN.GNS/18 of 29 November 1988, at para. 8.

4.2.5 Sovereignty Oh So Dear in the Hearts of Developing Countries

Developing countries reluctantly accepted services as a negotiating issue. At first, that is before the Ministerial Conference in Punta del Este, they refused to enter into any negotiation on this issue.[63]

The promoters behind this hard line were the countries forming the G-5 (or 'Gang of Five', as they were known), that is, Argentina, Brazil, Egypt, India, and Yugoslavia. They were hostile in the negotiation altogether and would not even bow to the temptation to use liberalization of their services markets as a *quid pro quo* for the opening up of the OECD countries' textiles markets: in their eyes, the multi-fibre arrangement, which essentially segmented national markets allowing only negotiated quotas in the importers' (OECD) markets was an illegal act altogether, and saw no reason to pay for its dismantlement.

They also feared that a negotiation on trade in services would divert the attention of negotiators from the true issues: the Tokyo Round left some unfinished business behind, in the sense that, farm and textiles trade continued to be non-liberalized. Developing countries, with typically scarce negotiating resources, would find it difficult to simultaneously follow negotiations on the traditional GATT agenda (which comprised farm and textiles goods) as well as on trade in services. As far as they were concerned, the latter could function as an undesired digression from their genuine priorities.[64]

Even in Punta del Este (1986), where they finally accepted to negotiate as we will see in section 4.3, they did so only as a means to explore to what extent an agreement was feasible. In the words of the Brazilian delegate:[65]

> The reluctance of developing countries was partially overcome in *Punta del Este* when they gave their assent to a beginning of this process, in a demonstration of good will, *by accepting to explore the possibility* of arriving at a 'set of multilateral rules on trade in services.

They did not want to enter, initially at least, into a wider bargaining game: they feared that their requests for opening up of the farms' and textiles'

---

[63] See GATT Docs. MDF/26 and 27. See also Hufbauer, G.C. and Schott, J., *Trading for Growth, The Next Round of Trade Negotiations*, Washington DC, Institute of International Economics, 1987, at p. 69 *et seq*.

[64] Developing countries voiced similar concerns when the EU in subsequent negotiations argued in favour of including new topics in the multilateral agenda, such as the elaboration of multilateral competition rules.

[65] GATT Doc. MTN.GNS/W/3 at para. 3, emphasis added.

markets of developed nations (for which they did not want to pay as we saw) would lead to the opening up of their services' markets, some sectors of which they considered of strategic importance and wanted for this reason alone to keep under their tight regulatory control. A firewall between the two negotiations should, in their view, be installed from day one.[66]

Their reluctance to participate overcome,[67] developing countries subsequently focused on limiting the immediate impact of liberalization of service activities (where policies in many cases had never been really developed due to the oft encountered perception that services cannot be traded internationally), and, as we will see *infra*, concentrated in advancing specific export interests (e.g. labour-intensive services).

Developing countries also advanced other, development-related concerns and invoked them as justification for their overall reluctance. In this vein, they made it clear time and again that the 'S' word should guide negotiations, it should be 'one fundamental principle to guide all phases in our collective endeavour', that is, 'solutions ... by definition must be compatible with ... *sovereignty*'.[68] In the words of the Brazilian delegate:[69]

> In the exercise of their sovereign right to regulate the services sectors, governments take actions essential for the promotion of vital national policy objectives. Such actions are by definition legitimate and cannot be submitted to international scrutiny. What flows from our decision in *Punta del Este* is solely a political willingness to consider incidental positive or negative effects such regulations might have on the implementation of the negotiating objectives. In other words, we would be prepared to consider such possible effects on the expansion of trade without in any manner putting into question the legitimacy of the ultimate aim, common to both our national regulations and to this process of negotiation, that of furthering the individual economic growth and development of our countries.

---

[66] The firewall, assuming one actually existed, was heralded as a Brazilian success: see Wahrendorff, C. R., *Brazil in the Uruguay Round of the GATT*, Aldershot, Ashgate, 1998. Paemen and Bentsch, *supra*, as we will see *infra* lead the voices arguing, quite persuasively in our view, that a firewall *de facto* never existed.

[67] There were nonetheless, voices in the academia urging them to do the opposite and use the services' negotiation as a *quid pro quo* for their requests for example in removing barriers for their exports of goods: see the analysis in Schott and Mazza, *supra*.

[68] GATT Doc. MTN.GNS/W/3 at para. 10, emphasis added. See also, Sapir, *supra*. Technological innovations do not only explain the growth of trade in services; they are also responsible for the erosion of the 'bite' of sovereignty (and ultimately, for the change in the attitude of developing countries).

[69] GATT Doc. MTN.GNS/W/3 at para. 17.

Through this attitude they wanted to signal their resolve to keep strategic sectors to themselves (national control) and avoid opening up their national markets to foreign companies.[70] Thus, they thought, they would avoid that their economies would be effectively controlled by foreigners.[71]

The picture painted so far is probably too absolute and need some refining: some (at least self-proclaimed) developing countries were quite favourable to the negotiation: Hong Kong, China and Singapore, financial centres of prominence welcomed the idea.[72] On the other hand, one should not neglect that developed countries did not always view with sympathy, never mind enthusiasm, the transformation of their economies from manufacturing to services economies, as the following passage from Shelp amply demonstrates:[73]

> Consider American reactions to the decline of the U.S. manufacturing base and the country's accelerating transformation into a service economy. Few welcome this change as a natural evolution into a higher stage of economic development. Instead, U.S. opinion makers unite in warning that dependence on services means economic decline and the loss of great-power status. The 1984 Democratic presidential nominee Walter Mondale captured this feeling when he spoke of a future in which America's children would be serving hamburgers and sweeping up around Japanese computers.

As things stood, domestic lobbies in the developed world were pushing for a services negotiation. There were no such lobbies in the developing world. Indeed, the only item that developing countries (eventually) pushed for during the Uruguay Round (as we will see *infra*) was migration. What is the domestic lobby pushing for this item though? Trade unions? Hardly so. Trade unions have other more pressing demands to push for. So while in the developed world American Express and the financial establishment was pushing for a multilateral negotiation, in the developing world the agenda was the exclusive privilege of the governmental bureaucracy. This is where ideology reigned, at least in the beginning.

---

[70] Paemen and Bentsch, *supra*, provide anecdotal evidence regarding the banking sector in African countries, p. 37 *et seq*. In general, see Riddle, *supra*.

[71] M. Gibbs and V. Ognitsev, 'International Trade', pp. 3–15 in *Beyond Conventional Wisdom in Development Policy, An Intellectual History of UNCTAD 1964–2004*, New York and Geneva, United Nations, 2004.

[72] See Rivers, Slater and Paolini, *supra*, at p. 19. The term 'developing countries' is conventionally used to describe non-OECD countries, but even so it comprises a highly heterogeneous group. On Singapore's strategy, see Mun Heng, T. and Low, L., 'GATT Multilateral Trade Negotiations: Singapore's Perspectives', *Asian Economic Journal*, Vol. 2, 1988, pp. 192–215.

[73] Shelp, *supra*, p. 65.

4.2.6 The Academia: Some Saw Potential

There were scarce academic voices arguing in favour of establishing a multilateral framework to liberalize trade in services.[74] Chief among them, the London-based Trade Policy Research Centre, founded by Australian economist, Hugh Corbet, one of the pioneers of the study for the necessity of an agreement on trade in services. In a highly influential report dating from 1972, this institution called for a negotiation of a global agreement on services.[75]

Other fora gradually developed. The Services World Forum (SWF), set up in Geneva in 1986, is worth mentioning in this regard for various reasons: it was an independent forum with idiosyncratic membership, since it provided academics, policy-makers, and members of the *GATT Secretariat* alike with a platform to discuss and indeed attempt to conceptualize the basic of a negotiation on trade in services.[76] This is how it described its role:

> The role of services in the world economy commands increasing attention among economists, business leaders and policy-makers. There is an absence, however, of a relevant body of theory, store of information, or independent forum for the exchange of ideas on these issues.
>
> To fill this gap, the Services World Forum (SWF) was established in 1986 in Geneva, the purpose of which was to facilitate the exchange of ideas among all those interested in the world services economy by facilitating dialogue among its members, publishing information on services in the world economy and organising conferences, symposia and similar meetings on services issues.

The agenda of the SWF is another reason for singling it out: a number of studies were prepared under its aegis by academics and policy-makers alike.

---

[74] Following the pioneering work of Deardorff, A.V., *Comparative Advantage and International Trade and Investment in Services*, Ann Arbor, Michigan, University of Michigan Press, 1984, a number of economists started working in this area exploring the applicability of trade theory to trade in services, see notably, Hindley, B. and Smith, A., 'Comparative Advantage and Trade in Services', *The World Economy*, 1984, Vol. 7, pp. 369–89; Ethier, W. and Horn, H., 'Services in International Trade', in E. Helpman and A. Razin (eds), *International Trade and Trade Policy*, Cambridge, Massachusetts, MIT Press, 1991, pp. 223–44; Richardson, J.B., 'A Sub-Sectorial Approach to Services' Trade Theory', in O. Giarini (ed.), *The Emerging Services Economy*, New York, Pergamon Press, 1987, pp. 59—82.

[75] See the appendix in Feketekuty, *supra*. The *Trade Policy Research Centre* published a number of services-related studies by influential analysts such as Robert Baldwin and Brian Hindley.

[76] See the discussion in Drake and Nicolaidis, *supra*, at p. 61 *et seq*. See also www.ucd.ie/sirc/swfintro.html.

Its President, Orio Giarini, managed to persuade people like Geza Feketekuty (USTR), Claude Barfield (Consultant, USTR, and then American Enterprise Institute (AEI)), Albert Bréssand (who later founded Prométhée, another forum that was active in the discussion of trade issues), but also Murray Gibbs (United Nations Conference on Trade and Development (UNCTAD)),[77] and GATT Secretariat members Mario Kakabadse, Raymond Kormmenacker, and Jacques Nusbaumer (acting as vice president).

It is difficult to establish with precision the influence that the epistemic community has had on the GATS. Indeed, although Drake and Nicolaidis[78] probably got it right when they conclude that the epistemic community did not substantially influence the drafting of specific GATS provisions, or even the basic GATS architecture, it did provide useful comments that helped negotiators in the initial stages of the negotiation to understand what was at stake.

4.3 THE GATS NEGOTIATION

4.3.1 The Road to Punta del Este

The Uruguay Round was launched in September 1986 in Punta del Este, near Motevideo. Here is how we got there:

- in 1982 the GATT Ministerial Decision allowed for national studies to be conducted by those willing and opened the door to their examination in the 1984 session;
- following the rejection of the US proposal to establish a Working Party on Services, the Jaramillo Group sees the light of day and it is in this context that national studies conducted in accordance with the 1982 Ministerial Decision were examined;
- in 1984, the contracting parties institutionalized the information exchange mechanism (in essence, the review of national studies) and *ipso facto* the Jaramillo Group.

Then, the US formally requested an extraordinary session of the GATT contracting parties in September 1985; the session was held between

---

[77] The UNCTAD prepared a number of major studies before and early on in the negotiation where trade in services was comprehensively discussed, the *Services and Development Process*, 1985 and the *Trade and Development Report*, 1988.

[78] Drake and Nicolaidis, *supra*, p. 97 *et seq.*

30 September and 2 October 1985.[79] During this session, it was decided to establish a Senior Officials Group (SOG) to discuss the modalities of a new round in which trade in services would have been included. This group met 11 times and although it did not manage to produce something concrete regarding trade in services it did keep the discussion regarding the new round alive.[80]

During the same time, the ECSG made its position regarding the ambit of the services negotiation in the next round clear to the EU Commission:[81]

> The ECSG sees the Services Agreement as the completion of an international framework of law for all trade. It should be designed to serve for decades to come, and be able to cope with the increasing pace of innovation in the creation and delivery of services.
>
> The ECSG affirms that it wishes to see a Services Agreement signed this year as the culmination of the four years of work by the GNS at GATT. The Agreement should include principles and rules for liberalisation of trade in services to apply to all service sectors and forms of services transactions.
>
> There should also be a clearly identifiable amount of liberalisation by central and local governments, and a standstill to prevent the imposition of any new restrictions and distortions inconsistent with the agreed principles.
>
> In order best to serve the needs of services users, the central issue for the providers is the creation of rules to provide certainty and predictability in gaining effective market access. This should include the necessary degree of establishment through local presence, and for access to local services and distribution networks and systems, under conditions of fair competition including the placement of qualified personnel and the use of proprietary business names.
>
> Beyond the Uruguay Round there should be periodic negotiations to increase liberalisation through further packages of concessions. Countries wanting to grant additional market access should be free to do so within the general coverage of the Services Agreement.

---

79 Bradley, J.A., 'Intellectual Property Rights, Investment, and Trade in Services in the Uruguay Round: Laying the Foundations', *Stanford Journal of International Law*, Vol. 23, 1987, pp. 57–98 at pp. 78 *et seq*. The GATT Council was an organ that had not been foreseen in the original GATT. It was established through a decision by the contracting parties (GATT Doc. BISD 9S at pp. 8–9). It was meant to undertake the tasks of the GATT contracting parties in between their (annual) sessions. Like the *GATT Council*, the GATT contracting parties was deciding by consensus. However, in theory at least, it could decide most issues by the majority of the votes cast (Article XXV GATT). It is impossible to know whether the United States would push for voting. It did nonetheless, signalled its interest to decide this issue at the highest level, and not simply in the context of an informal group.

80 Bradley, *supra*, at p. 79.

81 Quoted in Arkell, *supra*.

> Commitments undertaken initially should include transparency, mfn/nondiscrimination, and institutional provisions, together with additional commitments for specific sectors and/or transactions so as to yield increased effective market access either immediately or in a specified time scale of short duration.

So, while the momentum for the new round was building up, the trading partners needed to agree on how comprehensive the new round would be. Following encouragement by a number of delegations, Dunkel decided to turn to the experts in an effort to provide some extra intellectual legitimacy to the voices calling for a new round. He made appeal to a group of experts[82] with no affiliation to the GATT and asked them to provide a diagnosis of the major issues in trade relations and also suggest their medicine. The group was composed of seven personalities: Bill Bradley (US Senator and member of the SFC); Pehr Gyllenhammar (Chairman of Volvo); Guy Ladreit de Lacharrière (Vice President of the International Court of Justice (ICJ)); Fritz Leutwiler (Chairman of the Swiss National Bank, and President of the Bank for International Settlements); Indraprasad Patel (London School of Economics); Mario Henrique Simonsen (ex Minister of Finance for Brazil); and Sumito Djojohadikusumo (ex Minister of Trade and Industry of Indonesia). Leutwiler acted as chairman and the group produced the Leutwiler *report* to which we made reference *supra*. This was rather short report (roughly 50 pages) aimed at persuading governments about the merits of multilateralism. It did not address the merits of negotiating an agreement on liberalization of trade in services in meaningful detail. It did, however, provide those arguing in this sense with an encouragement through its statement to the effect: 'An attempt to extend a rule-based approach to new areas of economic relations while permitting the rules of trade in goods to continue to decay would lack credibility.'[83]

The next year, at the 41st session of the GATT Contracting Parties, a Preparatory Committee was established in order to prepare the next round

---

[82] This was only the second time in GATT history that the GATT turned to outside experts. In 1958, a group of experts was established under the Chairmanship of Gottfried Haberler (Harvard), Roberto de Oliveira Campos, a Brazilian economist and minister of state, and two Nobel prize winners in economics, James Meade and Jan Tinbergen. Together they produced a report called *Trends in International Trade* that discussed the state of international trade during that period. Meade was added as a fourth member, GATT Doc. L/794/Add. 1 of 14 March 1958.

[83] This passage is cited in Croome, *supra*, at pp. 19–20. Croome provides a comprehensive discussion of the report.

of multilateral trade negotiations.[84] The Preparatory Committee was mandated to determine the objectives, modalities, subject-matter and participation of the new round. Nothing substantial came from that body either, except for a separate decision to endorse the continued exchange of information on trade in services.[85] In his report to the Session of Contracting Parties at ministerial level, this is how Ambassador Jaramillo summarizes the state of the negotiations on the need to add trade in services in the agenda of the upcoming round:[86]

> In my own view, the meetings had gone a long way towards examining the relevant aspects of the issues under discussion and in addressing the themes and concepts to which various delegations had drawn attention. The discussions which had taken place in connection with the presentations by representatives of other international organizations had also provided an opportunity to deal with development aspects, with some key sectoral activities, and with the role, of transnational corporations in services. Clearly, however, in the absence of national examinations from developing Contracting Parties, and perhaps of some other elements of information on specific subjects which might be thought desirable, the documentation at hand could not be said to be exhaustive. Therefore, it would be wise at this stage to leave open the possibility for examining any new information which could be made available. Moreover, while the exchange of information had been useful, I did not find that there was a consensus on which to base recommendations to the Contracting Parties on the question of the appropriateness and desirability of multilateral action on services.
>
> A number of options were open under the terms of reference of the Decision of Contracting Parties of November 1985. Consultations were held among a large number of delegations and at informal meetings convened to discuss the matter. These consultations lead to the conclusion that an attempt to draft a text of agreed recommendations for adoption by Ministers would not be useful, given the divergences of views which existed.
>
> On the other hand, many delegations considered that a clear statement of positions by individual delegations would assist Contracting Parties in gauging the situation and in identifying some points of convergence concerning the central question of the appropriateness, desirability and modalities for any possible multilateral action on services.
>
> At the meeting of 29 August 1986, there were statements by some delegations in which they expressed their views on the state of the deliberations and indicated that -some elements of convergence between previously opposed views were emerging that seemed to show that a solution in the field of services might

84 GATT Doc. BISD 32, at p. 10.
85 Croome, *supra*, at p. 27.
86 GATT Doc. MIN(86)/4 of 15 September 1986.

be possible. Other delegations expressed scepticism about some aspects of these statements. In this situation I felt that it would be for Ministers at this meeting to tackle the issue in an effort to reach a solution satisfactory to all Contracting Parties. Accordingly, the meeting of 29 August 1986 recommended that Ministers take fully into account all statements made at that meeting (which are recorded in MDF/36), those made at the meeting of 27 and 30 June 1986 (MDF/35) as well as all the work undertaken under the Agreed Conclusions of 1984 and the November 1985 Decision of the Contracting Parties. I would suggest that all these elements might be used as a basis on which efforts way be undertaken at this Session to work towards consensus.

4.3.2 The Meeting in Punta del Este (1986)

The negotiation of the GATS was not completed until well after the advent of the WTO (1 January 1995).[87] Negotiators had not managed to agree on the disciplines on maritime transport, financial services and telecoms by the end of 1994. The general framework of the GATS nonetheless, that is the foundational agreement including the disciplines that are applicable across all sectors as well as those sectoral agreements that were finalized in time, entered into force on 1 January 1995. It all started with the Ministerial Conference held in Punta del Este in September 1986, where, amidst strong disagreements as explained above, the trading nations gathered in an effort to overcome their differences and agree on an agenda for the new round. The question we care about is whether trade in services would be integral part of this agenda. It was meant to be as we explain in what immediately follows. The ride, however, was far from smooth.

There the US adopted a very aggressive attitude threatening that absent inclusion of GATS in the new agenda it would have recourse to unilateral actions by virtue of its notorious section 301. Developing countries, and especially the G-5, stood their ground opposing any such negotiation and the EU was the accidental middle man. It was however, largely thanks to an idiosyncratic group that the situation was unblocked: the Café au Lait group owes its existence to the 1982 Ministerial Conference decision

---

[87] For a very concise history of the GATS, see Fuchs, C., 'GATS Negotiating History', pp. 1–16 in R. Wolfrum, P.-T. Stoll, and C. Feinäugle (eds), *WTO, Trade in Services*, Leiden, Martinus Nijhoff, 2008, Hoekman, B.M. and Kostecki, M.M., *The Political Economy of the World Trading System*, Oxford and New York, Oxford University Press, 3rd edn, 2009, p. 333 *et seq.* and Islam, R.M., *International Trade Law of the WTO*, South Melbourne, Oxford University Press, 2006 at p. 343 *et seq.* In anticipation of the Punta del Este meeting, the United States had put forward a draft *Ministerial Declaration* that included a passage on trade in services, see GATT Doc. PREP.COM(86)/w/34 of 11 June 1986.

discussed *supra*, calling for national studies and exchange of information on services: since there was no centralized mechanism to conduct such exchange of information due to the fierce opposition of the hardliners among developing countries, some developing countries decided to join forces with industrialized nations and pursue this mandate, albeit informally so.

It is Colombia's Ambassador, Felipe Jaramillo, who was presiding over the group's meetings. Jaramillo, at that time, while also serving as Chairman of the GATT contracting parties. Thus, a linkage of the group with the GATT was, de facto established.

Narlikar[88] mentions that two sets of developing countries were active in this process: the enthusiasts (her terminology), including exporters of services (typically, the east Asian newly industrialized countries), others that hoped to gain from issue linkage and trade-offs, such as Chile, Colombia, and Uruguay, and some, such as Jamaica, who was anticipating gains through services liberalization; a second group of countries, mainly small countries driven by the uncertainty of their own interests and by fears of the cost of exclusion. Under the leadership of Colombia and Switzerland, and combining the majority of developing and smaller industrial countries, the Café au Lait group emerged with the participation of members of both the G-20 and the G-9 group of countries. The Swiss–Colombian (revised) draft[89] became the basis for the talks during the Punta del Este Ministerial Conference where the decision to launch the Uruguay Round was taken with an agenda that would include international negotiations to liberalize trade in services.[90] This was aided by the fact that Argentina switched camps and this enfeebled the negotiating position of G-10.

The Uruguay Round agreements are often referred to in literature as a single undertaking: this term was conceived as the antidote to the GATT *à la carte* approach that was privileged in the Tokyo Round when trading nations could pick and choose the agreements that they wanted to join. Although not seriously discussed, it was agreed that WTO members should

---

[88] Narlikar, A., *International Trade and Developing Countries: Coalitions in GATT and the WTO*, New York, Routledge, 2003.

[89] GATT Doc. MTN.GNS/47/Rev. 2 of 30 July 1986.

[90] The Café au Lait group overcame the North-South divide, and in that it was unprecedented. It presented itself as a bridge-building coalition engaged in mediation-type diplomacy in the space provided by the EU–US rift on services and the extremes of the US position versus the G-10. Its alternative name, Friends of the New Negotiations, was indicative of this positive stance. It is not entirely surprising that the path of issue based diplomacy pursued by the G-10/Café au Lait was subsequently taken up by the Cairns Group of agricultural exporters.

avoid assuming asymmetric obligations in the WTO-era.[91] Multilateral trade negotiations (MTN) were covered by the single undertaking; MTN came under Part I of the Ministerial Declaration of Punta del Este that signals the beginning of the Uruguay Round; the GATS came under Part II and as such it was not part of the single undertaking approach.[92]

The decision to initiate the negotiations on liberalization of trade in services was taken in Punta del Este in an ad hoc intergovernmental meeting, parallel to the session of the contracting parties[93] where a decision on a new round of negotiations on trade in goods in the GATT was simultaneously adopted.[94] For Brazil, and India a separate track was the maximum they would accept.[95]

Note that the other contentious new issue, TRIPs, came under Part I that is it was formally part of the single undertaking. Trade in services was singled out and in what follows we explain how this compromise was reached and what it actually meant.

Paemen and Bentsch[96] conclude that the attempt to separate the two negotiations (goods, services) failed the moment when the Punta del Este Declaration was adopted.[97]

4.3.3 The EU between Punta del Este and Geneva

The EU negotiating position was uncertain at the moment the Uruguay Round was launched. It was clarified at the end of the round, when the EU

---

[91] Asymmetric obligations do exist however, in the WTO-era as well as a result of two factors: protocols of accession (where acceding countries often assume obligations that incumbents have not assumed), and the existence of plurilateral agreements, where participation was optional (four were signed during the Uruguay Round).

[92] GATT Doc. MTN.GNS/2 of 25 November 1986.

[93] Expressed in block letters this term refers to the highest organ of the GATT with the substantial authority to adopt acts by GATT organs, modify the agreement, launch trade negotiations etc.

[94] GATT Doc. MTN.GNS/W/3 at para. 4.

[95] Randhawa, P.S., 'Punta del Este and After: Negotiations on Trade in Services and the Uruguay Round', *Journal of World Trade Law*, Vol. 21, 1987, pp. 163–71 at p. 164 *et seq*.

[96] Paemen and Bentsch, *supra*, p. 56 *et seq*.

[97] Quite expectedly so. As McCulloch (*supra*, pp. 345 – 6) has argued, separation of the two tracks limits 'the efficiency gains attainable through multilateral negotiations, and especially potential North-South agreements to make liberalization in labour-intensive manufactured goods in the North the quid pro quo for high technology and services liberalization in the South.' On this score, see Conconi, P. and Perroni, C., 'Issue Linkage and Issue Tie-in in International Negotiations', *Journal of International Economics*, Vol. 57, 2002, pp. 423–47.

jointly requested an opinion from the ECJ to this effect. This meant that throughout the round the EU agent, the Commission was on a tight leash: its negotiating positions were not only *ex ante* decided but also *ex post* scrutinized by the EU Member states. This does not seem to have been such a decisive factor though: EU negotiators managed to advance common positions throughout the round and play a useful, a key role throughout the negotiation. There is no evidence of unpleasant back and forths between the EU agent and member states during the negotiation and all divergences managed to get resolved behind the scenes.

There was, moreover, a positive external effect stemming from the intra-EU distribution of competences: the common agent, the Commission, had to report back to ten member states with divergent interests. Sometimes it was participating in discussions next to them. It had to be in its best behaviour and provide the most detailed possible accounts as a token for continuing to enjoy the representation privileges. The EU delegates kept very comprehensive, details records of each and every discussion, participated in practically all meetings, and emerged, because of the information they had acquired during the process, as a key player in the negotiation.

The EU was in favour of a comprehensive agreement.[98] Its overall negotiating objective was to considerable extent function of its willingness to preserve its CAP. The farm lobby was, at the time at least, the one that in equilibrium the EU would defend over others. This led, as we shall see in more detail *infra*, the EU into reinventing itself as some sort of mediator between the US and the rest of the trading nations, developing countries included.

4.3.4 1986–88: Houston, We have a Problem

Negotiations went through many ups and downs. Schematically, this where countries stood at Punta del Este:

---

[98] A key negotiator for a member state (von Dewitz, Germany) went on record stating that 'from a negotiating point of view it is preferable to put as much as possible into the basket which contains the subjects for negotiations. The more comprehensive such subjects, the easier to reach a reasonably balanced exchange of concessions between the negotiating partners': von Dewitz, W., 'Services and the Uruguay Round: Issues Raised in Connection with Multilateral Action on Services: a Comment', in E.U. Petersmann and M. Hilf (eds), *The New GATT Round of Multilateral Trade Negotiations, Legal and Economic Problems*, Deventer, Boston, Kluwer, 1987, pp. 475–9 at p. 479.

		Forum	
		GATT	**Non-GATT**
Coverage	**Full**	Developed	
	Partial	Café au Lait	G-10

By the end of the round, the compromise reached by Uruguay Round participants could be described as follows:

		Forum	
		GATT	**Non-GATT**
Coverage	**Full**		
	Partial	Developed and Developing	

The first two years, however, were an education process for everybody (almost) as negotiators tried to get a good grip of the idea that they would be negotiating essentially regulatory barriers.

4.3.5 Mid Term Review at Montreal (1988)

As became the GATT practice, half way through the round (or around that time) negotiators would meet to take stock of the progress of negotiations and agree on whatever needed to be done in order to complete the round. Montreal welcomed the negotiators who, nonetheless, did not have much to report, not in services negotiations anyway. The basics had not been ironed out, never mind negotiating language that would find its way into the eventual agreement. The text that was submitted to the meeting[99] was heavily bracketed[100] to the point that Yeutter, the USTR, was quoted stating that it was: 'the worst I've ever seen coming to a ministerial meeting'.[101]

[99] GATT Doc. GNS/21 of 21 November 1988.

[100] By GATT custom, a bracketed text signals disagreements across the participants. Often, alongside the bracketed provision, one (or more than one) alternative will be mentioned in brackets of course.

[101] Capling, *supra*, at p. 156.

The EU essentially saw itself as mediator between the United States on the one hand and developing countries on the other. It tried to find a middle ground that would keep the negotiation on track and was probably hoping that its efforts would be recognized in other negotiating fora (such as farm talks, textiles trade) as well. Paemen[102] and Bentsch refer to a 'secret' meeting where delegates from the EU, Sweden and a host of developing countries (Argentina, Brazil, Egypt, India, Jamaica) participated where the so-called 'weekend text' was produced.[103] This text formed the basis of the Montreal Declaration.[104]

4.3.6 1988–90: Montreal–July Text

The main issues that occupied the negotiators during the post-Montreal period are:[105]

- the question whether the negotiation until the end of the Round should be limited to the provisions that would form integral part of the general framework, or, conversely, *initial liberalization commitments* would also have to be negotiated for the Round to be successfully completed;
- whether the *negative list-* or the *positive list* approach would ultimately carry the day;
- the manner in which the *initial liberalization commitments* would be entered (following the quick decision to reject a proposal by developing countries to limit the pre-Round negotiations to the shaping of the general framework). In this context, two questions emerged as the basic issues: *first*, the manner in which the *initial liberalization commitments* would be entered, that is, the subject-matter of what was eventually termed *specific commitments*; second, the manner in which services would be traded under the (eventual) GATS, that is, the *modes of supply*;
- the *GATT Secretariat* was asked to prepare documents to test the applica bility of GATT principles (such as NT, MFN, etc.) on specific sectors. The following sectors were chosen for this endeavour: telecommunications;

---

102 Hugo Paemen, a high EU Commission official, was one of the leading EU negotiators during the Uruguay Round.

103 Marconini, M., 'The Uruguay Round Negotiations on Services: an Overview', pp. 19–41 in B. M. Hoekman, P. Messerlin, and K. Sauvant (eds), *The Uruguay Round: Services in the World Economy*, Washington DC, The World Bank Group, 1990 goes so far as to describe the EU stance as that of a consistent mediator between the United States and developing countries throughout the process.

104 GATT Doc. MTN/TNC/7(MIN) of 9 December 1988.

105 Reyna, J.V., 'Services', in T.P. Stewart (ed.), *The GATT* Uruguay Round*: a Negotiating History*, Deventer, Boston, Kluwer, 1993.

> construction services; transportation; tourism; professional services; and financial services, including insurance.[106]

Between April and July 1990, the so-called July Text was prepared and circulated. This text was submitted by the Chairman of GNS and it is made clear in the text that there was no agreement on the provisions included therein. Additional negotiations would be necessary to this effect, especially concerning coverage (where, although Article II of the text made it clear that the text applied to all services, footnote 1 acknowledged the right to exclude specific sectors), MFN, and the negotiation of specific commitments. When presenting this document, Ambassador Jaramillo underscored that work had been done in this last aspect:

> 7. I also want to recall that under the auspices of the GNS, a number of sectoral working groups have held informal consultations on particular service sectors (i.e. on financial, telecommunications, transport, construction/engineering services as well as on issues relating to labour mobility). Such consultations will also be held with regard to professional, tourism and audiovisual services. The aim of these consultations is to arrive at sectoral annotations or annexes, where considered necessary, to interpret or effectively apply the provisions of the framework to specific sectors. These sectoral annotations, following agreement in the GNS, should then form an integral part of the framework.

The July Text is very interesting in several respects:

- It is made clear that the general obligations (including those on domestic regulation) will bind the discretion of signatories with respect to all services covered (by the eventual agreement), irrespective whether a specific commitment has been entered.[107] The bifurcation between general framework and specific commitments does not have only a time dimension anymore: the former can have *wider* coverage than the latter.
- It was foreseen at the time that specific commitments could be made not only with regard to market access and national treatment, but also with regard to 'any other provisions to be decided upon'.
- The text hints at the existence of four 'modes of delivery', as they used to be identified at the time, instead of 'mode of supply' that was

---

[106] GATT Doc. MTN.TNC/13 of 23 January 1990. Every sector had a different chair in an effort to speed up the process: Peter Gallagher, for example, an Australian official, chaired professional services (Capling, *supra*, p. 157 *et seq.*).

[107] This was made clear in Article XIX GATS, entitled 'Application'.

privileged later. Indeed, although Article I of the text made reference to cross-border supply, cross-border movement of consumers; and cross-border movement of factors of production (under the condition that the specificity of the purpose, discreteness of transactions, and limited duration); Article XX GATS on schedules of commitments identified four modes of delivery: cross-border delivery, movement of consumer, commercial presence, and movement of personnel.

- In line with the approach taken with regard to the application of the other general obligations, the provision on domestic regulation (now, Article VI GATS) does not distinguish between obligations in case a specific commitment has been entered and otherwise. It does, however, impose a necessity requirement with respect to requirements such as standards and qualifications.
- A framework is put into place with respect to restrictive business practices (RBPs), which requires from parties questioned to provide information about their own domestic economic operators whenever warranted.

Although the July Text was presented as a 'clean' text, it was clear, as indicated by Ambassador Jaramillo in his introductory note, that several key issues remained unresolved. Chief among them were the coverage (which was presented as universal in the text but where some delegations favoured the possibility of excluding sectors from the agreement's coverage); MFN and market access (where there were still proposals related to conditional MFN, relative reciprocity, or reciprocal market access); and the negotiation and application of specific commitments (where some delegations have taken the position that there should be a baseline for the future liberalization process).

Negotiations continued and, on the basis of the July Text and the progress made in the next six months, the trading partners met in Brussels at the end of that year where the next Ministerial Conference took place as scheduled. Between July and end of November 1990 (just before the date when the Brussels meeting took place), the July Text was not substantially altered, only refined. Negotiations in the period between July and end of November 1990 concentrated on MFN, the conceptualization of the provisions regarding specific commitments, US sub-federal taxation (the consistency of which with non-discrimination is heavily put into question), movement of physical persons, modification of schedules (where EU, and the United States wanted considerable flexibility), and subsidies.

4.3.7 The Brussels Meeting (December 1990)

Based essentially on the July Text, a text was prepared that was formally submitted to all trading partners when they met in Brussels (Brussels Ministerial Conference).[108]

The text was substantially *bracketed* but still even within brackets it provided more or less a meaningful basis for the GATS general framework. The text did not reflect a formal agreement between the trading partners. §1 of the Chapter on Services of the Brussels text reads:

> The draft text of the Agreement is submitted by the Chairman of the Group of Negotiation on Services on his own responsibility. There remain many divergences of views among participants, and most of these are reflected in square brackets in the text.

The Brussels text contained 35 provisions (just like the July Text). Basically all the GATS provisions as we know them, albeit not verbatim identical, are thematically there. The drafting however, is sometimes awkward. Moreover, there are some exceptions such as Article V*bis* GATS (Labour Market Integration Agreements), which was agreed at a later stage.

Nevertheless, several key features of the GATS took shape in this draft:

- it was the first time that the four modes of supply, with the distinction between presence of natural persons and juridical persons, were mentioned in Article I GATS;[109]
- the exclusion of services supplied in the exercise of governmental functions (now 'governmental authority') also appeared in the text for the first time;
- the provisions on increasing participation of developing countries in services trade and on economic integration agreements were beefed up, although there were two alternative texts for the latter;
- a provision on recognition and harmonization of regulations made its way to the text for the first time;

  specific negotiating mandates were drafted for safeguards and government procurement; and
- many of the provisions that were simply mentioned in the July text

---

[108] GATT Doc. MTN.TNC/W/35/Rev.1, Annex II of 3 December 1990.

[109] See the comment by Self, R.B. and Zutschi, B.K., 'Mode 4: Negotiating Challenges and Opportunities', pp. 27–59 in A. Mattoo and A. Carzaniga (eds), *Moving People to Deliver Services*, Washington DC, Oxford University Press and the World Bank Group, 2003, at p.33.

were actually developed, such as the ones on modification of schedules, and dispute settlement.

The issues however that remained open in the July Text were not resolved in Brussels either. One of those issues – the major one according to the commentary to the text – was MFN. The alternative text for Article II raised the question whether specific derogations from this principle should be provided for in sectoral annexes. In fact, one of the main objectives of the several sectoral annexes included in this text was to exempt those sectors from the application of MFN. The sectoral annexes included in the text dealt with telecommunications, maritime transport services, air transport services, road transport services, in-land water transport services, labour mobility, audio-visual services, and financial services. Regarding the latter, the commentary explained that 'while there was agreement on the need for a sectoral Annex on financial services, there was no agreement on its scope and content', which would 'again depend on the manner in which the MFN issue is settled'. The conditions for application of the balance-of-payments provisions, as well as the scope of exceptions, were also highlighted in the commentary as requiring further work.

The services negotiators managed to meet only once in Brussels and, thus, could make no substantial progress at all. It is in Brussels that the US backed definitively away from unconditional MFN, probably following pressure to this effect by Jack Valenti, the most important US lobbyist in the audio-visual sector, who was representing the Hollywood based *Motion Picture Industry Association* (MPIA) The coverage of the agreement remained unmodified, the Indian delegate (Zutshi) being now fully on board with respect to the right of establishment.

The Brussels meeting failed over disagreements regarding the transformation of the EU CAP. After all, it had been agreed that the package emerging from the Uruguay Round would be a single undertaking, that is, none of its constituents would become legally relevant if the whole itself had not become legally relevant: failure to agree on farm issues *ipso facto* led to general failure. The doom and gloom was back in Geneva.[110]

[110] In a way, the failure in Brussels was a blessing for services negotiators who now had more time to streamline the drafting of various provisions agreed as well as attempt an agreement on unresolved issues such as the ambit of MFN.

4.3.8 The Dunkel Draft

Back in Geneva delegates of the trading nations went back to the table of negotiations, following a decision of the TNC to this effect.[111]

In order to resolve the crisis, the GATT Secretariat prepared a series of confessionals, that is, meetings between members of the Secretariat and one delegation at a time, aimed at clarifying national positions. The round of confessionals started almost immediately after Brussels.[112] At the same time, negotiations in the GNS context continued: the so-called Room B meetings[113] multiplied and it is there that delegations attempted once again to iron out their differences and hammer the GATS general framework.

Intensive meetings were organized in Room B of the GATT building.[114] The meetings were of course, open to all GATT contracting parties. Only some of them were physically present almost all times. The rest were either participating by proxy or had decided not participate at all. The GATT contracting parties that were almost always present were: Australia; Bangladesh; Brazil; Canada; Chile; Colombia; Egypt; EU; Hong Kong, China; India; Japan; Korea; Malaysia; Mexico; New Zealand; Singapore; Sweden; Switzerland; Tanzania; Uruguay; United States. While Room B would normally host delegates with technical expertise on the issue, Green Room meetings would be organized where normally DG Dunkel and selected ambassadors would participate. The countries mentioned above were almost all present in these meetings.

Three delegates, nevertheless, almost monopolized the negotiations between Brussels and the preparation of the Dunkel Draft: Jonathan Scheele (EU), Dik Self (United States), and B.K. Zutshi (India) had many meetings with them and with the Secretariat (Mamdouh) and together managed to produce a number of drafts for various provisions that would ultimately be included in the Dunkel Draft.[115]

Based on input from the confessionals, as well as (some) progress made in the Room B meetings, DG Dunkel, put together a text which, its limited

---

[111] GATT Doc. MTN.TNC/19 of 1 March 1991.

[112] GATT Doc. MTN.TNC/19 of 1 March 1991.

[113] Room B is one of the meeting rooms in the main GATT, now WTO building in Geneva.

[114] Some negotiations took place in *Room F*. Irrespective of the room where they met, trading nations always tried to ensure that a balance between developed and developing countries participating was being kept.

[115] Brazil was concentrating in the goods negotiations, and India became the leading developing country in the services-negotiation.

legal value notwithstanding, provided content-wise the basis for the eventual agreement (the Dunkel Draft).[116] In prefacing his magnum opus, DG Dunkel described it as follows:[117]

> A complete and consolidate document bringing together the results of five years of effort. This document is the outcome both of intensive negotiations and of arbitration and conciliation: negotiations among you, the participants, and conciliation by the Chairmen when it became clear that, on some outstanding points, this was the only way to put before you a complete, consolidated text. It represents the global package of results of this Round.

It should be underscored that DG Dunkel did not think of services as a ground-breaker. From a moment onwards during the negotiations, he decided himself to chair the negotiating groups on Agriculture and on Textiles, obviously holding the view that these two groups held the key to the successful conclusion of the Uruguay Round.

4.3.8.1 The train leaves the station (December 1994)

Eventually, and after some self-imposed (unrealistic) deadlines had been violated, following a trade-off between EU concession in the farm sector against US additional opening of its services market,[118] and developing countries new offers in some sectors, the agreement on services was concluded. The new DG, Peter D. Sutherland, played an important role in bringing the overall package to a successful conclusion.

In his statement to TNC he highlighted the remaining issues to be resolved and requested from negotiators to focus there:[119]

> Yesterday's meeting of Heads of Delegation discussed the negotiations on Services, focusing on the few outstanding textual issues and on the remaining

---

116 Capling (*supra*, p. 163) reports that the services part of the text was the outcome of intense drafting by Ambassador Hawes, Ambassador Jaramillo, Charles Carlisle (through his aide, Abdel-Hammid Mamdouh) and Gary Sampson who at that time was still the Director of the Services Division.

117 GATT Doc. MTN.TNC/W/FA of 20 December 1991, (hereinafter 'the Dunkel Draft'). Hart (*supra*, p. 414) quotes Dunkel stating: 'This has not been a Round in which initial objectives have been steadily whittled away to produce 'diplomatic', but impractical solutions to difficult and complex problems. Quite the contrary; ambitions have risen with time, not fallen. The results we have already secured are relevant, precise, balanced and urgently needed answers to some of the biggest economic challenges of the day. They are results from which every trading nation will gain.'

118 *EC Hints at Agriculture Compromise Linked to US Action on Services*, Daily Report for Executives (BNA), 5 May 1992 at A-1.

119 GATT Doc. NUR 077 of 26 November 1993.

> problems in Maritime Transport, Audiovisual Services and in particular Financial Services. Quite apart from the substance of these problems, I was struck by the consciousness of the overwhelming pressure of time; however complex the substance may be, further delay will make their solution harder, not easier – because all solutions have to be multilateral.
>
> The time factor is particularly evident today, which is the deadline agreed by the GNS for the submission of draft final schedules and final lists of MFN exemptions. Revised schedules and exemption lists are being submitted and circulated every day, but many of these schedules are still heavily conditional often for perfectly understandable reasons and there are far too many outstanding. We have to remember the sheer logistical problems of circulating schedules which are submitted late, and of having them examined in capitals. I have asked Ambassador Hawes to focus on these questions at this afternoon's meeting of the GNS.

Focus there was, and it led to successful conclusion not without some late friction though: the EU, surprisingly for many, changed its attitude on maritime transport days before the final agreement, requesting now exclusion of this sector from the package. The rationale that the EU offered for its change of heart had to do with its disagreements with the United States regarding the extent of *cabotage*: in its view, the United States opted for a very expansive understanding of the term, making it impossible to successfully negotiate a compromise.

This led services negotiators back to the room where the Annex on Negotiations on Maritime Transport Services was concluded. For all practical purposes, negotiations on maritime transport were postponed for a later day, that is after the entry of the Uruguay Round package. It is thanks to this final compromise that reportedly was achieved one hour before the gavel in the hands of Peter D. Sutherland marking the end of the round went down, that the GATS had been finally agreed.[120]

Developed countries were in principle in favour of no exclusions. When it came however to negotiating the actual concessions disagreements across the trading nations appeared immediately even across developed countries. Except for the audio-visual sector,[121] the EU did not, in the initial phase at

---

[120] Negotiations on basic telecoms, financial services and maritime transport were concluded in the late 1990s. Mickey Kantor, the USTR, gave his own account of the last moments of the negotiation: see *The World Trade Agreement: The Turning Point; A Call from Clinton, and Then a Deal*, Business Day, 16 December 1993.

[121] The EU had enacted the Directive on the *Television Without Frontiers* whereby each EU member state could reserve a quota for 'European' programmes. France championed the cause opting for a 60 per cent quota. These quotas however did not stop the United States from conquering the EU audio-visual market:

least, have any sector that emerged as a 'no no' in the negotiation.[122] The EU was not alone in thinking that the audio-visual sector was idiosyncratic: Australia had, as we saw *supra*, local content requirements in broadcasting and lent a sympathetic ear to the EU's position in this respect. Japan was not unsympathetic either.

The United States on the other hand, had to deal with requests by powerful domestic lobbies against the opening of its maritime transport and the financial services markets. The position of the United States needs some further explanation here since it has moved a long during the negotiation: initially the United States (as we saw in the beginning of the chapter) adopted a universal approach, where all sectors would be included. After the Montreal Ministerial Conference, though, when the negotiation slowly moved into its final phase, lobbyists exercised pressure to exclude sectors:

- by letter of 1 August 1990, House Representatives Anderson and Hammerschmidt, requested from the Secretary of Transportation to exclude the airline industry from the coverage of the agreement;[123]
- a number of US Congressmen threatened to disrupt the fast track, that is, the US legislative procedure under which an international agreement will either be accepted as such and become US law or will be rejected but will not be modified, if the then USTR, Carla Hills, were to include maritime transport in the final package.[124]

The EU position needs some additional explaining. In its first comprehensive proposal, the EU had submitted that 'This Agreement covers all services. An illustrative list of sectors of services is provided in Annex (...) of this Agreement.'[125]

This would suggest that the EU favoured a negative list. In this vein, note that the EU did not share the belief of others that its position regarding the audio-visual sector was *ipso facto* an acceptance of the positive list approach: the EU believed that, in light of culture-related matters, the

---

Paemen and Bentsch (*supra*, p. 246 *et seq.*) cite evidence suggesting that the US had almost four-fifths of the EU market at that time.

[122] As we saw *supra*, the EU had a last-minute change of heart on maritime transport.

[123] *Inside US Trade*, Vol. 8, 10 August 1990 at p. 5.

[124] *Inside US Trade*, Vol. 8, 3 August 1990 at p. 4. Arkell (*supra*) states that the EU services lobbies were quite discouraged by the US change of heart (as well as the Japanese diffidence to go for a comprehensive, all-encompassing agreement).

[125] GATT Doc. MTN.GNS/105 of 18 June 1990.

audio-visual sector was idiosyncratic; it need not be excluded, it sufficed that its idiosyncratic elements were recognized.[126] However, in its first comprehensive proposal the EU did include provisions allowing for positive list: this is the only way one can meaningfully understand Artsicles XIX and XX of its submission (GATT Doc. MTN.GNS/W/105). And Falkenberg,[127] one of the EU negotiators, provided confirmation that for pragmatic reasons the EU was led to endorse the positive list:[128]

> Adopting a negative-list approach; I do not believe that countries will make commitments they do not intend to make by a simple presentational trick. I believe rather on the contrary that the approach followed in GATS has allowed many countries to list commitments which would otherwise have taken no commitment at all. It is the best means to achieve progressively higher levels of liberalization which is the major GATS objective.

In the same document, the EU accepted the idea that exceptions from MFN would be permissible to the extent that a PTA had been formed, or on non-application grounds (this provision should permit a signatory not to apply some of its liberalization commitments to another signatory when it considers that the level of commitment of the other signatory is not in keeping with the particular characteristics of that signatory's market and the degree of liberalization already achieved by that signatory, as well as its individual development situation in different sectors). The EU, with the benefit of its experience from its own internal market experience, made a series of proposals for a provision aiming to discipline domestic regulation.[129]

4.4 EU: WHAT IT ASKED, WHAT IT GOT

In general, as the table below shows, the EU was overall one of the four most active negotiators:

---

[126] Paemen and Bentsch, *supra*, at pp. 162 *et seq.* and 246 *et seq.*

[127] Falkenberg, K., 'Comments', in P. Demaret, J.F. Bellis, and G. Garcia-Jimenez (eds), *Regionalism and Multilateralism after the* Uruguay Round, Brussels, European University Press, 1997, pp. 457–64 at p. 461.

[128] It seems thus, fair to conclude that the EU wanted a negative list (minus air traffic and services in the exercise of governmental authority) as far as the general framework was concerned, and a positive list with respect to specific commitments.

[129] GATT Doc. MTN.GNS/105 is the most comprehensive. For example, Article VI.6 GATS is quite reminiscent of the notorious *Heylens* jurisprudence of the ECJ.

Table 4.3

	Brazil	EU[130]	India	US
General Individual	9	10	3	9
General Joint	1		2	
Sectoral Individual		10		8
Sectoral Joint			4	
Total	**10**	**20**	**9**	**17**

The EU had, as we saw, an originally negative attitude towards the Round in general, most probably because in the early and mid-1980s it was still a long way before seriously moving towards reform of its CAP: anticipating that the CAP reform would be the number 1 target of most participants, it attempted to stall the process. Eventually, however, that is, when it decided to go along with those requesting a new round, it became an influential player in this negotiation for a variety of reasons:

- its vulnerability (CAP) was also a huge asset: the EU realized that if it could 'tame', even to some degree, its farm lobby, it possessed automatically a very powerful tool to open up services markets abroad, since its consideration (opening up its farm market) was too good to turn down by the vast majority of trading nations;
- the EU further realized that it could play a useful role by positioning itself between the US requests to open up services markets across the board and the developing countries refusal to do so: siding with the latter could prove beneficial to its own unwillingness to open up its farm market while accepting at the same time limited liberalization of developing countries' services markets. The EU could thus, maximize its options and have more of a discretion to choose eventually whether it would side with its farm (defensive) or its services (offensive) lobby. The ultimate decision was not, of course, a unction of the international negotiation, but (also) very much the outcome of an internal struggle between the pro- and anti-CAP member states;
- the US later attitude (the request to exclude some services, such as maritime transport, and financial services from the coverage of GATS) provided the EU with an additional negotiating advantage since it would be in better position now to propose trade-offs;

130 We count EU-10, i.e. pre-accession of Austria, Finland, and Sweden.

- finally, one should not overlook the fact that the EU had a lot of technical expertise on the issue: the EU officials were well aware of problems associated with the opening up of national services market, as well as the usefulness (and the limits) of concepts such as MFN and NT in this endeavour.

The EU was in favour of a comprehensive negotiation, arguing that the non-inclusion of the audio-visual sector had to do with idiosyncratic elements inherent in this sector. The persuasiveness of this argument is, of course, debatable. As things stand nonetheless, nothing much has happened in this sector. The USTR, Mickey Kantor, and the Trade Commissioner for the EU, Sir Leon Brittan,[131] were locked into negotiations as of 13 December 1993, that is 48 hours before the agreed date for conclusion of the Uruguay Round. They did not manage to solve this issue (although they managed to save the round by agreeing that negotiations on telecoms, maritime transport, and financial services would continue after the entry into force of the Uruguay Round package). On 14 December 1993, Sir Leon Brittan[132] announced that the EU would not be making any commitments in the audio-visual sector.[133] This is how Sir Leon Brittan describes what happened:[134]

> On my return from lunch I found that Mickey had been in touch. The negotiations resumed, and indeed continued all night. Alternatively he threatened and pleaded and broke off from time to time to get fresh instructions from the President. But I was not prepared to budge, and in the end the US decided, rather foolishly in my view, that they would not accept our limited offer because that would 'legitimise' our current restrictions. Instead they got nothing at all. Their bluff had been called and the Round was concluded on the basis of a massive liberalisation of trade, but without any audio-visual commitment from Europe. The fact that I was willing to risk all in this way should convince even the most prejudiced person that I too could see that there were certain values which Europe was entitled to defend and that when they were under threat we should not roll over in the face of American pressure, however great.

[131] Brittan, L., *A Diet for Brussels, The Changing Face of Europe*, London, Little, Brown and Company, 2000.

[132] *Id*, at pp. 46–7.

[133] In fact, following the EU refusal to make commitments a number of countries withdrew the commitments made to the great disappointment of Jack Valenti.

[134] Mickey is of course, Mickey Kantor, the then USTR. In Brittan's account (*supra*, p. 46) the US film industry had at the time of the negotiation 80 per cent of the European market.

Overall, the EU delegates must have left the negotiating tables rather happy: they managed to keep out of the reach of GATS the sector where they were most defensive (audio-visual); the original pessimism (few commitments by its trading partners) gave its place to measured optimism since a framework for further liberalization was being slowly established while some of its partners increased their offers.

It is probably fair to conclude from the negotiating record cited so far that the EU was not instrumental in launching the negotiation on services, but very much so in shaping the final agreement. In what follows, we will invoke the main GATS provisions where the EU has had its hand.

The first EU comprehensive submission[135] is a far cry from the GATS as we know it:

- There is no clear distinction between general framework and specific commitments as we now know it: for example, NT figures as Article IV in the EU submission without specifying that it is applicable only to the extent a specific commitment has been made. Its function would be that of a general obligation from which, however, exceptions could be taken if so scheduled in national schedules (Article XIX of the EU proposal).
- The market access provision looks more like a standstill provision; three columns are provided (market access, NT/subsidies, and a third called effective market access: this last term covers additional measures to achieve effective market access through the modification or elimination of measures other than those which restrict the range of activities or otherwise deny service providers of other parties competitive opportunities on the market of the party concerned equal to those of its own providers).
- There is special emphasis put on the flexibility of the contract:
  - there are two provisions on non-application, one general, one specific between two parties;
  - there are provisions on balance of payments, and general exceptions (like in most proposals) but also on subsidies and countervailing measures, antidumping, and safeguards;
- There is finally, an elaborate provision on modification of schedules.
  - it is clear that the EU sides with those who believed that the forum to host the new agreement should be the GATT.

Hence, some notable differences exist were one to compare this vision of the agreement with the current GATS. Still, one can see that, abstraction

135 GATT Doc. MTN.GNS/W/105 of 18 June 1990.

made of contingent protection, the instruments used by the EU in order to achieve trade liberalization are those that were finally chosen by the trading partners. Their function however, was altered in the negotiation process.

The EU should be credited with the maternity (or paternity) of the transparency provision: it is the EU that proposed a comprehensive provision encompassing the duty to publish all relevant laws, to provide for enquiry points, and that allowed for counter-notification (or cross-notification, as the practice to report other members' laws is now usually referred to).[136]

The discussion *supra* points to the fact that EU also had a heavy hand in the drafting of other key provisions, such as the four modes of supply, domestic regulation, NT, and the modification of schedules.

The EU was quite vocal on institutional issues as well, such as dispute settlement. In fact, it is the EU and US that almost monopolized the discussion here. In their shared view, in case of retaliation (non compliance with a panel decision), appropriate compensation should be paid in the same sector, but the possibility for retaliating outside this sector should be left open.[137]

When it comes to specific sectors, the EU was in favour of market opening for the overwhelming majority of sectors: it was consistently defensive during the negotiations on the audio-visual sector, and suddenly at the end of the negotiation on maritime transport. While the rationale for its attitude in the former is well-documented (the EU arguing that there are idiosyncratic elements in this sector that make it a vehicle for transmission of cultural values), there is almost nothing on the record regarding its change of heart in the latter.

4.5 CONCLUDING REMARKS

The 1980s and 1990s is no time for exemplary statesmen like the post World War II period that saw the establishment of institutions such as the UN, the World Bank, the IMF, and closer to our discussion, the GATT. The study by Irwin et al.[138] shows that, individuals that marked the post World War II construction of international cooperation were behind a trade agreement as well. The (subsequent) Economics Nobel Prize winner James Meade was

---

[136] GATT Doc. MTN.GNS/W/65 of 20 July 1989.

[137] GATT Doc. MTN.GNS/34 of 16 July 1990 at para. 21 *et seq.*

[138] Irwin, D.A., Mavroidis, P.C., and Sykes, A.O., *The Genesis of the GATT*, New York, Cambridge University Press, 2008.

an active member of the UK delegation, as was the reputed economics professor Lionel Robbins, and the French philosopher Alexandre Kojève. The 1980s is a different world. It is now modern bureaucracies that drive the negotiation forward, and domestic inter-agency battles (like that between USTR and US Treasury on financial services) have had important repercussions on the shaping of the negotiating agenda and the eventual compromise.[139] The influence of the epistemic community is very limited indeed.

Against this background, it seems fair to conclude that the US provided the impetus to sign the agreement, and the EU in fine-tuning it. In a way, the Uruguay Round in this respect is not exceptional when compared to previous rounds: it is another version of US idealism against (or complemented by) EU pragmatism/realism. The United States started with a very ambitious agenda, and the EU tailored it down to what could realistically be achieved within a heterogeneous multilateral context.

The agreement as such is no monument of clarity. Indeed, it is very much the outcome of an elaborate political compromise. One might legitimately have a hard time trying to understand what purpose a rather empty general framework serves. Or, why Article VI GATS should be placed among the general obligations when its subject-matter relates to specific commitments. The language chosen is often awkward and it should come as no surprise that many of the disputes evolve around misunderstandings regarding the ambit of specific provisions. It is hard to imagine the GATS standing the test of time the way the GATT did, which goes strong more than 60 years after its original drafting. Yet, it is the negotiating history that we have discussed so far that explains why this has been the case: absent complex compromises, we would probably not have seen a GATS in the first place. Now, the first decisive step has been taken. Future experience can make it a better, more workable document.

[139] Although national delegations change over time and especially so in an eight year-period (that is, the time it took to complete the round), the reader can get a flavour of the individuals involved in the negotiation of the Uruguay Round by looking at GATT Doc. MTN.TNC/INF/1 of 27 October 1986. In this document the various delegations list their representatives to the negotiations.

5. Article IV of the GATT: an obsolete provision or still a basis for cultural policy?

Lothar Ehring*

This chapter is dedicated to Jacques Bourgeois in celebration of his 75th birthday. Since I have known Jacques only since 2003, I would like to extend my congratulations also on behalf of my late father, Hubert Ehring, who knew and worked with Jacques approximately half a century ago, and who appreciated him both professionally and personally as much as I do.

5.1 INTRODUCTION

Article IV of the General Agreement on Tariffs and Trade (GATT) 1994 of the World Trade Organization (WTO) has a prominent location in the text of the GATT 1994. It follows such fundamental provisions as Article I on most-favoured-nation treatment, Article II on scheduled tariff commitments, and Article III mostly on national treatment. It precedes Article V of the GATT 1994, another fundamental GATT article, not without reason, given that Article IV is connected to national and most-favoured-nation treatment.

Despite its prominent location, Article IV of the GATT 1994 is little known; even a very versed trade lawyer may not be able to spontaneously respond to the question of what this provision addresses. There is no GATT or WTO jurisprudence, and there is little literature touching on the content or interpretation of Article IV. This is probably because Article IV, contrary to most other GATT rules located in that article's neighbourhood, is not a fundamental obligation and does not have a broad scope of application. Rather, already the heading of Article IV, 'Special Provisions relating to

* This chapter expresses the author's views, and should not be attributed to the European Union or any of its member states.

Cinematograph Films', reveals that the rules contained in this Article are of a special nature in that they deal with a particular item only. They also deal with a particular type of national policy, namely regulations favouring the domestic film industry. Especially from a European perspective, this is precisely what makes it well worth knowing about the existence and content of Article IV, studying the history of the controversies surrounding the meaning of this provision and reflecting on the relevance that these have today in the light of the well-known changes in technology, social habits and commercial patterns that occurred in past decades and are ongoing today. For the same reason that Article IV addresses regulations favouring the domestic film industry and thus is related to the pursuit of cultural policies in potential contradiction to market forces, this provision has given rise to significant controversy over its interpretation especially in the 1960s and 1990s. None of these points of contention has so far been resolved authoritatively, whether by the GATT contracting parties, the WTO membership, or in dispute settlement by a panel or the Appellate Body.

Against this background, this chapter attempts to close a gap. It will first clarify issues of definition and the scope of application of Article IV, in particular in relation to television as well as modern forms of digital cinema. It will also explain the difference between trade in films within the meaning of Article IV and trade in goods as it is normally the subject of GATT rules. It will be seen that Article IV is peculiar in that it protects not just imported goods, or in fact not just trade in goods. The article then turns to the stipulations of Article IV themselves, addressing the introductory sentence and the four paragraphs of Article IV. The article finally deals with the nature of Article IV, specifically whether it is an obligation or an exception and the related question of the burden of proof, and sheds light on the relationship of Article IV to other provisions in the GATT 1994 and other WTO agreements.

5.2 THE SCOPE OF APPLICATION OF ARTICLE IV OF THE GATT 1994

For ease of reference, and because it will be seen that, as in many cases of legal interpretation, every word can matter, it is worth reproducing in full the text of Article IV:

Article IV
Special Provisions relating to Cinematograph Films

If any contracting party establishes or maintains internal quantitative regulations relating to exposed cinematograph films, such regulations shall take the form of screen quotas which shall conform to the following requirements:

(a) Screen quotas may require the exhibition of cinematograph films of national origin during a specified minimum proportion of the total screen time actually utilized, over a specified period of not less than one year, in the commercial exhibition of all films of whatever origin, and shall be computed on the basis of screen time per theatre per year or the equivalent thereof;
(b) With the exception of screen time reserved for films of national origin under a screen quota, screen time including that released by administrative action from screen time reserved for films of national origin, shall not be allocated formally or in effect among sources of supply;
(c) Notwithstanding the provisions of subparagraph (b) of this Article, any contracting party may maintain screen quotas conforming to the requirements of subparagraph (a) of this Article which reserve a minimum proportion of screen time for films of a specified origin other than that of the contracting party imposing such screen quotas; Provided that no such minimum proportion of screen time shall be increased above the level in effect on April 10, 1947;
(d) Screen quotas shall be subject to negotiation for their limitation, liberalization or elimination.

5.2.1 The General Scope of Application of Article IV of the GATT 1994

The introductory sentence of Article IV applies to 'exposed cinematograph films' relating to which members resort to 'internal quantitative regulations'. Article IV(a) to (c) seem to refer more broadly to 'cinematograph films' or 'films', but this does not lead to varying scopes of application within Article IV, as is clear from the fact that paragraphs (a) to (c) are requirements that a WTO member must satisfy if it applies internal quantitative regulations to exposed cinematograph films.

The concept of 'internal quantitative regulations' has not yet given rise to questions, in the limited practice of interpretation and discussion of Article IV to date. It also may be relatively straightforward to understand, at least regarding its main features, and the same concept is also used in Articles III:5–7. The first evident aspect to underline is that these regulations are 'internal' measures, as opposed to border measures in the form of quantitative or other restrictions on the *importation* of films. Secondly, they are imposed by the government or must at least be attributable to it for qualifying as 'regulations' that a WTO member 'establishes or maintains'. Thirdly, they must regulate the use or production of films in a *quantitative* manner.

At first sight, the concept of 'exposed cinematograph films' seems similarly straightforward. It is the type of films that so far has been the predominant medium shown in cinemas. 'Film' in the most ordinary meaning is a thin layer of any material, in Article IV and with the attribute 'cinematograph' it of course refers to the strip of transparent material covered with a photographic emulsion that allows the recording and reproduction of images. If it is 'exposed' it has content, and if it is developed (as well as transformed from the negative to a positive), the cinematograph film can also be exhibited. This product falls within heading 3706 of the Harmonized Commodity Description and Coding System and, at the time of the GATT 1947's drafting, it was *the* medium for the storage and exhibition of motion picture shows, whether with or without sound. Together with radio and newspapers, it was the most important mass medium of the time, as television had not yet emerged in force.

5.2.2 Post-1947 Changes in Technology and Commercial Patterns

Obviously, important technological changes have intervened since then and continue to take place today, bringing about new forms of media and more individual forms of viewing (television, video, internet etc.). Although films in the traditional sense as well as cinemas have not disappeared, the post-1947 developments raise the question of whether Article IV applies also to media other than those (still today, but possibly not for much longer) shown in cinemas. This question is relevant also because screen quotas applying to cinemas have lost a considerable part of their importance, given the developments that have taken place since 1947. Although some countries have kept their screen quotas in place or have newly introduced such quotas,[1] several other countries have abandoned the quotas that they had maintained over many years. At the same time, many countries have introduced quotas favouring domestic content in television broadcasting.

In summary, the following technological changes have occurred over time: first, the rise of television meant that viewers could see motion pictures no longer only in cinemas, but also in television broadcasts, even though originally this involved exhibiting the cinematograph film in the television studio, with a camera-type machine that transformed the picture and sound into broadcasting signals. Individual television sets would then transform those signals back into pictures and sound. Later, television broadcasters used tapes (and more recently other media), rather than exposed films, in order to play a motion picture in their programmes. The rise of television also brought about another form of production of motion

---

[1] For a list of such measures, see www.terramedia.co.uk/law/quotas_and_levies.htm (last visited 10 January 2011).

pictures not intended for cinemas, with the use of cameras that do not expose cinematograph films (but rather record on an electromagnetic tape or other medium). Simultaneously, motion pictures became available for private viewing from video tapes and then optical media such as digital versatile discs (DVDs). As far as motion pictures for cinemas are concerned, the high-end industry until these days continued to record the motion picture first on a negative cinematograph film. Since recently, the master negative is no longer multiplied and transformed into positives through analogue means, but digitised for the subsequent production of positives, as well as other, including digital, formats which can even be transmitted electronically across the world. At present, even the high-end motion picture industry is gradually migrating to a digital form of recording, and cinemas are – more slowly, but nevertheless also gradually – engaged in a process of installing digital exhibition equipment. These developments take time (also because of the costs involved), thus the 'exposed cinematograph film' has not yet disappeared from the market, even as far as new motion pictures are concerned. But this may happen at some point, at least to a large extent, namely when the recording of most or nearly all motion pictures occurs with digital cameras, and when cinemas are equipped with digital exhibition projectors and no longer can exhibit a film.

At that moment, Article IV of the GATT 1994 would become entirely obsolete, if its application was truly and definitively limited to 'exposed cinematograph films'. This would be a rather unusual proposition for an entire Article of the GATT 1994 and probably unprecedented, but of course unthinkable neither in law in general nor in WTO law. The following sections of this article will explore whether such redundancy is the inevitable fate of Article IV. The past advent and rise of television, as well as today's multitude and co-existence of analogue and digital formats, provide the perfect material for testing the ability of Article IV to adapt dynamically to different circumstances. Finally, the creation of the WTO General Agreement on Trade in Services (GATS) is also a change that intervened in the past and raises the question of whether it affected the scope of application or effect of Article IV of the GATT 1994.

5.2.2.1 Television in particular

The history of the debate The controversial question of the application of Article IV to television programmes first featured in a debate that took place in the early 1960s in the 19th and 20th sessions of the GATT contracting parties, and in a Working Party that they had established at the request of the United States. The United States at the time argued, rather plausibly to say the least, that tapes or films containing television programmes were goods that could be traded and that fell notably under Article III GATT 1947 but, less compellingly as this chapter will later explain, that Article IV did not or should not apply.[2] That entire debate is interesting from today's perspective in that a number of arguments made in support of distinguishing television from cinema seem contradicted at least by subsequent developments: namely that television broadcasters are not guided in their choice by the popularity of the programmes[3] or that cinemas, as opposed to television stations, compete with each other and that the consumer can choose the film and the time of viewing.[4] Often, the debate among the contracting parties or in the Working Party dealt more with the *lex ferenda*, i.e. the question of what guidelines the GATT should formulate and adopt for the content of television programmes, than with the *lex lata*, i.e. the question whether Article IV applies. The latter question, however, was always present as starting point or at least background, and the United Kingdom,[5] at the time not yet a member state of the European Economic Community, arguably deserves the prize for the sharpest and most convincing arguments in relation to distinguishing between television and cinemas and the question of Article IV applicability. The Working Party issued a report expressing totally opposing opinions regarding the applicability of Article IV to television programmes, namely the above view of the United States, then the contrary view that Article IV fully applies to television programmes, as well as finally the view that GATT 1947 does not apply at all to television broadcasting because this was a service. The latter argument is probably as plausible as saying that regulations governing the origin of passenger vehicles purchased by taxi companies fall outside the GATT because taxi transportation is a service. Whereas today a WTO member would have absolutely no chance of surviving with such an argument before a WTO panel or the Appellate Body (and the European

[2] Contracting Parties, Nineteenth Session, Application of GATT to International Trade in Television Programmes, L/1615, 16 November 1961; Contracting Parties, Nineteenth Session, Application of GATT to International Trade in Television Programmes, Statement Made by the United States Representatives on 21 November 1961, L/1646, 24 November 1961.

[3] Contracting Parties, Nineteenth Session, Application of GATT to International Trade in Television Programmes, L/1615, 16 November 1961, at pp. 1–2.

[4] Contracting Parties, Nineteenth Session, Application of GATT to International Trade in Television Programmes, Statement Made by the United States Representatives on 21 November 1961, L/1646, 24 November 1961, at p. 3.

[5] Contracting Parties, Nineteenth Session, Summary Record of the Ninth Meeting: Held at the Palais des Nations, Geneva, on Wednesday, 6 December, at 2.30 p.m., SR.19/9, 15 December 1961, pp. 148–50.

Union has in fact moved away from it),[6] such positions may have made some Realpolitik sense in a GATT where the work of dispute settlement panels was less legal and more political than today in the WTO, and most importantly could be blocked unilaterally by the responding party. The same held true for legal policy work undertaken by a GATT Working Party that could adopt any form of conclusion only on the basis of consensus. Consequently, the above-mentioned report of the Working Party proposed several (alternative) recommendations for adoption by the GATT contracting parties which, however, did not manage to reach consensus on any of those recommendations.[7] The United States subsequently proposed new draft recommendations,[8] but no agreement ever emerged.

The question of the applicability of Article IV to television programmes returned to the fore when the United States requested dispute settlement consultations under GATT 1947 with several European countries regarding European content rules in Article 10 of the European Convention on Transfrontier Television,[9] with the EEC regarding Articles 4 and 6 of the 'Television without Frontiers' Directive 89/552/EEC of 3 October 1989,[10] and with France regarding a decree on television broadcasting of cinematographic and audio-visual works.[11] The United States claimed that these measures constituted GATT breaches, whereas the EEC argued that they fell outside GATT 1947,[12] and that broadcasting, whether by television or by

6 See the European Union's written submission to the panel as a third party in the dispute *China – Publications and Audiovisual Products*, WT/DS363, 4 July 2008, para. 57, available at http://trade.ec.europa.eu/doclib/docs/2008/august/tradoc_140292.pdf (last visited 10 January 2011).

7 GATT, Application of GATT to International Trade in Television Programmes, Report of the Working Party, L/1741, 13 March 1962.

8 Contracting Parties, Twentieth Session, Application of GATT to International Trade in Television Programmes, Revised United States Draft Recommendation, L/1908, 10 November 1962; see also Application of GATT to International Trade in Television Programmes: Proposal by the Government of the United States, L/2120, 18 March 1964.

9 *Austria/Luxembourg/Netherlands/Norway/Spain/Sweden/Switzerland/United Kingdom – Measures to be Taken under the European Convention on Transfrontier Television*, Request for Consultations under Article XXII:1 by the United States, DS4/1, 11 September 1989.

10 *EEC – Directive on Transfrontier Television*, Request for Consultations under Article XXII:1 by the United States, DS4/3, 8 November 1989.

11 *France – Television Broadcasting of Cinematographic and Audiovisual Works*, Request for Consultations under Article XXII:1 by the United States, DS4/5, 8 May 1990.

12 *EEC – Directive on Transfrontier Television*, Response to Request for Consultations under Article XXII:1 by the United States, DS4/4, 8 November 1989.

any other means, belonged essentially to the area of services.[13] The dispute remained unresolved, and was merged into the Uruguay Round services negotiations, where new disciplines emerged for trade in services (subject to generous possibilities to schedule exceptions), while GATT disciplines remained unchanged. As a result, and in the absence of any dispute settlement decision by a panel, arbitrator or the Appellate Body, the question of the applicability of Article IV to television programmes remains controversial and unresolved to this date.

Analysis In the literature, the position that Article IV does not apply to television broadcasting is sometimes based on the subsequent practice of GATT contracting parties and WTO members.[14] It is, however, difficult to argue that the described practice satisfies the requirements of Article 31(3)(b) of the Vienna Convention on the Law of Treaties (VCLT), given the evident absence of an agreement of the parties regarding the treaty's interpretation. The dispute settlement practice of the Appellate Body and WTO panels suggests that a decision of this interpretative question would be made based on the ordinary language of Article IV as well as its context and object and purpose – as stipulated in Article 31 of the VCLT. The negotiating history of the GATT 1947, relevant in accordance with Article 32 of the VCLT, is unlikely to be of much assistance, as international trade in television content hardly existed at the time. The absence of such trade at the time, however, also means that the drafters of the GATT 1947 could not have the conscious intention to limit the scope of Article IV in such a fashion that it would not apply to television.[15] Such a limitation can in fact be said to be contrary to the drafters' objective, namely to allow a specific but effective method of protecting domestic film industries.[16] In that sense, the object and purpose of Article IV as well as the principle of effective treaty interpretation militate in favour of the application of Article IV beyond cinemas. In order to discern the precise extent of the coverage of television programmes, it is useful to take three different questions in turn.

---

[13] GATT Council, 11 October 1989, Minutes of Meeting held in the Centre William Rappard on 11 October 1989, C/M/236, 6 November 1989, p. 34.

[14] De Witte, B., 'Trade in Culture: International Legal Regimes and EU Constitutional Values', in G. de Búrca & J. Scott (eds.), *The EU and the WTO: Legal and Constitutional Issues*, 2001, p. 237, at pp. 245–6.

[15] The drafters of the GATT 1994 are arguably less relevant in this context, given that they did not modify the text of GATT 1947 and left the controversies over the interpretation of Article IV unresolved.

[16] See also *infra* section 5.3.

The first question is whether Article IV applies only to cinematograph films screened in cinemas, or whether it also covers the exhibition of the same exposed cinematograph films on television, which is how motion picture shows were initially broadcast on television. The terms 'screen quota' and 'screen time' in the introductory sentence, as well as in paragraphs (a) and (b), are not obstacles to the latter interpretation; on the contrary, television programmes are displayed on screens as well, albeit (so far) smaller ones than in cinemas. The Spanish version of the GATT 1994 does not speak of 'screen quotas', but of '*contingentes de proyección*' ('projection quotas'), which can equally apply to both cinemas and television. Less neutral is the stipulation in Article IV(a) that the screen quotas be 'computed on the basis of screen time per theatre per year', but since members can also use 'the equivalent thereof', it is arguable that the text of Article IV can apply to television programmes,[17] despite their (general) exhibition outside 'theatres'.

The mere fact that the drafters of the GATT 1947 did not have television programmes in mind is, of course, insufficient for ruling out the application of Article IV. That situation was different for the drafters of the GATT 1994 who incorporated the text of GATT 1947, but, more importantly, generic terms of the WTO Agreement that are not static are subject to a dynamic or evolutionary interpretation.[18] The terms of Article IV, whether 'cinematograph films', 'exhibition', 'screen quotas' or 'screen time', must therefore be interpreted in the factual contexts existing after 1947 and to this date. Hence, there is a solid basis for asserting that Article IV covers the exhibition of exposed cinematograph films on television.

The concept of dynamic or evolutionary interpretation is also crucial for the second question of whether Article IV applies to television programmes also when the object of the broadcast is not an exposed cinematograph film, but the same motion picture played from a videotape, an optical disk, hard drive or an electronically transmitted signal. All these situations nevertheless qualify as the (indirect) 'exhibition of cinematograph films', provided that the non-film medium was produced from a cinematograph film. It may be an indirect exhibition of that film, but an indirect exhibition is also an exhibition and therefore covered by the term 'exhibition' in Article IV. The motion pictures of the high-end industry so far have been first recorded on a negative cinematograph film, which then serves to produce other, including digital, formats. Where this is not the case, namely

---

[17] Opponents of this position would presumably argue that 'equivalent' does not allow switching to an equivalent of a 'theatre', but only to a different computation method producing a similar result.

[18] See Appellate Body Report, *US – Shrimp*, WT/DS58/AB/R, para. 130.

where motion pictures are originally recorded using video or digital cameras, as already the case in the more modest segments and increasingly now even in the high-end segment, it would seem arbitrary and wrong to rule out the application of Article IV just because a movie was never recorded on exposed film at the outset.[19] For this proposition, one can however no longer rely on the ordinary meaning of the terms stipulated in Article IV of the GATT 1994. Rather, one has to recall the principle of effective treaty interpretation, as well as the object and purpose of Article IV. In 1947, cinemas were the sole market for the products of the motion picture industries. If this has changed due to the advent of television, and other media have been added to the medium of 'exposed cinematograph film', then it is important to interpret Article IV in such a manner that it does not become partly, or one day even entirely, obsolete, and unable to fulfil its objective. These considerations not only should result in Article IV applying to motion pictures played on television from media other than exposed cinematograph film. They are even more compelling reasons to apply Article IV also when cinemas (partly already today and certainly even more in the future) play movies from such other media and no longer from cinematograph film.

Thirdly, it would seem consistent with the preceding analysis to apply Article IV also to recordings other than motion picture shows that are shown on television, e.g. television movies, television series, documentaries, game shows, music videos etc. Cinematograph films were by no means limited to motion picture shows in 1947, but could also be news shows (at the time called 'newsreels') that were indeed played in movie theatres in those days. On that basis, one could extend the scope of application of Article IV even to non-movie television programmes. On the other hand, such a broad scope of application of Article IV could be considered to go beyond what the object and purpose of Article IV call for, so that a *teleological reduction* or limitation may be warranted, at least so as to exclude documentaries, game shows, news programmes etc. Such a limitation would be compatible with the ordinary language of Article IV, given that the television programmes in question are typically not originally recorded on exposed cinematograph film. The non-application of Article IV to those television programmes even if they are recorded and transmitted with delay would also ensure that they are not arbitrarily differentiated

---

[19] Wright, C., 'Hollywood's Disappearing Act: International Trade Remedies to Bring Hollywood Home', *Akron Law Review*, Vol. 39, 2006, p. 739, at p. 766 concurs and even considers this to be the understanding of members (for which the basis does not seem apparent). See, however, the opposite opinion of Bhala, R., *Modern GATT Law*, London, Thomson Sweet & Maxwell, 2005, para. 44–013, p. 1188.

from the transmission of similar *live* programmes on television (which in practice are not movies and) which necessarily fall outside Article IV.

As a result, it is argued that television broadcasting of motion pictures falls under Article IV, no matter whether the exhibition of the movie is derived from a cinematograph film or from a videotape, DVD or other medium. In contrast, it is suggested that television broadcasting of non-movie programmes falls outside Article IV, in particular all programmes that can also be shown live. Moreover, the *private viewing* of a purchased or rented videotape escapes Article IV,[20] even if it contains a motion picture, as does the private viewing of a traditional cinematograph film. This is clear from the text of Article IV, given that the privately viewed film is not exhibited 'commercially', in a 'theatre' or 'equivalent'. The same applies to 'video on demand', whereas the internet television and non-television public viewing of motion pictures can fall under Article IV. Obviously, radio broadcasting does not fall under Article IV because the text of Article IV, i.e. the concept of 'cinematograph films', does not include the sound products broadcast on radio. Since radio existed at the time the GATT 1947 was negotiated, the drafters would have used other language had they wanted to cover radio broadcasting.

5.2.2.2 The applicability of Article IV without trade in goods, and without goods

It has been mentioned that it is technically feasible to exhibit (cinematograph) films based on an electronic cross-border transmission, e.g. the distributor can transmit the film to the television broadcaster via a satellite connection. In such a case, no film reel or other physical product needs to cross any borders. Yet, one should not assume that the applicability of Article IV depends on the importation of audio-visual products in the physical form of film reels, CDs, DVDs or tapes (of magnetic bands). A distinction on that basis would be not only arbitrary (not least from a teleological perspective), but also devoid of a textual basis. Although the GATT 1994 is a multilateral agreement on trade in goods, as part of Annex 1 A of the WTO Agreement, Article IV does not speak of '(imported) goods' or 'products', as do many other provisions of the GATT 1994, notably Article III. Nor does the GATT 1994 contain any general provision stipulating that the entire GATT 1994 applies only to goods. Rather, the scope of every GATT Article depends on its own stipulations. Cinematograph films of national and foreign origin in the sense of Article IV can be exhibited within a member independently of the presence of physical

---

[20] Bhala, *supra*, para. 44–005, p. 1184, and para. 44–013, p. 1188.

storage media. To reach this result, it is sufficient to understand an indirect exhibition of the exposed film as also qualifying as exhibition of that film. Thus, Article IV GATT 1994 can be argued to apply irrespective of the presence of internationally traded 'goods/products' and to have a broader scope than the GATT 1994 obligations contained in Articles I:1 and III.[21] For this reason, the complex and controversial question of when the products of electronic commerce fall under GATT and GATS rules, respectively, does not appear to be relevant for the interpretation of any of the terms contained in Article IV.

Based on the above reasoning regarding the applicability of Article IV to motion pictures originally recorded on digital media, one can go even one step further in concluding that Article IV does not even require the existence anywhere of a physical good incorporating an individual motion picture. The motion picture may be recorded digitally, then stored on a mass medium like a big hard drive and from there transmitted to cinemas and television stations worldwide with satellites or through other electronic means.

5.2.2.3 The origin of films

Interpreting Article IV in such a way that its applicability does not depend on the importation of foreign films in the form of physical goods also helps to resolve the question of what is a 'film of national origin', and what is a film of non-national origin. The above-mentioned fact that a film of foreign origin can find itself within the borders of a member in the absence of an imported physical storage medium, such as a reel, disc or tape, already shows that (non-preferential) rules of origin as defined in Article 1 of the WTO Agreement on Rules of Origin are ill-suited to determining this question.

The same is true even where films are stored and traded in the form of such physical media. Notably, the technical origin of these goods would otherwise depend on the country where they were wholly obtained or where their last substantial transformation occurred.[22] This would presumably be the country where the reel was developed and where the disc or tape was (manufactured and) recorded. Although this country may often be the

---

[21] But see the opposite assumption of Hahn, M., 'A Clash of Cultures? The UNESCO Diversity Convention and International Trade Law', *Journal of International Economic Law*, Vol. 9, 2006, pp. 515, 525, 527; *Idem,* 'Eine kulturelle Bereichsausnahme im Recht der WTO?', *Zeitschrift für ausländisches öffentliches Recht und Völkerrecht,* Vol. 56, 1996, pp. 315, 326–334; Wright, *supra*, pp. 739, 769, footnote 166, who posits that Article IV 'treats cinematographic films as goods'.

[22] Article 3(b) of the WTO Agreement on Rules of Origin.

same as that where the film was shot, the origin of the film and that of the media may also be different. Categorizing a film that was shot abroad as being of national origin due to the place where the reel was manufactured makes no sense within Article IV. In fact, the application of rules of origin could produce absurd results that would jeopardize the objective of Article IV, which is to allow the pursuit of cultural policy. It is noteworthy that the definition of rules of origin falling under the Agreement on Rules of Origin in Article 1 of that Agreement omits Article IV in the illustrative list of commercial policy instruments in Article 1.2. In contrast, this list expressly includes rules of origin used in the application of Articles I, II, III, XI and XIII.

The origin of a cinematograph film within the meaning of Article IV thus relates to the film itself in the sense of the content or movie, not to the physical product containing that film. This can sometimes make it difficult to determine the origin of films, the production of which may involve various countries. For instance, the director, actors and scriptwriter may be from different countries, and the shooting may take place, as well as the film studio be located, in yet other countries. One can argue, on the one hand, that the frequently occurring cross-boundary activity and cooperation of those involved in the production of motion pictures makes it increasingly difficult to say what a film 'of national origin' is.[23] On the other hand, it is clear that there are many examples where the determination of a film's origin is very straightforward because all or the most important elements that contributed to the film's production stem from the same country. Also, the absence of agreed special rules on the origin of films applying to Article IV arguably leaves members some leeway to define what they consider a film of national origin for the purposes of their screen quotas. A very strict definition of national origin will make the screen quota more difficult to satisfy and could also discourage cross-border co-productions. Unlike goods under traditional rules of origin, films can arguably also have two or more (foreign) origins within the meaning of Article IV, depending on a WTO member's definition and the film's place(s) of production. For the practical operation of the screen quotas, a WTO member's definitions, however, need to be clear on the question of whether the film is of national or of foreign origin.

5.3 BASIC OBLIGATION (INTRODUCTORY SENTENCE)

Article IV stipulates that if a member 'establishes or maintains', i.e. introduces or continues to apply, 'internal quantitative regulations relating

---

[23] Bhala, *supra*, para. 44–014, p. 1188.

to exposed cinematograph films' these must take the form of 'screen quotas'. They must also conform to the requirements set out in Article IV(a) to (c).[24] *Screen quotas* are internal regulations that apply where films are shown, i.e. in particular in cinemas,[25] and they limit the *extent* to which films of specified origins may be exhibited. Screen quotas therefore regulate the use of films at the stage of consumption. The introductory sentence, or *chapeau*, of Article IV prohibits internal quantitative regulations *other* than screen quotas, for instance a limitation on the sale or distribution of foreign films. In the light of the relationship particularly to Articles I:1 and III,[26] the Article IV *chapeau* simultaneously implies an authorization to apply internal quantitative regulations in the form of screen quotas which would otherwise be forbidden under GATT.

By virtue of Annex A to the GATT, '[t]he renters' film quota in force in New Zealand on April 10, 1947, shall, for the purposes of this Agreement, be treated as a screen quota under Article IV'. This stipulation extends the concept of the 'screen quotas' permitted by Article IV, but applies to only one Member, New Zealand, and only for any renters' film quota that is identical to that in force in 1947, which was considered equivalent to screen quotas.[27]

Although the object and purpose of Article IV is to allow certain forms of support or protection for domestic films as a means of cultural policy,[28] Article IV does not require the pursuit of any particular cultural or other policy as a condition of a screen quota's legality. This contrasts with exceptions in GATT like Article XX, which generally require that the domestic measure pursues the listed objective and that there is a risk for the value in question.[29] The actual policy a member pursues through recourse to screen quotas may therefore be the preservation of national culture, but it can also be the support of the domestic film industry for reasons of industrial policy, or the limitation of foreign film content to protect moral values or control political opinion etc. The latter conclusion that Article IV of the GATT 1994 allows WTO members to exercise political censorship is of course unpleasant, but seems inevitable, since Article IV restricts only

---

24 See *infra* sections III and IV.

25 On the scope of application of Article IV beyond cinemas see *supra* section 5.2.2.

26 See *infra* section 5.7.2.

27 WTO, *GATT Analytical Index, Guide to GATT Law and Practice*, Vol. I, 1995, p. 211.

28 De Witte, *supra*, p. 242.

29 See, e.g. Appellate Body Report, *EC – Asbestos*, WT/DS135/AB/R, paras 157–63.

the form of limitations on the exhibition of foreign films, and not the purpose which WTO members may pursue through such limitations. As indicated, this is different under Article XX of the GATT 1994, but under its paragraph (a), which allows the protection of public morals, a WTO panel and the Appellate Body unfortunately made rulings that could be understood as implying that this exception too permits political censorship.[30]

The underlying policy objective of Article IV, allowing Members to protect their film industries by reserving to them a share of the domestic market through screen quotas, explains the departure from the standard GATT structure: import tariffs, structurally the preferred and permitted form of protection, would not be able effectively to protect the domestic industry in the case of films.[31] The ineffectiveness of tariffs results not only from the possibility to show foreign films from physical media that have been manufactured domestically or otherwise to show foreign films without the importation of a dutiable product.[32] It is also because a single exposed film can be shown many times, whereas import tariffs are imposed only once on each imported product, be it in *ad valorem* terms or a specific amount.

5.4 NATIONAL TREATMENT DEPARTURE (ARTICLE IV(A))

Contrary to national treatment, screen quotas 'may require the exhibition of cinematograph films of national origin during a specified minimum proportion of the total screen time actually utilized'. Thus, screen quotas may *and must* take the form of rules that reserve a certain percentage or fraction of total screen time to domestic films. Article IV therefore outlaws regulations that limit the number of distinct foreign movies a cinema may show,[33] or require them to play a minimum number of domestic films. Also,

---

[30] See Panel Report, *China – Publications and Audiovisual Products*, WT/DS363/R, 12 August 2009, and Appellate Body Report, *China – Publications and Audiovisual Products*, WT/DS363/R, 21 December 2009.

[31] GATT, Report of the Working Party, *supra*, para. 8; Wilcox, C.A., *A Charter for World Trade*, 1949, p. 77.

[32] See sections 5.2.2.2 and 5.2.2.3.

[33] Bhala, *supra*, para. 44–010, p. 1186 and para. 44–017, p. 1190, who also points to the modest value of China's additional services commitment to increase the number of foreign movies allowed for importation to 20 per year, see: Trade in Services, The People's Republic of China: Schedule of Specific Commitments, GATS/SC/135, 14 February 2002, p. 21. See also the United States' request for the

a screen quota must not specify the number of hours or days on which domestic films or only domestic films must be shown.

The denominator of the screen quota is the total screen time actually utilized, rather than the time available, programmed or scheduled. It comprises the commercial exhibition of films of whatever origin; in other words, all films commercially shown. The screen quota must not apply to a period that is shorter than 12 months, giving cinemas seasonal flexibility within at least one calendar year to satisfy the national origin percentage.

Screen quotas must finally be 'computed on the basis of screen time per theatre per year or the equivalent thereof'. Except for the possibility to use an equivalent, the quota must thus apply to *theatres* on an individual basis. Strictly speaking, 'theatre' means an individual projection room, not a 'cinema', which may comprise several projection rooms. This is confirmed by the French and Spanish versions, which refer to '*chaque salle*' and '*cada sala*'. A more flexible screen quota that applies at the level of the cinema and leaves it flexibile to allocate films of national and foreign origin across its theatres of possibly different size would presumably also be compatible with Article IV(a), under the notion of 'equivalent'.

Although such difficulties have been argued to exist, there should be no problem or uncertainty in the calculation and application of a screen quota, if the quota applies as a proportion and on an ongoing basis in each period of 365 days or more. Such a quota adapts itself automatically to increases or reductions in the operating time of individual cinemas. It is only at the end of the year or the longer specified period that each theatre or cinema must ensure that it has shown at least the required minimum proportion of national films.[34]

It is important to realize that Article IV specifies *no limit* for the minimum proportion that a Member may prescribe for the showing of national films under a screen quota. It has therefore been posited that this minimum proportion may go up to 100 per cent.[35] One might call this position into question based on the textual argument that 100 per cent or

---

establishment of a dispute settlement panel, see below footnote 47, at pp. 2–3, which challenges under Article XI a different type of import restriction, namely that China reserves to certain enterprises the right to import films, video cassettes and DVDs. This claim raised the question of the relationship between Articles XI:1 and XVII of the GATT 1994.

34 But see Bhala, *supra*, para. 44–017, p. 1191, who assumes some uncertainty and wonders whether to use retrospective data from past periods and whether a carry-over to future periods may occur. Neither of these seems required by Article IV(a), nor necessary to operate the accounting under the screen quota.

35 Interestingly, this position has been expressed by the United States and the GATT Working Party. See Contracting Parties, Nineteenth Session, Application of

1/1 is not a 'proportion' or 'fraction' (the term used in the French and Spanish versions). Yet, this textual argument would not lead very far, given that it would not be valid in relation to very large percentages or fractions, such as 99 per cent or 19/20. Effectively, a WTO member is therefore entitled virtually to exclude foreign films from its market.

5.5 MOST-FAVOURED-NATION TREATMENT OBLIGATION AND EXCEPTION (ARTICLE IV(B) AND (C))

Article IV(b) establishes a most-favoured-nation treatment obligation for screen quotas, which is qualified by an exception in paragraph (c). For internal quantitative regulations relating to films, these two rules supersede Articles I:1 and III:7.[36]

Article IV(b) prohibits the allocation of screen time among sources of supply, with the exception of screen time reserved for films of national origin under a screen quota. As the French and Spanish versions set out with more clarity, Article IV(b) therefore deals with the screen time that remains after the subtraction of the time allocated to national films under a screen quota in the sense of Article IV(a). By definition, the sources of supply among which no allocation is permitted are foreign sources, which makes Article IV(b) an obligation of most-favoured-nation treatment.

Article IV(b) permits no allocation among foreign sources whatsoever, whether de jure ('formally') or de facto ('in effect'). This is a very strict and formal obligation on members to refrain from interfering with the competitive relationship between films of different foreign origins. A violation of this obligation does not depend on whether the allocation results in a disadvantage for a given source of supply. Such disadvantage would be absent where the allocation matches the market shares obtaining without governmental interference. In this sense, the obligation enshrined in Article IV(b) even reaches beyond most-favoured-nation treatment. Yet, Article IV(b) bans only allocations that are attributable to the government, whereas a de facto allocation that is the result of pure market forces would not be illegal.[37]

Article IV(c) provides for an exception to the prohibition on screen time allocation in Article IV(b). WTO members may maintain screen quotas

---

GATT to International Trade in Television Programmes, L/1615, 16 November 1961, p. 2; See also GATT, Report of the Working Party, *supra*, para. 13.

36 See *infra* section 5.7.2.

37 Bhala, *supra*, para. 44–020, p. 1192.

that 'reserve a minimum proportion of screen time for films of a specified [foreign] origin'. The condition however is that these minimum proportions favouring particular origins not 'be increased above the level in effect on 10 April 1947'. This is a grandfathering rule, which also covers exclusively screen quotas in the form of minimum proportions and in line with the other requirements of Article IV(a).

According to a strict reading, the prohibition on increasing any 'such minimum proportion' above the level of 10 April 1947 refers to the minimum proportions as they existed on that date. If they existed for individual countries, the prohibition of an increase would cover those individual quotas, and not the overall aggregate for foreign countries, taken together. In other words, Article IV(c) would not permit a re-adjustment among various sources in that case, even if the aggregate minimum proportion for foreign sources were not to increase. The contrary interpretation would of course give Members greater flexibility in the pursuit of cultural policies.[38] Both interpretations arrive at the same result where the 'specified [foreign] origin' in the screen quota in effect on 10 April 1947 related not to an individual country, but to a region, a culturally linked or other group of countries, and the WTO member in question subsequently decided to allocate the quota internally among the covered countries. This would be permitted, as long as the old aggregate quota is not surpassed.

5.6 MANDATE FOR NEGOTIATIONS (ARTICLE IV(D))

Although Article IV(d) explicitly subjects screen quotas to negotiations 'for their limitation, liberalization or elimination', no such modification of the applicable legal regime under Article IV actually occurred after 1947. Yet, the GATS has established a separate legal regime for services, including audio-visual services, which now overlaps with GATT. The following final section of this chapter will return to this question.

38 Voon, T., *Cultural Products and the World Trade Organization*, Cambridge, Cambridge University Press, 2007, pp. 160–2.

5.7 NATURE OF ARTICLE IV AND RELATIONSHIP WITH OTHER WTO RULES

5.7.1 Is Article IV an Exception (and who bears the Burden of Proof)?

Article IV grants WTO members a limited right to restrict the showing of films of foreign origin.[39] The effect of Article IV is *similar* to that of a qualified exception to the obligations contained in Article III (national treatment) and Article I:1 (most-favoured-nation treatment). Legally, however, Article IV is formulated not as an exception[40] of the same type as Article XX or XXI, but as a *lex specialis* dealing specifically with films. It imposes *obligations* on members that establish or maintain internal quantitative regulations. Article IV establishes a special legal regime for internal quantitative regulations relating to cinematograph films, which partly differs from general rules such as Articles I:1 and III. In contrast, Article III:10 is an exception in the technical sense, and it exempts measures that fall under, and comply with, Article IV from the disciplines of Article III, which may otherwise apply.[41]

Article IV is thus not an exception in the technical sense, which a respondent would have to invoke in a WTO dispute in response to a complainant's claim of a violation of other provisions of the GATT. Rather, the complainant would have to invoke Article IV as being violated and bear the burden of proof in that regard.[42]

---

[39] Bhala, *supra*, para. 44–005, p. 1184.

[40] But see *idem*, para. 44–003, p. 1181. Further Jackson, J., *World Trade and the Law of GATT*, Indianapolis, Bobbs-Merrill, 1969, p. 293; Voon, T., 'A New Approach to Audiovisual Products in the WTO: Rebalancing GATT and GATS', *UCLA Entertainment Law Review*, Vol. 14, 2007, pp. 1, 5; Voon, *supra*, p. 93; Neuwirth, R. J., *The Cultural Industries and the Legacy of Article IV GATT: Rethinking the Relation of Culture and Trade in Light of the New WTO Round*, Europe-Russia Working Paper, 2002, p. 9; *idem*, *The 'Cultural Industries': A Clash of Basic Values? A Comparative Study of the EU and the NAFTA in Light of the WTO*, European Diversity and Autonomy Paper 4/2004, p. 13; De Witte, *supra*, p. 242; See also The Uruguay Round, Group of Negotiations on Services, Working Group on Audiovisual Services, Matters Relating to Trade in Audiovisual Services: Note by the Secretariat, MTN.GNS/AUD/W/1, 4 October 1990, para. 2.

[41] On the applicability of Article III, see *infra* and *supra*, paras 14 and 36.

[42] Where Article III applies and is breached, the complainant could try to refrain from claiming a simultaneously existing Article IV breach, but rather leave it to the respondent to invoke the exception of Article III:10 and, as part of that task, demonstrate the observance of Article IV. It is uncertain whether panels and the Appellate Body would allow such a choice and its consequence on the burden of proof, which appears arbitrary. The situation is somewhat comparable to, e.g.

In theory, the general *exceptions* of Article XX are capable of justifying measures that fall foul of obligations contained in Article IV, just as they are in relation to obligations stipulated elsewhere in GATT. However, it is rather difficult to imagine a valid case of such a justification under Article XX.

5.7.2 Relationship to Articles I:1 and III of the GATT 1994

Article IV is *lex specialis* in relation to Articles I:1 and III, as is clear from the content of the provision and confirmed by the heading 'Special Provisions relating to Cinematograph Films'. By specifically regulating internal quantitative regulations on cinematograph films, Article IV takes precedence not only over Article III by virtue of Article III:10, but also over other rules of GATT such as Article I:1,[43] to the extent that there is a normative conflict. As a result, Articles IV and III:10 exempt cinematograph films from the most-favoured-nation and national treatment disciplines in Articles I:1 and III, respectively, provided that the disciplines of Article IV are respected.

Where the disciplines of Article IV are breached or Article IV does not apply because the measure at issue is not an internal quantitative regulation,[44] Articles III:10 and IV do not prevent the application of Articles III and I:1. A violation of these fundamental obligations however depends on the existence of discrimination against (physical) products imported from other members/a particular member, respectively. Imported goods containing movies would thus have to exist (potentially), and they would have to be e placed at a disadvantage,[45] in

safeguard measures, where legal challenges in practice are based on Article XIX, which could instead be considered an exception to the fundamental obligations in Articles II and XI.

[43] The question of whether Article I:1 applies at all where the discipline of Article III:4 is set aside by Article III:10 for an Article IV-compliant measure is similar to the question of whether Article III:8(b) excludes the applicability of Article I:1 to certain subsidies. A Panel has ruled that Article I:1 does not apply in such circumstances: see Panel Report, *EC – Commercial Vessels*, WT/DS301/R, paras 7.82–7.90.

[44] E.g., in the case of a non-quantitative internal distribution regulation, such as the Chinese restriction of the internal distribution of foreign films to two entities, challenged in *China – Measures Affecting Trading Rights and Distribution Services for Certain Publications and Audiovisual Entertainment Products*, Request for the Establishment of a Panel by the United States, WT/DS363/5, 11 October 2007, p. 7; see Panel Report, *China – Publications and Audiovisual Products*, WT/DS363/R.

[45] One should note that a disadvantage for foreign films in the form of an internal quota would not be a *de jure* disadvantage for imported products (see

comparison with either like[46] domestic products or like products imported from another member. Another difference from Article IV is that non-preferential rules of origin would be relevant to determine the origin of the products in question.

Within its scope of application, Article IV also makes ineffective the exemption in Article III:6 in favour of internal quantitative regulations in force on 1 July 1939, 10 April 1947 or 24 March 1948. Article III:6 is an explicit exception to the national treatment obligation for internal quantitative regulations contained in Article III:5. The latter rule is set aside by Article III:10 where a screen quota complies with Article IV. Where this is not the case, Article III:6 is unable to provide for an exception also to Article IV, both by virtue of its wording and because Article III:5 and III:6 are part of the *lex generalis* regime for internal quantitative regulations. Article III:7 belongs to the same regime and requires most-favoured-nation treatment. It is normatively similar to Article IV(b), with the important difference that the latter is qualified by an exception in Article IV(c). Article III:10 sets aside Article III:7 where an allocation is covered by Article IV(c).

The relationship between Article IV and the fundamental non-discrimination provisions of GATT reflects the respective scopes of application: Article IV can shield measures falling under Article IV against a breach of Article I:1 or III where these would otherwise apply. Conversely, Article IV arguably has a coverage that extends beyond that of Articles I:1 and III[47] and, as a rule of prohibition, not justification, Article IV may outlaw domestic measures that would not fall under Articles I:1 and III. Finally, where Article IV does not apply, the (internal) measure in question is legal, unless Article III or I:1 applies and is breached because of discrimination against imported physical goods and against imports from a particular member, respectively.

5.7.3 GATT 1994 and GATS

The special regime of Article IV of the GATT 1994 may prevail over contrary GATS stipulations. Namely, screen quotas that comply with

---

paras 14–16). Depending on the degree of the coincidence of the origin of films with that of the storage media, there may however be de facto discrimination against imports: see Ehring, L., 'De Facto Discrimination in World Trade Law: National and Most-Favoured-Nation Treatment or Equal Treatment?', *Journal for World Trade*, Vol. 36, No. 5, 2002, pp. 921–77.

[46] It is assumed that domestic and imported films generally are 'like products', even though responding Members might try to put forward arguments to the contrary.

[47] See *supra* section 5.2.2.2.

Article IV but conflict with the GATS may nevertheless be considered WTO-compatible. This may be a debatable proposition, though, since WTO members that have scheduled unlimited market access and national treatment commitments in audio-visual services or that have omitted to schedule an exemption to most-favoured-nation treatment may also be considered to have forgone parts of the policy space offered by Article IV.[48] In the opposite case of an Article IV violation and the absence of a GATS breach, it seems difficult to argue that the addition of the GATS would have reduced the scope of obligations under the GATT 1994 compared to that of the GATT 1947.

5.8 CONCLUSIONS

Taking the example of Article IV of the GATT 1994, the present article has attempted to trace a pragmatic line through the middle between the existing trenches in the controversy on cultural goods in international trade. Certainly, goods of culture are different to certain other products that are traded between countries under the rules of the WTO Agreement. It is also certain, however, that the WTO Agreement applies to cultural goods in each case that they fall under a general provision of the WTO Agreement applying to goods, which is notably the case whenever physical products like books or video tapes cross borders. The WTO Agreement even recognizes that cultural goods in certain respects have a special status. Article IV of the GATT 1994 is precisely a provision doing so, and it confirms that not only European members of the WTO, or the original contracting parties of the GATT 1947, but the entire WTO membership of 2011 and beyond recognize the legitimacy of certain policies designed to protect national cultures. Accepting the applicability of GATT rules to cultural goods, and using the flexibilities provided for by provisions such as Article IV, seems more promising than the doomed attempt of arguing that the GATT 1994 does not apply to cultural goods.

To allow Article IV of the GATT 1994 to be effective, one should interpret that provision in a sensible manner, also within the context of modern technological realities. This article has attempted to make a contribution to the pursuit of that objective. The technological changes intervening in the industry of motion pictures since the GATT's signature in 1947 confront the exercise of interpreting Article IV sensibly with significant challenges. Some of the proposals that the present article has made in such

---

48 See Voon, *supra*, p. 11.

respects may be quite debatable, for instance the fine line drawn between motion pictures shown on television and non-movie television programmes. While the argumentative basis for drawing that line would ideally be stronger, such line has the advantage of avoiding extreme results. Other interpretative proposals advanced in this chapter should be more easily acceptable, even though they might still surprise many readers, for example the proposition that Article IV of the GATT 1994 has a broader objective scope of application than many core GATT rules, by applying also where there are no physical goods that cross borders, and even where no physical products exist at all.

6. The debate continues: are border adjustments of emission trading schemes a means to protect the climate or are they 'naked' protectionism?

Reinhard Quick*

I have known Jacques for many years and always admired his intellectual curiosity and his enthusiasm, which go far beyond his professional activities. Over the years I had the privilege of discovering his manifold interests during lively and enriching conversations amongst colleagues and friends in professional meetings, as well as in the private gatherings of the 'Cercle Bourgeois'. It is a pleasure for me to honour Jacques with this contribution.

6.1 INTRODUCTION: THE EXTENSION OF ETS TO IMPORTS

Trade and climate change has been the subject of an intense political and academic debate in the last few years.[1] At the heart of the debate are unilateral trade measures against 'climate sinners'. Supporters of these measures consider them necessary for reasons of fairness.[2] The

* The views expressed in this chapter are those of the author.

[1] For an overview see Hufbauer, G., Charnovitz, S., Kim, J., *Global Warming and the World Trading System,* Washington, Peterson Institute for International Economics, 2009; or Cottier, T., Nartova, O., Bigdeli, S. (eds), *International Trade Regulation and the Mitigation of Climate Change*, Cambridge, Cambridge University Press, 2009; see also WTO/UNEP Report on Trade and Climate Change, Geneva, 2009, available at www.wto.org.

[2] In a letter to Commission President Barroso in April 2010, President Sarkozy of France and Prime Minister Berlusconi of Italy asked the Commission to

EU[3] has adopted far-reaching domestic legislation to mitigate climate change whilst in the United States discussions[4] on similar legislation are ongoing although it is questionable whether the United States will continue this path in the light of the results of the 2010 mid-term elections. A common feature of the European legislation and the draft US bills are their competitiveness-constraining effects on domestic industries; hence the calls for border adjustments of imports coming from countries with less ambitious climate change mitigation programmes.[5] The difficulty to agree at international level on a follow-up convention to the Kyoto Protocol with clear CO_2 reductions or other commitments also seems to strengthen the call for unilateral trade measures.

The debate has led to a rediscussion of the GATT rules on border tax adjustment.[6] At issue is not the adjustability of a tax imposed on a product (indirect taxes, e.g. VAT) but rather the potential adjustability of a tax imposed on an item that is consumed in the production process (energy) or a tax on carbon emissions during the production. How should these taxes be treated with respect to border tax adjustment rules developed by a GATT Working Party in 1970?[7] A different but related issue is whether the effects of the emission trading regulation (ETS) can be adjusted at the border. Existing and draft legislations so far favour emission trading schemes to combat climate change over carbon taxes. Therefore the present chapter will concentrate on the extension of ETS to imports (in the

consider such measures. See EurActiv.Fr of 16 April 2010, www.euractiv.fr/energie-climat/article/2010/04/15.

3 Directive 2003/87 of the European Parliament and of the Council of 13 October 2003 Establishing a Scheme for Greenhouse Gas Emission Allowance Trading within the Community, OJ L 275 of 25 October 2003 amended by Directive 2009/29 of 23 April 2009, OJ L 140 of 5 June 2009.

4 The US bills are mentioned by Hufbauer, *supra*, p. 22 *et seq*.; see also Maruyama, W., 'Trade and WTO Aspects of U.S. Climate Change Legislation: Cap-and-Trade or Carbon Tax?', A Study for the Fair Trade Center, Washington, 2010.

5 For an overview of other countries' initiatives see Dröge, S., 'Tackling Leakage in a World of Unequal Carbon Prices', 2009, pp. 12–13, available at www.climatestrategies.org.

6 For an analysis of the GATT rules on border tax adjustment see Hufbauer, *supra*, p. 39 *et seq*. See also Ruddigkeit, D., 'Border Tax Adjustment an der Schnittstelle von Welthandelsrecht und Klimaschutz vor dem Hintergrund des Europäischen Emissionszertifikatehandels', *Beiträge zum Transnationalen Wirtschaftsrecht*, No. 89, July 2009.

7 GATT Working Party on Border Tax Adjustment, BISD 18S/97.

following called the import measure) and will analyze its GATT compatibility building on two articles written on the same subject.[8]

Emission trading schemes create a price for carbon by establishing a 'cap-and-trade' system for covered industrial installations.[9] Within a given timeframe the maximum greenhouse gas (GHG) emissions output must be reduced (say from 100 to 80); covered installations receive (either free of charge or through auctioning) emission trading allowances according to their individual emissions and in relation to the overall GHG reduction goal (allowance limit). Companies that keep their emissions below the level of their allowances can sell their excess allowances on the market. Companies that have difficulties in keeping within their allowance limit have several options: they can buy the necessary certificates on the market, they can produce less, they can invest in GHG reduction technologies, or they can use a less carbon-intensive energy source. According to the European Commission 'this flexibility ensures that emissions are reduced in the most cost-effective way'[10]. The EU ETS scheme has been amended considerably in 2009.[11] The new scheme applicable from 2013 until 2020 provides for an ambitious Community-wide cap with a linear yearly reduction of 1.74 per cent resulting in a total GHG reduction of 21 per cent by 2020 (base year 2005). It also establishes the principle of auctioning of certificates but contains many exceptions, in particular for energy-intensive industries.[12]

The EU ETS scheme is an environmental regulation aiming at the reduction of GHG emissions (in the following, for simplification purposes, referred to as the reduction of CO_2 emissions) for covered installations; it does not cover products. The flexibility of the scheme can lead to considerable price variations for the finished product. In fact the owner of the installation will take an entrepreneurial decision on how best to comply

[8] Quick, R., 'Border Tax Adjustment in the Context of Emission Trading, Climate Protection or Naked Protectionism?', *Global Trade and Customs Journal*, Vol. 3, 2008, pp. 163–75, hereafter cited as Quick 2008; Quick, R., 'Border Tax Adjustment to Combat Carbon Leakage: A Myth', *Global Trade and Customs Journal*, Vol. 4, 2009, pp. 353–7.

[9] For an explanation of the European emission trading scheme see the European Commission's brochure, *EU Action Against Climate Change*, The EU Emissions Trading Scheme, 2009 edition, hereafter cited as Commission brochure. See also Ahner, N., 'Final Instance: World Trade Organization – Unilateral Trade Measures in EU Climate Change Legislation', *EUI Working Papers RSCAS* 2009/58, p. 2 *et seq*., available at: www.eui.eu/RSCAS/Research/.

[10] Commission brochure, *supra*, p. 9.

[11] EC Directive 2009/29, *supra*.

[12] See Commission brochure, *supra*, p. 11 *et seq*.

with the system taking into account the energy efficiency of the production process, the type of fuels and energy used and the energy mix in the country of production. As a consequence the cost of ETS on products could vary considerably.

For the time being the EU ETS scheme does not extend to imports. Yet it contains a reference to the fact that the Commission can make a proposal, in light of the outcome of the international negotiations, on how to extend the scheme to imported products from sectors 'that have been determined to be exposed to a significant risk of carbon leakage'.[13] The draft bills pending in Congress would also extend the future US ETS scheme to imports.[14]

In the preparatory work of the current EU ETS scheme a Commission service drafted a legislative text on how to extend ETS to imports, the so-called FAIR proposal.[15] Features common to FAIR and the US drafts are that they do not extend to all but only to some imports (energy intensive products) and that they do not extend to all countries but only to those that have not introduced a comparable emission trading system or that have not taken comparable emission reduction actions. They define how the calculation of the allowances surrendered upon importation should be made (actual CO_2 emissions or average CO_2 emissions during the production of the same product in the importing country) and stress incessantly that any action taken has to be in conformity with the country's international trade obligations.[16] In the logic of border tax adjustment FAIR considers the restitution of allowances upon exportation of energy-intensive goods, a possibility that has been described as 'environmentally perverse'.[17] Moreover it lays down rules on the proceeds from the sales of the allowances and contains a reference to the UNFCCC principle of 'common but differentiated responsibilities'.

The central provision of FAIR reads:[18]

---

[13] EC Directive 2009/29 Article 10 b, *supra*.

[14] See Hufbauer, *supra*, p. 22 *et seq*.; see also, Murayama, *supra*, p. 5 *et seq*.

[15] The so called Future Allowance Import Requirement (FAIR) was not incorporated in the Commission's final proposal. FAIR has been described in detail elsewhere, see Quick 2008, *supra*, p. 167.

[16] The European Parliament adopted a Resolution on trade and climate change on 25 November 2010, in which it suggested to extend ETS to imports provided that such proposal was WTO-compatible: see http://www.europarl.europa.eu/sides/getDoc.do?pubRef=-//EP//TEXT+TA+P7-TA-2010–0445+0+DOC+XML+V0//DE.

[17] Hufbauer, *supra*, p. 69. They clarify that symmetry is not necessary (p. 39); a state has a choice on whether to allow BTAs for imports only.

[18] See Quick 2008, *supra*, p. 168.

> Importers or exporters of goods shall be respectively required and entitled to surrender or receive allowances equivalent to the average level of green house gas emissions resulting from the production of those goods across the Community, reduced by the average transitional free allocation given in respect of the production of such goods, and multiplied by the tonnage of goods imported.

6.2 GATT ANALYSIS

6.2.1 Violation of Article I GATT

GATT Article I requires that any advantage in relation to 'charges imposed for imports and exports or internal taxes or other internal charges or regulations be granted immediately and unconditionally to like products originating in or destined for the territories of all other WTO members'. The extension of ETS to imports from some countries only (climate sinners) could constitute a violation of GATT Article I. It is not necessary to characterize the import measure as a charge, a tax or a regulation since Article I covers all of them. Exporting countries are treated differently when exporting energy-intensive products: some have to surrender ETS certificates at the border, some do not.

A possible argument could be made with respect to *like products:* could two products that are identical in all respects except for the production process or in this case the CO_2 emissions during this process be considered unlike? So far the discussion on likeness has taken place mainly in the context of GATT Article III. The Appellate Body has stated that 'a determination of likeness is fundamentally a determination about the nature and extent of a competitive relationship in the marketplace'.[19] In order to establish such relationship the four criteria mentioned by the GATT Working Party on Border Tax Adjustment[20] are used as a working tool, namely the product's properties, nature and quality, the product's tariff classification, the product's end-use and consumers' tastes and habits. In the case of products that are identical but for the CO_2 emissions in the production process the application of the first three criteria can only lead to a determination of likeness. The imported product's properties, nature and qualities, its end-use and its tariff classification do not differ whatsoever from the domestically produced product. It should be noted that the import measure is imposed for competitiveness reasons, therefore the importing

---

19 Appellate Body Report, *European Communities – Measures Affecting Asbestos and Asbestos-containing Products,* WT/DS135/AB/*R*, para. 99 (2001).

20 *Supra.*

country must therefore assume that a competitive relationship between these products exists. The only potential argument against likeness could be found in the fourth criterion. It has been argued[21] that a responsible consumer might indeed not buy a product if in its production process a considerable higher amount of CO_2 was emitted than in the production process of the same product domestically. However, we have argued elsewhere that a distinction between identical products on the basis of the fourth criterion alone should not be made for systemic reasons.[22] Besides, in the case before us, we do not even need an elaborate analysis of the fourth criterion as the ETS scheme covers installations emitting a large amount of CO_2. These installations are at the beginning of the value chain and produce products most of which are sold to industrial consumers. Industries, as 'consumers', will however predominantly decide on economic and not on societal grounds.[23] Thus, in this case a determination of likeness is unquestionable: the differences in CO_2 emissions in the production process of a product (e.g. steel) will not affect the determination of likeness.[24]

In the context of GATT Article III, some scholars suggest a different result with respect to non-product-related PPMs.[25] These suggestions have led to an intensive academic debate that many have considered to be closed

---

[21] See Howse, R. and Eliason, A., 'Domestic and International Strategies to Address Climate Change: an overview of the WTO Legal Issues', in Cottier, *supra*, p. 70.

[22] Quick, R. and Lau, C., 'Environmentally Motivated Tax Distinctions and WTO Law', *Journal of International Economic Law*, Vol. 6, pp. 419–58, 2003, at p.431.

[23] P. Vandenbossche, N. Schrijver and G. Faber, argue that even individual consumers are primarily guided by the price of a product. See Vandenbossche, P., Schrijver, N., Faber, G., 'Unilateral Measures Addressing Non-trade Concerns', Ministry of Foreign Affairs of the Netherlands, 2007, p. 64. It is interesting to note that Howse and Eliason discuss consumer awareness as the decisive criterion, yet the fail to take into account that in the case of ETS schemes the consumers are not private parties but industrial users of energy intensive products. The behavior of such consumers deserves a specific analysis, though. See Howse, Eliason, *supra*, p. 70.

[24] See Low, P., Marceau, G. and Reinaud, J., 'The Interface Between the Trade and Climate Change Regimes: Scoping the Issue', p. 8; preliminary draft paper written for the TAIT conference on Climate Change, Trade and Competitiveness, Issues for the WTO held in Geneva in June 2010, available at: www.graduateinstitute.ch/ctei.

[25] See for example, Regan, D., 'How to Think about PPMs and Climate Change', in Cottier, *supra*, pp. 97–123 with further references.

by the Appellate Body's rulings. We have argued elsewhere[26] that it can be dangerous to interpret a PPM-favourable solution into GATT Article III and continue to believe that the PPM issue should be solved via GATT Article XX, if the prerequisites of this article are fulfilled.

The discussion on likeness has centered on the Appellate Body's rulings concerning GATT Article III. In the *Japanese Liquor* case the Appellate Body has used the picture of an accordion in order to demonstrate that the term 'likeness' could have a different meaning in different GATT articles.[27] Whether the accordion is wide open or rather closed depends on the particular provision, the context and the circumstances in any given case to which the provision may apply. The question therefore arises whether the interpretation of likeness in Article III also applies to Article I. Articles I and III are key provisions containing basic obligations against 'discrimination'. Article I covers de jure and de facto origin-based discrimination. It has a broad scope that comprises, inter alia, measures falling within the scope of Article III. Its purpose is to ensure *equality of opportunity*[28] to import from, or to export to, all WTO members. Article III has a more limited scope, its purpose is to provide equality of competitive conditions for imported products in relation to domestic products.[29] In the *Banana* case the Appellate Body stated that the essence of the non-discrimination obligations is that like products should be treated equally, irrespective of their origin.[30] This reference to both non-discrimination obligations is an indication that the likeness concept of the two articles should be treated in the same way, at least as far as the issue at stake here is concerned, i.e. internal regulations. Equality of opportunity to import and equality of competitive conditions for imported products can only be achieved with one likeness concept. Also, context and circumstances in this case do not indicate a different likeness definition for the purpose of applying Article I.[31] Thus the Article III likeness concept can, in this case, also be applied with respect to Article I.

---

26 See Quick, Lau, *supra*, p. 448 *et seq.*; see also Crosby's response to Prof. Regan's paper, Crosby, D., 'Tilting at Conventional Wisdom', in Cottier, *supra*, p. 124 *et seq.*

27 Appellate Body Report, *Japan – Taxes on Alcoholic Beverages,* WT/DS8, 10, 11/AB/R, para. 114 (1996).

28 Vandenbossche, P., *The Law and Policy of the World Trade Organization*, Cambridge, Cambridge University Press, 2nd edn, 2008, p. 324.

29 See *Japan Alcohol*, *supra*, para. 109.

30 Appellate Body Report, *European Communities – Regime for Importation, Sale and Distribution of Bananas,* WT/DS27/AB/R, para. 190 (1997).

31 For a detailed 'like-product' analysis in GATT Articles I and III see Hudec, R., ' "Like Product": The Difference in Meaning in GATT Articles I and III', in

The extension of ETS to imports from some countries only therefore constitutes a violation of GATT Article I.

6.2.2 Border Measure or Domestic Measure Applied at the Border?

6.2.2.1 The problem: Article II (XI) or Article III GATT?

Article II:1(b) prohibits the imposition of other duties and charges on the importation of products in excess of bound MFN rates of custom duties. Translated to the trade and environment debate this provision seems to prohibit the imposition of a 'tax' at the border in order to equalize the compliance costs for domestic producers with an environmental command-and-control regulation (e.g. an industrial emissions' control regulation).[32] Such a 'tax' would be prohibited under Article II:1(b) since it only applies to imports and is not equivalent to an internal tax imposed on the like domestic product.[33] In fact there is no internal tax, there is 'only' an emissions' control regulation.

Article II:2(a) instead allows WTO members to impose at the border a charge equivalent to an internal tax imposed consistently with the provisions of paragraph 2 of Article III. It reads:

> a charge equivalent to an internal tax imposed consistently with the provisions of paragraph 2 of Article III in respect of the like domestic product and in respect of *an article from which the imported product has been manufactured or produced in whole or in part* (emphasis added)

The interpretation of the part of Article II:2(a) written in italics has led to an extensive legal debate on whether domestic carbon energy taxes can be adjusted at the border. The proponents argue that a tax on CO_2 emissions should be regarded as a tax on an article from which the imported product has been manufactured or produced. They propose to interpret the word 'indirect' in Article III:2 so as to cover taxes that are charged on inputs used

---

T. Cottier and P. Mavroidis (eds), *Regulatory Barriers and the Principle of Non-Discrimination in World Trade Law*, Ann Arbor, University of Michigan Press, 2000, p. 101 *et seq*. Hudec says on p. 108: 'With regard to internal measures covered by Article III, there really is no reason to distinguish between the Article I definition of 'like product' and the Article III definition of 'like product'. The basic policy of Article III is the economic policy to eliminate market distortions caused by internal measures, and that economic policy is just as compelling with respect to National Treatment-type discrimination as it is to MFN-type discrimination.'

[32] See for example the recently adopted European Directive 2010/75 on Industrial Emissions, OJ of 17 December 2010, L 334/17.

[33] This example is mentioned by Howse, Eliason, *supra*, p. 61.

during the production process. They refer to the Subsidy Agreement's rule on export subsidies that allows for the exemption of a prior stage cumulative indirect tax on goods that are consumed in the production process upon exportation of the final product and suggest to apply this rule *mutatis mutandis* also to border tax adjustment on imports.[34] Others defend the more traditional approach to border tax adjustment and express scepticism about such a creative interpretation.[35] The Appellate Body has not ruled on this specific issue yet. It has confirmed however the GATT Working Party's distinction between 'direct' and 'indirect' taxes for border tax adjustment purposes in the *FSC* case.[36]

The measure at issue is the application of an environmental legislation to imports. The ETS-scheme is not a tax. Yet what would happen if one were to consider the 'price' paid by an industry to participate in an emission trading scheme (namely the obligation to hold allowances) as an 'internal tax or other internal charge of any kind'?[37] Could one argue that the extension of ETS to imports is a 'charge' applied at the border that would be equivalent to an internal tax (the cost of the ETS scheme)? If so, the import measure would be covered by Article III.2. Yet, is this measure different from the example discussed above, namely a tax imposed on imports in order to equalize the compliance cost for domestic producers with a domestic environmental command and control regulation? The comparison of the two 'tax' examples leads to the following result: if the state chooses an environmental regulation with a market-based instrument, such as ETS, the compliance costs could be regarded as an adjustable 'internal tax'. If the state chooses an environmental command-and-control regulation the compliance costs could not be adjusted but would be considered a prohibited 'charge' under Article II:1 (b).

If one considered the import measure not a 'tax' but the application at the border of a domestic regulation then it would probably be covered by

[34] See Biermannand, F. and Brohm, R., 'Implementing the Kyoto Protocol without the USA: The Strategic Role of Energy Tax Adjustments at the Border', *Climate Policy*, Vol. 4, 2005, pp. 289–302; see also Pauwelyn, J., 'U.S. Federal Climate Policy and Competitiveness Concerns: The Limits and Options of International Trade Law', Working Paper for the Nicholas Institute, April 2007, www.nicholas.duke.edu/institute. For further references to this debate see GATT UNEP Report, *supra*, p. 103 *et seq*.

[35] Hufbauer, *supra*, at pp. 45–6.

[36] The Appellate Body ruled that the United States could not adjust its 'direct' FSC taxes at the border. The adjustment rather constituted prohibited export subsidies. Appellate Body Report *United States – Tax Treatment For Foreign Sales Corporations,* WT/DS108//AB/R (2000).

[37] Pauwelyn, *supra*, p. 21; see also the GATT UNEP Report, *supra*, p. 103.

GATT Article III.4. Given the fact that the ETS scheme is not a product regulation this approach leads to a discussion on the legal issues surrounding the GATT *Tuna* case.[38] Hence the importance of how to qualify such a measure in GATT terms: a border measure or an internal measure imposed at the border?

Let us recall the Note *Ad Article III*, which reads

> Any internal tax or other internal charge, or any law, regulation or requirement of the kind referred to in paragraph 1 *which applies to an imported product and to the like domestic product* and is collected or enforced in the case of the imported product at the time or point of importation, is nevertheless to be regarded as an internal tax or other internal charge, or a law, regulation or requirement of the kind referred to in paragraph 1, and is accordingly subject to the provisions of Article III (emphasis added).

The panel's conclusions in the *Tuna* case that Article III 'covers only measures affecting products as such' were heavily criticized.[39] Much of the criticism concerning the so-called product-process doctrine was addressed in later WTO dispute settlement cases regarding the substantive issues of Article III, in particular the definition of 'like products'. Professor Hudec writes[40] that the panel could have addressed the issue of the scope of the Ad Note quite easily instead of elaborating a conceptual architecture on the product-process doctrine: 'it required nothing more than a literal reading of the words of the Ad Note to say that the U.S. embargo did not qualify under the Ad note'.

The basic issue is whether one could regard the ETS-scheme as a regulation affecting the internal sale, offering for sale, purchase, transportation, distribution or use of products. How broadly should one interpret the word 'affecting'? It seems clear that this term covers more than 'regulations which directly govern the conditions of sale or purchase'[41] but does it also cover all the indirect effects on products that a domestic legislation can have? If a state tried to impose a measure at the border to compensate for the cost of compliance that its domestic industry has with legislation

38 GATT Panel Report, *United States – Restrictions on Imports of Tuna,* unadopted, BISD 39S/155.

39 On the criticism of the GATT *Tuna* case see Hudec, R., 'The Product-Process Doctrine in GATT/WTO Jurisprudence', in M. Bronckers and R. Quick (eds), *New Directions in International Economic Law, Essays in Honour of John Jackson*, The Hague, London, Boston, Kluwer, 2000, p. 187 *et seq*.

40 Hudec, *supra*, p. 194.

41 GATT Panel Report, *United States – Section 337 of the Tariff Act of 1930,* BISD 36S/345, 385.

regulating environmental media, such as air, water, soil would one read into the Ad Note that such legislations affected the internal sale of products and hence apply Article III? All legislative activities affect, to some extent, the internal sale of products, therefore some line must be drawn between a product regulation and a producer regulation.[42] ETS schemes require that installations reduce CO_2 emissions. They do not apply to products. They are therefore closer to a producer regulation than to a product regulation; indeed they are very similar to environmental media laws prescribing how to protect air, water and soil.

In its report *China – Measures Affecting Imports of Automobile Parts* the Panel observed that 'a charge cannot be at the same time an 'ordinary customs duty' under Article II:1(b) of the GATT and an 'internal tax or other internal charge' under Article III:2 of the GATT'.[43] The Appellate Body[44] accepted that the Panel had to begin its analysis by ascertaining which of these provisions applied in the circumstances of that dispute. In response to the substantive question the Appellate Body considered that charges covered by Article III are those imposed on goods that have already been 'imported' and that the obligation for these charges is triggered by an internal factor. It stated that:

> the key indicator of whether a charge constitutes an 'internal charge' within the meaning of GATT Article III para. 2 of the GATT 1994 is whether the obligation to pay a charge must accrue due to an internal factor (e.g. because the product was resold internally or because the product was used internally), in the sense that such 'internal factor' occurs after the importation of the product of one Member into the territory of another.[45]

With respect to Article II instead, the Appellate Body stated that for a charge to constitute an ordinary customs duty the obligation to pay must accrue at the moment and by virtue of, or, in the words of Article II:1 (b), 'on' importation.[46] In other words, a border measure specifies the amount to be paid in order for the good to be allowed into the market.

Under the import measure the importer would have to surrender a given amount of emission trading certificates upon importation, otherwise the product would not be allowed in the country. The obligation to surrender

---

42 Pauwelyn, *supra*, p. 24.

43 Panel Report, *China – Measures Affecting Imports of Automobile Parts,* WT/DS339/R, para. 7.105 (2008).

44 Appellate Body Report, *China – Measures Affecting Imports of Automobile Parts,* WT/DS339/AB/R, para. 139 (2008).

45 *Idem*, para. 163.

46 *Idem*, para. 158.

the certificates would therefore accrue 'on' importation. The reason for surrendering the emission trading certificates is due to an internal event, the domestic emission trading system. The import measure intends to create a level playing field between domestically produced and imported energy-intensive goods. It would be applied at the border in order for the products to be sold internally. One could therefore consider it as an internal measure applied at the border and therefore covered under Article III.

The import measure appears to have some features that could be categorized as a border measure and others that could be categorized as an internal measure applied at the border. The Appellate Body recognized this ambiguity. It said:[47]

> We consider that a panel's determination of whether a specific charge falls under Article II:1(b) or Article III:2 of the GATT1994 must be made in the light of the characteristics of the measure and the circumstances of the case. In many cases this will be a straightforward exercise. In others, the picture will be more mixed, and the challenge faced by a panel more complex. A panel must thoroughly scrutinize the measure before it, both in its design and in its operation, and identify its principal characteristics. Having done so, the panel must then seek to identify the leading or core features of the measure at issue, those that define its 'centre of gravity' for purposes of characterizing the charge that it imposes as an ordinary customs duty or an internal charge. It is not surprising, and indeed to be expected, that the same measure may exhibit some characteristics that suggest it is a measure falling within the scope of Article II:1(b), and others suggesting it is a measure falling within the scope of Article III:2. In making its objective assessment of the applicability of specific provisions of the covered agreements to a measure properly before it, a panel must identify all relevant characteristics of the measure, and recognize which features are the most central to that measure itself, and which are to be accorded the most significance for purposes of characterizing the relevant charge and, thereby, properly determining the discipline(s) to which it is subject under the covered agreements.

Emission trading schemes are environmental legislations to mitigate the effects of climate change. Like traditional command-and-control regulations they set a specific goal, for example the EU's goal of minus 21 per cent greenhouse gas emissions by 2020. In order to achieve this goal they apply a market-based instrument, the 'cap-and-trade' scheme. The certificates allow covered installations to emit CO_2 during the production process. Based on their actual CO_2 emissions the installations have to surrender a specific amount of certificates taking the 'cap' into account. The ETS scheme results in a reduction of CO_2 in a cost-effective way. Its core feature

[47] *Idem*, para. 171.

is the reduction of CO_2. ETS has been described as a hybrid system that combines traditional government regulation with an innovative trading scheme.[48] It covers installations, not products. The covered installations can comply with ETS in different ways so that it is not possible to know in advance the exact impact of ETS on product prices. This depends on the cost of the emission trading certificates and the risk that a domestic producer is willing to take (either to invest in new technologies and probably sell certificates, or to wait and buy certificates or to speculate with the certificates). The import measure on the other hand covers products. It requires importers to surrender a specific amount of CO_2 for a given quantity of products. The amount of certificates to be surrendered is calculated on the average CO_2 emission for a ton of a specific product in the importing country or on the specific CO_2 emissions of the installation exporting the product. The import measure does not oblige foreign producers to emit less CO_2. It is a charge added at the border and lacks the main feature of the domestic regulation, namely the reduction of CO_2. Furthermore it does not correspond to the 'charge' of ETS to domestic producers that differs from producer to producer.[49] For these reasons it is difficult to categorize the measure as a fiscal or a regulatory measure. Instead it seems to be a 'charge' accruing upon importation that would be covered by Article II 1(b). In fact the measure is similar to the above mentioned 'tax' to equalize a domestic command-and-control regulation.

6.2.2.2 Alternative I: The measure as a charge equivalent to an internal tax and applied consistently with Article III:2 GATT

In the previous section we have found the import measure to be a border measure. If one drew a different conclusion and were to consider such a measure as an internal measure applied at the border the question would arise whether it could be regarded as a charge equivalent to an internal tax. As mentioned above the cost of the import measure for imports and the cost of ETS for domestic production could differ considerably. Domestic producers can take an entrepreneurial decision on how to deal with ETS; their cost of production depends on the energy efficiency of the production process, the type of fuels and energy used and the energy mix in the country of production so that the cost of ETS on products can vary considerably. It is therefore questionable whether the import measure could ever be considered equivalent to an internal tax.

ETS schemes are environmental, not tax regulations. Some authors have nevertheless suggested that the obligation to hold emission certificates

---

48 Maruyama, *supra*, p. 15.

49 See Quick 2008, *supra*, p. 166.

could be qualified as a fiscal measure within the meaning of Article III.2.[50] They consider the effects of ETS tax-like, in particular if the ETS certificates are auctioned. At issue here is the question of when a regulation that is not a tax as such could nevertheless be considered a fiscal measure for border tax adjustment purposes.

A tax is commonly defined as a compulsory financial contribution imposed by a government to raise revenue, levied on the income or property of persons or organizations, on the production costs or sales prices of goods and services.[51] The requirement to hold certificates entails a cost for domestic producers: an opportunity cost in the case of a distribution free of charge and a specific price in the case of an auction. These costs could indeed be seen as a 'compulsory financial contribution imposed by government', yet do they also raise revenue? They do when the certificates are auctioned and the government receives the proceeds from such action. When the certificates are handed out *for free*, they entail an opportunity cost, but generate no revenue. One could therefore argue that a regulation could be considered a fiscal measure if it generates a revenue for the state. This revenue function could be the trigger to distinguish, for the purpose of border tax adjustment, between a regulation that can be adjusted and another that cannot. The revenue argument is not convincing though. The GATT rules on border tax adjustment distinguish between taxes directly levied on products and taxes that are not directly levied on products. Paragraph 14 of the Working Party Report reads:

> On the question of eligibility of taxes for adjustment under the present rules, the discussion took into account the term 'directly or indirectly' (inter alia Article III.2). The Working Party concluded that there was a convergence of views to the effect that taxes *directly* levied on products were eligible for tax adjustment. Examples of such taxes comprised specific excise duties, sales taxes and cascade taxes and the tax on value added … Furthermore, the Working party concluded that there was a convergence of views to the effect that certain taxes that were *not directly* levied on products were not eligible for tax adjustment. Examples of such taxes comprised social security charges whether on employers or employees and payroll taxes. (emphasis added)

There are taxes that cannot be adjusted and yet generate revenue. The trigger for adjustment is 'a tax directly levied on products', in other words

---

[50] See Ismer, R. and Neuhoff, K., 'Border Tax Adjustments: A Feasible Way to Address Nonparticipation in Emissions Trading', *European Journal of Law and Economics*, Vol. 24, 2007, p. 137 *et seq.*; see also Pauwelyn, *supra*, p. 21.

[51] *Collins English Dictionary – Complete and Unabridged*, Glasgow, Harper Collins, 2003.

there must be a direct relationship between the tax and the product. Such direct relationship does not exist in the case of ETS. Also *Murayama* considers that the effects of a regulation cannot be taken into account. Referring to the discussion between 'directly levied' and' not directly levied' and to the issue of 'hidden taxes' he argues that *the* Working Party showed no interest in exploring the unchartered waters of comparable tax effects and equivalent tax regimes.[52] The GATT Working Party knowing the language of GATT Article III.2 ('directly or indirectly') held the view that only taxes directly levied on products were adjustable.

The GATT Analytical Index suggests a broader reading. The term 'directly or indirectly applied' should be understood to mean 'applied *on or in connection with* products' whereas 'indirectly' means a tax applied, not on a product as such but on the processing of the product.[53] Could this broader reading mean that traditional command-and-control regulations, which entail a cost on business, could be adjusted at the border? Most probably not! One would have to establish a difference between ETS and typical command-and-control regulations. One difference could lie in the auctioning of the certificates but could this be considered as a 'tax' applied in 'connection' with products? Auctioning results in a specific price for certificates, yet the price of a finished product coming from an ETS installation depends on a variety of factors. Again, the 'tax' is not directly levied on products. In conclusion, since ETS cannot be distinguished from a traditional environmental command-and-control measure it cannot be considered a 'tax' in the context of GATT Article III.2.

Even if one were to regard ETS as a fiscal measure it would have to comply with the other requirements of Article III:2. Such compliance is questionable with respect to the obligation that taxes cannot be applied on imported products 'in excess' of those applied on products domestically. As has been explained above one cannot know beforehand the exact price of ETS on products. Depending on the specific facts of an individual case the argument could be made that the import measure resulted in taxation 'in excess of the taxes' applied to like domestic products.

6.2.2.3 Alternative II: Article III:4 GATT

Supposing that the ETS scheme was a regulation affecting the sale of products one could argue that the import measure is a measure applied at the border. To verify whether it is covered by Article III.4 the analysis will concentrate on the issue of 'less favourable treatment' since the question of

---

52 Murayama, *supra*, p. 15.

53 *Analytical Index: Guide to GATT Law and Practice*, WTO, 1995, p. 141.

'likeness' has already been answered in the affirmative. As the Appellate Body noted in the *Asbestos* case 'a complaining Member must still establish that the measure accords to the group of like imported products less favourable treatment than it accords to the group of like domestic products'.[54] The long-established interpretation of 'treatment no less favourable' is a treatment requiring effective equality of competitive opportunities.[55] Taking the environmental considerations into account the argument could be made that imported products subject to the import measure are not affected more heavily than the domestic production, they are just treated differently. Importers have to surrender ETS certificates on the basis of a specific calculation whilst domestic producers have quite a choice on how to deal with ETS. Yet a different treatment does not, *per se*, violate Article III.4. The measure has to accord to imported products conditions of competition no less favourable than the one it accords to like domestic products.[56] Could a less favourable treatment lie in the way the calculation of the CO_2 content is made for the surrender of the certificates? There are two conflicting cases. In the *Superfund* case the predominant method of production has been accepted as the basis for the calculation for a tax on chemicals whilst in the *Reformulated Gasoline* case the Appellate Body rejected this approach: if the domestic industry gets a specific treatment (individual baseline) it would be discriminatory not to give the same opportunity to importers. The difference in treatment however does not lie in the calculation of how many certificates have to be surrendered for a given product but rather in the choice the domestic producer has vis-à-vis the importer with respect to the product. The importer must surrender a specific amount of certificates that he has to buy on the market. The domestic producer must also have a certain amount of certificates but has the choice on how to comply with the obligation to reduce CO_2 emissions. It is this choice that results in different conditions of competition between the imported product and the domestic product even if it is taken into account that some certificates are given for free to energy-intensive installations.

6.2.2.4 Article II:1(b) or Article XI GATT

Assuming that the import measure is a border measure one still needs to establish which GATT provision is applicable: Article XI or Article II 1(b)? Article XI GATT has a broad scope. It does not refer to laws or regulations

---

[54] See *EC-Asbestos, supra*, para. 100.

[55] GATT Panel Report, *United States – Section 337 of the Tariff Act of 1930*, BISD 36S/345, para. 5.11.

[56] Appellate Body Report, *Korea – Measures Affecting Imports of Fresh, Chilled and Frozen Beef*, WT/DS161/AB/R, para. 135/136 (2001).

but more generally to measures thereby covering a whole range of cases such as minimum import prices, import measures made effective through an import monopoly or the US ban on shrimp because of non-product related PPMs. The extension of ETS to imports could be such an Article XI measure. The scope of Article XI, though broad, is limited. According to the principle of effective treaty interpretation Article XI cannot cover the items covered by Article II (i.e. 'duties, taxes or other charges') since otherwise the latter article would become redundant.[57]

Article II 1(b) distinguishes between 'ordinary customs duties' (first sentence) and 'other duties and charges' (second sentence). Article II 1(b) first sentence requires a WTO Member not to impose customs duties in excess of the duties set out in its schedule. Article II 1(b) second sentence provides that, on products subject to a tariff binding, no other duties or charges may be imposed in excess of those duties and charges that have been imposed at the date of the Agreement or which have been provided for by legislation in force on that date. The WTO does not define the term 'ordinary customs duty' nor term 'other duties or charges'.

Duties can be in the form of *ad valorem* duties (percentage of the value of the imported product), of specific duties (related to weight, volume, surface), of compound or alternative/mixed duties (combination of *ad valorem* and specific duty) and of technical duties (technical factors, e.g. sugar or alcohol content as the basis for the duty).[58] In the example discussed here, upon importation of an energy-intensive product two 'charges' are due: the MFN duty for the product as well as the surrender of ETS certificates. Added together these charges result in a financial burden that is in excess of the bound or applied tariff. One could regard the import measure as a technical duty, but then the duty calculation would have to be made on the basis of the CO_2 content of the imported product. This is however not the case in our example. To the duty calculated in the traditional way an additional charge is added, namely the surrender of the certificates. Therefore the Appellate Body's ruling concerning the *Chilean Price Band System* is not applicable here,[59] even if the exact difference between 'an ordinary

---

[57] See Mavroidis, P., *The General Agreement on Tariffs and Trade*, Oxford, Oxford University Press, 2005, p. 40.

[58] The examples are from Mavroidis, *supra*, p. 66.

[59] Appellate Body Report, *Chile – Price Band System,* WT/DS207/AB/R (2007). In this case Chile did not impose a fixed rate of duty but instead imposed on some imports a duty which was calculated on the basis of the world price of a given commodity and the corresponding domestic price. This calculation resulted in some cases in a duty beyond the bound level. The Panel interpreted the term 'ordinary customs duty' quite narrowly: a customs duty *senso strictu*, is to be understood as referring to a customs duty which is not applied on the basis of factors of an

customs duty' and 'other duties and charges' is not clear. The example discussed here shows that there is, at least in this case, a dividing line between Article II 1(b) first and second sentence.[60] Upon importation a duty is imposed and an additional charge is also due in the form of the surrender of certificates. The duty imposed is not applied in excess of the bound or applied tariff rate so the first sentence of Article II 1(b) is not applicable. The import measure could hence be regarded as another duty or charge. It is not reflected in the schedules of concessions of the importing country as required by the Understanding on the Interpretation of Article II 1(b) GATT and is therefore inconsistent with this article. The Understanding does not provide for a list of 'other duties and charges', in practice they are defined by exclusion.[61] Therefore one has to analyze whether the import measure could be an excluded item. A charge that is applied to domestic and imported products, in the logic of GATT Article II, cannot be a charge within the meaning of the second sentence.[62] The import measure is however not applied to domestic products but only to imports. As noted above the domestic ETS-scheme is much broader and applies to installations, not to products. Since other known exclusions are not applicable we conclude that the measure is a charge applied inconsistently with the provisions of Article II 1(b) second sentence.

6.2.2.5 Result: conditionality all over

In conclusion, the import measure is a border measure incompatible with the second sentence of Article II 1(b). The discussion shows however that this result is not crystal clear and that the GATT rules distinguishing between border measures and domestic measures applied at the border are in need of one or several authoritative interpretations by the Appellate Body. Taking the 'ifs' and 'buts' into account and looking at the import measure as a domestic measure applied at the border one could come to the

---

exogenous nature. The Appellate Body rejected this interpretation without giving its own definition of an 'ordinary customs tariff'.

[60] Mavroidis, *supra*, p. 58.

[61] Paragraph 4 of GATT Doc. MTN.GNG/NG7/W/53 of 2 October 1989 says: The definition of ODCs falling under the purview of Article II 1 (b) can only be done by exclusion – i.e. by reference to those categories of ODC not covered by it. It would be impossible, and logically fallacious, to draw up an exhaustive list of ODCs which do fall under the purview of Article II 1 (b) since it is always possible for governments to invent new charges. Indeed, an attempt to provide an exhaustive list would create the false impression that charges omitted from it, or newly invented, were exempt from the II 1 (b) obligation.

[62] See GATT Council Decision on the Introduction of a Loose Leaf System, BISD 27/22.

conclusion, if one were to interpret the term 'less favourable treatment' as extensively as *Howse* and *Eliason* seem to suggest,[63] that a violation of GATT Article III.4 cannot be demonstrated. Thus depending on the categorization of the import measure we might obtain an incongruous result: as a border measure there would be a violation of GATT Article II, whilst as a domestic measure applied at the border, consistency with GATT Article III.4 could at least be argued. For reasons of legal clarity one would therefore nearly wish that a country adopted the import measure and that another country instituted a WTO dispute settlement case against it. In any event, given the fact that the import measure is either inconsistent with Articles I and II 1(b) second sentence or is inconsistent with Article I alone it is in need of justification.

6.2.3 Article XX GATT

6.2.3.1 Article XX (g) GATT

Article XX paragraph (g) can be applied to measures protecting the global commons, that is, 'measures relating to the conservation of exhaustible natural resources if such measures are made effective in conjunctions with restrictions on domestic production or consumption'.

The first requirement of paragraph (g) is the conservation of exhaustible natural resources. The measure discussed here is part of a domestic regulatory programme to reduce CO_2 emissions aiming at protecting the climate. In view of the Appellate Body's dynamic evolutionary interpretation of the term 'exhaustible natural resource' it can reasonably be assumed that the planet's atmosphere is covered.[64]

The second requirement of paragraph (g) is that the measure at issue has to 'relate to' the conservation of an exhaustible natural resource. In its rulings, the Appellate Body[65] clarified the meaning of 'relate to' as requiring a substantial or a close and real relationship between the measure and

---

63 As Howse and Eliason seem to suggest; see Howse, Eliason, *supra*, p. 70.

64 It is interesting to note that almost all commentators consider that there is a sufficient nexus between the measure and the CO_2 emissions of the country concerned and therefore do not discuss the issue of an extra-jurisdictional limitation of GATT Article XX. See for example Pauwelyn, *supra*, p. 35; Ahner, *supra*, p. 12. Yet can one really assume that such a nexus exists if for example the EU with per capita CO_2 emissions of 8.9 tons per year were to apply the measure against a country with much lower per capita CO_2 emissions? I have raised this issue elsewhere: see Quick 2008, *supra*, p.170.

65 Appellate Body Report, *United States – Standards for* Reformulated and Conventional Gasoline, WT/DS2/AB/ R, p. 19 (1996); and Appellate Body Report, *United States – Import Prohibition of Certain Shrimp and Shrimp Products,* WT/DS58/AB/R, para. 141 (1998).

the policy objective. One could probably argue that the import measure is disproportionately wide with respect to the policy objective of mitigating the effects of climate change and that the means are not necessarily related to the ends. Actually this measure does not result in the reduction of CO_2 emissions abroad, it adds a charge on certain imports. Imagine the following situation: steel is produced in two installations in a country subject to the import measure. The first is a state-of-the-art installation from a CO_2 point of view, the second has an older production process that emits a considerable amount of CO_2. The import measure will encourage a steel importer only to import the steel from the highly environmental installation; steel produced in the other installation will most probably not be imported, but will be consumed domestically or exported to other countries. Would the required genuine relation of ends and means really be established? Could one argue that there exists a substantial relation between the domestic legislation (ETS plus the import measure) and the protection of the planet's climate? One would probably come to the conclusion that only the domestic regulatory program (ETS) has an effect on the planet's climate but not the measure. On the other hand, one could argue that the import measure is not insignificant in so far as it could be seen as an incentive to lower CO_2 emissions and to help to avoid 'carbon leakage', thereby genuinely contributing to the objective of mitigating the effects of climate change. Given the fact that the test should be applied to the legislation as such[66] we continue the analysis presuming that this requirement of paragraph (g) is fulfilled.

The third requirement is that the measure has to be made effective in conjunction with restrictions on domestic production and consumption. The Appellate Body interpreted this criterion to mean that the measures concerned impose restrictions not just on imported goods but also on domestic production and concluded that this criterion 'required even-handedness in the imposition of restrictions in the name of conservation upon the production and consumption of exhaustible natural resources'.[67] It has been argued above that there is quite a difference between the requirements of the ETS scheme for domestic producers and the requirements of the import measure. Yet this difference is not sufficient to put into question the notion of even-handedness. Even-handedness does not mean identical treatment of domestic and imported products.[68]

6.2.3.2 Article XX (b) GATT

Given the applicability of Article XX (g) to this case, a further analysis of GATT Article XX (b) does not seem necessary. One should point out

---

66 Pauwelyn, *supra*, p. 36.
67 *US-Gasoline*, *supra*, pp. 20–1.
68 *Idem*.

however that it could be difficult to justify the import measure as necessary in light of the Appellate Body's ruling in the *Brazilian Tyres* case. The Appellate Body required for a measure to be necessary within the meaning of Article XX (b) that it is apt to make a material contribution to the achievement of its objective.[69] Considering that the purpose of the import measure is the avoidance of carbon leakage for energy-intensive products and that an import ban will be imposed if the required certificates are not surrendered at the border, all these actions have little to do with the protection of the planet's climate and consequently of human health, in particular if the goods in the countries subject to the measure continue to be produced. The Appellate Body added:[70]

> We recognize that certain complex public health or environmental problems may be tackled only with a comprehensive policy comprising a multiplicity of interacting measures. In the short-term, it may prove difficult to isolate the contribution to public health or environmental objectives of one specific measure from those attributable to the other measures that are part of the same comprehensive policy. Moreover, the results obtained from certain actions – for instance, measures adopted in order to attenuate global warming and climate change, or certain preventive actions to reduce the incidence of diseases that may manifest themselves only after a certain period of time – can only be evaluated with the benefit of time. In order to justify an import ban under Article XX (b), a panel must be satisfied that it brings about a material contribution to the achievement of its objective.

The reference of the Appellate Body to *a* material contribution of the measure to the achievement of its objective and the additional *dictum* will provoke quite an interesting debate on whether the requirements of paragraph (b) are met with respect to the import measure. It seems to this author that such a material contribution cannot be established: The import measure consists in a financial burden that has to be paid at the border. Its effects on human health are at least questionable if not non-existent. The measure is necessary for the protection of the domestic industry, yet this is not an exception covered by Article XX.

6.2.3.3 The Chapeau of Article XX GATT

If a measure is covered by one of the paragraph of GATT Article XX it must nevertheless still comply with the requirements of the chapeau. In the

---

[69] Appellate Body Report, *Brazil – Measures Affecting Imports of Retreaded Tyres,* WT/DS332/AB/R, para. 150 (2007).

[70] *Idem,* para. 151.

Gasoline case the Appellate Body clarified the object and the purpose of the chapeau of Article XX as the search for a balance between the right of a member to invoke the exception and the rights of other members under the GATT.[71] In the search for a balance or the 'line of equilibrium'[72] the Appellate Body will, in the analysis of 'arbitrary or unjustifiable discrimination where the same conditions prevail' or of 'a disguised restriction on international trade', closely look at issues such as even-handedness, fairness and local conditions; in other words it will look at how the measure is actually applied. The Appellate Body also stresses that in the applying Article XX one cannot use the same standard as the one used in finding that a given measure is inconsistent with a respective GATT obligation.[73]

Without knowing the precise details of the import measure it is difficult to complete this analysis. The following arguments would anyway have to be taken into account when imposing such a measure:

First, in *US Shrimp* the Appellate Body made clear that measures that impose a single, rigid and unbending requirement on other countries could not be justified under Article XX:[74]

> However, it is not acceptable, in international trade relations, for one WTO Member to use an economic embargo to *require* other Members to adopt essentially the same comprehensive regulatory program, to achieve a certain policy goal, as that in force within the Member's territory, *without taking into consideration different conditions which may occur in the territories of those Members* (emphasis added).

The Appellate Body accepted however that a programme that is 'comparable in effectiveness' with a domestic measure could be justified under Article XX.[75] The import measure is intended to be applied against those countries that do not have a comparable ETS system or comparable emission reduction programmes as the country imposing it. Apparently the proponents of the import measure have carefully analyzed the Appellate Body's reasoning in *US Shrimp.* Yet are the comparability requirements

---

[71] *Idem.*

[72] *US-Shrimp*, *supra*, para. 159.

[73] The provisions of the chapeau cannot logically refer to the same standard(s) by which a violation of a substantive rule has been determined to have occurred. To proceed down that path would be both to empty the chapeau of its contents and to deprive the exceptions in paras (a)-(j) of meaning. See *US-Gasoline, supra*, p. 23.

[74] See *US Shrimp, supra*, para. 164.

[75] See Appellate Body Report, *United States – Import Prohibition of Certain Shrimp and Shrimp Products, Recourse to Article 21.5 of the DSU by Malaysia,* WT/DS257/AB/R (2001).

sufficient for the purposes of the chapeau of Article XX? It will be difficult to assess which countries are covered because of the complexity of determining the cost equivalence of different climate change policies of various.[76] Suppose a country has decided to achieve maximum CO_2 reductions in the housing and not in the industrial sector; further suppose that it has achieved a reasonable CO_2 reduction with such action: could this country not argue that the import measure is arbitrary? Could a country with a huge rain forest not argue that this is its major contribution to mitigate climate change and that therefore other measures (CO_2 reduction for the domestic industries) are not necessary?

Second, the import measure seems to have a coercive effect in so far as it puts pressure on the countries towards the future Kyoto II Protocol. Such behaviour contradicts Principle 12 of the Rio Declaration according to which 'environmental measures addressing transboundary or global environmental problems should, as far as possible, be based on an international consensus'. Instead a country adopting the import measure tries to impose its views on other countries twisting their position in its direction.

Third, the import measure would be in contradiction also with the approach followed by the UN regime (UNFCCC and/or Kyoto Protocol). Neither agreement provides for trade measures, the UNFCCC explicitly requires 'common but differentiated responsibilities' and the Kyoto Protocol exempts emerging and developing countries from CO_2 reductions commitments. If the international regime does not require from these countries specific CO_2 reductions possible domestic border measures imposed on them would be 'arbitrary'. Referring to the UN regime in the interpretation of GATT Article XX would be in line with the preamble of the WTO that refers to the objective of sustainable development. The Appellate Body has stated that the preamble adds 'colour, texture and shading' to the interpretation of the WTO.[77]

Fourth, arbitrariness could also lie in the domestic ETS scheme itself, in particular in the issuance of certificates free of charge. In the *Brazil Tyres* case the Appellate Body reiterated that 'the analysis of these measures under the chapeau focused on whether the discrimination that might result from the application of those measures had a legitimate cause or rationale in light of the objectives listed in the paragraphs of Article XX' (i.e. the environmental objective).[78] To avoid arbitrariness the allocation of certificates free of charge to certain domestic industries would have to be accommodated within the import measure as well.

---

[76] This difficulty has been amply demonstrated by Low, Marceau, Reinaud, *supra*, pp. 17–20.

[77] *US-Shrimp, supra*, para. 153.

[78] *Brazil-Tyres*, *supra*, para. 225.

Fifth, procedural shortcomings, such as lack of flexibility, transparency and verifiability of the proceedings, can also lead to a finding of arbitrary discrimination. At issue is, *inter alia*, the calculation of the certificates to be surrendered. If for example such calculation was based on the average CO_2 emissions of domestically produced goods this could be seen as arbitrary. In fact if the production process in the exporting country results in less CO_2 emissions than the average in the country taking the import measure the certificates to be surrendered can only be calculated on the actual CO_2 emissions.[79]

One of the most stunning aspects of the 'FAIR' proposal mentioned above[80] is that it was intended to apply to exports as well. Exporters, also on the basis of a Community average, would be entitled to receive allowances when exporting. Notwithstanding its ambitious climate change mitigation goals the European Union would exempt exports from the burden of the emission trading system so that these exports can compete 'fairly' on the global market. Even assuming that FAIR would cover exports only to those nations that are considered as not having adopted climate change measures comparable to those of the EU, the measure would not be taken for environmental reasons and could therefore be considered as a disguised restriction of international trade.

To sum up, it will be quite a challenge for a country imposing the import measure to demonstrate that its application is compatible with the requirements of the chapeau.

6.3 CONCLUSIONS

The analysis leads to the conclusion that the import measure will probably be considered WTO incompatible, in spite of the political statements of GATT-compatibility. In fact the measure is not taken for climate change but for competitiveness reasons. The latter are not protected by the WTO, and rightly so.

The protection of the global climate is a serious issue yet it must be resolved through multilateral negotiations and not through unilateral *dicta*. Although some countries would have liked a more ambitious outcome of the Copenhagen and Cancún negotiations, the non-binding commitments actually taken by almost all countries would make it difficult to categorize a country as not having done enough to mitigate climate change. It is

---

79 This reasoning is confirmed by the Appellate Body's ruling in the *Gasoline* case.

80 See *supra*.

questionable whether a country can require comparable reduction of CO_2 emissions if the international arrangements (UNFCCC and Kyoto Protocol) insist on 'common but differentiated responsibilities'. Therefore it would be politically impossible to impose the import measure against developing and emerging countries. The only countries that could be subjected to the measure would be the United States and, given its considerable CO_2 emissions, China. But would the EU be ready to risk a trade war with its most important trading partners?

Moreover a recent OECD study[81] has come to the conclusion that border adjustment measures imposed for climate change purposes actually have no or little economic effect. Hence the obvious conclusion: legal, political and economic reasons all speak against the import measure. There must be other, more successful ways to combat climate change.

---

[81] Burniaux, J.-M., Chateau, J. and Duvall, R., 'Is There a Case for Carbon-Based Border Tax Adjustment?', *OECD Economics Department Working Papers*, No. 794, 2010.

7. EU common commercial policy throwing off the shackles of 'mixity'

Inge Govaere

7.1 THE ECHTERNACH PROCESSION REVISITED

With his usual wit Jacques Bourgeois in 1995 pointedly identified the participation of the EU (then EC) in the WTO, as well as Opinion 1/94,[1] as an Echternach procession, meaning that 'for each three steps forward participants take two steps backward'.[2] Little did he know that from there on the procession would proceed painstakingly uphill, with successive Treaty revisions shedding thorns on the already slippery path. Right up until the Lisbon Treaty the process toward fully fledged participation of the EU in international trade relations indeed proved to be a long and difficult one. It might suffice here to point to the short-lived reference to 'joint' competence under the common commercial policy (hereafter CCP) heading, inserted by the Nice Treaty. This triggered Opinion 1/08, which was already, by the time it was rendered, historical in the sense of outlived, since the Lisbon Treaty entered into force the very next day.[3]

Fifteen years have gone by since Jacques wrote his critical paper. The time seems ripe to review the follow-up to two issues that he had identified as problematic immediately after Opinion 1/94, and that led the WTO to be concluded as a mixed agreement. First, he pointed to the 'inconsistent' off-hand limitation of the scope of the concept common commercial policy so as to exclude, for instance, transport policy.[4] Secondly, he put into

---

[1] CJEU, Opinion 1/94, WTO Agreement (GATS & TRIPS), 15 November 1994, [1994] ECR I-5267.

[2] Bourgeois, J., 'The EC in the WTO and Advisory Opinion 1/94: an Echternach procession', *Common Market Law Review*, 1995, pp. 763–87, at p. 763.

[3] CJEU, Opinion 1/08, GATS (Schedules of specific commitments), 30 November 2009, [2009] ECR I-11129. The Lisbon Treaty entered into force the next day, on 1 December 2009.

[4] *Idem*, at p. 776.

perspective the importance attached by the CJEU to the so-called 'institutional aspect', to the effect that the use of CCP as a legal basis should not lead to circumvent the internal constraints as to procedures and voting rules.[5]

We share Jacques' concern that the duty of cooperation might not be a sufficient bar against a cacophony resulting from the CJEU concluding to joint competence and thereby endorsing the mixed nature of trade related agreements, in particular the WTO Agreement.[6] To use his words '... experience shows that, when Member States promise to sing together in international negotiations, they more often than not produce a cacophony'.[7] The exclusive nature and scope of CCP determining the need, or not, for mixed agreements is a crucial given in this respect and also one that has received much attention in Jacques' academic oeuvre.[8]

7.2 THE SCOPE OF COMMON COMMERCIAL POLICY: NO GO AREAS?

It should be recalled that, quite paradoxically, it was in relation to the Agreement establishing the World Trade Organisation that the CJEU in Opinion 1/94 for the first time concluded to joint competence with respect to a trade agreement, holding that the Agreement was only partly covered by exclusive EU competence under CCP.[9] Other parts of the WTO, such as dealing with transport policy, continued to be subject to implied powers reasoning. This appeared to be a clear rupture with prior case law that

---

[5] *Idem*, at p. 783.

[6] *Idem*, at p. 784. Pieter Jan Kuyper has argued that joint competence should not necessarily imply mixed agreements, with most existing cases concerning 'voluntary mixity' '(because member states want it') as opposed to the few cases of 'necessary mixity' (because partly related to exclusive competence of member states), see Kuijper, P.J., *Of mixity and double hatting*, Vossiuspers, UvA, Amsterdam, 2008, p. 11. In practice, however, the CJEU conclusion that an agreement falls under joint competence will reinforce the position of the member states that a mixed agreement is in order.

[7] *Idem*, at p. 781.

[8] See Bourgeois, J., 'Mixed agreements: a new approach?', in J. Bourgeois, J.-L. Dewost, M.-A. Gaiffe (eds), *La Communauté européenne et les accords mixtes: quelles perspectives ?*, Bruxelles, Presses Interuniversitaires Européennes, 1997.

[9] Were held to come under exclusive CCP competence: the Multilateral Agreement on Goods, Cross frontier supply of services (GATS) and Counterfeit and Piracy (TRIPS). Shortly before that, the CJEU had concluded to joint competence under the implied powers doctrine in Opinion 2/91, ILO, 19 March 1993, [1993] ECR I-1061.

favoured a broad and dynamic interpretation of the concept of common commercial policy in keeping with the changing international trade context. Hence the intriguing question of what had changed and why it was precisely in relation to the WTO that the CJEU felt compelled to give a more restrictive interpretation of the EU trade concept. The weight of the political context should most likely not be underestimated, bearing in mind that eight out of 12 member states as well as the European Parliament opposed the finding of exclusive EU competence under CCP. But it is submitted that it was also possible to discern a legal rationale underlying Opinion 1/94, which is to a large extent lost today.

7.2.1 Exceeding the Limits to EU Competence: The 'Sweeping Approach' instead of 'Mixity'

The need for the EU to adhere to 'modern trade relations' at the risk of rendering the EU trade concept 'nugatory in the course of time' has always and systematically prevailed over a strict 'division of competence' logic. This became blatantly clear in particular with Opinion 1/78, where the CJEU set aside weighty arguments *inter alia* pertaining that member states economic and security issues, and thus their exclusive competence, were involved. The CJEU firmly introduced what could be called a 'sweeping approach' as it ruled that if the agreement was at least partly trade-related, then the whole Agreement could be based on the CCP legal basis alone.[10] As CCP is an exclusive competence of the EU,[11] a mixed agreement is not warranted in such a case. Similarly, when the argument as to a lack of EU competence in the field of development policy was put forward in the *GSP* case,[12] the CJEU did not hesitate to bring the measure under the sole CCP legal basis by reference to the international trade context that increasingly linked trade and development.

Less well known perhaps is that such a 'sweeping' logic was also consistently reiterated by the CJEU after Opinion 1/94. Whenever the argument was a lack of sufficient competence of the EC (under the former first pillar) because of exclusive competence remaining with the member states acting individually or jointly (under the former second and third pillars), the

---

[10] Opinion 1/78, International Agreement on Natural Rubber, 4 October 1979, ECR (1979) 2871.

[11] Opinion 1/75, Understanding on a Local Cost Standard, 11 November 1975, [1975] ECR 1355.

[12] Case 45/86, *Commission v Council (GSP)*, 26 March 1987, [1987] ECR 1493.

CJEU would apply such a 'sweeping' approach of the CCP legal basis.[13] This approach was later extended to new Treaty provisions giving express external competence to the EC also in other fields. As such, in the *Werner and Leifer* cases[14] the CJEU brought dual use goods firmly within the scope of CCP, whilst acknowledging the existence of security and foreign policy objectives.[15] The dual EC/EU regime for dual use goods accordingly had to be terminated in favour of a sole EC dual use measure with CCP as a legal basis.[16] A similar 'sweeping' logic was more recently used in the *ECOWAS* case,[17] whereby the CJEU ruled that an agreement relating to small arms should be concluded solely by the EC on the development cooperation legal basis (former first pillar) and not jointly or solely by the EU under the Common Foreign and Security Policy (former second pillar).[18] As a result, so-called 'inter-pillar mixity' was clearly excluded by the CJEU in favour of the first EC pillar, which, according to ex-Article 47 TEU, should not be affected by the EU pillars.

The Lisbon Treaty puts a severe break on the use of such a 'sweeping approach' in the face of security and foreign policy issues in general, thus also on the extensive use of CCP as a sole legal basis. Article 40 TEU replaces and modifies ex-Article 47 TEU to the effect that the CJEU will not only have to see to it that CFSP does not encroach on other external competence of the EU, but now also *vice versa*. With the formal abolishment of the pillar structure there is no longer a hierarchy between the different areas of EU external competence, so that preference may no longer systematically be given to the *acquis communautaire*. The crucial question is of course what legal criterion the CJEU will now use to delimit CFSP from other EU external action. This is not just an academic question in particular as the CFSP still obeys an inter-governmental logic and is still

---

13 See Govaere, I., 'External competence: what's in a name ? The difficult conciliation between dynamism of the ECJ and dynamics of European integration', in P. Demaret, I. Govaere, D. Hanf (eds), *European Legal Dynamics*, Bruxelles, P.I.E. Peter Lang, 2007, pp. 467–83.

14 Case C-70/94, *Werner*, 17 October 1995, [1995] ECR I-3189; Case C-83/94, *Leifer*, 17 October 1995, [1995] ECR I-3231.

15 For a detailed analysis of those cases, see Govaere, I., 'Case Comment on Werner and Leifer', *Common Market Law Review*, 1997, pp. 1019–37.

16 Schroeder, D. and Köhncke, N., 'Community regime for the control of exports of dual use goods', *International Trade Law Review*, 1995, pp. 101–4.

17 Case C-91/05, *Commission v Council (ECOWAS – Small arms)*, 20 May 2008, [2008] ECR I-3651.

18 Van Elsuwege, P., 'On the boundaries between the European Union's First pillar and Second pillar: a comment on the ECOWAS judgment of the European Court of Justice', *The Columbia Journal of European Law*, 2009, pp. 531–48.

not fully subject to judicial review by the CJEU.[19] It is no secret that the latter's role is crucial for establishing the autonomous EU legal order, characterized by uniform interpretation, direct effect and primacy. The choice of legal basis will therefore continue to determine whether the specific EU legal regime is applicable, or not, to the instrument or agreement at issue.

Bearing this in mind it would seem difficult for the CJEU to allow for the use of a double legal basis, such as CCP and CFSP.[20] Conversely, it no longer seems excluded that a 'reversed sweeping' approach be used, whereby preference is given to CFSP over CCP. The procedural provision for the conclusion of agreements, as modified by the Lisbon Treaty, expressly provides that the High Representative will lead the negotiations on agreements relating 'principally or exclusively' to CFSP.[21] It thus appears that CFSP action will not necessarily have to be restricted to 'pure' CFSP agreements as long as it 'principally' relates to CFSP, so that most likely EU agreements concluded on the CFSP legal basis may cover also (some) trade-related matters. The wording used in the Lisbon Treaty points to the need for a 'centre of gravity' test. However, as will be seen below,[22] the outcome of this test is not always satisfactory and it has up till now never been applied to delimitate the application, or not, of EU law. Keeping in mind the dual use goods cases, it may also not always be easy in practice to determine whether a subject-matter is 'principally' trade rather than foreign policy or security related.

7.2.2 Within EU Competence but outside CCP: The Special Case of Transport

In spite of the Commission's reliance on Opinion 1/78, Opinion 1/94 did not really fit the 'sweeping approach' as advocated there. This time the main argument was not a lack of sufficient EU competence to conclude the whole WTO Agreement.[23] Rather, divergences in views related to the nature

---

[19] Article 24 TEU, except for financial sanctions individuals under Article 275(2) TFEU and Article 40 TEU.

[20] For an opposite view, expressing 'cautious optimism' on the use of 'CFSP/TFEU mixity', see Dashwood, A., 'Mixity in the era of the Treaty of Lisbon', in C. Hillion and P. Koutrakos (eds), *Mixed Agreements Revisited,* Oxford, Hart Publishing, 2010, pp. 351–65, at pp. 354–5.

[21] See also Article 218 TFEU on conclusion of agreements.

[22] See *infra*, point C.

[23] Only with respect to Article 62 TRIPS did the member states argue that they retained exclusive competence, but this was firmly rejected by the CJEU, Opinion 1/94, *supra*, at para. 104.

of the EU competence, exclusive or concurrent, as translated in the choice of proper legal basis. The scarcity of Treaty provisions on external relations had led the CJEU early on to recognize external competence for the EU other than on the sole basis expressly laid down in the founding Treaties. In areas not already covered by CCP, the rationale of the doctrine of implied powers is to safeguard the internal legislative *acquis*. According to the *ERTA* test, member states may no longer act externally if and when their external action could affect internal measures or alter their scope.[24] Until then both the EU and its member states remain jointly competent.[25] The arguments pertaining to concurrent competence in particular for agriculture and transport ensued directly from the case law of the CJEU on implied powers.

Both CCP and implied powers are inherently dynamic in nature. It was thus inevitable that one day the question would arise at what point in time a subject-matter ceases to be regarded as implied powers in favour of the application of the CCP legal basis. With respect to agriculture, the CJEU in Opinion 1/94 gives the legally sound answer that the dynamics of the express CCP legal basis takes the upper hand against which implied reasoning, even if the latter was previously endorsed by the CJEU in that field, may not be opposed.[26] The outcome is, however, fundamentally different for transport. Here the CJEU specifically points to its prior case law to deny off-hand the inclusion of transport within the scope of CCP.[27] Not only does this present a major inconsistency in reasoning in Opinion 1/94 as compared to agriculture, it is also inconsistent with the very logic of implied powers reasoning as a second-best solution to express CCP competence.

The off-hand qualification of transport as a no-go area for CCP is most likely to be explained by the fact that the introduction by the CJEU of the

---

24 Case 22/70, *Commission v Council (ERTA)*, 31 March 1971, [1971] ECR 263. This test was later on extended to include the effect on foreseeable internal measures, see Opinion 1/03, Lugano Convention, 7 February 2006, [2006] ECR I-1145. In this Opinion the CJEU also strongly minimized the impact of Opinion 1/94 on implied powers by reducing the strict criteria advanced there to mere examples in the context of that case.

25 Opinion 2/91, ILO, *supra*, clarified that member states may continue to act externally if this does not affect the scope of the internal measures. This will be the case in particular if both contain only minimum rules. Joined Cases 3, 4 and 6/76, *Kramer*, 14 July 1976, [1976] ECR 1279, clarified that in the absence of EU measures the MS may continue to act on a transitional basis and respecting the solidarity clause of Article 4 TEU.

26 See Opinion 1/94, *supra*, para. 29.

27 See Opinion 1/94, *supra*, paras. 48–52.

doctrine of implied powers, in both *ERTA* and Opinion 1/76,[28] was precisely based on the transport chapter of the Treaty. As those two cases related to road transport and waterway transport respectively, it might appear that the very basis for implied power reasoning would be weakened in case transport was now brought within the scope of CCP. Unfortunately, this anomaly in the otherwise quite logical approach to EU external competence in the CJEU case law was subsequently codified by the Amsterdam Treaty and has also survived the revision of the CCP provision by both the Nice and the Lisbon Treaty. Article 207(5) TFEU unequivocally stipulates that 'The negotiation and conclusion of international agreements in the field of transport shall be subject to Title VI of Part Three and to Article 218'. In Opinion 1/08 the CJEU explained that the similar provision of the Nice Treaty[29]

> seeks to maintain, with regard to international trade in transport services, a fundamental parallelism between internal competence whereby Community rules are unilaterally adopted and external competence which operates through the conclusion of international agreements, each competence remaining -as previously- anchored in the title of the Treaty specifically relating to the common transport policy.

It thereby firmly cemented the no-go area for CCP in relation to transport at least for the years to come.

7.2.3 Multiplication of Legal Basis EU External Competence: The 'Centre of Gravity' Test

A combination of the 'sweeping approach' to CCP and the introduction of the implied powers doctrine has most likely also paved the way for the inclusion of new express legal bases for external EU competence in various fields. On the one hand, it became clear that the absence of Treaty provisions conferring express competence is no safeguard against the EU exercising competence externally. On the other hand, the advantage for the member states to expressly confer new external competence through Treaty revisions is that, in so doing, they can also determine in advance the nature of the competence. For instance, the inclusion of the environmental protection legal basis by the Single European Act was, in a Declaration, expressly

---

[28] Opinion 1/76, Laying up Fund for Waterway Vessels, 26 April 1977, [1977] ECR 741.

[29] Opinion 1/08, *supra*, at para. 164.

made subject to the *ERTA* logic with respect to the nature of the competence conferred. Member states' participation alongside the EU in environmental agreements is thereby guaranteed as long as this does not affect internal (environmental) measures.

The gradual insertion of new express legal bases for EU external action by successive Treaty revisions has proven to be an effective bar against the application of the 'sweeping approach' to CCP. Opinion 2/00 on the Cartagena Protocol was the first case whereby the CJEU acknowledged that CCP now had to be interpreted in a more restrictive way, and could even be totally discarded as a legal basis, so as to ensure that the new environmental protection provision could have a useful effect.[30] In that particular case, the absence of sufficient internal measures lead the CJEU to conclude to shared competence and thus implied the conclusion of a mixed agreement.[31] In a further series of cases equally concerning agreements with both an undisputed trade and environmental component alike, the CJEU has turned to the so-called 'centre of gravity test' to determine the proper legal basis for EU action. In the *Energy Star Agreement* case[32] it ruled in favour of CCP, and thus of sole EU exclusive competence, on the grounds that the effects of the agreement on trade, contrary to the effects on the environment, were direct and certain, whereas in content the agreement did not contain a new element proper to environmental protection. However, in the later *Rotterdam Convention* case it proved impossible for the CJEU to depart the two legal bases so that exceptionally, and contrary to Advocate General Kokott,[33] it ruled in favour of a double legal basis CCP and environmental protection. Also here the CJEU implied that a mixed agreement might be in order.[34]

The lesson to be learned from those cases is that it is no longer sufficient today to establish that an agreement relates to commercial policy in the

---

[30] Opinion 2/00, Cartagena Protocol on Biosafety, 6 December 2001, [2001] ECR I-9713.

[31] Opinion 2/00, *supra*, paras. 46–7.

[32] Case C-281/01, *Commission v Council (Energy Star Agreement)*, 12 December 2002, [2002] ECR I-12049.

[33] Advocate General Kokott had pointed to the procedural differences, and especially the fact that CCP merely requires qualified majority in the Council without implication of the European Parliament, to conclude to the incompatibility of both legal basis.

[34] Case C-94/03, *Commission v Council (Rotterdam Convention)*, 10 January 2006, [2006] ECR I-00001, see especially at para. 55, where the CJEU notes that the joint legal basis will give indications to the other parties to the Convention about the extent of EU competence and with regard to the division of competence between the EU and its member states.

sense of Article 207 TFEU for it to be automatically, let alone solely, adopted on that legal basis. Regard also needs to be had to the newer express legal bases for external EU competence, which may need to be put in the balance and may trigger a mixed agreement. Even a cursory look at the 'catalogue' of competence inserted by the Lisbon Treaty shows that the many areas of 'shared'[35] and 'special shared' competence,[36] listed in Article 4 TFEU, may well lead to further restrictions on the scope of CCP and support the plea for more mixed agreements in the future. The implications of such a development are of course potentially far more detrimental to the unitary and forceful representation of the EU in international trade-related negotiations than the clear exclusion of transport from the scope of CCP. Not in the least because one may expect that a further increase in internal bickering about the proper legal basis and internal procedures, whenever it does not concern a 'purely' trade issue (see below), may well trigger an increased pragmatic use of mixed agreements.[37]

7.3 INSTITUTIONAL CONCERNS AFFECTING CCP FROM WITHIN

Besides off-hand restricting the scope of CCP in relation to transport, Opinion 1/94 was also highly problematic in that, by taking into account institutional concerns, it imported what could be labelled as an 'implied powers rationale' into the concept of CCP. In Opinion 1/75 the CJEU had

---

[35] Article 2(2) TFEU stipulates that '(w)hen the Treaties confer on the Union a competence shared with the Member States in a specific area, the Union and the Member States may legislate and adopt legally binding acts in that area. The Member States shall exercise their competence to the extent that the Union has not exercised its competence. The Member States shall again exercise their competence to the extent that the Union has decided to cease exercising its competence.'

[36] Article 4(3) and (5) TFEU lays down 'special shared competence' for areas such as development cooperation and technological development, meaning that the exercise of that competence by the EU 'shall not result in Member States being prevented from exercising theirs'. This is to be distinguished from areas of complementary, supplementary or supporting competence in Article 6 TFEU, such as public health, which according to Articles 2(5) TFEU may not entail harmonization at EU level.

[37] On considerations of a more practical, general or strategic nature likely to fuel the conclusion of mixed agreements also after the Lisbon Treaty, see Rosas, A., 'The future of mixity', in Hillion and Koutrakos (eds), *supra*, pp. 367–74. He therefore argues that one should rather 'ponder what remedies are available to mitigate its negative consequences and also to limit its use to situations where mixity is absolutely necessary for legal or political reasons' (p. 371).

forcefully stated that CCP necessarily consists of a *'combination of internal and external measures, without priority being taken by one over the other'*.[38] It expressly added that it did not matter whether the external or internal measure was taken first. It will not go unnoticed that in the early case law of the CJEU this was an important factor differentiating CCP from implied powers reasoning. For the latter to apply, the CJEU consistently held that first an internal measure had to be adopted before the external measure (*ERTA*),[39] whereas only exceptionally the internal measure and the external measure could be adopted together (Opinion 1/76).[40] Totally excluded in the logic of implied powers is for the external measures to be adopted before the internal measures. In relation to GATS, and in particular to TRIPS, Opinion 1/94 created the impression that the CJEU had mixed up the CCP and implied powers principles together in a shaker, with as a result a difficult to digest cocktail. It was held, with respect to CCP, that

> (i)f the Community were to be recognized as having exclusive competence to enter into agreements with non-member countries to harmonize the protection of intellectual property and, at the same time, to achieve harmonization at Community level, the Community institutions would be able to escape the internal constraints to which they are subject in relation to procedures and to rules as to voting.[41]

Remnants of this mix up are still to be found in Article 207 TFEU today, but on the whole it appears that the Lisbon Treaty has attempted to come to terms with the confusion that Opinion 1/94 had thus created.

7.3.1 Blur of CCP and Implied Powers Doctrine Originating in Opinion 1/94

To try and come to terms with Opinion 1/94 it is important to take into account the dynamics and the broader context to the law. For over 30 years, the main focus of attention under the EU internal market rules, CCP and GATT alike, was to facilitate trade in goods. A certain 'natural' synergy in approach was thereby facilitated. This peaceful co-existence of systems was upset when the WTO Agreement extended the scope of the international

---

38 Opinion 1/75, *supra*, at pt. B1.

39 Case 22/70, *supra*.

40 Opinion 1/76, *supra*, this is only so if necessary to achieve an objective of the EU Treaty which could not be achieved through the adoption of unilateral measures.

41 Opinion 1/94, *supra*, at para. 60.

trade rules to include new fields, such as services and intellectual property rights, which had only received marginal attention from the EU legislator before. Services were of course covered by the internal market provisions already since the Rome Treaty of 1957. But the EU Services Directive[42] was nowhere in the pipeline, whereas the external frontier for persons was only later on established by the Amsterdam Treaty.[43] As for intellectual property rights, the CJEU was still to firmly acknowledge the competence for the EU to enact harmonization measures in that respect.[44] Besides for trade marks only few such EU measures had also effectively been adopted by 1994, mainly for lack of political willingness.

Against this context, the CJEU could be persuaded by the argument that CCP should not be used as a sole legal basis for GATS and TRIPS because it would upset the internal market institutional balance and 'circumvent' internal decision making procedures.[45] The qualification of the whole WTO Agreement as CCP indeed would not only have entailed far reaching exclusive competence for the EU, with application of the redelegation doctrine in case of EU inaction.[46] It also would mean proceeding through qualified majority voting in the Council without involvement of the European Parliament. In endorsing and even stressing the importance of the institutional argument, however, the CJEU created unwarranted confusion with implied powers reasoning. It suggested that in order to bring a new subject-matter within the scope of CCP, the existence of prior internal legislative *acquis* now had become a prerequisite. A slightly different formulation might have clarified that the CJEU's ruling on CCP was concerned more with the dynamics of the internal market project, and thus the broader contextual setting prevailing at that specific time, rather than the absence of more pointed internal measures that could be relevant in the framework of implied power reasoning. The rest of the story is well known. GATS and TRIPS were held to come only partly under CCP, whilst the internal legislative *acquis* was at that stage on the whole considered to be

---

42 Directive 2006/123 of the European Parliament and of the Council on services in the internal market Directive, OJ L 376/36 of 27 December 2006.

43 The Amsterdam Treaty added Articles 61–69 TEC (now Article 67 *et seq.* TFEU), which provided for the necessary flanking measures to the movement of persons to be established by 1 May 2004 (five years after the entry into force of the Amsterdam Treaty). The price to pay was the opt-out for the United Kingdom, Ireland and Denmark. This may explain why the three modes of service supply involving movement of persons were held by the CJEU in Opinion 1/94 not (yet) to be covered by CCP.

44 Case C-350/92, *Spain v Council*, 13 July 1995, [1995] ECR I-01985.

45 See Opinion 1/94, *supra*, at para. 60, quoted *supra*.

46 Case 41/76, *Donckerwolcke*, 15 December 1976, [1976] ECR 1921.

insufficient to confer exclusive EU competence by virtue of implied powers reasoning. The conclusion of joint competence thus led the WTO to qualify fully as a mixed agreement not just from a pragmatic but also from a legal perspective.

7.3.2 CCP and 'Mixity' according to the Successive Treaties: Now you see me, now you don't

Quite surprisingly, whereas eight member states had successfully blocked the inclusion of GATS and TRIPS in the scope of CCP before the CJEU, the Amsterdam Treaty on the face of it provided an opening by inserting the possibility for the scope of CCP to be extended by unanimity vote in the Council to those international negotiations and agreements on services and intellectual property not already covered.[47] But was such a construction really a step forward for CCP, in particular in view of its inherent dynamic nature? The underlying reasoning appears to be that the broader context is liable to change over time, so will the political willingness to proceed by virtue of exclusive CCP competence in new fields. Yet in case a qualified majority vote in the Council had been reached, would the EU Commission or the CJEU really have decided otherwise? Suffice it to point out that in all prior cases the party reluctant to interpret broadly CCP was precisely the Council and the member states. The Amsterdam Treaty in reality makes it more difficult than before to expand the scope of CCP through qualified majority vote or consensus building in the Council, as in practice it now gives a right of veto to each member state.

The Nice Treaty treaded further on the Amsterdam path by even more firmly anchoring the institutional concern in CCP. Unanimity in the Council now also became standard procedure for agreements containing trade-related provisions on services or intellectual property rights 'which require unanimity for the adoption of internal rules or where no internal rules have yet been adopted'. Furthermore, certain horizontal agreements warranted unanimity in the Council.[48] The most problematic feature of the Nice Treaty was, however, not only that it rendered EU decision-making procedures more difficult in more fields. It also undermined the very nature of CCP in case a decision could be taken by unanimity vote. Against all

---

[47] Article 133 (5) TEC, Amsterdam Treaty: 'The Council, acting unanimously on a proposal from the Commission and after consulting the European Parliament, may extend the application of paragraphs 1 to 4 to international negotiations and agreements on services and intellectual property insofar as they are not covered by these paragraphs'.

[48] Article 133(5) TEC, Nice Treaty.

prior logic that CCP should necessarily be exclusive in nature in order to preserve the internal level playing field,[49] the Nice Treaty makes important concessions to the member states. Member states could now maintain and even continue to conclude agreements in such fields as long the latter 'comply' with EU law 'and other relevant agreements'.[50]

The Nice Treaty will also be remembered as the first Treaty to openly endorse mixed agreements. Clearly there was a concern of the member states that CCP agreements might be used to go beyond internal competence, in particular in areas of so-called 'complementary' competence excluding EU harmonization.[51] It is in this respect that the Nice Treaty has the doubtful merit of expressly introducing the concept of 'shared competence'. Quite paradoxically it did so under the CCP heading that normally strives for uniformity.[52] In particular agreements relating to trade in cultural and audio-visual services, educational services and social and human health services were held to come within the 'shared competence' of the EU and its member states so that, according to the Nice Treaty, such agreements should be 'jointly concluded'.[53] This express Treaty obligation to conclude mixed agreements was interpreted by the CJEU in Opinion 1/08 as the expression of a balance between, on the one hand, the EU 'interest in establishing a comprehensive, coherent and efficient external commercial policy' and, on the other hand, 'the special interest which the Member States might wish to defend in the sensitive areas identified by that provision'.[54] Agreements to modify the schedules of specific commitments under GATS (WTO) necessitated by the 1995 and 2004 EU enlargements consequently had to be concluded under a mixed form.

Such an interpretation of the CCP Treaty provision was perhaps dictated by the Nice Treaty, but it was equally quickly dispelled by the entry into force of the Lisbon Treaty on 1 December 2009. As mentioned above, this was the very day after Opinion 1/08 was rendered. Advocate General Kokott had clearly pinpointed the short-lived nature of this anomaly in the CCP provisions in the twin case to Opinion 1/08 whereby the European Commission contested the mixed nature of the Approval, given on behalf

---

[49] As convincingly explained by the CJEU in Opinion 1/75, *supra*.

[50] Article 133(5) TEC, Nice Treaty.

[51] Such as in relation to public health. See Article 6 and 2(5) TFEU, see also *supra*.

[52] Article 207(1) TFEU, ex 133(1) TEC, 'The common commercial policy shall be based on uniform principles.'

[53] Article 133(6) TEC, Nice Treaty.

[54] Opinion 1/08, *supra*, para. 136. On this opinion, see the Case Comment by Adam, S., Lavranos, N., *Common Market Law Review*, 2010, pp. 1523–39.

of the EU and its member states, to the accession of Vietnam to the WTO. She succinctly summarized the situation as follows:[55]

> No doubt this legal position is not exactly conducive to the effective representation of Community interests in the area of external trade, particularly and precisely in the framework of the WTO. However, this disadvantage must be accepted as the Treaties stand at present. The far-reaching rights of joint decision which the Member States reserved for themselves in the Treaty of Nice in relation to the Community's new areas of external trade competence would otherwise be meaningless. In interpreting Treaty provisions, the Court may not exceed the limits on amending the Treaties laid down by Article 48 EU. The first and second subparagraphs of Article 133(6) EC have been removed only by the Treaty of Lisbon, with the result that the Member States' rights of joint decision are now confined to internal Community decision-making, but within the Council unanimity is required in areas which are regarded as being particularly sensitive (second and third subparagraphs of Article 207(4) TFEU).

The Lisbon Treaty indeed firmly replaces the notion of shared competence, coupled to the requirement of mixed agreements, by sole EU competence on the basis of unanimity decision in the Council.[56] It also meets the institutional concern with respect to the European Parliament which, pursuant to Article 207(2) TFEU, for the first time truly becomes co-legislator for CCP. Furthermore, it has the merit of expressly introducing trade in services, commercial aspects of intellectual property rights, as well as foreign direct investment, in the open-ended list of CCP measures of Article 207(1) TFEU. In so doing, it removes all ambiguity on the scope of CCP at least for some years to come.[57]

Read together, those provisions may nonetheless create a major problem, in that unanimity is now required for the 'exercise' of already acquired CCP competence, rather than for extending the scope of CCP to encompass new fields. The question is of course what will happen when unanimity is not achieved in the Council with respect to those sensitive areas, that remain of such a special interest to the member states that they warrant a veto right. A pragmatic, as opposed to legally necessitated, use of 'mixity' for such 'pure' trade agreements in order to convince the reluctant member states to sign, no longer seems very plausible. If it is at all possible to reach agreement on

---

[55] Case C-13/07, *Commission v Council (Accession of Vietnam to the WTO)*, Opinion of AG Kokott of 26 March 2009, at para. 124. The case was removed from the register on 10 June 2010.

[56] Article 207(4) TFEU.

[57] It is of course not to be excluded that with time new fields will be brought to the fore.

the content, the Lisbon Treaty unequivocally dictates the conclusion of an EU trade agreement rather than a mixed agreement. Not only the Commission, but now also the European Parliament, could thus quite easily contest a (pragmatic) use of 'mixity' before the CJEU. But if there is no unanimity in the Council and little or no possibility of a mixed agreement, what are then the chances of having a trade agreement relating to those sensitive fields at all?

8. The negotiations of a new anti dumping agreement (ADA) in the DDA – some observations

Hannes Welge*

The negotiations on antidumping of the Doha Round are ongoing. As negotiator for the EU it would probably be unwise to write extensively about the pros and cons of the positions of other WTO members or the ones of the EU. And of course, it is not possible to explain where everybody's bottom lines might be. However, in spite of these inherent restrictions, it may be interesting to read about some of the practical and structural difficulties and problems of these negotiations; how important organization and methods of negotiations are and which role the interaction of the negotiators play in finding compromises. At first, it might be useful to recall from where the positions originate and what this could imply when the negotiations progress.

8.1 WHY NEGOTIATE A NEW AGREEMENT?

One might ask why members in 2001 saw the need for renegotiations of an agreement, which had been completely rewritten just seven years ago. One most obvious and frequently mentioned reason for the inclusion of a variety of negotiating subjects into the negotiations of a new 'Round' was that many members at the time of the launch anticipated that this would facilitate cross-cutting deals at the end of the negotiations. This consideration is proved correct in previous Rounds and will eventually positively affect the capability of all participants to accept the results as a package.

On the other hand, there should be a motivation for choosing the Rules area with antidumping and subsidies, but not safeguards, or any other of the agreements forming part of the Uruguay Round (UR) package.

* The views expressed are those of the author and cannot be attributed to the European Commission.

Paragraph 28 of the Doha declaration started the negotiations on antidumping with the following text:

> In the light of experience and of the increasing application of these instruments by members, we agree to negotiations aimed at clarifying and improving disciplines under the Agreements on Implementation of Article VI of the GATT 1994 and on Subsidies and Countervailing Measures, while preserving the basic concepts, principles and effectiveness of these Agreements and their instruments and objectives, and taking into account the needs of developing and least-developed participants. In the initial phase of the negotiations, participants will indicate the provisions, including disciplines on trade distorting practices that they seek to clarify and improve in the subsequent phase ...

The declaration mentions 'experience' and 'increasing application' as reasons for renegotiation.

However, the experience with its implementation (newly initiated cases as from 1995) was thus limited: dispute settlement jurisprudence only began to emerge from the first cases (fewer than 20 cases decided by panels and the Appellate Body in the areas of subsidies and antidumping by the end of 2000). This would suggest that there was not a lot of experience with the implementation of the agreements by the time it was decided to review it.

The other reason '... the increasing application of these instruments by members ...' appears more convincing. Indeed, the number of AD/CVD investigations initiated worldwide had increased dramatically from 1995 to reach an all-time high between 1999 and 2001. This was most likely as a result of the impact of the Asian crisis, with the usual time-lag before trade defence cases are brought. However, the increase represented foremost the appearance of new users of the trade defence instrument: India, Brazil, Turkey, Argentina had become the most frequent users of the AD instrument. The numbers for the traditional users, i.e. United States, EU, Canada, Australia and New Zealand had remained rather stable and were about to decline.

In fact, the main push for the renegotiations of the AD/CVD rules came from those countries that later became known as 'friends of antidumping negotiations' (friends).[1] One might expect that their main focus would have been to address these cases opened by new users, often based on flimsy complaints and carried out, by inexperienced and understaffed authorities. But surprisingly, this was not the case. Brazil and Turkey even became

---

[1] For the development of the DDA Rules negotiations in its early phase and some details about the friends group, see: Kazeki, J., 'Antidumping Negotiations under the WTO and FANs', *Journal of World Trade*, 44, No.5, 2010, pp. 931–65.

members of the friends group. In reality, the driving force of the early years of the AD negotiations, the friends group, concentrated on the well-known laws and practices of the traditional users. In fact, their main focus was the US.

For those participants, who were involved during the Uruguay Round negotiations of AD, there was a remarkable *déjà vu* experience with regard to the proposals made by the friends and the arguments put forward to justify them. The main target of the proposals was Article 2 ADA, which deals with the calculation of the dumping margin. But the criticism centred on the United States' (and to a lower degree the EU's) methods, with little attention given to the way India or Brazil were doing their cases. Probably, the friends group were not even aware of how an antidumping margin was calculated in New Delhi or Brasilia.

Why was that? At least the circumstances would suggest that the increased use of AD measures by new users was not the only motivation for the demand of a renegotiation of the ADA. The suggestion that it was predominantly the US laws and practice on which the friends' proposals were focussed is supported by the way they were presented. In fact, the leadership of the friends used a Washington DC-based law firm to prepare their written submission and also their oral statements in the Negotiating Group (NG). It became quickly obvious that the arguments and proposals often only made sense with regard to the US system.[2]

In reality there was only little experience with the implementation of the UR Antidumping Agreement (ADA) in 2001and the practices of the new and most frequent users were not at all in the focus of the proponents for the renegotiation. Thus, it seems sufficiently clear that the reasons mentioned in Art 28 of the Doha Declaration are not exhaustive.

In my view, there are more reasons for the new negotiations which need to be recognized. The clear 'anti-US' (and anti-traditional user) thrusts can only be explained in two ways: The friends, or leading members of them, felt that they had not achieved the desired results on antidumping in the UR negotiations and therefore were looking for opportunity revise the AD Agreement in their direction. In fact, comparing the proposals made and the final results achieved in the UR, one has to admit that instead of a 'reform' it had become in large part a codification of existing US laws and practices into the ADA. It was therefore only natural that many participants of the UR were not at all happy with this end and were seeking revisions.

[2] As a side remark it may be interesting to note that this limited focus was probably the main reason why these friends' proposals were not very successful and convincing with the rest of the membership.

The second hidden reason for the particular way in which the antidumping negotiations were started might rather be a defensive function. Quite a few members of the friends group were not really affected a lot by AD measures, or they were even active users themselves. For them the aggressive demands in antidumping were made in order to protect them against potential demands against them in other areas of the DDA. It is not too far fetched to assume that these areas might have been agriculture and NAMA (non agricultural market access). In fact, some of the membership of the friends can almost only be explained with this consideration.

Both additional motives, revision and tactical defence, are perfectly legitimate.

The simple reason for their exploration here is the anticipation of whether the participants might lose interest in the negotiations under certain circumstances. At the end of the chapter, I will try to argue that lack of interest is the major threat to the AD negotiations, and for this, the excursion into past motives might proof useful.

8.2 HOW TO NEGOTIATE?

Now, I would like to turn to what can be called negotiating methods or techniques. This is about the question of how negotiators come from a variety of different and differing proposals to a text, which can be agreed on. The DDA negotiations on AD have some 40 active participants and potentially 110 who only watch what happens but could intervene as soon as something happens that they do not like. In the worst case scenario this could happen at the very end, when everybody thinks 'the deal is done'. It goes without saying that 40 negotiators with their support staff sitting in a large meeting room normally do not know how to find agreement on approximately 100 conflicting proposals. Among them reasonable and unreasonable, knowledgeable and not so knowledgeable ones – negotiators as well as proposals. Some way has to be thought out, how the differing positions can be brought together.

In principle, negotiators could sit down and agree sentence by sentence, article by article until a new agreement is completed. GATT veterans can remember that such a traditional way of negotiation might have worked last in the Tokyo Round negotiations in limited areas. However, today this is a theoretical possibility given the numbers of issues and, in particular, the number of participants. The traditional approach can only be successful, if there are not too many participants (best no more than four), nobody is playing tactical games, all want to agree, at the time; all know the subjects well and have an overview of what they could trade against what, etc. In today's WTO reality almost all the above conditions are absent. It follows that a different negotiating method has to be found. Since the negotiations of the Uruguay Round (UR) draft texts prepared by the chairpersons of the negotiating groups has become the method of choice.

For the Rules area, the Hong Kong Ministerial meeting in December 2005 was not a very important milestone. The Rules part of the final declaration had been prepared beforehand and almost all negotiators tried to keep Rules well away from controversies at Ministerial level. However, one important decision in the declaration went through without creating any controversy:

> 11. mandate the Chairman to prepare, early enough to assure a timely outcome within the context of the 2006 end date for the Doha Development Agenda and taking account of progress in other areas of the negotiations, consolidated texts of the AD and SCM Agreements that shall be the basis for the final stage of the negotiations.

From this moment onwards, negotiators had to try to convince the chair of the value of their proposal(s). At the same time, the chair had to find a modus operandi for the group that allowed him to do substantive work with a limited number of delegations without upsetting the rest.[3] Of course every proposal had to be presented and discussed in plenary (called 'open-ended session') first. After this it would go to a small group of some 15 participants, which were still somehow representative of the actively negotiating membership. Here, the size of delegations would be limited to two or maximum three persons.

While in the plenary often (unfortunately) the interventions are made on the basis of prepared written statements and normally every delegation would only speak once, in the small group the communication became more interactive. There were real discussions, with questions and answers (including questions from the chair), which brought about some more clarity. The small group format also had some immediate impacts on the dynamics of the negotiations:

The negotiators got to know each other much better than through just listening to speeches in plenary. The discussions became more open and direct, because of the more intimate setup.

[3] Woznowski gives a very good overview about the different negotiating techniques and the ways in which the Group proceeding after the Hong Kong Ministerial. Woznowski, J., 'Antidumping Negotiations in the GATT and in the WTO', in T.P. Stewart, *Opportunities and Obligations*, Leiden, Martinus Nijhoff Publishers, 2009, pp. 89–109.

On the other hand, negotiators with insufficient preparation and/or knowledge of the subject had obvious difficulties in convincing others and the chair of their case.

The small group format favoured the experienced, knowledgeable and well-prepared negotiators. This turned out to be a clear disadvantage for some delegations.

8.3 WHO NEGOTIATES FOR A COUNTRY?

At this point, the question, who negotiates, became important. Negotiations of a technical area such as antidumping require expertise of the subject. Obviously, those members who do not have their own investigating authority would need to operate only on the basis of the experience of cases against their exports and/or rely on external expertise. In spite of this structural disadvantage, some negotiators learned quickly. However, capitals that changed during the negotiations their negotiators, who had just learned the issues, weakened their capability, as the new incoming negotiator would not always have sufficient time to catch up. Of course, active users of the antidumping instrument have sufficient technical expertise. However, the technical experts for trade defence are not necessarily skilful negotiators.

In fact, some countries that actually have their own investigating authorities give the responsibility for the negotiations to other agencies, often the foreign ministries. The decisions not to give the investigating authority the lead might also be based on the fear that the technical experts would be more interested to agree on new provisions, which make the lives of investigators easier, at the expense of the positions of exporters.[4] Since the beginning of the work in small groups, the process favoured the technical experts over the more political negotiators. This will probably last for the phase in which solutions for complex technical problems have to be developed. At a later stage, when on higher hierarchical levels cross-cutting deals beyond the narrow negotiating areas have to be made, remains to be seen.

8.4 THE DELICATE WAY TO A NEGOTIATED CHAIR'S TEXT

When negotiations intensify and the work takes place in small and smaller groups, the interaction between negotiators becomes more important.

---

[4] Unfortunately, often the communication between the agencies and the negotiator does not work well. This leads to a lack of expertise and often positions taken by the negotiators simply contradict the well-established and known practices of its own country.

Knowledge, credibility, reliability are values associated with the negotiator personally. A process of confidence building has to develop. Negotiators need to know and trust their counterparts. Among other things, this process takes time and opportunity to test each other in various situations.

While negotiations progressed after the Hong Kong Ministerial during the years 2006 and the first part of 2007, the main group of active negotiators remained rather stable and the type of chemistry as described above could develop. Of course, the chairman and the advising WTO secretariat played an important role during this period as well.

The trustful interaction between negotiators is so important because today's WTO is far more a 'member-driven organization' than the old GATT used to be. The understanding seems to be that members will have to develop solutions through agreements among themselves. The role of the WTO secretariat is very constrained. In GATT times this was different. For example, it was normal that members of the secretariat staff could chair meetings of negotiating groups. Also, the final draft text, which became the basis of the conclusion of the UR, was elaborated on the basis of direct bilateral discussions of secretariat staff with the members. Such approaches might not remain unthinkable for the future, but for the time being it does not appear to be an option.

Therefore, the chair, when preparing for his text, needs to try and generate a process by which the members themselves produce the necessary compromises. If the members are unable to do so, which is almost always so, the chair must at least create a process which keeps members informed about what might be coming in his text. For this purpose, every small group process has to be followed by a transparency exercise for all participants (open ended session) in which the chair, at least in summary form, reports about the conduct and result of the small group's work. On the other hand, even a small group of some 15 delegations is not yet the forum in which constructive and confidential discussions can be expected easily. This is why, on an ad hoc basis, the chair would convene even fewer delegations or negotiators to consult with them on particular issues. These meetings are based on work done in the larger configurations and might be prepared by himself or a 'friend of the chair', which he would appoint for this purpose. This friend of the chair (or facilitator) might organize the discussion, prepare outline papers summarizing the positions and options for solutions, or perhaps even produce draft texts, which could represent compromises. Of course, such a process cannot be binding for any of the participants (including the facilitator) and would not commit their countries, but it can lead to a situation in which all participants have some idea of what might be coming when the chair actually tables his text.

Such process of these ever smaller groups was carried out throughout the year 2006 until the chair took the decision that it was now the right time to table his text.[5] It is well known that when the text came out, it triggered immediately very strong criticism and, in effect, basically stalled the negotiations. If the chair's text was based on such careful negotiating process as described above, why could things go so wrong then?

8.5 WHY THE CHAIR'S TEXT FAILED

The first answer to the question is that is does not take a lot to make things go wrong in such a complicated and politicized environment, as existed in 2007. Actually, the chair had prepared his text relatively well in most areas, but unfortunately not all. Knowing that his text was only the first complete draft text in this round of negotiations (the UR for antidumping saw more that half a dozen), he did not, for example, make the mistake of using the best language for the first draft. A first draft never survives the following debate and any best solution presented in a first attempt automatically goes down with it. Also, the chair took many decisions on what to retain in his text and what to disregard, which proved to be by and large acceptable. Of course, everything was criticized, but this is part of the game, no country will ever openly give up on an issue before the very end.

While the chair carried out intensive consultations on possible solutions (see above) on almost all important issues under negotiation, he apparently shied away from doing this for zeroing as well. Zeroing had been made the most important point for resolution by the United States after they had lost a number of dispute settlement cases on this subject. On this most prominent issue of zeroing, the chair took a higher risk than in other areas. Whatever the reasons for the chair were to try to draft a text on zeroing without testing it with negotiators, he took the risk of coming with a surprise.

The main reason, however, for the apparent failure of his text, in my view, was an error in judgement with regard to the ability of negotiators to move to compromises in the prevailing political atmosphere. Presumably, the chair had calculated that if he gave to the United States more on zeroing than they actually needed, but at the same time gave to the *friends* a number of issues that they had demanded, but which were completely indigestible for the United States, both sides would sit down and trade one against the other. What the chair underestimated was the political publicity that his

---

[5] Woznowski, *supra,* pp. 101–4.

text and the issue of zeroing attracted immediately. During the first discussion of his draft in the negotiating group, many countries were represented by their ambassadors or senior officials, who made strong statements against the chair's draft and in particular the legalisation of zeroing in it. From then on, it was almost impossible to have discussions among negotiators that were only technical. Of course, no negotiator could be seen as compromising on such a highly political issue as zeroing. The rather confrontational attitude and the speeches for the galleries continued throughout the first reading of the rest of the chair's text.

Although the rules negotiators managed to go through the failed Ministerial meeting in July 2008 without becoming subject of controversial discussions among ministers, the chair had to withdraw his 2007 text with regard to the most contentious issues, which he put into brackets.

Since December 2008 not much was happening. The negotiating group did another full reading of the 2008 text, in plenary session only, with the repetition of the positions known from the reading of the 2007 text. Unfortunately, the chair did not allow smaller group to address the issues in a more technical and constructive way and therefore, the negotiations on antidumping saw no development for about three years.

8.6 PROSPECTS, CHALLENGES AND RISKS

At the time when this chapter was written, at the end of 2010, the DDA is about to wake up again. A serious attempt shall be made to reach agreement on all important elements of this Round, including Rules, by the summer 2011. New texts shall be tabled in all areas until the end of the first quarter of the year, in order to refine these texts further for the final deal a few months later. This puts considerable pressure on the negotiating group and its new chairman, Ambassador Francis (Trinidad and Tobago). During a period of only three months, solutions will have to be developed in the four subgroups of Rules under his chairmanship, antidumping, general subsidies, fish subsidies and regional trade agreements. This task appears to be even more challenging since most of the present negotiators are relatively new and were not around during the years 2006 and 2007, the last period of intensive negotiations. As explained above, the constructive interaction between the negotiators is a necessary condition for successful negotiations and can normally only be created over time.

However, at this juncture, in early 2011, this process has to be jump-started. The chairman has decided to intensify the activities by convening more and longer meetings in multilateral and plurilateral format and to appoint *friends of the chair* to facilitate the elaboration of compromises.

In the area of antidumping solutions have to be found for the remaining differences on a large number of mostly procedural changes to the ADA, which represent the so-called non-bracketed issues, i.e. from part of the 2008 text, but which are not yet agreed. They relate to issues of transparency and due process, which are naturally more difficult to accept for those members who belong to the new user countries and are partly still lacking expertise and resources.

The most important work has to be done in the area of the so-called 'bracketed issues'. These issues are the most contentious ones, for which the former chair had to withdraw his proposed solutions in his 2007 text. In the 2008 text the brackets only contained an outline of the problem with the different positions taken on it.

The issues are: Zeroing, Causation of injury, Material retardation, Exclusion of producers who are related to exporters or who are themselves importers, Product under consideration, Information requests to affiliated parties, Public interest/Lesser duty, Anti-circumvention and Sunset reviews.

Not all these points have the same weight and not all of them are equally contentious. As a matter of fact, the former chair had increased the number of bracketed issues in order to facilitate trade-off between them. Of course, in the middle of negotiations, it is not possible for the negotiator to anticipate the likely results in each area without compromising on his negotiating tactics and strategies. Therefore, I cannot give any assessment of the chances and merits of the different demands. However, some general comment might be possible by pointing to the structural difficulties the negotiators will face in the coming months.

Filling all brackets with compromise text, which is more acceptable to members than the 2007 text, in the time available, might be regarded an almost impossible task. Thus there might be a call to lower the ambition; to put up with less in order not to jeopardize the overall deal.

In my view, this is unlikely to work for a new ADA. A low ambition deal would most likely only consist of additional rules on due process and transparency, demands from the friends as well as from the traditional users, in particular the United States and the EU. These additional disciplines in the procedural field would not necessitate big changes for the traditional users, since their processes are already on a high level of procedural fairness (with differences, of course). On the other hand, for the new user countries and those who only intend to use the AD instrument in the future, the increased disciplines, on top of the existing ones, would be an extra burden. There is no reason for them to agree to this. At least, inside the new negotiations on antidumping there would be no incentive for this deal.[6]

The issue of zeroing has dominated the AD debate for long. Its importance for the outcome of AD cases was probably overestimated. How far the United States will insist on some authorization of zeroing has to be seen.

One bracketed issue deserves particular attention. This is the question of special and differential treatment for developing countries (SDT), which could become a critical element for the negotiations. The issues of SDT in the context of the use of AD/CVD laws are not new. Already in the UR it was discussed whether under certain circumstances developing countries (DCs) could benefit from more favourable treatment in cases carried out against their exporters. Typically, higher thresholds for *de minimis* margins for dumping and injury were discussed. This issue is still under consideration in the present Round. However, a new aspect of SDT has appeared recently. This is the demand from DCs to be put into a position to be able to use the instruments. Their argument is that the traditional users have set the rules for the trade defence instruments in the UR, which are already too demanding for many DCs with their limited resources and lack of administrative experience. In view of the current negotiations, it appears that the standards for due process and transparency, which are the most demanding disciplines for the proper administration of AD/CVD cases, will be again increased. This would make it even more difficult for DCs to 'exercise their rights under the agreement' to carry out trade defence cases. Therefore, DCs are requesting lower standards with regard to the administrative burden for their investigating authorities. There is no obvious solution for this dilemma, because some DCs are the most active and frequent users of AD laws and much of the increased discipline on transparency and due process is meant to apply to them in particular. Whether other criteria and conditions can be found, or new and more efficient ways and means of technical assistance can be developed, has not even been discussed in depth in the negotiations. Therefore, this problem needs urgent and extensive preparation on the level of technical experts. It is clear, however, that a solution for this new SDT demand has to be found before the end of the negotiations, since the new agreement needs support from all participants.

---

6 In this context, some statements by the former chair that large parts of his text (due process and transparency issues) are more or less agreed have to be seen with great caution.

8.7 THERE IS A REAL CHANCE OF NO DEAL AT THE END

Many positions in the AD negotiations have been developed for tactical, defensive reasons (as explained in the first part of this article) and, if the tactical needs have disappeared, there might be very few participants left who actually need a new agreement. Most users can live with the existing rules and use the DSU in case of conflict.

With regard to the very demanding positions of the friends group and its most ambitious proponents such as Switzerland, Norway, Hong Kong, Chile and Japan as coordinator, it must be taken into account that their demands are not matched by any possible concession from their side. In other words, they have nothing to pay with inside the antidumping negotiation. Whether they are eventually prepared to offer compensation in other areas has to be seen.

By the time when this chapter is published, we might know more.

9. The EU and free trade: can we still afford it?

Gérard Depayre*

Born under the auspices of free trade, and a key actor with the United States in the post World War II efforts to liberalize international trade, the European Economic Community (EEC), now the European Union,[1] has been one of the main beneficiaries of the liberalization of trade.

9.1 BORN UNDER THE AUSPICES OF FREE TRADE

The very creation of the European Coal and Steel Community (ECSC) in 1952 and of the EEC in 1958, which required the elimination of restrictions on trade among the six original members, involved a liberalization without precedent of international trade in Europe.

This coincided with the major effort undertaken since 1945 by a number of countries, led by the United States – as part of the broader plan to rebuild the international economic system (Bretton Woods agreement of 1944) – to liberalize trade and create a more open international trading system through the establishment of the General Agreement on Tariffs and Trade (GATT 1947).[2]

* The author wishes to express his gratitude to members of the law firm Gide Loyrette Nouel for their support.

[1] First called the European Economic Community by the Treaty of Rome, then referred to as the European Communities following the Merger Treaty of 1965, it became the European Community in 1993 and the European Union in 2009 with the entry into force of the Lisbon Treaty. For the sake of simplicity, we shall refer here to the EC for developments relating to the past, and to the EU for recent ones.

[2] The original intention behind the negotiations on the International Trade Organization, that eventually lead to the birth of GATT, was to create a third institution to handle the trade side of international economic cooperation, joining the two 'Bretton Woods' institutions, the International Monetary Fund and the World Bank.

While having different purposes, these initiatives had their common roots in the memories of the 1930s and of the protectionist trade policies that contributed to worsen the Great Depression, and led to the dreadful consequences that followed. They were inspired by the belief that, not only liberalization of trade would lead to increased collective wealth for the countries concerned, but also that it would create conditions conducive to closer economic solidarities between countries and peoples, and could thus help avoid the recurrence of the disorders that preceded, and directly led to World War II.

This belief in the benefits of the liberalization of trade is reflected in one of the objectives set out in the preamble to the Rome Treaty, which states: 'Desiring to work, by means of a commercial policy, to the progressive abolition of restrictions on international trade.'

This makes the EC probably the only economic entity having an organic law that sets the liberalization of international trade as one of its key objectives.

The EC, which has been, and continues to be, a key actor in the liberalization of international trade, has, over the years, remained committed to this objective.

9.2 THE EC HAS BEEN A KEY ACTOR IN THE LIBERALIZATION OF TRADE

First, it has expanded and deepened the area of free trade in Europe.

This was done by the gradual incorporation in the EEC of 21 new members with which, and among which, trade was consequently liberalized. Not only were some of the new members, like the United Kingdom, Spain, Poland, large economies or, like Sweden or Denmark, affluent ones, but others, the East European states, had been until then largely closed to external trade. The effect of liberalization resulting from the enlargement of the EEC was thus significant.

The deepening of the integration of the economies of EC members has also been an important factor of liberalization. Following the progressive elimination of tariffs and quantitative restrictions, it became apparent that the integration of national economies into one single market required more than the elimination of traditional protections. There remained indeed many obstacles hampering the free circulation of goods, services, capital and workers. This led J. Delors, then President of the Commission, to launch the single market project with the White Paper on 'Completing the internal market' of June 1985, which asked 'the European Council to pledge itself to completion of a fully unified market by 1992…'. Meeting this objective involved massive efforts to eliminate a wide variety of obstacles to free circulation, the cost of which was convincingly demonstrated in the so-called Cechini Report (1988). While, as can be seen from the recent Monti Report,[3] these efforts have not been successful in all areas and a lot still remains to be done, the EU has achieved a high degree of integration of its economies, particularly with respect to goods, and of liberalization of its internal trade, that few – if any – other regional groupings have reached. For instance, the EU has a central system of control of state aids, aimed at avoiding distortions of competition among member states, which, to our knowledge, no other regional groupings or states have.

To this should be added the creation of the euro, an indispensable complement to the single market, and a factor of reduction of transaction costs between member states.

Thus, through its successive enlargements and the completion of its internal market, the EC has contributed significantly to the development of free trade. It did not, however, confine itself to the practice of free trade internally. It also played a crucial role in the liberalization of international trade through its external action:

First, when it established the common external tariff, it did it at a level that was a compromise between the high tariffs of some members and the lower ones of others: tariffs on more than 80 per cent of the tariffs lines were set at the level of the arithmetic average of national tariffs.

Since its inception, the EC, in the field of trade, has had to accommodate two opposite camps: those who favored protection of the EU market, and those who, to the contrary, wanted complete free trade. In most cases, as it did at the outset, the EC chose the middle road, and, in so doing, resisted any backtracking on existing liberalization.

This policy line was further confirmed when, in the framework of the completion of the internal market, the EC had to adopt common external regimes in areas where it had developed new internal policies. This raised the question of what level of protection of its market the EC should adopt. Should it adopt protective regimes or liberal ones? A heated debate ensued, of which the issue of access to the EC market for financial services and capitals was a telling example. When the then Trade Commissioner, W. De Clercq, raised the issue of reciprocity in a speech, implying that the EU could condition access to its financial market on the treatment granted by other countries to EU financial operators and investments, it provoked such negative reactions that the idea was quickly abandoned for what is

3 'A new strategy for the single market', Report to the President of the European Commission José Manuel Barroso by Mario Monti.

essentially a liberal regime. The same was generally true of other areas where the EU could have through specific rules or standards created barriers to entry into the EU market. In the definition of the new common external policies that it had to adopt in the framework of the completion of the external market, the EU thus confirmed its free trade orientation, the rationale being that what was good internally should also be good externally. The fears of foreign countries that raised the spectrum of 'fortress Europe' did not materialize.

In line with this orientation, the EC has been an active participant in all the Rounds of multilateral trade negotiations that took place since its creation. While it usually took, in these Rounds, more moderate positions than the US, it played an active role in negotiations to insure their successful conclusion and the further liberalization of trade. The EC was particularly instrumental in the gradual build up of what is now the multilateral trading system. In particular, it supported actively the development of rules, as well as the reinforcement of the dispute settlement mechanism, with the objective of changing the system from one largely based on balance of power to one more closely based on legal rights.

While globalization, and the trade liberalization that has led to it, are often blamed for a number of the problems that affect European economies, the EU has in the course of the pending Doha Round continued to defend the principle of additional liberalization and has offered significant contributions to the further lowering of trade barriers, including in agriculture.

In addition to the part it played in multilateral negotiations, the EU has unilaterally reduced or eliminated the protection of its market *vis-à-vis* imports from developing countries under the Generalized System of Preferences, and for the ACP countries under the Lomé/ Cotonou preferences scheme that granted non-reciprocal preferential market access to these countries. The EU, in order to conform to WTO rules, has been for some years now negotiating with ACP countries new Economic Partnership Agreements (EPA) that differ from the Cotonou/Lomé regime in two important respects: EPAs are FTAs that are based on reciprocity and cover services. Finally, for least developed countries, the EU has offered them unrestricted assess to its market for all products but arms (the so called 'Everything but arms initiative').

The EU has also, embarked in a broad effort to negotiate bilateral agreements, including free trade agreements (FTAs), with a number of countries. Until recently, these agreements had been with smaller, developing countries. The EU is now engaged in FTA negotiations with large countries, such as India and Canada, and large groupings of countries, such as Mercosur or Asean. It recently concluded an agreement with South Korea.

In these efforts to liberalize trade, one sector, however, has lagged behind: agriculture. In this sector, EU priority objectives, inherited from the post-war period marked by painful shortages, have been the expansion of production and exports and the defense of EU farmers' income. This translated into a policy involving a high level of protection of the EU internal market and high subsidies that has made the EC the subject of sharp attacks by its trading partners.[4]

Since 2003 the EC has been engaged in a major reform of its Common Agricultural Policy (CAP) marking a turning point towards a more market-oriented agriculture. Following this reform, the EU has offered in the Doha negotiations to abandon all export subsidies by 2013 and to reduce considerably its domestic support, as well as the level of protection of its market. While agriculture would still be subject to specific rules, these commitments, if and when fully implemented, would reduce the gap between the very liberal trade policy of the EU regarding industrial goods, services and capital, and its policy on agriculture.

On the whole, it is thus fair to say that the EU has kept faithfully its commitment to the liberalization of international trade. Not only did it, over the years, resist protectionist pressures, particularly in times of economic slow down, but it further liberalized access to its market – making it probably the most open in the world. And it will make a very significant further step in the direction of liberalization if Doha is successfully concluded.

9.3 THE EC HAS BEEN ONE OF THE MAIN BENEFICIARIES OF THE LIBERALIZATION OF TRADE

Since the war and, subsequently, the creation of the EEC, European countries have increased their external trade by massive amounts and managed to capture a major share of world trade, in particular in manufactured goods, and in services. Between 1963 and 2008 – the year where world trade reached its highest level before being hit by the Recession – the value of the exports of merchandise of the four largest European economies, Germany, the United Kingdom, France and Italy (including trade between each other) increased nearly eighty-fold. The EU countries share of total

4 It is fair to say, however, that the EC has not been the only one to practise such policies. At one point or another all major agricultural producers have protected their market and subsidized their agriculture.

world exports of merchandise (in value, and intra EU trade included) increased from 24.5 per cent in 1963 to 42.4 per cent in 2003 and 37.7 per cent in 2009.[5] Even allowing for the loss of value of currencies and other factors that distort comparisons, this reflects an enormous growth in volume.

In addition, over these years, the composition of EU trade has evolved: a large proportion (65 per cent in 2005)[6] of its imports of goods now consists of components and capital goods that are subsequently used for the production in the EU of finished products. This allows EU businesses to continue producing goods for which otherwise they could not be competitive, and allows EU consumers to benefit from cheaper and more diversified goods.

The expansion and diversification of the trade of European countries, which can, in large part, be attributed to the liberalization of trade that has taken place since 1945, has been a key factor in the spectacular growth from which these countries have benefited in the 30 years that followed the war. While there are, as always, dissenting opinions, numerous studies have demonstrated the essential contribution of trade to the growth of economies in general, and of EU economies in particular.

This, however, corresponded to a long period of uncontested economic domination of the EU and the United States that has come to an end. In the course of the last 20 years, we have indeed seen a considerable change in the conditions of competition on the world market with the rapid emergence of China, India and Brazil.

9.4 IN THESE CIRCUMSTANCES, CAN THE EU AFFORD TO MAINTAIN THE LIBERAL ORIENTATION OF ITS TRADE POLICY?

While rare in trade policy circles are those that would dare ask such an iconoclastic question, the issue of free trade, and more broadly that of globalization, which is indissociably linked to it, have for sometimes been the subject of a heated debate in public opinions and in the media. The recent financial crisis and economic recession have further increased the intensity of this debate.

---

5 Source: *WTO Trade Statistics 2009 and 2010*; Eurostat.

6 Source: *Global Europe – EU performance in the Global economy – 2008.*

9.4.1 A Deeply Changed Trading Environment

The EU and the United States, who had a clear competitive edge over the rest of the world in a number of sectors, have since the mid 1990s lost that advantage, and find it now harder and harder to compete with emerging countries, even in areas such as certain high tech products and services that previously seemed beyond the reach of these countries. The phenomenon is far less pronounced in the EU than in the United States, but the fact that EU economic operators are losing ground to companies from emerging economies both in their own markets and in third country's markets is indisputable. While the EU share of world trade in manufactures has remained more or less stable over the last decade, at between 14 and 15 per cent, there are some ominous signs: the deterioration of the EU trade balance from a small surplus in 2000) to a negative €255 billions in 2008. Even more worrying are: the fast-rising deficit of the EU trade balance with China; the reduction of the gap between the EU and China total exports of merchandise, which has gone down from an advantage of 67 per cent in 2000 to 15 per cent in 2008; the losses suffered by the EU on some of the most dynamic importing markets (India, Russia, and to a lesser extent Brazil); as well as the relatively low level of the EU share of the world market for high tech products (18.5 per cent in 2005), still higher than that of the United States and Japan, but for which the EU is losing more market share than in other product categories.

It should moreover be kept in mind that Germany's high competitiveness in goods somewhat hides the serious deterioration of the performance of most other members of the Union, which is far worse than global figures for the EU as a whole would suggest.

The increasing difficulty in competing with goods from emerging countries, in the first place those from China, translates into increasing rates of penetration of the EU market by imports. In France, for instance, between 1999 and 2009 the share of products made in France in the French total consumption has gone down from 67 per cent to 64 per cent, with far higher decreases for sectors like textiles, garments, products related to health, or cars. To this should be added that the share of imported components in French made products has increased from 25 per cent to 31 per cent.[7] Such trends, which can also be observed in the EU as a whole, will continue, as will the erosion, particularly spectacular for certain sectors,[8] of the manufacturing base of the EU.

---

[7] *Observatoire du Fabriqué en France*, Ministry of Industry.

[8] One should keep in mind that statistics on production and trade, as presently recorded, offer a completely distorted picture of the reality of trade flows and of what is produced where, by whom. Indeed, many businesses now rely on global

This evolution has been accompanied by sharp increases in levels of unemployment in most member states, a trend that has been further amplified by the recession. While a number of economists argue that the main factor in the present high levels of unemployment is not foreign trade, but technological progress and the inability of countries to replace, through the creation of new activities, the jobs thus gone, it remains that EU economies have lost ground to emerging economies and are, and will continue to be, in all sectors where international competition can play freely, under considerable pressure from the exporters of goods and, to a lesser extent, providers of services of these countries.

And, rightly or wrongly, this has led to the perception among large segments of public opinion in Europe, particularly in the southern member states of the Union – a perception that cannot be ignored by governments – that free trade and, more generally, economic liberalism are to be blamed for the economic problems faced, albeit to different degrees, by EU countries: outsourcing, delocalizations, erosion of the manufacturing base, low growth, deterioration of the purchasing power of certain socio-economic groups, unemployment and the social ills that result from it. There is a widespread feeling that free trade has left European businesses wide open to unfair competition by foreign companies which, in areas such as labour laws, environmental standards and control of aids, benefit from much more lenient standards than those applied in the EU. Such feelings are widespread and particularly strong among members of the European Parliament, a body that, as a result of the Lisbon Treaty, will play a considerably increased role in determining EU trade policy. While some would only want to see a hardening of the policy *vis-à-vis* countries like China, and generally, more reciprocity in our relations with our trading partners, others want more radical changes that would require the reopening of existing international agreements, or even their denunciation. Among the many ideas floating around, some advocate selective protectionism to defend key sectors; others would want to take agriculture out of the WTO on the ground that, as shown by the recent episodes of speculation on basic products, this sector cannot be managed by relying solely on the free play of market forces.

---

supply chains, and products registered, for their whole value, as exported by a given country may only have been assembled in that country from imported components, with little value added. As a result, the level of value added in a given country may not be what trade statistics would suggest. Pro trade advocates argue that official statistics underestimate local production, but one cannot exclude either that the opposite would be true.

9.5 WILL THE EU STAY THE COURSE OR YIELD TO SUCH PRESSURES?

While a complete change of direction in EU trade policy seems out of question, some shift towards more restrictive policies cannot be excluded.

9.5.1 A Complete Change of Direction of EU Trade Policy seems out of Question

A complete change of direction of EU trade policy seems out of question, first because, as the world biggest trading block, the EU has an objective interest in a stable and open multilateral trading system. Dependent on foreign sources to meet its needs for a number of basic products, and in the first place energy, it has a vital interest in unhampered access to the markets of its trading partners for its exports.

In addition, any radical change of its policy that would restrict access to its market would put it at odds with the extremely dense array of commitments that it has taken in the framework of the many multilateral and bilateral agreements to which it is a party – and, in the first place, the WTO. Trying to reopen such agreements would meet with the strongest resistance inside as well as outside the EU. It would unavoidably trigger retaliations by the EU trading partners and throw the world trading system into chaos.

It is all the more unlikely that the EU would embark on such a course as interests among member states are very diversified. Users, consumers, in addition to importers, wholesalers and retailers, now represent large and powerful interest groups that in some member states and for certain sectors dominate those of producers. With some variations depending on the issue, the two camps are now more or less of equal force in the Council, and, thus, in a position to neutralize each other. Given the decision-making system of the EU, and in particular the voting procedure in the Council, it is thus very unlikely that, barring catastrophic circumstances, there could be, in the near future, enough support for a radical change of direction in EU trade policy. It is of course conceivable that member states could take individual initiatives, but European treaties leave very little, if any, leeway to member states in the field of trade policy.

Thus, the very dense corpus of binding commitments that members of the Union have taken *vis-à-vis* the rest of the world as well as *vis-à-vis* each others creates a situation that practically rules out the kind of fundamental changes of direction in EU trade policy that the most extreme elements of public opinions claim is necessary.

9.5.2 EU Trade Policy Cannot Continue Unchanged

That does not mean, however, that EU trade policy can continue unchanged. Indeed, given the very high and persistent level of unemployment, the prospects that this situation may last, and the social damages resulting from it – of which the signs are becoming more and more evident – pressures for a tightening of EU trade policy will increase regarding both the access of foreign goods and services to the EU market and the treatment of EU exports on third country markets.

On the import side, there are a number of areas that, without changes to existing international rules, would lend themselves to such tightening:

The prime candidate would be government procurements, an area where there is a strong imbalance between the access that the EU grants to foreign producers and the access that other countries grant to EU businesses. For its own reasons, the EU has made the choice to offer nearly unlimited access to its procurements to foreign businesses. It consequently finds itself with practically no leverage to obtain from other countries reciprocity of treatment for its companies. This has led some member states and businesses to demand a revision of the existing EU directive to condition access to EU procurements on reciprocity of treatment for EU businesses in third countries. The EU, while it has commitments in the WTO Government Procurement Agreement (GPA), has a certain leeway to adopt a more restrictive policy *vis-à-vis* other members, and has it hands free *vis-à-vis* countries that have not joined the GPA. As in other areas, however, there are very different views on this subject among member states and changes to the existing directive may prove extremely difficult, if not impossible. In that case, the only possibility left to member states that are opposed to the present situation would be to instruct their purchasing entities to reject offers from certain countries, which would put them at odds with EU law.

Another area where we could see a tightening of EU trade policy is the use of contingent protection: antidumping, countervailing duties. Already, the Commission, departing from a long-standing policy, and following the example of the United States, has initiated anti-subsidy cases against China in parallel to anti-dumping investigations. We can expect that the present series of cases, anti-dumping and anti-subsidy, against China will continue and even, possibly, increase. We can also expect a more aggressive policy, including through recourses to the WTO dispute settlement, towards subsidies or practices akin to subsidies, such as export restrictions, including export taxes, or dual pricing of energy and raw materials that benefit transformers in resources-based economies.

Excluding completely the most advanced developing countries from the benefits of the GSP scheme is also a possibility that is sometimes mentioned, but this would probably only have a very limited economic impact while raising very negative reactions on the part of those concerned.

Regulations can also be a means of protection. Tariffs having been reduced to very low levels and quantitative restrictions eliminated – in particular in developed countries – ,regulatory barriers have become the main obstacles to access to major markets. The adoption by an importing country of new regulations that differ significantly from those of major exporters has by itself protective effects. This is all the more so when regulations are adopted with a protectionist objective, a possibility left open by the relative looseness of WTO provisions in this area. While for instance, the Sanitary and Phytosanitary (SPS) agreement, specifies that 'measures necessary to protect human, animal and plant life should not constitute a disguised restriction on international trade', it leaves members free to regulate as they see fit. The line between measures that are disguised restrictions on trade and measures necessary to protect human, animal, or plant life being sometimes very fine, tracking down and preventing such abuses is not an easy task. The EU, which is one of the principal world regulators, if not the main one, has clearly the power to use regulations as a protective device, and some foreign countries consider that it already does. For instance, serious objections have been raised against REACH on the ground that it creates unjustified obstacles to the access to the EU market for foreign chemical products.

There are a number of other tools that could be used to curtail access to the EU market for foreign goods. One of them would be, if discussions on climate change did not lead to an agreement or if they led to an unbalanced agreement, the imposition of taxes at the border on imports from countries applying lower environmental standards than the EU. However, this idea, which could take different forms, would raise serious practical and legal difficulties, and it seems that it has been, at least temporarily, put on the backburner.

Critics will argue that retrenchment of EU businesses behind their borders will not help correct trade imbalances. Not only will it not improve their competitiveness, but it may even hurt it, particularly in those cases, which are more and more frequent, where their production process relies on supplies from other countries outside the EU (global supply chain). It may also lead EU trade partners to retaliate and further restrict access to their markets at the expense of European exporters. The solution to the current jobs and competitiveness problems of Europe does not thus appear to lie in an increased protection of the EU market.

Rather, it would seem that fundamental EU interests would be better served by concentrating efforts on improving the access of EU goods, services and investments to third country's markets, in particular those of the emerging ones. There is a variety of actions that can be taken to that effect:

- improving access of EU firms to foreign procurements;
- putting pressure, through all legal and diplomatic means available, on foreign countries to eliminate the innumerable non-tariff obstacles that they maintain and that hamper the access of EU exports and investments to their markets;
- ensuring better protection of intellectual property rights;
- promoting regulatory cooperation, either by trying to find ways to overcome discrepancies between existing regulations or by associating trading partners to the elaboration of new regulations.

However, for such efforts to lead to tangible results, adequate leverage on foreign governments is indispensable. Ideally, multilateral negotiations, in the framework of which concessions can be exchanged on a large variety of subjects, would be the best format. The reality, however, is that, as experienced in the Doha Round, multilateral negotiations have become extremely difficult, if not impossible, with 153 participants. In addition, as is certainly true in the present case, they often fail to address new, emerging issues that are of immediate importance to business.

The solution therefore would appear to be, in addition to a continuing commitment to the multilateral system, the active pursuit of bilateral negotiations. In such negotiations, the EU not only has more leverage to obtain specific concessions from its partners through offers of improved access to its market, but it has also more direct support from EU industries, which can see in a more tangible way the benefits they could draw from such agreements.

The logic would thus be that we see intensified efforts on the part of the EU to negotiate bilateral agreements and that the agreements it negotiates be more ambitious. Already it is engaged in the negotiation with a large number of countries of various types of agreements, including FTAs. An agreement has been recently concluded with South Korea; negotiations are under way with India, Canada, Pakistan, Ukraine, Asean and Mercosur, to which should be added the partnership agreements under negotiation with the former members of the Cotonou Agreement. Negotiations have also been under way for several years with China to update the 1985 EU–China Trade and Cooperation agreement. It is also not a mystery that some in the Commission have been giving thoughts to the possibility of a free trade agreement with Japan, and not unlikely that we could see a reactivation of negotiations with the United States on some form of agreement aimed at eliminating the remaining obstacles to transatlantic trade.

To the initial question as to whether the EU could still afford free trade, the answer is thus clear: There is no alternative to free trade for the Union. But, particularly if the employment situation was to remain bleak, the Commission will have difficulty escaping demands of public opinions for a significant hardening of its trade policy. In its recent Communication on its future trade policy (Trade, Growth and World affairs), made public shortly after this paper was initially written[9], the Commission undertakes to launch a number of actions – some of which similar to those discussed above – that would go in this direction. It remains to be seen, however, whether the Commission will actually be able to implement this somewhat more aggressive line. Differences of views and interests among Member States on trade are indeed so strong that any proposal considered as deviating from the traditionally moderate stance taken by the EU would be hard to sell.

In addition, one should be under no illusion that a more active trade policy, while it could bring benefits, could by itself correct the large imbalances that affect the international trading system. The correction of such imbalances, and of the economic and social problems that they cause, will come in the first place from policies addressing macroeconomics factors, such as rates of savings, and investments, relative role of consumption, investments, and exports in the growth of economies, as well as parities of currencies. It will also, and even more importantly, come from internal policies creating the right environment for growth: better education and training for workers, encouragement to R&D, better infrastructure, lower taxes, smart regulation and the preservation of local industrial clusters of large and small firms that feed off one another.

---

[9] Trade, Growth and World affairs – Com(2010) 612 – September 2010.

Interpretation and dispute settlement

10. Modern approaches to treaty interpretation

John H. Jackson

10.1 INTRODUCTION: ADDING TO THE LIST OF USEFUL TREATY INTERPRETATION CONCEPTS

It is a distinct privilege and honour to participate in this well-deserved *Festschrift* honoring Jacques Bourgeois. We have a long history together, and many times have discussed important directions of international law. Jacques has always maintained true scholarly rigour in such discussions, and he has had a remarkable and varied career contributing to the theory and institutions of international law. I remain always an admirer of him for that and many other reasons.

Those thoughts lead me in this brief chapter to focus on a critical and often troublesome aspect of international law, namely treaty interpretation. This is a huge subject, and cannot be extensively explored in the context of this work, but by examining a few particular and currently critical subjects of treaty interpretation, perhaps I can contribute to further exploration of the broader landscape of the general subject that I hope will stimulate Jacques to continue his many discourses and searches for clarity and truth that I have been privileged to share.

Some of the concepts that underpin my thoughts expressed below have been partly explored in my 2006 book published by Cambridge University Press.[1] In addition, many works of other important scholars and professionals relevant to international law have influenced me and

[1] Jackson, J.H., *Sovereignty, the WTO and Changing Fundamentals of International Law*, Cambridge, Cambridge University Press, 2006 (paperback edition published 2009).

enhanced my thinking. Among these I would mention the 2009 book by Isabelle Van Damme.[2]

Needless to say, my thoughts have been influenced by my years of attention to the major trade treaties, WTO (World Trade Organization) and its predecessor GATT (General Agreement on Tariffs and Trade). Indeed since the WTO came into force on 1 January 1995, its newly constructed dispute settlement system has often deeply engaged numerous issues of treaty interpretation with unparalleled depth of analysis, and intense struggle in that context with the tensions imposed by the proponents of maintaining national government 'sovereignty', as opposed to other advocates who urge the necessity of creating operational international institutions of cooperation and coordination. This constant reasoning tug of war occurs in most of the WTO cases now on the books, as part of the WTO elaborate jurisprudence relating to over 400 cases brought, with over 100 case reports adopted, and approximately 60,000 pages of those jurisprudence reports, an incredible record for the brief 15 years of WTO existence.

10.2 THE VIENNA CONVENTION ON THE LAW OF TREATIES: ROLE AND FUNCTION

As a further part of introducing this subject I will mention only a few concepts and propositions, which clearly can be contested, but which deserve attention directed to clarifying and thus making more useful such concepts. In particular I note that the Vienna Convention on the Law of Treaties (VCLT), although very influential in WTO/GATT history and in the context of treaty interpretation, does not operate as binding treaty obligation, because more than 60 WTO members out of a total membership of over 150 are not official parties to the VCLT. There exists some opinion that at least the treaty interpretation articles of the VCLT (Articles 31 and 32) may be considered binding international 'customary law' but, as usual with customary international law, there is at least some ambiguity about that. In addition, even assuming (as I do) that the VCLT 31 and 32 are a good starting point for treaty analysis, nevertheless it seems clear that the VCLT does not impose a limit on the potential for adding interpreting concepts that are not unambiguously included in the VCLT set. Some of the potential additions should, in this author's view, include

[2] Van Damme, I., *Treaty Interpretation by the WTO Appellate Body*, Oxford, Oxford University Press, 2009.

'evolutionary' interpretation, rethinking the traditional views of preparatory work usefulness, a broader 'purposeful' approach to interpretation and finally the very important questions surrounding concepts (plural) of 'precedent'.

10.3 NEEDED ADDITIONAL CONCEPTS FOR BETTER TREATY INTERPRETATION

In this section I put forward four treaty interpretation concepts (mentioned above) that are among those that I believe merit emphasis and attention. In the view of some international law professionals some or maybe all four of these can be based on language already in the VCLT. However, I differ from those who believe that to 'shoe horn' the concepts into the VCLT would be wise or optimal. In some cases there are major ambiguities involved with that approach, and in other cases it is simply better and clearer to recognize some concepts separately from the sometimes constraining context of VCLT language. For example, some international tribunals (including the WTO Appellate Body) have at least in the past put much emphasis on 'textual analysis' (partly influenced by the language in VCLT Article 31) that arguably led to reasoning and conclusions that some argue are not appropriate or at least not optimal. And when recognizing the 'non-party' status of the VCLT WTO membership, it seems quite appropriate to take advantage of the freedom from VCLT problems, by utilizing other potential approaches. So I now look briefly at four concepts, which can benefit from such freedom.

Concept 1: Preparatory Work: It is well known that the application of preparatory work has been something of a puzzle in the light of VCLT 31 and 32. It is often argued that preparatory work is only allowed under Article 32, and then only when the language of 31 cannot solve an interpretive question. (I am purposely condensing this discussion, which involves many pages of controversial material.) Thus it is argued that preparatory work holds a lower rank in interpretation. Yet it can be argued that preparatory work in many cases truly provides the most significant insight to the intention of the treaty draftsman.

In addition, we have seen cases where a tribunal (especially the WTO) has utilized preparatory work without attempting to justify its need because of Article 31. Most particularly, and very interesting was one such WTO AB report, which did not mention the words 'preparatory work', but nevertheless turned quickly to such history on the grounds that a clause in Article 31 called for attention to the 'object and purpose' of a treaty clause. This report then included a footnote that clearly cited preparatory work for the

ITO draft charter and the GATT.[3] This approach could make Article 32 irrelevant for using preparatory work.

Concept 2: Evolutionary Interpretation: This approach seems very necessary in the context of treaty language that often cannot be changed or amended, whereas events in the world (especially perhaps economic developments) change very quickly. It is necessary to allow an interpretation to prevent absurdities in treaty application, which sometimes can even defeat important activity designed to enable an institution to carry out the mission delegated to it by the treaty goals. In the famous *Shrimp Turtle* case of the WTO, the Appellate Body expressly adopted the concept of the evolutionary approach to treaty interpretation.[4]

Concept 3: Purposeful Interpretation: Sometimes termed 'teleological', this approach enables a tribunal to focus more strongly on the purpose of a treaty or an international institution. This can be tricky and indeed controversial, of course. But many members of major tribunals, including the US Supreme Court,[5] express views that favour this approach as better able to carry out the goals of the treaty makers. We can see influence in this direction in the *Shrimp Turtle* case, especially in the discussion that mentions 'balancing goals'.

Concept 4: Precedent: Although some argue that precedent is not applied in international tribunals, it is abundantly clear that major tribunals do apply it. But they do not apply *stare decisis*. It is vitally important not to mix up the concepts of *stare decisis* and precedent. Precedent, in this author's approach, has a number of different levels. We know from members of the World Court that, despite the influence of Article 59 of the Statute of the ICJ (which states that a Court opinion is binding only on the parties to the case, and only in that case), nevertheless precedent is commonly utilized.[6] In addition the European Court of Justice clearly uses precedent, and members have written so. Finally, the WTO AB does in effect (without mentioning the word precedent) apply the concept of

---

[3] This is reflected in several parts of the AB report in DS8, Case on Japan-Taxes on Alcoholic Beverages, 1996. See especially text at footnote 20 and the detail in footnote 39 referring to GATT 1947 preparatory works in an EPCT document.

[4] United States – Import Prohibition of Certain Shrimp and Shrimp Products, DS 58, AB report 1998 at para. 30 (evolutionary) and paras. 157–9 (balancing).

[5] EU e.g. Justice Bryer's recent book *Making our democracy works: A Judge's view*, United States, Knopf, 2010.

[6] Judge Buergauthal's address in April 2009 to the annual meeting of the American Society of International Law.

precedent, noting the importance of predictability and security (WTO Dispute System Understanding, Article 3, para. 2).[7]

Indeed, the use of some level of precedent, whether soft or strong, is a very important characteristic of 'rule of law' concepts, and clearly should be central to the work of tribunals. The concept is notable also for its absence in the VCLT.

There are a number of other troublesome concepts relating to treaty interpretation, but I will not weigh this short chapter down with more than expressed above.

10.4 IMPORTANCE OF THE CONSTITUTIONAL TREATY CONCEPT

To reinforce the appropriateness of the concepts discussed in section 10.3 above, if any more support is needed, it is useful to explore their institutional context. In particular, it is useful to appreciate the importance of the treaty context of many interpretative problems that arise.

To many international law observers, scholars, and professionals, it is reasonable to recognize that not all treaties should be treated the same with regard to interpretation principles and guiding rules. For example, note the situation of a treaty that has a large number of members and that is designed to establish an international law institution (e.g. UN, or WTO, etc.) to which the treaty creators (draftsmen) have delegated certain powers that are designed to enable the institution to carry out the missions and goals that are assigned to it. Such a treaty, I have suggested, could be called a 'constitutional treaty'. I use the term 'constitution' in a very norm-neutral sense, as being an institutional framework for the ongoing activity of the institution. Some scholars and even important judges have said that the word 'constitution' can only be used for the structure of a nation state. I (and many others) disagree, since we see the word used in a wide variety of contexts, including many institutional structures both national and international, and even referring to relatively informal structures like a neighbourhood group, or an economic structure such as city ordinances. Here I use the word 'constitutional' to mean only a set of procedural-type rules that provide relatively permanent or long-term rules about how to conduct the activity of the institution.

---

7 See especially the AB report in DS344 United States – Final Antidumping Measures in Stainless Steel from Mexico, 20 May 2008 at paras. 160–2. The AB directly discusses these issues of precedent (while not using that word).

When an institutional framework created by international treaty has characteristics, such as large membership, and long-term goals and procedural rules, often certain characteristics will be part of the institutional structure. In many treaty cases, rules for changing the institutional structure require super-majority procedures, or otherwise make it difficult for the institution to create or amend rules. This can be termed 'treaty rigidity'. Such rigidity can be troublesome in a world of changing circumstances that require changing responses and therefore often call for rules that can cope with such circumstances.[8]

One way to address this rigidity problem, it would seem to this author, is to have a system for definitively interpreting treaty language that has enough flexibility to allow responses that can better carry out the mandate and mission of the institution. It can be argued that the creators of the institution have explicitly or implicitly agreed to that approach by agreeing to the dispute settlement system that embodies these characteristics.

Then the logic seems to lead to the ideas of treaty interpretative approaches that understand and accommodate these flexibility needs. Arguably the concepts elaborated in the text of section 10.3 above can contribute in that way to a more stable international institutional structure, as needed in the 'globalized' world of change, particularly with regard to economic activities and measures.

10.5 RISKS AND DANGERS OF THE ADDED FLEXIBILITY CONCEPTS FOR TREATY INTERPRETATION

Clearly the flexibility and extra-VCLT methods of treaty interpretation may not be appropriate in some circumstances, and inevitably there will be proponents of a strictly 'textual' interpretation. Some will turn to rules such as *in dubio mitius* to fend off any attempts to use flexibility constructively. The argument will be that the dispute resolution body or treaty-interpreting processes are 'exceeding' their mandate, or using judicial overreach. And to some extent this may be true. But too much rigidity has its defects. Also often there will be a balancing process in the minds of the decision-makers. There is no easy answer to how these balances should be undertaken, except to try to establish institutions that can ably follow general 'rule-oriented' approaches, free of bias, taint or corruption.

---

[8] See Jackson, *supra*, Chapter 2 at 2.3(c), pp. 42–5.

10.6 PERSPECTIVES

The chain of logic outlined in the paragraphs above has enormous importance in some contexts, as well as posing some risks. No significant human endeavour or institutions is likely to avoid these risks and, indeed, when the history of national institutions as well as international treaty structures is considered, it is clear that such human institutions will inevitably evolve and accommodate change in the circumstances that they face.

11. WTO dispute settlement: promise fulfilled?

William J. Davey

I have known Jacques for many years – initially on a personal level as a fellow alumni of the University of Michigan Law School and as a co-attendee of numerous conferences on international trade law topics – and later professionally at the WTO while I was Director of the Legal Affairs Division and Jacques served as a panel chair and legal advisor to disputing governments. Indeed, since so much of my professional contact with Jacques has concerned international trade law, and in particular the WTO dispute settlement system, I thought it appropriate to write a few words on that subject in this book honouring Jacques. This seems particularly appropriate given Jacques' active role in the operation of both the WTO system and its GATT predecessor.

The first five years of the dispute settlement under the WTO's Dispute Settlement Understanding (DSU) (1995–99) were noteworthy because of the high volume of cases, brought predominantly by the United States and the EU; the controversial nature of many of the cases, which ultimately, however, did not preclude their solution; and the development of the Appellate Body.[1] The second five years (2000–04) were noteworthy by the decline in the number of cases, although the system remained relatively active; by an increase in the time needed to process cases; and by the noticeable and significant increase in the use of the system by developing countries as complainants.[2] The third five years (2005–July 2010), which is the subject of this chapter, are noteworthy because of a continued decline in the number of new cases brought; the continued broad diversity of complainants and respondents, including the much more active involvement of China, mainly as a respondent; and by the system's continuing success in

[1] The first five years are discussed in more detail in Davey, W.J., 'The WTO Dispute Settlement System: The First Ten Years', *Journal of International Economic Law*, Vol. 8, No. 1, 2005, pp. 17–23.

[2] Davey, *supra*, pp. 24–5.

ultimately resolving cases. Delays remain a problem, however, which detracts from the system and may serve to undermine its effectiveness over time.

11.1 ACTIVITY LEVELS IN WTO DISPUTE SETTLEMENT: 2005–10

In terms of the number of cases brought, in the first few years' operation of the WTO dispute settlement system, the system was quite active in terms of consultation requests. In 1995, there were 25 consultation requests; in 1996, the number increased to 39; and in 1997, it peaked at 50 consultation requests.[3] This rate declined significantly in the second five years. For example, the number of new consultation requests was 26 in 2003 and only 19 in 2004. It has fallen further in recent years:

2005	12 requests
2006	20 requests
2007	13 requests
2008	19 requests
2009	14 requests
As of July 2010	9 requests

or an average of about 16 consultation requests a year.

Despite the decline in the number of consultation requests, the system has remained active, however, because of several complex cases that have taken a very long time to process (e.g. in particular the US/EU aircraft subsidy cases)[4] and because of disputes over compliance with past rulings.[5] In terms of the number of panel reports adopted, there was an average of

[3] This number of consultation requests per year is derived from the WTO website's chronological list of disputes, which can be found at: www.wto.org/english/tratop_e/dispu_e/dispu_status_e.htm. In this chapter, I have referred to individual WTO cases by DS numbers and short names. Detailed information about an individual dispute can be found by selecting that dispute in the chronological list of disputes referenced above.

[4] In the US complaint against the EU, the panel report was issued four years and 11 months after its establishment. As of this writing, the panel in the EU complaint against the United States has not issued its report.

[5] There were 15 compliance panel reports adopted in the 2005–09 period, compared to 11 in the preceding ten years. Appellate Body: Annual Report for 2009, WT/AB/13, p. 59 (17 February 2010).

13 a year in the 2000–04 period, but only nine a year in the 2006–09 period.[6] The level of activity at the Appellate Body remained largely constant over the two five-year periods; it averaged eight reports adopted in each period.[7]

This continued high level of activity may also reflect that the cases being brought in recent years are more carefully selected than perhaps were some of those brought in the first years of the system's operation. This can be seen in the US Trade Representative's snapshot of US WTO dispute settlement activity, where almost all of the pending cases that are listed as inactive or under monitoring were started in the first few years of the system. More recently, it would seem, at least from the perspective of the US administration, the cases that are brought are resolved – either through the panel process or settled.[8] They do not simply hang around in limbo.

There continues to be considerable diversity in complainants.[9] During the 2005–July 2010 period, the United States and the EU were the most frequent complainants, with 14 consultations requests each, but together they initiated less than a third of the cases. The consultation requests in this period were filed by:

EU	14
United States	14
Mexico	9
Canada	7
Argentina	6
China	4

Brazil, India, Norway and Panama each filed three cases, while Indonesia, Korea and Thailand each filed two cases. Chile, Chinese Taipei, Colombia, Costa Rica, Ecuador, Guatemala, Japan, New Zealand, Peru, Philippines, Ukraine and Vietnam each filed one consultation request.

---

6 Appellate Body: Annual Report 2009, *supra*, p. 59. There were 20 panel reports issued in 2005, which was an unusual number – roughly twice the number of the following years. If 2005 is included, the average number of panel reports adopted annually for the five-year period 2005–09 would increase to 11.

7 See Appellate Body: Annual Report for 2009, *supra*, p. 59.

8 The US snapshot as of 30 July 2010 can be found at: www.ustr.gov/webfm_send/2120. Most of the cases brought by the US that are listed as 'monitoring progress or otherwise inactive' are from the early years of WTO dispute settlement. Indeed, all but two of the 16 cases so listed, were commenced more than ten years ago; and the two more recent cases date from 2002. All other cases brought by the United States are listed as having been resolved, litigated or in litigation, save one pending consultation request that involved a partially litigated case (DS295 – Mexico Beef & Rice).

9 This data comes from the WTO website's chronological list of disputes, *supra*.

There is less diversity in respondents, as the United States (22), the EU (17) and China (17) are by far and away the main targets of consultation requests.[10] Indeed, they represent almost two-thirds of such requests. The next main targets were Chile and India, subject to three requests each, while Argentina, Brazil, Canada, Colombia, the Philippines and Thailand were each subject to two such requests. Armenia, Australia, Dominican Republic, Egypt, Guatemala, Korea, Mexico, Panama, Turkey and South Africa each received one consultation request.

The regional distribution of disputes has continued more or less as before.[11] Africa is almost uninvolved in disputes (Egypt and South Africa were each the subject of one consultation request during the period). While a wide range of Asian countries have appeared as complainants or respondents, they tend to make fairly restrained use of the system, with China accounting for half the cases involving Asian countries. India and Thailand account for half the remaining Asian cases. Latin American countries continue to make disproportionate use of the system, with 11 countries involved, often in cases against each other.

Thus, although overall use of the WTO dispute settlement system seems to have declined somewhat over time, the system remains active and is used by a broad range of countries. It remains the case, however, that poor developing countries and least developed countries have very little involvement in the system.

11.2 SUCCESSFUL RESOLUTION OF CASES IN THE WTO DISPUTE SETTLEMENT SYSTEM: 2005–10

The WTO dispute settlement system continued to be an effective resolver of inter-governmental disputes in its third five-year period. There were 38 cases initiated through consultation requests in the 2005–07 period.[12] The cases can be categorized as follows:

---

[10] This data comes from the WTO website's chronological list of disputes, *supra*.

[11] This data comes from the WTO website's chronological list of disputes, *supra*.

[12] I have grouped consultation requests involving the same measures and counted them as one case for this part of my analysis. I have looked at only the first three years of the period since many of the cases initiated in the 2008–09 period were still pending before panels or involved reasonable periods of time for implementation that had not expired.

Settled or challenged measure withdrawn[13]	14	
Panel established, but lapsed after suspension[14]	2	
Apparently abandoned[15]	2	
Total settled/abandoned	18	47.5%
Pending consultations[16]	1	2.5%
Panel proceedings	19	50%
Pending[17]	4	10%
Panel report implementation due	15	40%
Implemented[18]	12	80%
Not implemented[19]	3	20%

[13] DS326 (EC Salmon Safeguard Chile); DS327 (Egypt Matches); DS328 (EC Salmon Safeguard Norway); DS329 (Panama Milk); DS330 (Argentina Olive Oil CVD); DS333 (Dominican Republic Forex Fee); DS338 (Canada Corn CVD); DS346 (US OCTG AD Argentina); DS348 (Colombia Customs Measures); DS354 (Canada Wine & Beer); DS355 (Brazil Resins); DS358 & 359 (China Tax Refunds); DS361 & 364 (EC Bananas); DS368 (US Coated Paper AD China).

[14] DS351 & 356 (Chile Milk Safeguard); DS352 (India Wines & Spirits).

[15] In one case (DS349), consultations were held in 2006, but there has been no follow-up. That case involved Argentine objections to the administration of the EU's TRQ for garlic in connection with the EU's enlargement. In the other case – a Brazil/Canada challenge to US agriculture subsidies, a panel was established in 2007, but it has never been composed (DS357 & 365). Given that the facts underlying the complaint would have changed significantly since the panel was established, it seems that if the complainants were to decide to pursue this matter, they would have to start afresh to obtain any meaningful result.

[16] In this case (DS369), Canada had requested consultations on an EU measure prohibiting the import and marketing of seal products. The challenged measure was replaced by another measure and a new set of consultations was commenced in November 2009 (DS400).

[17] Three cases are still in the litigation process or related to a case still in that process – DS347 – EC Aircraft (panel authority lapsed, but related to DS316, which is on appeal); DS353 – US Aircraft (panel report expected in 2010); DS367 – Australia Apples (panel report issued, appeal possible at this writing). In one case – China – AV (DS363) – the reasonable period of time has not yet expired.

[18] DS331 (Mexico Steel Pipes AD); DS332 (Brazil Tyres); DS334 (Turkey Rice); DS335 (US Shrimp AD – Ecuador); DS336 (Japan DRAMS); DS337 (EC Salmon AD); DS339, 340 & 342 (China Automobiles); DS 341 (Mexico Olive Oil CVD); DS345 (US Customs Bond); DS360 (India Additional Duties); DS362 (China IP); DS366 (Colombia Ports of Entry). In the latter two cases, there may an implementation issue, but so far it does not seem to have been pursued.

[19] These three cases – DS343, 344 & 350 – involve US failure to change its zeroing practices in administrative reviews on a prospective basis. The measures actually challenged in the cases were revised or are no longer in effect.

These results are not that dissimilar to what I found in 2005, when I looked at the results of cases from the first seven and a half years of the system's operation.[20] There has been an increase in the number of consultation requests that result in panel reports. In my prior analysis of the system's operation through July 2002, I found that close to 60 per cent of the cases did not result in a panel report. In the three-year period being examined in this chapter, the comparable figure is 50 per cent. That is an increase, but not a huge increase. This may reflect, as noted above in the case of the United States,[21] that countries are taking more care in their selection of cases. That is to say, that they are more likely to start consultations only when they are sure that they have a case to go forward with, which would be expected to lead to a higher level of litigated cases. In any event, it remains the case that a significant percentage of consultation requests lead to settlement or withdrawal of the challenged measure.

As to implementation of the cases that proceed to panel, the recent experience is comparable to what I found earlier. In the prior period, I counted a successful implementation rate of 83 per cent; in the current period, the rate appears to be 80 per cent. The main implementation problem in the current period is that the United States has not changed its zeroing practices prospectively with respect to annual reviews in antidumping cases. The United States views this issue as one under negotiation in the Doha Round and may well not take any action until those negotiations are completed. The United States arguably does implement panel/Appellate Body reports where it has been found to have violated WTO rules in specific cases, but because of the annual review process, by the time such a review is successfully challenged, it is likely that it is no longer in effect.

Of the ten cases I considered to present implementation problems in my prior analysis,[22] it is noteworthy that almost all of those cases can now be viewed as resolved.[23] Thus, over time, implementation tends to occur in

---

[20] See generally Davey, *supra*, pp. 45–9.

[21] See *supra*.

[22] Davey, *supra*, p. 47, n. 115.

[23] Nine of the cases seem to have been resolved or effectively abandoned: EC Hormones (DS26 & 48); Brazil Aircraft (DS46), Canada Aircraft & Canada Aircraft Guarantees (DS71 & 222, also 71), US FSC (DS108); US 1916 Act (DS136 & 162); Chile Price Band (DS207); US Countervailing Measures (DS212); US Offset Act (Byrd Amendment) (DS217 & 234) (implementation has largely, but not completely, been phased in over time); Japan Apples (DS245). Thus, one case remains unresolved: US Copyright (Irish Music) (DS160), plus two other US cases from this period in which the US had obtained extensions of the reasonable periods of time at the time of the writing of the previous article. In those cases, implementation would have been due but for the extensions and the extensions are no longer

almost every case. But as discussed in the next section, the system often takes a long time to produce results. As of July 2010, the DSB was receiving status reports on non-implementation from the United States in respect of three long-standing cases plus three zeroing cases and from the EU in one case.[24]

11.3 THE TIMELINESS OF WTO DISPUTE SETTLEMENT PROCEEDINGS: 2005–10

While the activity level of the WTO dispute settlement system has moderated somewhat and the settlement/implementation record remains strong, the timeliness of the system has continued to decline. This decline is most noticeable in panel proceedings, as the Appellate Body in the vast majority of cases is able to meet its goal of getting its report circulated to WTO members 90 days after an appeal is filed. In the case of panels, the median elapsed time from panel establishment to circulation of the final report to WTO members was 12.5 months for reports circulated in the 1995–2006 period, but for those circulated at the end of that period (2003–06), the median time had grown to almost 15 months.[25] For the 19 panels that arose out of consultation requests filed in the 2005–07 period, the median time from panel establishment to circulation of the panel report to WTO

---

in effect for US Hot Rolled Steel (DS184) and US Section 211 (DS176). Three of the cases seems to have been abandoned as opposed to having been truly settled. The Canada–Brazil aircraft dispute seems to have been 'settled' with each side continuing not to implement. In the Chile Price Band case, Chile continues to apply that system, but it appears that high commodity prices in recent years have meant that the system has not led to particularly high tariffs. Secretariat Report on Chile, Trade Policy Review, WT/TPR/S/220/Rev.1, p. viii. In any event, Argentina has not pursued further dispute settlement procedures in the case.

[24] DSB Proposed Agenda for 20 July 2010, WT/DSB/W/430 (16 July 2010). The three long-standing US problem cases are listed in the prior footnote. They involve relatively minor matters, but implementation requires Congressional action that has not been forthcoming. The three 'zeroing' cases are DS 294, 322 & 350, but as noted in note 19 *supra*, there are other 'zeroing' cases where implementation is questioned. The EU case is EC Biotech – DS291. There are two cases in the 'retaliation' stage that have not been resolved – US Gambling (DS285) and US Cotton (DS267), although there is a temporary settlement of sorts in Cotton, where Brazil has delayed taking retaliatory action in return for certain US commitments. Antigua has not sought DSB authority to retaliate, although an arbitration on the permitted level of retaliation was completed in 2007.

[25] Davey, W.J., 'Expediting the Panel Process in WTO Dispute Settlement', in M. Janow, V. Donaldson and A. Yanovich (eds), *The WTO: Governance, Dispute Settlement and Developing Countries,* New York, Juris, 2008, p. 416.

members was 18 months.[26] This represents a considerable increase over the times achieved in the first years of the system's operation. I have discussed elsewhere how timeliness might be improved – both in terms of the panel process itself[27] and in terms of more prompt compliance.[28] Suffice it to say here, that this is a serious and growing problem that the system needs to address more forcefully than it has to date. To the extent that members believe that the system takes too long, they will make less use of it notwithstanding the existence of outstanding disputes that need resolution.

11.4 CONCLUSIONS

The Uruguay Round negotiators who agreed on the reforms to the GATT dispute settlement system that resulted in the WTO Dispute Settlement Understanding doubtless had various goals, depending on the particular concerns of their countries. Nonetheless, it seems clear that there were a number of goals that they broadly shared.

First, it is often said that the EU and Japan, both of whom had traditionally preferred a less judicial approach to dispute settlement in GATT, agreed on the more judicial approach largely in return for a commitment by the United States to bring its WTO-related disputes to the WTO multilateral dispute settlement system in lieu of pursuing them unilaterally under section 301 of the US Trade Act of 1974. It seems that this goal was achieved. There was one incident of US unilateralism shortly after the WTO came into being at the beginning of 1995 – involving US threats to impose severe trade restrictions on Japanese automobile imports – but the matter was resolved when the United States backed down. Indeed, it did so in part because Japan commenced a case in the WTO, which it undoubtedly would have won (DS6). A later instance of US unilateralism occurred in connection with the *Bananas* case (DS27), where the US took retaliatory action against EU non-implementation without DSB authorization. That authorization was received about two months later and the United States adjusted the level of its retaliatory measures in line with the DSB authorization. The EU brought a case against the United States for its premature action, which it won (DS165). But overall, US unilateralism has been tamed by the DSU.

---

26 Based on dates reported in Dispute Settlement Body – Annual Report (2009) – Overview of the State of Play of WTO Disputes – Addendum, WT/DSB/49/Add.1, Annex II (5 November 2009).

27 Davey, *supra*.

28 See, e.g. Davey, W.J., 'Comment: Compliance Problems in WTO Dispute Settlement', *Cornell International Law Journal*, Vol. 42, No. 1, 2009, p. 119.

Second, the negotiators wanted to eliminate the problems of delays caused by blockages of the process as a result of one or more parties refusing to join the consensus necessary to move a dispute forward procedurally. Under GATT practice, the establishment of a panel, the determination of its terms of reference, its composition, and the adoption of its report could be blocked in that way, as could a request for authorization to take retaliatory measures for non-compliance with a panel ruling. These problems were essentially eliminated with the advent of the DSU. Establishment of panels, adoption of their reports and authorization of retaliation all take place automatically – the DSB is required to act in these matters unless there is a consensus not to do so, which cannot happen if the party requesting the action persists in its request. In January 1999, during the week-long DSB meeting dealing with the US request for authority to retaliate in the *Bananas* case, one potential loophole in the DSU automaticity was firmly closed. That potential loophole arose from the fact that the practice of WTO bodies calls for them to adopt the proposed agenda for each meeting at the beginning of the meeting. An attempt to have the US request removed from the agenda was rejected. The objector tried to argue that the meeting could be blocked absent a consensus to adopt the agenda, which it would not join unless the US request was deleted from the agenda. If this argument had succeeded, any of the automatic actions required of the DSB could be blocked through invocation of this procedural device. Fortunately, the DSB chair ruled the attempt out of order.[29]

Third, there was a feeling that because the possibility of blockage existed and because it had been used in some cases, there was a hesitancy to bring important but controversial cases to GATT dispute settlement because of fear that there would be no result achieved. This problem was also one that negotiators wanted to solve. As I have detailed elsewhere,[30] the WTO system has not wanted for controversial cases. Particularly in the first five years of the system's operation, the issues that had led to blocked panel requests or reports in the GATT years were presented in WTO dispute settlement and were generally resolved, albeit in some cases after considerable delay. Thus, I have generally concluded here and elsewhere that the system has worked well, particularly given the difficulties inherent in trying to resolve disputes between sovereign states.

Two caveats should be expressed. First, as noted above, the system has not eliminated delays. While the process moves forward, it often does so at a

[29] See generally Minutes of DSB Meeting held on 25, 28 and 29 January and 1 February 1999, WT/DSB/M/54 (20 April 1999).

[30] Davey, *supra*, pp. 18–21.

rather slow pace – far slower than foreseen in the DSU. This can be explained by many reasons – the complexity of some cases and the related need to select and use outside experts to advise the panel; scheduling difficulties inherent in relying on ad hoc panellists; participants who like the idea of speedy proceedings in the abstract, but want the maximum amount of time they can negotiate when required to file written submissions; the need to translate voluminous reports; and so on. As noted above, these delays could undermine the system if they cause countries to make less than optimal use of the system. My impression is that delays have caused some concern in the business community, but there is no sign that countries are becoming profoundly dissatisfied with the system. In the end, delay is not necessarily a bad thing if the correct outcome – more or less faithful implementation of adopted reports – becomes viewed as inevitable. In the grander scheme of things, delays can simply be viewed as transition periods that will expire sooner rather than later. Nonetheless, in my view, the system could profitably make greater efforts to reduce delays.

The second caveat has to do with the overall success rate of the system. While the vast majority of disputes are resolved, it is the case that in some cases, the prevailing party either receives far less than it is entitled to receive or receives it only after a very long delay. The latter issue I have noted already, but the quality of implementation is also an important consideration. In another paper, I have examined that issue and found that in some areas, it is not clear that complainants ultimately receive what they merit.[31] This has been particularly true in safeguard cases, where implementation has been timely, but where WTO-illegal safeguards have nonetheless remained in place for two or three years. It is also a problem, I found, in trade remedy cases, where the challenged measure is only modified. One can imagine that Canada – despite having won numerous WTO and NAFTA dispute settlement cases against the United States in the *Softwood Lumber* matter – did not view its ultimate settlement with the United States as representing the vindication of its position that the case results suggested was appropriate.

Ultimately, however, I think that the WTO dispute settlement system has worked well – in no small part because of the important role that Jacques played as a participant in multiple roles over many years.

[31] Davey, W.J., 'Evaluating WTO Dispute Settlement: What Results Have Been Achieved Through Consultations and Implementation of Panel Reports?' in Y. Taniguchi et al. (eds), *The WTO in the Twenty-First Century: Dispute Settlement, Negotiations, and Regionalism in Asia,* Cambridge, Cambridge University Press, 2007, pp. 102–7.

12. Consolidation of WTO dispute settlement proceedings before panels and the Appellate Body

Raimund Raith*

12.1 INTRODUCTION

The issue of consolidation of WTO Dispute Settlement Proceedings rose to a certain degree of prominence when the Appellate Body launched the process for amendments of the Working Procedures for Appellate Review (AB Working Procedures) in December 2009.[1] The appellate procedure is laid out in Articles 17–18 of the Understanding on Rules and Procedures governing the Settlement of Disputes (DSU). Given the more general character of these provisions in the DSU, the Appellate Body has been obliged, pursuant to Article 17(9) of the DSU, to draw up working procedures. The process for drawing up its working procedures is a bit peculiar from a procedural point of view. While working procedures for panel procedures are set up on an ad hoc basis by each panel, AB Working Procedures apply to all appellate procedures in the same way. Therefore AB Working Procedures follow a more formal path. The Appellate Body consults the Dispute Settlement Body (DSB) chair on the intended modifications of the AB Working Procedures and the DSB chair in turn consults the membership in the DSB and conveys members' views and comments back to the Appellate Body chair.[2] The Appellate Body is not bound by members'

* The views expressed are those of the author and cannot be attributed to the European Commission.

[1] Letter from the Appellate Body chairman to the chairman of the Dispute Settlement Body of 16 December 2009, document WT/AB/WP/W/10.

[2] The DSB has adopted Additional Procedures for Consultations between the Chairperson of the DSB and the WTO Members in relation to amendments to the Working Procedures for Appellate Reviews on 19 December 2002, document WT/DSB/31.

views and may proceed with a modification even in the light of widespread opposition from members, but has in the past refrained from doing so.

12.2 MULTIPLE COMPLAINANTS AT THE PANEL STAGE

For the panel stage Article 9 DSU gives some guidance. This provision reads:

Article 9
Procedures for Multiple Complainants

1. Where more than one Member requests the establishment of a panel related to the same matter, a single panel may be established to examine these complaints taking into account the rights of all Members concerned: A single panel should be established to examine such complaints whenever feasible.
2. The single panel shall organize its examination and present its findings to the DSB in such a manner that the rights which parties to the dispute would have enjoyed had separate panels examined the complaints are in no way impaired. If one of the parties to the dispute so requests, the panel shall submit separate reports on the dispute concerned. The written submission by each of the complainants shall be made available to the other complainants, and each complainant shall have the right to be present when any one of the other complainants presents its views to the panel.
3. If more than one panel is established to examine the complaints related to the same matter, to the greatest extent possible the same persons shall serve as panellists on each of the separate panels and the timetable for the panel process in such disputes shall be harmonised.

Article 9 DSU does not create an obligation for complainants to follow the consolidation options set out in paragraphs 1, 2 and 3 respectively, but makes these options available on a voluntary basis. Indeed India tried to argue in *India – Patents (EC)* that the EC's case should be dismissed as inadmissible on the ground that since it was feasible for the EC to have brought its complaint simultaneously with that launched by the US, the EC's conduct did not conform to the requirements of Article 9(1) DSU. The panel turned India's contention flatly down.[3]

Article 9 DSU contemplates two different situations: paragraphs (1) and (2) contemplate the establishment of a single panel to deal with disputes brought by several complainants against the same respondent.

---

[3] Panel Report, *India – Patents (EC)*, paras. 7.9–17.

The possibility to extend one single panel in cases where one complainant brings a case against several respondents is not foreseen in the DSU.[4] In the *Canada/US – Continued Suspension (Hormones)* cases the EC went against the United States and Canada with identical claims and completely identical timing from the outset; however, separate panels were established. The separate panels were composed of the same panellists and they held joint hearings. Neither in the panel requests nor in the panel reports can any reference to Article 9 DSU (or by analogy) be found.

The other alternative, which is foreseen in Article 9(3), DSU contemplates a situation where several panels have already been established on the requests of several complainants against the same respondent. Here the provision recommends having the same panellists serve on each of the separate panels and to have the timetables of the several panels harmonized wherever possible.

12.2.1 The Single Panel Alternative

The requirement that the panel requests have to be related to the same matter has been interpreted by panels in a broad way. The claims and arguments do not have to be identical; neither do the targeted measures need to be identical. For example, in *EC – Approval and Marketing of Biotech Products* the three co-complainants complained about deficiencies in relation to different applications for marketing approval for their respective biotech products.[5] In other cases however, the subject matter was strictly identical.[6]

The key to having a single panel is timing, because the panels have to be established at the same meeting of the DSB[7]. This does not of course mean that consultations pursuant to Article 4 DSU also have to be carried out in tandem. In *EC – Trademarks/GIs* the US consultation request preceded the Australian request by almost four years.[8]

---

[4] In national laws on civil procedure such possibilities to join multiple defendant cases are common: see for example Rules 18 and 19 of the Federal Rules of Civil Procedures for the United States.

[5] US panel request, document WT/DS/291/23 of 8 August 2003, Argentina's panel request, document WT/DS/293/17 of 8 August 2003 and Canada's panel request, document WT/DS/292/17 of 8 August 2003.

[6] See e.g. *EC – Chicken Cuts*, *EC – Export Subsidies on Sugar*, *US – Steel Safeguards*.

[7] A recent example is the case *China – Raw Materials*.

[8] The US consultation request is dated 1 June 1999, while the Australian consultation request is dated 17 April 2003.

In any event, the co-complainants have to make sure that their respective panel requests are on the agenda[9] of the same DSB meeting, if they want to get a single panel. While panel composition is a joint exercise by all parties, each co-complainant has the right of objections under Article 8 DSU. In this context it has to be mentioned that each co-complainant (and of course the respondent) have the individual right to ask the Director General of the WTO to compose the panel pursuant to Article 8(7) DSU.

It is standing practice that each co-complainant seeks third party status in the case(s) of the other co-complainant(s).[10] Several cases that are before a single panel remain fundamentally separate cases, which may have different destinies. This means for example that one co-complainant may find a mutually satisfactory solution with the respondent pursuant to Article 12(7) DSU, thus ending the dispute, while the other co-complainants will continue the dispute. This also applies to the suspensions of the panel's work pursuant to Article 12(12) DSU, thus effectively leading to a split of the single panel process.

In terms of substance, the cases of the different complainants may fare differently. For example, one panel request may be found to be deficient under Article 6(2) DSU, while the other request(s) may be considered compliant. This applies equally to claims, arguments and facts presented by the individual co-complainants. This is linked to the fact that co-complainants regularly make their own individual submissions to the panel. While the individual submissions are normally – more or less – co-ordinated among the co-complainants, it is generally difficult to agree on single submissions, in particular when a large number of co-complainants exists.[11]

That said, in practice 'weaker' co-complainants tend to benefit from 'stronger' co-complainants, who have prepared and argued their cases more thoroughly. In any event the implementation of adverse findings by the respondent has to occur in full respect of the most-favoured-nation principle.

As to the presentation of the panel reports, the basic assumption appears to be that there shall, in the absence of requests to do otherwise from the parties, be only one single panel report. In practice issuing a single report is

---

9 In order to be certain that such a panel is established by the DSB, the requests have to be for the second time on the agenda (Article 6(1) DSU).

10 However they do not normally make third party submissions or statements at the first meeting with the panel.

11 In *US – Steel Safeguards* there were eight co-complainants and in *US – Offset Act (Byrd Amendment)* there were 11 co-complainants.

exceptional.[12] Regularly panels issue separate panel reports either within the same document[13] or in different documents.[14]

12.2.2 The Several Harmonized Panels Alternative

This alternative contained in Article 9(3) DSU essentially intends to catch cases where the strict parallelism of timing for the establishment of panels sought by different complainants has not been followed. This may be based on political considerations when one of the complainants considers that it still wants to wait a bit (e.g. because of an imminent state visit or summit) or because the minimum consultation deadlines contained in Article 4(7) DSU have not yet lapsed for one complainant.

The standard concerning 'the same matter' in Article 9(3) DSU is identical to the standard contained in Article 9(1) DSU.

The application of the procedure contained in Article 9(3) DSU is entirely in the hands of the parties and, if only one party opposes, Article 9(3) DSU cannot work.

The appointment of the same panellists to the subsequent panel is not, strictly speaking, time bound. Practical problems that might arise in this situation may concern the availability of panellists. But also the nationality of the panellists can create obstacles because Article 8(3) DSU forbids panellists holding the nationality of a party to serve on the panel. That way, a panellist from the earlier panel may be precluded from a subsequent panel.

While this alternative gives a certain degree of flexibility from a timing point of view, some inherent limits exist. The identity of the panellists can of course only be achieved if the subsequent panel has not yet been composed. In addition, the harmonization[15] of the panels' timetables depends on how far the first-in-time panel has advanced its work prior to the harmonization attempt. Indeed, at least one panel under Article 9(3)

---

[12] In *US – Offset Act (Byrd Amendment)*, the Appellate Body upheld the Panel's decision not to issue separate panel reports, see paras. 305–17 of the AB Report.

[13] See Panel Reports in *EC – Biotech Products*, *Canada – Wheat* and *US – Steel Safeguards*.

[14] See Panel Reports in *EC – Trademarks/GIs* and *US – Customs Bonds.*

[15] The Appellate Body noted that 'harmonised' rather than 'synchronised' gives the panels some degree of judgement and practicality. See Appellate Body Report, *EC – Bananas III (Article 21.5 – Ecuador II)* , paras. 187–98.

DSU has refused to harmonize timetables[16] and the Appellate Body confirmed that this panel had not infringed the EC's due process rights.[17] There have also been cases of a partial harmonization of the panels' timetables.[18]

It is obvious that in this scenario, divergences of the destinies of the several panel proceedings are more probable than under the single panel approach. For example, in *India – Additional Import Duties* the EC and US Panels did indeed harmonize the timetables, but on the EC's request, the EC Panel in this case suspended its work indefinitely pursuant to Article 12(12) DSU.[19] Under this option, panels issue separate panel reports in separate documents.

The issue of so-called enhanced third party rights of one complainant in the other complainant's case[20] has also arisen.

12.3 CONSOLIDATION OF PROCEEDINGS BEFORE THE APPELLATE BODY

12.3.1 Current Practice

Neither the DSU nor the AB Working Procedures contain provisions such as Article 9 DSU for appellate procedures. This said, the lack of guidance in the DSU and AB Working Procedures did not prevent the consolidation of appellate procedures in the past. There were indeed about 20 instances when multi-party appeals were in effect consolidated. Such consolidation occurred both in the situation of multiple appellants[21] or in a situation of multiple appellees.[22] It is particularly interesting to note that consolidated appeals did not only occur when there was a single panel pursuant to

---

16 Panel Report, *EC – Bananas III (Article 21.5 – US)* paras. 1.2, 1.8–1.16 and 7.1–7.11.

17 Appellate Body Report, *EC – Bananas III (Article 21.5 – Ecuador II)*, paras. 187–98.

18 Panel Report, *India – Additional Import Duties*, para. 1.9.

19 *Ibid.*

20 While Article 10 DSU gives third parties to a dispute only limited rights of participation (one submission and partial participation at first hearing), panels have repeatedly granted, upon duly motivated requests, so-called enhanced third party rights which give the third parties more participation possibilities than foreseen in Article 10 DSU. See for example *EC – Export Subsidies on Sugar* where all 27 third parties obtained enhanced third party rights.

21 E.g. *US – Steel Safeguards*, *EC – Export Subsidies on Sugar*, *EC – Chicken Cuts*.

22 E.g. *US – Offset Act (Byrd Amendment)* and *China – Auto Parts*.

Article 9(1), (2) DSU or previously harmonized panels pursuant to Article 9(3) DSU, but also in cases where the panels did not even share the same timetable.[23]

Even more so than for panel proceedings, the fundamental consideration for allowing or disallowing consolidation is timing, because of the extremely tight schedule for appellate proceedings.

Therefore in all consolidated appellate proceedings all appellants filed the notice of appeal on the same day, even in the case mentioned in footnote 24 where the panel reports were issued two months apart.

It is obvious therefrom that a consolidation of appellate proceedings will generally only be possible for consolidated panels pursuant to Article 9(1) or (3) DSU and will only in exceptional circumstances be possible in cases where panel reports are issued at different points in time. It is equally obvious that consolidation is only possible where the parties to the dispute so wish.

In all consolidated appellate proceedings the Appellate Body essentially followed the Article 9(1) DSU approach. The cases were dealt with by one division of the Appellate Body with an identical timetable. The Appellate Body has tried to ensure that the distinct aspects of the dispute were properly dealt with too. For example, third participants have been invited to limit their participation to issues raised in the specific dispute to which they were third party before the panel.

As to the presentation of the reports issued by the Appellate Body following a consolidated procedure, the Appellate Body has in some cases issued a single report setting out the specifications of each appeal; in other instances it has issued separate reports in one or in separate documents.

12.3.2 Proposed Changes to the AB Working Procedure

The Appellate Body complained that: 'To date, decisions to consolidate appellate proceedings have been made on an *ad hoc* basis in consultation with the parties.'[24] It went on to say that: 'We consider it appropriate to codify this practice by adding a rule on consolidation to the Working Procedures'[25] and proposed a new Rule 16(1) *bis* of the Working Procedures, as follows:

> When more than one panel report is circulated and/or appealed at or around the same time and there is substantial overlap in the content of those reports, the

---

23 E.g. *US – 1916 Act (Japan)*.

24 Document referred to *supra*.

25 *Ibid.*

> Appellate Body may, upon request by a party or on its own initiative, and after consultations with the parties, decide to consolidate the appellate proceedings before a single division. The Appellate Body may take such a decision if it considers that a substantial overlap in the content of the appeals is likely, and provided that consolidation of the appellate proceedings can be done consistently with due process and with the requirements of the DSU. Unless the participants agree otherwise, third participants will address only the issues arising in the dispute(s) to which they were third parties in the panel proceedings. The single division will organize its examination of the appeals in such a manner that the time-limit described in Article 17.5 of the DSU is respected for each dispute. Upon completion of the consolidated appellate proceedings, the Appellate Body will issue a single report, unless, following a request of a participant, it considers that there are good reasons to issue separate reports. Separate reports may be issued in a single document, or in multiple documents.

This proposal by the Appellate Body has received almost unanimous criticism from WTO members, and the Appellate Body has eventually abandoned its proposal by saying:[26]

> We have decided not to pursue our proposed amendment regarding consolidation of appellate proceedings, although we may revisit this issue at a later date … We will thus continue to take decisions on consolidation in appropriate cases on the basis of Rule 16(1), after consulting with the participants.

The single most contentious issue related to the new powers that the Appellate Body wanted to obtain. While consolidations have so far only occurred when all parties to the dispute were agreeable to such a course of action, the language in the proposed new Rule 16(1) *bis* would have allowed the Appellate Body to make such a decision, *in extremis* against the declared intention of all parties. In practice such a right would appear to be of little, if any, usefulness, because different appellants can undermine such a right by simply filing their appeals sufficiently staggered, thus not allowing the Appellate Body to meet the 90-day timeframe set out in Article 17(5) DSU for the appeal filed first in time.

There were other issues that WTO members considered as lacking exhaustive reflection by the Appellate Body.

- How can the Appellate Body get involved in appellate proceedings and take decisions before it has been seized through the notice of appeal by an appellant?

---

[26] Working Procedures for Appellate Review, document WT/AB/WP/W/11 of 27 July 2010 at p.7.

- How can the Appellate Body form a view on the existence of 'substantial' overlap in the content of the reports at a point in time when not all reports have been circulated?
- How can the Appellate Body reasonably form a view on whether 'substantial overlap in the content of the appeals is likely' when it does not have all concerned panel reports leave alone all relevant notices of appeal?

Many more open questions have been put forward by WTO members. While it has happened in the past that the Appellate Body has, in the light of WTO members' comments, refrained from pursuing its original proposal, it is somewhat unusual that it had to backtrack on a more substantive issue.[27] It is also interesting to note that the Appellate Body did not engage in a discussion of the concerns and objections raised by members during the consultation process when it issued the final version of the new Working Procedures.

The Appellate Body might have wished to sound out members' views informally beforehand and thus benefit at an earlier stage from the extensive doubts and concerns raised by members subsequently.

In any event, the old American saying: 'If it ain't broke, don't fix it' would seem to have maintained its relevance.

12.4 CONCLUSIONS

The consolidation of panel and appellate proceedings is a frequent event and it would appear to be generally appreciated by WTO members as a tool to guarantee consistency in the Dispute Settlement System and to use limited resources in the most efficient manner.

The consolidation of dispute settlement proceedings, however, entails additional challenges both for the parties and the adjudicators.

In order to be 'happy' co-complainants, they need to have a certain degree of commonality, be ready to consult with the other co-complainants and accept compromises for example as to timing, panel composition and

---

27 In 2004 the Appellate Body had also launched a consultation procedure in the context of intended modifications to the AB Working Procedures. As one of the planed modifications it was foreseen to introduce special timing arrangements for appeals, which may be affected by summer and end of year holiday periods (see document WT/AB/WP/W/8 of 8 April 2004, pp. 6–7. Following relatively mild criticism from only some members, the Appellate Body did not follow through on this intended modification.

panel working procedures. Also as to the substance of the case they need to have a common denominator, which does not mean that everything has to be fully co-ordinated, but outright contradictions should be avoided. The latter may particularly be a challenge when 'big players', who hold – diverging – convictions on particular issues of legal policy, are involved on the same side. Additional complexities might occur when co-complainants are represented by outside legal advisers, such as private law firms or the Advisory Centre on WTO Law.

While it is generally beneficial for the respondent to defend several complainants 'in one go', its defence may become more complicated when the several complainants pursue different chains of arguments. Also in cases where there are a particularly large number of complainants, such as in *US – Steel Safeguards* or in *US – Offset Act (Byrd Amendment)*, it appears that certain co-complainants would, in the absence of the numerous other complainants, not have brought a dispute by themselves.

Finally the consolidation of dispute settlement procedures also presents certain challenges for the adjudicators. While it appears reasonably simple in theory to distinguish the arguments made by the different complainants, particularly as far as their written submissions are concerned, such a distinction becomes much more difficult when it comes to discussions in the framework of oral hearings, which are of particular importance before the Appellate Body.

As pointed out above, the consolidation of WTO dispute settlement proceedings is a popular practice for WTO members and it would appear that the mentioned challenges are considered worthwhile in the light of the efficiency and consistency gains and there are indeed very few instances where a complainant could have been seen as sabotaging the consolidation because they only wished to avoid such consolidation.

13. Can the EU's disregard for 'strict observance of international law' (Article 3 TEU) be constitutionally justified?

Ernst-Ulrich Petersmann

During his many years as legal advisor in the EU Commission, Jacques Bourgeois contributed to the revolutionary transformation of EU law from an international treaty among states into 'a Community based on the rule of law, inasmuch as neither its member states nor its institutions can avoid a review of the question whether the measures adopted by them are in conformity with the basic constitutional charter, the Treaty'.[1] Yet, like other advocates of the EU and EU diplomats representing the EU in the GATT and World Trade Organization (WTO), Jacques welcomed the now established jurisprudence of the ECJ exempting the EU institutions from legal and judicial accountability *vis-à-vis* EU citizens for the frequent violations of the EU's GATT/WTO obligations, as formally established in more than 40 GATT and WTO dispute settlement rulings. From my perspective as a former legal advisor in GATT and the WTO and representative of Germany in European and international institutions, I have argued long since[2] that the unnecessary, frequent disregard in EU trade policy-making for the EU's constitutional obligation of 'strict observance of international law' (Article 3 TEU) lacks a constitutional justification

[1] ECJ, Case 294/83, *Les Verts* [1986] ECR 1339, para. 23.

[2] Cf. Petersmann, E.U., 'Application of GATT by the Court of Justice of the European Communities', in *Common Market Law Review*, Vol. 20, 1983, pp. 397–437. This article criticized the legally unconvincing 'GATT arguments' of the ECJ against 'direct applicability' of precise and unconditional GATT prohibitions of tariffs and of non-tariff barriers, without addressing the question under which conditions judicial self-restraint by the ECJ might be justifiable.

vis-à-vis EU citizens. Moreover, rather than relying on the misleading interpretations of GATT/WTO rules advanced by the EU advocates as justification of the EU's claim to 'freedom of manoeuvre'[3] in the sense of 'freedom to violate WTO law', the ECJ should recognize and protect the constitutional rights of EU citizens rather than 'Westphalian claims' to power politics that have no legitimate basis in EU and WTO law. This contribution in honour of Jacques explores whether the Lisbon Treaty has changed the legal conditions under which welfare-reducing violations of international law by EU institutions to the detriment of EU citizens, and the ECJ's denial of judicial remedies of both EU citizens and EU member states, are legally consistent with the EU's constitutional identity as a rule-of-law community with constitutionally limited powers. My conclusion remains that EU law requires not only legal and judicial protection of EU citizens' reasonable reliance on the EU's compliance with 'the rule of law' (Article 2 TEU), including 'strict observance of international law' (Article 3 TEU) and of 'the freedom to conduct a business in accordance with Union Law' (Article 16 EU Charter of Fundamental Rights). As stated in Article 21 TEU, the EU's respect for international law is also necessary to 'ensure consistency between the different areas of its external action and its other policies' (like respect for the customs union principle of GATT/WTO law, as incorporated into Articles 28–32, 206 TFEU) in order to protect interdependent public goods (PGs) for the benefit of EU citizens.

13.1 LACK OF JUDICIAL PROTECTION OF RULE OF LAW IN THE EU'S EXTERNAL TRADE RELATIONS UNDERMINES THE EU'S INTERNAL MARKET AND RULE OF LAW

The 'Union is founded on the values of respect for human dignity, freedom, democracy, equality, the rule of law and respect for human rights' (Article 2 TEU). It has nowhere been granted powers to violate its international legal obligations ratified by parliaments and thereby harm EU citizens and engage the international responsibility also of EU member states. The recent *FIAMM* and *Intertanko* judgments[4] of the ECJ suggest that –

[3] This term continues to be used by both the political EU institutions and the EU Court of Justice (e.g. in Joined cases C-120 and C-121/06 P, *FIAMM* [2008] ECR I-6513, para. 119) as the main justification for their disregard of legally binding WTO rules and WTO dispute settlement rulings.

[4] Joined cases C-120 and C-121/06 P (n. 3); C-308/06, *Intertanko,* [2008] ECR I-4057.

contrary to the constitutional mandate of Article 21 TEU that the 'Union's action on the international scene shall be guided by the principles that have inspired its own creation, development and enlargement, and that it seeks to advance in the wider world', as convincingly defended in the recent *Kadi*-judgments[5] – the ECJ has decided to grant legal and judicial immunity to violations by the EU of its obligations under WTO law and the UN Convention on the Law of the Sea, without offering adversely affected EU citizens and EU member states judicial remedies. As neither EU constitutional law nor WTO law provide for any freedom of EU institutions to violate its international legal obligations, the ECJ justifies its refusal to review the legality of alleged EU violations of GATT/WTO obligations as 'integral parts of the Community legal system'[6] by relying on claims by the political EU institutions that they need 'freedom of *manoeuvre*'. Yet, in contrast to the *Kadi*-judgment's defence of the 'autonomy of the EU legal order' in order to *enhance* legal protection for individuals and respect for human rights, the ECJ's refusal to cooperate with WTO and UNCLOS dispute settlement bodies in protecting 'strict observance of international law' *undermines* the EU's rule of law system even if there would be no adverse impact on the EU's participation in the WTO dispute settlement system.

The successful realization of the EU's internal market was to a large extent due to the legal and judicial protection of the EC Treaty's 'common market freedoms' as individual, enforceable rights by national and European courts. Arguably, the ECJ's interpretation and enforcement of the EU's customs union rules in conformity with the EU's obligations under GATT law could have protected EU citizens in their trade relations with third GATT contracting parties against many of the GATT/WTO dispute settlement findings of EU violations of international law. In case of pending GATT/WTO disputes (e.g. on EC restrictions on imports of bananas, hormone-fed beef and biotech products), the ECJ could have exercised judicial self-restraint on political grounds until the 'reasonable period' for implementing WTO dispute settlement rulings had expired. Yet, such a 'political question doctrine' could not have justified denying EU member states judicial remedies against EU majority decisions violating

---

5 Joined cases C-402/05 P and C-415/05 P, *Kadi* [2008] ECR I-6351.

6 According to the ECJ, international agreements concluded by the EC become an 'integral part of the Community legal system' (Case 181/73, *Haegeman* [1974] ECR 449). In *International Fruit Company* (Joined Cases 21–24/72, [1972] ECR 1219), the ECJ recognized that – due to the legal succession of the EC to the GATT rights and obligations of EC member states – also GATT law had become an integral part of the Community legal system.

WTO obligations.[7] Nor would the bureaucratic self-interests of EU institutions in avoiding legal and judicial accountability for their illegal redistribution of domestic income for the benefit of protectionist interest groups (like certain European banana trading companies), nor the EU's misleading claims regarding the alleged 'flexibility' of GATT/WTO rules, have offered convincing justifications of disregarding 'strict observance of international law' (Article 3 TEU) and domestic compliance with WTO obligations (as required by Article XVI:4 WTO Agreement).

In *International Fruit Company*, the ECJ accepted the claim by the EU Commission and EU Council that the flexibility of GATT provisions, GATT's safeguard clause, reciprocity principle and dispute settlement system excluded invocation and enforcement of GATT rules in European courts. This legal reasoning was widely criticized in view of the fact that most GATT prohibitions are drafted in more precise and unconditional terms than the often vague customs union rules of the EC Treaty and related exceptions. The more the ECJ recognized the 'direct applicability' of free trade provisions in reciprocal agreements with third countries and preferential trade agreements without effective dispute settlement and enforcement systems (e.g. in the Yaundé Convention), and admitted that 'the fact that the courts of one of the parties consider that certain of the stipulations in the agreement are of direct application whereas the courts of the other party do not recognize such direct application is not in itself such as to constitute a lack of reciprocity in the implementation of the agreement',[8] the more the ECJ's GATT/WTO jurisprudence revealed its true nature as a 'political question doctrine' lacking a convincing constitutional foundation. This became obvious when – in *Commission v Germany* – the Court had no hesitation to enforce GATT rules at the request of the EU Commission against an EC member state failing to implement its GATT obligations. In *Chiquita v Commission* and *Van Parys*, the ECJ once again relied on obvious misinterpretations of GATT/WTO rules as a justification of the EU's disregard for 'strict observance of international law'.[9] In

7 In Case C-280/93, *Germany v Commission* [1994] ECR I-3989, the outvoted EU member state was left without judicial remedies against the EC's violations of WTO law to the detriment of German importers and consumers and Germany's international legal responsibility in the WTO.

8 Case 104/81, *Kupferberg* [1982] ECR 3641, paras. 13–21 ('the mere fact that the Contracting Parties have established a special institutional framework for consultations and negotiations *inter se* in relation to the implementation of the agreement is not in itself sufficient to exclude all judicial application of that agreement').

9 In these judgments (Cases T-19/01,[2005] ECR II-315; C-377/02, [2005] ECR I-1465), the Court offered no convincing justification of why – after the end of the

FIAMM, the ECJ confirmed its jurisprudence rejecting private actions for damages caused by EU non-compliance with WTO obligations (e.g. the illegal restrictions on imports of bananas notwithstanding 15 GATT/WTO dispute settlement rulings between 1993 and 2009). Even though a few ECJ judgments interpret national and secondary EC rules in conformity with pertinent WTO obligations, the Court often disregards the 'consistent interpretation requirement' of EU and WTO law if complainants invoke WTO dispute settlement rulings against the EU or interpret general principles of EU primary law (like non-discrimination) in conformity with the pertinent WTO obligations of the EU. The ECJ never offered a convincing 'constitutional justification' of why the 'Community interest' could justify violating 'strict observance of international law' (Article 3 TEU) and denying judicial remedies to EU member states and EU citizens contrary to the EU principles of rule of law, access to justice and 'freedom to conduct a business in accordance with Union law' (cf. Articles 19 TEU, 6 and 13 ECHR, 16 and 47 EU Charter of Fundamental Rights).

In *Intertanko*, the ECJ extended its judicial refusal to review the legality of EC acts in the light of WTO law to the EC's obligations under the UN Convention on the Law of the Sea: 'UNCLOS does not establish rules intended to apply directly and immediately to individuals and to confer upon them rights or freedoms capable of being relied upon against States, irrespective of the attitude of the ship's flag State'.[10] As in its WTO jurisprudence, the ECJ's acceptance of the EU Commission's claims to 'judicial immunity' inside the EU is unconvincing in terms of EU constitutional law. The ECJ's refusal to cooperate with worldwide economic courts might be justifiable in individual cases if EU institutions can demonstrate that EU compliance with rule of law, and its judicial protection for the benefit of EU citizens, could undermine legitimate 'Community interests' in WTO and UNCLOS dispute settlement proceedings (e.g. if individual complaints could prejudge intergovernmental dispute settlement proceedings). Yet, as EU law prevents EU member states from invoking the WTO judicial remedies against EU majority decisions violating WTO obligations to the detriment of legal and trading interests of outvoted EU member

---

'reasonable period' granted for complying with WTO dispute settlement rulings – European courts should not construe EU law in conformity with the EU's commitments under the WTO legal and dispute settlement system. The judicial reference to Article 21.6 DSU (concerning the possibility of preventing lawful sanctions by third countries by additional trade concessions of the EU) cannot justify EU violations of precise and unconditional WTO and EU legal obligations to terminate illegal trade restrictions.

[10] Case C-308/06, [2008] ECR I-4057, para. 64.

states, the ECJ's refusal to review complaints by EU member states challenging EU violations of international law denies 'access to justice' and 'rule of law'; as the legitimacy of EU law derives from respect for constitutional rights of EU citizens, manifestly illegal trade protectionism by the EU at the expense of EU citizens undermines also the constitutional legitimacy of the EU.[11] From a citizen perspective, the self-interests of the EU's political institutions (e.g. in avoiding legal, judicial and financial liability *vis-à-vis* EU citizens) and of EU courts (e.g. in limiting the influence of WTO and ITLOS jurisprudence on the ECJ's jurisdiction) should not prevail over the constitutional rights of EU citizens to transnational rule of law and judicial remedies against arbitrary EU violations of international law to the detriment of EU citizens. Protection of the rule of law in conformity with international treaty obligations ratified by all parliaments inside the EU for the benefit of their citizens would not only better respond to the explicit rule-of-law requirements in EU and WTO law (e.g. in Article XVI:4 WTO Agreement and the WTO guarantees of individual access to domestic legal and judicial remedies). As discussed in the next section, it would also enhance the legitimate 'soft power' and leadership role of the EU for protecting international PGs.

13.2 WHY EU LEADERSHIP FOR PROTECTING 'INTERDEPENDENT PGS' REQUIRES RULE OF LAW FOR THE BENEFIT OF CITIZENS

During the first year after the entry into force of the Lisbon Treaty in December 2009, the 27 EU member states agreed on a vast range of additional fiscal, monetary and financial disciplines, procedural safeguards (e.g. for supervision of national budgets) and new institutions (like the Financial Stability Facility, the European Systemic Risk Board and three separate EU agencies to monitor securities, banks and insurance companies) aimed at strengthening 'rule of law' in the EU's 'management' of international financial crises. The fact that the EU succeeds more quickly

---

[11] Cf. Dani, M., 'Remedying European Legal Pluralism: The *FIAMM* and *Fedon* Litigation and the Judicial Protection of International Trade Bystanders', in *European Journal of International Law*, Vol. 21, 2010, pp. 303–40 (discussing various ways of promoting 'indirect effect of WTO rules' based on consistent treaty interpretation of EU law in conformity with the corresponding WTO rules and principles, 'judicial comity' between the ECJ and other international courts, a new EU liability regime for lawful conduct, or by enabling EU member states to challenge EU breaches of WTO rules in the ECJ).

and more comprehensively than other regional or worldwide organizations in using crises as opportunities for improving multilevel governance raises the broader question: Does the *European laboratory* for multilevel governance offer more general policy lessons for the biggest policy challenge of the twenty-first century, i.e. to protect international PGs more effectively?

The increasing participation of EU citizens in the worldwide division of labour illustrates that national, regional and worldwide markets enabling and protecting mutually beneficial trade are 'interdependent PGs' beneficial for all consumers. Like the collective protection and distribution of common natural resources (like clean air, bio-diversity, climate, the ozone layer), man-made 'collective goods' – like rule of law, an efficient financial and world trading system – raise 'collective action problems' and multilevel governance problems affecting billions of people. By granting and protecting equal rights of citizens, multilevel regulatory approaches can set incentives for stakeholder participation, decentralized surveillance and enforcement of rule of law and other 'checks and balances'. 'Governance failures' in the collective supply of *international* PGs, and their harmful 'externalities', can often be 'internalized' most effectively by providing adversely affected citizens and states with 'countervailing rights' and institutional and judicial remedies, thereby promoting synergies between individual pursuit of self-interests and public interests (e.g. in rule of law). 'Westphalian conceptions' treating citizens as mere objects rather than subjects of international economic law (IEL), including also international 'market freedoms' and non-discrimination requirements, run counter to the ever more comprehensive constitutional guarantees in European law of equal individual freedoms as 'first principle of justice' (e.g. in terms of Kantian and Rawlsian legal theories) and of non-discriminatory access to transnational PGs. The ever more comprehensive legal obligations of all governments to respect, protect and promote inalienable human rights entail that 'community interests' – e.g. in preventing the 'tragedy of unregulated commons' by regulating the underlying 'market failures', 'governance failures' and 'discourse failures' caused by information asymmetries and 'rational ignorance' of individuals *vis-à-vis* systemic risks (e.g. of climate change, complex financial instruments or tobacco consumption) – must be defined in terms of equal constitutional rights of citizens and other 'principles of justice'. Hence, Article 205 TFEU rightly prescribes that the EU's action on the international scene, including its common commercial policy, shall be guided by the EU's constitutional principles and objectives as defined in Article 21 TEU, such as 'democracy, the rule of law, human rights and the principles of international law'. Article 206 TFEU likewise emphasizes the close legal and economic interrelationships between the citizen-oriented, rights-based regulation of the EU's internal customs union (pursuant to GATT Article XXIV and GATS Article V) and the EU's common commercial policy based on respect for GATT/WTO law. The more EU citizens participate in the global division of labor, the stronger becomes their reasonable self-interest in transnational rule of law and judicial remedies against arbitrary violations of WTO guarantees of freedom, non-discrimination and rule of law in international trade among citizens.

International PGs are often composed of corresponding *national* PGs and overlap among each other. For instance, the PG of an efficient international trading system overlaps with regulation of other PGs like international food security, energy security, protection of the environment and transnational rule of law. The more EU violations of WTO obligations are decided by majority voting (cf. Article 207 TFEU), the stronger is the need for legal and judicial remedies against such decisions whose harmful effects may go far beyond trade. As EU law nowhere transfers powers to the EU institutions to violate international law, claims of EU institutions to 'freedom of *manoeuvre*' for violating GATT/WTO obligations – without legal and judicial accountability *vis-à-vis* EU citizens and individual EU member states that are internationally responsible for such violations of WTO law – require constitutional justification. Judicial self-restraint by the ECJ on political grounds (like the 'institutional balance' *vis-à-vis* the political EU institutions) offers no constitutionally convincing justification of manifest violations by EU institutions of the rule of law.

13.3 LESSONS FROM THE EU'S 'RULE OF LAW COMMUNITY' FOR REGULATING GLOBAL PGS?

The multilevel regulation and judicial protection of PGs inside the EU, the European Economic Area (EEA) and the European Convention on Human Rights (ECHR) confirms the experience of constitutional democracies that 'collective action problems' in protecting PGs require constitutional and judicial protection of rights and responsibilities not only of governments, but also of citizens. Hence, the prevailing conceptions of 'international law among sovereign states', 'global administrative law' and multilevel economic regulation must be 'embedded' – as in European integration law – by multilevel constitutional restraints consistent with the human rights obligations and constitutional restraints of UN and EU member states.[12] Even if the 'internal constitutional pluralism' inside the diverse European legal regimes (e.g. EU law) may legitimately differ from the 'external constitutional pluralism' (e.g. in EEA and WTO law), the EU's multilevel governance of interdependent markets derives its legitimacy from multilevel protection of transnational rule of law protecting constitutional rights of EU citizens.

The financial crises since 2008 and climate change illustrate increasing governance failures to protect international PGs. These failures are closely linked to the systemic failures of the 'Westphalian international law among states' adequately to regulate the 'collective action problems' impeding supply of PGs. Examples include the lack of US trade legislation enabling conclusion of the WTO Doha Round negotiations, the lack of US environmental legislation enabling US leadership for preventing climate change, and the inadequate cooperation among international and domestic courts in protecting transnational rule of law for the benefit of citizens. The effective supply of international PGs in the framework of the diverse forms of European integration law empirically refutes 'realist' claims that the anarchical structures of international relations make collective supply of international PGs legally and politically impossible. European integration confirms that collective supply of international PGs depends on multilevel rules, institutions and governance mechanisms limiting the five main 'collective action problems'[13] impeding multilevel governance of interdependent PGs:

The *jurisdictional gap*, i.e. the incapacity of every state to provide global public goods without international cooperation, requires delegation of additional governance powers to international organizations as international 'guardians of PGs' so as to limit 'prisoner dilemmas' in international cooperation among states and citizens.

The *governance gap*, i.e. the inability of most intergovernmental organizations to protect, regulate and govern collective supply of international PGs effectively, requires new forms of multilevel rule-making, administration and judicial protection of rule of law and constitutional rights. Democratic governance requires that rules must be justifiable – at all levels of multilevel governance – in terms of satisfying the reasonable interests of all affected citizens.

---

[12] Cf. Petersmann, E.U., 'The Future of International Economic Law: A Research Agenda', in C. Joerges and E.U. Petersmann (eds), *Constitutionalism, Multilevel Trade Regulation and International Economic Law*, Oxford, Hart Publishing, 2011, ch. 15.

[13] For detailed analysis see: Petersmann, E.U., *International Economic Law in the 21st Century. Constitutional Pluralism and Multilevel Governance of Interdependent Public Goods*, Oxford, Hart Publishing, 2011.

The *incentive gap*, i.e. the inherent temptation of free-riding in collective supply of international PGs, requires common, but differentiated responsibilities not only among states but also for civil society and business. Multilevel regulation of citizen-driven market competition should provide for stronger participation rights and legal remedies of private actors, for instance by empowering citizens to enforce international trade, competition and investment rules in domestic courts as decentralized incentives for 'internalizing harmful externalities'.

The *participation gap*, i.e. the need for inclusive consensus-building and worldwide participation, requires leadership, incentives and financial assistance for 'capacity building' by 'coalitions of the willing' so that all relevant public and private actors cooperate in the collective supply of global public goods. Citizen-driven economic and environmental systems cannot function legitimately and effectively without rights of all affected citizens to participate in multilevel decision-making and have recourse to legal and judicial remedies against unjustified restrictions of individual rights and market distortions.

The *rule-of-law-gap* results from the inevitable *legal fragmentation* among hundreds of national, international and transnational legal regimes interacting in the supply of global public goods. Legal predictability, transnational rule of law and legal protection of legitimately diverse conceptions of justice, human rights and 'constitutional pluralism' are essential for the collective supply of global public goods. Transnational rule of law must be promoted by 'balancing' and reconciling competing rights and constitutional principles. 'Freedom to violate international law' may lack democratic legitimacy and undermine individual rights. As illustrated by the ECJ's *Kadi* judgment as well as by the *'solange'* jurisprudence of the German Constitutional Court, domestic courts should act as 'guardians of the rule of law' and protect constitutional rights of EU citizens against intergovernmental power politics.

13.4 EU LEADERSHIP FOR A 'PARADIGM CHANGE' IN MULTILEVEL GOVERNANCE OF INTERDEPENDENT PGS?

Globalization promotes increasing shifts of regulatory power to diplomats and 'member-driven governance' in worldwide organizations operating on the basis of the 'Westphalian international law among sovereign states' without effective parliamentary and judicial constraints. Also IEL continues to be analyzed in most textbooks and in the jurisprudence of WTO dispute settlement bodies as a part of public international law regulating the international economy. Such 'Westphalian paradigms' risk undermining transnational rule of law for the benefit of citizens and other interrelated PGs, especially if newly emerging powers (like China) continue emulating 'US exceptionalism' and power politics.

Most governments outside Europe remain unwilling to follow the diverse 'multilevel constitutional conceptions' of IEL applied in the EU, the EEA as well as in the ECHR based on the constitutional insight that the legitimacy and effectiveness of multilevel economic regulation need to be enhanced by multilevel judicial protection of constitutional rights of citizens and transnational rule of law. Yet, the increasing cooperation among international, regional and domestic courts and investor-state arbitral tribunals – notably in human rights, trade, investment, economic integration and labour law – increasingly requires courts to clarify the common 'constitutional principles' underlying human rights, constitutional law and the law of international organizations, like limited delegation of powers, due process of law, access to justice, and rule of law. For instance, the more courts acknowledge the customary law requirement (as codified in the Preamble and Article 31 of the 1969 Convention on the Law of Treaties) of interpreting international treaties, and settling international disputes, 'in conformity with principles of justice' and the human rights obligations of governments, the more national and international courts engage in 'balancing' of competing rights and legal values in interpreting IEL. WTO jurisprudence confirms that the customary rules of treaty interpretation offer sufficient flexibility for interpreting IEL in conformity with legitimately diverse conceptions of human rights, 'principles of justice' and 'constitutional pluralism'.

European integration law has offered a uniquely successful framework for multilevel governance of interrelated PGs by integrating the diverse international, transnational, constitutional, administrative and private law conceptions of IEL so as to better secure overall coherence of multilevel rule-making, administration and adjudication. In their review of intergovernmental regulation and judicial protection of the constitutional rights of citizens, both national and international courts should cooperate by insisting on common constitutional principles, like respect for human rights and transnational rule of law for the benefit of citizens in areas that – as international trade – are driven by autonomous decisions of billions of citizens. The EU should lead by example – as mandated by the Lisbon Treaty's commitment to 'strict observance of international law' and human rights also in the EU's external relations – in promoting the European policy experience that the democratic legitimacy of IEL and effective protection of international PGs depend on transnational rule of law for the benefit of citizens as 'democratic owners' of multilevel governance institutions. Respect for human rights requires empowering citizens by multilevel legal and judicial protection of their constitutional rights and of their mutually beneficial economic cooperation across state borders based on reasonable expectations of transnational rule of law, as mandated by the Lisbon Treaty. Rather than shielding bureaucratic self-interest in avoiding legal and judicial accountability for illegal trade protectionism at the expense of EU citizens (as in the *FIAMM* and *Fedon* cases), European courts and EU lawyers should demonstrate more courage in defending 'strict observance of international law' (Article 3 TEU) in conformity with international treaty obligations ratified by all parliaments in the EU for the benefit of EU citizens. The ECJ's denial of remedies of adversely affected 'innocent bystanders' against EU non-compliance with legally binding WTO dispute settlement rulings should be limited to the very rare situations where 'Community interests' can be shown to prevail over legitimate EU citizen interests in transnational rule of law.

14. The effect of WTO dispute decisions in EU law – autonomy or autarky?

Piet Eeckhout*

14.1 INTRODUCTION

Article 38 of the ICJ's Statute refers to judicial decisions as a source of international law. It is clear of course that such decisions are of a different nature than the other sources: conventions, customs, and general principles of law. International courts and tribunals interpret and apply the norms of international law produced by those other sources. Moreover, they do not have inherent jurisdiction. Their authority to hear and decide cases is usually conferred by an international agreement, and requires the consent of states. As international law is fragmented, there is no complete and coherent system of jurisdiction and remedies. In some areas of international law litigation is rare. In others it is highly developed. Moreover, there is great diversity in the systems of dispute settlement, and the extent to which those systems are judicial in character.

Although Article 38 ICJ Statute mentions judicial decisions as a separate source of law, it makes more sense to discuss the legal effect of such decisions in EU law under the broader heading of agreements concluded by the EU. It is within the setting of such agreements that dispute settlement systems have been created, which may lead to judicial – or quasi-judicial – decisions, involving the EU. The question of the effects, in EU law, of international litigation has so far mainly arisen in the context of the EU's WTO membership. Jacques Bourgeois has always been a lawyer of many trades. An excellent practitioner, he is in equal measure a leading academic voice in a range of areas of EU law, and indeed also in matters of GATT

* This contribution is based on material developed for P. Eeckhout, *EU External Relations Law*, Oxford, Oxford University Press, 2nd edn, 2011.

and WTO law. His analysis of the Court of Justice's approach towards the WTO, even if written at an early stage, continues to stand out as one of the most refined and knowledgeable contributions to the debate.[1] It is therefore with great intellectual debt, and with enormous admiration, that the following analysis of the legal effect of WTO dispute decisions is dedicated to this most distinguished jurist and scholar.[2]

The Court of Justice already considered the question of the legal effect of international judicial decisions, in outline, in its first Opinion on the EEA Agreement.[3] In that Opinion the Court intensely scrutinized, and rejected, the judicial system that had been set up to interpret and apply the agreement. The envisaged EEA Court was considered a threat to the autonomy of Community law, because notwithstanding the parallelism between the EEA Agreement and Community internal market law, the objectives of the agreement and of the Treaty were different. One of the Court's objections concerned the effect that the decisions of the envisaged EEA Court could have on the interpretation of Community law. The Court referred to the binding effect of agreements, which became an integral part of the Community legal order when they entered into force. Where an international agreement provided for its own system of courts, including a court with jurisdiction to settle disputes between the contracting parties to the agreement, and, as a result, to interpret its provisions, the decisions of that court would be binding on the Community institutions, including the Court of Justice. Those decisions would also be binding in the event that the Court was called upon to rule, by way of preliminary ruling or in a direct action, on the interpretation of the international agreement, in so far as that agreement was an integral part of the Community legal order. An international agreement providing for such a system of courts was in principle

---

[1] Bourgeois, J., 'The European Court of Justice and the WTO: Problems and Challenges', in J.H.H. Weiler, *The EU, the WTO and the NAFTA*, Oxford, Oxford University Press, 2000, pp. 71–121.

[2] See also Mendez, M., 'The impact of WTO rulings in the Community legal order', *European Law Review*, Vol. 29, 2004, p. 517; von Bogdandy, A., 'Legal Effects of World Trade Organization Decisions Within European Union Law: A Contribution to the Theory of the Legal Acts of International Organizations and the Action for Damages Under Article 288(2) EC', *Journal of World Trade*, Vol, 39, 2005, p. 45; Bronckers, M., 'The Relationship of the EC Courts with Other International Tribunals: Non-Committal, Respectful or Submissive?', *Common Market Law Review*, Vol. 44, 2007, p. 601 and 'From 'Direct Effect' to 'Muted Dialogue' – Recent Developments in the European Courts' Case Law on the WTO and Beyond', *Journal of International Economic Law*, Vol. 11, 2008, p. 885.

[3] Opinion 1/91 re Agreement on the European Economic Area [1991] ECR I-6079.

compatible with Community law. The Community's competence in the field of international relations and its capacity to conclude international agreements necessarily entailed the power to submit to the decisions of a court that was created or designated by such an agreement as regards the interpretation and application of its provisions.[4]

These statements show that the Court is in principle receptive towards international judicial decisions. However, what the Court did not discuss in Opinion 1/91 was whether the binding nature of an international judicial decision is dependent upon the direct effect of the international agreement within the setting of which the decision is made. If an agreement lacks direct effect, does that mean that also judicial decisions reached under the agreement are not binding? Neither did the Court analyse the requirements for a system of dispute settlement to be considered to be of a judicial character, or the extent to which a fully judicial system is required for the relevant decisions to be binding.

Both those issues came up in case law on the WTO agreements. This author was one of the first to suggest a distinction between the lack of direct effect of WTO law, in general, and the binding effect of WTO dispute decisions. The argument was that the Court's reasons for the lack of direct effect of WTO law, such as the agreement's flexibility or the scope for negotiations, could not justify not giving effect to a final, binding dispute decision, which established that the Community (now EU) had violated WTO law. In cases where there was such a decision, the principle of *pacta sunt servanda* should trump the lack of direct effect.[5]

To cut a long story short, the EU courts have not accepted this distinction. Their rejection of any self-standing effect of WTO dispute decisions is partly based on doubts about the judicial character of those decisions: the courts emphasize the never-ending scope for negotiations in the WTO. What follows is a survey of the courts' reasoning in the relevant case law, followed by some dissenting statements by Advocates General. The next section will offer a critique of the rulings on the effect of WTO dispute decisions.

14.2 THE CASE LAW

Judicial developments took off with the *Biret* case, on non-contractual liability for failing to comply with WTO law and dispute rulings as regards

---

[4] *Idem,* paras. 37–40.

[5] Eeckhout, P., 'The Domestic Legal Status of the WTO Agreement: Interconnecting Legal Systems', *Common Market Law Review*, Vol. 34, 1997, pp. 51–5.

legislation on beef treated with hormones. On appeal, the Court established that the CFI (now the General Court) had made an error of law by not addressing the argument of the applicants that the legal effects of the Dispute Settlement Body (DSB) decision in the hormones case called into question the lack of direct effect of WTO law and provided grounds for a review by the Community courts of the legality of the relevant EC legislation.[6] The Court thus suggested that there was at least reason for a separate examination of the legal effects of WTO dispute decisions. Its statements were in the nature of *obiter dicta*, however, because on the facts the CFI's error turned out to be irrelevant.

Where the Court appeared to leave the door open in *Biret*, it firmly closed it later on. In *Chiquita* the CFI made some statements on the nature of WTO dispute settlement. It considered that the Dispute Settlement Understanding (DSU) did not establish a mechanism for the judicial resolution of international disputes by means of decisions with binding effects comparable with those of a court decision in the internal legal systems of the member states. To support this, it referred to the Court of Justice's analysis of the WTO dispute settlement system in *Portugal v Council*, in particular the scope that that system offers for negotiated arrangements.[7] The Court of First Instance added that that analysis was not confined to cases where the reasonable period laid down by Article 21(3) DSU for implementing DSB recommendations or rulings had not yet expired. Even at the expiry of that period and after the introduction of measures under Article 22 DSU to offer compensation or suspend concessions, the DSU continued to reserve an important place for negotiation between the parties. In this respect, the Court referred to Articles 21(6) and 22(8) DSU, which in essence instruct the DSB to keep the implementation of its rulings under surveillance. It then established that, at the time, the WTO dispute was still pending and on the agenda of the DSB. The Community judicature could not therefore review the legality of the Community measures in question without depriving Article 21(6) DSU of its effectiveness, for as long as the question of implementing the recommendations or rulings of the DSB was not resolved.[8]

In *Van Parys* the Court of Justice confirmed this type of analysis of WTO dispute settlement. It had to be noted that even where there was a decision of the DSB holding that the measures adopted by a member were incompatible with the WTO rules, the WTO dispute settlement system

---

6 Case C-93/02 P, *Biret International v Council* [2003] ECR I-10497, para. 57; see also Case C-94/02, *Etablissements Biret v Council* [2003] ECR I-10565, para. 60.

7 Case C-149/96, *Portugal v Council* [1999] ECR I-8395.

8 Case T-19/01, *Chiquita v Commission* [2005] ECR II-315, paras. 162–6.

nevertheless accorded considerable importance to negotiation between the parties. It was true that, according to Articles 3(7) and 22(1) DSU, compensation and suspension of concessions were temporary measures available in the event that the recommendations and rulings of the DSB were not implemented within a reasonable period of time, the latter of those provisions showing a preference for full implementation of a recommendation to bring a measure into conformity with the WTO agreements in question. However, Article 22(8) provided that, if the member concerned failed to enforce those recommendations and decisions within a reasonable period, it was to enter into any negotiations with any party having invoked the dispute settlement procedures with a view to agreeing compensation. If no satisfactory compensation was agreed, the complainant could request authorization from the DSB to suspend the application of concessions. Furthermore, Article 22(8) provided that the dispute remained on the agenda of the DSB, until it was resolved. Where there was no agreement as to the compatibility of the measures taken to comply with the DSB's recommendations and decisions, Article 21(5) of the understanding provided that the dispute had to be decided 'through recourse to these dispute settlement procedures', including an attempt by the parties to reach a negotiated solution. In those circumstances, the Court concluded, to require courts to refrain from applying rules of domestic law that were inconsistent with the WTO agreements would have the consequence of depriving the legislative or executive organs of the contracting parties of the possibility, afforded by Article 22 DSU, of reaching a negotiated settlement, even on a temporary basis. The Court then described the negotiations, at WTO level, that had taken place between 1997 and 2001, leading to agreements with the United States and Ecuador. Such an outcome could be compromised if the Community courts were entitled judicially to review the lawfulness of the Community measures in question upon the expiry of the time-limit granted by the DSB. The expiry of that limit did not imply that the Community had exhausted the possibilities under the DSU of finding a solution; judicial review could have the effect of undermining the Community's position in its attempt to reach a mutually acceptable solution to the dispute.[9]

In *Ikea Wholesale* the company, which had instituted proceedings for the recovery of anti-dumping duties, relied mainly on the WTO bed linen ruling,[10] but the Court chose to ignore that ruling on the ground that the

---

[9] Case C-377/02, *Van Parys v Belgisch Interventie- en Restitutiebureau* [2005] ECR I-1465, paras. 42–51.

[10] WTO Appellate Body, *EC – Bed Linen*, WT/DS141/AB/R, adopted on 12 March 2001.

so-called *Nakajima* principle did not apply.[11] Paradoxically, that worked to the advantage of Ikea Wholesale. The Court decided that the EU's basic antidumping regulation had been violated through the use of the so-called zeroing technique. In substance, therefore, it arrived at the same conclusion as the WTO Panel and Appellate Body, without however basing its finding on their reports. The advantage for Ikea Wholesale was that the challenged antidumping regulation was considered null and void *ab initio*, leading to a ruling that the duties paid should be reimbursed. It is less clear that such a conclusion could have been reached if the Court had applied the WTO ruling, since WTO rulings are considered to be prospective.[12]

It may further be noted that in *Ikea Wholesale* there was an Opinion of Léger AG, which was very negative about the effect of WTO dispute decisions. The Advocate General urged the Court not to accept such decisions as binding, claiming that to do so would constitute a threat to the autonomy of Community law.[13]

The last set of cases involved actions in damages of a peculiar kind. They were brought by companies whose exports to the United States were affected by the WTO-authorized trade sanctions ('suspension of concessions') in the bananas and hormones disputes. They claimed damages, contending that those sanctions resulted from the Community's failure to comply with WTO law and with the WTO dispute rulings, and that this failure constituted unlawful conduct as from the expiry of the reasonable period of time granted under WTO law to comply with the rulings. The Court of First Instance rejected the actions, and as regards the effect of WTO dispute rulings essentially repeated *Van Parys*. Two of the judgments were appealed.

In the appeal in *FIAMM and Fedon* Maduro AG examined whether WTO dispute decisions could justify a modification to the principle that WTO law cannot be relied upon, because it lacks direct effect. The test was whether the ability for the appellants to rely on such decisions would affect neither the scope for negotiations, nor the reciprocity and balance in the application of the commitments undertaken. To perform that test required an examination of whether the institutions' political freedom continued to exist in the specific circumstances of the cases in point. The debate ultimately hinged on the binding force of the DSB decision: did the DSU

---

[11] Case C-351/04, *Ikea Wholesale v Commissioners of Customs & Excise* [2007] ECR I-7723.

[12] For a further discussion of this principle, see Eeckhout, P., 'Remedies and Compliance', in D. Bethlehem, D. McRae, R. Neufeld, and I. Van Damme (eds), *Oxford Handbook of International Trade Law*, Oxford, Oxford University Press, 2009, pp. 448–51.

[13] *Ikea Wholesale*, paras. 77–89 of the Opinion.

require the rulings and recommendations of the DSB to be implemented in full? To answer this question the Advocate General recalled the analysis of the DSU that the Court made in *Van Parys*. He considered that the Community remained free to make the political choice to lay itself open initially to retaliatory measures, and an important place continued to be reserved at all events for negotiation between the parties to the dispute. Whether one viewed the perennial possibility of reaching a negotiated solution to the dispute as a freedom limited to the choice of the means of implementing DSB decisions or as the freedom to prefer an alternative to implementation of the decision, it still constituted freedom of choice. That freedom would be undermined, also by a ruling of unlawfulness in an action for damages. It was true that such a ruling would not lead formally to either the annulment or the invalidation of the legislation in issue, which thus remained an integral part of the legal order and theoretically applicable. The finding of unlawfulness nevertheless constituted *res judicata*, and the political organs of the Community could not allow such unlawfulness to persist, short of disregarding the principle of a Community based on the rule of law. Moreover, the prospect of the financial burden that successful actions in damages would entail would likewise force the political organs of the Community to eliminate the incompatible measure. The scope for political manoeuvre would thus undeniably be jeopardized.[14]

The Court of Justice started its analysis in *FIAMM and Fedon* by referring to its established case law on WTO law. The focus here is on the additional points that the Court made. It had to be remembered, the Court emphasized, that the decisive factor was that the resolution of disputes concerning WTO law was based, in part, on negotiations between the contracting parties. Withdrawal of unlawful measures was admittedly the solution recommended by WTO law, but other solutions were also authorized. There was no reason to draw a distinction according to whether the legality of the Community action was to be reviewed in annulment proceedings or for the purpose of deciding an action for compensation. First, the prospect of actions for damages was liable to hinder exercise of the powers of the legislative authority. Second, any determination by the Community courts that a Community measure was unlawful was inherently liable to have repercussions on the conduct required of the institution that adopted the measure in question. The Court thus confirmed the

[14] Opinion of Maduro AG in Joined Cases C-120/06 P and C-121/06 P, *Fiamm and Fedon* [2008] ECR I-6513, paras. 42–50.

analysis by Maduro AG of the effects of an unlawfulness ruling in an action for damages.[15]

There was also no basis for the distinction between the 'direct effect' of the WTO rules imposing substantive obligations and the 'direct effect' of a decision of the DSB. A DSB decision, which had no object other than to rule on whether a WTO member's conduct was consistent with the obligations entered into, could not in principle be fundamentally distinguished from the substantive rules that conveyed such obligations. A recommendation or ruling of the DSB was no more capable than the substantive rules of conferring upon individuals a right to rely thereon before the Community courts for the purpose of having the legality of the conduct of the Community institutions reviewed. To support this finding the Court again referred to the general reasons for the lack of direct effect of WTO law (nature of the WTO agreements; reciprocity and flexibility; room for discretion and scope for negotiations). It further referred to Article 3(2) DSU, according to which recommendations and rulings of the DSB cannot add to or diminish the rights and obligations provided in the agreements concerned.[16] The Court also rejected the claim that the cases called for the application of a principle of no-fault liability.

As can be seen, the Court's rejection of any independent or binding effect of WTO dispute decisions is founded on two main considerations. The Court considers that the WTO dispute settlement system continues to provide room for negotiations, even after the expiry of the reasonable period of time that the WTO grants for implementing dispute decisions. As pointed out by Maduro AG, this involves an assessment of the binding effect of WTO dispute decisions, and construes the latter as leaving perennial room for political manoeuvre. The second consideration is that the effect of WTO rulings in EU law is inextricably bound up with the lack of direct effect of WTO law in general. Dispute decisions cannot be relied upon, simply because WTO law as a whole cannot be relied upon.

Before moving on to a further assessment of the case law on direct effect of agreements concluded by the EU, it is useful to point out that the above case law on WTO dispute decisions did not come about with the unanimous support of the Advocates General involved.

In *Biret* Alber AG made a strong plea in favour of recognizing the binding effect of WTO dispute settlement. He started with an analysis of the WTO dispute settlement system that reached radically different conclusions from those the Court arrived at. The Advocate General considered

---

15 *Idem*, paras. 122–4 of the judgment.
16 *Idem*, paras. 125–31.

that, once a recommendation or ruling had been adopted, it had to be 'unconditionally' accepted (Article 17(4) DSU). The parties were no longer free to reach a settlement and could only agree on the period of time within which to comply with the DSB ruling (Article 21(3)(b) DSU) or the terms of a mutually satisfactory solution (Article 22(8) DSU). Mutually agreed solutions had to be consistent with the WTO agreements (Article 3(5) DSU). The DSU also provided that 'prompt' compliance was 'essential' to ensure effective resolution of disputes (Article 21(1) DSU). Compensation and suspension of concessions were 'temporary measures' (Article 22(1) DSU) and neither of them was preferred to full implementation of a recommendation to bring a measure into conformity (Article 22(1) DSU). The fact that the DSB kept implementation under surveillance meant that, even where compensation had been paid or concessions had been suspended, there was still a duty to comply with the DSB recommendations or rulings. It therefore had to be concluded that there was ultimately no alternative but to implement the recommendations or rulings of the DSB, which could not be circumvented by negotiation between the parties.[17]

The Advocate General further considered that non-compliance with a DSB recommendation or ruling could be a commercial policy option. However, it was clear that it was not a lawful option. Under WTO law, the legislative and executive bodies no longer had any discretion that could be reduced by recognizing dispute decisions to be directly applicable. He urged the Court to support the principle of legality after the expiry of the reasonable period allowed to comply, rather than the commercial option of non-compliance. The latter was a commercial policy option only because there was no means of enforcing WTO recommendations or rulings. This was bound up with their nature as instruments of international law. There was in principle no way of enforcing international law, and the Advocate General finely remarked that the position in Community law had in fact been the same before the introduction of (current) Article 260 TFEU on penalties that a member state may incur for failure to comply with its obligations. Unenforceability was therefore no reason to disregard DSB recommendations and rulings.[18]

The Advocate General also took the view that recognizing the direct applicability of WTO law as a basis for a claim in damages did not reduce the discretion of the legislative and executive bodies in deciding how to implement a DSB recommendation. The end of an action for damages was

---

[17] Case C-93/02 P, *Biret International v Council* [2003] ECR I-10497, paras. 74–81 of the Opinion.

[18] *Idem*, paras. 82–8.

not the abolition of a particular measure but compensation for damage caused. It did not therefore open the way for Biret to demand a particular form of conduct on the part of the Community in implementing DSB recommendations.[19]

As regards reciprocity, Alber AG considered that this was really a commercial issue, decked out in the legal trappings of a 'principle of reciprocity'. There appeared to be considerable doubt as to whether the Community's trading position might be weakened at all by recognizing the direct applicability of WTO law as a basis for a claim in damages.[20]

In *Van Parys*, Tizzano AG agreed with the analysis by Alber AG in *Biret*.[21] He concluded that in a 'Community governed by law' DSB decisions had to be considered as a criterion of the legality of Community measures and that the Court consequently should not, on grounds of doubtful legal merit, give clear approval to legal arguments that would lead to the opposite conclusion.[22]

14.3 A CRITICAL REVIEW

In *Portugal v Council*, where the Court established the lack of direct effect of WTO law, it referred to the nature of the WTO dispute settlement system as a reason for denying direct effect. That analysis of the WTO dispute settlement system was justified, in the strict sense in which it was employed by the Court: its purpose was simply to examine whether the WTO Agreement *mandates* direct effect.[23] The fact that the DSU envisages cases in which compliance with a dispute ruling is not forthcoming, and thus provides for remedies and mechanisms to secure such compliance (compensation and suspension of concessions), presupposes that WTO law does not require direct effect. If it did, and all WTO members accepted that WTO law was enforceable before their domestic courts, then there would arguably be no need for these international law mechanisms.

However, by extending that reasoning to non-compliance at the expiry of the reasonable time granted under WTO law, the Court has moved from a position in which WTO law is construed as not requiring direct effect – which is correct – to one in which compliance with WTO law is legitimately subject to perennial political negotiations. That position, it is submitted, is

19 *Idem*, paras. 93–4.
20 *Idem*, para. 102.
21 *Van Parys*, paras. 63–73 of the Opinion.
22 *Idem*, para. 73.
23 Cf. Bourgeois, *supra*, at 109.

an incorrect understanding of the dispute settlement mechanism, and one that is not in accordance with international law principles.

The case against the Court's reading of the DSU was convincingly made by Alber AG in *Biret*. On balance, the relevant provisions of the DSU, even if couched in language and terms that are not wholly conclusive, leave little room for doubt that dispute rulings are binding, and that the mechanisms for ensuring such compliance, in those cases where it is not forthcoming, are simply temporary alternatives. But there is more. Looked at from a broader international law perspective, the Court puts the aim and function of the dispute settlement mechanism on its head. In international law circles the WTO dispute settlement system is generally regarded as among the most sophisticated and advanced such systems in the international law universe. It is a system of compulsory jurisdiction (in itself rare), and in contrast with most other systems it contains at least some specific mechanisms to secure compliance. Suspension of concessions (often referred to as trade sanctions), in particular, offers members of the WTO at least some enforcement tool, even if it is a crude one, with many defects, to secure compliance by members failing to comply with dispute rulings. They are an attempt to respond to one of the greatest deficiencies of international law: its lack of enforcement. They are advanced by comparison with other subsystems of international law, or with other international agreements, including agreements that the Court recognizes as having direct effect. As a minimum this means that the WTO members sought to emphasize the need for compliance with dispute rulings when concluding the WTO agreement. It is this emphasis that the Court effectively turns on its head, by characterizing it as an acceptance of perennial negotiations, and as weakening (if not denying) the binding character of WTO dispute decisions. The fact that WTO law provides for at least some mechanisms to secure compliance – some penalties for those breaking the law – is regarded as weakening the legal nature of the norms which are enforced.

It is true that the actual provisions of the DSU are not without ambiguity. There is more than those provisions, however. Under Article 31(3)(b) VCLT, 'any subsequent practice in the application of the treaty which establishes the agreement of the parties regarding its interpretation' shall be taken into account in the interpretation of treaties. What does that practice of the WTO members, together with the case law that has developed as part of that practice, tell us?

Pursuant to Article 21(5) DSU disagreements 'as to the existence or consistency with a covered agreement of measures taken to comply with the recommendations and rulings … shall be decided through recourse to these dispute settlement procedures, including wherever possible resort to the original panel'. Such a compliance panel will look at the measures adopted to comply with an earlier ruling. A substantial number of WTO members – including the EU – have used this opportunity. A mere cursory examination of the panel reports adopted in such compliance cases shows that, routinely, (1) complainants claim that the defending party has failed to comply with the rulings and recommendations of the DSB, and (2) panels confirm or deny such claims, depending on the outcome of their substantive examination. Compliance panels may be appealed. The Appellate Body has not as yet squarely been asked whether rulings and recommendations of the DSB are 'binding'; WTO members simply accept that they are bound to comply. Nevertheless, the Appellate Body has been faced with several tangential issues and arguments, and its response to those arguments is straightforward and telling. In *EC – Bed Linen*, for example, the issue was whether it was possible, in a compliance case, to re-examine an unappealed finding by the original panel; a finding, therefore, adopted by the DSB. The Appellate Body's reply is worth quoting in full:[24]

> in our view, an *unappealed* finding included in a panel report that is *adopted* by the DSB must be treated as a *final resolution* to a dispute between the parties in respect of the *particular* claim and the *specific* component of a measure that is the subject of that claim. This conclusion is supported by Articles 16.4 and 19.1, paragraphs 1 and 3 of Article 21, and Article 22.1 of the DSU. Where a panel concludes that a measure is inconsistent with a covered agreement, that panel shall *recommend*, according to Article 19.1, that the Member concerned bring that measure into conformity with that agreement. A panel report, including the *recommendations* contained therein, shall be *adopted* by the DSB within the time period specified in Article 16.4 – unless appealed. Members are to *comply* with recommendations and rulings *adopted* by the DSB promptly, or within a reasonable period of time, in accordance with paragraphs 1 and 3 of Article 21 of the DSU. A Member that does not comply with the recommendations and rulings adopted by the DSB within these time periods must face the consequences set out in Article 22.1, relating to compensation and suspension of concessions. Thus, a reading of Articles 16.4 and 19.1, paragraphs 1 and 3 of Article 21, and Article 22.1, taken together, makes it abundantly clear that a panel finding which is not appealed, and which is included in a panel report *adopted* by the DSB, must be accepted by the parties as a *final* resolution to the dispute between them, in the same way and with the same finality as a finding included in an Appellate Body Report adopted by the DSB – with respect to the particular claim and the specific component of the measure that is the subject of the claim. Indeed, the European Communities and India agreed at the oral hearing that both panel reports and Appellate Body Reports would have the same effect, in this respect, once adopted by the DSB.

---

[24] Appellate Body Report, *EC – Bed Linen (Article 21.5 – India)*, at paras. 92–3, emphasis in the original.

There is clearly a big gap between that assessment by the WTO's highest adjudicator and the EU courts' emphasis on perennial room for negotiation, even after the expiry of the period for implementing a WTO ruling. Even more straightforward is the following statement of the arbitrator in *EC – Chicken Cuts*. The arbitration award related to the reasonable period of time for implementing the ruling in that case, which concerned the customs classification of chicken cuts. The EC argued that, in order to comply, it first needed to obtain a new decision by the World Customs Organization on the classification issue. The arbitrator was concerned that this could mean that implementation would become conditional on such a decision. In response, he stated:[25]

> It is axiomatic that alleged violations of the covered agreements must be redressed exclusively through the procedures set out in the DSU, providing for examination of such allegations by a panel and possibly the Appellate Body, and that, if violations are found and the relevant reports are adopted by the DSB, the respondent Member is obliged to implement promptly the recommendations and rulings of the DSB. These recommendations and rulings are *binding* on implementing Members, and give rise to an *obligation* to bring their WTO-inconsistent measures into conformity with their obligations under the covered agreements.

The conclusions to be drawn from the above analysis are obvious. Adopted panel and Appellate Body reports create a clear, unconditional obligation to comply with the recommendations they contain (namely, for the responding party to bring its measures into conformity) within a reasonable period of time. If correct implementation is lacking, it is possible to agree on compensation, or to suspend concessions. These remedies, however, are not an alternative to compliance. Rather, they seek to induce compliance. The fact that these remedies exist should not be seen as in any way diminishing the obligation to comply, but as enhancing it. They show the importance that WTO Members attach to an effective and efficient system of dispute settlement.[26]

The Court's analysis of the dispute settlement is therefore misguided. However, in *FIAMM and Fedon* the Court has advanced a further argument against recognizing the direct effect of WTO dispute decisions: the apparently straightforward point that, if WTO law as such does not have

---

[25] Award of the Arbitrator, *EC – Chicken Cuts,* at para. 55 (emphasis added). The arbitrator was James Bacchus, former member and Chairman of the Appellate Body.

[26] Cf. Bronckers, *supra*, at pp. 616–8.

direct effect, WTO dispute decisions that simply apply such law cannot be relied upon either. Again, though, a different approach is called for. The Court's argument works to the extent that the reasons for rejecting direct effect of WTO law as such are equally valid for dispute decisions. It is not clear that that is the case. The political room for manoeuvre for the EU's political institutions that the Court sought to safeguard by denying direct effect should no longer be protected in the face of an adverse WTO dispute ruling that establishes that the EU has violated WTO law. Where there is such an adverse ruling, allowing parties to rely on it does not turn the EU courts into day-to-day enforcers of WTO law. Nor does it turn those courts into adjudicators on merely presumptive violations of WTO law. Furthermore, the argument that there should continue to be room for political manoeuvre, even after an adverse ruling, and the expiry of the reasonable period, fails to understand the nature of WTO dispute settlement and violates the binding effect of dispute rulings. Ultimately, it is inconsistent with the core international law principle of *pacta sunt servanda*.

14.4 CONCLUSIONS

It is easy to sum up the basic argument of this short chapter. The EU courts' refusal to recognize the effect, in EU law, of WTO dispute decisions is difficult to justify. The general reasons for denying WTO law direct effect, be it the nature of the WTO dispute settlement system, or the need to safeguard the EU institutions' room for manoeuvre, do not extend to final WTO dispute decisions. Those reasons must in any event be balanced against the key international law principle of *pacta sunt servanda*. The EU is ill served by a failure by its highest judicial organs to respect the rule of law in international affairs. In fact its constitutional charter now provides, post-Lisbon, that the EU shall contribute to 'the strict observance and the development of international law' (Article 3(5) TEU).

It was precisely in one of its most significant decisions aimed at safeguarding the autonomy of EU law, Opinion 1/91, that the Court of Justice accepted that international judicial decisions arrived at under an agreement concluded by the EU are binding on the EU institutions, including the courts. This autonomy is an important value, which the courts must indeed protect. It is not, however, threatened by showing respect for dispute decisions such as those arrived at by the WTO's adjudicators, when they have dutifully identified the legal obligations to which the WTO members, including the EU, have consented. There is a danger that autonomy may turn into autarky if there were too much disconnect between EU law and international law.

15. The domestic law effect of the WTO in the EU – a dialogue with Jacques Bourgeois

Marco Bronckers*

Jacques Bourgeois has been a professional mentor for me ever since I became his stagiaire in 1981 when he was a prominent member of the external relations division of the European Commission's Legal Service. He taught me the intricacies of European trade policy, as well as the vicissitudes of the Community's membership of the GATT and subsequently the WTO. His blend of intellectual rigour and forward thinking, coupled with an eye for the possible, has always held special appeal for me. On a wide variety of issues we have thought alike, that is to say I have come to think like him. I cherish the fact that over the years we have become good personal friends too and so have our families.

On this happy occasion of Jacques' *Festschrift*, I want to revisit a topic that has preoccupied me on and off for many years, and see how the position where I have ended up compares with that of Jacques'. That topic is the domestic law effect of the WTO in the European legal order. It is a topic that has intrigued scores of European scholars and practitioners. In fact, in this volume Piet Eeckhout and Ernst-Ulrich Petersmann devote chapters to it as well.

Bourgeois has addressed this topic on many occasions, at conferences, seminars and in papers. To compare our views, I will notably refer to a comprehensive and admirable contribution he published in the year 2000: 'The European Court of Justice and the WTO'.[1]

* Subject to the usual disclaimer, I express my appreciation for the excellent research assistance of my law firm colleagues Marie Boscher and Tomas Silla, and my helpful discussions with Natalie McNelis.

[1] See Bourgeois, J.H.J., 'The European Court of Justice and the WTO', in J. Weiler (ed.), *Towards a Common Law of International Trade*, Oxford, Oxford University Press, 2000 (hereafter 'Bourgeois').

15.1 THE LAW AS IT STANDS

To start with, Bourgeois recalls that the European Court of Justice (ECJ) refuses to grant direct effect to the WTO.[2] According to the ECJ (now renamed the Court of Justice of the European Union), the WTO's dispute settlement system is fundamentally diplomatic in nature, and gives members who have been found to infringe a WTO obligation other options in addition to compliance. Furthermore, the ECJ has noted that in none of the EC's major trading partners do courts allow private parties to challenge domestic measures by reference to WTO law. As a result, according to the ECJ, private parties cannot directly challenge the validity of national or EC[3] measures on the basis of GATT/WTO obligations. Bourgeois adds that the Court has made some kind of an exception, in that it will admit such direct challenges in those instances where the European legislator has indicated that it intended to implement WTO law (the so-called *Nakajima* doctrine).[4]

This case law of the Court is unchanged, at the time of this writing in early 2011. No provision of the WTO has been found to have direct effect;[5] the *Nakajima* doctrine is still good law.[6]

Bourgeois then makes a number of important points. He argues that WTO law contains no obligation on members to grant direct effect to WTO provisions on their domestic legal order.[7] That view is commonly held nowadays.

He also argues that there is no principle in EC law according to which the European Courts must take certain WTO obligations into account in the interpretation of EC law, notably its foreign trade law.[8] As Bourgeois notes, whenever the European Courts *did* decide to grant direct effect to other

[2] Case C-149/96, *Portugal v Council* [1999] ECR I-8395.

[3] As Bourgeois was writing in 2000, he still referred to the European Community (EC). Ten years or so later, at the time of this writing, we speak of the European Union (EU) since the entry into force of the Lisbon treaty. I will use both pre- and post-Lisbon terminology, generally depending on when a particular argument was made, by him or others.

[4] Case C-69/89, *Nakajima v Council* [1991] ECR I-2069.

[5] E.g. Case C-428/08, *Monsanto Technology LLC v Cefetra BV, Cefetra Feed Service BV, Cefetra Futures BV, Alfred C. Toepfer International GmbH*, judgment of 6 July 2010 (not yet reported), paras. 71–2; Case T-237/08, *Abadía Retuerta, SA, v Office for Harmonisation in the Internal Market (Trade Marks and Designs) (OHIM) (Cuveé Palomar)*, judgment of 11 May 2010 (not yet reported), para. 66.

[6] E.g., Case T-45/06, *Reliance Industries v Council* [2008] ECR II-2399.

[7] See Article XVI.4 WTO.

[8] Bourgeois, at p. 110.

international treaties this was judge-made law as well.[9] In other words, the European courts did not feel compelled to do so either on the basis of the international treaty at issue or on the basis of equivalent principles in the European treaties. I see nothing in the Lisbon Treaty, which entered into effect in December 2009, to have changed this approach. While the European Union is committed 'to contribute to … the strict observance and the development of international law',[10] the decision whether or not to grant domestic law effect (including direct effect) to international treaty obligations has been left to the courts.

From an international law perspective the distinctions drawn by the European courts between the WTO treaty and other international agreements are 'puzzling', as Bourgeois has written.[11] The European courts do not seem to have given the correct interpretation of the changes wrought in the WTO framework, compared to the predecessor agreement the GATT. In particular, as Bourgeois points out, the WTO's dispute settlement system has been substantially reinforced compared to the old consensus-based GATT system.[12] One might add that the WTO's dispute settlement system is also unusually compelling compared to other international agreements to which the European Court of Justice *did* grant direct effect.[13] Bourgeois and I agree therefore that the reasons advanced by the ECJ to deny direct effect to the WTO are not legally persuasive.

15.2 LEGAL POLICY ASSESSMENT

Yet while it is of interest to debate the merits of the legal arguments that the European Court of Justice in its judge-made law has used to deny direct effect to the WTO's provisions so far, the bottom line question is whether the Court reached the right result.

---

[9] E.g., Case C-303/08, *Bozkurt*, judgment of 22 December 2010, not yet reported, at para. 31; C-372/06, *Asda Stores* [2007] ECR I-11223, at para. 91 (regarding the direct effect of a Decision taken pursuant to the EEC – Turkey Association Agreement).

[10] See Article 3 TEU.

[11] Bourgeois, at p. 107.

[12] Bourgeois, at p. 108.

[13] M. Bronckers, in Kuijper, P.J. and Bronckers, M., 'WTO Law in the European Court of Justice', *Common Market Law Review*, Vol. 42, 2005, pp. 1313, 1344.

15.2.1 Bourgeois' Views

Bourgeois fundamentally takes issue with the denial of direct effect to WTO law:[14]

> [A]t the end of the day there is something wrong with a system that on the one hand generates rules designed to regulate international trade, even if it is supposed to regulate what states are supposed to do or not to do in matters of trade, but on the other, denies people, affected by what states do or not do in matters of trade, the possibility of relying on these rules to protect their interests.

He also believes it is preferable from a WTO perspective to allow private parties to bring WTO-based challenges in national court, rather than allowing private parties access to the WTO's own dispute settlement process, as he considers the latter overburdened.[15]

Characteristically, however, Bourgeois does not close his eyes to political realities. Governments keep more discretion to deviate from WTO rules for as long private parties cannot challenge such deviations in court. It would be politically difficult for the EU to stomach that its courts would grant direct effect to WTO law, whereas none of its trading partners are inclined to give courts this role. And Bourgeois echoes the concern that, given the diverging positions of the member states on trade issues (he recalls the *Bananas* dispute) any grant of direct effect to WTO law by the European courts could be internally divisive within the EC (and now the EU).[16] Accordingly, Bourgeois does not plead for an unconditional grant of direct effect to WTO provisions. Instead, he formulates a rather nuanced proposal.

First, courts should test whether their grant of direct effect would upset the balance of rights and obligations of the EC, not in respect of one particular WTO member or all the members, but in respect of a relevant cross-section of the WTO's membership. Furthermore, the test should be limited to the WTO agreement in question, rather than to the WTO package of agreements as a whole. In order for the European courts to reach an informed opinion on this question, Bourgeois envisages that they ask the defending institutions (the Commission, the Council of Ministers) whether granting direct effect would upset the balance of the EC's rights and obligations under that agreement.

---

14 Bourgeois, at p. 113.

15 Bourgeois, at p. 116.

16 Bourgeois refers to Thomas Cottier as a scholar who shared this concern in a 1997 paper. Bourgeois, at p. 117.

Second, and in addition to this inquiry, Bourgeois would not want the European courts to recognize the enforceability of a WTO rule in the absence of a WTO panel or Appellate Body ruling condemning the EC's measure that is being litigated before the European courts. He argues that before such a ruling is issued the EC has different ways to avoid or resolve an incompatibility with WTO law, such as a negotiated solution, including the 'unbinding' of a tariff concession.

Ultimately, then, Bourgeois would allow a private litigant to challenge the validity of an EC measure on the basis of a WTO rule, and thereby grant this rule 'direct effect', in the limited circumstance that (1) the EC measure had already been condemned in WTO dispute settlement proceedings *and* (2) granting the private litigant this opportunity would not upset the balance of rights of obligations of the EC under the relevant WTO agreement.

15.2.2 Bronckers' Views

I believe that Bourgeois' proposal represents a creative attempt to reconcile his fundamental starting position, that the WTO's rules should somehow also be meaningful to private parties in order to be meaningful at all, with the political realities of the day. Expressed differently, in my view any useful proposal on the WTO's domestic law effect must give a place to the *conviction* that international economic law is to be meaningful to private parties, as well to the *responsibility* the EU and its institutions have to manage this international system sensibly in a way that takes the effects on European interests overall duly into account.[17]

What I find more problematic are the two conditions that Bourgeois wants to impose on the European courts before they should grant direct effect to provisions of the WTO package of agreements: the prior condemnation of the EU's measure, and the balance of rights and obligations (reciprocity). I would rather impose a different condition: allowing the political institutions to suspend the interpretations of WTO law to which the European courts have given direct effect for as long as they believe the imbalance continues.

[17] This proposition echoes one of the main themes in Max Weber's lecture *Politik als Beruf* (1919): '[A]n ethics of conviction and an ethics of responsibility are not absolute antitheses but are mutually complementary, and only when taken together do they constitute the authentic human being who is capable of having a "vocation for politics".' (this translation is from Livingstone: *Max Weber: The Vocation Lectures* 92 (Owen and Strong (eds), Hackett, 2004)). Thanks to Thierry Gontier (Lyon III) for pointing this reference out to me.

15.2.2.1 Prior WTO condemnation

As is well known, only governments can bring a dispute to the WTO, and so far only governments can be actively involved (as a party or an intervener) in litigation before the WTO.[18] Accordingly, requiring that an EU measure first be condemned by a WTO tribunal before the relevant WTO obligations can be given direct effect by the European courts puts a considerable burden on private litigants. They would have to go through a foreign government first.

Except for the unusually well-connected private industry, seeking the endorsement or espousal of its claim by a government will be a challenge for a private party. Government-to-government litigation has a dynamic of its own and often imposes diplomatic costs on the relations between governments. These political costs, as well as the resources (manpower and expenses) required to bring a case to a successful conclusion, will be factored in before one government decides to sue another government at the WTO. Such considerations severely limit the protection private parties can derive from WTO rules in disciplining unwelcome regulatory activities of a member, in case a prior WTO ruling were to become a condition precedent to a WTO rule being granted direct effect by the European courts. In fact, with this condition it would become pretty unpredictable when these rules might have a beneficial effect for private parties, thereby weakening one of the basic rationales for the move of a power-based to a rule-based system.[19]

Furthermore, this condition of a prior WTO condemnation of the controversial EU measure will be particularly difficult to satisfy for *European* interest groups who want to rely on a WTO obligation to correct or invalidate that EU measure. A sizable number of WTO obligations constitute principles of good governance, which can protect domestic production as much as foreign trade against misplaced regulation. For example, the WTO principle that restrictions on the sale of food ought to have a scientific basis, and cannot be based merely on speculative health concerns, has been pertinent not only to European importers of US hormone-treated

---

[18] Even the very limited possibility for private parties to support as *amicus curiae* a government's written submissions in a WTO dispute remains controversial. See, e.g. Panel Report, *Thailand – Customs and Fiscal Measures on Cigarettes from the Phillipiness*, WT/DS371/R, at para. 2.5, circulated on 15 November 2010.

[19] Jackson, J.H., 'Governmental Disputes in International Trade Relations: A Proposal in the Context of GATT', *Journal of World Trade Law*, Vol. 13, 1979, pp. 1–21.

beef,[20] but also to European producers of vitamin-enriched cornflakes or fruit drinks.[21]

In most cases, chances are that European interest groups will not find a foreign government willing to assume the political and litigation costs to challenge the EU measure. Moreover, in accordance with the EU's solidarity rule, no EU member state – although all are members of the WTO and entitled to bring cases to the WTO – can challenge an EU measure before the WTO.[22] Consequently, this 'exhaustion of *international* remedies' rule effectively deprives European citizens from the possibility to rely on WTO principles before the European courts in a case not involving imported goods or services. I find that unacceptable.

In addition, it is not always necessary to wait until a WTO tribunal has had occasion to adjudicate a dispute on a WTO measure in order to have a pretty good idea whether that measure runs foul of WTO law. Thus, a WTO ruling involving a similar measure of another WTO member country may make it pretty clear that an EU measure, when challenged before a WTO tribunal, will be held to infringe WTO law too. Without going so far as to say that WTO rulings constitute binding precedents for WTO tribunals in other disputes,[23] in such cases it could make good sense for the EU (including the European Courts) to draw the consequences in order to

---

[20] Appellate Body Report, *EC Measures Concerning Meat and Meat Products (Hormones)*, WT/DS26/AB/R, WT/DS48/AB/R, adopted 13 February 1998; see also 'Joint Communication from the European Communities and the United States' in *EC Measures Concerning Meat and Meat Products (Hormones)*, WT/DS26/28, from 30 September 2009.

[21] See Bronckers, M., 'Exceptions to Liberal Trade in Foodstuffs: The Precautionary Approach and Collective Preferences', in C. Baudenbacher, P. Tresselt, and T. Orlygsson (eds), *The EFTA Court: Ten Years On EFTA*, Oxford, Hart, 2005, pp. 105–6 (commenting on Case E-3/00, *EFTA Surveillance Authority v Norway*, 2000–2001, EFTA Ct Rep 75, and ECJ, Case C-192/01, *Commission v Denmark* [2003] ECR I-9693).

[22] See Article 4.3 TEU.

[23] In the successive stages of the long-running saga on zeroing in antidumping law, the US Government fiercely resisted any reference to earlier WTO rulings, in which various measures of the US and other Members involving zeroing had already been condemned, on the grounds that these rulings did not constitute binding precedent. The most recent Panel report in this case asserted that prior Appellate Body rulings do create 'legitimate expectations' that they will be followed; see Panel Report, *United States – Use of Zeroing in Anti-Dumping Measures Involving Products from Korea*, WT/DS402/R, at paras. 7.28–7.35, circulated on 18 January 2011. See generally McNelis, N., 'What Obligations Are Created by World Trade Organization Dispute Settlement Report?', *Journal of World Trade*, Vol. 37, 2003, pp. 647–72.

avoid the domestic cost of unnecessary litigation and/or to improve the integrity of the international system.[24]

In sum, I find the condition that WTO obligations should only be given direct effect by the European courts in the event a disputed EU measure has been condemned by a WTO tribunal too limiting. Moreover, even a WTO ruling condemning an EU measure does not provide the certainty that Bourgeois is looking for to make sure that a European court will not unnecessarily condemn the EU for an action for which the EU might still obtain legal cover. After all, following a WTO ruling condemning its action the EU could still decide for example to ask for a waiver,[25] or renegotiate a concession.[26] Expressed differently, the European courts will always have to think for themselves and interpret WTO obligations to which they give

---

[24] It is of some interest that the EU legislature, in the trade remedies area, has already recognized that WTO rulings involving trade remedies of other WTO countries can be a good reason for the EU to amend a trade remedy measure of its own without waiting for a WTO ruling specifically condemning the EU's measure. See Council Regulation (EC) No. 1515/2001 of 23 July 2001 on the measures that may be taken by the Community following a report adopted by the WTO Dispute Settlement Body concerning anti-dumping and anti-subsidy matters, OJ (2001) L 201/10.

[25] The EU was already in a similar situation during the Bananas saga, where it obtained a 'Cotonou Waiver' (European Communities – the ACP-EC Partnership Agreement, Decision of 14 November 2001, WT/MIN(01)/15, accessible at: www.wto.org/english/thewto_e/minist_e/min01_e/mindecl_acp_ec_agre_e.htm) *after* the early rounds of the 'Bananas III' WTO dispute settlement rulings, such as the Appellate Body Report, *European Communities – Regime for the Importation, Sale and Distribution of Bananas*, WT/DS27/AB/R, adopted 25 September 1997, DSR 1997:II, 591.

[26] This is exactly what the United States did following the condemnation by the WTO Appellate Body of a restriction it had imposed on electronic gambling. See Appellate Body Report, *United States – Measures Affecting the Cross-Border Supply of Gambling and Betting Services*, WT/DS285/AB/R, adopted 20 April 2005, DSR 2005:XII, 5663; followed by USTR, *Statement of Deputy United States Trade Representative John K. Veroneau Regarding U.S. Actions under GATS Article XXI,* 3 May 2007 (available at: www.ustr.gov/about-us/press-office/press-releases/archives/2007/may/statement-deputy-united-states-trade-represen). The US move was considered controversial. See Ruse-Khan, H., 'A Pirate of the Caribbean? The Attractions of Suspending TRIPS Obligations', *Journal of International Economic Law*, Vol. 11, 2008, p. 313, at pp. 323–4. The US renegotiation of its concessions apparently also did not come cheap. See King, K.F., 'Geolocation and Federalism on the Internet: Cutting Internet Gambling's Gordian Knot', *Columbia Science and Technology Law Review*, Vol. 11, No. 41, 2010, at pp. 55–6.

domestic law effect as best as they see fit.[27] Prior WTO rulings are helpful, but neither necessary nor decisive to the outcome of a European Court case.

Bourgeois does make a sensible point though by recalling that the WTO régime, like many other treaties, offers governments the possibility to claim exceptions.[28] Therefore, private claims that a government has violated WTO principles should not be taken at face value. Governments should be offered the possibility to decide whether they want to invoke such an exception. I would therefore like to slightly reformulate Bourgeois' suggestion to say that, before condemning an EU measure on the basis of a WTO principle, the European courts should first request the institutions whether they want to avail themselves of any of the exceptions or exceptional remedies the WTO is providing for; and, if so, demonstrate that the required steps have been taken (it would not be a good enough for the EU's political institutions, by way of a defense in a court action, merely to claim or speculate that they *might* appeal to an exception to escape or cover a WTO violation).

15.2.2.2 Reciprocity

As to the *reciprocity* condition that Bourgeois has formulated, this is problematic for different reasons. One first will recall, as does Bourgeois, that the ECJ, in its seminal *Kupferberg* judgment of the early 1980s, dismissed reciprocity as a relevant criterion when determining whether or not a prohibition on tax discrimination in a bilateral trade agreement (between the then EEC and then non-member Portugal) ought to be given direct effect. According to the ECJ, the implementation of the treaty by the third country, and notably whether the courts of the other party recognized direct effect, was not relevant to determine whether this treaty could be granted direct effect in the EU legal order.[29]

With the passage of time, the Court's refusal to take the practice of other countries into account has been criticized, essentially as being politically naive. Bourgeois echoes this criticism, when he argues that it does not seem

---

[27] See generally Bronckers, M., 'The Relationship of the EC Courts with Other International Tribunals: Non-Committal, Respectful or Submissive?', *Common Market Law Review*, Vol. 44, 2007, pp. 601–27.

[28] Incidentally, the fact that governments might occasionally avail themselves of such a rule-based exception following a particular dispute settlement ruling does not make that dispute settlement system diplomatic in nature, as the ECJ may have thought in respect of the WTO.

[29] Case C-104/81, *Hauptzollamt Mainz v C.A. Kupferberg & Cie. KG a.A.* [1982] ECR-3641, at para. 18.

'out of order' for a court to take into account 'manifest and substantial' non-performance by the other party. He believes that a court must not only have regard to the lack of direct effect but also more broadly to the overall behaviour of the other state.[30] He would want a court to test whether enforcing a WTO rule would 'on the whole', not just in respect of a particular WTO member, upset the balance of the EC's rights and obligations. That test should be limited to the WTO's rule in question, not to the EC's position in the WTO as a whole. Bourgeois submits that this condition should not present a court with too many difficulties, as it could ask the defendant institutions to state why granting 'direct effect' to a provision of a given WTO agreement would upset the balance of the EC's rights and obligations under that agreement.[31]

Preliminarily, I do not see the relevance here of whether the courts in another country allow the WTO to have 'direct effect', i.e. allowing private claimants to rely on WTO law in a challenge of domestic measures or legislation. As the European Court pointed out in *Kupferberg*, while being bound under public international law to perform its treaty obligations in good faith, each country remains free to determine the legal means to do so.[32] Some countries, it will be recalled, allow at least certain provisions of public international law to enter directly into the domestic legal order, allowing national courts to refer to these provisions in resolving private challenges of domestic measures (so-called *monist* countries); other countries only allow public international law to enter into the domestic legal order after and through transformation of these international law provisions into a domestic statute (so-called *dualist* countries).[33] As it is accepted that each country has the basic constitutional freedom to choose the system it prefers of giving effect to public international law, I do not see how the

30 Bourgeois, at p. 118.

31 Bourgeois, at p. 119.

32 See ECJ, *Kupferberg*, *supra* n. 29, at para. 18.

33 In reality, few countries opt for a purely dualist or a monist system, and virtually all countries find themselves on a spectrum tending more or less towards one or the other pole. In the period of decolonization more countries moved towards dualism, as a means to underscore their sovereignty. In more recent times a trend towards monism has been discerned, for instance in central and eastern countries as a means to distinguish themselves from their history in the Soviet Union, which was very much dualist in nature, and where international law could never be invoked let alone enforced before national courts. See Franckx, E. and Smis, S., 'Doorwerking van Internationaal Recht in de Belgische en Russische Nationale Rechtsorde: een rechtsvergelijkende analyse', in J. Wouters and D. Van Eeckhoutte (eds), *Doorwerking van internationaal recht in de Belgische rechtsorde*, Antwerpen–Oxford, Intersentia, 2006, pp. 123–5.

European courts (who operate in a monist-type system) could draw any negative inferences for the direct effect of WTO law in the EU legal order from the fact that courts in a more dualist country will not entertain direct appeals to WTO law of private claimants.

Whether or not other countries do not effectively perform their substantive obligations under an international treaty that a European Court is called upon to apply is a different matter. Yet at least in respect of certain treaties I have difficulties accepting that reciprocity could become relevant at all. In particular, where the enforcement of human rights treaties are concerned, it is not at all obvious why reciprocity should matter. For instance, should a Belgian court really inquire before granting direct effect to a human rights treaty at the request of a Chinese individual who feels harmed by aggressive police behaviour in Brussels, whether China's human rights record under that treaty is up to par? In this context it is to be noted that in France, where the Constitution in general terms imposes a reciprocity condition before a court can grant domestic law effect to international agreements,[34] the courts in more recent times have determined that the rule of reciprocity does *not* apply with respect to international human rights treaties.[35]

A French author, Bechillon, eloquently observed:[36]

> If there is one category of international agreements to which the application of a reciprocity principle really is incongruous it is human rights treaties – or, more generally, those treaties which create subjective rights for private parties … these treaties do not have as their primary objective the establishment of a legal framework contributing to peaceful relations between nations, but are designed

---

[34] See Article 55 of the French Constitution: 'Les traités ou accords régulièrement ratifiés ou approuvés ont, dès leur publication, une autorité supérieure à celle des lois, sous réserve, pour chaque accord ou traité, de son application par l'autre partie.'

[35] *Cour de cassation* in 1989 (Civ, 1ère, 15 November 1989, Bulletin civil I, n° 346, p. 233); *Conseil Constitutionnel* in 1999 (Décision n° 98–408 DC, 22 January 1999, *Traité portant statut de Cour Pénale Internationale*). The European Court of Human Rights had previously come to the same conclusion in *Ireland v the United Kingdom* (App. No. 5310/71) (1978) Series A no. 25, at para. 239 ('Unlike international treaties of the classic kind, the [European] Convention on [Human Rights] comprises more than mere reciprocal engagements between contracting States. It creates, over and above a network of mutual, bilateral undertakings, objective obligations which, in the words of the Preamble, benefit from a "collective enforcement"…').

[36] De Bechillon, D., 'De quelques incidences du contrôle de conventionalité internationale des lois par le juge ordinaire (Malaise dans la Constitution)', *Revue Française de Droit Administratif*, 1998, p. 225, at p. 235 (my translation).

to offer to a State that so wishes the means to commit itself, before the international community, to recognize and protect the rights it intends to grant to private persons residing in its territory and a fortiori to its citizens. Accordingly, there is absolutely no reason why the violation of a treaty by a third State could justify that a State rids itself of the constraints it has imposed on itself.

WTO agreements do not create human rights, nor more generally subjective rights for individuals. At the same time, as Bourgeois[37] has noted, many of the WTO's rules do benefit private parties directly; and the WTO's objectives of increasing economic welfare could not be realized without the very activities of private parties. A well-known WTO panel report put it this way:[38]

> [I]t would be entirely wrong to consider that the position of individuals is of no relevance to the GATT/WTO legal matrix. Many of the benefits to Members which are meant to flow as a result of the acceptance of various disciplines under the GATT/WTO depend on the activity of individual economic operators in the national and global market places. The purpose of many of these disciplines, indeed one of the primary objects of the GATT/WTO as a whole, is to produce certain market conditions which would allow this individual activity to flourish. Providing security and predictability to the multilateral trading system is another central object and purpose of the system which could be instrumental to achieving the broad objectives of the [WTO's] Preamble ... The security and predictability in question are of 'the multilateral trading system'. The multilateral trading system is, per force, composed not only of States but also, indeed mostly, of individual economic operators. The lack of security and predictability affects mostly these individual operators ... Trade is conducted most often and increasingly by private operators. It is through improved conditions for these private operators that Members benefit from WTO disciplines.

Moreover, the WTO's rules are 'colour-blind': they can be as relevant to domestic parties as to foreign trade or traders.[39] From this perspective, the application of a reciprocity condition in respect of the direct effect of the WTO's principles seems inappropriate.

Yet all our experiences show it is politically not palatable that treaty partners are perceived not to play by the same rules and create economic disparities. This is illustrated, for example, by the outcry these days over China's currency policy. Now one could argue that WTO principles are no

---

[37] See his observation cited *supra* n. 14.

[38] WTO Panel Report, *Section 301–310 of US Trade Act of 1974*, WT/DS152/R, adopted 27 January 2000, at paras. 7.73, 7.75–7.

[39] See text *supra* nn. 20 and 21.

longer exclusively based on reciprocal trade concessions (consider the rule-based parts in the GATT, GATS and TRIPS treaties), and that trade disequilibria do not justify trade wars or judicial 'tit for tats'. However, these finer points will not diminish the sense of political frustration if the other side is seen not to be a good citizen and our own courts continue to give direct effect to these same rules to the benefit of trade and traders from the other side. The EU's negotiating power with third countries to remedy an economically unbalanced situation is likely to suffer in the event the European courts were to continue to allow foreign traders the benefit of challenging EU measures, including EU trade retaliatory measures, on the basis of WTO rules (From this perspective as well, international economic law seems different from international human rights law. There is no reason to assume that the negotiating power of the EU to improve human rights protection in a third country would suffer in the event the EU courts continue to protect the human rights of that country's citizens. On the contrary, the EU's moral authority might suffer if EU Courts were seen to suspend human rights protection of foreign citizens.) Bourgeois is right not to close his eyes to this political reality. The European courts' own credibility, if not legitimacy, would come under considerable strain if they were to ignore strong political sentiments about foreign economic policy. But I cannot follow him when he assigns an essentially political question to the courts.

Bourgeois concedes that the European courts are ill-equipped to decide whether or not there is a 'disequilibrium' in the EU's rights and obligations under a WTO agreement. He would encourage them to ask the EU's defending institutions for advice. This is a tricky suggestion, unless one ensures that the private litigant can meaningfully contest the views put forward by the institutions on this issue. Otherwise, the independence of the European courts is put at risk. Courts cannot depend on the views of another branch of government, and certainly not when this other branch is one of the litigating parties, when resolving a dispute. That would be a violation of the fundamental right to an 'independent tribunal', enshrined in Article 6 of the European Convention on Human Rights, as well as in Article 47 of the Charter.

Again, recent French experiences illustrate this point. When private parties appealed to international treaties other than human rights treaties, the *Conseil d'Etat* before entertaining such pleas routinely asked the French Foreign Ministry for advice whether the treaty partner of France had implemented the obligation at issue, and the *Conseil d'Etat* considered this advice binding. This practice was challenged before the European Court of Human Rights, which ruled that it violated the right of the private plaintiff to have access to an independent tribunal.[40] Recently, the French *Conseil d'Etat* formally accepted this ruling of the European Court of Human Rights.[41]

In other words, I agree with Bourgeois that the European courts should not ignore, when faced with private appeals to international economic agreements like the WTO, whether the EU's treaty partner(s) is substantially not performing its treaty obligations towards the EU. Yet I do not believe courts are well placed to make this assessment. This puts them in a difficult position, as their role of an independent tribunal does not allow them to defer to the views of one of the litigating parties (i.e. a defending EU institution). I am also sceptical of EU political institutions that only 'discover' when called upon to defend themselves in a particular piece of litigation that there is a substantial lack of reciprocity in the implementation of an international agreement.

The mere fact that an EU measure would be invalidated by the EU courts on the basis of an international agreement to which they granted direct effect is unlikely to create a substantial imbalance in the implementation of that agreement to the detriment of the EU.[42] There would have to be other, rather more serious accompanying circumstances. These would have to be identified by the political branches of government. They should have determined that there is a substantial lack of reciprocity in the implementation of a particular agreement in a *regular* review, outside the context of litigation; and they should have indicated that certain steps were needed to redress that situation (which might include the suspension of direct effect, or even domestic law effect generally of that agreement in the EU). I also expect that governments will be more careful when attributing a substantial lack of implementation to another country in a general rule-making type of decision, duly published, than in largely confidential court pleadings in a specific case. Such a public decision will have to withstand the scrutiny of the other country, and of other interested parties.

It is true that, following such a rule-making type review, the courts would be bound by the assessment of reciprocity by another branch of government as well. But, as I have argued, there is a difference with the courts

---

[40] ECHR, *Chevrol v France*, No. 49636/99 (Sect. 2), ECHR 2003-III, 13 February 2003.

[41] CE, 9 July 2010, No. 317747, *Cheriet-Benseghir*: JurisData No. 2010–011132; Rec. CE 2010.

[42] In that particular case, the EU may simply have erred and infringed the international agreement at issue, without there being any indication that the EU's treaty partner (or the EU itself for that matter) is failing to implement the agreement on any significant scale.

relying on, and deferring to a reciprocity assessment that is made by another government branch within the context and for the specific purpose of litigation.[43] In short, in the event and for as long as the EU political institutions properly establish that there is a serious lack of reciprocity in the implementation of an international economic agreement, I would find it perfectly acceptable for the EU courts to decline or suspend any direct effect of that agreement. But how does one get to this result?

The key problem is that, pursuant to standing case law of the European Court of Justice, such a political assessment on lack of reciprocity would be frustrated as soon as and whenever the European courts have given direct effect to provisions of the international (e.g. WTO) agreement at issue. The reason is that the Court of Justice has normally coupled direct effect of international agreements with supremacy.[44] Expressed differently, once an international treaty provision has been given direct effect, the EU's legislature can no longer overrule or suspend that interpretation of the European courts through later legislation or decisions.

It should also be noted that the EU courts to date have given no indication that they would be willing to suspend the direct effect of an international agreement only *temporarily*, for as long as the state of a substantial disequilibrium continues. Yet the recognition of a temporary suspension is essential if one wants to deal with a lack of reciprocity. After all, one would like to think that the EU will normally be able to resolve serious imbalances in an international agreement to which it is a party or withdraw.

15.3 CONCLUSION

I agree with Jacques Bourgeois that one must give meaning to international economic agreements like the WTO by allowing private individuals to appeal to them in order to discipline domestic regulation. I also appreciate his concern that the benefits private individuals can draw from such agreements need to be circumscribed though, notably in the event that there

---

[43] This distinction was also recognized in the Opinion of the *Commissaire du Gouvernement* Schwartz of 9 April 1999 on the reciprocity principle, but not followed by the *Conseil d'Etat*, in the original *Chevrol*-litigation preceding the European Court of Human Rights judgment referred to *supra* p. 40. The importance of Mr Schwartz's Opinion was recognized by Rogoff, M.A., 'Application of Treaties and the Decisions of International Tribunals in the United States and France: Reflections on Recent Practice', *Maine Law Review*, Vol. 58, 2006, pp. 406, 460–61.

[44] E.g. Case C-549/07 *WallentinHermann* [2008] ECR I-11061, at para. 28.

is a substantial imbalance in the implementation of the agreement by the EU and its treaty partners.

In order to arrive at this balanced outcome, Bourgeois would be prepared to recognize in principle that the WTO can have direct effect, but then attach certain conditions narrowing this grant of direct effect. These conditions contain elements I find useful, and others with which I have more difficulty. Fundamentally, I do not believe that courts are well placed to assess whether the EU suffers from a substantial lack of reciprocity in the economic relations with its treaty partners. I also have a problem with the concept of direct effect, given its linkage with supremacy in the case law of the European courts. This has turned direct effect into an inflexible instrument.[45] In particular, once a treaty provision has been granted direct effect by the EU courts, the EU's political (and democratically elected) institutions are no longer allowed to suspend the benefits of this international economic agreement temporarily, when they determine that there is a substantial lack of reciprocity in its implementation by the EU's treaty partner(s).

Until we have found ways to turn direct effect into a more flexible instrument where international economic agreements are concerned, I am happy to see that the EU courts have developed techniques to pay respect to international rules and rulings without granting them direct effect. One important principle they have developed is that of treaty-consistent interpretation: whenever an EU measure permits several interpretations the courts feel obliged to choose the interpretation that is consistent with a relevant international agreement. Another fledgling technique developed more recently by the EU courts has been to transform international legal principles into an interpretation of EU law. In this way they can avoid inconsistencies with international rules or rulings of a competent international tribunal, while not being bound to always follow them. Through these techniques the European courts are creating a balance between private interests and overall European interests in giving domestic law effect to international economic law. This is still a work in progress.[46]

I believe it would be desirable for the EU political institutions to engage with these fundamental issues. The European Parliament made an effort in

---

45 See Bronckers, M., 'From "Direct effect" to "Muted dialogue": Recent developments in the European Courts' case law on the WTO and beyond', in M.K. Bulterman et al. (eds), *Views of European Law from the Mountain: Liber Amicorum Piet Jan Slot*, Austin et al., Wolters Kluwer, 2009, p. 403, at p. 414.

46 See generally Bronckers, *idem.*

a report of some years ago for instance,[47] and would be well placed to reinitiate a debate. The domestic law effect of international agreements like the WTO should not be left to the hazards of case-by-case court judgments with an occasional reflection by some interested private commentators.

[47] European Parliament – *Report of the Committee on Legal Affairs and Citizen's Right on the relationships between international law, Community law and the constitutional law of the Member States*, 24 September 1997, A4–0278/97, at pp. 13–14.

16. The Court of Justice and unrecognized entities under international law

Pieter Jan Kuijper

16.1 INTRODUCTION

Jacques Bourgeois was a mentor to many in the Legal Service of the Commission in the early 1980s – a status that did not rest on any formal arrangement. It was simply a matter of fact that, especially as a young Dutch-speaker in the Service, you inevitably gravitated towards this jovial and generous person for legal and personal counsel from time to time. Moreover, because of our temperaments and the force of circumstances we were professionally interested in the same issues, in particular competition and trade policy. And, within those fields, we suffered from the same fatal attraction to issues with a high political content.[1]

[1] A good example was the Siberian pipeline issue. Nordstream, Nabucco and Southstream, the controversial pipelines of today, had their antecedent in the Siberian gas pipeline of the early 1980s, despised by the Reagan administration as creating a dangerous dependence of western Europe on USSR gas deliveries. Accordingly the pipeline project was subjected to US export controls that not only curtailed US exports of oil and gas technology, but also purported to impede extraterritorially any such exports from the European Economic Community, as it then was, to the 'Soviet bloc'. This was considered unacceptable in the Community and soon Jacques and I were attending meetings of a special Council working group on the issue. Here the idea ripened that the Community might send a legal memorandum on the illegality of such extraterritorial export controls under international law to the United States, in order to make use of the opportunity to make public comments on the draft export controls. This was the summer of 1983. The Commission was charged with writing a draft of these comments. Jacques was called as a kind of legal firefighter to another big 'dossier'. It was then that he showed me great trust and let me fend for myself, while benignly looking at my drafts and steering me from a distance. Thus I found myself alone defending my successive drafts in what was a kind of COJUR, the group in which the legal

For that reason it is appropriate that an international law problem with high political content should be the subject of this contribution to the book honouring Jacques. Since the European Court of Justice has recently, once again, given an interesting judgment on the question of the treatment of unrecognized or contested entities or situations in international law,[2] it was not necessary to search very long.

16.2 COURTS AND UNRECOGNIZED OR CONTESTED ENTITIES IN INTERNATIONAL LAW

As in respect of all issues relating to the effect of international law and international agreements, the Court of Justice of the European Union (ECJ) operates in questions of recognition of entities whose status under international law is uncertain or contested as a kind of national supreme court. It is a sort of gatekeeper in charge of determining where and how far international law should enter the legal order of the Union[3] and, in cases involving the treatment of unrecognized entities, how far recognition, if any, should go.[4] As a starting point it is necessary to have a quick look at how national (supreme) courts have behaved in questions of recognition of contested entities or territories. This will make it possible to place the practice of the ECJ in such matters within a frame of reference that will give us the possibility to assess critically the practice in question.

From authoritative manuals of international law one may conclude that, though national courts have often hewn to the line of the executive in matters of recognition, they have also maintained a certain independence.

---

advisers of the ministries of foreign affairs of the member states meet, some 20 years before it actually came into existence. Since Jacques was the beneficiary of the same trust he showed me from the side of Claus Ehlermann, the extra-ordinary Director-General of the Legal Service in those days, in the end the draft resulting from the discussion with the member states in the Council was sent to the US government. This episode created a bond with Jacques that I have always cherished, even in periods that we did not see much of each other.

2 Case C-386/08, *Brita v Hauptzollamt Hamburg-Hafen*, Judgment of the Court of Justice of 25 February 2010, not yet reported.

3 As far as the use of the terms Union/Community, EU/EC etc. is concerned, this chapter follows the historical use of term of the ECJ, which even after entry into force of the Lisbon Treaty still uses the historical terms, if they are the official terms used in the acts of the EU at the time.

4 Snyder, F., 'The Gatekeepers: The European Courts and WTO Law', *Common Market Law Review,* Vol. 40, 2003, pp. 313–67.

In many instances, especially where the private legal situation of individuals was concerned (marriage, inheritance, property claims etc.), national courts have often been more inclined than national governments to accept the factual authority of states or governments over specific territories and to accept the consequences of such authority.[5] Thus the courts in the United States and the United Kingdom already began to give effect to nationalization decrees of the Soviet Union in the 1930s, even before the two countries had recognized the Soviet government.[6]

On the other hand, the United Nations has had great influence on the position of the governments, but also on the courts, of its Member States by taking strong positions on the non-recognition of the acts of governments or authorities that were considered illegitimate, and even outright illegal in certain circumstances.[7] The position of different UN organs in respect of the unilateral declaration of independence of Southern Rhodesia,[8] the continued presence of South Africa in Namibia,[9] the 'Turkish Republic of Northern Cyprus'[10] and the way in which Israel carries on the continued occupation of the West Bank, Gaza and East Jerusalem[11] are cases in point. These positions of the UN have been confirmed in advisory opinions of the International Court of Justice (ICJ) on the Legal Consequences for States of the Continued Presence of South Africa in Namibia[12] and on the Legal Consequences of the Construction of a Wall constructed

---

[5] See for instance Sir Robert Jennings and Sir Arthur Watts (eds), *Oppenheim's International Law*, London, Longman, 9th edn, Vol. I, pp. 201–2.

[6] *Idem*, pp. 202–3 and accompanying footnotes.

[7] See Dugard, J., *Recognition and the United Nations*, Cambridge, Grotius Publications, 1987, in particular ch. V.

[8] The Security Council ruled in SC Res. 216 (1965) and 217 (1965) that the unilateral declaration of independence should not be recognized.

[9] The Security Council in SC Res 276(1970) decided that South Africa's de facto rule over Namibia should not be recognized.

[10] The Security Council has called upon all States not to recognize the TRNC, which is considered the illegal fruit of the Turkish occupation of the northern part of Cyprus. S.C. Res. 541(1983) and 550 (1984).

[11] There are numerous UN resolutions condemning the continued occupation of these areas, for example SC Resolution 242 (1967), SC Resolution 605 (1987), AG Resolution ES – 10/15 (2004) on the ICJ Advisory Opinion on the Legal Consequences of the Construction of a Wall in the Occupied Palestinian Territory.

[12] Advisory Opinion on the Legal Consequences for States of the Continued Presence of South Africa in Namibia (South-West Africa) notwithstanding S.C. Resolution 276(1970), ICJ Reports 1971, p. 16.

by Israel with the aim to cut off the West Bank from Israel and protect certain communities of Israeli settlers.[13]

In particular the Advisory Opinion on Namibia spelled out in some detail which legal consequences UN members should draw from the situation in Namibia. The Court said that member states should be extremely careful in their diplomatic, consular, economic and treaty relations with South Africa not to do anything that could lead to implicit acceptance of the assertions of authority of South Africa over Namibia. The Court also notes that in principle the power to spell out specific consequences from SC Resolution 276 (1970) falls to the 'appropriate political organs of the United Nations acting within their authority within the Charter.'[14] Moreover, the Court also signals that the Security Council itself had already spelled out some specific consequences of such continued presence in its Resolution 283 (1970).[15] It would seem, therefore, that the ICJ was conforming in the Namibia case to the practice of national courts mentioned above of following the guidance of the political organs, in this case of the UN.[16] However, just as national courts, it was not doing so in an uncritical manner, in particular where it concerned the consequences for individuals. It moderated its rejection of any and all implicit recognition of South African authority over Namibia in the following manner:[17]

> In general, the non-recognition of South Africa's administration of the territory should not result in depriving the people of Namibia of any advantages deriving from international co-operation. In particular, while official acts performed by the government of South Africa on behalf of or concerning Namibia after the termination of the Mandate are illegal and invalid, this invalidity cannot be extended to those acts, such as, for instance, the registration of births, deaths and marriages, the effects of which can be ignored only to the detriment of the inhabitants of the Territory.

As we will see, this pronouncement of the ICJ played a role in later case law of the Court of Justice.

---

[13] Advisory Opinion on the Legal Consequences of the Construction of a Wall in the Occupied Palestinian Territory, ICJ Reports 2004, p. 136.

[14] See ICJ Reports 1971, p. 55, para. 120.

[15] *Ibid.* Resolution 283 mentioned *inter alia* the interruption of al diplomatic, consular and other official relations with South-Africa insofar as they related to Namibia; it also contained a call to all States to stimulate their private sectors not to begin or maintain economic relations with Namibia which would recognize the South African authority over the Territory.

[16] See in general ICJ Reports 1971, p. 55, paras. 120–24.

[17] ICJ Reports 1971, p. 56, para. 125.

16.3 HOW THE ECJ CONFRONTS UNRECOGNIZED AND CONTESTED ENTITIES

16.3.1 Miscellaneous Cases

First of all, it is interesting to note that the Court has never been put in a position to express itself on the situation of the German Democratic Republic during the period that it was not recognized by the member states (1958–72). During that period as well as when it was so recognized (1972–89), the GDR was in a rather peculiar situation as the 'hole in the internal market'.[18] There have been cases where issues arose that were linked to the unification of Germany, but none that placed the Court before the necessity to determine its position in respect of the GDR as an entity, the status of which was controversial.[19]

It is not surprising that the territories and states resulting from the break-up of the former Yugoslavia caused some problems to the ECJ. First there was the special case of Macedonia that even before its status had been determined to the full satisfaction of all member states, in particular Greece that contested its very right to bear the name 'Macedonia' without qualification, was already being protected by the Commission in a case before the Court. In this way the Commission reacted to what it considered to be the abuse by Greece of its right under what is presently Article 347 TFEU to take unilateral measures that Greece felt 'called upon to take' as a reaction to 'serious international tension constituting a threat of war'.[20] The Commission accompanied its submission to the Court by a request for interim measures. That request was rejected, as it was in the Court's view impossible to allow the interim measures without prejudicing the substance of the case.[21] After some kind of compromise had been reached between Greece and Macedonia (which was officially to be indicated by the acronym

---

[18] De facto the GDR constituted a hole in the internal market, as there were no tariffs in operation between the GDR and the FDR during the period from the beginning of the EEC. In reality, however, the consequences of this hole remained limited because of other obstacles to intra-German trade.

[19] See for example Case T-99/98, *Hameico v Council and Commission* [2003] ECR II-2195 concerning the succession of certain companies in the territory of the former GDR to EC banana quotas allegedly held by their predecessor companies.

[20] Article 348 TFEU allows the Commission to bring a case against a member state that in the Commission's view abuses the power of Article 347directly before the Court without a reasoned opinion as is required in the normal infringement procedure under Article 258.

[21] Case C-120/94R, *Commission v Greece,* Order of the Court [1994] ECR I-3037.

FYROM) and Advocate General Jacobs had published a fairly sceptical opinion,[22] the case was abandoned by the Commission and removed from the Court's docket.

Later on, Macedonia came back to haunt the ECJ in an antidumping case.[23] In this case the question arose whether antidumping duties could be imposed on sheets and plates of iron and steel from Macedonia under the authority of an ECSC antidumping decision of the Commission, which imposed such duties on the same products from Yugoslavia and which had not yet been adapted to the break-up of that country. It was argued by those who were struck by the antidumping duties that, in the succession between Yugoslavia and its successor states, the Federal Republic of Yugoslavia (Serbia and Montenegro) had been recognized as the sole successor state to the former Yugoslavia. Hence the duties could only be imposed on that state and not on imports from Macedonia.

The Court, largely following Advocate General Jacobs, decided, however, that considerations of state succession under international law could not determine the outcome of the case due to the specific function of antidumping duties. The function of such duties was to provide protection to a Community industry in response to a threat of unfair trade in products produced by specific companies in a specific territory. In the light of this function and as long as the unfair trade competition continued coming from those companies in the specific territory, it mattered little that the international status of that territory had changed in the meantime. Moreover arguments of state succession could not be of any avail as antidumping duties were not levies on the exporting state but on the companies concerned.[24] Hence sheet and plates of iron and steel from Macedonia could lawfully be hit by the antidumping duties on the relevant products from 'Yugoslavia'.

A similar problem, but with a different outcome, concerned the special preferential levies granted to so-called 'baby beef' from Yugoslavia, but in reality coming from Macedonia.[25] After the EC Cooperation Agreement with Yugoslavia was first suspended and then denounced in November 1991 upon the outbreak of large-scale hostilities inside the former Yugoslavia, this also spelled the end of a special regime of reduced levies on baby

---

[22] Because the case was removed from the docket of the ECJ at the request of the Commission, there is no official publication of the opinion of A-G Jacobs in the ECR.

[23] Case C-177/96, *Belgium v Banque Indosuez et al. and European Community* [1997] ECR I-5659.

[24] *Idem*, paras. 18–25.

[25] Case C-230/98 *Amministrazione delle Finanze dello Stato and Schiavon* [2000] ECR I-3562.

beef imported from Yugoslavia. In the course of 1992 that system was replaced by an autonomous regime in favour of baby beef imported from Bosnia-Herzegovina, Croatia, Macedonia and Slovenia. However, such baby beef had to be accompanied by a certificate of origin from specifically mentioned issuing bodies for Slovenia and Croatia. For Macedonia initially no issuing body was fixed. There was only a retroactive tolerance of certificates of origin issued by an entity operating in Beograd, the capital of Serbia (which itself was not allowed to profit from the autonomous regime for baby beef) for the first three months of 1992. A new issuing authority for Macedonia was only established by the Commission regulation relating to the baby beef regime for 1993.

Schiavon, an Italian importer had requested preferential treatment for baby beef imported from Macedonia after March 1992, relying on certificates issued by the entity from Beograd. The Court, following Advocate General Colomer, rejected this on the ground that it was important that all the conditions for importation under the preferential levies were strictly adhered to. In the absence of an issuing agency for certificates of origin having been appointed in the Commission Regulation, such reliance on certificates of the Beograd agency was not justified after March 1992. This was in particular important, according to the Court,[26] since a system for establishing the origin of products

> is founded on the principle of mutual reliance and cooperation between the authorities of the exporting State and those of the importing State. A system of that kind cannot therefore function properly unless the procedures for administrative cooperation are strictly complied with.

In such a situation, therefore, no flexible and broad interpretation on the basis of the function of the rules in question as in the case of the antidumping duties on products from Macedonia. However, it is possible to argue that the same technique of functional interpretation in respect of certificates of origin leads just as naturally to a narrow interpretation, excluding the issuance of Macedonian certificates of origin by an entity not from Macedonia, as it led to a broad interpretation in the case of the antidumping duties regarding iron and steel products from Macedonia as falling under rules relating to the same products from Yugoslavia. In both cases the result is a strong protection of the EU market.

---

[26] *Idem*, para. 53, referring to Case C-432/92 *Anastasiou I* [1994] ECR I-3087, paras. 38 and 40, see *infra* and accompanying text.

16.3.2 Cases concerning Northern Cyprus

16.3.2.1 The Anastasiou cases

There are three *Anastasiou* cases concerning the recourse to various techniques employed by the customs and phyto-sanitary authorities of member states and of Turkey to place the so-called Turkish Republic of Northern Cyprus (TRNC) in a position to export its agricultural produce to the EC at preferential rates laid down in the Association Agreement. They all date from before the accession of the Republic of Cyprus to the European Union in 2004. The separation between North and South dates back to 1973, when an attempt to force a unification between Greece and Cyprus by the dictatorship of the Greek colonels ended in an intervention by Turkey as one of the 'guarantor' states and finally in the drawing of the 'green line' patrolled by a UN peace-keeping force. The other guarantor power, the United Kingdom, continued its important military presence on the island. In 1983 the Turkish North proclaimed the TRNC – a declaration of independence that was declared illegal by the Security Council, which also enjoined all states not to recognize the TRNC.[27]

The *Anastasiou I* case[28] was the consequence of a policy of the Commission and a number of member states of the Union to accept certificates of origin and phyto-sanitary certificates issued by the de facto authorities of the TRNC (as long as they were not referred to by name) declaring Cyprus origin and phyto-sanitary safety and thus ensuring agricultural products from the North entitlement to these preferential rates. This policy was based on the notion that all the inhabitants of the island should be able to reap the fruits from the Association Agreement without discrimination, as prescribed by the non-discrimination clause of the Association Agreement (Article 5). In particular the United Kingdom and the Commission argued that such de facto acceptance of such certificates issued by the TRNC did not amount to recognition of the TRNC, but was simply a way to guarantee that the interests of the whole population of Cyprus was taken into account.

The Court, however, rejected this point of view out of hand on the basis that it did 'not warrant a departure from the clear, precise and unconditional provisions of the 1977 Protocol [to the Association Agreement] on the origin of products and administrative cooperation'.[29] It was of the view that the EC system of accepting movement certificates as certificates of

27 See S.C. Res. 541/83 and S.C. Res. 550/1984.

28 Case C-432/92 *R v Minister of Agriculture, Fisheries and Food, ex parte S.P. Anastasiou(Pissouri) et al.* [1994] ECR I-3087.

29 *Idem*, para. 37.

origin was based on complete confidence in the authorities of the exporting state. This can only function if the procedures for administrative cooperation are strictly complied with. In the Court's view such cooperation is excluded with the authorities of the TRNC 'which is recognized neither by the Community nor by the Member States'. In those circumstances accepting movement certificates not issued by the Republic of Cyprus would amount to a denial of the object and purpose of the 1977 Protocol.[30] This cannot be counterbalanced by the alleged breach of Article 5 of the Association Agreement. In the final analysis Article 5 cannot confer on the Community the right to interfere in the internal affairs of Cyprus.[31]

The Court also rejected the Commission's reference to the Advisory Opinion on Namibia, and in particular its statement to the effect that 'the non-recognition of South Africa's administration of the territory should not result in depriving the people of Namibia of any advantages deriving from international cooperation'. In the Court's view the special situation of the two territories was not comparable both as to the law and the facts.[32]

The reasoning relative to the issuance of phyto-sanitary certificates was based on fundamentally the same arguments. Nevertheless the Court recognized that such certificates theoretically could be replaced by controls at the border, though in reality this was not feasible, since such border checks had serious limitations.[33]

It is remarkable that at the time the Court's judgment was reasonably well received by Community lawyers, who noted that it was based on a very strict interpretation of the relevant provisions, which depended on some basic assumptions, such as the view that the clear words of the 1977 Protocol were basically incompatible with the interpretation of Article 5 on non-discrimination advanced by the Commission and the United Kingdom. In spite of what was perceived as the Court's somewhat cramped style of argumentation, most Community lawyers could not really find fault with the Court's tendency to literal interpretation, especially in the highly charged political climate surrounding the case.[34]

International lawyers, however, were relatively critical of the case. They pointed to a trend in state practice and case law from national courts away from regarding non-recognized governments as non-existent and towards accepting their day-to-day acts in so far as they were in line with public

---

30 *Idem*, paras. 38–9. See also *supra* and accompanying text.

31 *Idem*, paras. 40–41.

32 *Idem*, para. 49.

33 *Idem*, paras. 56–64.

34 See for example M. Cremona, Annotation of Case C-432/96, *Common Market Law Review*, Vol. 33, 1996, pp. 125–35.

policy. They argued that the ECJ was insufficiently aware of this trend both in US and UK case law. They also argued that the Court's rejecting the Namibia precedent overlooked the fact that the ICJ's core point had been that non-recognition should not be applied to the detriment of the local population. They felt that the ECJ thus was de facto instituting an economic sanctions regime to which the Security Council had never acceded.[35]

The *Anastasiou II* case[36] followed six years later and continued where the *Anastasiou I* case had left off, namely with the possibility that phyto-sanitary certificates required for the importation of fruit into the EU could be issued by a third country through which such fruit transited and not just by the country of origin. This was a possibility of obvious interest to the TRNC exporters of citrus fruit who could probably obtain such certification from authorities in Turkey.

The ECJ admitted that it did not necessarily flow from its judgment in *Anastasiou I* to the effect that member states were not allowed to accept phyto-sanitary certificates issued in the country of origin by authorities that were not recognized, that such certificates could not be validly issued by a non-member consignor country. The basic objective of the relevant EU directive is to protect the territory of the EU from the introduction and spread of organisms harmful to plants. This objective can also be achieved by certificates issued by the authorities of third consignor countries, in spite of the fact that the place of production remains the most appropriate place. The required close collaboration between the EU authorities and the country issuing a phyto-sanitary certificate can take place with the consignor country.[37] The Court did subject this acceptance of the authority of a non-member consignor country to a few conditions such as: the plants have been imported in the consignor country before being exported from there to the EU; the plants have remained in that country long enough to enable the proper checks to be carried out; and the plants are not subject to special requirements that can only be satisfied in their country of origin.[38]

Three years later *Anastasiou III*[39] dealt precisely with this situation, namely that in so far as Cyprus had been recognized under EC legislation as

---

[35] Greenwood, C. and Lowe, V., 'Unrecognized States and the European Court', *Cambridge Law Journal,* Vol. 54, 1995, pp. 4–6. See also Talmon, S., 'The Cyprus Question before the European Court of Justice', *European Journal of International Law,* Vol. 12, 2001, pp. 727–50, who pointed to other precedents of states accepting export certificates from non-recognized entities.

[36] Case C-219/98, *R v Minister of Agriculture, Fisheries and Food, ex parte S.P. Anastasiou (Pissouri) Ltd and others* [2000] ECR I-5241.

[37] *Idem*, paras. 31–2 and 37.

[38] *Idem*, para. 38.

[39] Case C-140/02, *R on the application of S.P. Anastasiou (Pissouri) Ltd. and others v Minister for Agriculture, Fisheries and Food* [2003] ECR I-10635.

being free of certain noxious pests, the special origin mark linked to the determination that indeed the goods were free from such pests had to be affixed in the country of origin, *in casu* Cyprus, by the recognized authorities of the Republic of Cyprus. The Court felt obliged, however, to go through a long and painstaking analysis of the relevant Community directive 77/93 and its annexes before arriving at this outcome.[40]

Analysing the three *Anastasiou* cases, it is relatively easy to arrive at the conclusion that the Court indeed did not pay attention to international law and how it was being applied more and more by national courts in the member states and the United States, as well as by the International Court of Justice, in cases concerning unrecognized or contested entities and their 'governmental actions'. The Court felt not much inclined to follow their example and to accept and recognize such actions as long as they did not seem clearly contrary to the public policy of the forum, while affecting the subjective rights of its citizens and long-term residents. To the contrary, the Court seemed to feel compelled to go for an extremely analytical and strongly literal interpretation of the EU legislation and the Union's international agreements at issue. The ECJ probably believed that in this way it would shield itself against any assertion that it was being 'too political' in these cases.

16.3.2.2 The Orams case

This case concerns the story of the Orams family from the United Kingdom who bought land in northern Cyprus from a private party who in turn had bought it from the TRNC government. The land had belonged to the Apostolides family before the Turkish invasion of northern Cyprus in 1974, but the purchase of the land was claimed to have occurred in good faith and in conformity with TRNC law. The Orams family built a villa on the land and use it frequently as their holiday home.

Meletidis Apostolides sued the Orams family in a Nicosia court and succeeded to have a default judgment entered against them ordering the villa and swimming pool to be demolished, the land delivered to Mr Apostolides and various sums paid to him constituting damages, rent for use of the land and cost and expenses of the proceedings. All appeals by the Orams family were rejected by the higher courts of the Republic of Cyprus. As the case arose after the accession of Cyprus to the EU in 2004, Mr Apostolides then attempted to have the judgment of the Cyprus Court recognized and enforced in England in accordance with the relevant procedures of Regulation No. 44/2001, the so-called Brussels I Regulation. After

[40] To arrive at this relatively straightforward result, the Court needed no less than 76 paragraphs.

further procedures in the English courts this led to preliminary questions asked by the Court of Appeal (England and Wales) to the Court in Luxembourg.[41]

Thus the ECJ found itself once more confronted with the status of the acts of an unrecognized entity, but now one which in principle is regarded as being an integral part of a member state of the EU and whose authority is essentially upheld by the troops of a country that is engaged in accession negotiations with the Union. Even more than in earlier cases the acts of the unrecognized entity were relied upon by individuals and contested by other individuals, all of them Union citizens. All this against the background of a settlement of the Cyprus question in which both the UN and the EU had heavily invested, only to see it shot down with the active encouragement of the government of the Republic of Cyprus of the day, whilst the unrecognized entity and the occupying candidate country, after initial and possibly too long hesitations, were supporting it.[42] This in turn resulted in the law of the Union being suspended 'in those areas of the Republic of Cyprus in which the Government of the Republic of Cyprus does not exercise effective control'.[43]

This toxic mix of political elements might well have inspired many courts to throw up their arms and declare 'a political question' and thus injusticiability of the case, but not so the Grand Chamber of the European Court of Justice. It continued on the road it had taken before in the *Anastasiou* cases, namely with a highly technical, black letter approach to the interpretation of Protocol 10 and of the relevant provisions of the Brussels I Regulation, strongly relying on the fact that the TRNC had not been recognized by the EU or by any country of the world except Turkey. The case is too complicated to do justice to all aspects here, but the main steps of the Court's approach will be recalled.[44]

First of all, the ECJ, following Advocate General Kokott, interpreted Article 1 of Protocol 10 restrictively, since it was an exceptional measure. The fact that the litigation was about land in an area over which the authorities of the Republic of Cyprus exercised no effective control and

---

41 Case C-420/07 *Meletidis Apostolides v David Charles Orams and Linda Elizabeth Orams* [2009] ECR I-3571.

42 See for more detail, Hoffmeister, F., *Legal Aspects of the Cyprus Problem, Annan Plan and EU Accession*, Nijhoff, Leiden, 2006.

43 Article 1(1) of the Protocol 10 on Cyprus to the Act of Accession, OJ (2003) L 236, p. 955.

44 For an exhaustive and excellent comment on the case see Geert de Baere, Annotation of Case C-420/07, *Common Market Law Review*, Vol. 47, 2010, pp. 1123–59.

that the land thus was not subject to such control mattered less than the fact that the judgment for which recognition and enforcement was sought came from a court sitting in the government-controlled area. If the English courts apply the rules of Regulation No. 44/2001 to such a judgment, this does not imply that the Regulation is being applied in the northern part of Cyprus.[45]

Secondly, the Commission raised the question of whether a judgment the material facts of which rest ultimately on the exercise of authority by the de facto government in the North, namely its nationalization/ confiscation of Greek Cypriot property, remains 'a civil or commercial matter' and thus might not be covered by the Regulation. This was dismissed by the Court on the basis of the formal argument that the case in question is purely one between individuals and not brought against conduct which involves the exercise of public authority and thus was a case concerning 'civil and commercial matters'.[46]

Thirdly, the Court was confronted by questions about the fact that the judgment related to land over which the government of the member state did not exercise effective control could be an obstacle to recognition and enforcement under Regulation No. 44/2001. The ECJ ruled that these circumstances were no reason to argue that the national court had infringed the rule of jurisdiction of Article 22 of the Regulation, since in the present case it was a question not of excess of international jurisdiction, but a question of the internal jurisdiction of the Cypriot courts, which was a prerogative of the member state to decide. [47]

Moreover the lack of effective control over the North in practice could also be an obstacle to the enforcement of the judgment there. Could this be a reason to refuse recognition for reasons of public policy under Article 34 of the Regulation? In this respect the Court recalls that the courts in the member state in which enforcement is sought cannot refuse such enforcement simply because they are of the view that the case has been wrongly decided as a matter of Community law (or, for that matter, national law). In such situations the system of legal remedies in the member states combined with the preliminary question procedure gives a sufficient guarantee to individuals that the requesting state will not ask for enforcement of judgments that include misapplications of Community law.[48]

However – and here the ECJ itself extracts a new element from the questions of the Court of Appeal – it could be argued that the practical lack

---

45 Case 420/07, *supra*, paras. 36–9.
46 *Idem*, paras. 40 and 43–6.
47 *Idem*, paras. 48–52.
48 *Idem*, paras. 59–62.

of possible enforcement in the North would create an obstacle to enforcement in England under Article 38(1) of the Regulation. This provision has been interpreted by the Court as implying that the enforceability of the judgment in the member state of origin is a condition for its enforcement in the member state where enforcement is sought. In the end the Court's position is summarized in the following pithy statement:[49]

> The fact that claimants might encounter difficulties in having judgments enforced in the northern area cannot deprive them of their enforceability and, therefore, does not prevent the courts of the Member State in which enforcement is sought from declaring such judgments enforceable.

Fourthly, the Court was confronted by the question whether the lack of proper service of the court documents on the Orams family before the default judgment was an obstacle to enforcement of the judgment in England. Here the Court, for once in this case, went to the substance of the rights in question, basing itself on earlier case law. Accordingly it decided that since the Orams later on in the procedures before the Cyprus courts had been able to carry on a proper defence of their interests and had actually done so after instituting appeal, there had been no abridgement of the rights of the defence.[50]

There can be little doubt that the *Orams* judgment of the ECJ is in line with the Anastasiou cases in respect of the approach followed by the Court to a highly controversial and *politically*-loaded case, namely to hew strictly to a non-political line, to stick to Community/Union law and to interpret it strictly, basing itself on the wording and on its own case law, while not paying attention to broader developments in international law. Thus from reading the judgment one would never learn that the TRNC 'government' had created a compensation mechanism for confiscated 'Greek' property in the North as from 2005. This mechanism has recently received some kind of benediction from the European Court of Human Rights, which has accepted that those who have had no recourse to this mechanism have not exhausted all local remedies and are, therefore, not admissible in their claims against Turkey under the European Convention of Human Rights.[51] Only the Advocate General dealt with this question and dismissed it.[52] It

---

49 *Idem*, para. 70.

50 *Idem*, paras. 76–9.

51 See Judgment of the Grand Chamber of the ECtHR of 1 March 2010, *Demopoulos and Others v Turkey.*

52 For a more thorough treatment of this aspect of the case, see De Baere, *supra*, pp. 1138–43.

remains typical for the Court's fixation on Union law and nothing but Union law that it does not evoke the question in its judgment, if only to follow the Advocate General and say something to the effect that the existence of the compensation scheme is no bar to civil claims in the courts of the Republic of Cyprus and any consequent requests for enforcement elsewhere in the Union. Although there is no conflict between the two courts on the issue, a softer landing would have been possible.

16.3.3 The Rights to Preferential Treatment as between Israel and Palestine: The Brita Case

16.3.3.1 Background

The basic question underlying the *Brita* case[53] had been brewing for a long time between the Commission and the Government of Israel in discussions carried on in the framework of the organs of both the old and the new Association Agreement between the EU and Israel.[54] The discussion concerned the territorial scope of the Agreement, which on the Israeli side was simply described as 'the territory of the State of Israel'. It was also about the quality of the cooperation between the two parties in the framework of the administrative cooperation procedure instituted under Article 32 of the Fourth Protocol to the Agreement on the rules relating to originating products.

The EU view was that products that originated in Jewish settlements on the West Bank did not have Israeli origin, whereas the Israeli authorities were of the opposite view. There was a third opinion, namely that this difference of opinion was without real object, since both the Association Agreement with Israel and the EC–PLO Association Agreement provided for free trade in industrial products. Thus goods, whether they originated in Israel or in the West Bank, were always entitled to freedom of tariffs.[55]

The Commission had already openly complained about the lack of cooperation from the Israeli side, when determining the origin of goods from the occupied territories and published a notice to importers and

---

[53] Case C-386/08, *Brita v Hauptzollamt Hamburg-Hafen*, Judgment of the ECJ of 25 February 2010, not yet reported. See also my annotation in *Legal Issues of European Integration*, Vol. 37, No. 3, 2010, pp. 241–51.

[54] The new Association Agreement was approved by Decision 2000/384/EC, ECSC of 19 April 2000, OJ (2000) L 147/1. It was one of the new generation of so-called Mediterranean Agreements. These agreements have now become part of the so-called Neighbourhood Policy.

[55] This was the view of the *Finanzgericht* Hamburg which referred the case to the ECJ.

raised the issue in the EU Council in the years 1997 and 1998 respectively. When a thorough discussion in the Association Council EU–Israel in the presence of the then Israeli Minister of Foreign Affairs, Shimon Peres, had once again not led to much improvement, the Commission again published a notice to importers that constituted a clear warning to those who imported goods from Israel. The notice stated that Israeli authorities also issued certificates of origin for goods imported from the settlements in the occupied territories. The Commission expressed the view that the Israeli authorities were not entitled to do so. Consequently importers could not claim preferential tariff rates for such goods under the Association Agreement. Importers were clearly warned of the risk that they could incur customs debt, if they did not take precautions in this matter.[56]

16.3.3.2 The case

Matters came to a head, when Brita, a company that is best known for its water filters, imported a number of sparkling water drink-makers produced by Soda-Club Ltd in Mishor Adumin, an Israeli settlement on the West Bank close to Jerusalem. On the customs declarations and the invoices, the origin of these goods was declared to be Israel. Although the German customs authorities provisionally accepted these customs declarations and initially let the goods enter without levying any duties in conformity with the EU–Israel Association Agreement, they started a long procedure of verification and exchanges with the Israeli customs authorities. When the Israel authorities in the end did not reply to a pointed question whether the goods came from Israeli settlements in the occupied territories, this clinched the question for the German customs service and it imposed payment of the applicable customs duties on Brita to the tune of some €20,000. Brita then started procedures in the German customs courts, which led to the reference from the Hamburg *Finanzgericht* to the ECJ. This account will concentrate on the question whether the customs authorities of the importing member state should refuse preferential treatment under the Association Agreement where the goods originate in the occupied West Bank.

The crucial and somewhat daring aspect of the ECJ's approach to this question is how the Court in its interpretation of the relevant provisions of the EU–Israel Association Agreement, and in particular the article referring to the 'territory of the State of Israel', has recourse not just to the usual

---

[56] Notice to Importers – Imports from Israel into the Community, of 23 November 2001, OJ (2001) C 328/6. See also more generally the excellent account of the factual and legal background to the case in the Opinion of Advocate General Bot, see paras. 9–58, especially pp. 26–31.

articles on treaty interpretation in the Vienna Convention on the Law of Treaties 1969, which it often refers to, namely Articles 31 and 32, but also to Article 34, the so-called *pacta tertiis* rule.[57] In order to give colour and texture to what the 'territory of the State of Israel' in Article 83 of the EC–Israel Agreement is supposed to mean, the court draws into the balance the EC–PLO Association Agreement. Just as it flows from the relevant provisions of the EC–Israel Agreement and the relevant protocols that the Israeli authorities are competent to issue certificates of origin for goods from the exporting state, similarly the EC–PLO Agreement and its protocols state clearly that if products can be regarded as originating in the West Bank and the Gaza strip, the customs authorities of the West Bank and the Gaza Strip have sole competence to issue a movement certificate EUR 1 bestowing that origin.[58]

Thus, the Court arrives at the conclusion that the authorities both of the State of Israel and of the Palestinian Authority have the exclusive power within their own jurisdiction to issue certificates of origin. If the Israeli interpretation were to be followed and the Israeli authorities would have that power in the occupied territories as well, the Palestinian customs authorities would be bereft of their power recognized by the EC–PLO Agreement. That in the eyes of the Court would constitute a clear case of *pacta tertiis*. As a consequence Article 83 of the EC–Israel Agreement has to be interpreted 'as meaning that products originating in the West Bank do not fall within the territorial scope of that agreement and do not therefore qualify for preferential treatment under that agreement'.[59]

As to the theory of the *Finanzgericht* according to which goods from Israel and the West Bank should always profit from one of the two agreements and hence should always receive preferential treatment: in the eyes of the Court, however, this reduces the issuing of certificates of origin by a competent authority to a mere formality. This is not acceptable – and here the ECJ reverts to its judgment in *Anastasiou I* – since the Court has already stated that certificates of origin issued by authorities other than those indicated by name in the relevant association agreement cannot be tolerated.[60]

The crucial question with respect to the approach followed by the Court, when it takes into account the *pacta tertiis* rule in the interpretation of the territorial scope of the EC–Israel Association Agreement, is of course

57 From the Latin maxim *pacta tertiis nec nocent nec prosunt,* i.e. agreements cannot be to the detriment or to the advantage of a third party.

58 Case C-386/08, paras. 43–50.

59 *Idem*, paras. 51–3.

60 *Idem*, paras. 55–7.

whether the Court in doing so has not exposed Israel to having to accept an obligation derived from an agreement between third parties, namely the EC–PLO Agreement. There are several considerations that mitigate this objection.

First of all, purely from the viewpoint of the Court, it was incumbent on it to act in line with the presumption against conflict between two international agreements concluded by the same state or international organization and hence to apply a harmonizing interpretation between the two international commitments undertaken by the EU.

Secondly, it is not as if Israel was totally unaware of the consequences of the Oslo Accords and subsequent agreements for the international status of the Palestinian Authority; it is natural that third states and organizations such as the EC would conclude agreements with the PLO or the Palestinian Authority and that these needed to link in with the consequences of the Oslo Accords in respect of the transfer of powers. It is probably for this reason that the Court puts emphasis on the identical objective of the two association agreements, respectively with Israel and the PLO.

Thirdly, as Advocate General Bot pointed out at length, Israel also has concluded in the framework of the Oslo process a so-called Interim Agreement with the Palestinians, which transferred powers in the field of commerce and industry, including import and export, to the Palestinian authorities, even in areas, such as where Mishor Adumin was located, in which Israel would retain exclusive competence in matters of security. Moreover, the Palestinians would have the right to export their industrial products without restrictions, on the basis of certificates of origin issued by the Palestinian Authority.[61]

It was possibly too difficult and too awkward for the ECJ, as Court of an international organization of which Israel was not a member, to confront that country with an agreement to which the EC was not a party, but there is little doubt that Bot's information on this agreement formed an important background against which the Court's judgment should be read since it related to obligations accepted by Israel itself, which tended to corroborate the Court's approach to the interpretation of the EC–srael Agreement in the light of the EC–PLO Association.

16.4 CONCLUSIONS

The *Brita* case is somewhat of a departure, but at the same time also a continuation in a different form of the earlier case law of the ECJ in respect

---

[61] Case C-386/08, Opinion AG Bot, paras. 38–48.

of unrecognized or contested entities or situations under international law. In none of the cases discussed above has the Court substantially deviated from the line of action broadly laid out by the relevant UN organs. However, nowhere in these judgments has the Court expressly referred to the relevant decisions of the UN bodies, except to say in passing in the Cyprus cases that no country, including the members of the Union, had recognized the TRNC. To the contrary, the Court has stuck very closely to the law of the Union to the point even, as we saw in the Macedonian cases, to rely on the function of the Community rules in question such as antidumping rules in order to interpret the origin of the products subject to an antidumping decision.

The same can be said of the Cyprus cases, where the Court refers neither to any appreciable degree to the international context, nor to the evolution of case law elsewhere in the world where it concerns the question what attitude to take if normal actions of unrecognized governments affect individuals. The ECJ in such cases insists on a very literal and strict interpretation of the relevant Community law and does so with great precision and effectiveness. In this way it seeks to avoid being seen to be 'playing politics' in such cases. It would seem that it has largely succeeded at that, but one may ask the question whether as a result of this approach the Cyprus question is being fought in the Court at the expense of and over the backs of individuals who happen to have been caught between the two parties, whilst relying on de facto situations that had seemed stable over a long period of time and were relying on actions of the authorities both in Cyprus and in the Union of the authorities which seemed to enhance this stability.

The *Brita* case is different for two reasons. First of all, the reaction of the international community embodied by the UN to the two cases was very different. The Palestinians had always profited from a modicum of international support for their position (although honoured more in words than in deeds), expressed for instance by their special enhanced observer status in the UN General Assembly. On the other hand the TRNC 'government' had always suffered unmitigated official opprobrium from the same world community. Secondly in *Brita*, perhaps for the reason just explained, the Court could be more bold and innovative than in the other cases in its interpretation of the relevant legal instruments of the Union, introducing interpretation in the shadow of *pacta tertiis.* Moreover, the Union instruments referred to were all international agreements and hence the Court seemed more open than in the other cases here discussed. On the other hand the international agreements in question were all agreements of the Union so that the Court could show again that in politically loaded questions it restricted itself to the handiwork it knew best, interpreting Union law.

17. The *Brita* ruling of the European Court of Justice: a few comments

Marc Maresceau

17.1 INTRODUCTION AND BACKGROUND

In his introduction to a volume on the phenomenon of rules of origin in international trade law published in 1994,[1] Jacques, after recalling the purpose of rules of origin and the different methods to establish origin, moved on to more existential questions such as the legitimacy of preferential rules of origin and the relationship between rules of origin and the international division of labour. While at first sight rules of origin appeared 'as an exclusively technical, albeit practically important, subject matter', it was evident for him that they rapidly also took on both a legal and, often, perhaps a political dimension. The recent *Brita* ruling of the European Court of Justice is perhaps the most perfect illustration of this point and explains the choice of this contribution for Jacques' *liber amicorum*.

On 25 February 2010 the Court of Justice of the European Union for the first time provided an interpretation of the Association Agreement between the EC and its Member States and Israel signed in 1995 (hereafter the 'EC–Israel Association Agreement') in the aftermath of the Oslo Peace Process and ratified in 2000 when, unfortunately, the momentum of that process had already largely vanished.[2] The case had been brought before the Court of Justice following a reference for a preliminary ruling by a

---

[1] Bourgeois, J., 'Rules of Origin: An introduction', in E. Vermulst, P. Waer, J. Bourgeois (eds), *Rules of Origin in International Trade: A Comparative Study*, Ann Arbor, The University of Michigan Press, 1994, pp. 1–5.

[2] For the text of this agreement, see OJ (2000) L 147/3. The association agreement needed the assent of the European Parliament. This and the mixed nature of the agreement requiring ratifications by the EU member states combined with the deteriorating political climate in the Israeli–Palestinian relations, caused considerable delay in its entry into force. Where possible, alongside mixed agreements, often an interim agreement is signed incorporating the trade and trade-related provisions of the mixed agreement. Such an interim agreement between the EC and Israel entered already into force in 1995. The first questions relating to the

German Court after a dispute had arisen when a German importer (Brita GmbH) challenged customs duties imposed on imports of drink-makers for sparkling water manufactured in an Israeli settlement in the West Bank. These products had received a EUR 1 certificate attesting Israeli origin from the Israeli customs authorities, while the German customs considered these products not to originate in Israel and therefore refused to recognize the origin as stated in the documents. As a consequence, the imported goods in Germany could not benefit from the free trade provisions of the EC–Israel Association Agreement.

The case raised various questions regarding the legal effect of a declaration of origin by the authorities of the exporting country and the possible role of the Customs Co-operation Committee as established under Protocol 4 to the EC–Israel Association Agreement in solving disputes between the parties concerning verification of origin. Needless to say, however, the case also went far beyond the technical aspects of a mere judicial interpretation of the EC–Israel Association Agreement and quickly – how could it otherwise? – assumed a broader trade policy and indeed important political dimension. In particular, it soon appeared that the question could not be dealt with without also considering the Interim Association Agreement on trade and co-operation between the EC and the Palestine Liberation Organization (PLO) for the benefit of the Palestinian Authority of the West Bank and the Gaza Strip (hereafter the 'EC–PLO Interim Agreement') concluded in 1997.[3]

The relevant provisions of the two bilateral agreements should be recalled briefly. Article 7 of the EC–Israel Association Agreement stipulates that the provisions on trade liberalization apply to products originating in the Community and 'in Israel'. Customs duties on imports and exports and charges having equivalent effect are prohibited between the Community and Israel. Article 75(1) of the Agreement allows each of the parties to refer to the Association Council any dispute relating to the application or interpretation of the agreement. Article 83 defines the territorial scope of the agreement and reads as follows:

> This Agreement shall apply, on the one hand, to the territories in which the Treaties establishing the European Community and the European Coal and Steel Community are applied and under the conditions laid down in those Treaties and, on the other hand, to the territory of the State of Israel.

---

certification of origin in the relations EC–Israel emerged under the regime established by the Interim Agreement.

[3] For the text of this agreement, see OJ (1997) L 187/3.

Protocol 4 to the EC–Israel Association Agreement (hereafter the 'EC–Israel Protocol') contains the definition of the concept 'originating products' and lays down the methods of administrative cooperation. Products 'originating in Israel' are defined as products 'wholly obtained in Israel within the meaning of Article 4 of this protocol'. Also products containing products not wholly obtained in Israel may be considered as 'products originating in Israel' on condition that the products in question have undergone sufficient working or processing in Israel. This formulation of the criteria of origin in the protocol is identical to that in many free trade agreements concluded by the EU with third states. It should be noted that neither the agreement nor the protocol define the expressions 'territory of the State of Israel' or 'in Israel'. For the EU it was evident that the expressions 'territory of the State of Israel' or 'in Israel' were to be understood as not comprising the occupied territories since 1967: any attempt by Israel in the negotiation to include within the territorial scope of the 1995 Agreement and Protocol territory beyond the 1967 border of the State of Israel would certainly have encountered insurmountable difficulties and would simply have prevented the signature of the agreements. From an Israeli perspective the West Bank and Gaza Strip do not form part of the 'territory of the State of Israel' but Israel has annexed East Jerusalem and the Golan Heights. Regarding the West Bank and Gaza Strip, an Israeli–Palestinian Interim Agreement was signed in 1995 providing *inter alia* a scheme for the transfer of powers and responsibilities from the Israeli military authorities and civil administration to the Palestinian authorities, and allowing the latter to conclude economic agreements with other parties. The military occupation of the Gaza Strip ended as a result of Israel's unilateral disengagement in 2005, but Israel continues to control access to and exit from that territory. For Israel the delimitation of the border of the occupied territories, the question of the settlements and also that of the goods exported from these settlements have to be part of a global agreement with the Palestinians.[4] In any such a global political solution for the Israeli-Palestinian conflict, security considerations must of course have a prominent place.

Concrete implementation of the free trade principles is organized through the issuance of a EUR 1 certificate for the movement of goods. As a general rule, and again the EC–Israel Association Agreement is no exception to this, it is the customs authorities of the exporting state that certify the origin of the products in question. With regard to the methods of administrative cooperation

---

[4] For an overview of the different approaches, see Pardo, S. and Peters, J., *Uneasy Neighbors. Israel and the European Union*, Lanham, Lexington Books, 2010, in particular pp. 47–68.

between the parties, the agreement provides that if an importing state has doubts about the precise origin it may request further information from the authorities of the exporting state. Should no adequate response or no response be provided by the exporting state within ten months, the importing state shall, except in case of *force majeure* or in exceptional circumstances, refuse entitlement to trade preferences. The protocol also provides that where disputes arise regarding the verification of proof of origin procedure that cannot be settled between the customs authorities requesting a verification and those responsible for carrying out the verification, they shall be submitted to the Customs Co-operation Committee.

The EC–PLO Interim Agreement and relevant protocol (Protocol 3) contain very similar provisions as those just mentioned. It is not the place here to examine the unique legal character of that agreement in detail.[5] Suffice it to recall that the party contracting with the EC is not a state[6] but the PLO, that the agreement is an interim agreement to soon be followed by a Euro–Med Association Agreement proper, something which, fifteen years later, has not yet happened and that the legal basis for the conclusion of the agreement was not (the then) Article 310 EC concerning association agreements, but rather Article 133 EC concerning trade agreements. In addition, the agreement, contrary to the EC–Israel Association Agreement, was non-mixed, which made a rapid conclusion and swift entry into force possible. On the basis of the EC–PLO Interim Agreement, the 'free movement of goods' provisions apply to products originating or having undergone sufficient working or processing, 'in the West Bank and Gaza Strip'. The administrative cooperation indispensable to apply these provisions relies on the issue of the movement certificate EUR 1 'by the customs authorities of the exporting country' (Article 16(1) of the EC–PLO Agreement). Certainly at first sight, the formulation 'exporting country' is somewhat astonishing since the territory for which the Palestinian Authority has competence is not yet that of an internationally recognized state. But Article 16(4) of the Agreement removes any ambiguity as to the territorial scope of the Agreement by holding that this certificate is to be issued by 'the

---

[5] So far, little legal analysis has been made of this agreement. One of the rare in-depth legal studies remains that of Lannon, E., 'L'accord d'association intérimaire: Communauté européenne-OLP: l'institutionnalisation progressive des relations euro-palestiniennes', *Revue des affaires européennes*, 1997, pp. 177–90; for a more concise legal comment, see Maresceau, M., *Bilateral agreements concluded by the European Community*, Recueil des Cours de l'Académie de droit international, Leiden-Boston, Nijhoff, 2006, Vol. 309, pp. 400–07.

[6] On 'unrecognized entities' in EU law, see contribution by P.J. Kuijper in this volume.

customs authorities of an EC Member State or the West Bank and Gaza Strip if the products concerned can be considered as products originating in the Community, the West Bank and Gaza Strip'; in other words, as far as products originating in the West Bank and Gaza Strip are concerned, by the Palestinian authorities.

As already mentioned, German customs authorities had serious doubts that goods imported by Brita into Germany and certified by the Israeli customs as 'originating in Israel', satisfied the conditions for preferential treatment under the EC–Israel Association Agreement since the goods concerned were manufactured in the Israeli settlement Mishor Adumin in the West Bank. Requests for additional information by the German authorities to the Israeli authorities had resulted in a statement by the latter that 'verification has proven that the goods in question originate in an area that is under Israeli Customs responsibility'. For the Israeli authorities the goods 'were originating products pursuant to the EC–Israel Association Agreement and are entitled to preferential treatment under that agreement'. A subsequent additional German request as to whether the goods were manufactured in the West Bank or Gaza Strip, East Jerusalem or the Golan Heights had remained unanswered by the Israeli side. Consequently, the German authorities refused preferential treatment for the import of the goods in question and this led Brita to bring an action before the *Finanzgericht* Hamburg.

17.2 THE COURT'S REPLY AND SOME COMMENTS

17.2.1 The Territorial Scope of the Free Trade Provisions

In its preliminary ruling the Court first establishes the territorial scope of the EC–Israel Association Agreement and, in order to do so, seeks support in the Vienna Convention on the Law of Treaties. The Court is of the opinion that the general principle of international law, incorporated in Article 34 of that convention according to which a treaty does create neither obligations nor rights for a third state without its consent (*pacta tertiis nec nocent nec prosunt* or principle of the relative effect of treaties) needs to be applied. In the question before the Court there are two distinct bilateral agreements to be considered and each of which has its own territorial scope. While it is true that both agreements pursue the same objective of favouring free trade and trade liberalization, the declaration on the origin of the goods that is necessary to allow preferential treatment should be made by the customs authorities of the exporting country. This declaration is a crucial intervention in the organization of a free trade framework and for the Court, the customs authorities of the exporting states 'have exclusive competence – within their territorial jurisdiction – to issue movement certificates EUR 1 or to approve exporters based in the territory under their administration'.[7] The consequence of this approach is evident and in the words of the Court, Protocol 3 to the EC–PLO Interim Agreement implies that, if the products can be regarded as products originating in the West Bank or the Gaza Strip, it is the customs authorities of the West Bank and Gaza Strip that have 'sole competence to issue a movement certificate EUR 1'.[8]

In order to sustain this view the Court explicitly invokes the *Anastasiou* ruling of 5 July 1994, which concerned the legal effect of certificates issued by the authorities of the Turkish Republic of Northern Cyprus certifying Cypriotic origin of goods produced in the Northern part of Cyprus. In that case the Court held that the validity of proof of origin issued by authorities other than those designed by name in the relevant association agreement could not be accepted: only movement certificates EUR 1 issued by the customs authorities of the Republic of Cyprus could be used within the framework of the Association Agreement with the Republic of Cyprus.[9] The rationale behind the reasoning in the *Anastasiou* case is easy to understand: a system which allows preferential treatment 'is founded on the principle of mutual reliance and co-operation between the competent authorities of the exporting State and those of the importing State'. This implies that acceptance of certificates by the customs authorities of the importing state 'reflects this total confidence in the system of checking the origin of products as implemented by the competent authorities of the exporting State'.[10] In *Brita*, the Court emphasizes that the origin of goods is in principle established by the authorities of the exporting state since they are 'best placed to verify directly the facts which determine origin'.[11] Such a system can indeed only function properly if the customs authorities of the importing state can accept the determinations legally made by the authorities of the exporting state.

But the question in the *Brita* case was not whether the goods were wholly obtained in a certain location or whether they had undergone sufficient processing there, but whether the imported goods 'fell within the territorial

---

[7] Para. 51.

[8] Para. 50.

[9] Case C-432/92, *R v Minister of Agriculture, Fisheries and Food, ex parte S. P. Anastasiou (Pissouri) Ltd and others* [1994] ECR I-3087.

[10] *Anastasiou, supra*, paras. 38 and 39.

[11] *Brita*, para. 61. The Court relied for this statement on Case 218/83, *Les Rapides Savoyards and others* [1984] ECR 3105, para. 26.

scope of the EC–Israel Association Agreement'. As Advocate General Bot rightly observes in his Opinion on this case 'the main proceedings are not concerned with verifying the accuracy of information relating to the product origin that creates entitlement to preferential treatment, since the origin is known and is not contested' but '[t]hey are in fact concerned with ascertaining whether that origin falls within the scope of the EC–Israel Agreement'.[12] Hence, the dispute could not be seen as a question of fact or as a technical verification issue but was in essence one regarding the territorial application of the EC–Israel Association Agreement. As a direct consequence, the Court of Justice had to reject the so-called 'elective determination' approach as to the classification of the imported goods. The referring court had drawn the attention of the Court to the fact that 'in any event' both agreements aimed to achieve the same objective of establishing free trade with the Community and that, ultimately, preferential treatment was granted for goods originating in territory of the State of Israel *and* of the West Bank. However, as a result of the territorial scope approach followed by the Court, such a reasoning had no chance of being accepted and this had also been made unequivocally clear by the Advocate General in his Opinion where he held that 'it would not be consistent for the preferential treatment established by that agreement to be applied to a product for which a EUR 1 certificate has been issued by authorities other than the Palestinian authorities'.[13]

Consequently, applying the *Anastasiou* ruling in the *Brita* case was a logical move in the reasoning of the Court and the Advocate General but an additional question still needed to be answered. Article 33 of the EC–Israel Protocol provides that where disputes arise in relation to the verification procedure or where questions arise as to the interpretation of that protocol, 'they shall be submitted to the Customs Co-operation Committee'. Therefore, regarding the territorial scope of the EC–Israel Agreement, the Court was of the opinion that the existence of Article 33 of the EC–Israel Protocol did not affect the competence of the German authorities to refuse certification of origin provided by the Israeli customs authorities. According to the Court, the Customs Co-operation Committee is only an administrative body entrusted with the performance of a technical task in the customs field and 'it cannot be regarded as having competence to settle disputes concerning questions of law such as those relating to the interpretation of the EC–Israel Association Agreement itself'.[14] Of course, it is true that questions of such a nature can always be brought

---

[12] Opinion, Case C-386/88, para. 86.
[13] Opinion, para. 131.
[14] Para. 69.

before the Association Council but dispute settlement procedures formally foreseen in bilateral agreements concluded by the EU with third states have only very rarely been used in practice and as a matter of fact, not one of the consultations initiated on the basis of these procedures has ever resulted in a final decision on the dispute. Clearly, diplomatic channels to settle disputes between parties are preferred and the EC–Israel Association Agreement is no exception to this practice. Thus, notwithstanding the existing divergence of views as to the territorial scope of the agreement, there was never an initiative before the Association Council to take a decision settling the dispute on the basis of Article 75 of the Agreement. On the basis of that provision the Association Council may settle a dispute by means of a binding decision and in the event no such decision can be taken there is the possibility to appoint arbitrators. But all this would in practice have been difficult to achieve since a decision of the Association Council can only be taken by 'common agreement' of the parties.[15] Also the fact that the dispute had not been referred to the Association Committee, an emanation of the Association Council, could, according to the Court, not be used as a justification to derogate from the system of cooperation as foreseen in the agreement.[16] However, not making use of the dispute settlement procedure and/or trying through diplomatic channels to find a solution does not mean that any judicial intervention is *a priori* to be excluded. A particular interpretation by national authorities of an agreement concluded by the EU can be contested before a national court of the EU member states. Already in early case law on the effect of bilateral agreements, the Court of Justice has emphasized that 'the mere fact that the Contracting Parties have established a special institutional framework for consultations and negotiations *inter se* in relation to the implementation of the agreement is not in itself sufficient to exclude all judicial application of the agreement'. Moreover, 'the fact that a court of one of the parties applies to a specific case before it a provision of the agreement involving an unconditional and precise obligation and therefore not requiring any prior intervention on the part of the joint committee does not adversely effect the powers the agreement confers on that Committee'.[17] In other words, the existence of a dispute settlement procedure in an agreement does not prevent national courts from applying provisions of the agreement on condition of course that these provisions have direct effect.

15 Article 10 of Decision No. 1/2000 of the EU–Israel Association Council adopting its rules of procedure.

16 Para. 72.

17 Case 104/81, *Kupferberg* [1982] ECR 3641, paras. 19 and 20.

17.2.2 The Wider Legal and Political Context

It is useful to place the Court's ruling in *Brita* against the broader legal and political context of the relations between the EU and Israel and the EU's position towards the Israeli–Palestinian conflict. Of course, within the framework of this chapter, only a few brief comments can be made. The EU, together with most of its partners in the world, is in favour of a two-state solution for this conflict. The Israeli settlement policy in the Occupied Territories combined with the separation wall built on occupied territory has always been rejected by the EU since it results 'in confiscation of Palestinian land'.[18] Israeli settlements in these territories pose a significant obstacle to peace, prejudge the outcome of final status and render more difficult if not impossible the establishment of a viable Palestinian state.[19] Of course, the recent policy of the Israeli Government to support the building of new housing units in East Jerusalem and the Government's intention to favour further settlement development instead of a continuation of the settlement freeze, have also been firmly condemned by the EU.[20] In the wording of the 'Declaration on the Middle East Peace Process' of the European Council of 16 September 2010 this is formulated as follows: 'The European Union recalls that settlements are illegal under international law and calls for an extension of the moratorium decided by Israel.' The EU has also consistently held that it will not recognize any changes to the pre-1967 borders other than those agreed between the parties themselves[21] and has refused systematically to accept that territories placed under Israel administration since 1967 qualify for preferential treatment under the EC–Israel Association Agreement.[22]

The *Brita* case was certainly not the first dispute regarding the application of the rules of origin in the EU–Israel relations. The deterioration of

---

[18] See, for example, GAERC Conclusions 22 March 2004.

[19] There are innumerable EU declarations and statements in this respect. For a selection, see for example Declarations by the EU Presidency of 14 July 2008, 11773/08 (Presse 210) or of 18 December 2009, 17698/09 (Presse 385); also statements in External Relations Council meetings, see 2951st meeting, 15–16 July 2009, Presse 174 (10939/09) or 2817th meeting, 23 July 2007, Presse 171 (11914/07); and by the EU at the EU–Israel Association Council, Luxembourg 16 June 2008.

[20] See, for example, Declarations of the Presidency of 9 September 2009 and 18 December 2009, 13044/1/09 (Presse 262) and 17698/09 (Presse 385); also Declaration of HR Ashton of 10 March 2010, 7374/10 (Presse 58) and 27 September 2010, A 190/10.

[21] See, for example, Euro–Mediterranean Mid-term Meeting of Ministers of Foreign Affairs, Dublin 5–6 May 2004.

[22] See, for example, Answer by Mr Kovács on behalf of the Commission on Written Question by M. De Rossa, European Parliament, 29 August 2005, E-2427/2005.

the peace process from 1995 onwards has also accentuated the rules of origin issue. Already soon after the signature of the 1995 EC–Israel Agreement, questions had arisen regarding the application of these rules.[23] In 1997 the European Commission published a Communication on the Implementation of the Interim Agreement on trade and trade related matters between the European Community and Israel[24] stating that there were a number of obstacles that stood in the way of the correct implementation of the EC–Israel Interim Agreement. The Commission noted that the Israeli view, according to which there should be Israeli jurisdiction in the Israeli settlements in the West Bank and Gaza Strip, was not in conformity with international law and various UN Security Council resolutions were invoked in support of the Commission's approach. The Commission also reiterated in clear terms the EU view that the EC–Israel Association Agreement did not cover exports originating in Israeli settlements in the West Bank and Gaza Strip nor exports originating in East Jerusalem and the Golan Heights. In the Communication the Commission further drew attention to the fact that for exports of products from the Occupied Territories there was a tendency to contract Israeli exporters. The reason for that were the many obstacles imposed upon such exports by Israeli authorities. Particularly, security checks often damaged or delayed Palestinian traded products and made them more expensive. Moreover, in Israeli ports and airports, the Commission noted that in general priority was given to Israeli shipments. With regard to exports from the Israeli settlements the Commission urged the European Community to take action to bring the violation of the rules of origin to an end. On 8 November 1997, a few months after the publication of this Communication, the Commission published a *Notice to importers. Importations from Israel into the Community*, expressing grounds for doubt regarding the validity of EUR 1 certificates for importations in the Community and regretting the lack of effective administrative cooperation with the Israeli customs authorities.[25] While initially the Commission was targeting fraudulent exports of Brazilian orange juice to the EC under Israeli certificates of

---

[23] For an analysis of the legal background, see Paasivirta, E., 'EU trading with Israel and Palestine: Parallel legal frameworks and triangular issues', *European Foreign Affairs Review*, 1999, pp. 305–26; for a trade policy background, see Sadeh, T., 'Israel and a Euro-Mediterranean Internal Market – A survey of existing barriers to trade and possible remedies', in P. Xuereb (ed.), *Euro-Mediterranean Integration – The Mediterranean's European challenge*, Malta, European Documentation and Research Center, 2002, Vol.III, pp. 182–243.

[24] SEC (1998) 695 final, 12 May 1998.

[25] OJ (1997) C 338/13.

origin, the question soon moved on to the issue of origin of goods produced in Israeli settlements in Palestinian Occupied Territory. An important follow-up to this notice – which obviously had not produced the desired results – was a new notice of 23 November 2001, this time aiming more specifically at the origin of products from the settlements.[26] This notice informed the economic operators 'that Israel issues proofs of origin for products coming from places brought under Israeli administration since 1967, which, according to the Community, are not entitled to benefit from preferential treatment under the Agreements'. Consequently

> Community operators presenting documentary evidence of origin with a view to securing preferential treatment for products originating from Israeli settlements in the West Bank, Gaza Strip, East Jerusalem and the Golan Heights, are informed that they must take all the necessary precautions and that putting the goods in free circulation may give rise to a customs debt.

Notwithstanding this unequivocal EU position, difficulties continued to arise and it was only in 2003 that there were signs of a possible 'technical solution' to this legal and also highly political dispute. In November 2003, Israeli authorities announced that they were prepared to indicate the city of origin on the label of the exported goods.[27] Through the channels created by the EC–Israel Association Agreement – that is for this question the Customs Co-operation Committee – the parties were able to arrive at a 'technical arrangement' on the implementation of Protocol 4 to the EU–Israel Association. Legally speaking, the arrangement was not a decision of the Association Council but whatever the legal nature of the arrangement, the good thing was that a 'practical solution' had been found. Afterwards, economic operators were informed through a notice to importers on imports from Israel into the Community that all movement certificates EUR 1 and invoice declarations made out in Israel 'will bear, as from 1 February 2005 the name of the city, village or industrial zone where production conferring originating status has taken place'.[28] The notice also made clear that goods indicating that production conferring origin status

---

[26] OJ (2001) C 328/6. The need for a Commission clarification on the matter had also been triggered following a ruling of the Court of First Instance of the European Communities in *Importation of Television Sets from Turkey* in which the Court had emphasized the Commission's duty to informing economic operators on the legal uncertainty about the regularity of certain Turkish customs certificates: Case T-186/97, *Kaufring v Commission* [2001] ECR II-1337.

[27] See 'Exports to EU will indicate whether from territories', *Haaretz*, 25 November 2003.

[28] OJ (2005) C-20/2.

had taken place 'in a city, village or industrial zone which is brought under Israeli Administration since 1967' would not be granted preferential status.

After the 2005 Notice, there have been a number of complaints that the technical arrangement has not always been applied properly[29] and regularly parliamentary questions on this have been raised in the European Parliament: the *Brita* case is a clear example of a disfunctioning of the established rules but on the whole, it appears that the Commission is satisfied with the application of the arrangement.[30] A number of complaints tend to focus on the question of labelling. Certainly, the issue of proper labelling in general is a matter of concern for the Commission but the 2005 Notice deals with the rules of origin and verification procedures aiming to establish the appropriate tariff on imports originating in Israel and it does not, as such, aim to regulate labelling issues. Labelling rules and procedures 'are meant to provide correct information to the customer'.[31] Consequently, the *Brita* ruling does not concern the labelling of products imported from Israel and the Court does not deal with this question but, that said, on imports also

---

[29] For example, it has been alleged that some companies in settlements use their units located in Israel or 'invent' within the 'Green line' an address to conceal the real origin of the product, see BBC News, 11 May 2008, 'Concern over Israeli Settlement exports'. It also appears that some national administrations of the member states have discussed with the European Commission certain aspects related to the implementation of this arrangement. For example, the Dutch Minister of Economic Affairs has informed the Dutch 'Tweede Kamer' that a suggestion implying a change of the burden of proof of origin had been discussed with DG TAXUD but that the Commission had rejected such an idea as non-realistic and lacking a legal basis: see Letter of 11 June 2010, Ministry of Economic Affairs, addressed to the President of the Second Chamber on 'Follow-up kamerdebat over invoer van producten uit door Israël bezette gebieden'.

[30] Answer by Mrs Ferrero-Waldner on behalf of the Commission on Written Question by Mrs McCarthy, European Parliament, 4 May 2009, E-1242/2009; also Mr De Gucht on behalf of the Commission on Written Question by Göran Färm a.o., European Parliament, 27 July 2010, E-4237/2010. It has also been alleged that exporters from Israeli settlements in the occupied territories were being compensated by the Israeli treasury if preferential status on their exports was being refused in the EU. In 2008 the Commission acknowledged that she was aware of this practice and that the Israeli authorities 'have established a budget line to compensate exporters producing in the occupies territories for not being eligible to preferential access to the EC market': see Answer by Mr Mandelson on behalf of the Commission on Written Question by Erik Meijer, European Parliament, 15 February 2008, E 6033/2007. It is not clear whether this practice has led to formal complaints by the European Commission.

[31] Answer by Mr De Gucht on behalf of the Commission on Written Question by Eva-Britt Svensson, European Parliament, 21 June 2010 E-226/2010; also Mr Füle on behalf of the Commission on Written Question by Franz Obermayer, European Parliament, 1 July 2010, E-2605/2010.

from Israel, EU consumer law applies. For foods imported in the EU, this means among others Directive 2000/13/EC on the labelling, presentation and advertising of foodstuffs.[32] That directive provides that if in principle the indication of the place of origin of goods is voluntary, consumers may not be misled as to the true origin or provenance and for a number of agricultural products such as wine and fresh fruits – not irrelevant in EU–Israel trade relations – even more strict rules apply. For these goods the labelling of the country of origin is obligatory. The Commission takes the view that such goods, if they originate in settlements in the West Bank and Golan Heights, 'should be in line with Security Council Resolutions and the 1949 Geneva Convention, that these settlements are not part of the State of Israel'.[33] The Commission is also of the opinion that it remains within the competence of the authorities of the member states and the national courts to apply the national laws implementing EC law. It should be noted that some national administrations in the member states have made suggestions for economic operators regarding labelling of produce from the West Bank. Perhaps the best known example of such an intervention is that of the British Department for Environment, Food and Rural Affairs. In a recent Technical Advice from these authorities it is stated that the label may indicate whether the product originates from an Israeli settlement or from Palestinian producers.[34] In addition, the advice also holds rather outspoken views on the matter where it is stated 'that traders would be misleading consumers, and would therefore almost be certainly committing an offence, if they declare products from the OPT (including from the West Bank) as *Produce of Israel*', but on this issue no cases before British courts seem so far to have been reported.

17.3 CONCLUSION

Allowing Israeli customs authorities competence to deliver movement certificates for goods manufactured in the occupied territories and exported to the EU would implicitly have extended the territorial scope of the EC–Israel Association Agreement beyond the internationally recognized borders of the State of Israel. For legal as well as political reasons this would have been a bridge too far and it is not astonishing that the *Brita*

---

32 OJ (2000), L 109/29.

33 Answer by Mr Mandelson on behalf of the Commission on Written Question by Charles Tannock, European Parliament, 4 June 2007, E 1725/2007.

34 See 'Technical Advice' on the labelling of produce grown in the Occupied Palestinian Territories, 10 December 2009.

ruling has been warmly welcomed by the EU. European Commissioner De Gucht has observed that the Court's ruling 'convincingly confirmed the relevance and correctness of the Commission's policy on the import of Israeli settlement products, which had been consistently applied since 2004'.[35] At the moment of writing there seems to be no official reaction from the Israeli authorities to the Court's judgment and it is still early for comments on the Court's ruling in legal writing. One of the annotations soon to be published is that of Harpaz and Rubinson.[36] Drawing inspiration from the writings from M. Hirsch,[37] it makes a more than laudable attempt to understand and explain the Court's approach. On the one hand the authors convey the message that the Court's ruling 'is well-founded in legal terms and inevitable in political terms' but they also argue that the Court's reliance on international law nevertheless remains 'one-dimensional, incomplete and selective'. The author of the present contribution, however, does not share the criticism that the Court did not sufficiently address the primary object and purpose of the EC–Israel Association Agreement and therefore did not sufficiently adopt a 'trade-practical approach'. On the contrary, the Court was right to emphasize why the examination of the territorial scope of agreements was not only unavoidable but also so crucial in providing an answer to the German Court. A main aspect in this respect was the fact that the EC had next to an agreement with Israel also concluded an agreement with the PLO. Both agreements have their own territorial scope and, of course, it must be said that it is also true that the final outcome of the Court's ruling, whatever the reasoning might have been to reach this, fits perfectly well with the EU's and member states' approaches to the Israeli Palestinian conflict as a whole. It would have been totally unrealistic to have expected a different outcome than that which results from the Court's *Brita* ruling.

---

35 See Answer to Written Question by Göran Färm a.o., European Parliament, 27 July 2010, E-4237/2010.

36 I am grateful to the authors of the annotation: 'The interface between trade, law and politics and the erosion of normative-power Europe: Comment on *Brita*', which was sent to me before its publication. The annotation was published in *European Law Review*, 2010, pp.551–70, after the completion of this text.

37 Hirsch, M., 'Rules of origin as foreign policy instruments?', *Fordham International Law Journal*, 2002–03, pp. 572–94. Professor Hirsch was one of the first to present an in-depth comparative analysis of the application of rules of origin in territorially disputed areas and his study is required reading for any further research on this topic.

18. The standing requirements for bringing a direct action before the General Court in the field of trade defence and customs following the entry into force of the TFEU

Philippe De Baere

18.1 INTRODUCTION

Companies importing products originating in third countries into the EU customs territory may be confronted with an increase in the import duties payable upon importation due to a reclassification of the imported product under a new tariff line or as a result of the imposition of trade defence measures such as antidumping duties. In certain cases, the new duty level may even make the continuation of the import activity commercially non-viable and force importers to close their business. Yet, the judicial remedies available to such importers under the EC Treaty used to be limited, costly and time-consuming. In fact, under the rules applicable before the entry into force of the Treaty on the Functioning of the European Union (TFEU), importers had to challenge the application by the customs authorities of the measure imposing the higher duty, in most cases a Commission or Council regulation, before the national courts of each member state of importation and invoke in the context of this national procedure the illegality of the underlying Community act. Importers then had to hope that at least one national court would eventually refer the question on the legality of the classification or antidumping regulation to the Court of Justice[1] by means of a request for a preliminary ruling.[2]

[1] The Court of Justice of the European Communities has been renamed the Court of Justice of the European Union since the entry into force of the TFEU. It embodies the Court of Justice, the General Court (formerly, the Court of First Instance) and the Civil Service Tribunal. When referring to these courts generally,

The inability of importers to bring a direct action for annulment against Commission regulations reclassifying a product in the Combined Nomenclature or against a Council regulation imposing antidumping measures has led to a multiplication of national court proceedings. In each member state of import the importer will need to go through the national administrative procedures before being able to bring a national court challenge. These national court procedures will continue in parallel until one court eventually decides to refer a question on the validity of the regulation underlying the contested customs decision to the Court of Justice. Only then will the importer be able to ask for the suspension of the other court procedures until the Court of Justice issues its preliminary ruling. This whole process normally takes at least four years and often even longer. During this period, the importer will either need to pay the higher customs or antidumping duties or stop importing as long as no final judgment is issued.

The complexity of bringing an indirect challenge is particularly frustrating in the field of antidumping since regulations imposing antidumping measures normally have a period of validity of five years only. This means that the most an importer is likely to achieve is the annulment of a measure that has either already expired or has been replaced by a new measure following an expiry or interim review investigation. Since antidumping duties are frequently set at a level that makes any further imports commercially impossible, a successful court challenge in such circumstances will be perceived by the importer as meaningless. It is probably for this reason that indirect actions brought by importers against antidumping regulations are very rare.[3] Although this problem does not pose itself to the same extent in the field of customs duties, it is clear that the protracted uncertainty about the legality of a classification regulation and the corresponding level of the customs duties due has a negative impact on business.

Many of these problems would not arise if importers had the right to bring a direct action for annulment against classification and antidumping

---

the term 'European Union Courts' or 'CJEU' will be used. This new terminology will be used also for cases before the entry into force of the TFEU.

2 Article 234 EC Treaty, now Article 267 TFEU. Private applicants may also bring actions for failure to act (Article 265 TFEU) or for damages (Article 340 TFEU). Moreover, an incidental claim of illegality may be raised before the CJEU on the basis of Article 277 TFEU.

3 Most such references are brought where due to a reclassification or a change in the origin determination, antidumping duties become due and not as an alternative to a direct action. See, e.g. Case C-373/08, *Hoesch Metals and Alloys GmbH v Hauptzollamt Aachen* [2010] ECR 0000 and Case C-56/08, *Pärlitigu OÜ v Maksu- ja Tolliameti Põhja maksu- ja tollikeskus* [2009] ECR I-6719.

regulations. The strict interpretation given by the CJEU to the requirements that private applicants must meet before they can bring a direct action for annulment against a Community act of general application such as a regulation excludes, however, most importers from this direct route. The following analyses the standing requirements applicable to importers that wish to bring an action for annulment against a regulation imposing an antidumping duty or against a customs classification regulation before and after the entry into force of the fourth paragraph of Article 263 TFEU.

18.2 THE STANDING REQUIREMENTS UNDER THE FOURTH PARAGRAPH OF ARTICLE 230 EC TREATY

18.2.1 General

Pursuant to the fourth paragraph of Article 230 EC Treaty, a direct action can only be brought against a decision[4] which, although in the form of a regulation or a decision addressed to another person, is of direct and individual concern to the applicant.

'Direct concern' has been interpreted as requiring that the measure directly affects the legal situation of the applicant and leaves no discretion to the addressees of the measure, who are entrusted with its implementation. This implementation must be automatic and result from Community rules without the application of intermediate rules.[5]

The second, cumulative, requirement, namely that the measure must also be of individual concern to the applicant has led to more discussion and criticism. Under the interpretation adopted by the Court of Justice in *Plaumann,*[6] it is required that a decision not addressed to the applicant nevertheless affects him individually by certain attributes that are peculiar

---

4 Since Case C-309/89, *Codorniu SA v Council*, [1994] ECR I-1853, if a regulation satisfies the test for individual concern, no further proof of its 'true' nature as a 'decision in disguise' will be required.

5 Case T-243/01, *Sony Computer Entertainment Europe v Commission* (SCEE) [2003] ECR II-4189, para. 62; Case C-152/88, *Sofrimport v Commission* [1990] ECR I-2477, para. 9. The same applies where the possibility for addressees not to give effect to the Community measure is purely theoretical and their intention to act in conformity with it is not in doubt: Case 11/82, *Piraiki-Patraiki and Others v Commission* [1985] ECR 207, paras. 8–10; Joined Cases C-68/94 and C-30/95, *France and Others v Commission* [1998] ECR I-1375, para. 51 and Case T-80/97, *Starway SA v Council* [2002] ECR II-0001, paras. 61–9.

6 Case 25/62, *Plaumann v Commission* [1963] ECR 95.

to him or by reason of circumstances in which he is differentiated from all other persons and by virtue of these factors distinguishes him individually just as is the case of the person addressed by the decision. Moreover, this requirement must also be met in the abstract. It is not sufficient that the applicant is the only company concerned in practice at the time the decision was taken. It must also be demonstrated that it is theoretically impossible that other applicants at an undefined time in the future will be concerned by the measure.

Likewise, where an applicant wishes to challenge a regulation rather than a decision, it is not sufficient for the applicant that the regulation in fact applies only to a limited number of parties and that it is possible to determine the number or even the identity of the parties affected by the regulation. The measure will not be considered as being of individual concern to the applicant where it applies to objectively determined situations and produces legal effects with regard to categories of persons described in a generalized and abstract manner.[7]

Both antidumping measures and classification regulations are measures of general application. Nevertheless, the CJEU has much more frequently concluded that private applicants had standing to challenge antidumping regulations than in cases where classification regulations were challenged. This seems to be due to the fact that in antidumping cases several distinct categories of applicants can be distinguished, namely complainants, exporting producers and importers and that the CJEU's interpretation of the standing requirement has been less strict for the former two categories only. This different approach has on occasion been justified by the fact that importers could bring an indirect action through the national courts as an alternative to a direct action for annulment.

18.2.2 Admissibility of a Direct Action for Annulment against an Antidumping Regulation

The imposition of antidumping measures on imports of products originating in certain third countries is the trade defence measure most frequently applied by the EU. Antidumping measures are adopted following an investigation initiated at the request of a complaining EU industry that

---

[7] Case 790/79, *Calpak SpA v Commission* [1980] ECR 1949, para. 9: 'the measure applies to objectively determined situations and produces legal effects with regard to categories of persons described in a generalized and abstract manner. The nature of the measure as a regulation is not called in question by the mere fact that it is possible to determine the number or even the identity of the producers to be granted the aid which is limited thereby'.

submits evidence showing the existence of injurious dumping. The measures themselves are imposed by Council Regulation upon proposal of the Commission and apply to all imports of the product concerned having the origin of the third country investigated. Depending on their price and cost data, company-specific antidumping duties may be imposed on third country producers together with a countrywide residual duty. Importers will have to pay upon importation the antidumping duty at the rate applicable to their third country supplier or, in case no individual rate has been determined for the supplier, the residual duty.

Direct challenges against the imposition of antidumping measures have been brought by foreign exporting producers, unrelated importers and the complaining Union industry. Although antidumping measures are clearly measures of general application that are applicable indiscriminately to all importers of the product concerned, several of these challenges have been declared admissible.

Starting with *NTN Toyo Bearing*[8] and *Allied Corp.*,[9] the Court of Justice has accepted that measures imposing antidumping duties are liable to be of direct and individual concern to those producers and exporters who are able to establish that they were identified in the measures adopted by the Commission or the Council or were concerned by the preliminary investigations.

This decision seems at least partially to have been motivated by the fact that a refusal to grant standing could have conflicted with the EU's international obligations since such a refusal would have left exporting producers that were not at the same time importers without means of legal redress.[10]

---

[8] Case113/77, *NTN Toyo Bearing Company and Others v Council* [1979] ECR 1185.

[9] Joined Cases 239/82 and 275/82, *Allied Corporation and others v Commission* [1984] ECR 1005.

[10] See *Allied Corp., supra*, para. 9: '[the Commission] was in favour of the admissibility of direct actions brought by undertakings from non-member countries and, in any event, of those brought by the applicant undertakings on the ground that they were expressly mentioned in the statement of the reasons for, and in the provisions of, the contested measures. The Commission considers that such an approach would have a beneficial effect on the interests of Community undertakings in non-member countries in the event of the initiation of antidumping proceedings against them, particularly in the United States of America where the means of redress are to a large extent available to undertakings from other countries. The Commission takes the view that, in the interests of reciprocity, it is appropriate to provide similar guarantees under the judicial system of the Community.' See also the obligation contained in Article 13 *'Judicial Review'* of the

Likewise, the Court of Justice in *Timex*[11] declared admissible an action brought by a complaining producer because the objections submitted by Timex, at that time the only manufacturer of the product in question in the United Kingdom and the leading manufacturer in the Community, lay at the origin of the complaint made by the association that led to the opening of the investigation procedure. Moreover, Timex' views were heard during the procedure and the antidumping duty had at least partially been determined in the light of the injury caused to Timex. Finally, Timex, not being an importer, would have found it impossible to bring an indirect action through the national courts.

The more economic analysis made by the Court of Justice in *Timex* was unfortunately not followed when the Court came to analyse the standing of unrelated importers. The Court considered in *Alusuisse*[12] that the fact that there were only a limited number of identifiable importers of the product concerned and that the applicant had participated in the procedure leading up to the imposition of the measures was insufficient to obtain standing since 'the distinction between a regulation and a decision may be based only on the nature of the measure itself and the legal effects which it produces and not on the procedures for its adoption'.[13] The Court also emphasized that such a conclusion was in conformity with the system of remedies provided for by Community law since importers may contest before the national courts individual measures taken by the national authorities in application of the Community regulations.

The fact that the Court of Justice examined each time whether or not the applicant had the possibility of bringing an indirect action before the courts of the member state of import suggests that the Court interpreted the standing requirements for private applicants differently depending on the availability of alternative means of legal redress.[14]

This approach was abandoned by the Court of Justice in *Extramet Industrie SA v Council (Extramet)*.[15] As argued by Advocate General Jacobs in his Opinion, the economic situation of Extramet was not unlike

---

Uruguay Round Agreement on Implementation of Article VI of the General Agreement on Tariffs and Trade 1994.

11 Case 264/82, *Timex Corporation v Council* [1985] ECR 0849.

12 Case 307/81, *Alusuisse Italia SpA v Council and Commission* [1982] ECR II-3463.

13 *Idem*, para. 13.

14 Case C-50/00 P, *Unión de Pequeños Agricultores v Council* [2002] ECR I-6677, para. 44: '[...] this last condition must be interpreted in the light of the principle of effective judicial protection by taking account of the various circumstances that may distinguish an applicant individually'.

15 Case 358/89, *Extramet Industrie SA v Council* [1992] ECR I-3813.

that of Timex and as he stated, 'it is not easy to see any justification for distinguishing in this respect between the position of complainants and independent importers'. He therefore defended acknowledging the admissibility of an action brought by any undertaking whose participation in the proceedings before the Commission can be regarded as having affected their outcome.[16]

As in *Timex,* the Court of Justice in *Extramet* based its decision to declare the application admissible on economic considerations:[17]

> [t]he applicant has established the existence of a set of factors constituting such a situation which is peculiar to the applicant and which differentiates it, as regards the measure in question, from all other traders. The applicant is the largest importer of the product forming the subject-matter of the anti-dumping measure and, at the same time, the end-user of the product. In addition, its business activities depend to a very large extent on those imports and are seriously affected by the contested regulation in view of the limited number of manufacturers of the product concerned and of the difficulties which it encounters in obtaining supplies from the sole Community producer, which, moreover, is its main competitor for the processed product.

Unlike in *Alusuisse*, the Court of Justice did not consider that the standing criteria for private applicants should be the applied more strictly for importers because they, unlike exporters and complainants, could bring an indirect action via the national courts and that this different treatment was therefore in conformity with the system of remedies provided for by Community law.

Advocate General Jacobs had argued in his Opinion that such an interpretation of the standing requirements would not be in conformity with the Court's previous case law on standing since importers related to exporters had been granted standing in the past even though they could have challenged the validity of the antidumping measures by means of the preliminary reference procedure.[18] The possibility that this could lead to

---

16 Opinion of Advocate General Jacobs in Case 358/89, *Extramet Industrie SA, supra*, para. 66.

17 Case 358/89, *Extramet Industrie SA, supra* note 16, para. 17; see, however, Case T-138/98, *ACAV and Others v Council* [2000] ECR II-341, para. 66: '[as] to the arguments going to the serious economic impact which the contested regulation has on the applicants' business, the fact that a legislative measure may have specific effects which differ according to the various persons to whom it applies is not such as to differentiate them in relation to all the other operators concerned where that measure is applied on the basis of an objectively determined situation.'

18 Opinion of Advocate General Jacobs in Case 358/89, *Extramet Industrie SA, supra*, para. 70.

dual actions had not been considered by the Court as a sufficient reason for refusing standing to related importers. As the Court of Justice stated 'there is no risk of conflicting decisions in this area since, by virtue of the mechanism of the reference for a preliminary ruling under article 177 of the EEC Treaty, it is for the Court of Justice alone to give a final decision on the validity of the contested regulations'.[19]

In an Opinion that foreshadowed his Opinion in *Unión de Pequeños Agricultores v Council,*[20] Advocate General Jacobs further argued that preliminary reference proceedings, as an alternative to a direct action, present serious disadvantages to importers subject to antidumping measures.[21]

Unfortunately, *Extramet* has remained the exception and, in its subsequent case law, the CJEU has reaffirmed its strict interpretation of the standing requirements as they apply to unrelated importers.[22]

In conclusion, the CJEU has not hesitated to grant standing to private applicants other than unrelated importers where they could demonstrate that they had participated in the proceedings and that the measure would have a serious economic impact on them. For unrelated importers, participation in the proceeding or the fact that the measure would have a serious economic impact on their business has generally not sufficed to have standing. This distinct application of the standing criteria to the different categories of applicants has been motivated in several cases by the fact that unrelated importers have the possibility of bringing an indirect action by means of the preliminary reference procedure. The exception to this rule is *Extramet*, where the Court of Justice applied the standing criteria in a similar way to an unrelated importer as it would have done for a complainant.

18.2.3 Admissibility of a Direct Action for annulment against a Commission Regulation Classifying a Product in the Combined Nomenclature

Companies importing products into the customs territory of the EU need to declare the imported product to the customs authorities of the member

[19] Joined Cases 239/82 and 275/82, *Allied Corporation and others v Commission, supra*, para. 13.

[20] Case C-50/00 P, *Unión de Pequeños Agricultores v Council, supra.*

[21] Opinion of Advocate General Jacobs in Case 358/89, *Extramet Industrie SA, supra*, paras. 71–4.

[22] Case T-598/97, *British Shoe Corporation Footwear Supplies Ltd and Others v Council* [2002] ECR II-1155 and Joined Cases T-74/97 and T-75/97, *Büchel & Co. Fahrzeugteilefabrik GmbH v Council* [2000] ECR II-3067.

states under a specific product code. Depending on the applicable product code a specific customs tariff will apply. The product codes applicable in the EU (the Combined Nomenclature or CN) and the corresponding Common Customs Tariff (CCT) rates are contained in Regulation (EEC) No. 2658/87 of 23 July 1987 on the tariff and statistical nomenclature and on the Common Customs Tariff.[23] The nomenclature itself is set out in Annex I to that regulation and is replaced annually by an updated version.

It is possible, however, that the customs authorities of the various member states classify the same product under different customs codes. In order to ensure the uniform application of the Combined Nomenclature in the EU, the Commission, with the assistance of a committee of representatives of the member states (the Nomenclature Committee), may adopt a number of measures that are set out in Article 9 of Regulation (EEC) No. 2658/87. One of the measures most commonly used by the Commission is the adoption of a regulation classifying a specific good in the Combined Nomenclature.

These measures are normally adopted in order to solve a specific classification problem and it is therefore almost always possible to identify precisely the importer and the product concerned by the classification decision. Such classification decisions are, however, adopted in the form of a regulation and, therefore, of general application to all importers of the specific product classified by that regulation.[24] In view of this, the CJEU has consistently rejected the admissibility of direct actions brought against classification regulations.[25] This has even been the case where the importer had participated in the procedure leading up to the adoption of the regulation and there could be no doubt that the product classified was in fact the product imported by him. The CJEU has, consequently, treated importers confronted with a reclassification of their product as a result of a classification regulation in the same way as unrelated importers wishing to bring a direct action against a regulation imposing antidumping measures.

As was the case with *Extramet*[26] in the area of challenges against antidumping measures, the CJEU has exceptionally declared a direct

---

23 OJ (1987) L 256/1.

24 Case 40/84, *Casteels v Commission* [1985] ECR 667, para. 11; Case C-130/02, *Krings GmbH and Oberfinanzdirektion Nürnberg* [2004] ECR I-2121, para. 33; see, however, Opinion of Advocate General Mischo in Case C-119/99, *Hewlett Packard* [2001] ECR I-3981, para. 17 *et seq.*

25 Case 40/84, *Casteels v Commission, supra* and the orders in Case T-120/98, *Alce v Commission* [1999] ECR II-1395 and Case T-49/00, *Iposea v Commission* [2001] ECR II-163.

26 Case 358/89, *Extramet Industrie SA, supra.*

application by an importer for the annulment of a Commission classification regulation admissible. In Case T-243/01 *Sony Computer Entertainment Europe v Commission* (SCEE), the General Court found that in the exceptional circumstances of that case, the contested regulation affected the applicant 'by reason of certain attributes which are peculiar to it and by reason of circumstances in which it is differentiated from all other persons'.[27]

Among the exceptional circumstances relied upon by the General Court, special emphasis was placed on the fact that the product description could only apply to the PlayStation®2 game console and that SCEE was the only company authorized to import the PlayStation®2 into the EU.

The judgment of the General Court in *Sony Computer Entertainment Europe v Commission* thus constituted a departure from the previous case law on standing whereby it had been consistently held that for a trader to be deemed individually concerned by a regulation it is not sufficient that he belongs to a closed class of traders.[28]

This less restrictive interpretation of the standing requirements for importers challenging classification regulations was not followed by the General Court in later cases. The applicant in *Apple Computer International v Commission*[29] found itself in circumstances that were very similar to those of SCEE in *Sony Computer Entertainment Europe v Commission*. Yet, the General Court rejected the application as inadmissible and reaffirmed its previous more restrictive case law.

Compared to the reasoning followed in antidumping cases, it is noticeable that the CJEU does not enter into an economic analysis of the impact of the measure on the applicant. No references are made to the serious economic impact of the classification measure on the applicant.

Also, there is hardly any discussion on the relevance of the fact that importers can bring an indirect challenge of the classification regulation before the national courts. Again, *Sony Computer Entertainment Europe v Commission* is the exception where the General Court suggested that the standing criteria should be applied more restrictively to unrelated importers since they have access to other legal remedies.[30]

---

[27] Case T-243/01, *Sony Computer Entertainment Europe v Commission, supra*.

[28] Case T138/98, *ACAV and Others v Council, supra*, para. 64; Case T-482/93, *Weber v Commission* [1996] ECR II-609, para. 64.

[29] Case T-82/06, *Apple Computer International v Commission* [2008] ECR II-0279.

[30] Case T-243/01, *Sony Computer Entertainment Europe v Commission, supra*, para. 57: '[i]n a case such as the present one, where the applicant is not even alleging that there are no legal remedies, but rather merely that those remedies are not

18.3 THE CHANGES INTRODUCED BY ARTICLE 263 TFEU

18.3.1 The Need for Reform: Unión de Pequeños Agricultores v Council

The CJEU has repeatedly reaffirmed[31] that the combination of the various ways in which private applicants can obtain judicial redress makes the Community system

> a complete system of legal remedies and procedures designed to permit the Court of Justice to review the legality of measures adopted by the institutions. Natural and legal persons are thus protected against the application to them of general measures which they cannot contest directly before the Court by reason of the special conditions of admissibility laid down in the second paragraph of article 173 [now Article 263 TFEU] of the Treaty.

The above analysis of the case law on standing in the field of antidumping measures has shown that this theory has occasionally served as a justification for applying the criteria on standing more strictly to private applicants that could rely on ways of judicial redress other than direct actions under Article 230 EC Treaty.

The theory that the EU system of legal remedies was a complete system offering effective judicial protection to all natural and legal persons affected by general measures did not, however, withstand close scrutiny.[32] As demonstrated by the situation of the applicants in *Unión de Pequeños Agricultores v Council*[33] and in *Jégo-Quéré & Cie SA v Commission,*[34] there are situations in which a private applicant does not have access to an effective means of judicial redress against Community measures of general application. Secondly, it overlooks the fact that an indirect action whereby the national court refers the question on the legality of the Community

---

appropriate and cause it greater financial loss because of their length, there is all the more reason for the Court not to declare the action admissible when the applicant is not directly and individually concerned by the contested act.'

[31] Case 294/83, *Les Verts v Parliament* [1986] ECR 1339, para. 23.

[32] Craig, P., 'Legality, Standing and Substantive Review in Community Law', *Oxford Journal Legal Studies*, Vol. 14, 1994, pp. 507–9 and more in general, Craig, P. and De Burca, G., *EU Law, Text, Cases and Materials*, Oxford, Oxford University Press, 4th edn, 2007, pp. 525–7.

[33] Case T-173/98, *Unión de Pequeños Agricultores v Council* [1999] ECR II-3353.

[34] Case T-177/01, *Jégo-Quéré et Cie SA v Commission* [2002] ECR II-2365.

measure to the Court of Justice does not offer the same guarantees to applicants as a direct action.[35]

In order to overcome these deficiencies, Advocate General Jacobs proposed to interpret the words 'direct and individual concern' as requiring that the measure had a 'substantial adverse effect' on the applicant. The General Court in *Jégo-Quéré* also proposed a less strict interpretation whereby a natural or legal person would be regarded as individually concerned by any Community measure of general application that concerns him directly if the measure in question affects his legal position, in a manner that is both definite and immediate, by restricting his rights or by imposing obligations on him.[36]

Both suggested interpretations would not only have avoided situations where no indirect action was possible due to absence of a national implementing measure but would also have given standing to other categories of applicants that wished to bring a direct action for annulment and thereby to avoid the need to rely on the circuitous and uncertain indirect route.[37]

The Court of Justice in *Unión de Pequeños Agricultores* refused to take up these suggestions. It would be wrong to conclude from this that the Court of Justice favoured a more limited definition of the standing criteria than the criteria proposed by the Advocate General or the General Court. In particular, the Court of Justice expressly rejected an interpretation to the effect that a direct action for annulment before the General Court should be allowed where it can be shown, following an examination by that Court of the particular national procedural rules, that those rules do not allow the individual to bring proceedings to contest the validity of the Community measure at issue. As the analysis of the case law has shown, the possibility for an applicant to bring an indirect challenge had repeatedly been taken in consideration by the CJEU when assessing the standing requirements for bringing a direct action. The Court of Justice now rightly held that such an interpretation would require the CJEU, in each individual case, to examine and interpret national procedural law and that this would go beyond its jurisdiction when reviewing the legality of Community measures.

Rather, the reason for the rejection of the suggested solutions was the Court of Justice's reticence to rewrite the wording of Article 230 of the EC Treaty by an overly broad interpretation of the terms 'direct and individual

---

35 Opinion of Advocate General Jacobs in Case C-50/00 P, *Unión de Pequeños Agricultores v Council, supra*, para. 41 *et seq*.

36 Case T-177/01, *Jégo-Quéré et Cie SA v Commission, supra*, para. 51.

37 European Convention, Working Group II, Francis G. Jacobs, 'Note for the Working Group on the Charter/ECHR: Necessary Changes to the System of Judicial Remedies', WGII-WD020 (27 September 2002) at p. 4.

concern'. For that reason the Court of Justice enjoined the member states to amend the treaty rules restricting the possibility for private applicants to bring direct actions. The new standing criteria in the fourth paragraph of Article 263 TFEU can be seen as a response to this latter suggestion.

18.3.2 The Amendment of the Standing Requirements: Article 263 TFEU

The fourth paragraph of Article 236 TFEU now reads:

> [a]ny natural or legal person may, under the conditions laid down in the first and second paragraphs, institute proceedings against an act addressed to that person or which is of direct and individual concern to them, *and against a regulatory act which is of direct concern to them and does not entail implementing measures.* (emphasis added).

Besides the widening of the type of legal act that can be challenged to all types of legal acts intended to produce legal effects *vis-à-vis* third parties, the main change compared to the wording of the fourth paragraph of Article 230 of the EC Treaty concerns the addition of the words 'and against a regulatory act which is of direct concern to them and does not entail implementing measures'.

This new wording raises several questions of interpretation. The term 'regulatory act' is not defined in the TFEU and could refer either to regulations only or to all non-legislative acts of general application or to all acts of general application including legislative acts. Several authors have defended an interpretation that would restrict the notion of regulatory acts to non-legislative acts. Although the dichotomy legislative/regulatory act played a role in the drafting history of the comparable provision by the Convention on the Future of Europe (the Convention), this distinction was abandoned in the TFEU. The latter no longer differentiates between legislative acts, on the one hand, and regulatory acts, on the other hand. It would also make little sense to introduce such a distinction by analogy if the purpose of the amendment was, *inter alia*, to ensure that private applicants could bring a direct action to the CJEU in situations where no other judicial remedy was open to them.[38] As pointed out by several commentators, an interpretation restricting 'regulatory acts' to non-legislative acts of general application would still have left the applicants in

---

[38] Van Waeyenberghe, A., Pecho, P., 'L'arrêt UNIBET et le Traité de Lisbonne – Un pari sur l'avenir de la protection juridictionnelle effective', *Cahiers de Droit Européen*, 2008, p. 123, at p. 151 *et seq.*

Unión de Pequeños Agricultores[39] without means of judicial review since the Community measure challenged would have been qualified as a legislative act under the criteria contained in Article 289(3) TFEU.[40]

There exists even more interpretative uncertainty regarding the meaning of the words 'and does not entail implementing measures'. A straightforward interpretation suggests that the regulatory act must be directly applicable without it being necessary that either the EU institutions or the member states adopt further implementing measures. In other words, it is merely required that the act can be applied as it stands. This still leaves the question open whether the need for implementing measures must be assessed in fact, namely whether implementing measures have already been adopted, or in the abstract, namely whether the regulatory act itself requires member states or other EU institutions to adopt further measures.

A restrictive reading of the new standing requirement has been defended in the light of the drafting history of the draft Treaty establishing a Constitution for Europe.[41] According to such interpretation, a direct action against a regulatory act that is of direct concern would not be admissible if the legality of the regulatory act can be challenged indirectly by an action brought before the national or EU courts against a measure implementing or applying the regulatory act. Under this interpretation, any measures based on the regulatory act that allow an importer to bring an indirect challenge before the national courts should be considered as implementing measures. The new wording of the fourth paragraph of Article 263 TFEU would thus merely aim at plugging the holes in the system revealed by cases such as *Jégo-Quéré* and *Unión de Pequeños Agricultores*. In this logic, if a further measure has been adopted that is based on the regulatory act, it should be possible to bring an indirect action before the national courts challenging the validity of the regulatory act itself and there would therefore be no need to grant private applicants the right to bring a direct action.

This reductionist interpretation is difficult to accept. The CJEU would need to examine each time the admissibility is in doubt whether under the national rules of the member state a measure has been adopted that would allow the applicant to raise the invalidity of the regulatory act indirectly as part of its challenge of the national measure or decision. This could lead to

---

[39] Case C-50/00 P, *Unión de Pequeños Agricultores v Council, supra*.

[40] Lenaerts, K., 'Le Traité de Lisbonne et la protection juridictionnelle des particuliers en droit de l'Union', *Cahiers de Droit Européen*, 2009, p. 711 at p. 728, footnote 70.

[41] Lewis, X., 'Standing of private plaintiffs to annul generally applicable European Community measures: if the system is broken where should it be fixed?', *Fordham International Law Journal*, Vol. 30, p. 1496.

a situation where in certain member states an applicant would be required to bring an indirect action while in other Member States the applicant would have the possibility of bringing a direct action. For instance, under Article 12(5)(a)(i) of the Community Customs Code,[42] a classification regulation has the automatic effect of invalidating conflicting Binding Tariff Information (BTI) which has been issued by the customs authorities of the member states for the product concerned.[43] In some member states though, a specific decision of the national customs authorities is issued to the BTI holder, while in other member states there is no such specific action.

This can hardly be considered a satisfactory situation and is in fact similar to the approach which was rejected by the Court of Justice in *Unión de Pequeños Agricultores*:[44]

> it is not acceptable to adopt an interpretation of the system of remedies, such as that favoured by the appellant, to the effect that a direct action for annulment before the Community Court will be available where it can be shown, following an examination by that Court of the particular national procedural rules, that those rules do not allow the individual to bring proceedings to contest the validity of the Community measure at issue. Such an interpretation would require the Community Court, in each individual case, to examine and interpret national procedural law. That would go beyond its jurisdiction when reviewing the legality of Community measures.

A more natural reading of the words 'and does not entail implementing measures' is that the regulatory act itself does not require further implementing measures and, as such, affects directly the legal situation of the applicant. The condition that no further implementing measures must be necessary should therefore be read as a codification of the rule proposed by the General Court in *Jégo-Quéré*.[45] This implies that a private applicant's action for annulment must be declared admissible 'if the measure in

---

[42] Council Regulation (EEC) No. 2913/92 of 12 October 1992 establishing the Community Customs Code, OJ (1992) L 302/1.

[43] Case T-243/01, *Sony Computer Entertainment Europe v Commission, supra*, para. 62.

[44] Case C-50/00 P, *Unión de Pequeños Agricultores v Council, supra*, para. 43. A similar difficulty would have arisen if the proposal by Advocate General Jacobs would have been followed. This would have required that the CJEU analyses in each case the economic impact of a measure and whether such impact could be qualified as a 'substantial adverse effect'.

[45] Van Waeyenberghe and Pecho, *supra*, at p. 150.

question affects his legal position, in a manner which is both definite and immediate, by restricting his rights or by imposing obligations on him'.[46]

Also, it is the regulatory act that must entail implementing measures. The word 'entail' is defined in the *New Shorter Oxford Dictionary* as, *inter alia*, 'attach inseparably to; attach, associate' and 'necessitate as a consequence; have as an inevitable accompaniment, involve'. The use of the word 'entail' and of the present tense thus imply that the wording of the contested act must itself cause or require the adoption of further measures.

Such an interpretation would make it possible for the CJEU to examine on the basis of the challenged measure itself if the requirements for standing are met. Moreover, it will make it unnecessary to examine whether implementing measures have actually already been adopted in practice, thereby removing any temporal uncertainty as to when a regulatory act becomes challengeable or stops being directly challengeable.

18.3.3 Will the New Standing Requirements of Article 263 TFEU facilitate Direct Challenges by Private Applicants against Antidumping and Customs Classification Regulations?

Neither Council regulations imposing antidumping measures nor Commission regulations classifying a product in the Combined Nomenclature are adopted by legislative procedure. Their status as regulatory acts within the meaning of the fourth paragraph of Article 263 TFEU is therefore not in doubt.

Also, both types of measures affect the legal position of importers in a manner that is both definite and immediate by restricting their rights or by imposing obligations on them. Antidumping measures have as their immediate and direct effect that importers must pay antidumping duties on the products they import without that there is left any discretion to the member state of import in this regard. The obligation to pay the additional antidumping duty flows from the regulation itself, not from any subsequent implementing measure.

Likewise, classification regulations have as their immediate and direct effect that importers must declare the imported product under the tariff code prescribed by the classification regulation. Importers who would continue importing under another tariff code would be considered to have made a false import declaration and expose themselves to sanctions. Moreover, Binding Tariff Information that is not in accordance with the classification given in the classification regulation will be invalidated automatically by the classification regulation.

---

[46] Case T-177/01, *Jégo-Quéré et Cie SA v Commission, supra*, para. 51.

The new wording of the fourth paragraph of Article 263 TFEU makes it thus possible for importers affected by an import duty increase, either by the imposition of antidumping measures or as a result of a classification regulation, to challenge immediately and directly the legality of the regulation before the General Court. Previously, importers, other than in very exceptional cases, could bring such a challenge only by raising an indirect illegality claim before the courts of the member states. This not only created the risk of differences in the judicial protection of importers depending on the member state of import, it also led to a multiplication of national court proceedings.[47] Article 263 TFEU has removed these disadvantages by giving the competence to review actions by importers for the annulment of antidumping and classification regulations to the jurisdictional level best suited for such an analysis, namely the CJEU.[48]

The improved access to the CJEU for importers does not come without a price. Actions for annulment pursuant to Article 263 TFEU need to be brought within two months of the publication of the measure. Moreover, failure to bring a direct action may make it impossible to challenge at a later time the legality of the regulation by bringing an indirect action before the national courts.[49]

18.4 CONCLUSIONS

By removing the requirement that private applicants must be individually concerned before they can bring an application for annulment of a regulatory act before the General Court, Article 263 TFEU has removed one of the main obstacles that importers faced in obtaining an effective means of judicial redress against regulations imposing antidumping measures or reclassifying products in the Combined Nomenclature. The CJEU will now need to define in its case law the precise boundaries of this right. Many commentators have criticized in the past the restrictive interpretation by the CJEU of the notion of 'individual concern' in Article 230 of the EC Treaty as being both unjustified and unnecessary. Now that this requirement is no longer applicable to actions against regulatory acts, it is to be hoped that the CJEU will interpret the new conditions contained in Article 263 TFEU in a manner that facilitates the rapid and efficient resolution of any doubts

---

47 European Convention, Working Group II, Francis G. Jacobs, *supra*.

48 Van Waeyenberghe and Pecho, *supra*, at p. 155.

49 Case C-188/92, *TWD Textilwerke Deggendorf* [1994] ECR I-833, para. 23; Case C-233/99, *Nachi Europe* [2001] ECR I-1197, para. 36; Case C-550/09, *E and F*, 2010, ECR (not yet reported; judgment of 29 June 2010).

regarding the legality of regulatory acts in the areas of trade defence and customs classification.

PART III

Competition

Agreements

19. Vertical restraints and online sales in the era of modernization: is the new regime 'modern' enough?

Massimo Merola and Leonardo Armati

19.1 INTRODUCTION

Initiated in the late 1990s, the modernization of European competition law is a complex process that was born out of several historical factors. While the prospect of enlargement by itself triggered the modernization process, other factors also played a crucial role. Among these were, namely, the increasing globalization of the economy and the need to promote integration, efficiency and competitiveness within the single market. These factors drove the Commission to abandon some of its previous dogmas on anti-competitive practices and use economic theory as a source to develop its policy and rules, and employ thorough factual analysis as a primary tool for the enforcement of these rules.

The effects-based approach is an essential component of the moderniza-tion of European competition law and encompasses action in all its fields, from state aid to restrictive agreements, from abuse of dominance to merger control.

Vertical restraints, in particular, were an ideal candidate for an early application of the new approach and the Commission's 1996 Green Paper on vertical restraints, which preceded the adoption of Regulation No. 2790/1999,[1] represents a milestone in the modernization process. As a result

[1] Commission Regulation (EC) No. 2790/1999 of 22 December 1999 on the application of Article 81(3) of the Treaty to categories of vertical agreements and concerted practices (Text with EEA relevance), OJ (1999) L 336/21. For a thorough analysis of the application of Article 101 TFEU (formerly Article 81 EC) to vertical agreements, see: Whish, R., Bailey, D., 'Regulation 330/2010, The Commission's new block exemption for vertical restraints', *Common Market Law Review*, Vol. 47, No. 6, 2010, pp. 1757–91; Marco Colino, S., *Vertical agreements and competition*

of the early application of this approach, it is now an accepted fact that vertical restraints raise less competition concerns than horizontal agreements, as they are often pro-competitive in nature.

Modernization, enforcement priorities, and the increasing focus on effects have driven the Commission's actions and resources away from these kinds of agreements and towards more serious restrictive practices (e.g. cartels). Since the entering into force of Regulation No. 1/2003 and the abolition of the prior notification requirement, the Commission's decisions on vertical agreements have been few and far between, and litigation before the Court of Justice on this issue almost non-existent.

Given these premises, and in the absence of major case law developments, when adopting the new framework for vertical agreements the Commission rightly assumed that the system set up by Regulation No. 2790/1999 was working smoothly. Therefore, Regulation No. 330/2010 granting a block exemption to certain categories of vertical agreements (the Block Exemption Regulation or BER),[2] which was accompanied by new Guidelines on vertical agreements (the Guidelines)[3] that replaced the 2000 Vertical Guidelines (the Old Guidelines),[4] broadly confirmed the rules and the effects-based approach on which Regulation No. 2790/1999 was based.

The main principle underlying the new BER therefore remains the same: vertical agreements that are concluded between companies with limited market power (i.e. a market share not exceeding 30 per cent) and do not contain hardcore restrictions of competition, are presumed to be pro-competitive and are therefore covered by a general exemption. Agreements not qualifying for a block exemption are not automatically prohibited but

law: a comparative study of the EU and US regimes, Oxford, Hart, 2010; Lugard, P., *Vertical restraints under EC competition Law*, Oxford, Hart, 2006; Wijckmans, F., Tuytschaever, F., Vanderelst, A., *Vertical agreements in EC competition law*, Oxford, Oxford University Press, 2006; Goyder, J., *EU distribution law*, Oxford Portland, Hart, 2005; Kerber, W., Vezzoso, S., 'EU competition policy, vertical restraints, and innovation : an analysis from an evolutionary perspective', *World Competition*, Vol. 28, No. 4, 2005, pp. 507–32; Verouden, V., 'Vertical agreements and article 81(1) EC : the evolving role of economic analysis', *Antitrust Law Journal*, Vol. 71, No. 2, 2003, pp. 525–75; Korah, V., O'Sullivan, D., *Distribution agreements under the EC competition rules*, Oxford, Hart, 2002; Mendelsohn, M., Rose, S., *Guide to the EC block exemption for vertical agreements*, The Hague, Kluwer Law International, 2002; Pappalardo, A., 'Les nouvelles règles de concurrence applicables aux accords "verticaux" ', *Revue du droit de l'Union Europeenne*, No. 1., 2000, pp. 151–67.

2 Commission Regulation (EU) No. 330/2010 of 20 April 2010 on the application of Article 101(3) of the Treaty on the Functioning of the European Union to categories of vertical agreements and concerted practices, OJ (2010) L 102/1.

3 Commission Notice – Guidelines on Vertical Restraints, OJ (2010) C 130/1.

4 Commission notice – Guidelines on Vertical Restraints, OJ (2000) C 291/1.

an individual assessment must be carried out to weigh up the restrictive effects and efficiencies.

Only some aspects of the previous framework have been modified or updated, most notably to take into account the growing concerns on the market power held by distributors and the need to protect the development of online sales. This issue, in particular, has formed the subject-matter of a heated debate before the adoption of the new package, most notably due to some industries' concerns that, without any restrictions, free riding would proliferate.

This chapter will devote particular attention to the issue of online sales in the new Guidelines and try to address its most controversial aspects. After giving a very broad overview of the main changes introduced in the general framework for vertical restraints in the first section, focusing in particular on the Commission's more economic approach and the increasing recognition of the free-riding problem, the second section will review the application of this approach to online sales. The aim is to analyse, in this respect, whether the Commission has managed to strike the right balance between the need to enhance this fast-growing area of commerce and the legitimate interests of manufacturers to limit free riding and maintain sufficient incentives for their bricks-and-mortar distributors.

19.2 MAIN CHANGES IN THE GENERAL FRAMEWORK FOR VERTICAL RESTRAINTS

19.2.1 The new BER

Very few changes can be identified in the text of the new BER, as the Commission's approach has been to leave the law basically as it was while developing its interpretation and policy in the Guidelines. The two main changes in the regulation relate to its scope of application but go in opposite directions: on the one hand, the 30 per cent threshold used as safe harbour now applies to both the supplier's and the distributor's market share, which results in a restriction in scope of the block exemption; on the other, the BER abolishes the turnover threshold in relation to agreements between competitors, with the consequence of extending the scope of the exemption.

19.2.1.1 Safe harbour

The BER confirms the 30 per cent market share threshold below which vertical agreements are exempted. Experience under the previous regime has confirmed that this threshold represents a good proxy to presume a net positive balance of the effects arising from vertical agreements. An important change, however, concerns the extension of this threshold to the buyers' market position on the purchasing market, which is now taken into account irrespective of the vertical agreement being assessed (Article 3 of the BER). As a result, the buyer's market share will have to be considered in all vertical agreements (single branding, exclusive distribution, selective distribution etc.) and not only in the case of exclusive supply obligations, as provided under Regulation No. 2790/1999.

This change is due to the increasing pressure, most notably from national competition authorities, to tackle vertical restraints induced by distributors or retailers with considerable market power (e.g. large supermarket chains). The stated purpose is the protection of both consumers and small and medium enterprises, by ensuring that the latter are not denied sufficient access to the market and that the choice for consumers is not unduly limited by distributors.

While the motive of the amendment is certainly laudable, arguably the extension of the market share threshold to the purchasing market will complicate the self-assessment that undertakings are called on to carry out in the application of the BER. Indeed, such an assessment is generally carried out by suppliers in respect of their overall distribution system(s). While they are (or at least should be) fully aware of their own market position, it may prove very difficult, if not impossible, except when counterparties are very large distributors, to obtain accurate and updated information on the buying power of each reseller within their network. The market share threshold introduced in the BER will therefore certainly increase the burden of the self-assessment (which will have to be individual for each distributor) and risks frustrating one of the aims of the BER itself, i.e. providing clear limits and legal certainty as to the application of the exemption.

In addition to the increased complexity of the self-assessment, another potential negative effect of this amendment is the discrimination of distributors with more than 30 per cent share of purchases, which may be excluded from a distribution system so as not to lose the benefit of the exemption.[5] Of course, it is always possible to carry out an individual assessment of the economic impact of the agreement based on Article 101(3) of the Treaty and the Commission's Guidelines, but in fact this analysis can never provide the same legal certainty as the application of a

---

[5] See Vilmart, C.,'La nouvelle exemption des accords de distribution: une insécurité grandissante', *Journal of Computational Physics – La semaine juridique*, No. 23, 2010, pp. 17–22.

block exemption. For practical reasons, a cautious supplier may therefore decide that it is easier, for instance, simply not to allow a reseller in its selective distribution system, when it doubts the latter's market share.

Rather than imposing double thresholds to all kind of agreements, the Commission could have better explained the situations where it is either the buyer's or the supplier's, or both of their market shares, that are relevant. Based on that, the Guidelines could have pointed to the threshold(s) to be applied with reference to specific agreements according to the foreclosure risk arising, similarly to the Commission's Notice on non-horizontal mergers.[6] A more analytical and targeted application of the thresholds would in fact seem more consistent with the economic-based approach of the framework for vertical restraints.[7]

The restriction of the safe harbour's scope may result in de facto withdrawing the block exemption from agreements that benefited from it under Regulation No. 2790/1999: in this event, Article 9 of the BER provides for a one-year transition period during which the prohibition laid down in Article 101(1) of the Treaty shall not apply, with the aim of ensuring sufficient time to review the distribution systems concerned by this change.

19.2.1.2 Vertical agreements between competitors

While narrowing the scope of the new BER from the standpoint of the market share thresholds, the Commission widens the scope of the exemption in relation to vertical agreements between competitors. Article 2(4) of the BER confirms that the exemption applies only to non-reciprocal vertical agreements between competitors where the buyer is not active at the supplier's upstream level of trade (a competition relationship is instead admissible at the downstream level), but eliminates the turnover threshold provided under the previous regime (a maximum of €100 million). As a result, non-reciprocal vertical agreements entered into by large companies with competitors can also benefit from the exemption, provided of course they fulfil the requirements laid down in the regulation. This amendment is

---

6 Guidelines on the assessment of non-horizontal mergers under the Council Regulation on the control of concentrations between undertakings, OJ (2008) C 265/6.

7 It is, however, positive that the Commission departed from its original proposal to set a 30 per cent threshold related to the buyer's shares 'on any of the relevant markets affected by the agreement', i.e. including the downstream markets, which are seldom relevant for foreclosure issues.

particularly welcome, as given the beneficial effects of vertical agreements, the turnover and undertakings' size should not be a cause for different treatment.

19.2.1.3 Hardcore restrictions untouched

Finally, it should be mentioned that the new BER leaves the list of hardcore resale restrictions (Article 4) essentially unaltered. A presumption of harm to competition exists for these restrictions, which therefore prevent the block exemption from applying. The Commission did introduce a number of new elements of interpretation, including objective reasons capable of justifying these restrictions (most notably as regards resale price maintenance) in the Guidelines, that will be briefly discussed below.

19.2.2 Main Changes or Clarifications in the New Vertical Guidelines

The Guidelines do not depart significantly from their predecessor. Only a few points can be regarded as a real evolution in policy or a significant development deserving to be commented on here.

As regards *agency agreements*, it is confirmed that obligations related to the contracts negotiated by an agent on the principal's behalf, such as resale price fixing or territorial restrictions, which would amount to intra-brand restrictions in normal distribution agreements between independent undertakings, are not caught under Article 101(1) of the Treaty, as the principal and the agent act as a single economic entity.[8] The agreement will qualify as an agency agreement, however, only in the absence of significant financial or commercial risks being taken by the agent. Paragraph 14 of the Guidelines introduce a new category of risks to be taken into account, i.e. risks related to activities that the principal requires the agent to undertake in the same relevant market, not as an agent on behalf of the principal but at its own risk (for instance, the purchase of demonstration vehicles as imposed on car dealerships).

In relation to *exclusive distribution agreements*, the Guidelines resolve a number of doubts that arose under the Old Guidelines and overall set out a clearer framework for exclusive suppliers. First, reference to the fact that restrictions of active sales may bind direct buyers only has been deleted. This results from the new Article 3(2) of the BER, which enables the

---

[8] Para. 12 *et seq.* of the Guidelines. It should be noted that para. 19 confirms that restrictions concerning the relationship between the agent and the principal impacting on inter-brand competition, such as single branding obligations, may conversely infringe Article 101(1) of the Treaty.

conclusion of multi-level agreements with more than one buyer.[9] Second, the Guidelines state that sales by the supplier are irrelevant for the qualification of a distribution system as being exclusive. The exclusive distributor is accordingly protected against active selling in its territory or to its customer group inside the EU by all the buyers of the supplier, even if the latter makes sales in its territory.[10]

As regards *selective distribution systems,*[11] the Guidelines state that restrictions of (active and passive) sales to unauthorized distributors (Article 4(b)(iii) of the BER) are allowed not only in the territory where the system is operated but also in territories where the supplier does not yet sell the contract products.[12] The Guidelines further clarify that it is possible to combine selective distribution with exclusive distribution systems within the EU. This is implicit in paragraph 56, which states that restrictions of sales to end-users by dealers in a selective distribution system are permitted if they are aimed at protecting an exclusive distribution system operated elsewhere.[13]

Another area of significant development in the Guidelines relate to 'permitted' hardcore restrictions. The Guidelines offer some examples where even the restriction of passive sales can: (1) be objectively necessary for the existence of an agreement of a particular type or nature and fall short of Article 101(1) of the Treaty; (2) generate efficiencies and fall within the scope of Article 101(3) of the Treaty. This may be the case, for instance,

---

[9] Compare para. 50 of the Old Guidelines with para. 51 of the Guidelines. The former text was 'there are four exceptions to the hardcore restriction in Article 4(b) of the Block Exemption Regulation. The first exception allows a supplier to restrict active sales by *his direct buyers* to a territory or a customer group which has been allocated exclusively to another buyer or which the supplier has reserved to itself.' The current wording is '... The first exception allows a supplier to restrict active sales *by a buyer party* ...'(emphasis added).

[10] Guidelines, para. 51.

[11] Pursuant to Article 1 of the BER, selective distribution system means 'a distribution system where the supplier undertakes to sell the contract goods or services, either directly or indirectly, only to distributors selected on the basis of specified criteria and where these distributors undertake not to sell such goods or services to unauthorised distributors within the territory reserved by the supplier to operate that system'.

[12] Guidelines, para. 55.

[13] Para. 57 of the Guidelines however clarifies that, within the same territory, a selective distribution system may not be combined with exclusive distribution as that would lead to a restriction of active or passive selling by the dealers. These amendments are a clarification of the Old Guidelines, which only stated that 'distribution may be combined with exclusive distribution provided that active and passive selling is not restricted anywhere' (para. 53).

where a distributor incurs sunk investments to launch a new brand or product on the market, which he would not have borne without having absolute protection from active and passive sales for a certain period (two years). Similarly, the restriction of active sales can either not be caught by Article 101(1)[14] or be justified under Article 101(3)[15] in the cases where a high risk of free riding exists.

These interesting developments testify that the Commission is increasingly open to accept justifications of sale restrictions based on the risk of free riding. These are also possible grounds to justify, in exceptional circumstances, resale price maintenance (RPM). According to the new paragraph 225 of the Guidelines, efficiencies may arise where the extra margin originating from RPM may allow retailers to provide additional pre-sales services, in particular in case of so-called 'experience' products or technically complex products, which would be jeopardized if free riding by discounters was allowed. Other efficiencies may arise where there is a need to support the launch of new products, as RPM may provide the distributors with the means to increase sales efforts, or in the case of coordinated low price advertisement campaigns in franchise networks. The Commission's new approach is in line with the judgment delivered by the US Supreme Court in 2007 in the *Leegin* case,[16] which reversed long-settled case law that considered vertical price fixing as illegal *per se*, and established instead a rule of reason assessment on a case-by-case basis. It remains to be seen if the Commission is ready to follow the American example in an individual case. The impression is that it is still too early and that no undertaking would be ready to take the risk of setting up a RPM policy only based on the examples of the Guidelines. Still, this more open view of hardcore restrictions is certainly to be welcomed, as it reflects the Commission's interest to look at the real effects of these agreements. The Commission seems to encourage the analysis of all possible implications of restrictive agreements and the recognition of legitimate interests to fight free riding. This new approach emerges clearly from the new Guidelines and is key even in respect to its new policy on internet sales, which is discussed below.

---

[14] This may occur for instance in the case of a genuine testing of a new product (para. 62 of the Guidelines).

[15] For instance, where wholesalers are required to invest heavily in promotion in a selective distribution system. This exception, set out in para. 63 of the Guidelines, represents an exception to the rule set out in para. 57, that it is not possible to combine selective and exclusive distribution within the same territory.

[16] US Supreme Court, 28 June 2007, *Leegin Creative Products, Inc. v PSKS, Inc.*

19.3 THE COMMISSION'S POLICY IN RELATION TO E-COMMERCE

In contrast to the skeletal references in the old Guidelines, online sales are now the subject of extensive analysis by the Commission, which recognizes them as an area of major change since the adoption of the previous regime. This is not surprising, considering that this trade channel is growing at a very steady pace, having reached between 5 and 10 per cent of the overall retail sales in the European Union, a trend that is expected to consolidate in the current situation of economic stagnation.[17]

With the progressive development of e-commerce, a number of legal issues connected thereto have emerged as a source of growing controversy, including in the field of competition law. In particular, the battle between online traders and luxury brands has increasingly drawn the attention of competition law practitioners to the difficult issue of how to strike a balance between, on the one hand, consumers' interests to find deals on the internet and, on the other, manufacturers' interests to protect their investments and brand reputation.

When adopting the new package on vertical restraints, the Commission had this and other challenging issues in mind, such as the treatment of exclusive distribution through the internet. Although the matter could have called for innovative solutions, however, after having extensively consulted with stakeholders,[18] the Commission confirmed its choice under the former regime not to lay down specific rules for online distribution in the new BER. It decided instead to continue to treat this trade channel using the existing legal categories, while providing additional interpretations specific to internet distribution in its Guidelines.

As will be seen below, the Guidelines do not significantly depart from the former treatment of internet distribution, the general rule being that the limitation of online sales is prohibited, although some restraints can be

---

[17] See Mardsen, P. and Whelan, P., 'Selective Distribution in the Age of Online Retail', *European Competition Law Review*, Vol. 1, 2010, pp. 26–37, who quote Mintel study *E-commerce-Europe retail intelligence*, 2006, Frontier Economics, *Economic Study of the Consumer Benefits of eBay*, 2008, and Dellner, *European E-commerce*, 2007.

[18] Not only did the Commission conduct a public consultation open to all stakeholders, as it usually does before adopting new legislation, but former Competition Commissioner Kroes also personally met with several high-profile representatives of luxury industries and online traders, so as to understand their position on internet sales of branded goods.

justified, most notably in the framework of exclusive distribution or selective distribution systems.

19.3.1 New 'Soft' Hardcore Restrictions

The first important development in the Guidelines is that the Commission eliminated the sentence 'an outright ban on internet or catalogue selling is only possible if there is an objective justification'.[19] On the other hand, the new Guidelines maintain in paragraph 52 the principle that 'every distributor must be allowed to use the internet to sell products' and set out a list of hardcore restrictions specific to internet sales, which add up to those listed in the BER.

The Guidelines thus seem to mark the beginning of a 'zero tolerance' policy where outright bans on online sales will be considered *per se* illegal – no room seems to be left in the Guidelines for any objective justification – while partial limitations can be accepted if one of the circumstances described therein occur.

Of course, being contained in a 'soft law' document, this list is nothing other than an interpretation of Article 4 of the BER by the Commission and is not binding. In practice, however, the effect is similar as undertakings will regard the Commission's Guidelines as compulsory requirements when they self-assess their distribution arrangements. This raises the question as to whether the Guidelines are the right instrument to introduce hardcore restrictions that represent extensive interpretations of those set out in the BER.[20]

Paragraph 52 lists the following as restrictions to passive sales: (1) an agreement that the (exclusive) distributor will prevent customers located in another (exclusive) territory from viewing its website; (2) automatically rerouting customers to the website of another distributor; (3) terminating a sales transaction if the credit card data shows an address outside the area to which a given distributor has been assigned; (4) the limitation of the proportion of overall sales made over the internet, without prejudice, however, to the possibility of the supplier to require a certain absolute amount of offline sales to ensure an efficient operation of its 'bricks and mortar' shop; (5) so-called dual pricing, i.e. agreeing that the distributor has to pay a higher price for products intended to be resold online than for products resold offline, without prejudice, however, to agreeing to a fixed fee with the buyer to support the latter's offline or online sales efforts.

---

19 Old Guidelines, para. 51.

20 See, for a critical view, Vilmart, *supra*.

While restraints (1) to (3) are particularly (although not exclusively) relevant to exclusive distribution agreements, as they clearly draw the line between active and passive sales through the internet, restraints listed under (4) and (5) are of particular interest for selective distribution, as the Guidelines explicitly recognize some possible limitations aimed at protecting investments in the offline trade channel.

19.3.2 Allowed Restrictions in Exclusive Distribution

In so far as it grants a certain degree of territorial protection, exclusive distribution is strictly linked to the notion of territory. Needless to say, this notion is not easily reconcilable with that of the internet, by definition a virtual place that is unsuitable to be split and apportioned.

Despite the intrinsic difficulty of the exercise, the Commission endeavours to pigeonhole internet sales in the traditional macro-categories of active and passive sales by providing a few examples of these types of sales applied to the internet.

The main assumptions are the same as in the Old Guidelines and are therefore particularly restrictive for suppliers. Having a website is thus considered a form of passive selling. The fact it may have effects outside one's own territory or customer group is considered the result of the technology rather than of the dealer's willingness to directly reach other territories/groups of customers. As a consequence, if a customer visits the website of a distributor and this contact leads to a sale, including delivery, then that sale is considered as passive.[21]

The decisive element for distinguishing active sales from passive sales is, like under the Old Guidelines, the action of targeting specific customers or territories with active promotional initiatives. In an effort to build general categories suitable to e-commerce, the Guidelines consider that an advertisement that is specifically addressed to certain customers, for instance through territory-based banners or, more generally, efforts to be found specifically in a certain territory or by certain customer group, amount to active selling. This is for instance the case when the distributor pays a search engine or other provider to have its advertisement displayed specifically to users in a particular territory.[22]

While *prima facie* the distinction between active and passive sales over the internet may seem straightforward, in fact it may prove very tricky in light of the several advertising options possible over the internet, which

---

[21] Old Guidelines, para. 51 and Guidelines, para. 52.
[22] Guidelines, para. 52.

may involve a more or less active intervention by the dealer. As a result, a number of 'grey' forms of advertising would be difficult to include in one or the other category.

For instance, imagine that a customer visits a website that is not registered in its territory and opts to be kept automatically informed by the distributor, and a subsequent contact that originated from the dealer leads to a sale: does this amount to an active or passive sale? The Guidelines solve this specific issue by classifying the sale as passive.[23] This is not uncontroversial. The example in the Guidelines goes much further than what could be implied *a contrario* from the statement in the Old Guidelines that 'unsolicited e-mails sent to individual customers or specific customer groups are considered active selling'.[24] Based on the Commission reasoning, would the fact that a customer more or less deliberately clicked on the 'keep me informed' option (which very often is a default option) justify any advertisement being sent in furtherance of this contact, even if this is customized to meet the particular tastes of its addressee? This would be in plain contradiction with the notion of active sales set out above, but still an online retailer may claim that it is permitted under the Guidelines.

The same applies to the language options used on a website, which are not considered by the Guidelines as a way of targeting specific customers. This is, however, debatable and should be subject to careful analysis. Imagine that by visiting a 'dotcom' website you are automatically directed, based on your country of origin, to the language version corresponding to this country: is this still a passive act? Considering the ease with which one could reach any website, it may be argued that the fact that this is available in multiple languages is a way to target customers abroad. More generally, it has been observed that transposing the distinction between active and passive sales to the creation of websites gives rise to difficulties and appears as an oversimplification. Indeed, by creating a website, the distributor is aware that it can reach customers everywhere in the world and, by using specific languages, it is aware that it will enable customers from territories assigned to other distributors to view and purchase from its site: this could therefore be interpreted as a sort of invitation to purchase.[25]

On the other hand, it has been argued that targeting may result from an automated selection of the online advertising displayed to a user on the basis of anonymized information about past use of the website. Accordingly, in these circumstances targeting in the sense of the BER would not

---

[23] Guidelines, para. 52.

[24] Old Guidelines, para. 51.

[25] See Ottimi, O.B., 'Réseaux de distribution et réseau internet', *Les Petites Affiches*, No. 243, 2007, pp. 3–10.

arise, as it would not be based on an individual, active decision by the online retailer but rather on an automated categorization by the online advertiser.[26]

The above examples show that the Guidelines may create arbitrary categories of legal and illegal online practices that do not necessarily reflect the principles enshrined in the BER as regards territorial restrictions and the concept of active and passive sales.[27] These principles, however, should always been borne in mind when assessing the countless situations made possible by technological developments.

The policy choice of the Commission, however, is clear. By conservatively classifying most internet sales as passive, it creates a sort of presumption that internet sales are passive, unless the contrary is proven.

This has of course important implications, as restrictions to passive sales are hardcore restrictions under Article 4(b) of the BER. Suppliers should therefore in principle be prevented from restricting these types of sales made by their distributors through limiting the quantities sold or charging higher prices.

As mentioned above, the Guidelines set out a few examples of the specific forms these hardcore restrictions may take, such as agreeing that the (exclusive) distributor: prevents customers located in another (exclusive) territory from viewing its website; automatically reroutes customers to the website of another distributor; or terminates a sales transaction if the credit card data shows an address outside the area to which a given distributor has been assigned. Although this list of territorial restrictions is not exhaustive, it is surprising that the Guidelines do not mention other very common – and unsophisticated – practices of internet retailers, such as the refusal to deliver the requested goods in territories other than their country of establishment. Should this occur as a result of an agreement restraining the retailers' ability to deliver goods, and in the absence of objective reasons, this will be considered as a hardcore restriction of passive sales under the BER despite the silence of the Guidelines in this respect.

---

[26] See eBay's response to the Commission's public consultation on the review of competition rules applicable to vertical agreements, on: http://ec.europa.eu/competition/consultations/2009_vertical_agreements/index.html.

[27] With regard to para. 51 of the Old Guidelines, Dethmers and Posthuma had criticized the lack of examples for distinguishing active and passive internet sales and the Commission's assumption that, as a result, internet sales are almost always passive sales (Dethmers, F., Posthuma, P., 'Ten Years On: Vertical Agreements under Article 81', *European Competition Law Review,* Vol. 9, 2009, pp. 424–39). The new Guidelines do not seem to have decisively improved the situation on this specific issue in terms of clarity, as set out above.

In light of the very restrictive approach of the Commission in respect of active sales, very few restrictions can be safely imposed on exclusive distributors: the ability to restrict active sales will be confined to the prohibition to send unsolicited emails to customers exclusively allocated to other distributors, or to target them with specific advertising, as explained above. Online traders will on the other hand profit from the possibility to favour all possible 'grey' practices, and so lead customers to make purchases in territories other than their own.

19.3.3 Allowed Restrictions in Selective Distribution

Although the last two hardcore restrictions listed at paragraph 52 of the Guidelines, i.e. partial limitations to online sales and dual pricing, are generally applicable to all distribution systems, they are understood as being particularly relevant for selective distribution systems. In fact they reflect the debate taking place before the Commission between on the one hand, the champions of online retail, and on the other, the luxury manufacturers and other suppliers that use selective distribution systems.

The latter argue with conviction that the limitation of internet sales is necessary to contrast free riding, i.e. the practice whereby consumers test and choose products in traditional 'bricks-and-mortar' stores, taking advantage of the service provided therein, before purchasing the goods online.[28] This is especially the case with certain products, so-called 'experience products' (such as perfumes or cars) that are normally tested before the purchase, the online purchase of which would therefore seem logically inconceivable. The reasoning goes even further, as luxury brands for instance[29] fear that internet sales may ultimately put their physical distribution networks at risk, and cause the deterioration of the prestige of the product and the brand image they have continuously heavily invested in.

Supporters of online distribution, on the other hand, argue that consumers who prefer buying online should not be forced to pay a premium for a pre-sale service they do not need or request. It is argued that the internet

---

[28] A notorious advertisement by the UK electrical retailer Dixons is particularly illustrative of this phenomenon: 'Step into middle England's best loved department store, stroll through the haberdashery to the audiovisual department where an awfully well brought up young man will bend over backwards to find the right TV for you …then go to Dixons.co.uk and buy it.'

[29] See, for instance, LVMH's response to the Commission's public consultation on the review of competition rules applicable to vertical agreements, available on: http://ec.europa.eu/competition/consultations/2009_vertical_agreements/index.html.

nowadays is the most convenient source to get complete information on products and consumers increasingly make their purchase choice on the internet without the need for window shopping.[30] The conclusion is that online and offline distribution is largely complementary and that one should not exclude the other.

The Guidelines are the result of a compromise between these opposite positions. However, they take as a starting point a significant statement in favour of online retailers, i.e. that 'in principle, every distributor must be allowed to use the internet to sell products', and the consequent prohibition of outright bans discussed above.

In this respect, it should be noted that a reference for a preliminary ruling from the Paris Court of Appeal is pending before the Court of Justice on the question whether a general and absolute ban on selling via the internet, imposed in the context of selective distribution network, constitutes a hardcore restriction of competition by an object that cannot be covered by the BER.[31] This reference follows a decision by the French Competition Council to fine Pierre Fabre, a supplier of pharmaceutical and personal care products, for including in its selective distribution agreements a provision to prohibit the online sale of its products. Interestingly, prior to this Decision, the Court of Appeal of Versailles, many years before, had ordered one of Pierre Fabre's distributors to cease the internet sale of its products, on the grounds that these sales did not meet the selective distribution system criteria, and undermined the supplier's corporate image as well as the guaranteed security and quality of its products.[32] The position of the claimant in that case was that sales on the internet should be classified as sales from an unauthorized (virtual) establishment. There are very high expectations on the preliminary ruling of the Court of Justice, especially from the supporters of selective distribution, who see this as an opportunity for the Court to clarify the relationship between selective distribution and the limitation on the use of the internet as a requirement to meet quality standards.[33]

---

30 See eBay's response to the Commission's public consultation, *supra*.

31 Reference for a preliminary ruling from the Cour d'appel de Paris (France) lodged on 10 November 2009 – Case C-439/39 *Pierre Fabre Dermo-Cosmétque AAS v. Président de l'Autorité De la Conourrence, Ministre de l'Economie de l'industrie et de l'Emploi*, OJ C 24/27 of 30 January 2010.

32 Cour d'appel de Versailles, 13th Chamber, 2 December 1999. See for a commentary, Ottimi, *supra*.

33 In its opinion delivered on 3 March 2011 in Case C-439/39, A.G. Mozak seems to endorse the Commission's position that an outright ban on internet sales acts as a limitation on active and passive sales and therefore amounts to a hardcore

Until the Court of Justice delivers its judgment, it would be prudent however to rely on the Commission Guidelines and, therefore, consider an outright ban on internet sales as a hardcore restriction. Equally, it has been rightly observed that this conclusion makes sense anyway in a selective distribution system, to the extent that retailers are normally all required to have a physical store. Since there are no pure internet players, there is no risk of free riding, without of course breaching the agreement made by a supplier or a retailer.[34] This should lead to the acceptance that internet sales must be allowed even in a selective distribution system. The real problems arising with selective distribution would therefore be: (1) how much online sales can be limited; (2) the quality standards of the sales made on internet; and (3) the price of the products sold over the internet.

As regards the first point, the Commission has made it clear that the proportion of overall sales made over the internet cannot be limited. However the Guidelines allow for the supplier to require a certain *absolute* amount of offline sales to ensure the efficient operation of its 'bricks and mortar' shop. This provision is consistent with the 'brick and click' principle, already recognized by the Commission in the *Yves Saint Laurent* case,[35] whereby within a selective distribution system a supplier may require its distributors to have one or more physical stores or showrooms as a condition to become a member of the system.[36] The exclusion of pure internet players is therefore allowed in the Guidelines and the possibility to require a minimum amount of offline sales is nothing else than a way to ensure that the supplier may effectively take advantage of this possibility. Otherwise, a distributor may overturn its requirement by setting up an 'alibi shop' with virtually no sales. Although the quantification of a minimum amount of offline sales seems to be the most proportionate way to pursue the above aim, in practice the criterion seems difficult to implement, as absolute quantities are always hard to establish. The approach taken by the German Federal Supreme Court on a case regarding perfumes in 2003,[37] whereby a supplier could require that turnover from sales made online did not exceed that from offline sales, certainly seems easier to apply. However,

restriction, without prejudice, however, of the possibility for such a ban to benefit from an individual exemption, if the conditions laid down in Article 101(3) TFEU are fulfilled.

[34] See Mardsen and Whelan, *supra*.

[35] See IP/01/713 of 17 May 2001.

[36] Guidelines, para. 54.

[37] File No.KZR 2/02. See Held, M., 'The More Lenient Approach Of German Courts Towards Prohibition Of Distribution Via Internet Auction Platforms – Recent Developments', *European Competition Law Review*, Vol. 9, pp. 343–8.

it is debatable that the latter approach represents an economically accurate and proportionate method.

The supplier may also require that its distributor meets quality standards for the use of internet sites, like for a shop. Of course, these standards cannot be identical to those required for a shop, as the characteristics of a shop are not necessarily replicable in the virtual world of the internet. Paragraph 56 of the Guidelines provides, however, that quality standards in the two trade channels should pursue the same objectives and achieve comparable results. Any difference between the criteria must therefore be justified by the difference of these two distribution modes. For instance, if instant delivery is required for offline sales, since the same requirement cannot be imposed on online sales, certain reasonably prompt delivery times may be accepted instead.

As regards pricing, while it is not possible for the supplier to set different prices for products to be sold online and offline, the Guidelines specify that it is possible to agree to a fixed fee with the buyer to support the latter's offline or online sales efforts (paragraph 52). The reason for this exception is similar to that justifying the exclusion of internet-only dealers, i.e. to ensure that investments are made on the physical network (or, less likely, on online infrastructure/services). However, this exercise must be made in the least restrictive way possible and obey solid economic principles.

The Guidelines further set out an exceptional example where dual pricing does not amount to a hardcore restriction: when online sales cause the supplier to incur substantially higher costs (for instance because they lead to more complaints and warranty claims), imposing a higher price in relation to products to be sold online can be justified (paragraph 64). However, this is believed to be a rare occurrence.

Finally, the Guidelines briefly treat the question as to whether sales on a third party online platform, such as, for example, the eBay auction site, can be restricted within a selective distribution system.[38] This issue has given rise to much controversy in the last few years in Germany, where several courts have ruled in cases relating to sales on the eBay platform.[39] While an

---

[38] Guidelines, para. 54.

[39] The Higher Regional Court of Karlsruhe in 2009 upheld the decision in first instance that the disruption by a school bag manufacturer to supply an eBay online distributor was legitimate. Similarly, in the same year, the Higher Regional Court of Munich upheld the first instance judgment finding that this restriction was justified due to the damage to the manufacturer's reputation. The District Court of Berlin, however, held in two judgments in 2007 and 2008 that an outright prohibition of sales through eBay is not admissible; this can be allowed only if quality standards are disregarded. See Held, *supra*.

outright ban to use third party platforms seems not to be allowed according to the Guidelines, a supplier may require that its distributors use them only in accordance with the standards and conditions agreed between the supplier and its distributors for use of the internet (paragraph 54). It is not very clear to what extent a third party platform may offer to meet exactly the same requirements as an agreed distributor's website. eBay claims, in its response to the Commission's consultation, that a distributor may set up a customised eBay shop that suits the product display and information requirements or needs specified by the supplier.[40] If this is really the case, then preventing distributors from using such a site would be difficult to justify. The Guidelines, however, specify that if a distributor uses a third party platform, the supplier may require that customers do not visit the distributor's website through a site carrying the name or logo of the third party platform. This restriction seems reasonable and legitimate as, in the absence of it, a customer may be inclined to think that the third party is in fact a member of a selective distribution system.

To conclude, the Commission seems to have listened to the reasons of luxury/appliance manufacturers and taken appropriate steps, at least in theoretical terms, as to permit sufficient protection of their investments in brand image and pre-sale (physical) service. It remains to be seen if the criteria set out in the Guidelines work in practice, and if suppliers are able to elaborate the right parameters to warrant that restrictions are suited to ensure the viability of their offline networks, without going beyond what is strictly necessary to achieve this result.

19.4 CONCLUSION

While not revolutionary, the new package on vertical restraints does represent a meaningful evolution of the Commission's practice and shows a more open approach to the review of these types of agreements.

The Commission has opened the door to several potential justifications to hardcore restrictions, and has paid particular attention to the suppliers' legitimate concerns regarding free riding. This phenomenon, which is typical of internet discounters, is used as the main grounds to allow partial restrictions on internet sales.

Overall, the solutions offered by the Guidelines appear to be a balanced result. The main objective of the Commission, to enable the full development of online sales, appears to have been achieved, while at the same time

---

40 See eBay's response to the public consultation, *supra*.

investments in brand image and pre-sale service in 'bricks-and-mortar' shops are protected.

The way in which the Commission obtains this result, though – i.e. mainly by assuming that internet sales are almost always passive sales – does not always seem to be suitable and probably suffers from the choice of treating sales in the virtual world with instruments (such as the legal categories applicable to territorial restrictions) that were created to govern 'physical' sales. It can therefore be asked whether a less conservative approach would have been more appropriate in this important and ever-evolving area of business.

The inconsistency highlighted above may in future give rise to interesting legal issues should the Court of Justice rule negatively on whether an outright ban on selling over the internet in a selective distribution system amounts to a hardcore restriction, an early revision of the Guidelines would be warranted.

20. Parallel trade: econ-oclast thoughts on a dogma of EU competition law

Nicolas Petit

20.1 INTRODUCTION

With an unparalleled ability to explain complex legal issues in a catchy and creative manner, Professor Jacques Bourgeois has set a high standard for legal scholars. This short chapter modestly attempts to pay tribute to his academic brilliance, in shedding new light on the European Union (EU) competition law principle that firms' attempts to block parallel trade from 'low price countries' to 'high price countries' in the EU are akin to 'hardcore' restrictions of competition infringing Articles 101 and 102 of the Treaty on the Functioning of the European Union (TFEU). The choice of a topic that lies at the intersection of competition and trade policies will not come as a surprise to readers familiar with Professor Bourgeois' work. And since Professor Bourgeois is a man of many languages, this study uses the words of economics to review this remarkably stable issue, at least in the case-law of the European courts.

In the past decades, the European Court of Justice (ECJ) has repeatedly upheld European Commission (the Commission) decisions against firms that had sought to limit parallel trade within the EU. This is because parallel trade is deemed to improve consumer welfare, through downward price equalization. The leading cases involve sectors where goods/services are subject to price differentials across countries and/or intellectual property rights (IPRs), such as pharmaceuticals, cars, luxury goods and branded products, etc. In *GlaxoSmithKline*, for instance, the ECJ held that an agreement intended to limit parallel trade must in principle be considered to have as its object the restriction of competition.[1] In *Sot. Lélos kai Sia*, it explained clearly that 'parallel trade is liable to exert pressure on

[1] ECJ, C-501/06 P, *GlaxoSmithKline Services Unlimited v Commission and Others*, not yet reported para. 43.

prices and, consequently, to create financial benefits' for consumers.[2] Finally, in sectors involving IPRs, the EU courts have consistently ruled that once a particular product/service is sold into a low price country, the IPR holder can no longer prevent imports of this particular product/service into the high price country.[3] His rights are exhausted.

Against this background, this chapter seeks to demonstrate that whilst parallel trade (also referred to as 'grey market trade' in the United States, or as 'arbitrage' in economic theory) in the EU is subject to a remarkably sympathetic and protective legal regime, the economic case supporting this approach remains to be made. To this end, it shows that in at least four respects, the position of the EU courts, and more generally of the EU institutions, is far from unquestionable. First, there is no undisputed theoretical or empirical evidence that parallel trade improves short-term consumer welfare (section 20.2). Second, parallel trade may harm long-term consumer welfare, through a detrimental effect on commercial and technological innovation (section 20.3). Third, parallel trade shares many analogies with speculation and other wasteful economic activities (section 20.4). Fourth, parallel trade may generate a host of collateral welfare-reducing effects on society at large (section 20.5).

20.2 THE POSITIVE EFFECTS OF PARALLEL TRADE ON THE SHORT-TERM WELFARE OF CONSUMERS HAVE NOT BEEN ESTABLISHED

Proponents of parallel trade often intuitively argue that it leads to downward price equalization,[4] and increased intra-brand competition (competition between perfect substitutes, i.e. products/services of a same brand) to the benefit of consumers.[5] Upon closer examination, this view deserves to be seriously nuanced. The short-term benefits of parallel trade on consumer welfare are indeed poorly documented in the empirical economic

---

[2] ECJ, C-468/06 to C-478/06, *Sot. Lélos kai Sia EE and Others v GlaxoSmith-Kline AEVE*, 2008, ECR I-7139, para. 56.

[3] In the field of trademarks, see, ECJ, C-355/96, *Silhouette International Schmied GmbH & Co. KG and Hartlauer Handelsgesellschaft mbH* [1998] ECR I-4799.

[4] Parallel trade leads in principle to price equalization (in case of perfect arbitrage) or price approximation (in case of imperfect arbitrage: when transaction costs are >0).

[5] Abbot, F.M., 'Parallel Importation: Economic and Social Welfare Dimensions', Study prepared for the Swiss Agency for Development and Cooperation, June 2007.

literature (20.2.1). Rather, from an economic standpoint, parallel trade may almost equally be seen as detrimental to short-term consumer welfare, in that it prevents suppliers from engaging into socially efficient price differentiation (20.2.2). More specifically, parallel trade may decrease the satisfaction of positional goods consumers (20.2.3).

20.2.1 The Short-Term Welfare Effects of Parallel Trade on Consumers have not been Empirically Proven

To date, the very few *empirical* economic studies devoted to the effects of parallel trade on consumer welfare have reached inconsistent results. To focus only on the EU internal situation – where parallel trade is lawful[6] – a first strand of studies have invalidated the perception that parallel trade enhances consumer welfare in the short term through price reductions. In 1999, a survey conducted in relation to a wide range of trademarked products (e.g. compact discs, cars, cosmetics and perfumes, soft drinks, clothing, etc.) reported for instance that the 'effect of [parallel trade] on retailers and consumers was largely seen as neutral',[7] and consequently that the case for parallel trade is 'simply stated and rests on the assumption that this will deliver lower prices to consumers'.[8]

In the same vein, a 2004 London School of Economics (LSE) study empirically tested the effects of parallel imports on six pharmaceutical product categories in six EU member states.[9] It found that[10]

> the hypothesis that pharmaceutical parallel trade stimulates price competition and drives prices down in destination (importing) countries over the long-term is rejected. There is also very little evidence lending support to the argument that parallel trade stimulates (price) competition among exporting and importing countries. Thus, the arbitrage hypothesis of price equalisation or price approximation is also rejected.

---

[6] The situation of the EU provides what economists call a good 'natural experiment'.

[7] National Economic Research associates (NERA), SJ Berwin & Co et IFF Research, 8 February 1998, p. 17.

[8] *Idem*, p. 8.

[9] Accounting for 21 per cent of the retail market.

[10] Kanavos, P., Costa-I-Font, J., Merkur, S., and Gemmill, M., 'The Economic Impact of Pharmaceutical Parallel Trade in European Union Member States: A Stakeholder Analysis', *MA Special Research Paper*, LSE Health and Social Care London School of Economics and Political Science, January 2004, p. 13.

A similar finding was reached in a 2003 study, which demonstrated that parallel imports of pharmaceutical products in Finland had not intensified price competition, and has thus only generated nominal savings.[11]

A second strand of empirical studies has, however, pointed out to a contrary conclusion. In 2001, a study showed that the price of drugs subject to parallel imports in Sweden had risen less than the price of other drugs.[12] Similarly, a 2003 study focusing on patented drugs in Denmark, the United Kingdom, Germany, Sweden and the Netherlands found that prices had decreased with competition from parallel trade between 1997 and 2002.[13] In the same vein, another study covering 50 pharmaceutical products in Denmark, Germany, the United Kingdom and Sweden found in 2006 that parallel imports competition had exercised a downward effect on prices.[14]

Finally, a third strand of studies has offered nuanced, ambiguous results. For instance in 1999, a report of the Swedish Competition Authority indicated that the magnitude of the price increases arising from a prohibition of parallel imports was at best limited.[15] To add even more confusion to this complex state of affairs, an academic paper argued that the price pressure exerted by parallel imports was highly product-specific and often immaterial.[16]

Overall, the empirical economic literature provides little conclusive evidence that parallel trade delivers lower prices to consumers. In addition, most of the above-mentioned studies relate to pharmaceutical products, subject to patents.[17] One may thus wonder whether their findings are valid across the board, to other industries and other forms of IPR. Finally, from

---

[11] Linnosmaa, I., Karhunen, T., Vohlonen, I., 'Parallel importation of pharmaceuticals in Finland. Effects on markets and expenditures', *Pharmaceutical Development and Regulation*, Vol. 1, 2003, pp. 67–74.

[12] Ganslandt, M. and Maskus, K., 'Intellectual property rights, parallel imports and strategic behaviour', *Working Paper Series 704*, Research Institute of Industrial Economics.

[13] West, P. and Mahon, J., 'Benefits to Payers and Patients from Parallel Trade', *Health Economics Consortium*, York, 2003.

[14] Enemark, U. Møller Pedersen, K., and Sørensen, J., 'The economic impact of parallel import of pharmaceuticals', University of Southern Denmark, 2006.

[15] Swedish Competition Authority, 'Parallel Imports-Effects of the Silhouette Ruling', Report Series, Vol. 1, 1999.

[16] Persson, U., Anell, A., and Persson, M., 'Parallel Trade with Medicines in Sweden'An Economic Analysis', Swedish Institute for Health Economics, Lund, 2001.

[17] The specifics of the pharmaceutical sector have been acknowledged, and discussed at lenghth by Advocate General Jacobs in his Opinion in the *Syfait* case. C-53/03, *Synetairismos Farmakopoion Aitolias & Akarnanias (Syfait) and others v GlaxoSmithKline AEVE* [2005] ECR I-04609 (para. 96, in particular).

a purely methodological standpoint, the robustness of those empirical studies is not entirely convincing because they either: (1) rely on unverifiable proprietary information; (2) are based on unreliable stakeholders surveys;[18] or (3) have been financed by industry stakeholders.[19]

20.2.2 Parallel Trade injures Short-Term Consumer Welfare by removing the Ability of Producers to engage into Socially Efficient Price Differentiation

In addition to the lack of clear-cut empirical evidence in support of (or against) parallel trade, economic theory puts another dent in the blanket intuition that parallel trade improves short-term consumer welfare. From an economic perspective, parallel trade may in fact well be detrimental to consumer welfare because it prevents firms from charging different prices in countries where consumers have different preferences.[20]

The core of this idea revolves around the fact that in real world markets, consumers often exhibit a different ability or willingness to pay. This may be due to differences in wealth, taste, brand perception, taxes, cultural differences, local purchasing power, insurance system, etc.[21] For instance, a bottle of Polish-branded vodka might be perceived as a special product in Western Europe – hence western EU consumers are ready to pay a high price for this product – and by contrast, be perceived as a relatively standard product in Poland – hence Polish consumers are only willing to pay a low price for this product. In a setting of this kind, the vodka producer will charge different prices in Poland and in western European countries.[22]

Many economists consider that there is 'nothing intrinsically bad' about such forms of 'price discrimination'.[23] On the contrary – as long as production costs are covered – differential pricing entitles firms to serve markets where consumers' ability to pay is limited. Those consumers would

---

[18] Ganslandt and Maskus, *supra.*

[19] Many studies are based on surveys because data on parallel trade is often confidential.

[20] Malueg, D. and Schwartz, M., 'Parallel Imports, Demand Dispersion and International Price Discrimination', *Journal of International Economics*, Vol. 37, 1994.

[21] NERA, SJ Berwin & Co et IFF Research, *supra*; Swedish Competition Authority, Parallel Imports-Effects of the Silhouette Ruling, *supra.*

[22] According to the consumers' ability to pay (economists talk of consumer elasticity). See Heimler, A., 'Competition Law Enforcement and Intellectual Property Rights', 2008, mimeo.

[23] NERA, SJ Berwin & Co et IFF Research, *supra.*

possibly not be served if producers had to set a uniform EU-wide price.[24] Price differentiation thus allows producers to make some consumers better off (those of the low price country), without making other consumers worse off (those of the high price country). As long as consumption (and with it, output) increases, price differentiation is thus a 'Pareto-efficient', welfare-enhancing practice.[25] In addition, in industries where fixed costs are high (e.g. in R&D or advertisement-intensive sectors), any increase in the quantities produced (and sold) generates economies of scale. Hence, price differentiation also improves the welfare of producers.[26]

By contrast, in a legal system that forbids all restrictions of parallel trade, a producer can no longer price discriminate, absent means to close off parallel imports from low price to high price countries. If parallel trade undermines his profitability in the high price market,[27] the producer will thus choose to sell at a single price across all markets, possibly leaving some markets unserved.[28] The producer may even decide to shut down distribution activities in low price markets.[29] This, in turn, is likely to trigger a spate of other harmful economic side-effects (e.g. job losses, etc.), particularly if the low price country is a developing economy.[30] Of course, dominant producers can exceptionally be forced to sell under the competition rules. However, the current approach under the EU competition rules is ambiguous,[31] and regulators seem reluctant to delve into such matters, which often involve complex price regulation issues. In summary, parallel trade is likely to discourage manufacturers from selling in low price countries.

From a public policy standpoint, the upshot of the above analysis is that rules forbidding price differentiation (such as the above-mentioned case-law or the so-called principle of 'international exhaustion' may well yield

---

24 Ganslandt and Maskus, *supra*, p. 21.

25 Heimler, *supra*; Kanavos, Costa-I-Font, Merkur and Gemmill, *supra*, p. 41.

26 See, for a similar argument, Hilke, J.C., 'Free-trading or free-riding: An Examination of the Theories and available Empirical Evidence on Grey Market Imports', *World Competition*, Vol. 32, 1998, p.75. See also NERA, SJ Berwin & Co et IFF Research, *supra*, p.6.

27 Not because prices will decline, as explained in §I, but because parallel importers reduce the quantities sold by the producer, and reduce its market share.

28 Valletti, T. and Szymanski, S., 'Parallel Trade, International Exhaustion and Intellectual Property Rights: A Welfare Analysis', *Journal of Industrial Economics*, Vol. 54, No. 4, 2006, pp. 499–526.

29 Grossman, G.M. and Lai, E.L.-C., 'Parallel Imports and Price Controls', *RAND Journal of Economics*, Vol. 39, No. 2, Summer 2008, pp. 378–402, fn 4.

30 Kenny, P. and McNutt, P., 'Parallel Imports & Trademark Exhaustion: Two Wrongs from a Trademark Right', Irish Competition Authority' Discussion Paper No. 8 Competition, 1 December 1999.

31 ECJ, C-468/06 to C-478/06, *supra*, paras. 68–9.

welfare-reducing effects for consumers.[32] In particular, such rules could likely lead to increased, uniform prices or alternatively to reduced products/services availability in low price countries.[33] Conversely, from a welfare-oriented perspective, rules maintaining some wiggle room for producers to price discriminate may be socially more beneficial to consumers. This is all the more true when consumers across markets exhibit heterogeneous characteristics.[34]

20.2.3 Parallel Trade may reduce the Satisfaction of Customers on Specific Product Markets

Parallel imports may reduce the satisfaction which consumers derive from certain products/services (often, trademarked products/services) in the case of positional goods (or 'Veblen goods'), such as luxury cars, high-end wines, etc. In a system of unfettered parallel trade, the influx of low-price imports (1) will indeed decrease in the short term the personal satisfaction of consumers located in the high price country;[35] and (2) might in the long term dry out demand for the product/service, which will no longer be perceived as an exclusive or high status good.

20.3 PARALLEL TRADE MAY HARM THE LONG-TERM WELFARE OF CONSUMERS, THROUGH A DETRIMENTAL EFFECT ON COMMERCIAL AND TECHNOLOGICAL INNOVATION

The argument that parallel trade chills producers and retailers' incentives to innovate has often been challenged as intuitive and exaggerated. Yet, it seems a reasonable assumption that *producers* take the anticipated profitability of future products/services into account when devising their R&D or advertising programmes. Hence, the very fact that parallel imports may depress *ex post* profit margins, should logically reduce producers' *ex ante*

---

32 Kanavos, Costa-I-Font, Merkur and Gemmill, *supra*, p. 41.

33 Gallini, N. and Hollis, A., 'A Contractual Approach to the Grey Market', *International Review of Law & Economics*, Vol. 19, No. 1, 1999, p. 17.

34 Malueg and Schwartz, *supra*, p. 22. To date, only a few, solitary studies have challenged the view that price discrimination is socially efficient. See Abbott, *supra*, pp. 5–7.

35 Kenny & McNutt, *supra.*

incentives invest in costly R&D,[36] advertising campaigns or product-quality improvement programmes.[37]

Interestingly, in *GlaxoSmithkline*, the EU General Court (GC) seemed, albeit implicitly, open to the view that restrictions on parallel trade did not necessarily have the object to restrict competition, and could in fact stimulate R&D financing.[38] This case concerned a distribution agreement between a pharmaceutical firm and its Spanish wholesalers that sought to limit parallel trade from Spain to high-price countries. In a 2001 decision, the Commission had refused to admit that the agreement contributed to R&D funding, and denied the benefit of the exception rule enshrined in Article 101(3) TFEU. On appeal, the Court vacated the Commission's decision. It considered in particular that the Commission should have more intensively scrutinized whether the agreement gave rise to an 'economic advantage' by contributing to the financing of pharmaceutical innovation. This ruling was however struck down at a later stage by the ECJ, on the ground that restrictions to parallel trade ought to be presumed unlawful under Article 101(1) TFEU.[39] However, the ECJ upheld the analysis of the GC in relation to Article 101(3) TFEU, thereby implicitly confirming that restrictions to parallel trade could benefit from the exception rule upon proof of efficiency benefits.

The negative effects of parallel trade on incentives to invest also extend to other sides of the market. Parallel trade may indeed undermine *retailers'* incentives to invest into before-sale (e.g. marketing, promotional advertisement, product information, websites), sale (e.g. testing, advice, etc.) and after-sale (e.g. technical assistance, service workshops, etc.) services.[40] On close examination, this chilling effect of parallel trade on retailers' *ex ante* incentives to invest has two facets. First, the fact that *retailers'* investments will help parallel traders to increase sales without incurring similar costs

---

[36] Li, C. and Maskus, K.E., 'The impact of parallel imports on investments in cost-reducing research and development', *Journal of International Economics*, Vol. 68, 2006, pp. 443–5.

[37] Valletti and Szymanski, *supra*. Rey reaches the same conclusion in a scenario of government price regulation and finds that parallel trade reduces incentives to invest in R&D. See Rey, P., 'The impact of Parallel Imports on Prescription Medicines', *IDEI*, Toulouse, 14 October 2003, mimeo. *See* also Danzon, P., 'The Economics of parallel trade', *Pharmacoeconomics*, Vol. 13, 1998, pp. 293–304, p. 32.

[38] CFI (now GC), T-168/01, *GlaxoSmithKline Services v. Commission* [2006] ECR II-2969.

[39] ECJ, C-501/06 P, *supra*, paras. 62–4.

[40] Yonatan, E., 'Appropriability, First Sale & Exhaustion', 28 September 2008, mimeo.

(and procure the goods at a lower price) is perceived by the latter as 'free-riding' on their investments.[41]

Second, in a regime of unfettered parallel trade, the influx of low price imports may induce official dealers to focus on price reductions and neglect service.[42] Of course, this is likely to introduce a jolt of intra-brand competition in the market. Meanwhile, however, this may reduce inter-brand competition, which crucially hinges on the ability of market players to promote their brands through efficient retail services.

Unfortunately – and despite their immediate impact on consumers – retailers' investments are often overlooked because unlike producers' costly R&D and advertisement programmes, they often involve less significant numbers.

20.4 PARALLEL TRADE SHARES ANALOGIES WITH SPECULATION AND OTHER WASTEFUL ECONOMIC ACTIVITIES

20.4.1 The Intriguing Analogies between Parallel Trade and Speculation

Like most, if not all, economic operators, parallel traders are profit-maximizers. Yet, unlike a majority of economic operators, parallel traders must make little, if any, investments in the course of their business.[43] They simply hedge against transport, transactions and pure regulatory costs, as well as exchange rates differentials.[44] In plain language, parallel traders are akin to speculators. They buy and sell products with the sole purpose of taking advantage of price differentials. Their business model is devoid of any value-adding, innovative activity.

---

41 Kanavos, Costa-I-Font, Merkur and Gemmill, *supra*.

42 Yonatan, *supra*, p. 66.

43 In their daily business, parallel traders incur essentially two types of costs. First, they support indirect costs, which consist in search costs in low price countries. Second, they incur direct costs, which are the costs associated with the satisfaction of regulatory requirements in export countries (e.g. safety, repackaging, etc.). See Kanavos, Costa-I-Font, Merkur and Gemmill, *supra*, p. 88.

44 Economic studies demonstrate that parallel trade is boosted in times of rapid changes in currency exchange rates (see, for instance, the survey of Hilke in the United States, *supra*).

With this in mind, it becomes obvious that parallel traders have significant incentives to keep their purchasing price secret from their clients;[45] charge high prices; and pocket-in the widest possible profit margin when exporting products/services. Moreover, parallel traders' ability to speculate is magnified when end-consumers are not price sensitive, such as when their purchases are refunded by national healthcare systems (for instance, through social security schemes).[46]

Against this background, and provided that the existence of parallel trade does not improve the welfare of end-consumers,[47] the question whether a system of unrestrained parallel trade is desirable revolves around what economists term a 'distributional' (or transfer) issue. Put simply, governments should decide whether they want (1) to give preference to producers that have incurred investments (and their official retailers) by affording them a degree of protection against parallel imports; or; (2) to confiscate part of their revenue, and distribute it to parallel traders.[48] In the latter case, a system of parallel trade is tantamount to a tax on investments.

The resolution of this issue involves a discretionary policy choice. This being said, any such decision ought to be based on a comparative assessment of the contribution that parallel traders and producers respectively bring to economic welfare. In this regard, the very fact that long-term innovation strategies and investments are critical to economic growth should steer public policy choices towards increased protection of inventive firms. By contrast, governments should resist the temptation to assist operators who may widespread speculate on short-term imbalances between markets, on pain on promoting free-riding on others' investments

20.4.2 Parallel Trade may encourage Inefficient and Wasteful Economic Behaviour

Some proponents of parallel trade have argued that besides improvements to short-term consumer welfare, parallel trade also yields additional welfare-enhancing effects. In the normal course of their business, parallel

---

45 Kanavos, Costa-I-Font, Merkur and Gemmill, *supra*, p. 88. It ought to be noted here that parallel trade only rarely occurs at the retail level. See NERA, SJ Berwin & Co et IFF Research, *supra*.

46 Kanavos, Costa-I-Font, Merkur and Gemmill, *supra*.

47 The majority of benefits arising from arbitrage accrue to those who perform it. See Danzon, *supra*.

48 Along those lines, unbridled parallel trade favours jobs in unofficial outlets, and hinders jobs in official distribution channels. See NERA, SJ Berwin & Co et IFF Research, *supra*, p. 26.

traders must indeed proceed to repackaging, relabelling, marketing and other handling activities.[49] Arguably, those activities give rise to job opportunities, and should thus be encouraged. Moreover, parallel trade would arguably allow retailers subject to cyclical demand vacillations on their home market (fluctuations in fashion, for instance), to offload inventory on other markets, thereby encouraging timely rationalization measures.[50]

On close examination, those allegations deserve to be mitigated. The first argument is economically disputable. As a general principle, mainstream economic theory teaches that welfare is maximized when as little of society's scarce resources (capital and labour) are consumed to produce a given good/service. This means that the ratio between input and output is optimized. When a parallel trader engages in repackaging, relabelling, marketing, and handling activities, he consumes additional scarce society resources, without however, increasing output. From this perspective, parallel trade is socially inefficient.

The second argument can be equally challenged. Virtually all business management textbooks teach that efficient operators seek to anticipate demand fluctuations, and accordingly adjust their procurement needs. Rules entitling firms to freely offload quantities on external markets fare poorly with this principle. They are likely to trigger input overconsumption dynamics (thereby misallocating scarce resources within society). Anticipating that there will be external markets on which they can sell whenever they want, retailers will be less cautious when placing orders.

20.5 PARALLEL TRADE MAY TRIGGER A HOST OF ADVERSE COLLATERAL EFFECTS

20.5.1 Parallel Trade is Likely to Generate Welfare-Reducing Effects on Other Products/Services

A first harmful collateral effect of parallel trade may arise when the supplier is active on several markets, where he provides a range of complementary products/services (e.g. a car manufacturer that provides also credit and financial services to customers). Faced with parallel imports with respect to one product/service but not to others, the supplier holder may seek to recoup the profits lost on the product subject to parallel imports

[49] Swedish Competition Authority, Parallel Imports-Effects of the Silhouette Ruling, *supra,* p. 28.

[50] *Idem*, p. 30.

through price increases on the other product/service. This is clearly detrimental to short-term consumer welfare in the market for the product not subject to parallel imports. Alternatively, the supplier may decide to cut down on investments in other products/services,[51] thereby again harming the 'interests of consumers' in terms of quality and choice.[52] For instance, the car manufacturer may decide to cease providing credit and financial services.

20.5.2 Parallel Trade exacerbates the Costs of Fighting Against Counterfeiting and Piracy

Parallel trade may facilitate counterfeiting. An OECD report noted that in the area of sportswear, 'it is not uncommon for parallel traders to send genuine samples to the importer and mix the consignment with counterfeits'.[53] Because parallel imported product consignments sometimes conceal pure counterfeits, it is critical that suppliers holding IPR can avail themselves of border controls and import suspension measures against parallel imported products/services. Such protections are generally absent from countries endorsing a full parallel trade regime. This is why it is generally considered that 'allowing parallel imports would weaken a number of defences against counterfeiting and piracy'.[54]

Besides this, economic literature suggests that in industries subject to counterfeiting, an optimal response for suppliers holding IPR is to keep their product distinct from (potential) counterfeiters. The maintenance of distinctiveness is seen as a 'prerequisite' for effective anti-counterfeiting strategies.[55] To this end, IPR holders must invest significant resources into branding and other market promotional activities. However, the fact that parallel trade reduces the profitability of IPR holders limits the resources that can be devoted to the fight against counterfeiting.

20.5.3 Parallel Trade may promote Socially Wasteful Behaviour from Manufacturers

A system of unlimited parallel trade is likely to prompt suppliers to adopt a range of private remedies in order to curtail parallel trade. From an

---

51 *Idem*, p. 21.

52 NERA, SJ Berwin & Co et IFF Research, *supra*, p. 6.

53 'The Economic Impact of Counterfeiting', OECD, 1998, p. 13, available at www.oecd.org/dataoecd/11/11/2090589.pdf.

54 NERA, SJ Berwin & Co et IFF Research, *supra*, p. 7 and 14.

55 Bosworth, D. and Yang, D., 'Conceptual issues of global counterfeiting on products and services', *Journal of Intellectual Property Rights*, Vol. 11, 2006, pp. 15–21.

economic perspective, such remedies are socially wasteful because they consume resources which could otherwise be allocated to productive and innovative investments. Illustrations of such practices include: relabelling on export markets; change of the product specifications in export markets; adoption of different trademarks in each country to discourage gray trade; modification of product/service characteristics across countries.[56]

20.5.4 Parallel Trade can lead to Inefficient Distribution Structures

Systems of parallel trade limit the dissemination of products/services throughout society. A certain degree of protection against parallel imports might be necessary to increase the density of a distribution network (and in turn, foster intra-brand service competition). A prospective distributor contemplating the decision to join a distribution network will typically request assurances from the supplier that he will not be confronted with cut-throat price competition from parallel importers. Absent such assurances, he might be reluctant to join the distribution network in the first place.[57]

20.5.5 Parallel Trade conflicts with Other Global Policy Goals

20.5.5.1 Parallel Trade is not Congruent with Sustainable Development

In recent years, many of the world's nations have repeatedly insisted on promoting economic strategies which 'meet the needs of the present without compromising the ability of future generations to meet their own needs'.[58] Worldwide, this commitment has led governments to encourage – and sometimes coerce – economic operators to optimize energy generation and consumption patterns.

---

[56] Hilke, *supra*, p. 6.

[57] A somewhat similar argument applies to technology transfer agreements and the dissemination of information. See Fink, C., 'Entering the Jungle of Intellectual Property Rights Exhaustion and Parallel Importation' in C. Fink and K. E. Maskus (eds), *Intellectual Property and Development: Lessons from Recent Economic Research*, Washington, DC, The World Bank and Oxford University Press, 2005; Conley, C., 'Parallel Imports: The Tired Debate of the Exhaustion of Intellectual Property Rights and Why the WTO Should Harmonize the Haphazard Laws of the International Community', May 2008. IP holders might be reluctant to transfer technology, if this leads at a later stage to parallel imports.

[58] 'Our Common Future', Report of the World Commission on Environment and Development, World Commission on Environment and Development, 1987. Published as Annex to General Assembly document A/42/427, Development and International Co-operation: Environment 2 August 1987.

A salient, often overlooked, feature of parallel imports is to trade off the long-term preservation of natural resources against the short-term economic benefits arising from intra-brand competition. This is because parallel trade duplicates transport flows, for instance through 'reimports'. In addition, parallel trade may lead suppliers to relocate their production facilities towards low-costs, energy-inefficient countries. This, in and of itself, is wholly inconsistent with the current fervour for sustainable development and the use of eco-friendly production techniques.[59]

20.5.5.2 Parallel trade is not Congruent with Economic Development

From the standpoint of low price, developing countries, 'it is unclear whether parallel trading brings net benefits to the economy'.[60] To draw a glaring – yet controversial – analogy, in a parallel trading ecosystem, developing countries are akin to large shopping malls, where massive quantities of products/services can be sourced under attractive conditions. As a result, an increasing number of parallel traders source products/services from developing countries, and one cannot exclude that the needs of the local populations will not be fully ensured. Albeit not a developing country, it has been reported that Greece – a low-price country that has positioned itself as a primary source of parallel trade in the EU – has experienced shortages in pharmaceutical products.[61] This, in fact, was the factual situation that triggered the *Syfait* and *Sot. Lelos kai Sia EE* cases, which were later ruled upon by the ECJ.[62]

In this regard, some observers have, however, contended that this issue was not a cause of concern.[63] They argue that in a system of parallel trade, welfare is 'additive'.[64] The gains of consumers located in the import country would allegedly be greater than the losses for consumers located in the export country, because the former value the product/service more. Hence, from a welfare-oriented standpoint, parallel trade would be beneficial, regardless of the fact that consumers in the low price country are no longer served.

It is submitted that this argument is wholly unpersuasive, and contrary to basic principles of economics and natural justice. Under mainstream

---

59 Swedish Competition Authority, Parallel Imports-Effects of the Silhouette Ruling, *supra*, p. 40.

60 World Bank Discussion Paper No. 412, IPRs and Economic Development, 2000, p. 36.

61 Kanavos, Costa-I-Font, Merkur and Gemmill, *supra*, p. 85.

62 ECJ, C-53/03, *Syfait & ors v GlaxoSmithKline*, *supra*; CJ, Joined Cases C-468/06 to C-478/06, *Sot. Lelos kai Sia EE v GlaxoSmithKline AEVE*, *supra*.

63 Kenny and McNutt, *supra*, p. 11.

64 It draws on what economists generally label a 'total welfare' perspective.

economic theory, a welfare-optimizing outcome arises when all the customers that are ready to pay the producer's costs are served. In the above setting, consumers in the export country are not served, regardless of their ability to pay a price which compensates the producer's costs. Economic welfare might thus not be maximized.[65]

20.6 CONCLUSION

Legal standards often have a profound impact on economic growth. They should thus be based, and selected, on the basis of sound economics, and in particular following an objective cost/benefit assessment (including the assessment of alternative legal principles).

In light of the above, the EU institutions' firm stance in favour of unbridled parallel trade seems questionable. Beyond the intuitive, perfunctory view that parallel trade stimulates intra-brand competition to the benefit of consumers, a significant number of economic studies shed light on the fact that parallel trade wields welfare-reducing effects. The current legal paradigm has thus apparently more to do with politics – the commitment to market integration inherited from the late 1950s – and/or legal conservatism – the Court's reluctance to recast entrenched legal standards – than with sound economics.[66]

[65] A more optimal outcome could, however, be attained with international price discrimination. The producer would set its price above costs, but would serve consumers in the export and the import countries at different prices (Kenny and McNutt, *supra*, p. 32).

[66] To date, most if not all attempts to soothe this principle have failed. See CFI, T-168/01, *GlaxoSmithKline Services v Commission* [2006] ECR II-2969. Or they have been left unanswered by the EU institutions. See ECJ, C-53/03, *Syfait & ors v GlaxoSmithKline*, *supra*.

Abuses and mergers

21. How to treat aftermarkets under Article 102 TFEU

Hendrik Bourgeois

Many of the contributors to this *Festschrift* are in a better position than I to give direct testimony of Jacques Bourgeois' outstanding qualities as a teacher, academic, mentor, legal counsel, advocate, colleague, and friend. Be that as it may, I am quite confident that it is as a father that he really surpasses himself. My contribution addresses a question that he and I some time ago discussed. At the end of that discussion, as happens more often than not when I debate all sorts of things with him, I was left with a lingering feeling that some of my arguments had not quite convinced him. This is a modest attempt to set the record straight.

21.1 INTRODUCTION

The manufacturing and sale of durable equipment that requires ongoing maintenance, spare parts, or related consumables once the durable equipment has been purchased, constitutes an important part of Europe's economy.[1] I refer to the first type of equipment as 'primary equipment' (including, for instance, mechanical, electronic goods and IT products, covering everything from kitchen appliances to automobiles, from cameras to printers, and from computers to healthcare equipment). I refer to the maintenance servicing, spare parts or consumables (for instance the cartridge in a printer), add-on products, applications and upgrades related to primary equipment as 'complementary products and/or services'. The market for these products and/or services is often referred to as the

[1] In terms of number of enterprises, turnover, value added, or persons employed, roughly 15 per cent of the European non-financial economy could be defined to consist of primary equipment as defined in this chapter. See for instance, Eurostat Statistical Books, *European business – Facts and figures*, 2009, available at http://epp.eurostat.ec.europa.eu/cache/ITY_OFFPUB/KS-BW-09–001/EN/KS-BW-09–001-EN.PDF.

aftermarket of the market for the primary equipment (presumably because purchasing decisions relating to, or supply of, these products and/or services take place after the purchase decision relating to, or supply of, the primary equipment). Obviously, primary equipment manufacturers are often extremely interested in the quality of the maintenance, spare parts and/or consumables for primary equipment. This is because complementary products and/or services impact the level of customer satisfaction for the primary equipment products during these products' useful life, and hence the primary equipment manufacturers' commercial success. A complex piece of durable equipment that does not work well or performs badly or that is very costly to maintain once it has been sold, is also likely to sell poorly in the future. Hence, manufacturers of primary equipment are usually actively involved in providing maintenance services for their primary equipment products (either directly or by relying on carefully vetted and appointed third parties), and typically will also manufacture and sell products/or services complementary to the primary equipment.

However, in periods of economic downturn and reduced access to finance, the pools of commercial opportunities for suppliers to sell, often expensive, durable equipment may become fewer. When faced with budget cuts and fewer euros to spend, customers will often try to extend the lifetime of their primary equipment, and as a result generate increased demand for complementary products and/or services. In addition, when confronted with fewer opportunities to sell primary equipment, suppliers may either seek to increase their offer and sales of complementary products and/or services, to meet an expected customer demand.

Under these circumstances, issues of contention may increasingly arise from a competition law perspective when a manufacturer of primary equipment is perceived either to attempt to reserve the business for the complementary products and/or services for itself, or when a manufacturer amends its commercial policies relating to services/spare parts/consumables.[2] Similarly, when faced with economic constraints, purchasers of complementary products and/or services may inappropriately try, on alleged competition law grounds, to renegotiate the long-term contractual conditions of (relatively high-value) complementary products and/or services supply agreements that have been entered into at arm's length in a competitive environment. Such agreements are often entered into at the

[2] European competition law issues could arise when a primary equipment manufacturer would either engage in exclusionary behaviour, for instance by refusing to supply the necessary inputs to independent service providers, denying them the ability to effectively compete for complementary goods and/or services, or engage in exploitative pricing behaviour.

time when the purchasing decision for the primary equipment was made (at competitive prices), but on terms that some customers may, *ex post*, perceive to be too favourable to the supplier.

These practices and issues can and sometimes have caused some to conclude, probably too hastily, that a primary equipment manufacturer can abuse a dominant position in the aftermarket for the provision of its own branded replacement parts or services, even in a situation where the manufacturer faces fierce competition in the market for the primary product.[3] Indeed, as described in more detail below, this seems to be the case under (old but settled) jurisprudence of the European Court of Justice (ECJ).[4]

This conclusion is often troubling and worrying to primary equipment manufacturers and their legal advisors, since primary equipment manufacturers often have a very high share in the servicing and/or the supply of spare parts on/or consumables for the installed base of their own products. This is often because these original equipment manufacturers typically will start off with 100 per cent share of the servicing, spare parts or consumables delivery of newly introduced primary equipment products, and will only lose share in response to new entry from independent service providers or self-service done by the customers. Indeed, firms that are less successful in the primary equipment market often continue to maintain a very high percentage of the sales of spare parts and service for their brand of equipment because third parties typically will focus on the equipment brands with the largest installed base and the higher primary equipment market share, since they offer the greatest commercial potential for alternative providers. Hence, even a manufacturer with an extremely low share of the primary equipment market could in theory be held to be a monopolist in the aftermarket for the equipment in question. The observation is also disconcerting because customers are often willing to pay a premium for servicing or parts provided by the original equipment manufacturer, who is typically perceived – rightly or wrongly – as being able to provide

---

[3] When the manufacturer has significant market power in the primary market, conduct by that manufacturer that is geared towards reducing competition in the aftermarket may constitute illegal tying. Under that scenario, the manufacturer tries to reserve the aftermarket to itself by leveraging a dominant position in the primary equipment market into the aftermarket and tying the sales of the tied products, the complementary products and/or services, to the sale of the tying product, the primary equipment.

[4] See *infra*. Although older cases may be of reduced utility to anticipate how today's Article 102 enforcement *policy* would or should be pursued in dealing with abuses of dominance in so-called aftermarkets, primary equipment manufacturers cannot afford to ignore these.

better quality spare parts and servicing, and as having a greater expertise in, and incentives to ensuring that the primary equipment performs well during its lifetime. So the combination of high market shares and customers willing to pay a premium (which can wrongly suggest that the supplier is extracting rents) can cause competition law concerns if it is possible to be dominant in the aftermarket for one's own brand of primary equipment, even in a situation where the manufacturer faces fierce competition in the market for the primary product. The issue for companies becomes then to try to anticipate *when* these concerns will give rise do liability under Article 102 TFEU.

This chapter briefly looks at how these issues are likely to be dealt with under Article 102 TFEU, based on the relatively limited number of recent cases and European Commission guidance in this area. It first looks at the question of how aftermarkets are likely to be defined under EU and European competition law. The next section analyzes the circumstances under which, assuming an appropriately defined aftermarket, aftermarket suppliers are likely to be viewed dominant in that market. Finally, the last section of the chapter provides some reflections on the issue of consumer harm, assuming the existence of a dominant position in an appropriately defined aftermarket.

21.2 MARKET DEFINITION ISSUES

Aftermarket definition issues have received greater attention under US antitrust law than under EU competition law. In the United States, the famous Supreme Court decision in *Kodak*[5] – which stands for the proposition that market power and anticompetitive conduct in an aftermarket cannot be excluded as a matter of law, even if the primary market is competitive – has given rise to a significant amount of cases analyzing plaintiffs' antitrust claims against anticompetitive conduct of primary equipment manufacturers (operating in competitive primary markets) in alleged aftermarkets. However, it seems that in most of these cases, defendants have prevailed against such claims.[6] US courts often rely, among other arguments, on the non-existence of an aftermarket as the basis for rejecting plaintiffs' claims, as opposed to invoking the lack of market power in a

---

[5] *Eastman Kodak Co. v Image Technical Services Inc.*, 504 U.S. 451 (1992).

[6] For a survey of the treatment of Kodak following the Supreme Court's decision by lower US courts up to 2004, see Goldfine, D.A.J. and Vorrasi, K.M., 'The Fall of the Kodak Aftermarket Doctrine: Dying a Slow Death in the Lower Courts', *Antitrust Law Journal*, Vol. 72, 2004, pp. 209–231.

relevant aftermarket. In doing so, courts identify the interconnections between the alleged primary market and the relevant aftermarket(s), hold that customers either assess or should be able to adequately assess lifecycles costs for the primary products, so that knowledge of a supra-competitive price in the aftermarket will result in increased sales for competitive primary products. This is another way of holding that there is positive cross-elasticity of demand between the alleged primary market and the aftermarket, which is the same thing as saying that the aftermarket and primary market are in fact the same market, or saying that there is no aftermarket at all, but a 'systems market'.[7] This approach to dealing with aftermarkets by the majority of US courts has perhaps been the reason why in the 18 years since the *Kodak* judgment was rendered, there has not been a single Sherman Act section 2 case in which the US Department of Justice (DOJ) or the Federal Trade Commission (FTC) alleged monopolization of a single-brand aftermarket, notwithstanding the US Supreme Court's judgment in *Kodak*.

The EU Notice on the definition of relevant market for the purposes of Community competition law suggests that this approach, resulting in defining systems markets as opposed to aftermarkets, could also be followed under EU competition law, but rather on an exceptional basis.[8] The starting point of the EU market definition analysis appears to consist in assessing whether a price increase of complementary products and/or services can be profitable, as a result either of the fact that consumers can only purchase complementary products that are compatible with the primary equipment (leading thus a narrow aftermarket definition), and/or of the fact that the primary equipment products have a long lifetime (providing for greater opportunities to increase prices for complementary products and/or services than in a situation where primary equipment products have a short lifetime). Only if the characteristics of the primary equipment products enable quick and direct consumer responses to price increases of the complementary products would a broader system market definition seem to be warranted under the EU approach.[9] Hence, it is unclear whether previous competition for the primary equipment resulting for instance in infra-competitive primary equipment prices (pointing to the existence of cross-elasticity in demand) would, pursuant to an EU approach suggested by the Commission's Notice on defining relevant markets, be viewed as

7 Or, in other words, an aftermarket would exist only if exploitation would be profitable for a primary equipment manufacturer controlling its own aftermarket.

8 Commission Notice on the definition of relevant market for the purposes of Community competition law, OJ (1997) C 372, 09.12.1997.

9 *Idem* at para. 56.

sufficient to conclude that a separate, single-brand aftermarket does not exist. In *Hugin*, the ECJ concluded that there was a separate market for spare parts, notwithstanding the existence of effective competition in the market for the primary equipment, based partly on the fact that the category of clients requiring the parts were different from the clients requiring the primary equipment.[10] In *Hilti*, the Court of First Instance (CFI) also reached the conclusion that a separate market for spare parts existed, since the complementary products were specifically manufactured, and purchased by users for a single brand of primary equipment, and since there existed independent producers of complimentary products.[11] In *Hilti*, however, the manufacturer was found to have significant shares of the primary equipment market. In *Tetra Pak*, the CFI rejected the applicant's arguments that the markets for primary equipment and consumables were inseparable, based on the fact that there had been independent manufacturers of consumables (who did not themselves manufacture the primary equipment) designed for use in the primary equipment.[12] In *Digital*, the European Commission (the 'Commission') also concluded that there existed a separate proprietary aftermarket for Digital hardware and software maintenance services, notwithstanding the existence of a competitive primary equipment market.[13] Another good example of how swiftly a relevant aftermarket definition can be adopted from a European competition law perspective, notwithstanding the existence of competition in the primary product market, is presented by the *Italian elevators* case: different categories of customers (elevators are purchased by construction companies, maintenance services are purchased by the real estate owners, and spare parts are purchased by maintenance companies), and different categories of suppliers (some suppliers are integrated, offering elevators, maintenance and spare parts, other smaller suppliers offer either only maintenance services or only spare parts) were found by the Italian Competition Authority to be sufficient to justify the existence of separate markets, notwithstanding the existence of strong links between these markets, and strong competition in the primary equipment market.[14] These market

---

10 Case 22/78, *Hugin v Commission* [1979] ECR 1869, at para. 6.

11 Case T-30/89, *Hilti v Commission* [1990] ECR II-1439, at paras. 66–7.

12 Case T-83/91, *Tetra Pak v Commission*, 1994, ECR II-755, at paras. 82–6.

13 Although the Commission acknowledged that, at the time, Digital was one of the largest hardware and software suppliers in the world, the product line of which includes VAX and Alpha computer systems. IP/97/8681997.

14 Otis-Kone Italia-Schindler, *Provvedimento n. 8272*, L'Autorità Garante della Concorrenza e del Mercato (2000), paras. 25–28. The French *Conseil de la Concurrence* has adopted a number of decisions taking the existence of an aftermarket

definition approaches appear to be incomplete. The presence of independent suppliers on an 'aftermarket' only and their absence on the 'primary market' does not necessarily imply that there is a separate aftermarket and that these suppliers could not exercise a competitive constraint on the primary market and hence create a degree of cross-elasticity of demand between primary and purported aftermarket. Accordingly, these approaches may have led to the adoption of incorrect market definitions in specific cases.

Nevertheless, the above-described market-definition approach seems somewhat in line what the Commission's DG Competition discussed around this topic a few years ago in its discussion paper on the application of Article 82 of the Treaty to exclusionary abuses.[15] This document suggests that the Commission, in trying to respond to the question whether a separate aftermarket exists, normally will/does not take into account the effects on sales of the primary equipment to deny the existence of a particular aftermarket (or at least not to a significant extent). Although the discussion paper appears to recognize the theoretical possibility of the existence of an overall systems market as a result of complementary product customers switching to another primary equipment product when faced with price increases of complementary products, the discussion paper seems to stress that this switching is normally difficult to achieve.[16] However, in a recent case, the European Commission appears to have taken the view that a/the relevant aftermarket did not exist. In particular, the Commission reached *a prima facie* conclusion that two after-sales markets, for spare parts and for repair and maintenance services in connection with luxury and prestige watches, do not constitute markets distinct from the primary market for luxury and prestige watches.[17] What motivated the

virtually for granted, without any detailed market analysis. See for instance, Décision n. 95-D-50 *relative à des pratiques relevées sur les marches de l'installation et de la maintenance des extincteurs*; Décision n.05-D-46 *relative à des pratiques mises en œuvre par la société Jaeger Lecoultre*; Décision n. 00-D-50 *relative à des pratiques mises en œuvre par la Société Française des Jeux dans les secteurs de la maintenance informatique et du mobilier de comptoir*; and Décision n. 93-D-36 *relative à des pratiques relevées dans le secteur de la vente de pièces détachés pour appareils photographiques*.

[15] DG Competition discussion paper in the application of Article 82 of the Treaty to exclusionary abuses, Brussels, December 2005, at para. 247, noting that 'the full effects of "bundle" or "systems" competition will [thus] be taken into account in the dominance analysis'.

[16] *Idem*, at para. 249.

[17] Commission Decision SG-Greffe (2008) D/204448 C (2008) of 10 July 2008 in Case COMP/E-1/39097, *Confédération Européenne des Associations d'Horlogers-Réparateurs*, not published. Reportedly, the contested decision made clear that,

Commission to reach this conclusion in this case is, however, questionable. The fact that in this case, the size of the after-sales service related to luxury/prestige watches apparently amounts to an insignificant part of the general turnover achieved in the sale of these watches, and that the case involves a market of limited size and of limited economic importance, may have been the determining factor in the Commission's desire to take the view that the aftermarket for spare parts, taken in isolation, is not the market on which the effects of competition are to be assessed.[18] If true, this would not seem a proper basis for reaching that conclusion: the higher the value of the complementary products *vis-à-vis* the primary equipment products, the lower the costs to switch to other primary equipment products, and thus the greater the likelihood of the existence of a systems market. Unfortunately, at the time of writing this chapter, the Commission's decision is not yet published, and the General Court has not yet adopted a judgment in this case.

21.3 DOMINANCE ISSUES

Hence, the general approach followed under EU and European competition law practice seems to consist more in analyzing the potential effects of competition in the primary equipment market on aftermarkets within the context of the question of dominance, rather than as part of a market definition analysis.[19] This may be related to the fact that under EU and European competition law, it is not only in itself not illegal to be in a dominant position, but also not illegal to attempt to gain a dominant position (unless as a result of a concentration or of leveraging an existing dominant position in a related market).[20] In the United States, attempted

since the primary market is competitive, the aftermarkets are likewise competitive. See Case T-427/08, *CEAHR v Commission*, 2008, Report for the Hearing, paras. 26 and 69.

[18] *Idem,* at paras. 8 and 44.

[19] From a practical perspective, there may be not a lot of difference between looking at competitive effects either within a market definition analysis or as part of a dominance analysis. The greater the influence of the primary equipment market competition on the aftermarket, the more likely the primary equipment market and the aftermarket constitute a single market.

Conversely, if an aftermarket is deemed to exist, very high market shares would normally be sufficient to conclude that the aftermarket supplier is dominant.

[20] Case C-333/94, *Tetra Pak v Commission* [1996] ECR I-5951, where the ECJ found that the CFI was right to accept the application of Article 86 EC on a distinct but closely associated market but in which the firm in question did not hold a dominant position (paras. 30–2).

monopolization is caught by section 2 of the Sherman Act, and hence may cause courts to focus more on the issue of market definition when finding in favour of defendants. But assuming the existence of an aftermarket separate and distinct from a primary equipment market, economic theory suggests that the existence of strong competition in the primary equipment market would normally, barring exceptional circumstances, exclude the possibility of having a dominant aftermarket position. This is because the primary equipment market competition often disciplines and exercises competitive constraints on commercial conduct in the connected aftermarket, denying the supplier the power to behave to an appreciable extent independently of its competitors, its customers and ultimately of consumers in the aftermarket. The following paragraphs discuss (1) why and how primary equipment market competition disciplines behavior in the alleged aftermarket, (2) the European Commission's likely approach when assessing this issue.

21.3.1 Why and How

The above-mentioned competitive constraints can be exercised because of two phenomena. First, customers who know, at the time when the initial primary equipment purchasing decision is made, that they will have to purchase the complementary products and/or services from the primary equipment manufacturer, will be able to obtain reduced primary equipment prices to balance higher prices for complementary products and/or services (or obtain contractual protection against complementary product and/or services price increases). Second, even when customers are uninformed about the fact that they will have to purchase complementary products and/or services from the primary product manufacturer, informed primary equipment manufacturers who operate in a competitive primary equipment market will normally be forced to offer competitive primary equipment prices. In a competitive primary equipment market, manufacturers that do not offer competitive primary equipment prices will risk losing sales to their primary equipment competitors who are willing to offer lower priced primary equipment products as a result of their perceived ability to obtain higher prices for complementary products and/or services. Accordingly, even charging high prices for complementary products and/or services to uninformed customers may not result in overall consumer harm where the market for primary equipment products is competitive.[21]

---

[21] Carl Shapiro, the Deputy Assistant Attorney General for Economics of the Antitrust division of the US Justice Department, finds this 'a very compelling

There are thus a number of ways in which primary equipment market competition often prevents a primary equipment manufacturer to be dominant in the aftermarket, even if that primary equipment manufacturer has high shares of the aftermarket, and even if prices in the aftermarket are perceived to be high.[22]

First, a primary equipment manufacturer who attempts to raise aftermarket prices at supra-competitive levels may cause the aftermarket customer to switch to another brand of primary equipment. The higher the switching cost, the greater the opportunity to increase prices on the aftermarket. However, even in situations in which switching costs are relatively high, increasing aftermarket prices may constitute a risky strategy for primary equipment manufacturers. Aftermarket customers often have varying switching costs (for instance, some customers may have amortized their primary equipment more than others, or the prices of the complimentary products and/or services may constitute a significant proportion of the value of the primary equipment), and being able to identify a group of customers with sufficient switching costs may not be an easy task. Moreover, in industries characterized by rapid technological development, a switching cost may be overly compensated by the prospect of obtaining the benefit of another, and more performing, competing brand of primary equipment. Accordingly, aftermarket price increases may, particularly in these industries, create a 'tipping effect', leading customers to switch, where switching would not have occurred in the absence of the aftermarket price increase.

Second, and probably more importantly, even in markets where switching costs are high, primary equipment manufacturers should normally internalize the loss of *future* primary equipment sales caused by harming the interests of aftermarket customers facing high switching costs. Indeed,

---

argument, that goes a long way towards showing that substantial on-going consumer injury from exclusionary aftermarket policies is unlikely to occur in competitive equipment markets, even if consumer information is poor'. Shapiro, C., 'Aftermarkets and Consumer Welfare: Making Sense of Kodak', *Antitrust Law Journal*, Vol. 63, 1995, p. 483. See also in this respect, Klein, B., 'Market Power in Aftermarkets', *Managerial and Decision Economics*, Vol. 17, 1996, pp. 143–164, at pp. 147–148. For a view supporting the notion that equipment market competition does not prevent service market exploitation, see Borenstein, S., MacKie-Mason, J.K., and Netz, J.S., 'Exercising Market Power in Proprietary Aftermarkets', *Journal of Economics & Management Strategy*, Vol. 9, 2000, pp. 157–88.

[22] Obviously, the primary equipment manufacturer may face effective competition from independent service providers in the aftermarket. This will be often the case when the complimentary products offered by other suppliers are sufficiently interchangeable with those of the primary equipment manufacturer.

companies that attach commercial value to their reputation, will generally restrain from adopting policy changes leading to supra competitive aftermarket prices. As a hypothetical example, one could think of the sale of primary equipment marketed as energy efficient that requires servicing and spare parts over its lifetime. If a short-sighted primary equipment manufacturer, not fearing immediate switching in view of the high switching cost of the customers, changes its spare parts policies and increases the prices of the spare parts (either directly or by refusing to sell original spare parts to independent service providers) after the initial purchase of the primary equipment, the increased aftermarket prices may well nullify the savings the customer was expecting to achieve from the energy-efficient nature of the primary equipment. If so, primary equipment manufacturers risk losing future sales of the energy efficient primary product to competitors that have not increased their aftermarket prices.[23] For companies that offer different types of primary equipment, sometimes to identical customers, these considerations may be of increased importance, as a policy change with respect to a product that is complementary to primary equipment A, may cause losses in the future sales not only for that primary equipment A, but also for primary equipment B, C, and D.

Third, particularly in relation to high-value primary equipment, customers can be protected from the primary equipment manufacturer's policy change as a result of contractual provisions negotiated at arm's length in a competitive setting when the initial primary equipment purchase decision was made. These contractual provisions can be effective mechanisms to prevent the primary equipment manufacturer to act to a significant extent independently from competitive pressures in the aftermarket. The provisions typically will provide for guaranteed supplies of complementary products, price protections, or 'most favored nation' clauses promising a customer not to be charged more than other customers. Such provisions often result from broader negotiations than take place in connection with the purchase of the primary equipment, where the primary equipment manufacturer will sometimes grant these protections to give the customer the necessary incentives to purchase the primary equipment.

21.3.2 European Commission Approach

In *Pelikan/Kyocera*, the European Commission looked at the relationships between the primary equipment market for printers with that of the

---

[23] For an explanation of how to ascertain whether the equipment manufacturer controlling aftermarkets can profitably raise prices in the aftermarket see Shapiro, S. and Teece, D.J., 'Systems Competition and Aftermarkets: An Economic Analysis of Kodak', *Antitrust Bulletin*, Vol. 39, 1994, pp. 135–62.

aftermarket of toner cartridges.[24] The Commission ultimately concluded that because potentially abusive behaviour in the aftermarket would have impacted Pelican's position on the primary market, there were sufficient constraints on Kyocera on that aftermarket to consider that Kyocera was not dominant in the aftermarket. The Commission apparently reached that conclusion for a number of reasons, but essentially because (1) switching in primary market was relatively easy, (2) consumers made life cycle cost calculations, (3) prices for cartridges were publicly available, and (4) prices for cartridges represented approximately 70 per cent of the total system costs.

DG Competition's discussion paper concedes that either because customers may base their choice on accurate life cycle calculations, or because suppliers are able to make such calculations (and hence suppliers will cause potential high aftermarket profits to be competed away in their attempts to secure the sales of the primary products), it is unlikely that a supplier can be considered dominant in an aftermarket when competition is strong in the primary market.[25] However, the discussion paper suggests that only a certain category of aftermarket customers would/could benefit from competition in the primary equipment market, namely only those who may buy the primary equipment product in the future, and not those who have already bought the primary product. Aftermarket customers who have already bought the primary equipment can become the victims of so-called 'installed-base opportunism' when the primary equipment manufacturer changes his policies (increasing prices or reducing quality or choices) after the initial primary equipment purchase decision has been made. This distinction between future and existing customers does not appear to be sound. Every 'existing' customer was by definition a 'future' customer at the time when the first purchase was made. Competition in the primary market should normally cause (or will have caused) this category of customers (the 'existing' customer) to protect themselves against installed-base opportunism either by demanding and obtaining contractual protection against potentially harmful future policy changes, or by obtaining reduced prices for the primary equipment. In addition, even if an existing customer did not negotiate sufficient protection, customers are often protected against policy changes because these customers may be repeat customers in the primary equipment market and/or that any policy change will harm the supplier's reputation in the primary equipment or in other markets.

---

[24] XXVth Report on Competition Policy, 1995, paras. 86–7.

[25] Discussion paper, *supra*.

The more recent Communication from the Commission containing guidance on the Commission's enforcement priorities in applying Article 82 EC Treaty to abusive exclusionary conduct by dominant undertakings (hereafter Guidance document) provides virtually no guidance on how the Commission will apply Article 102 TFEU in aftermarkets.[26] It contains one footnote, in which the Commission simply suggests that it will normally take action against tying or bundling not only when the firm is dominant in the tying primary equipment market, but also on the condition that the firm in question is dominant in the tied aftermarket, presumably even if the firm in question is not dominant in the tying market for primary equipment.[27] As such and of itself, this somewhat cryptic footnote does not give particularly transparent guidance on how the Commission intends to enforce Article 102 TFEU to aftermarkets, and seems to cover the rather exceptional situation of competitive harm resulting from increased barriers of entry in the primary equipment market derived from dominance in the tied aftermarket. The absence of a section on aftermarkets, may simply mean that the Commission agrees with the general proposition that when primary equipment markets are competitive, aftermarket conduct that may lead to increased aftermarket prices (for instance by limiting access to independent service providers) is unlikely to be harmful to consumers, and therefore should not constitute an enforcement priority. However, the Commission may of course adapt the approach set out in its Guidance document to the extent that this would appear to be reasonable and appropriate in a given case. The Commission may have just done so in a recent case, and has opened on its own initiative an investigation into IBM's alleged discriminatory behaviour towards competing suppliers of mainframe maintenance services, in particular by restricting or delaying access to spare parts for which IBM is the only source.[28] Currently, not much is known about this investigation, but if IBM faces effective competition in its primary equipment market, then one could clearly question why the Commission would be pursuing an aftermarket case as a matter of priority and

[26] Communication from the Commission – Guidance on the Commission's enforcement priorities in applying Article 82 of the EC Treaty to abusive exclusionary conduct by dominant undertakings, OJ (2009) C 45/7.

[27] Footnote 34 states 'that [t]he undertaking should be dominant in the tying market, though not necessarily in the tied market. In bundling cases, the firm needs to be dominant in one of the bundled markets. In the special case of tying in after-markets, the condition is that the firm is dominant in the tying market and/or the tied aftermarket.'

[28] IP/10/1006 (26/07/2010).

on its own initiative, if the pursuit of such cases was not identified in its Guidance document.

21.4 HARM TO COMPETITION

Assuming the primary equipment manufacturer (operating in a competitive primary equipment market) is found to be dominant in a relevant aftermarket, Article 102 TFEU will prohibit the manufacturer from trying to exclude competition in that aftermarket (for instance either by refusing to deal with downstream competitors, tying, bundling, or by engaging predatory pricing), unless the manufacturer can provide an objective justification for the conduct in question, or can demonstrate that the conduct generates efficiencies that outweigh the negative effect on competition.

A primary equipment manufacturer, deemed to be dominant in a relevant aftermarket, refusing to make its own complementary products available (or inputs to complementary products such as technical information) where independent providers service the primary equipment products, may often find it very difficult successfully to invoke objective justifications to avoid liability under Article 102 TFEU.[29] This is probably mainly because of the fact that the conduct in question must be according to the Commission indispensable in order to achieve the justifiable objective.[30] Examples of such objectives would include the need to have the primary equipment manufacturer's installed base serviced by experienced service providers, to ensure that the primary equipment functions well or is safely maintained and serviced. Arguably, primary equipment manufacturers can achieve these aims using less restrictive ways, for instance by selecting service providers on the basis of more or less objective criteria of quality and experience, and limiting the sale of complementary products or their inputs to a limited number of recognized service providers. Whilst refusing to deal with non-recognized service providers who do not meet these objective criteria may, at least in theory, constitute a valid objective justification under Article 102 TFEU, doing so may not eliminate competition

---

29 There is not a single EU court case in which this defence was successfully invoked by a dominant undertaking.

30 See *supra*. The Commission takes the view that the community courts apply strictly the condition of indispensability. However, others believe that a survey of case law shows that indispensability would not be a requirement imposed by the courts. See for instance Loewenthal, P.J., 'The Defence of 'Objective Justification' in the Application of Article 82 EC', *World Competition*, Vol. 28, 2005, pp. 455–77, at p. 465, identifying three requirements: (1) it needs to pursue a legitimate aim, (2) be reasonable, and (3) proportionate to the aim sought.

law risks for the primary equipment manufacturer. This is because primary equipment manufacturers will often have shares in excess of the 30 per cent threshold in the aftermarket for their own proprietary primary equipment, and will thus normally not be able to obtain the benefit of the presumption of legality created by the Vertical Block Exemption Regulation,[31] and hence may be exposed to Article 101 TFEU liability. But even primary equipment manufacturers authorizing only a specific set of service providers to be active in the aftermarket with less than 30 per cent share may not benefit from the presumption of legality in situations where the nature of the product does not necessitate a selective distribution system to preserve the quality of the primary equipment and ensure its proper use.[32] Accordingly, a successful defence invoking objective justifications may in reality be limited to circumstances where the primary equipment supplier is facing real practical difficulties to supply, such as a straightforward genuine capacity limit, or to similar situations where for instance the customer lacks creditworthiness. However, interpreting the law in this narrow manner may cause suppliers simply to align their aftermarket practices in a manner that is responsive to the desires of their competitors, rather than to allowing suppliers to choose the most efficient way of serving their customers' needs in the aftermarket. Accordingly, a standard of 'reasonableness' would seem more appropriate to recognize objective justifications than the 'indispensability' criterion advocated by the Commission.[33]

However, conduct of dominant primary equipment manufacturers that limits commercial opportunities for independent service providers in the aftermarket should also escape the Article 102 TFEU prohibition when the conduct generates efficiencies that are sufficient to guarantee that no net harm to consumers is likely to arise in the aftermarket. Refusals to deal or tying and bundling practices can generate important economic efficiencies, even when the firms that engage in these practices have market power. These include, for instance in connection with refusals to supply, the protection of intellectual property rights for innovative firms, and the protection of the incentives of the requesting and dominant firms to invest, or, in connection with tying practices, economies of scale and scope in production and distribution. However, as many have rightly observed, issues of standards and burdens of proof, probably resulting from a

---

[31] OJ (2010) L102/1.

[32] European Commission Guidelines on Vertical Restraints, OJ (2010) C130/1, at paras. 175 and 185.

[33] See *supra*.

prosecutorial bias, may unfortunately reduce the practical availability of the efficiency defence.[34]

When analyzing possible efficiencies, it is important to consider the extent to which the exclusionary conduct in the aftermarket may generate pro-competitive outcomes not only in the aftermarket, but also in the primary equipment market. In view of the strong links that often exist between the primary equipment market and the aftermarket, it would be inappropriate to limit the analysis of efficiencies in the aftermarket only (to the same extent as it would be inappropriate to conduct a market definition analysis or a dominance analysis without taking these links into account). For instance, Carlton and Waldman developed three economic models suggesting that exclusionary conduct in an aftermarket may not be the result of a desire to earn monopoly profits in the aftermarket, but rather an attempt to avoid inefficiencies in the primary equipment market.[35] The most basic of these models assumes a primary equipment market that is perfectly competitive but characterized by high switching costs, and shows that when the primary equipment is priced above the marginal cost of production, aftermarket customers will over-maintain the installed base of primary equipment. When the aftermarket is monopolized, consumers will make more efficient maintenance decisions and generate more competition for primary equipment.[36] In the same vein, Laussel and Resende found that exclusionary behaviour in the aftermarkets induces firms to compete more fiercely in the primary market, in order to create a durable basis of costumers and increase the future size of that aftermarket, leading to the conclusion that supra-competitive pricing the aftermarket may not necessarily be welfare detrimental. This model shows, among other things, that there is a trade-off between competition in the aftermarket and competition for the primary equipment market, and that the absence of competition in the aftermarket leads firms to invest in price-cutting strategies in the primary equipment market, and, as a consequence, to innovate.[37] Accordingly, attempts to increase aftermarket competition, may lead to a reduction in primary market competition. As a final example, Chen and Ross

---

[34] See for instance O'Donoghue, R. and Padilla, J., *The Law and Economics of Article 82 EC*, 2006, Oxford, Hart Publishing, at pp. 229–34.

[35] Carlton, D.W. and Waldman, M., 'Competition, Monopoly, and Aftermarkets', *Johnson School Research Paper Series*', Cornell University, 2006.

[36] The second model involves primary equipment with product improvements and upgrades, and the third model deals with remanufactured parts.

[37] Laussel, D. and Resende, J., 'Does the Absence of Competition in the Market Forster Competition for the Market? A Dynamic Approach to Aftermarkets', *CORE Discussion Paper* 2008–33, Leuven, Département des Sciences Economiques de l'Université catholique de Louvain, 2008.

explain that higher aftermarket prices, achieved for instance via a refusal to deal, charged to some customers who use the installed base primary equipment more intensely and heavily than other customers may be efficient responses to recover the higher cost associated to the increased usage for original equipment manufacturers, without the need to increase the primary equipment prices *ex ante* when primary equipment-purchasing decisions are made, leading to an overall more efficient market organization.[38]

Commenting on the value or reliability of these economic models is beyond the scope of this chapter. However, these models highlight the need to be very careful when intervening against alleged abuses of dominant positions in aftermarkets. After all, common sense suggests that approaches that excessively focus on deeming aftermarkets to constitute separate product markets or finding market power in single-branded aftermarkets may result in inappropriate enforcement actions, since firms that have larger shares in their aftermarket usually tend to have smaller positions in the primary market or in the 'systems' market. This is because third party suppliers and independent service providers (ISP) or other primary market firms will focus their efforts on those aftermarkets for the most successful primary products. Hence, pursuant to this approach, it would often be the smaller firms (who usually derive more revenues from aftermarket sales than larger firms operating in competitive primary markets) that would face the prospect of being found dominant. In addition, approaches that signal that competitive harm to consumers through actions of a supplier in the aftermarket would be very rare and exceptional when there is effective competition in the primary market, would encourage primary product manufacturers to adopt open and flexible aftermarket policies in the first place. If a primary equipment manufacturer has a genuine commercial interest in providing spare parts or service to an ISP to make the product more attractive by providing the customer various service alternatives (which may provide incentives to new entry), a misguided aftermarket antitrust approach, exposing the supplier to the risk of being found to abuse a dominant position, and to the risk of fines, would prevent (or reduce the incentives of) the supplier from adopting pro-competitive conduct in the first place. In addition, although a restrictive spare part policy may harm intra-brand competition for these spare parts, it may in reality, in a situation where there is fierce competition in the primary

---

38 Chen, Z., Ross, T., and Stanbury, W.T., 'Refusals to Deal and Aftermarkets', *Review of Industrial Organization*, Vol. 13, 1998, pp. 131–51, at p. 140.

market, promote inter-brand competition, as highlighted in the above economic models.

21.5 CONCLUSION

There is no clear EU competition law enforcement policy with respect to unilateral conduct in so-called aftermarkets. European authorities and courts, more likely than not, will take primary equipment market competition into account when assessing the potential dominance of the primary equipment manufacturer, and not at the market definition stage. This probably allows for greater enforcement flexibility and for following a case-by-case approach, to support the result that the authority or court desires to achieve. Categorically precluding the possible existence of market power in an aftermarket because a manufacturer lacks dominance in the primary equipment market may be a bridge too far, in light of the existing case law of the European courts, and since at least in theory it would be possible for a firm to be dominant in such circumstances. However, where there is vigorous competition in the primary market, for a variety of reasons, supplier behaviour in an alleged aftermarket can only raise legitimate competition concerns and create anticompetitive foreclosure in very exceptional circumstances. Before concluding to an Article 102 TFEU infringement, enforcement authorities and courts would need to (1) correctly address the problem of market definition, (2) properly analyze the links and interactions between the primary equipment market and the aftermarket, and (3) carefully assess the extent to which objective justifications or efficiencies would demonstrate that the conduct in the aftermarket would not be, on balance, welfare enhancing. A clearer and less equivocal enforcement policy statement confirming these requirements would be helpful to avoid unjustified and counterproductive deterrent on undertakings wishing to implement flexible and/or customer-friendly aftermarket polices at initial stages of a commercial relationship.

22. The British Airways judgment – what are the 'underlying factors' in exclusionary abuses?

John Temple Lang

In its decision in *British Airways* (hereafter 'BA'),[1] the Commission found that by paying increased commissions to travel agents who increased their sales of BA tickets over their sales in previous years, BA had abused its dominant position. The Commission found that BA had illegally rewarded loyalty with the object and effect of excluding BA's competitors from the UK markets for air transport, and had discriminated between travel agents. In short, BA had committed an exclusionary abuse and a discriminatory abuse, in the view of the Commission.

The Court of First Instance[2] upheld the Commission's decision, and BA appealed to the Court of Justice. BA argued, in effect, that conduct could constitute an exclusionary abuse under what is now Article 102 TFEU only if the conduct came under Article 102(b) TFEU, which prohibits: 'limiting production, markets or technical development to the prejudice of consumers'.

BA then argued that offering extra commission to travel agents who increased their sales did not 'limit' the possibilities open to BA's competitor airlines, and that therefore BA had not abused a dominant position.

22.1 THE OPINION OF THE ADVOCATE GENERAL

This argument was dismissed by Advocate General Kokott. She said:[3]

> suffice it to say that that provision [Article 102(2) (b) TFEU] merely gives an example of an abuse of a dominant position. Rebates and bonuses by dominant

[1] OJ (2000) L 30/1.
[2] Case T-219/99 [2003] ECR II-5917.
[3] Paras. 35, 40, 41, 42, 44, 48, 69: except for the words 'underlying thoughts', all emphasis in the original.

> undertakings can infringe Article 82 EC even if they do not correspond to any of the examples contained in that second paragraph ... this case-law does not indicate any closed categories of abusive bonus and rebate schemes ... The decisive factor is rather the underlying thoughts which have guided the previous case-law of the Court of Justice and which can also be transposed to a case such as the present. It therefore needs to be examined first whether the rebates or bonuses granted by an undertaking in a dominant position can give rise to a foreclosure effect, i.e. whether they are capable of making it difficult or impossible for the competitors of the dominant undertaking to have access to the market and for the business partners of the dominant undertaking to choose between various sources of supply; secondly, it needs to be examined whether there is an objective justification for the rebates or bonuses granted ... Rebate schemes may infringe Article 82 EC even if they are not ... linked to a condition of exclusivity ... the foreclosure effect of a rebate or bonus scheme may arise from the other circumstances of the particular case ... a foreclosure effect may arise from rebates and bonuses the granting of which is linked to the fulfillment of individually defined sales targets ... The conduct of the dominant undertaking is not, therefore, to be regarded as abusive within the meaning of Article 82 EC only once it has concrete effects on individual market participants, be they competitors or consumers. Rather, a line of conduct of a dominant undertaking is abusive as soon as it runs counter to the purpose of protecting competition in the internal market from distortions (Article 3(1)(g) EC)...

22.2 THE JUDGMENT OF THE COURT OF JUSTICE

The judgment of the Court[4] agreed with the Advocate General. The Court said: 'The list of abusive practices contained in Article 86 EC is not exhaustive, so that the practices there mentioned are merely examples of abuses ... discounts and bonuses granted by undertakings in a dominant position may be contrary to Article 82 EC even where they do not correspond to any of the examples mentioned.'

After referring to the *Hoffmann-La Roche*[5] and *Michelin*[6] judgments, the Court went on:

> Contrary to BA's argument, it cannot be inferred from those two judgments that bonuses and discounts granted by undertakings in a dominant position are abusive only in the circumstances there described. As the Advocate General has stated in paragraph 41 of her Opinion, the decisive factor is rather the underlying

[4] Case C-95/04P [2007] ECR I-2331, para. 57.
[5] Case 84/76 [1979] ECR 461.
[6] Case 322/81 [1983] ECR 3461.

factors which have guided the previous case-law of the Court of Justice and which can also be transposed to a case such as the present.[7]

22.3 THE PREVIOUS CASE LAW AND TYPES OF ABUSIVE CONDUCT

It is clear that conduct can be illegal and contrary to Article 102 TFEU even if it does not fall within the literal words of the four kinds of conduct set out in that article. That has been clear since *Continental Can*,[8] *Commercial Solvents*,[9] and *Hoffmann-La Roche*.[10] These three cases, and a number of other cases under Article 102 TFEU, are all examples of exclusionary abuses, rather than any other kind of abuse. However, there must be some limiting principle that defines or sets boundaries to the kinds of conduct that are prohibited by the Article.

For a considerable time practising lawyers have used a classification of abuses into four categories. The first is 'exploitative' abuses, taking undue advantage of market power to impose for instance excessive prices on buyers. These are considered to be contrary to Article 102(a) TFEU, which prohibits 'unfair' prices. Another category is 'reprisal' abuses, conduct intended to harm another company in order to warn or punish it because it competed too aggressively or because it complained to a competition authority. The third category is 'discriminatory' abuse, contrary to Article 102(c) TFEU.

It is the fourth category of abuse that is relevant to the conduct of BA and to the statements of the Court and of the Advocate General. The fourth category is 'exclusionary' or anticompetitive abuse, which is conduct limiting competition further than it is already limited as a result of the existence of the dominant position, but which is not legitimate or 'normal' competition, such as offering lower prices, better quality, or both.

BA argued, in effect, that Article 102(b) TFEU provided the Treaty definition of 'exclusionary' abuses, and that if conduct was said to be illegal only because it was exclusionary, it had to fall under Article 102(b) TFEU. Conduct such as BA's clearly does not come under any of the other

---

[7] Para. 64, emphasis supplied.

[8] Case 6/72 [1973] ECR 215, acquisition of a competitor by an already dominant enterprise.

[9] Cases 6 and 7/73 [1974] ECR 223, refusal to supply a downstream competitor with an essential raw material or intermediate product.

[10] Rebates granted on condition that the customer bought exclusively from the dominant enterprise.

clauses in Article 102 TFEU, so that if it is illegal, it must either fall under Article 102(b) TFEU or there must be some other principle, not stated in the Treaty, that makes some other broader kind of conduct an abuse of a dominant position. That kind of conduct, whatever it may be, must be different from legitimate or 'normal' competition, so there must be some way of distinguishing between them.

The difficulty of distinguishing between exclusionary conduct and legitimate competition is greater than it may appear at first sight, both in law and in economics. No generally accepted distinction has emerged from the extensive legal and economics literature in the United States, and this failure does not seem to be explained by the different wording of section 2 of the US Sherman Act and Article 102(b) TFEU. The difficulty can be explained simply. If a dominant company offers products or services at a very low price or of very high quality, its conduct may make it difficult or impossible for any competitors to sell their products, but its conduct is obviously lawful and indeed desirable competition. So the test of exclusionary abuse cannot be whether the conduct makes life difficult or even impossible for competitors of the dominant enterprise, since clearly legitimate competition may do that. The test suggested by the Advocate General and repeated by the Court in *British Airways* 'whether those discounts or bonuses can produce an exclusionary effect, that is to say whether they are capable of making market entry very difficult or impossible for competitors of the undertaking in a dominant position'[11] fails to distinguish between lawful competition and exclusionary conduct. The proposed test applies equally to both.

22.4 'UNDERLYING FACTORS'

The next question that needs to be considered is whether the phrase 'underlying factors' used by the Court and the phrase 'underlying thoughts' used by the Advocate General resolve the ambiguity. Neither of these phrases seem to have been used previously in the case law on Article 102 TFEU, and neither the Court nor the Advocate General cited any publication in which the phrase was used. They are not found in the judgment of the Court of First Instance. The phrase does not seem to occur in any of the official comments on Article 102 TFEU or the case law on Article 102 TFEU, and it does not occur in the Commission's Discussion Paper on Article 82 of 2005 or in the Commission's Guidance Paper on Exclusionary Abuses in 2008.

---

11 At para. 68.

What kind of conduct would not be legitimate competition, but creates difficulty or impossibility for competitors and is wider than Article 102(b) TFEU, and what kind of 'underlying factors' might enable lawyers and economists to identify it? The rest of the judgment of the Court, the Opinion of Advocate General Kokott, and the judgment of the Court of First Instance in *British Airways*, throw no light on the question. The Court of Justice said that the Court of First Instance was right to examine 'whether the bonus schemes at issue had a fidelity-building effect capable of producing an exclusionary effect'.[12] However, the phrase 'fidelity-building' is no more helpful than 'underlying factors'. If a dominant enterprise offers products or services that are very much better bargains than those offered by any of its competitors, the result is likely to be that customers will buy exclusively from it, and that the effect will in that sense be 'fidelity'. But this is, once again, legitimate competition. The phrase 'fidelity-inducing' suffers from the same fundamental ambiguity as the phrases about making difficulties for competitors.

The word 'fidelity' in this context applies, or might be thought to apply, in two different kinds of situations. A rebate that is given on the express condition that a buyer has bought large quantities from the dominant enterprise may amount to a significant sum of money, and this may make it likely that the customer will buy only from that source. If the customer ultimately fails to reach the quantity that entitles it to the rebate, it has lost a benefit, but it has not suffered any penalty. On the other hand, if a rebate is given on condition that the customer buys only from the dominant company, the customer suffers a penalty (the loss of the rebate) if it buys even a small quantity from any other supplier at any time during the relevant period. In the second situation, the dominant enterprise has imposed a fine or cost on the buyer for buying elsewhere, and this is clearly exclusionary. The dominant enterprise has created an obstacle or handicap for competitors, to which they would not otherwise have been subject: it has 'limited' their 'market' contrary to Article 102(b) TFEU. This basic distinction is well-established (if not always correctly understood), but it does not clarify the phrase 'underlying factors'.

What could 'underlying factors' mean? It is difficult to think of any kind of conduct that should be prohibited by competition law that is not exploitative, exclusionary, discriminatory, or a reprisal. Conduct that is contrary to Article 102(b) TFEU is exclusionary because it limits competitors' production (e.g. by depriving them of access to a factor of production), limits their markets (e.g. by preventing customers from buying from

---

12 At para. 77.

them), or limits their technical development (e.g. by depriving them of access to new technology). That seems to cover all the kinds of undesirable conduct that create difficulties, obstacles or handicaps for competitors that are due only to the conduct in issue, and that they would not have had to deal with if that conduct had not occurred. Offering better bargains does not 'limit' the ability of competitors to offer their products or services, although it may make it unlikely that customers will buy them. Consumers are not harmed, of course, if they are free to choose. Their freedom to choose is not restricted because one company offers better bargains than another. Article 102(b) TFEU therefore provides a way of distinguishing between desirable competition and anticompetitive conduct.

Parret lists as possible objectives: market integration, 'economic freedom', economic efficiency, industrial policy, protection of small and medium sized enterprises, 'fairness, justice and non-discrimination', and consumer protection.[13] These objectives are not necessarily consistent with one another, and are certainly not equally firmly based on the words of the Treaties. As Parret stresses, and as explained by Giorgio Monti,[14] the competition law of the EU is not based on any single theory of economics. But that makes it more necessary, not less, to know what 'underlying factors' might be.

22.5 COULD THERE BE ANOTHER CATEGORY OF ABUSE?

Might there perhaps be some principle to the effect that a dominant company should not compete so vigorously, or offer such generous rebates or agents' commissions, that there is a risk of competitors being pushed out of the market? This idea, although it may sound vaguely Ordoliberal, has never been suggested in connection with Article 102 TFEU, and it does not stand up to scrutiny. It is inconsistent with what the Court has consistently said, that abuse is conduct other than normal competition. It is inconsistent with the Commission's Guidance paper, which distinguishes (though not clearly) between 'foreclosure' of competitors by legitimate competition and 'anticompetitive foreclosure', only the latter being unlawful. The idea would imply that even otherwise legitimate competition might be illegal if competitors were too weak, which seems absurd. It would be unworkable,

---

[13] Parret, 'Shouldn't we know what we are protecting? Yes we should! A plea for a solid and comprehensive debate about the objectives of EU competition law and policy', *European Competition Journal*, August 2010, Vol. 6, No. 2, pp. 339–76.

[14] *EC Competition Law*, Cambridge, Cambridge University Press, 2007.

because a dominant company could not foresee how much competition its rivals would be able to withstand, or how many rivals it should protect, or for how long. Abuse has been repeatedly said by the Court to be an objective concept, so it could not vary with the vulnerability of competitors. The idea would be bad policy, since it would reduce the incentives for the rivals to become more efficient. It would also be positively harmful for consumers, because the competitors could be protected only by the dominant company raising its prices to consumers, or reducing the quality of its products. It would also reduce the incentives of the dominant company to innovate, in case it innovated too successfully. The idea is also contrary to what has always been believed, that a dominant company is entirely free to compete legitimately, and has no duty to subsidize its competitors or to compensate them for their weaknesses (unless, of course, it has caused them). The Commission could not impose a rule that would eliminate or reduce legitimately acquired dominance. Even the Commission's Guidance Paper refers only to the possibility of Commission intervention in favour of a not-yet-as-efficient competitor, and the suggestion is unexplained, and difficult to understand, at least as a matter of competition law. (It might be different in a regulatory regime, but EU competition law is not a regulatory regime, and nothing in the case law cited by the courts in *British Airways* suggests that it could be.)

The Court said that conduct was exclusionary if it makes it 'more difficult or impossible for its co-contractors to choose between various sources of supply or commercial partners'.[15] Unfortunately, this phrase repeats the ambiguity caused by the judgment. Agents do not find it 'difficult or impossible ... to choose' merely because the dominant company is offering better incentives than its competitors. That only makes it less likely that they will choose to promote the competitors' products. But that is legitimate competition. A competitor's difficulty is not necessarily harm to competition, and it is important not to imply that it is. The Court of First Instance had also referred to conduct 'preventing customers from obtaining supplies from rival producers',[16] and to 'fidelity-building', but had not explained these ideas more clearly than the Court of Justice.

Neither the Commission, the Advocate General or the Court suggested that there is a finite demand for travel (probably untrue for leisure travel), that this demand cannot be increased by airlines offering travel to additional destinations (probably untrue), and therefore any payments conditional on travel agents increasing their sales each year tends to lead to a

---

15 In para. 68.

16 Paras. 244–8 of the judgment of 2003.

greater share of a limited market. Offering incentives likely to increase a dominant company's share of even a market of limited size is not necessarily exclusionary, of course. It might be pro-competitive, for instance if travel agents share their increased commissions with travellers. But the theory would have been intelligible, if the facts supported it, even if ultimately it might not have withstood scrutiny. It is unfortunately difficult to escape the conclusion that the *British Airways* judgment missed an opportunity to clarify the law, and indeed by hinting at unexplained influences made the rules on exclusionary abuses less clear than they were. It also made it more difficult for the Commission to persuade the Court to change the law, and to put it on a sounder and clearer economic and legal basis. The judgment also made it more difficult to advise dominant companies.

22.6 THE COMMISSION'S GUIDANCE DOCUMENT, AND THE FUTURE

The Commission's Guidance Paper on its enforcement priorities on exclusionary abuses under Article 102 TFEU is not entirely satisfactory from a legal or economic viewpoint, in connection with rebates. It also adopts an approach that is entirely different from that in the Court's case law. The Commission's explicit approach, in essence, is to say that rebates are illegal when they are conditional on exclusivity, or when they involve sales below cost of some of the quantities subject to the rebates. Neither the Court's judgment nor the Commission's Guidance Paper rely on the language of the Treaty. The Commission told the Court in *British Airways* that the law on exclusionary abuses needs to be reconsidered, but the Commission did nothing to explain to the Court what might be done, and its arguments in *British Airways* show no signs of new legal thinking, or of the 'economic approach' to Article 102 TFEU that the Commission claims to have adopted. Whatever the merits of the Guidance approach may be, the *British Airways* judgment seems to have made it less likely that the Court can be persuaded to adopt it.

Neither did the Guidance document do anything to clarify or resolve the issues raised by the *British Airways* judgment, although it was issued long after the judgment. The Guidance does not discuss the legal basis for exclusionary abuses, or try to define exclusionary abuse or foreclosure. On the basis of statements made by officials involved in the drafting of the Guidance, it was apparently assumed in effect that any conduct harmful to or inconveniencing competitors of a dominant enterprise is illegal unless it benefits consumers. This surprising proposition (which clearly needs to be explained in connection with, e.g. pricing below cost, or refusal to contract, or obtaining patents for inventions by the dominant enterprise, or indeed any pro-competitive conduct that strengthens the dominant firm in the longer term) is not, however, stated in the Guidance Paper, either as a proposition of law or of economics. If this proposition were applied to the facts of *British Airways*, they might well be considered lawful, since increased incentives for travel agents tend to benefit travellers by offering them more information and more choice. There is nothing in the Guidance Paper to suggest that any of the statements in it are intended to explain the 'underlying factors' referred to by the Court. The only proposition in the Guidance Paper that might be considered as an 'underlying factor' is that conduct is abusive only if it harms consumers, which is no doubt correct (it is said in Article 102(b) TFEU) but does nothing to clarify the legal position. Even more seriously, the Guidance does not say whether and if so how far the Commission wishes the Court to modify its case law to bring it into line with the Guidance Paper. The Guidance does not mention that in a number of respects it is inconsistent with the Court's case law. Indeed, the Guidance gives the impression that it was written by economists who were not basing themselves primarily on the judgments of the Court, and who were not setting out to give 'guidance' to companies or their lawyers, but merely to indicate what the Commission might do, or try to do.

If there is a solution to the difficulty that the Commission has created for itself and for the Court of Justice, it presumably will need to be on the following lines. The Commission should rely on the words of Article 102(b) TFEU whenever it can. It could certainly do this in cases where rebates are given on condition that the buyer buys exclusively from the dominant enterprise. It is less obvious that the Commission could do this in the other circumstances described in the Guidance document, where there are sales of certain quantities at prices artificially calculated as being below cost. But this Guidance theory is not based on the wording of the Treaty or on any judgment or case law of the Court, so it will have to be defended, if possible, on other grounds. In the case of any other conduct regarded as exclusionary but neither prohibited by Article 102(b) TFEU nor clearly within the case law of the Court, the Commission would need to produce a wholly new theory. It is difficult to imagine what it might be. In other words, all kinds of exclusionary conduct is illegal if it is contrary to Article 102(b) TFEU, and certain rebates and agents' commission are apparently illegal because the case-law has said so, but the category of unlawful exclusionary conduct probably cannot be widened further. In any future case in which the words of the Treaty do not apply, the Court would be unwise to base any judgment on 'underlying factors' that are unexplained, unknown, difficult to identify, and impossible to reconcile with the principle of legal certainty.

23. Magill revisited

Ian S. Forrester*

Jacques Bourgeois, when last I spotted him, arrived at my house beautifully dressed and elegantly accompanied (by two good-looking ladies), with vivacity, polyglot humour and gentle charm. Just a normal encounter with Jacques. In many, many years, I have seen him pressed and stressed and challenged, but never less than courteous, interesting, and well-informed.

To say that I was His Lawyer, once, is a point of pride, and to say that 'We Won' is a point of honour. This affectionate essay will tell the *Magill* story, warts and all.[1] In the process, I will draw your attention, gentle reader, to the truth that famous cases look easy once they have been decided; and that once a seed has been sown, it can grow into something huge and surprising.

23.1 THE PHENOMENON

Television broadcasters want to attract viewers, which they do by offering good programmes at the right times. Today, public service television competes for attention with video games, social networking sites, personal computers and the many ways of accessing internet content. A satellite dish can offer hundreds of television channels, but last century, in 1985, viewers seated in front of a television screen had only a small selection of channels from which to choose. The BBC weekly magazine, the *Radio Times*, was the largest-selling publication in the UK and a substantial source of revenue for the BBC. It told viewers about BBC radio and television programmes for the week ahead. It related gossip, hints about the story-line, published interviews with stars, all material likely to attract viewers to BBC programmes, which were competing with those of ITV and RTE, the BBC's then rivals in the United Kingdom and Ireland.

* The opinions expressed are wholly personal.

[1] Oliver Cromwell allegedly declined the portrait painter Sir Peter Lely's offer to depict him favourably, saying that he wished the picture to show him 'warts and all'.

The BBC published details of every BBC programme scheduled for the next week, drawn up in 'listings'. The listings were sent every week to all magazines and newspapers, which were thus encouraged to publish daily the programmes of that day. But they were forbidden to reproduce them on a weekly basis, since each of the three broadcasters preferred to have no competitor offering a multi-channel weekly guide.

23.2 THE BETTER MOUSETRAP

Magill was a weekly magazine that built up a reputation as a sharp commentator on political affairs in the Republic of Ireland. It was founded by Vincent Browne and others in 1977. Publication ceased in the late 1990s; the magazine was relaunched in 2004 but closed in mid-2009 despite cutting costs by dropping from weekly to bi-weekly to monthly; another relaunch is rumoured for the near future. It is fair to say that it has become more famous to competition lawyers than to Irish aficionados of political scandal. Back in 1985, the publisher of *Magill* had the idea of producing something new – a weekly guide to the forthcoming programmes of the three broadcasters (BBC, RTE, ITV) whose channels were received in Ireland. The *Magill TV Guide* would not contain as much information about the next week's programming as the in-house television guides, but it would be a multi-channel weekly. The price would be 82 pence. (The Irish viewer who wanted to be well-informed about favourite programmes, interesting drama or good sport would be buying three weekly magazines costing a total of 124 pence.)

The first issue was published in May 1985. But the first issue was also the last. The three broadcasters separately but simultaneously, applied to the Irish High Court to enjoin further publications, and succeeded.

Magill complained to the European Commission in April 1986, asserting that the three broadcasters had cooperated with each other in breach of Article 85 of the EC Treaty to stifle the *Magill TV Guide* in the cradle. Magill was unable to produce a weekly magazine giving details of all forthcoming programmes, though it could have produced a daily one, since the information was sent to every newspaper in the country to advertise the television programmes on offer each day. The view within the Commission was that Article 86 was the sounder route: thus the accusation was that each of the three plaintiff broadcasters had separately abused its dominant position by refusing to license Magill to reproduce on a weekly basis listings of forthcoming television programmes.

In those days, there was a rush of competition decisions at the end of each year, and an exceptional rush at the end of a Commission mandate, when long-blocked dossiers would get unblocked as policy deals were traded between different Commission services. After much internal debate, the Commissioners and their staff were able to unblock the controversial *Magill* dossier. And the unfortunate official in charge, Karen Williams, was given the job of drafting the Decision in a very few days, since the Commission would run out of mandate very shortly.

The Decision was adopted three days before Christmas 1988.[2] It said that the three broadcasters 'use copyright as an instrument of the abuse, in a manner which falls outside the scope of the specific subject-matter of that intellectual property right'.[3] Indeed, the Commission expressed doubt as to whether copyright existed in the controversial material, since the times and names of the programmes were mere utilitarian facts, like a railway timetable, and their arrangement in chronological order involved no 'sweat of the brow' which could in the United Kingdom and Ireland justify a copyright claim. The Commission ordered the three broadcasters to license Magill and others, on reasonable and non-discriminatory terms, to reproduce lists of future programmes on a weekly basis.

23.3 CHOOSING COUNSEL

In March 1989, when the inevitable appeal arose, Jacques Bourgeois, then leading the Commission Legal Service competition team, elected to recruit the services of outside counsel, and was imprudent enough to retain a Scot. Of course, as a youngish and hungry practitioner, I was delighted to have such an exciting mandate and began to think of irresistible arguments, powerful ripostes and sound policy themes. My ardour was somewhat dampened when a very senior member of the Legal Service told me that the *Magill* Decision had been a 'disgrace' and that he 'very much hoped' the Commission would lose on appeal. (Passion is still engendered by all encroachments on IP rights.) The immediate procedural challenge was to survive interim measures, suspending the effectiveness of the duty to comply with the operative of the Decision. They had been requested at the same time the appeal on the merits was submitted.

Before that, we had to agree on a fee. As best I can recall, the fee was 1,400,000 Belgian francs per case, or 4,200,000 Belgian francs (about \$80,000 for the four years of litigation) for the three – the Commission tariff was not generous but its lawyers do not complain. Certainly this one was content.

---

[2] Commission Decision of 21 December 1988 – *Magill TV Guide/ITP, BBC and RTE*, OJ L 78 (1989) 43 (Magill Decision).

[3] *Idem,* recital 23.

Then came the argument on interim measures before President Koopmans. My instructions had been to focus on the procedural question: no one could suffer irreparable harm from negotiating with potential licensees. The Decision had ordered the three broadcasters to explore licensing terms with Magill. Whether the Decision was good or bad was not the point. The negotiations might lead to an agreement on terms agreeable to all parties. My instructions from Jacques were that we should 'keep our powder dry', that is to say we should not commit ourselves to any precise theory of the case. The relevant market was slippery, the nature of the abuse was not yet well defined, the Decision had been written at high speed, Irish copyright law was not clear, better not exclude or include any theory. Better to focus on the prematurity of seeking a suspension of the Commission Decision. The judge, however, had other ideas. He insisted on knowing what the infringement was. Blushing counsel said without fierce conviction that there had been an abuse. The bench asked for a little more detail. Counsel offered a litany of possibly relevant wickednesses, but declined to be too specific; possibly it was discrimination, possibly it was unjustified refusal to supply, possibly it was other things also. The judge sniffed, as judges do, a whiff of lack of precision. What were the big principles at stake? How far did the Decision go? Was the Commission suggesting that if Samuel Beckett refused to allow someone to perform his plays, this was illegal? That Samuel Beckett was not dominant in the market for theatrical performances was brushed aside. What was the precise nature of the abuse? Why was a copyright holder not free to choose how to exploit his right? Jacques Bourgeois sat silent in the safety of the seats behind and wriggled sympathetically as Commission counsel endured heavy punishment. Jeremy Lever (no less), for the BBC, trumpeted with satisfaction, and lamented the feebleness of the Commission's case.

In May 1989, the President granted interim measures, ordering the suspension of the compulsory licence.[4] Things got worse. Two months later, in July 1989, the Irish High Court found that the claimed copyright, contrary to the Commission's doubts, did exist.[5] So the outcome was

---

[4] Order of the President of the Court of 11 May 1989, Joined Cases C-76, 77, 91/89 R, *Radio Telefis Eireann and others v Commission* [1989] ECR 1141, para. 20.

[5] Lardner J. declined to recognise a difference between the work of drawing up the day's viewing and the factual record of that effort. He reasoned as follows: 'I am satisfied by the evidence that the BBC's weekly TV programme schedules as published in Radio Times are the end product of a long process of planning, preparation, arrangement and revision which involves a great deal of work and experience and the exercise of skill and judgment. They are the creation of the BBC and in my judgment they constitute an original literary work in the sense of a compilation within Sections 2 and 8 of the Copyright Act 1963 in which the BBC

anything but certain. The Commission had invested some intellectual capital in doubting if the right existed. There were sceptical articles.[6]

The appeal before the freshly-hatched CFI then proceeded on the merits. Magill was granted leave to intervene in support of the Commission's conclusions. On the one hand, there was the common-sense observation that the broadcasters were delivering to hundreds of newspapers, free-of-charge, advertising materials about their own programmes and were claiming a semi-sacred copyright entitlement to block the weekly reproduction of that material. They were claiming that they were free to use their copyright rights without constraint, even where the only motive was to prevent competition with their single-channel guides. But they correctly observed that any IP right includes the power to exclude: the right-holder has a right that it can invoke or not invoke. What would be the limiting factor? What would be the criteria to examine future refusals to license? Did the nature of the content mean that other utilitarian works like maps and recipes were liable to a compulsory licence? Where were the governing principles? The Commission argued that consumers had to buy three television guides if they wanted to plan a week's viewing. Does that mean that saving money is a reason for ordering a compulsory licence?

There was a lot of debate about whether the encroachment on the broadcasters' rights went to the 'specific subject-matter' of the right. This notion had arisen in the free movement IP cases of the 1970s, when the European Court, rationalizing the obligation on right-holders to tolerate unwelcome trade in genuine goods between member states, asserted that the then Articles 30 to 36 left the core rights ('specific subject-matter') of patentees and trademark-holders intact while encroaching on other peripheral ('exercise') rights. Those arguments never seemed very troubling to me since the few authorities (notably *Volvo/Veng*) did not suggest that the distinction was relevant in cases of abuse.[7] *Volvo/Veng* suggested that the rule was that most invocations of IP rights are legitimate, but can be an abuse in specific circumstances. The *Volvo/Veng* judgment said that an IP right could be invoked without thereby being abusive, but that it could become abusive if there were aggravating factors (one example was denying Veng's right to manufacture Volvo parts that Volvo itself would not supply).

---

and BBC Enterprises Limited have shown that they are entitled to copyright in the Republic of Ireland.' (*RTÉ & ors v Magill TV Guide Ltd & ors* [1990] ILRM 534, at p. 550).

[6] Porter, V., 'The copyright protection of compilations and pseudo-literary works in EC member states', *Journal Business of Law*, 1–23 January 1993, at p. 18; Perkins, D., 'Foreign principles of Intellectual Property/Antitrust: the EEC', *Pragmatic Language Impairment*, Vol. 339, p. 279.

[7] Case 238/8, *AB Volvo v Erik Veng (UK) Ltd.* [1988] ECR 6211.

On the other hand, what was the exact nature of the abuse? One infelicitous justification offered by the BBC for taking action in the Republic of Ireland was a fear that exports of the *Magill TV Guide* would spread contagion in England, which was free of multi-channel guides. This seemed to be a damaging concession at a time when parallel trade was celebrated as a civil religion by the European Commission and Courts. There were dozens of multi-channel guides in continental Europe, so it seemed frivolous for the broadcasters to say their public mission obligations were under threat due to the emergence of a multi-channel weekly guide. The companies invoked high moral principles and the Commission replied that the precious material was freely-distributed advertising. The Commission stressed the nature of the material, the lack of R&D or research effort involved in producing it, and the sharing free-of-charge with allies but not competitors. Was it a refusal to supply, or a discrimination? What were the limits to the duty?

The argument before the CFI went better for the Commission. Antonio Saggio presided over a chamber formed of Judges Yeraris, Briët, Barrington and Biancarelli. They seemed sympathetic to the practical absurdity being remedied. The unhappy counsel for ITP mistook his time to plead and, after two warnings, was ordered to sit down in mid-speech. The Commission conceded that copyright existed in the material and argued that although there was an encroachment on the rights of the copyright-holders, the burden was very modest and the required licence could be remunerated. As to the suggestion that the *Magill* case might be invoked to justify shocking encroachments yet undreamt of, these were qualified as 'fevered imaginings'. I received a kind letter from one judge after the argument. The bruises of interim measures faded.

The Court of First Instance very strongly upheld the Commission's Decision, reasoning that the circumstances of the case warranted subjecting the refusal to license to scrutiny under EU competition rules:[8]

> Conduct of that type ... *clearly goes beyond what is necessary to fulfil the essential function of the copyright as permitted in Community law*. The applicant's refusal ... was ... arbitrary ... as ... not justified either by the specific needs of the broadcasting sector ... or by those peculiar to ... publishing television magazines ... The applicant's conduct cannot, therefore, be covered in Community law by the protection conferred by its copyright in the programme listings.

---

8 Case T-69/89, *Radio Telefis Eireann v Commission* [1991] ECR II-485, para. 73 (emphasis added).

And[9]

> ... while it is plain that the exercise of the exclusive right to reproduce a protected work is not in itself an abuse, that does not apply when ... that right is exercised in such ways and circumstances as in fact to pursue an aim manifestly contrary to the objectives of Article 86. *In that event, the copyright is no longer exercised in* a manner which corresponds to *its essential function*, within the meaning of Article 36 of the Treaty, which is to protect the moral rights in the work and ensure a *reward for the creative effort* ...

The judgment from the CFI went too far in support of the Commission in asserting that there had been no encroachment on the essential rights conferred by copyright, thus forgetting the right of first publication which the copyright-holder enjoys. As we will see, it was left to the ECJ to find the best formulation of the abuse.

The argument in Luxembourg on 21 February 1991 was not without drama and uncertainty. Julian Currall was the agent of the Commission as Jacques had moved on to other duties. The hearing coincided with thickly-snow-blocked roads, abandoned cars and more than the usual level of doubt. Before the argument, the President asked the Juge Rapporteur (Judge Rodriguez Iglésias) if he had any questions to counsel, and received the provocative reply that the case was clear and straightforward, so no questions were necessary. Opposing counsels' eyes met under collectively-raised brows. The argument was lively and thorough. At the end, the various counsel (Willy Alexander and Gerard van der Wal (RTE), Alan Tyrrell (ITP), Julian Currall and me (European Commission), Jeremy Lever and Christopher Bellamy (BBC), John Cooke (Magill), David Vaughan (the intervening Intellectual Property Owners)) each felt they had done respectably and that it was impossible to tell which way the case would go.

Advocate General Gulmann felt the Decision should be annulled.[10] His opinion was very long but contained well-stated elements of the 'conservative' approach:

Paragraph 13: 'The copyright laws of the Member States have thus duly balanced the various interests that must be protected by society ... In principle, where copyright law confers an exclusive right, that must be respected by competition law.'

---

9 Case T-69/89, *Radio Telefis Eireann v Commission*, *supra*, para. 71 (emphasis added).

10 Opinion of Advocate General Gulmann, delivered on 1 June 1994, Joined Cases C-241/91 and C-242/91 P, *RTE and ITP v Commission* (Court of Justice *Magill* Judgment) [1995] ECR I-743.

Paragraph 26: '... the judgments of the Court of First instance drew criticism from academics.'[11]

Paragraph 38: 'It is plain that a corollary of an exclusive right to reproduce the protected work is the right to refuse licences. Accordingly the right to refuse licences forms part of the specific subject-matter of copyright.'

Paragraph 39: '... it is thus not disputed that the exercise of the exclusive right of reproduction by refusing to grant licences does not in itself constitute an abuse of a dominant position. The Commission has stressed that it agrees.'

Paragraph 40: 'The question is whether there may exist such special circumstances in connection with a refusal to license that it can no longer be regarded as a refusal to licence in itself.'

Paragraph 44: 'the Court of Justice's case law shows ... that it is possible to identify a number of core rights which the owner of an intellectual property right enjoys under national law and whose exercise is not affected by the Treaty rules on the free movement of goods and undistorted competition.'

Paragraph 67: 'The Court of First Instance's premiss seems to be that the aim pursued by Article 86 outweighs the aim of copyright. As I understand the case-law of the Court of Justice, the contrary premiss is the right one.'

Paragraphs 79–80: 'The determination of which rights fall under the specific subject-matter depends on a balancing of on the one hand of the concern of protecting the intellectual property right in question and on the other the concern for free movement of goods or undistorted competition ... The fact that there is a balance does not signify that both interests must be given equal weight. The balance must always be in favour of the intellectual property rights. The starting point set out in the Treaty is that intellectual property rights can be exercised even if that leads to obstacles to trade or restrictions on competition. Consequently if an exercise of a given intellectual property right is necessary in order for that right to be able to fulfil its essential function, that exercise is not affected by the Treaty rules. It

[11] See *inter alia* Bonet, G., *Revue Trimestrielle de Droit Européen*, 1993, pp. 525–33; Desurmont, T., *Revue Internationale du Droit d'Auteur*, 151, January 1992, pp. 216–72; Forrester, I.S., *European Competition Law Review*, 1992, pp. 5–20; Françon, A., *Revue Trimestrielle de Droit Commercial et de Droit Economique*, 1992, pp. 372–6; Hermitte, M.-A., *Journal du Droit International*, 1992, pp. 471–7; Myrick, R.E., *European Intellectual Property Review*, 1992, pp. 298–304; Smith, J., *European Competition Law Review*, pp. 135–8; Subiotto, R., *European Competition Law Review*, 1992, pp. 234–44; Vinje, T.C., *European Intellectual Property Review*, 1992, pp. 397–402; Waelbroeck, M., *Annual Proceedings of the Fordham Corporate Law Institute*, 1992, pp. 134–7.

is only where an exercise is not necessary in order to fulfil the essential function that the interest of free movement of goods or the interest of free competition must prevail over the interest of the owner of the right to engage in that exercise.'

Paragraph 87: 'As regards in particular the right to refuse licences, it is clear that a requirement to grant licences constitutes a serious interference in copyright since it would be reduced merely to the right to receive an economic reward. There must therefore exist particularly substantial and weighty competition grounds for the right to refuse licences to be regarded as having been exercised in circumstances signifying that that exercise cannot be regarded as necessary for copyright to fulfil its essential function.'

Paragraph 127: '... the fact that the programme listings are less deserving of protection is also not a circumstance that can justify interference with the exercise of copyright therein.'

The Court of Justice did not follow the Advocate General. It confirmed the lower court's decision, but did so in more scientific language that could more comfortably be applied in future.[12] It stated that 'the exercise of an exclusive right by the proprietor may, in exceptional circumstances, involve abusive conduct'.[13] Such circumstances were present because:

(1) the refusal to license concerned a product (the weekly programme listings) the supply of which was *indispensable* to the publication of a multi-channel weekly television guide[14] (necessity not desirability must indeed be the right test);

(2) the refusal *prevented the appearance of a new product*, a comprehensive weekly guide to television programmes, which the television companies in question did not offer and for which there was potential consumer demand.[15] The broadcasters reserved for themselves a secondary market, the market for weekly television guides, by excluding all competition on that market: the right was being used to prevent the emergence of something desired by the public that the broadcasters could have made but did not.[16] This second test was a good rationale: it potentially offered a way to distinguish bad refusals from good refusals, and it rooted the abuse in consumer harm;

---

[12] Court of Justice in Joined Cases C-241/91 P and C-242/91, *Radio Telefis Eireann v Commission, supra.*

[13] Court of Justice *Magill* Judgment, para. 50.

[14] *Idem,* para. 53.

[15] *Idem,* para. 54.

[16] *Idem,* para. 56.

(3) the refusal was *not justified* (not very persuasive, since the broadcasters had a right that conferred on them a valuable monopoly: this criterion seems to be more or less meaningless).[17]

So the Decision of the Commission was upheld on appeal, but on narrower grounds. There was a chorus of expressions of dismay, grave predictions, triumph and other contrasting views. One eminent German professor said to a mutual friend 'It is the end of copyright in Europe.' But things went quiet for about ten years.

23.4 CHILDREN OF MAGILL?

The next case of compulsory copyright licensing in EC competition law was *IMS*. IMS is the world leader in gathering and supplying data on deliveries to pharmacies by wholesalers of pharmaceuticals. Pharmaceutical companies use this data to measure the effectiveness of their promotional efforts in each town and district. On the German market a geographic format for presenting this data had been developed by IMS and its customers and had become the de facto industry standard. The format divided Germany into 1,860 geographic zones, based on postal codes, each containing at least three pharmacies, by reference to which marketing data describing deliveries, prices and volumes in those zones is compiled and analysed. The precise frontier of each zone was agreed between IMS and its pharmaceutical customers, who drew the lines taking account of the location of bridges, hospitals, pharmacies, doctor's premises and the like. When a breakaway competitor, NDC, appeared on the German market, IMS relied on copyright to preclude it from presenting sales data, independently captured by NDC, using the same map of Germany as had been used for over a decade by IMS. Customers said to NDC that presenting the marketing data in any other way was not acceptable. NDC challenged the use by IMS of copyright before the German courts, and also complained to the Commission.

The Commission found that there was no practical possibility for companies wishing to compete with IMS to offer pharmaceutical sales data in any other format than that used by IMS. There were no alternatives to reporting the sales of pharmaceutical products in Germany other than the geographic lines delineating 1,860 regions following postal codes, which IMS was successfully claiming constituted a breach of its copyright.

[17] *Idem*, para. 55.

The 1,860 zone map was a de facto industry standard. IMS had developed the map together with its customers to match their needs and then invoked copyright to prevent NDC from offering its services in that format. Thus, the Commission could have based its case on the theory that IMS was claiming IP rights over a standard developed with the client industry for the abusive purpose of excluding competition by preventing its competitors from using the standard.[18] The Commission, however, never pursued this avenue. I would have felt more confident of the soundness of the attack in this case.

The President of the Court of First Instance suspended the Commission Decision ordering the grant of a licence by IMS.[19] The Commission did not ultimately rule on the merits, so there was no appeal. Instead, the Court of Justice gave a preliminary reference ruling in response to questions from a German court before which the national case was pending.[20] The *IMS* judgment came out just one month after the Commission's next adventure in compulsory licensing, *Microsoft*. The Court of Justice, building on and referring to *Magill*, held that a refusal to license will be deemed abusive if four conditions are satisfied: (1) the protected product or service is '*indispensable*' for carrying on a particular business; (2) the refusal is '*such as to exclude any competition on a secondary market*'; (3) the refusal prevents the emergence of a new product for which there is a potential consumer demand; and (4) the refusal is not justified by any '*objective considerations*'.[21]

The access to the material had to be *indispensable* for carrying out business on a particular market. It must be, in other words, absolutely necessary. As the Court clarified, the indispensability condition would not be satisfied if there are '*alternative solutions, even if they are less advantageous*'.[22] Thus a licensee who wished to bring out a copy of the original product with purple stripes or with added chlorophyll or at a lower price would not be making something new. The party requesting the licence would need to launch something wholly different from the product offered by the owner of the right, and plan to produce new goods or services not offered by the owner of the right and for which there is a potential consumer demand.

Magill and *IMS* provoked a stream of lively academic and policy debate. So much concern was generated that when the Department of Justice held

[18] On this point see Killick, J., 'IMS and Microsoft Judged in the Cold Light of IMS', *Competition Law Review*, Vol. 1, No. 23, 2004, pp. 30–32.

[19] Case T-184/01, *IMS Health v Commission* [2001] ECR II–3193.

[20] Case C-418/01, *IMS Health Inc. v Commission* [2004] ECR I-5039.

[21] *Idem,* paras. 37–8.

[22] *Idem,* para. 28.

hearings in 2002 on competition and intellectual property law and policy in the knowledge-based economy, it devoted a portion of the debate to *Magill* and *IMS*.[23] Having been involved in both cases, I felt qualified to speak:

> It would be unimaginable to me that a truly innovative piece of technology (a pharmaceutical patent or novel software code, for example) would be treated in such a manner. [This just shows how naïve advocates can be!] Thus the Magill and IMS cases can be seen as remedies to aberrations in the application of national copyright laws.
>
> Predictions of dire consequences for IP rightholders due to the uncertainties created by Commission decisions have not been borne out in practice. In substantive result I think the current situation is thus far not alarming. Other than those exceptional cases … compulsory licensing of IP rights on competition grounds is almost unknown in European law. These cases probably represent a corrective reaction by competition authorities to a national right covering questionable or doubtful subject matter, coupled with discriminatory use of the IP right …

Did *IMS* mean that no right-holder could sleep easily in his bed because the Commission was uncaged again and roaming the world in search of plunder? Or was *IMS* a one-off remedying of erroneous interlocutory decisions in national courts? Whatever the answer, it is reasonable for any operator, dominant or not, to operate in a legally stable and predictable environment.

I argued that it was vain to pretend that every European IP right is equally precious and that in both *Magill* and *IMS* there was a clear imbalance between the creative effort of the right-holder and the economic advantages flowing from its exercise of the right. The result in *Magill* and *IMS* would have been the same in US law, in that an American court would not have found that the aggregation of five postcodes into a single area conferred copyright over marketing data describing sales in that area.

The big surprise was the next compulsory licensing case, *Microsoft*.[24] Microsoft was ordered to draw up a detailed description of how certain features of the operating system for its servers (which coordinate networks of personal computers) functioned. The objective was to allow Sun and other competitors of Microsoft to offer servers that would interact perfectly in 'native' mode in a network of servers running Microsoft software.

---

[23] Forrester, I., 'Compulsory Licensing in Europe: a rare cure to aberrant national intellectual property rights?', Department of Justice/Federal Trade Commission Hearings on Competition & Intellectual Property Law & Policy in the Knowledge-Based Economy: Comparative Law Topics, 22 May 2002. See www.ftc.gov/opp/intellect/020522forrester.pdf.

[24] Case T-201/04, *Microsoft Corporation v Commission* [2004] ECR II-2977.

The prize at stake was Microsoft's newly-developed directory technology, called Active Directory. Viewed from one perspective, this was an engineering innovation that was very attractive to users, as it reinforced the ease and convenience of choosing Microsoft software to control large networks of PCs. Viewed another way, the complex interactions between servers performing directory functions (every Active Directory server acted like a perfect replica of every other one) tended to exclude or make less attractive to customers servers from Microsoft's competitors. The remedy imposed was intrusive: several hundred Microsoft engineers had to research how the relevant server software functioned, describe that in some 10,000 electronic pages, and then license it. This would allow competitors to write a new software program where the electronic zeroes and ones were different to the Microsoft software thus described, but the functionality of the program would be identical. Thus what the Commission said was unthinkable in *Magill* came to pass some 15 years later in *Microsoft*.

23.5 ENVOI

There are very few formal decisions by the European Commission and European courts on the desirability of compelling an allegedly dominant player to deal against its will. The law on refusals to deal has developed in a jerky, uneven fashion. In less than 20 years, we have moved from anything being surprising (*Magill*) to everything being possible (*Microsoft*). This difficulty of predicting outcomes is reinforced by the difference between how the law is promulgated by the European Court of Justice to courts making references (principled, rather cautious), and how the European Courts perform their appellate function (deferential, confined to a review of the legality of the act). The courts are much more cautious in the former cases and much less critical in the latter.

So where does the story leave us? Who won? Who lost? Did it matter? Well, in a technical sense, the European Commission won the litigation and Magill got some financial compensation for its lost opportunity. The lawyers had a wonderful tussle, as the case presented fundamental legal questions, arguing which was an honour. (I was approached in October 2010 in New Delhi by a bright young lawyer who seemed to regard my having participated in the *Magill* case as being as remarkable and as temporally remote as having survived the Battle of Trafalgar.) The *Magill TV Guide* never emerged from the cradle in which it was untimely stifled. Its counsel, John Cooke, became a judge of the Court of First Instance; Karen Williams became the Commission's Hearing Officer. The world continued to turn. Listeners in Ireland and the United Kingdom gained access to multi-channel guides. Multi-channel guides therefore competed more directly with each other since they had become substitutes for each other. I expect that the BBC's *Radio Times* was the principal commercial winner in the circulation war, as it offered a better and richer publication than the other guides, so I suspect that it became stronger for eschewing its monopoly.

23.6 WHERE DO WE STAND NOW, LEGALLY SPEAKING?

Now that the dust of *Microsoft* has settled, it is appropriate to consider where we stand as to compulsory licences. The right-holder should, in principle, be allowed to exclude others from using its IP and should be able to choose freely whom to license. Only truly egregious circumstances should create a need for antitrust intervention. I suggest that the following list of considerations, some rooted in case law, all based on common sense, should be helpful.

Is the requested input objectively essential for entering the market, or would it just be very convenient? Is the concession necessary to do business, or is it only necessary for doing the business in a particular way favoured by the complainant? Does the lack of the IP right offer the would-be licensee absolutely no alternative?

Proper consideration should be given to the circumstances preceding the creation of the protected subject-matter. How big has been the investment in time, skill, effort and in resources to create the protected subject-matter? How much investment went into developing it? Is it a fruit of skilled or laborious efforts? Is its real value as a gatekeeper or is it intrinsically valuable? A patented cure for cancer that is the fruit of years of research and huge financial expenditure should not, I suggest, be treated in the same way as television listings, but the law at this stage does not clearly say so.

The presumption of legality should be rebutted more easily in cases where the encroachment on the IP rights and the commercial freedom of the right-holder is relatively minor. Notably, both in *Magill* and in *IMS*, the copyrighted subject-matter was widely reproduced and, at least under certain constraints, available free of charge. Is the input secret or is it widely dispersed? If it is already widely accessible, perhaps free of charge, it seems less justified to restrict access to it, less shocking to compel its wider reproduction. Again, the law does not clearly say so, as can be seen from the *Microsoft* case.

Is the compulsory licence likely to create specific benefits for consumers? This condition is most likely to be satisfied when, as a result of the compulsory licence, the consumer would obtain access to a completely new product that the dominant company perhaps may, but does not, offer.

I would hope that such mushy, adjectival concepts as 'exceptional circumstances' or 'objective justification' may become obsolete, if the foregoing factors were prudently analysed. Economic crimes demand articulated and foreseeable criteria.

23.7 FINALLY …

Contrary to my predictions, the law changed immensely due to *Magill*. The *Microsoft* case was a child of *Magill*. Far from being a circumscribed European law corrective for an aberrant national IP right, the notion of compulsory licensing spread after *Magill*, to be adopted in most surprising circumstances.

Jacques Bourgeois, who performed the delicate function of being the Commission's lawyer in a fiercely controversial case, did not change, however. He remained as ever. Calm, cheerful, positive, and sympathetic to his counsel, in good times and in adversity, a man who knows the wisdom of an English poet.[25]

> But this I know:
> From quiet homes and first beginning
> Out to the undiscovered ends,
> There's nothing worth the wear of winning
> But laughter and the love of friends.

[25] Hilaire Belloc, 'Dedicatory Ode', 1910.

24. Refusal to supply and margin squeeze: a discussion of why the '*Telefonica* exceptions' are wrong

Damien Geradin

24.1 INTRODUCTION

In its Guidance Paper on Article 102 of the Treaty on the Functioning of the European Union (TFEU),[1] the Commission established three conditions that in its view must normally be satisfied before a 'refusal to deal'[2] or 'margin squeeze'[3] may be considered contrary to Article 102 TFEU. These

[1] Guidance on the Commission's enforcement priorities in applying Article 82 of the EC Treaty to abusive exclusionary conduct by dominant undertakings issued in December 2008, OJ (2009) C45/7.

[2] 'Refusal to deal' cases typically arise where a vertically-integrated dominant firm refuses to grant access to an input that is essential for a rival to compete with the dominant firm on a downstream market. The conditions under which a refusal to supply can infringe Article 102 TFEU have been set by the EU courts in the following cases: See Cases 6 and 7–73, *Commercial Solvents and Others v Commission* [1974] ECR 223; Case T-69/89, *Radio Telefis Eireann v Commission of the European Communities* (the '*Magill*' case) [1991] ECR II-485; C-7/97, *Oscar Bronner v Mediaprint* [1998] ECR I-7791; Case C-418/01, *IMS Health GmbH & Co. OHG v NDC Health GmbH & Co. KG* [2004] ECR I-5039; Case T-201/04, *Microsoft Corp. v Commission* [2007] ECR II-3601. For a discussion of the refusal to supply case law of the ECJ, see Geradin, D., 'Limiting the Scope of Article 82 of the EC Treaty: What can the EU Learn from the US Supreme Court's Judgment in Trinko in the wake of Microsoft, IMS, and Deutsche Telekom', *Common Market Law Review*, Vol. 41, 2004, p. 1519.

[3] 'Margin squeeze' cases arise when a vertically-integrated dominant firm sells an essential input to a downstream rival at a price that leaves a margin between the upstream input price and the downstream retail price that is insufficient to allow this rival to operate profitably on the downstream market. The conditions under which margin squeeze can infringe Article 102 TFEU have been set by the ECJ in the following cases: Case T-5/97, *Industrie des Poudres Sphériques SA v Commission* [2000] ECR II-3755; Case T-271/03, *Deutsche Telekom AG v Commission* [2008]

conditions mirror those established by the European Court of Justice (ECJ) in the *Bronner* case:[4]

> The refusal relates to a product or service that is objectively necessary to be able to compete effectively on a downstream market;
> The refusal is likely to lead to the elimination of effective competition on the downstream market; and
> The refusal is likely to lead to consumer harm.[5]

However, in its *Telefónica* decision,[6] the Commission took the view that in the circumstances of that case it did not have to prove that these conditions were satisfied before concluding that there was an abusive margin squeeze. The Commission argued that the particular circumstances of the *Telefónica* case were fundamentally different from those in *Bronner*. These purportedly fundamental differences were that:[7]

> Spanish and EU telecommunications law already imposed on *Telefónica* an obligation to supply and it was clear, from the considerations underlying such regulation, that the necessary balancing of incentives had already been made by the public authority when imposing such an obligation to supply ; and
> Telefónica's infrastructure was to a large extent the fruit of investments that were undertaken well before the advent of broadband in Spain and were undertaken in a context where Telefónica was benefiting from special or exclusive rights that shielded it from competition.

Against this background, this short chapter seeks to demonstrate that what I will refer to as the '*Telefónica* exceptions' do not make sense and are not justified from an EU law standpoint. On the contrary, their application could lead to negative consequences in particular by forcing a vertically-integrated dominant firm to give access to its infrastructure even when this access is not 'essential' within the meaning of the refusal to deal case law of the ECJ. This chapter is divided into four sections. Following this introduction, section 24.2 reviews the *Telefónica* case and the exceptions to the

---

ECR II-477. For a discussion of the margin squeeze case law and decisional practice of the Commission, see Geradin, D. and O'Donoghue, R., 'The Concurrent Application of Competition Law and Regulation: The Case of Margin Squeeze Abuses in the Telecommunications Sector', *Journal of Competition Law and Economics*, Vol. 2, 2005, p. 355.

[4] See Bronner, *supra*.

[5] Guidance Paper, *supra*, at para. 80.

[6] See Case COMP/38.784, *Wanadoo España v Telefónica*, Commission decision of 4 July 2007.

[7] *Idem*, at para. 302.

conditions set in the *Bronner* case law it contains. It also shows that these exceptions were taken on board by the Commission in its Guidance Paper on Article 102 TFEU, as well as referred to by Advocate General Mazák in its Opinion in the *TeliaSonera* case.[8] Section 24.3 explains why these exceptions are fundamentally flawed. Section 24.4 provides a short conclusion.

24.2 THE TELEFÓNICA EXCEPTIONS

This part successively describes the main aspects of the *Telefónica* decision and the exceptions to the conditions set in the *Bronner* case law it contains (24.1.1). It then shows that these exceptions were confirmed by the Commission in its Guidance Paper on Article 102 TFEU (24.1.2), as well as referred to by Advocate General Mazák in its Opinion in the *TeliaSonera* case (24.1.3).

24.2.1 The Telefónica Decision

In *Telefónica*, the Commission found that from September 2001 to December 2006 the margin between Telefónica's retail prices and the prices for wholesale access at national and regional levels were insufficient to cover the costs that an operator as efficient as Telefónica would have to incur.[9] The Commission ruled that, by imposing a margin squeeze on its competitors, Telefónica's behaviour amounted to an abuse of dominant position contrary to Article 102 TFEU.[10]

Because a margin squeeze is nothing less than a 'constructive' refusal to supply,[11] it appears logical that the conditions that have been set by the ECJ in *Bronner* should be met to establish a margin squeeze infringement. Hence, in its Reply to the Statement of Objections, Telefónica argued that the Commission should prove that the upstream input (i.e. its DSL network) is 'indispensable' for the provision of the downstream service. In this respect, Telefónica alleged that the conditions set by the ECJ in *Bronner* were not met in its case because (1) there were real and/or potential

---

[8] Opinion of Advocate General Mazák in Case C-52/09, *Konkurrensverket v TeliaSonera AB*, 2 September 2010.

[9] See *Wanadoo España v Telefónica, supra*, at para. 7.

[10] *Idem,* at para. 9.

[11] While access to the requested input is not formally refused, the price at which the input is sold does not allow the vertically-integrated firms' downstream competitors to operate profitably.

alternatives to the regional and national wholesale access services of Telefónica, (2) the regional and national wholesale access services of Telefónica could be replicated and (3) the alleged conduct was not likely to eliminate all competition on the downstream market. Telefónica concluded that given the fact it was not obliged under Article 102 TFEU to grant access to its own network, it was illogical, and legally unjustified, to maintain that its pricing policy concerning its national and regional wholesale products was nonetheless subject to Article 102 TFEU on the mere ground that these wholesale products had been offered to competitors as a result of a regulatory obligation.[12]

The Commission, however, argued that the particular circumstances of this case 'fundamentally differed' from those in *Bronner*.[13] First, Telefónica has a duty to supply the upstream inputs in question and it was clear from the considerations underlying both the EU and Spanish law that[14]

> Telefónica's duty to supply the relevant upstream products results from a balancing by the public authorities of the incentives of Telefónica and its competitors to invest and innovate. This is because the need to promote downstream competition in the long term by imposing access to Telefónica's upstream inputs exceeds the need to preserve Telefónica's ex ante incentives to invest in and exploit the upstream infrastructure in question for its own benefit.

Second, the Commission estimated that 'Telefónica's *ex ante* incentive to invest in its infrastructure [we]re not at stake in the present case.'[15] Indeed, Telefónica's infrastructure[16]

> was to a large extent the fruit of investments that were undertaken well before the advent of broadband in Spain and that thus bore no relation to the provision of broadband services (but for the provision of traditional fixed telephony services). Also, those original investments were undertaken in a context where Telefónica was benefiting from special or exclusive rights that shielded it from competition. The investment criteria used by the former monopoly at that time would have led to the investment being made even if there would have been a duty to supply.

In *Telefónica*, the Commission could have demonstrated that the conditions set in *Bronner* were present as there did not seem to be a serious

---

12 See *Wanadoo España v Telefónica, supra*, at para. 301.
13 *Idem*, at para. 302.
14 *Idem*, at para. 303.
15 *Idem*, at para. 304.
16 *Idem*

alternative to Telefónica's DSL network, hence these exceptions merely allowed the Commission to take a shortcut in its analysis. As will be discussed below, applied to other cases these exceptions could have a greater impact than allowing the Commission to realize a shortcut. In fact, it could lead to unjustified finding of infringements (i.e. Type I errors or 'false positives') based on the misguided view that access to a vertically-integrated firm's infrastructure is essential for one or several rivals to compete on a downstream market.[17]

24.2.2 The Commission Guidance on Article 102 TFEU

In its Guidance Paper on Article 102 TFEU, the Commission analysed refusal to supply and margin squeeze under the same section, which is the analytically correct approach. It also recognized that for these practices to be prohibited under Article 102 TFEU, the conditions defined by the ECJ in *Bronner* must be met, including a determination that the refusal in question 'relates to a product or service that is objectively necessary to be able to compete effectively on a downstream market'.[18]

The Commission, however, observed that 'in certain specific cases, it may be clear that imposing an obligation to supply is manifestly not capable of having negative effects on the input owner's and/or other operators' incentives to invest and innovate upstream, whether *ex ante* or *ex post*'.[19] The Commission considers that this is particularly likely to be the case when the particular circumstances it identified in *Telefónica* are present, i.e. where:

- 'regulation compatible with Community law already imposes an obligation to supply on the dominant undertaking and it is clear, from the considerations underlying such regulation, that the necessary balancing of incentives has already been made by the public authority when imposing such an obligation to supply' (first exception); or
- 'the upstream market position of the dominant undertaking has been developed under the protection of special or exclusive rights or has been financed by state resources' (second exception).

[17] On the notions of Type I and Type II errors, see Frank Easterbrook, 'The Limits of Antitrust', *Texas Law Review*, Vol. 63, 1984, p. 1.

[18] Guidance Paper, *supra*, at para. 80.

[19] *Idem*, at para. 81.

The Guidance Paper, an otherwise well-reasoned document,[20] accepts therefore uncritically the above exceptions, hence making them part of its 'official' enforcement policy on Article 102 TFEU. That should, however, not come as a surprise since at the time of writing of the Guidance, Telefónica had appealed the decision of the Commission before the General Court. Even if the drafters of the Guidance Paper could have easily perceived that the *Telefónica* exceptions were fundamentally misguided, they may have estimated that the Commission was bound to remain consistent with what it said in the decision.

24.2.3 The Opinion of Advocate General Mazák in the TeliaSonera Case

The Opinion of AG Mazák in the *TeliaSonera* case originated in a reference for a preliminary ruling made by Stockholm District Court in which it asked the ECJ a series questions on the interpretation of Article 102 TFEU concerning an alleged abuse of a dominant position in the form of a margin squeeze.[21] The reference was made in the course of proceedings between TeliaSonera Sverige AB ('TeliaSonera') and the Konkurrensverket (the National Competition Authority, the NCA).

TeliaSonera is the incumbent operator of the fixed telephone network in Sweden. Apart from providing broadband services to the benefit of end-users (retail market), TeliaSonera offered access to its metallic access network to other operators (wholesale market), which were also active on the end-user market. The NCA alleges that TeliaSonera abused its dominant position on the wholesale market by applying a margin – between the wholesale price for ADSL products and the retail price for ADSL services it offers to consumers – which would not have been sufficient to cover TeliaSonera's incremental costs on the retail market.

Against that background, the Stockholm District Court decided to stay the proceedings in the case and to refer ten questions to the ECJ, one being whether to constitute abuse under Article 102 TFEU, the product supplied by the dominant undertaking on the wholesale market must be 'indispensable' to downstream competitors. To this question, AG Mazák answered that the indispensability of TeliaSonera needed to be established (which was an important issue in this case since some alternative technologies were apparently available to provide broadband services to end-users), except 'where the dominant undertaking is subject to a regulatory obligation compatible

[20] With some exceptions, however, notably rebates and discounts. See Geradin, D., 'A Proposed Test for Separating Pro-competitive Conditional Rebates from Anti-competitive Ones', *World Competition*, Vol. 32, 2009, p. 41.

[21] Opinion of Advocate General Mazák , *supra*.

with EU law to supply the wholesale products.'[22] AG Mazák, without any form of critical analysis, took therefore on board the first *Telefónica* exception.

AG Mazák took, however, a more cautious attitude towards the second *Telefónica* exception. The NCA and the Commission had argued that TeliaSonera's situation was special because its upstream market position had allegedly been developed under the protection of special or exclusive rights or had been financed by state resources. Echoing AG Jacobs in its Opinion in the *Bronner* case,[23] AG Mazák acknowledged the importance of the fact that basic property rights affect incentives to make investments, as well as the fact that such rights are recognized in the legal systems of the member states and in some they have constitutional status.[24] In addition, AG Mazák noted that it had been argued that it was not clear why a public source of funding for property should lead to a stricter legal standard. The reason is that Article 102 TFEU does not allow a distinction to be made between public and private funding.[25]

Moreover, AG Mazák correctly observed that it might not always be easy to determine whether the source of funds is clearly public in nature as much of the infrastructure of former state monopolies may have been the subject of significant improvements following privatization with the result that sources of funding are now substantially mixed.[26] Without taking a firm position on the second *Telefónica* exception, he concluded his reasoning by stating that the relevance of the argument that a dominant undertaking's position has been developed under the protection of special or exclusive

---

22 *Idem*, at para. 58.

23 *Bronner*, Advocate General Jacob's Opinion, para. 58 ('[The]… justification in terms of competition policy for interfering with a dominant undertaking's freedom to contract often requires a careful balancing of conflicting considerations. In the long term it is generally pro-competitive and in the interest of consumers to allow a company to retain for its own use facilities which it has developed for the purpose of its business. For example, if access to a production, purchasing or distribution facility were allowed too easily there would be no incentive for a competitor to develop competing facilities. Thus while competition was increased in the short term it would be reduced in the long term. Moreover, the incentive for a dominant undertaking to invest in efficient facilities would be reduced if its competitors were, upon request, able to share the benefits. Thus the mere fact that by retaining a facility for its own use a dominant undertaking retains an advantage over a competitor cannot justify requiring access to it.').

24 Opinion of Advocate General Mazák, *supra*, at para. 27.

25 AG Mazák also noted that Article 345 TFEU would preclude discrimination between property rights along these lines.

26 *Idem*

rights or has been financed by state resources 'will depend on the specifics of a given case'.[27]

In sum, AG Mazák seems to accept the first *Telefónica* exception without identifying its serious flaws. As far as the second *Telefónica* exception is concerned, AG Mazák identifies the implementation difficulties it is likely to create without however ruling out entirely its application.

24.3 ANALYSIS OF THE TELEFÓNICA EXCEPTIONS

The Commission's view that it is not necessary to demonstrate that the conditions established in the *Bronner* case are satisfied when a dominant firm is under a regulatory obligation to supply its upstream input to downstream competitors (the first exception) or when it's upstream market position has been developed under the protection of special or exclusive rights or has been financed by state resources (the second exception) is wrong for the following reasons.

24.3.1 The First Exception is Unjustified and Wrong

First, there is no trace of any such exception in the case law of the ECJ on refusals to deal and it is not for the Commission to set aside the legal tests adopted by the Court. This case law is based on the premise that as a matter of law an obligation to deal can only be imposed in 'exceptional circumstances'. Nothing in the case law suggests that the strict conditions imposed in *Bronner* and previous and subsequent refusal to deal cases may be disregarded when an obligation to deal has been imposed by a regulatory authority based on a different set of objectives, pursuant to different standards, and to which is attached different consequences.

First, EU competition law and national regulatory laws have different objectives irrespective of whether the latter implements secondary EU law. As expressly stated by the CFI, national regulatory authorities apply a different set of principles and assumptions.[28] The objective of EU competition law is to prevent anticompetitive behaviour so as to maintain a competitive market structure to the benefits of consumers.[29] Regulation and regulators must balance a broader set of objectives including not only the protection of competition, but also the creation of competitive market

---

27 *Idem*, at para. 28.

28 See *Deutsche Telekom*, *supra*, at para. 113 ('Sector-specific regulations 'have objectives that differ from those of Community competition policy.')

29 See Geradin and O'Donoghue, *supra*.

structures, the promotion of investments in the telecommunications sector, and the maintenance and improvement of universal service.[30] Hence, the imposition of an obligation to deal by regulators may serve to achieve objectives that are broader than those pursued under Article 102 TFEU.[31] An obligation to deal may thus be imposed by national regulatory authorities in circumstances where the Commission would not be entitled to impose such an obligation. The Commission is not entitled to use Article 102 TFEU to enforce regulatory obligations.

In this regard, it is irrelevant that a national regulator may be required to balance incentives to invest and/or innovate before imposing regulatory obligations on a given operator as the Commission alludes to in the first *Telefónica* exception. Since regulatory authorities and competition authorities pursue different objectives, their balancing of a firm's incentives to innovate with the benefits of an obligation to deal may be entirely different. In addition, the Commission's approach in *Telefónica* assumes that the indispensability condition enshrined in the *Bronner* case law serves only to protect investment incentives.[32] This view is unfounded. While incentives to invest and innovate are relevant factors, the analysis is broader and strongly influenced by fundamental principles of law. In fact, the case law strikes a

---

[30] For a similar view, see Faella, G. and Pardolesi, R., 'Squeezing Price Squeeze under EC Antitrust Law', September 2009, available at http://papers.ssrn.com/sol3/papers.cfm?abstract_id=1478937 ('The balancing carried out by a regulatory authority does not necessarily coincide with the same assessment made by an administrative or judiciary authority in charge of applying antitrust rules. Regulatory authorities may impose obligations to supply beyond the limits set by competition law.'); Gonzalez-Díaz, E. and Padilla, J., 'The *Linkline* Judgment – A European Perspective', *Global Competition Policy*, April 2009.

[31] See, for instance, recital 25 of Directive 2002/21/EC of the European Parliament and of the Council of 7 March 2002 on a common regulatory framework for electronic communications networks and services (Framework Directive), 0.J. (2002) L 108/33: 'There is a need for ex ante obligations in certain circumstances *in order to ensure the development of a competitive market*.' (emphasis added) See also Article 12 of Directive 2002/19/EC of the European Parliament and the Council of 7 March 2002 on access to, and interconnection of, electronic communications networks and associated facilities (Access Directive'), OJ (2002) L 108/7: 'A national authority may, in accordance with the provisions of Article 8, impose obligations on operators to meet reasonable requests for access to, and use of, specific network elements and associated facilities, inter alia in situations where the national regulatory authority considers that denial of access or unreasonable terms and conditions having a similar effect *would hinder the emergence of a sustainable competition market at the retail level, or would not be in the end-user's user interest*.' (emphasis added).

[32] See *Bronner*, *supra*, para. 41.

delicate balance between the public interest in protecting the competitive process and the fundamental right to property.[33]

Even if a national regulatory authority and the Commission did pursue the same objectives, the Commission would still not be entitled to pursue a margin squeeze case without satisfying the strict conditions established by the ECJ for a finding an abusive refusal to deal. These strict conditions are not reflected in the regulatory framework and are not necessarily taken into account by regulatory authorities when imposing access obligations.[34] Moreover, the verification of the strict obligations imposed in *Bronner* cannot be delegated to national regulatory authorities. Given the serious consequences attached to findings of abuse of dominance under Article 102 TFEU, including the imposition of behavioural and/or structural remedies, and of very high fines, the Commission must conduct its own analysis on the basis of criteria that are unrelated to the existence of regulatory obligations.

Second, the dynamics relating to the imposition of obligations to deal are very different under regulatory law and EU competition law. For instance, a finding of significant market power (SMP) on the basis of Article 14(2) of the Framework Directive automatically leads to the imposition of one or more remedies,[35] whereas a finding of dominance under Article 102 TFEU does not in itself lead to the imposition of remedies. Remedial action requires a prior finding of abuse.[36] Thus, while the imposition of an obligation to grant access may be quasi-automatic when a

---

[33] *Bronner*, Advocate General Jacob's Opinion, para. 57 ('it is apparent that the right to choose one's trading partners and freely to dispose of one's property are generally recognised principles in the laws of the Member States, in some cases with constitutional status. Incursions on those rights require careful justification.')

[34] Article 12.2 of the Access Directive, supra note 31, does not require that the strict conditions set by the ECJ in *Oscar Bronner* be met to impose an access obligation on the SMP firm.

[35] See Article 16(4) of the Framework Directive, *supra*: 'Where a national regulatory authority determines that a relevant market is not effectively competitive, it shall identify undertakings with significant market power on that market in accordance with Article 14 and *the national regulatory authority shall on such undertakings impose appropriate specific regulatory obligations* referred to in paragraph 2 of this Article or maintain or amend such obligations where they already exist.' (emphasis added).

[36] In addition, an investigation of abuse of dominance is based on a set of findings reflecting the undertaking's position and behaviour in a market over a given period of time in the past, while under the new regulatory framework ex ante obligations arise (and are withdrawn) as a result of forward-looking market analysis based on existing market conditions. Given its forward-looking nature, the analysis of SMP will often work on the basis of predictions or speculations than on existing evidence.

vertically-integrated telecommunications operator is identified as having SMP on a wholesale market, an obligation to deal under EU competition law can be imposed only in 'exceptional circumstances'.

Finally, a potentially serious problem when the Commission decides not to apply the strict obligations imposed in *Bronner* on the ground that the vertically-integrated operator is subject to a regulation obligation to supply on the basis of an SMP analysis is that there may be an important time lag between the period during which this analysis was made (e.g. one or two years earlier) and the moment the competition analysis made by the Commission takes place. During the interval, market circumstances may have considerably changed with, for instance, the entry of one or more facilities-based competitors with the consequence that the Commission could mandate access to infrastructure, which even under a regulatory analysis is no longer essential.

24.3.2 The Second Exception is Unjustified and Wrong

The second exception whereby there would be no need for the Commission to satisfy the *Bronner* conditions for imposing an obligation to deal when the 'firm's upstream market position has been developed under the protection of special or exclusive rights or has been financed by state resources' is equally misguided for the following reasons.

First, there is also no trace of this exception in the case law. It has not and should not play a role in how a given piece of property has been obtained. In *Magill* – which involved TV listings required to produce TV guides – the property rights in question were bi-products of the broadcasters' main activity, namely broadcasting.[37] No investment was made in developing the listings. Yet, the ECJ insisted that an obligation to deal could only be imposed on strict conditions.

Second, as observed by AG Mazák in its *TeliaSonera* opinion, this exception is difficult to apply in practice and is likely to lead to unpredictable and erroneous results. Whether or not the 'firm's upstream market position has been developed under the protection of special or exclusive rights or has been financed by state resources' may not be clear cut. Some of the network assets required to provide a wholesale product may have been paid in large part after market liberalization and it may be difficult to determine which parts of the assets have been paid for pre-liberalization and post-liberalization. Incumbent operators may have to upgrade very significantly the networks inherited from the pre-liberalization/pre-privatization periods to make such networks usable for the provision of end user services.

---

[37] See *Magill*, *supra*.

Third, the Commission's approach ignores the adverse effects of obligations to deal on future incentives to invest. Once the obligation has been imposed, both the dominant firm and its competitors may have less incentive to invest. The dominant firm may derive less benefit from its own infrastructure and hence have less incentive to invest in it. Competitors are able rely on the dominant firm's network instead of investing in their own. When the conditions established in *Bronner* are satisfied, this is not an issue since it is not viable for competitors to create their own infrastructures. However, when these conditions are not satisfied, this becomes a real issue. In *Bronner*, the ECJ proceeded on the basis of the premise that it was in the consumer interest that competitors created their own country-wide distribution system. Hence, by creating an exception where no exception has been recognized, the Commission is undermining a rule that has been created in the interest of competition and consumers, even if it may reduce the scope for Commission action. However, enforcement action is not an aim in itself.

24.4 CONCLUSION

The analysis conducted in section 24.3 *supra* shows that the two *Telefónica* exceptions, whereby there would be no need for the Commission to satisfy the *Bronner* conditions for imposing an obligation to deal, are fundamentally flawed. As pointed out by some authors 'they seem to open for a remarkable intrusion into the commercial freedom of dominant firms, which could negatively affect their incentives to invest and innovate'.[38] They could also lead to fundamentally misguided Article 102 decisions either when national regulatories have not conducted a proper regulatory analysis or when there is an important time lag between the moment this analysis was conducted and the moment at which the Commission's assessment of a dominant firm's conduct takes place with the consequence that market circumstances may have significantly changed.

---

[38] See Faella and Pardolesi, *supra*.

25. Making sense of the reactions to the 2010 US Horizontal Merger Guidelines

Barry E. Hawk and James A. Keyte

25.1 INTRODUCTION

In once describing why he would not join his teammates for dinner at a popular restaurant, baseball legend Yogi Berra famously quipped, 'Nobody goes there anymore, it's too crowded'.[1] The same could be said about trying to comment on the revised Horizontal Merger Guidelines (RMGs), issued by the Antitrust Division of the Department of Justice (DOJ) and the Federal Trade Commission (FTC) (collectively, Agencies) in August 2010.[2] The RMGs explain enforcement policy for two of the most important antitrust and competition regulators in the world, which makes the RMGs one of the most potentially influential documents in today's antitrust world. Recognizing this importance, in 2010 alone, commentators have put out (by our count) more than 120 articles or shorter analyses discussing the RMGs. In other words, seemingly anyone who considers themselves an expert on antitrust law and/or economics has felt compelled to weigh in on the RMGs.

Recognizing this rising cacophony, we offer this chapter – particularly for readers who typically have a European focus – as a starting point for understanding the positions on the RMG taken by authors across disciplines, economic perspectives, and continents. Thus, our purpose is two-fold. First, this chapter is descriptive, surveying the commentary to date on the RMGs. Second, although we acknowledge a number of widely accepted positives in the RMGs, the incredible variance in opinions demonstrates

[1] Pepe, P., *The Wit and Wisdom of Yogi Berra*, Chicago, Triumph Books, 2002, p. 186.

[2] US Department of Justice & Federal Trade Commission, *Horizontal Merger Guidelines*, 2010 (hereinafter *2010 Guidelines*).

one of the RMGs' primary weaknesses: its lack of substantive guidance. To this end, we offer a brief explanation of how the Agencies' decision in the RMGs to choose enforcement flexibility over guidance strikes many observers as questionable, and we contrast this decision with the EU's approach as embodied in the 2004 EC Merger Regulation.

25.2 CONSENSUS: THE NEED FOR NEW GUIDELINES

One area on which almost all commentators seem to agree is that the United States was overdue for new merger guidelines. Two related factors likely motivate this general consensus. First, there was a growing sense that the 1992 Horizontal Merger Guidelines (1992 Guidelines) no longer accurately described what the Agencies actually did when they evaluated proposed mergers for anticompetitive effects. Second, the significant efforts and advances in economics research since 1992 resulted in many economic tools that were simply unavailable the last time the Agencies engaged in a full revision of the Guidelines.[3]

That the literature has converged on the idea that merger guidelines should accurately describe the Agencies' review is no surprise. To the extent that a business understands how the Agencies review proposed transactions, it is then able to plan those transactions accordingly and is in a better position to challenge the Agencies if it thinks they are overreaching or taking actions contrary to their own guidelines.[4] Updating the merger guidelines also serves to memorialize agency policy and confirm minor changes in policy that the Agencies have made without issuing formal guidance.[5] Likewise, courts are able more accurately to assess the Agencies' actions if they have a clear picture of the Agencies' guiding principles in merger review.[6]

Commentators also have supported updating the 1992 Guidelines because of the magnitude of change in economic theory in the intervening

---

[3] E.g. American Antitrust Institute, HMG Revision Project Comments – Comment Project No. P092900, 4 June 2010, pp. 1–2, to be found at www.ftc.gov/os/comments/hmgrevisedguides/548050–00025.html.

[4] See, e.g., American Bar Association Section of Antitrust Law, HMG Revision Project Comments – Comment Project No. P092900, 4 June 2010, pp. 1–2, to be found at www.ftc.gov/os/comments/hmgrevisedguides/548050–00026.pdf.

[5] Leonard, G.K., 'The 2010 Merger Guidelines: Do We Need Them? Are They All We Need?', *CPI Antitrust Journal*, Vol. 10, No. 2, 2010, p. 3.

[6] See, e.g., Federal Trade Commission, *Federal Trade Commission Seeks Views on Proposed Update of the Horizontal Merger Guidelines*, Press Release, 20 April 2010, to be found at www.ftc.gov/opa/2010/04/hmg.shtm.

18 years. It is true, as we describe below, that these advances aggravate the tension between fact-specific economic analysis and clear, predictable legal rules (i.e. flexibility and guidance).[7] However, merger guidelines must not be so economically anachronistic as to fail to describe the Agencies' techniques for analyzing potentially anticompetitive mergers. Thus, the RMGs' inclusion of diversion ratios and upward pricing pressure (UPP) analyses, for example, reflects changes in economic thinking regarding unilateral effects developed since 1992.[8]

Our review of the commentary on the Agencies' decisions in drafting the RMGs shows that it is really only the need for new guidelines that has generated near-universal agreement. In almost every other aspect of the RMGs, commentators have laid out well-argued positions either supporting or criticizing choices that the Agencies made in revising the 1992 Guidelines.

25.3 DIVISION: EVERYTHING ELSE

Nearly every substantive issue in the RMGs has generated at least some debate. Indeed, whereas some commentators have suggested that the RMGs are only incrementally different from the 1992 Guidelines and what the Agencies have been doing anyway,[9] other authors reject this 'no-big-deal' attitude toward the RMGs. This latter group of authors claims instead that such a *laissez-faire* view misses important changes in how the Agencies will conduct merger review under the RMGs, or at least understates significant differences between the RMGs and the 1992 Guidelines.[10] Thus, focusing on the degree of difference between the arguments of critics and supporters of the RMGs on particular issues can be useful. Such an exercise allows a determination on whether the Agencies have gently

---

[7] See *infra*, section 25.4.

[8] Leonard, *supra*, p. 2.

[9] Doane, M., Froeb, L., and Tschantz, S., 'Warning: Improper Use of the *New Horizontal Merger Guidelines* Can Result in Overly Narrow Markets, Mistaken Inferences of Market Power, and Wrong-Headed Analysis', *CPI Antitrust Journal*, Vol. 10, No. 2, 2010, p. 6; Leonard, *supra*, p. 2; McDavid, J. and Stock, E., 'New Horizontal Merger Guidelines Indicate Greater Scrutiny of High Tech and Pharmaceutical Transactions', *CPI Antitrust Journal*, Vol. 10, No. 2, 2010, p. 2.

[10] Wellford, H. and Wells, G., 'The 'Litigation Mulligan' in the 2010 Merger Guidelines: Better Economics but Not (Necessarily) More Clarity Before the Agencies and the Courts', *CPI Antitrust Journal*, Vol. 10, No. 2, 2010, p. 2; Langenfeld, J., '2010 Horizontal Merger Guidelines: Changes in Policy, Transparency, & Predictability', *CPI Antitrust Journal*, Vol. 10, No. 2, 2010, p. 2.

nudged antitrust enforcement in the Agencies' preferred direction on specific issues, or whether they have instead sought a significant break from past practices, perhaps exceeding the courts' guidance in particular areas.

Of course, examining every change from the 1992 Guidelines to the RMGs is well beyond the scope of this chapter, and we limit our focus to some of the areas that have generally garnered the most ink: the RMGs' de-emphasis of market definition and market concentration, as well as effects issues in the RMGs, such as margins, unilateral effects analysis, and UPP.

25.3.1 Market Definition and Market Concentration

We begin our discussion with market definition, which traditionally has been the starting point for analyzing purportedly anticompetitive mergers.[11] The wide-ranging debate on the RMGs' de-emphasis of market definition is one of the most hotly contested changes in the RMGs.[12] Moving from our starting point to the Agencies', the RMGs state that market definition 'is not an end in itself, but is useful to the extent it illuminates the merger's likely competitive effects'.[13]

Most commentators recognize that the RMGs do not dispense with market definition all together – section 4 of the RMGs is, after all, entitled 'Market Definition'. Some commentators have thus downplayed the extent to which the role of market definition is truly reduced in the RMGs.[14] However, more commentators have drawn a heavier line, recognizing that by making a defined market unnecessary in a particular case, the RMGs do in fact present the Agencies with the opportunity to do away with market definition in particularly difficult cases.[15] These commentators tend to view the RMGs as directly conflicting with recent court decisions requiring the government to sufficiently define a relevant market.[16]

In responding to these criticisms, government officials have primarily argued that characterizations of the RMGs' treatment of market definition

---

[11] See US Department of Justice & Federal Trade Commission, *Horizontal Merger Guidelines*, 1992 (revised 1997), para. 1.

[12] See, e.g., Sohn, M.N., 'Pricing of Differentiated Products in the 2010 Horizontal Merger Guidelines: Some Unanswered Questions' (to be published in *2010 Fordham Competition Law Institute* (B. Hawk (ed.) 2011)).

[13] *2010 Guidelines*, *supra*, para. 4.

[14] McDavid and Stock, *supra*, p. 2.

[15] See Wellford and Wells, *supra*, p. 4.

[16] *Idem,* pp. 7–8 (citing *FTC v Whole Foods Market, Inc.*, 502 F. Supp. 2d 1, 8 (D.D.C. 2007); *United States v Oracle Corp.*, 331 F. Supp. 2d 1098, 1131 (N.D. Cal. 2004)).

as a major change are overblown. Carl Shapiro, Deputy Assistant Attorney General for Economics at the DOJ Antitrust Division, has addressed this criticism of the RMGs, noting that 'this concern is not well-founded' because the DOJ 'recognizes the necessity of defining a relevant market as part of any merger challenge we bring'.[17] The FTC Commissioner, J. Thomas Rosch, echoed this view, recently stating that market definition is 'a necessary prerequisite' to the government bringing any antitrust litigation.[18] In recognizing the criticism that the RMGs no longer require the type of market definition that courts have required, Rosch stated that the market definition 'requirement has gotten lost in translation'.[19]

Despite these competing views on what the RMGs do with market definition, a survey of the literature reveals that most commentators would agree that what was a fairly linear process under the 1992 Guidelines now provides the Agencies with more discretion to begin their analyses where they deem appropriate. However, whether this is a major change or just a matter of recognizing what the Agencies had already been doing is contested.

Moving from how the RMGs treat market definition to whether such treatment is sound policy enters an even more crowded node in the literature. Professor Hovenkamp has explained that the RMGs 'suggest use of a broad array of tools, in which [m]arket delineation plays a smaller role', because 'the enforcement agencies are increasingly sensitive to the problem of excessive reliance on market definition mechanisms that are, at best, rough approximations of reality'.[20] Hovenkamp thus appears to represent a group of commentators that are sympathetic to the reduced role of market definition in the RMGs, at least at the stage of agency review.[21]

---

[17] Shapiro, C., Remarks for the American Bar Association Section of Antitrust Law Fall Forum, Washington, D.C., 18 November 2010, pp. 14–15, to be found at www.justice.gov/atr/public/speeches/264295.pdf. However, one of Shapiro's argument regarding the importance of market definition in the Guidelines is too simply note how many pages the Guidelines devote to product and market definition (12 out of 37 by Shapiro's count).

[18] Rosch, J.T., Remarks the American Bar Association Section of Antitrust Law Fall Forum, Washington, D.C., 18 November 2010, pp. 2–3, to be found at www.ftc.gov/speeches/rosch/101118fallforum.pdf.

[19] *Idem,* p. 18.

[20] Hovenkamp, H.J., *Merger Policy and the 2010 Merger Guidelines*, University of Iowa Legal Studies Research Paper, December 2010, p. 42, to be found at http://ssrn.com/abtract=1693246 (follow download hyperlink).

[21] Accord McDavid and Stock, *supra*, p. 2 (citing *FTC v Lundbeck, Inc.*, Nos. 08–6379, -6381 (JNE)(JJG) (D. Minn. 31 August 2010)); *idem,* p. 3 (noting that while market definition has been useful 'as a restraint on … challenging mergers based on insignificant anticompetitive effects', the RMGs' 'de-emphasis of market

These authors often begin by claiming that economists have generally rejected market definition as a necessary component of merger evaluation because it requires drawing artificial lines, particularly in differentiated product markets. Other commentators have argued against the use of market definition even more forcefully, though even among those who believe that market definition is an unsound economic tool, there is recognition of the practical necessity of its inclusion in merger analysis.[22]

Of course, many commentators are significantly more sceptical regarding the desirability of the reduced role of market definition in the RMGs. In commenting on the draft RMGs, the American Bar Association (ABA) took the strong position that '[a] reduction in the role of market definition in merger analysis would be wrong as a matter of policy, as a matter of law, and as a matter of international competition norms that the Agencies and others have espoused'.[23] Like-minded commentators frequently point to the statutory 'line of commerce' language and the US Supreme Court's decisions requiring market definition.[24] Others note that the RMGs' tests generally create even narrower markets than those that courts have already rejected in earlier cases.[25] The commentators who are the most sceptical about the reduced role of market definition in the RMGs often take the position that this change is a response to (and push-back against) recent government losses on market definition in high-profile cases.[26] One article has derisively stated that 'it is not immediately apparent how codifying the Agencies' disagreement' with the courts in the recent section 7 cases the Agencies have lost, 'would make courts more receptive', regardless of what 'assistance' the RMGs claim to be offering.[27]

Turning to market concentration, the recent commentary tracks the literature on the RMGs' treatment of market definition: the RMGs lessen

---

definition provides increased legitimacy to a trend at the Agencies to focus mainly on the likely real-world "competitive effects" of mergers').

[22] See Stelzer, I., *Merger Policy and Schumpeter's Creative and Destructive Gale*, Lecture Delivered at the 15th Annual EU Competition Law and Policy Workshop, Florence, Italy, 12 November 2010, to be found at www.hudson.org/files/documents/Florence%2012–13%20November,%20Hudson.pdf.

[23] American Bar Association Section of Antitrust Law, *supra*, p. 6.

[24] See, e.g., Denis, P.T., 'The Framework of the 2010 Horizontal Merger Guidelines', *CPI Antitrust Journal*, Vol. 10, No. 2, 2010, p. 6; Keyte, J., Dick, A., and Schwartz, K., 'Tally Ho: The 2010 Horizontal Merger Guidelines' (to be published in the *Antitrust Law Journal*, Vol. 78, 2011) (collecting the statutes and cases requiring market definition).

[25] Wellford and Wells, *supra*, p. 8.

[26] See Sohn, *supra*.

[27] Wellford and Wells, *supra*, p. 8.

the historical importance of concentration, but claims of the elimination of concentration analysis, so says the majority position in the literature, are somewhat exaggerated.

Reaction to the elimination of any concentration threshold or safe harbour, for example, has been mixed. It is fair to say that economists have more broadly supported this change while lawyers have generally opposed it.[28] One exception is Professor Hovenkamp, who has lauded the RMGs for their abandonment of the 35 per cent safe harbour in favour of the Agencies' willingness to examine a merger of two less-concentrated firms that are each others' closest competitors. Hovenkamp has called this choice 'clearly correct' because, he explained, '[e]ven two firms with relatively small market shares can effect a price increase provided that they are sufficiently close in product space while most other firms are more remote'.[29] A view more typical of those questioning the removal of the safe harbour is that of Paul T. Denis, a principal draftsman of the 1992 Guidelines, who has questioned whether the elimination of safe harbours and bright line tests leaves the RMGs providing inadequate guidance. He has argued that 'for those looking for standards that can be applied rather than directional indicators, the new text is unsatisfying'.[30]

These differing perspectives also carry over into the more general question regarding the proper role of market concentration data under the RMGs. Government commentators have explicitly recognized that the RMGs 'downplay the role of market concentration' by focusing more closely on other evidence of effects.[31] Shapiro, however, has claimed that 'there is a rather broad consensus about the desirability of supplementing evidence about market structure ... with other forms of evidence'.[32]

We are less certain that any consensus is actually so broad. One commentator, for example, while recognizing the role of diversion ratios and UPP, argues that the RMGs may overstate these tools' importance because courts have generally considered Herfindahl-Hirschman Indices (HHIs) and seemed less receptive to moving towards these other analyses.[33] Likewise, there is evidence in the literature of concern that by allowing the Agencies to exclude 'smaller rivals' from a calculation of concentration, the

---

28 Compare Shapiro, Remarks, *supra*, p. 23, with Hawk, B.E., 'A Tale of Two Cities: Washington and Brussels Face the Courts', p. 3 (to be published in the November 2010 Fiesole proceedings of the European University Institute).

29 Hovenkamp, *Merger Policy*, *supra*, p. 25, n. 12.

30 Denis, *supra*, p. 5.

31 Shapiro, Remarks, *supra*, p. 15.

32 *Ibid.*

33 Langenfeld, *supra*, p. 16.

RMGs 'appear to discount a competitive fringe that could expand substantially if there were an attempt to raise price after the merger'.[34]

Such disagreements aside, there are few aspects of market concentration for which we found something approaching consensus. There is a general consensus in favour of increasing the HHI thresholds in the RMG. This decision has generally been well received,[35] and as Professor Hovenkamp has explained, there is agreement that the HHI levels in the 1992 Guidelines no longer reflected Agency practice.[36] There also is a general recognition that whatever else the RMGs may do or not do with concentration, its importance is diminished in the RMGs. Even those answering criticisms about too little focus on concentration recognize that the RMGs have moved away from market concentration to a more eclectic approach,[37] and commentators have noted that the RMGs' sections on market definition and concentration are now dwarfed by the RMGs' discussion of effects.[38]

25.3.2 Effects Theories and Evidence of Anticompetitive Effects

Like other areas in which commentators have sought transparency in the RMGs, there has been broad support for the Agencies' valuing transparency in their efforts to describe the types of effects evidence they consider in the merger review process.[39] Unsurprisingly, commentators have taken sharply different tacks when arguing whether the RMGs reflect the correct choices regarding theories and evidence of anticompetitive effects. The literature also is characterized by contrasting arguments when considering whether the newly described tools for making effects determinations are appropriate and, if so, in what contexts. Given the space constraints of this chapter, we focus in particular on margins, unilateral price effects, and UPP, which have generated significant commentary in response to the RMGs. In terms of effects, a review of the commentary suggests that critics and supporters of the RMGs agree that they place increased emphasis on the merging firms' margins compared to the 1992 Guidelines. Any margin-related disputes, therefore, concern whether such enforcement policy is desirable.

---

34 *Idem,* p. 11.

35 Hawk, *supra*, p. 2; Wellford & Wells, *supra*, pp. 6–7.

36 See Hovenkamp, *Merger Policy*, *supra*, pp. 40–41; see also Langenfeld, *supra*, p. 10.

37 See Lubell, K.B., 'International Convergence and the New Horizontal Merger Guidelines: Summary of a Fordham Law School Panel Discussion', *The Threshold*, Vol. 11, No. 1, 2010, pp. 4–5.

38 Wellford & Wells, *supra*, p. 7.

39 See, e.g., American Bar Association Section of Antitrust Law, *supra*, p. 4.

Critics have levelled margin-based attacks against the RMGs on two bases. First, commentators have noted that the RMGs in effect equate larger margins with market power (or an implication that there is already coordinated behaviour).[40] Some commentators have been especially critical of this reliance on margins evidence because its use by the Agencies, they claim, is new and essentially untested outside of limited factual scenarios.[41] The ABA has seconded this criticism.[42] Similarly, commentators have expressed concerns that the RMGs indicate the Agencies' greater willingness to pursue theories of harm to competition based on narrow categories in which sellers are able to price discriminate.[43] This issue, these commentators note, likely overlaps with firms characterized by high R&D and low manufacturing costs (and often high margins). The overlap exists because such firms have an incentive to offer discounts to consumers who are identifiably unable to pay the high price necessary to support the R&D – pharmaceuticals being the paradigmatic example.[44] Compounding the matter, some commentators have argued that high margins in the pharmaceutical and high tech markets 'typically have nothing to do with whether a particular market is competitive or whether a manufacturer has market power'.[45]

The second basis for criticizing the RMGs' use of margins is not a concern with the use of margins qua margins, but rather whether data related to margins (and diversion ratios) are reliable. In particular, commentators have questioned whether sufficient information on margins and diversion ratios really exists for the Agencies to engage in the robust effects calculations envisioned in the RMGs.[46] The lack of data to perform these calculations, critics note, may be particularly problematic because of the weight that the RMGs seem to place on margins and diversion ratios for ferreting out anticompetitive effects via UPP.[47]

In response to these claims, commentators supportive of the RMGs appear confident that margins data exist even outside the retail merger area

40 Langenfeld, *supra*, p. 4.

41 Coate, M.B and Simons, J.J., 'Continuity and Change in the 2010 Merger Guidelines', *CPI Antitrust Journal*, Vol. 10, No. 2, 2010, p. 2.

42 See American Bar Association Section of Antitrust Law, *supra*, p. 17.

43 See, e.g., McDavid and Stock, *supra*, p. 4; Wellford and Wells, *supra*, pp. 4, 9.

44 *Ibid.*

45 McDavid and Stock, *supra*, p. 5.

46 Hawk, *supra*, p. 7.

47 See Langenfeld, *supra*, p. 7.

where scanner data may be plentiful.[48] As for whether margins, even if calculable, are rightly elevated to this central role in the RMGs, economists in particular have filled the literature with defences of the use of margins, noting that high margins tend to imply that actual loss from raising prices will be small and that economic theory strongly supports this focus on margins.[49] Other commentators also have defended the Agencies, claiming that the RMGs do not act as a categorical bar to a merger in the face of high margins but that such margins should lead to further study.[50] Related to margins, there also is broad disagreement apparent in commentators' statements regarding the RMGs' treatment of unilateral price effects and UPP. These disagreements may be of particular importance because there is at least some consensus that the RMGs are characterized by a shift in the Agencies' emphasis from coordinated effects to unilateral effects.[51]

Critics of the RMGs' effects explanation and use of UPP point to a number of potentially serious weaknesses. Initial objections to UPP, for example, include the claim that any tool that is as new as UPP has no place in the RMGs.[52] Supporters of such a claim (or critics of UPP more broadly) have pointed to arguments from prominent economists claiming that UPP poses a 'serious concern' since it can be used to allege an anticompetitive effect in any merger.[53] Such attacks are magnified by the fact that UPP is one area in which commentators have criticized the RMGs for providing the Agencies with an enforcement tool without adequately delimiting its use.[54] Further, critics have insisted that the Agencies' assurances that UPP will not be used to challenge all horizontal mergers rings

---

48 See Remarks of Alison Oldale, Chief Economist, UK Competition Commission (to be published in *2010 Fordham Competition Law Institute* (B. Hawk (ed.) 2011)).

49 See, e.g., Katz, M.L. and Shapiro, C., 'Critical Loss: Let's Tell the Whole Story', *Antitrust Magazine*, Vol. 17, No. 2, 2003, pp. 49–50; Proposed Horizontal Merger Guidelines: Economists' Comment, 4 June 2010, pp.2, 6, to be found at www.ftc.gov/os/comments/hmgrevisedguides/548050–00017.pdf.

50 American Antitrust Institute, *supra*, p. 3.

51 See, e.g., McDavid and Stock, *supra*, p. 4.

52 See Wellford and Wells, *supra*, pp. 4–5.

53 Simons, J.J. and Coate, M.B., 'Upward Pressure on Price Analysis: Issues and Implications for Merger Policy', *European Competition Journal*, Vol. 6, No. 2, 2010, p. 379. In discussing the RMGs' treatment of UPP, one commentator has noted that 'this is a case where a little additional complexity is worse than no complexity at all' because 'UPP does not translate to a predicted post-merger price increase' without knowing the 'curvature of the demand functions'. Leonard, *supra*, p. 4; see also Epstein, R.J. and Rubinfeld, D.L., 'Understanding UPP', *The B.E. Journal of Theoretical Economics*, Vol. 10, No. 1, 2010, p. 8.

54 Hawk, *supra*, pp. 3–4.

hollow because the Agencies provide no guiding statement describing when a merger will in fact be challenged on the basis of UPP.[55]

Effects criticisms of the RMGs, however, are by no means limited to UPP. Commentators also have voiced particular concern with the decision in finalizing the RMGs to exclude any credit for efficiencies and synergies. Such a decision is especially problematic, critics claim, in the face of statements from chief economists at the Agencies that efficiencies can offset an upward pressure on prices.[56] To this end, the ABA has criticized the draft RMGs as embodying a 'static approach to unilateral effects analysis'.[57] Similar concerns related to effects in the previously discussed high-margin industries are also commonplace as an example of economic theory having moved too quickly past business realities in particular industries.[58] Defenders of these aspects of the RMGs are represented most vocally by the government economists who are largely credited with devising UPP. They have focused on effects analyses in particular, claiming that the economic theories underlying the RMGs do not involve novel or distorted application of economics and are, essentially, 'just arithmetic'.[59] A number of economists outside the government have similarly supported UPP.[60]

The plurality of commentators see more shades of gray in the RMGs' effects analyses, discussions of unilateral effects, and use of UPP. Professor Hovenkamp, for example, has expressed some support for the RMGs, noting that '[t]he unilateral effects analysis provisions in the [RMGs] certainly do not reflect any more speculation or uncertainty than is present in the more traditional analysis depending on coordinated interaction, notwithstanding that the latter has been in use far longer'.[61] For Hovenkamp, '[t]he fact is … that the diversion ratio analysis is much better suited for assessing market power in product differentiated markets than are traditional market definition criteria'.[62] Yet Hovenkamp also has provided one of the most pointed critiques of unilateral effects analysis in the RMGs, illustrating a basic limit to the RMGs' explanatory force: a lack of

55 *Idem,* p. 4.

56 American Bar Association Section of Antitrust Law, *supra*, p. 17.

57 *Idem,* p. 13.

58 McDavid and Stock, *supra*, pp. 4–5.

59 See, e.g., Shapiro, C., 'The 2010 Horizontal Merger Guidelines: From Hedgehog to Fox in Forty Years', *Antitrust Law Journal*, Vol. 77, No. 3, 2010, p. 724.

60 See, e.g., Moresi, S., 'The Use of Upward Price Pressure Indices in Merger Analysis', *Antitrust Source*, Vol. 9, No. 3, 2010, pp. 8–9.

61 Hovenkamp, H., *Harm to Competition Under the 2010 Horizontal Merger Guidelines*, University of Iowa Legal Studies Working Paper, November 2010, p. 10, to be found at http://ssrn.com/abtract=1702843 (follow download hyperlink).

62 *Idem,* p. 15.

reasoning to explain why non-merging firms are unable (particularly over time) to discipline predicted price increases that will result from a merger.[63]

Other commentators have similarly taken a more ambivalent approach than either the strongest critics, or the defenders and drafters, of the RMGs. These middle-ground authors have recognized that leading Agency economists essentially proposed UPP as a tool to allow the Agencies to challenge mergers in difficult-to-define markets. However, these commentators view the RMGs as taking a 'step back from this linkage' and 'as only one of many tools that the agencies will use' depending on their needs.[64] Whether one is satisfied with this grayscale view of the merger control world may have more to do with one's view of the proper role of flexibility versus guidance in the RMGs, to which we now turn.

25.4 THE REVISED MERGER GUIDELINES' PRIMARY CHOICE: FLEXIBILITY VERSUS GUIDANCE

A tension between flexibility and guidance is present in many areas of antitrust and competition law and reflects a decades old debate about legal structural presumptions.[65] Considering how this tension plays out in the RMGs, and how the RMGs compare to the EU approach, sheds light on both the utility of the RMGs as the primary source of merger guidance and their likely reception in court.

25.4.1 The Revised Merger Guidelines Favour the Agencies' Flexibility

The inherent tension in the RMGs between flexibility and guidance has at once generated substantial agreement and heated conflict in the literature. Except for the concurrence among commentators that new guidelines are a positive when the old ones no longer reflect agency practice, there may be no area over which commentators agree more than the following: the RMGs reduce the specific level of guidance on how the Agencies conduct merger review in favour of a more flexible approach, through which the Agencies conduct fact-specific inquiries and use different analytical tools depending upon the merger under review. But whether this change is the RMGs' greatest strength or its fatal weakness (or something in between) is

63 Hovenkamp, *Merger Policy*, *supra*, pp. 29–30.
64 Doane, Froeb and Tschantz, *supra*, p. 3.
65 Hawk, *supra*, p. 1.

a subject that commentators have debated vigorously since the Agencies issued the RMGs.

We briefly described above the state of the debate in the literature. In this section, we indulge in the normative, suggesting that the RMGs' choice of agency flexibility over substantive guidance may be a regrettable decision that limits the usefulness of the RMGs for practitioners and courts – i.e. everyone except the government.

To some, the balance the Agencies struck with the RMGs is reasonably correct. Hovenkamp, for example, has praised the RMGs' flexibility, focus on different types of anticompetitive harm, and less-detailed treatment of market delineation.[66] Flexibility is beneficial, in Hovenkamp's view, because the '[o]lder Guidelines were overly technocratic and excessively wed to methodologies that were at the forefront of applied merger analysis when they were drafted, but that tended to make the Guidelines obsolete as new methodologies became available'.[67] Hovenkamp also recognizes, however, that '[t]o be sure, there is a tradeoff between flexibility and guidance. Often we can have more of one only by giving up some of the other, and that tradeoff is clearly present in the [RMGs]'.[68] Unsurprisingly, government economists such as Shapiro and Richard Feinstein, Director of the Bureau of Competition at the FTC, have gone further. They have defended the Agencies' discretionary 'toolbox', as well as the Agencies' judgment in using the appropriate tool in the appropriate instance.[69] Still other commentators find the criticism of excess flexibility surprising since, in their view, the Agencies have been conducting analyses in this manner for years.[70]

Another group of commentators sees the RMGs quite differently. To some authors (primarily legal in training), perhaps the single major criticism of the RMGs is that they increase the mystery of US merger review despite the purported goal of increasing transparency.[71] Some of these critics note that the RMGs provide a list of what are essentially advocacy tools, allowing the Agencies to select the particular tool of analysis that will provide them with the best chance to win in litigation. Similarly, Paul T.

---

66 Hovenkamp, *Harm to Competition*, *supra*, p. 1.

67 *Ibid.*

68 *Ibid.*

69 Shapiro, C., Remarks, *supra*, pp. 16–20; Lindell, C.K., 'Regulators Defend Revised Merger Guidelines', *The Deal Pipeline*, 21 September 2010.

70 American Antitrust Institute, *supra*, p. 2.

71 See Arquit, K.J., 'Unilateral Effects Analysis in the 2010 Horizontal Merger Guidelines: The Beginning of the End of the Age of Restraint?', pp. 3–4 (to be published in *2010 Fordham Competition Law Institute* (B. Hawk (ed.) 2011)).

Denis has noted that he is troubled by the 'enormous amount of flexibility the government has given itself' because 'you don't know what they'll do'.[72] Even Commissioner Rosch registered his criticism of the RMG – albeit in concurring with the RMGs' issuance – calling the guidelines 'flawed' and noting that they did not deliver on what the antitrust 'bar and their clients deserve': complete transparency and guidance.[73]

An even more sceptical group of authors has questioned not only the Agencies' prospective choice of tools, but its retrospective stocking of the toolbox. Some commentators note that what the Agencies call 'flexibility' – 'the use of broader types of evidence, economic tools that operate at a more minute level of detail (as [UPP] does), a greater focus on price discrimination, and identification of smaller or 'targetable' groups of customers whom the Agencies will attempt to protect not only from pricing harm, but also from harm involving hard-to-quantify factors such as preferences over differentiated products' – may be viewed by firms as involving 'a higher risk of subjectivity and speculation'.[74] Under this view, the RMGs 'appear indifferent, or even defiant, to the foregoing court loses'.[75]

As we stated earlier, we find it fair to conclude that the philosophy underlying the RMGs falls well on the side of flexibility and fact-specific merger analysis. In the best case, this eclectic approach amounts to the Agencies asking parties whom they are reviewing to 'trust us' when it comes to methodology. In the worst case, the toolbox approach is a tactical response to litigation losses and a misunderstanding of the very purpose of guidelines in general. Thus, it does not surprise us when we read another commentator predicting that the RMGs' abandonment of the structured framework of the 1992 Guidelines 'probably spells an earlier obsolescence for the final document'.[76]

---

[72] Greene, J., 'Antitrust Bar Reacts to New Merger Guidelines', *The National Law Journal*, 21 April 2010.

[73] Statement of Commissioner Thomas J. Rosch on the Release of the 2010 Horizontal Merger Guidelines, Project No. P092900, 19 August 2010, pp. 1, 4, to be found at /www.ftc.gov/os/2010/08/100819hmgrosch.pdf.

[74] Wellford and Wells, *supra*, p. 9.

[75] *Idem,* p. 8.

[76] Denis, *supra*, p. 2; see also Lubell, *supra*, pp. 6–7 (describing the statement of Janusz Ordover, Professor of Economics at New York University, questioning whether courts will accept the RMGs).

25.4.2 The Agencies' Approach to the RMGs Contrasts With the EU Commission's 2004 Merger Regulation

Given the disputes in the literature over whether the Agencies made good choices in drafting the RMGs, it is revealing to compare the US's new guiding document to the 2004 EC Merger Regulation, its transatlantic cousin.

Interestingly, in September 2010 a key EU competition official offered a negative assessment of the RMGs, a somewhat rare occurrence in the world of US–EU antitrust and competition relations. The EC's Chief Economist, Damien Neven, stated that the RMGs suffered from several 'missed opportunities' and 'criticized the shift away from market definition'.[77] Neven explained 'that while "convergence is not a goal in itself" the refined US approach "might lead to different outcomes" '.[78] At least one commentator has highlighted Neven's statement that ordinarily ' "Guidelines act mostly as an intellectual discipline on the authority" – a pre-commitment constraint on the Agencies'.[79] In highlighting this aspect of Neven's comments, the implication is that the RMGs do not inflict such intellectual discipline on the US Agencies. The concomitant unanswered question is: if not constraint on the Agencies, for the RMGs' drafters, what other purposes might the RMGs serve?

But perhaps this reaction from European enforcement officials is unsurprising when one considers the approach the EU took with the 2004 EC Merger Regulation.[80] Specifically, following a series of losses before the Court of Justice, the Commission significantly reformed its procedures, substantive test, and institutional mechanisms to address the court's criticisms.[81] As one of us has previously pointed out, this reaction arguably contrasts with the US Agencies' reaction to a number of litigation losses involving mergers in US courts, if one assumes that the RMGs reflect (at least to some extent) an attempt to strengthen the Agencies' litigation position in future cases before the courts.[82] If this is indeed a partial motivation for the choices the Agencies made in drafting the RMGs, it is

---

[77] Vascott, D., 'Neven Criticises New US Guidelines', *Global Competition Review*, 29 September 2010.

[78] *Ibid.*

[79] See Wellford and Wells, *supra*, pp. 10–11.

[80] See Council Regulation (EC) No. 139/2004 on the Control of Concentrations Between Undertakings, OJ (2004) L 24/1.

[81] See generally Horner, N., 'Unilateral Effects and the EC Merger Regulation – How the Commission Had Its Cake and Ate It Too', *Hanse Law Review*, Vol. 2, No. 1, 2006 (describing the EC Merger Regulation).

[82] See Hawk, *supra*, p. 2.

not difficult to make the case that the EU approach is superior. In keeping with the historical tradition of the Guidelines, they should reflect clarity, transparency, and provide businesses (and, we would add, courts) with a better understanding of how the Agencies review transactions.[83] Responding to judicial dictates by incorporating judicial directives (arguably the EU approach), rather than using guidelines as advocacy (arguably the approach in the RMGs) would be better aligned with the RMGs' self-identified goals.

25.5 CONCLUSIONS

Most of us in the antitrust community welcomed the idea of new guidelines that could accurately reflect what the Agencies have been doing for years, but whether the RMGs took optimal advantage of the opportunity is hotly debated. Although the consensus among commentators is that any new guidelines should incorporate up-to-date, accepted economic thinking, it remains to be seen whether courts will view the RMGs as a neutral updating of agency policy or as a process that occurred with one eye trained on former litigation losses, and as part of an effort to create rules more favourable to their drafters. Either way, in our view, the Agencies could have done more to serve the core function of any guidelines: provide guidance. On this score, the RMGs may prove to fall short of similar efforts in the EU. Of course, only months into the application of the RMGs, it is impossible to know which commentators are correct, and only time (and courts) will prove whether the RMGs' flexibility for the Agencies is accompanied by sufficient guidance for parties considering horizontal mergers.

---

[83] See US Department of Justice, *Department of Justice and Federal Trade Commission Issue Revised Horizontal Merger Guidelines*, Press Release, 19 August 2010, to be found at www.justice.gov/atr/public/press_releases/2010/261642.htm.

State aid

26. From trade to tutelage: state aid and public choice in the European Union

William Bishop*

26.1 GENESIS

European state aid control is an odd constitutional entity. Such control is *not* found in other economic federations. For example in the United States, Canada or Australia there is no control of the equivalent of state aid. NAFTA too knows nothing of state aids, or at least has implemented nothing. In these economic unions, state aid is commonly practiced, is ubiquitous even, yet nobody much worries about it. Every now and then the state of Washington, say, pays a lot of money to, say, Boeing not to move its manufacturing facilities away. The state of Alabama tries to attract a chemical company to locate even more plant in Mobile Bay. And Ontario and New South Wales offer similar inducements. It happens all the time. It is also true that public discussion does sometimes come to the conclusion that these subsidies are ill judged. The various states and provinces reach this conclusion without the wise of any outside agencies – such as their own federal governments or European Commission – standing in an examination over them.

The microeconomics and industrial economics now standard antitrust analysis is of little help in understanding state aid. But one branch of economics that does help – the economics of politics and public decision-making, called 'public choice'. In particular there are three useful concepts from that branch of economics: the self-enforcing constitution, side payments and blame-shifting (or 'shift of responsibility'). These three concepts

* I have benefitted from the guidance of Jacques Bourgeois, Leigh Hancher, Claus-Dieter Ehlermann, Rainer Nitche and Tom Ottervanger, and from the research assistance of Nonthika Wehmhorner – none of whom bears any responsibility whatsoever for the views expressed.

I think do help us understand something about the economics of state aid and about the prospects for any real reform.

26.2 THE PECULIAR HISTORY OF A UNIQUE INSTITUTION

European state aid control as we know it today did not just fall out of the sky – it happened for a reason. We need to go back in time to understand something about the process. The origins go back, surprisingly and interestingly, to the original GATT treaty – the General Agreement on Trade and Tariffs – in 1947. If you look at the drafting of the Treaty of Rome you find that Article 30 and following on free movement of goods and Article 92 on state aids have language reminiscent of the GATT treaty of 1947. In particular, note GATT Article XVI on subsidies, Article XIX on emergency actions, Article XX on exceptions. It is clear that the concern in GATT '47 and in Rome '56 is a concern about *export subsidies* and about *strategic trade* in general, and especially about attempts to defeat imports by subsidizing home producers.

The threshold concept adopted in the Treaty of Rome is *effect on trade between member states*. That treaty was the first constitution of the European community and the foundation of any power that the Commission has. What was intended by Article 92 was that member state governments should not by their domestic actions unduly impede imports or promote exports. The threshold concept of 'effect on trade between member states' was essential to the functioning of Article 92. If evidence of this is wanted note a commentary on the Treaty of Rome published in 1957 by a pair of German scholars who were also high officials of the early EC, Von der Groeben and Von Boeckh,[1] where the co-authors say that the concept of effect on trade under Article 92 can be expected to be more restrictive than that under Articles 85 and 86. It is interesting to note that this is exactly the opposite of the way things have developed under the jurisprudence of the European Court of Justice.

Article 92 was *not* – and this is extremely important – *not* a licence for the European Commission to second-guess member states' domestic policies. In 1956 the notion that the member state governments might set up an

---

[1] Von der Groeben, H. and von Boeckh, H. (eds), *Kommentar zum EWG-Vertrag*, Baden-Baden, Bonn, Frankfurt, Verlag August Lutzeyer, 1st edn, 1958.

external authority to judge their own *internal* actions within France, Germany, the Netherlands etc. – as some sort of super-policeman over their own internal affairs – would have seemed bizarre.

26.3 THE SELF-ENFORCING CONSTITUTION

Now I want to turn to the first of the three key concepts that I think illuminate the state aid issue – the concept of the 'self-enforcing constitution'. Why is it that some constitutions are self-enforcing and some are not? Some constitutions are set up, work more or less as intended – they become stable even though there is no outside authority to enforce them. There is a considerable economic literature on this topic. For example, in 2005 Professor Barry Weingast of Stanford, a leading scholar on public choice, published a paper on the American constitution and with the unusual claim that it really only became stable and self-enforcing in 1877.[2]

One strain in that literature considers the idea of leaving enforcement to some supreme court. Tullock, long ago, pronounced this 'naive'. Who will make the supreme court honour the original constitutional deal, he asks? They will just interpret it to suit their own political preferences. The ancient question '*quis custodiet custodes ipsos*?' still cries out to be answered.

26.4 'INTERPRETATION' AND THE EMERGENCE OF THE TUTELAGE MODEL

Let us examine what actually happened to the Treaty of Rome at the hands of the European institutions. Crucial here is that for, purposes of day-to-day administration, interpretation is in the hands of the Commission. If someone wants to challenge what the Commission does, then ultimately interpretation is in the hands of the European Court of Justice. In the nature of things both of these institutions are staffed by people who are bound up with the 'European project'. Naturally they tend to see the 'European project' as a good thing and wish to advance it. Moreover, they have an in-built career interest in moving more power to the centre.

Unsurprisingly, this has led to a 'reinterpretation' of 'effect on trade' away from the original intention – at least as expounded by Von der

---

2 Weingast, B., 'The Constitutional Dilemma of Economic Liberty', *Journal of Economic Perspectives*, Vol. 19, No. 3, 2005, pp. 89–108.

Groeben and Von Boeckh – in the direction of greatly increased power for the European Commission. That this happened was *not* for want of articulate attempts by member states to argue to the contrary. Several member states have tried to claim in particular cases before the Court that there was no effect on trade of the state aid they had granted because 'nothing is exported', or because 'the market is not liberalized'.

Philip Morris (1979) is a pivotal case.[3] There the European Court of Justice faced a straightforward matter in which a member state was paying a chunk of money to the famous tobacco company to induce it to site a plant in its country rather than somewhere else. The court said (approximately):

> This is certainly an aid. There is no need for the Commission to define the relevant market for purposes of talking about effect on trade. *That the firm is receiving an advantage is eo ipso an aid.* And that is true even if the aid itself is very small and consequently the effect on trade too very small.

In other words, the ECJ was saying, the key threshold condition was effectively to be read out of the Treaty. The power of the central authority was thereby expanded well beyond what was ever agreed or intended by the contracting member states in 1956 or later.

Moving on 23 years, *Altmark* in 2003 was a case about a modest regional bus company.[4] Paragraph 81 is the key. The court says that there is no threshold percentage too small to count as a distortion of trade between two states. Again, this amounts to even further weakening of 'effect on trade' as the threshold condition under Articles 92, indeed not so much weakening as de facto removal. It is the opposite of what Von der Groeben and Von Boeckh, and presumably others, understood at the foundation of the Community.

In consequence of the Courts' 'interpretation' we have numerous more-or-less absurd cases: the regional bus company in provincial Germany in the *Altmark* case; a swimming pool in the city of Dorsten;[5] ski-lifts in the

---

3 *Philip Morris Holland BV v Commission of the European Communities*, Case 730/79, Judgment of the Court of 17 September 1980. This decision confirmed the case 79/743/EEC, OJ L 217, 25 August 1979, pp. 17–19.

4 Altmark Trans GmbH, *Regierungspräsidium Magdeburg v Nahverkehrsgesellschaft Altmark GmbH*, Case C-280/00, Judgment of the Court of 24 July 2003, OJ C 226, 20 September 2003, pp. 1–2.

5 Commission Decision of 21 December 2000, N 258/2000 – Germany (Leisure Pool Dorsten), OJ C 171, 16 June 2001, p. 16.

Trento region of Italy; and even the zebra cage at the Rotterdam Zoo.[6] Aid in all these cases is something that now the European Commission opines on. They are not matters solely for the jurisdiction of the member state. I call this the *tutelage model* – the wise Commission as schoolmaster and disciplinarian of the venal member states – even in their own internal affairs.

26.5 SUBSIDIARITY AND THE ZEBRA CAGE AT THE ROTTERDAM ZOO

Subsidiarity was constantly talked of in Europe in the 1990s. It was even said to be a key idea for the new federal future of the European community. Reassurance was offered to sceptics that subsidiarity would guarantee in future that the institutions of the centre would handle only those things appropriate to the centre. In particular decisions would be taken *at the lowest possible level*, at the level nearest to the people. And yet today we have the zebra cage at the Rotterdam zoo as a matter within the jurisdiction of the European Commission. How is that possible? How did it happen? Why has it not been changed? If the tutelage model of state aid is allowed to stand then the idea that subsidiarity is Europe's fundamental principle is simply not credible.

26.6 HOW REFORM HAPPENS IN THE EUROPEAN UNION

Let us now turn to the prospects for reform. First, let us ask: how does reform happen in the European Community? I think we can draw a lesson from the way that reform has happened in antitrust. Beginning in 1997, there has been sweeping and continuing reform of competition policy, led by the European Commission. The Commission in October of 1997 issued its notice on the definition of the relevant market, a notice that adopted economic criteria for market definition. The Commission was not at all shy about saying, in so many words, that it was going to ignore 30 years of ECJ jurisprudence, as, in the Commission's (correct) opinion, the jurisprudence was vague and unhelpful.

---

6 Written question P-1907/05 by Kartika Liotard (GUE/NGL) to the Commission, Investigation by Commissioner Kroes into subsidization of the Artis and Blijdorp Zoos, OJ C 299, 8 December 2006.

What then happened? Did the courts take issue with the Commission on this? Not at all. The courts of the European Community, themselves unsettled by previous confusion, fell into line, grateful to the Commission for the lead that it was giving. Exactly the same happened in the United States in the 1980s and early 1990s with the DoJ guidelines. The guidelines were quickly adopted by US courts, even though they impugned, or departed from, all kinds of jurisprudence. The courts saw that the guidelines were rational and had some sensible purpose – as opposed to the intellectual mess that they knew their own jurisprudence had created. One of the reasons that there is a lot of vagueness and confusion in the difficult, especially, Article 82 cases is that the judges themselves are afraid of doing something really stupid. Judges are intelligent people well aware that they have no magic wand to solve difficult problems. When a judge sees sensible ideas coming along he does not reject them; instead he is more likely to cleave to them like a drowning sailor to a lifeboat. The lesson from antitrust reform is that the Commission can change bad policy if it wishes to change. But does it wish to change?

26.7 PUBLIC CHOICE EQUILIBRIUM AND THE PROSPECTS FOR REFORM

If there is going to be any change in state aid policy we need to consider whether the Commission is going to change, whether the Court is going to change or whether the member states are going to change. Equilibrium in a political market shifts only if something changes. Change only happens if someone wants it, if someone propels it. So our first a question: Is the Court going to change?

First, note that court control of the Commission operates over two very different aspects of Commission action. The first is the definition of what constitutes a state aid. On that issue there is close control of the Commission by the Court. The Court developed the market economy investor principle. It demands clear analysis by the Commission of whether or not something is an aid – even for little things like aid to a parking garage in the Netherlands. So there is close control of the Commission on the definition of aid.

The second aspect of state aid is exemption decisions, that is the Commission's decision to exempt a particular aid from the provisions of the treaty. Here there is almost no control of the Commission. The court has, quite deliberately, said that the Commission has a very wide discretion – it is subject only to control based on 'unreasonableness'.

Contrast this to court control of the Commission's decisions in competition law. Take for example, *Tetra Laval v The Commission* in both the CFI[7] and the ECJ.[8] There we find careful control of the Commission – in effect elaborate second-guessing by the Court. The Commission will not be allowed to block mergers, or indeed grant merger clearances, without being able to justify itself in fine detail to the court. DG Enterprise in 2005 issued a 50-page booklet of guidance on where the lightning of Commission generosity might strike in state aid exemption decisions.[9] It gives no real guidance at all because you cannot really predict it – there are no true principles. All the booklet does is give an account in the many instances in which exemption has happened.

26.8 SIDE PAYMENTS

What is one to make of these developments? The first point is that this 'settlement' – i.e. the tutelage model – is in the interest to both the Court and the Commission. The Court has residual power and it has a continuing task in supervizing the definition of state aid. And, the Commission has the power to use its state aid power of exemption, de facto, *for any purpose it likes*, in particular for deals with the member states.

Side payment is the second key concept, derived from public choice theory, that I think is helpful here. The idea of a side payment is that an official (or legislator) exercises his power, not solely on objective or official legal criteria, but partly in return for a concession or agreement that advances his personal or institutional aims. Side payments have been studied since the emergence of public choice theory 50 years ago.[10]

What happens with state aid is simple. Nearly everything *can* count as a state aid. Where there is state aid the Commission has essentially unfettered discretion to grant exemption or not. The Commission uses its unfettered

---

7 *Tetra Laval BV v Commission of the European Communities*, Case T-5/02, CFI's judgment of 25 October 2002, [2002] ECR II-04381.

8 *Commission v Tetra Laval*, Case C-12/03, ECJ's Judgment of 15 February 2005, [2005] ECR I-987.

9 'Innovation market failures and state aid: developing criteria', November 2005, Oxera. See http://ec.europa.eu/enterprise/newsroom/cf/_getdocument.cfm?doc_id=412 (accessed 14 January 2011).

10 See, e.g., Bailey, M.J., 'Implementation of the Thompson mechanism', *Public Choice*, Vol. 89, No. 3, 1996, pp. 231–43; or for an overview of the early literature on the Clarke-Groves mechanisms see *Public Choice*'s special supplement in its Spring 1977 issue.

discretion as a bargaining chip, to be traded off to achieve the Commission's other institutional and political objectives. Everyone, without exception, observes that 'state aid is highly political'.

Let me give you a small example of this in practice. Consider the *Air France* case in the mid 1990s.[11] The aid was allowed by the Commission – exemption was granted – on condition that the French Government agreed to the privatization of Air France. But, the Commission has no constitutional power to order privatization in a member state – and no legitimate role in any 'federal' structure. This was, in a straightforward sense, an abuse of power. No doubt it was done with the best intentions but it was an abuse of power nonetheless.

26.9 BLAME-SHIFTING

Next let us turn from the Commission and the Court to the member states. Do the member states want to change? Do they want to go back to the constitution as originally agreed? Are they happy with this general tutelage of member state actions by the Commission? First, note that the sanction in state aid cases is repayment. But repayment actually happens only in a tiny percentage of cases. Even in those cases, the average delay is 54 months. Little repayment and long delays are the rule – at least in large part because the enforcer is the miscreant himself. The criminal is his own policeman. The government collects the money back from the company to whom the government itself illegally granted the money in the first place.

I now want to observe something that might seem at first surprising: it might suit member states to play this sort of game. Here I come to the third concept of 'shift of responsibility' or 'blame-shifting', again much studied in public choice. Morris Fiorina, of Harvard and Stanford, is the leading scholar in the area.[12] Fiorina studied the question of why it is that a legislature *ever* hands power over a certain area of economic life to an independent regulatory agency. After all, the *raison d'être* of the politician is to seek power, not to give it away. Fiorina's theory is that giving power away happens when individual legislators calculate their personal advantage over two dimensions. First, can they, by transferring control to independent regulators, *shift the blame* away from themselves for unfavourable decisions? Second, will they suffer *loss of credit* for future favourable

---

[11] Case 94/653/EC, OJ L 254, 30 September 1994, pp. 73–89.

[12] See, e.g., 'Legislative choice of regulatory forms: Legal process or administrative process?', *Public Choice*, Vol. 39, No. 1, 1982, pp. 33–66; or 'Rational Choice and the New(?) Institutionalism', *Polity*, Vol. 28, No. 1, Autumn 1995, pp. 107–15.

regulatory decisions? If the gain through shifting blame is greater than the loss through credit slippage then a legislator will cast his vote for creation of an independent regulator. There has been some testing of this hypothesis and it is claimed that it has some power to predict instances of shifts of responsibility to independent regulatory agencies.

This mechanism is common in other contexts. Officials at the IMF and the World Bank will tell anyone that it is accepted as a matter of course that 'client' governments will use the IMF as an excuse, as a blame-shift device. The IMF teams and the client governments even go to the extent of planning together the timetable of austerity and blame. For example:

> Our (IMF) team will fly in on such and such a date – lets call it D-Day. We will meet on D+1 and D+2. On D+3 an announcement will be made about an IMF austerity package. Or D+4, you (client government) will issue your press release and give interviews condemning us, saying that these are harsh terms and very much not what you want to do, but that we, the IMF, are nasty people and that, reluctantly, you have no choice, blah, blah. We'll dine together that night. Then, both sides happy, the IMF team will fly out on D+5.

This is understood by all those in the know to be a pantomime. The client government knows perfectly well that it has to do something drastic about the many importunate constituencies who wish for something from the taxpayers' purse. But it does not want to say that to its electoral clients. So it tries to go in for blame-shifting to the IMF.

This is an all-too-plausible model for much state aid activity in Europe. It is attractive for a politician in a member state to have a ready, all-purpose excuse for his various constituencies: 'The European Commission is to blame'.

But note that EC state aid control is not a major deterrent if the member state government really wants to grant state aid. Remember that repayment happens in only the tiniest fraction of cases. Moreover, the government itself recollects the money and can delay until the next government has been elected before anything is collected. It is, however, a sometimes effective pantomime to mislead the voters.

26.10 IS TUTELAGE THE FINAL EQUILIBRIUM?

All things considered the European tutelage model of state aid control is a sorry confection. There is little in it to admire or to defend. I think it is a system that no constitutional convention of a federation ever would have adopted deliberately. The Lisbon agenda said 'less and better targeted state aid'. A better slogan would be 'less and better targeted intervention against state aid'.

Will we get reform any time soon? I think not. It seems to me that the current state of affairs is a stable equilibrium. Equilibrium in political markets is like equilibrium anywhere else: something has got to shift – either supply or demand – before you get a change in the equilibrium. First consider the Commission. The Commission loves the wide power and the side-payment value – and, everyone agrees, state aid is heavily political. It is a source of real power for the European Commission.

Next consider the Court. The Court does not seek to control Commission deal-making power. And it is not at all averse to power for the EU's central institutions, of which the Court itself is one. It has no reason to change anything.

Next, consider the Council of Ministers and the member states. They are rather attracted by blame-shifting, I conjecture. In any case, getting unanimity to amend the Treaty would be difficult. Note that, properly speaking, unanimity should *not* be necessary. It should require unanimity to move *to* the tutelage model that we now have – i.e. the Commission's wide discretion to review almost any spending policy of member states – not unanimity to move *away* from it. But Europe did not have a self-enforcing constitution.

I conclude that this is a stable equilibrium, one that no one wants to change enough to make reform happen. I predict that any reforms for the foreseeable future will be a petty reform, not fundamental reform – good house keeping, not revolution.

26.11 CONSTITUTIONAL DYSPEPSIA

My final observation is that the story of state aid is a microcosm of Europe's constitutional ills. First, solemn agreements cannot be trusted. Agreements are not self-enforcing: they are undermined by 'interpretation' on the part of institutions with an in-built interest in centralization. Second, deals between sovereign member states are changed without going through the treaty amendment procedure. Important amendments, such as doing away with the effect on trade provision, are made without unanimity – and unanimity is the only amending formula that member states have ever agreed to. Third, unelected officials at the centre interfere in democratic decisions in member states. They, not the voters, tell the citizens of (say) France what industries may be supported by the French taxpayer and they do this even if no other country is adversely affected. Fourth, while there has been a lot of solemn talk about subsidiarity, in state aids, at least, the talk is just rhetoric. Subsidiarity simply does not exist and apparently will not be brought about. Fifth, domestic elected officials in member states use

'Europe' and the European Commission to deflect criticism by shifting blame for unpopular decisions. Instead of taking the unpopular decision to confront what they know to be harmful policies, they duck. The result, effectively, is the misleading of the public and a small 'European' contribution to reducing the transparency of democratic public discussion around Europe.

Enforcement and litigation

27. Public and private enforcement of competition law

José Rivas

27.1 INTRODUCTION

I first met Jacques back in 1986 when I was a student at the College of Europe (Bruges, Belgium) and he was my professor. Never in my wildest dreams could I have imagined then that one day I would be contributing to Jacques' *liber amicorum*! More recently, I have had the personal and professional pleasure of interacting with Jacques as members of the Executive Committee of the Global Competition Law Centre. As a newcomer to this group it is a privilege to be guided and inspired by Jacques' observations and remarks. In between these two dates, I have come across Jacques at conferences (on both sides of the Atlantic), at academic events, as a Commission official, as a practitioner, etc. I have also had the pleasure of meeting members of his family (all eminent lawyers), notably Hendrik, who is also a contributor to this well-merited book.

I will not dwell on the high caliber of Jacques as an academic and practitioner. Others have already done so much better than I could aspire to. However, I want to highlight one of Jacques' unique features, in which he truly excels: he is the best 'cultural interface' I have ever met and an unrivalled linguist; a 'true European' as Salvador de Madariaga would put it.

At the beginning of 2010 Jacques contacted me because he was working on an article that he was considering publishing in *World Competition*. The article (written together with Stéphanie Strievi) was published in the June 2010 issue under the title: 'EU Competition Remedies in Consumer Cases: thinking out of the shopping bag.'[1] In essence, in this article Jacques (and Stéphanie) support the view that compensation for the damages

[1] Bourgeois, J.H.J. and Strieve, S., 'EU Competition Remedies in Consumer Cases: Thinking Out of the Shopping Bag', *World Competition*, Vol. 33, No. 2, June 2010, pp. 241–56.

suffered by the victims of competition law infringements can be improved in Europe with the use of two existing public competition law tools. Compensation of victims could be accepted by competition authorities, notably the European Commission (the 'Commission'), as an undertaking in the framework of a commitment procedure under Article 9 of Regulation 1/2003 and compensation could be treated as a mitigating circumstance when setting the level of the fine under Article 23 of Regulation 1/2003.

In the following pages I consider these creative propositions (hereinafter, Jacques Bourgeois' proposal) in light of the recent Opinion of Advocate General Mazák in Case C-360/09 *Pfleiderer AG v Bundeskartellamt*, and conclude that Jacques Bourgeois' proposal to increase voluntary compensation of victims of competition law infringements remains perfectly valid.

Indeed, as identified by Jacques Bourgeois in his article, in the same way as an efficient system of private enforcement can contribute to the public policy objective of deterring infringement, a well-designed system of public enforcement can – and should – contribute to compensating business, and indeed any victim of anticompetitive practices.

27.2 A QUICK SUMMARY OF JACQUES BOURGEOIS' PROPOSAL

In view of the existing hurdles to bringing successful damages actions in the EU[2] Jacques Bourgeois proposes that the Commission provide a strong incentive for infringers to compensate consumers at the stage of public enforcement.

Ideally, such compensation would become part of the public enforcement procedure. During the investigating phase regarding a possible termination of the investigation, competition authorities could accept undertakings to compensate consumers as a special kind of commitment and put an end to the investigation. Or, once an infringement has been established, they could reward such compensation with a fine reduction.[3] In

---

2 An exploration of the hurdles to be overcome in order to bring a successful damages claim has been undertaken at length by the European Commission in its public consultations on damages actions, and is beyond the scope of this article. For details of these please consult the European Commission's webpage on Damages Actions (http://ec.europa.eu/competition/antitrust/actionsdamages/index.html).

3 Bourgeois and Strievi, *supra*, p. 243.

his article; Jacques lists examples of national and EU precedents where compensation has been taken into consideration.[4]

This way, the public enforcement process would achieve several goals at once: ensuring effective enforcement and deterrence; and promoting a culture of compensation at a time when the Commission's initiatives in this area appear to be stalled amid controversy with regard to the legal and policy implications of its proposals concerning damages actions.

It is clear that, in the context of EU competition law, the interplay between the public policy objectives sought via competition law enforcement and the individual redress sought via damages actions is a complex one, and one must tread carefully to ensure that they do not undermine each other.

This requires a delicate balancing act between public interest and the interests of those directly affected by the anticompetitive behaviour, and one in which competition law authorities will naturally tend to grant more weight to the public good. But do they go too far? And could this concern interfere with the implementation of Jacques Bourgeois' proposal? Interestingly, the potential pitfalls of this interplay were recently assessed by Advocate General Mazák in his Opinion in *Pfleiderer AG v Bundeskartellamt,*[5] in a way that sheds light on some of the potential tensions that could arise when implementing this form of compensation 'mechanism' as part of public enforcement proceedings.

27.3 THE OPINION OF AG MAZÁK IN PFLEIDERER AG V BUNDESKARTELLAMT

The Opinion of Advocate General Mazák, delivered on 16 December 2010, concerned a preliminary ruling from the Amtsgericht Bonn (Germany). In the national proceedings, Pfleiderer AG sought redress from members of a cartel of producers of décor paper, which had been fined by the National Competition Authority (Bundeskartellamt) for breach of Article 101 TFEU and the German national equivalent.

Pleiderer AG requested access to the leniency applications and the documents voluntarily submitted by the leniency applicants in the context

---

[4] *Idem*, footnotes 25–32. See also further examples in footnotes 96–104, Wills, W., 'Public antitrust enforcement and private actions for damages', *World Competition*, Vol. 32, No. 1, March 2009, pp. 1–26.

[5] Opinion of Advocate General Mazák of 16 December 2010 in Case C-360/09, *Pfleiderer AG v Bundeskartellamt*.

of a leniency programme. The German National Competition Authority, however, only allowed for limited access.

The referring court sought clarification as to whether, and if so to what extent, a national competition authority may disclose information, voluntarily communicated to it by members of a cartel pursuant to the authority's leniency programme, to an aggrieved third party for the purpose of the preparation of an action for damages in respect of alleged injury caused by the cartel.

It was in seeking to answer this question, that the Advocate General undertook an analysis of the merits of damages actions, and their interplay with public enforcement programmes. This analysis is highly relevant to Jacques Bourgeois' proposal.

27.4 THE MERITS OF DAMAGES ACTIONS

The Advocate General highlights the key role of actions for damages, both as an essential right of the aggrieved party, and as a method of enforcement. In doing so, the Advocate General underscores the fundamental right to an effective remedy in civil proceedings for breach of competition law stands on its own merits, and is guaranteed *inter alia* by Article 47 in conjunction with Article 51(1) of the Charter of Fundamental Rights of the European Union.[6]

He further notes that the role of damages actions as a method of enforcement was fundamental to the European Court's judgment in *Courage v Crehan*,[7] which clearly stated that '*the full effectiveness*' of Article 101 TFEU[8] – and by extension EU competition law as a whole – would be put at risk if it were not open to victims of competition law infringements to bring damages actions for loss caused by the infringement.

In that case, the Court added that[9]

> the existence of such a right strengthens the working of the Community competition rules and discourages agreements or practices, which are frequently covert, which are liable to restrict or distort competition. From that point of view, actions for damages before the national courts can make a significant contribution to the maintenance of effective competition in the Community.

---

[6] *Idem*, paras. 37 and 48.
[7] *Idem*, para. 26.
[8] At the time, Article 85 EC Treaty.
[9] *Idem*, para. 27.

On this basis, the Advocate General determines that, where there is an action that not only may lead to the determination of the right to compensation of an injured party, but also to the application of Article 101 TFEU, a competition authority[10]

> should not in the absence of overriding legitimate reasons of public or private necessity deny an injured party access to documents in its possession [. . .] as this could de facto interfere with and diminish the party's right to an effective remedy which is guaranteed by Article 101 TFEU and Article 47 in conjunction with Article 51 of the Charter and Article 6(1) of the ECHR.

One can derive from this that the right to seek fair compensation is of paramount importance. The question then becomes what factors could constitute 'overriding legitimate reasons' in this context.

27.5 DAMAGES ACTIONS AS A DETERRENT TO LENIENCY

Of principal concern to the Advocate General and to the Commission, an intervener in this case, was the effect of access to documents on the leniency programmes, as it was deemed that such disclosure could 'seriously undermine the attractiveness and therefore the effectiveness of the leniency programme'.[11]

In this regard the Advocate General considers that, whilst Regulation 1/2003 and the case law of the Court have not established a de jure hierarchy between public enforcement of EU competition law and private actions for damages, 'at present, the role of the Commission and national competition authorities is [. . .] of far greater importance than private actions for damages in ensuring compliance with Articles 101 and 102 TFEU'.

Critically, the Advocate General's Opinion makes an initial distinction between access to documents by an aggrieved party where (1) such access is requested *following the adoption of a decision* imposing a fine which is no longer subject to judicial review; and (2) those cases where an injured third

---

[10] *Idem*, para. 37.

[11] For a dissenting view, see Wills, *supra*, pp. 1–26, footnote 95: 'The mere fact that disclosure of corporate statements in private actions for damages may make leniency programmes less attractive is not a sufficient reason for granting protection against disclosure. Indeed, the right of victims to claim damages from leniency recipients is the main potential disincentive to leniency applications. Nevertheless, leniency recipients are not granted immunity from liability in damages.'

party seeks access to information held by a national competition authority *prior to the adoption of a decision by such an authority.*[12]

In the Advocate General's view, in the latter situation access to the contentious information could undermine the investigation of the infringement or influence the outcome of the investigation. Put more simply, the rights of third parties must be respected unless they can potentially affect the outcome of the public enforcement process, as will likely be the case before a final decision is taken.

27.6 THIRD PARTY INFLUENCE IN PUBLIC ENFORCEMENT

To interpret this Opinion as contrary to any third party participation on the grounds that it will necessarily influence the investigation or its outcome would appear to be excessive, and contrary to applicable legislation.

Interested third parties are entitled to and actually play an active role in Commission investigations, one that is often highly supportive of the Commission's investigative efforts. Furthermore, their legitimate interest in the conduct of the investigation has given rise to a right to participate in the proceedings, codified in Regulations and Notices.

Regulation 1/2003 on the implementation of the rules on competition laid down in Articles 81 and 82 of the Treaty[13] states at Article 27(3), when discussing the Commission's discretion to hear 'other natural or legal persons' states that 'applications to be heard on the part of on the part of such persons *shall*, where they show sufficient interest, be granted' (emphasis added). This right to be heard accorded to third parties whose interests may be affected by a decision is further set out at recital 32 of the preamble.[14]

Further, Commission Regulation 773/2004 relating to the conduct of proceedings by the Commission pursuant to Articles 81 and 82 of the EC

---

[12] *Idem*, para. 20.

[13] OJEC L1/1 of 16 December 2002.

[14] Recital 32 of Regulation 1/2003 states: 'The undertakings concerned should be accorded the right to be heard by the Commission, third parties whose interests may be affected by a decision should be given the opportunity of submitting their observations beforehand, and the decisions taken should be widely publicised. While ensuring the rights of defence of the undertakings concerned, in particular, the right of access to the file, it is essential that business secrets be protected. The confidentiality of information exchanged in the network should likewise be safeguarded.'

Treaty[15] states at its Article 13(1) that if natural or legal persons other than complainants and addressees of the statement of objections 'apply to be heard and show a sufficient interest, *the Commission shall* inform them in writing of the nature and subject matter of the procedure and set a time-limit within which they may make known their views in writing' (emphasis added). In practice, the way in which these interested third parties are informed of the nature and subject matter of the procedure varies from case to case. It ranges from a very short document (e.g. a couple of pages) to an abridged version of the non-confidential version of the statement of objections, and there are even instances where they receive a full non-confidential version of the statement of objections (see below for complainants). In any event, nothing prevents the Commission from informing interested third parties of the nature and subject-matter of the procedure by disclosing a non-confidential version of the statement of objections to them. It is submitted that, in the interest of implementing Jacques Bourgeois' proposal, it should do so.

It is possible that a third party injured by a competition law infringement is also a complainant to the European Commission.[16] In cartel cases where the normal procedure is applied, the complainant is entitled to receive a non-confidential version of the statement of objections and to participate at the oral hearing.[17]

Such rights confirm that there is room for interested third parties affected by anticompetitive behaviour to participate actively in Commission proceedings and for their legitimate interest to be recognized, for example, by allowing for consideration of their compensation to be encouraged and taken into account within the proceedings.

27.7 MORE RESTRICTED ACCESS

Having said this, in recent times Commission policy seems to have moved towards limiting the participation of third parties in Commission proceedings, and their influence over the process, to the extent the influence is not deemed in the clear interest of the public enforcement proceedings.

---

15 OJEC L123/18 of 7 April 2004.

16 Article 7 of Regulation 1/2003 and Articles 5 and 6 of Regulation 773/2004. See also Commission Notice on the handling of complains (OJEU C101/65 of 27 April 2004).

17 See Article 6(1) of Regulation 773/2004. In cases decided under the settlement procedure, the complainant is only entitled to be 'informed in writing of the nature and the subject matter of the procedure', see Article 6 of Regulation 773/2004 as amended by Article 1(2) of Regulation 662/2008 of 30 June 2008 (OJ L 171/3).

Indeed the Commission's recent Guidance on procedures of the hearing officers in proceedings relating to Articles 101 and 102 TFEU[18] ('the Guidance') appears overly to limit the presence of interested third parties in Commission proceedings. Hopefully, this will be rectified in the final version of the Guidance, as the observations made during the consultation period will be taken into account by the Commission.

Paragraph 33 of the Guidance states that:

> In assessing a request for third party status, the Hearing Officer *will take into consideration in particular the contribution the party has made or is likely to make* to establish the truth and relevance of the facts and circumstances pertinent to the proceedings, *as opposed to an exclusively private interest, which would normally not be considered as sufficient*. If necessary, the Hearing Officer may request any further information from the party in order to assess the application to be admitted to the proceedings (our emphasis).

Though it follows on from the statement in the preceding paragraph that 'The Hearing Officer has the responsibility to admit natural or legal persons with a sufficient interest to proceedings before the Commission' this paragraph would appear to make the admission of third parties dependent exclusively on the value they bring to the procedure, as determined by the hearing officer. The extent of their interest in proceedings, which in many cases will be a private interest, would furthermore 'normally not be considered as sufficient'.

This threshold clearly subsumes the interests of third parties to the interest of the investigation. Under this admission threshold, presumably third parties would still need to demonstrate an interest in the proceedings. However, in itself this would not be sufficient to determine whether they should be admitted to the procedure. Instead, the determining factor would be the hearing officer's view as to whether the relevant party has made or is likely to make a contribution towards establishing the truth and relevance of the facts of the proceedings.

In my view this presents an unnecessary barrier to third party access to proceedings, and one that is not supported in law.[19] Its restrictive effect on

---

[18] See http://ec.europa.eu/competition/antitrust/legislation/legislation.html.

[19] Further clarity in this regard is provided in recital 11 of the preamble to Regulation 773/2004 where it states that provision should be made for the hearing of persons who are neither complainants nor addressees of the statement of objections but who can nevertheless show sufficient interest. It then adds that 'Where it considers it to be useful for the proceedings, the Commission should *also* be able to invite *other persons* to express their views in writing' (our emphasis).

rights of access and participation are not merely theoretical given that, as indicated on the Commission website, such best practices are applicable provisionally,[20] and we have understood this to have indeed been applied in certain cases.

The importance of the right to be heard, a fundamental principle of Community law, was acknowledged in paragraph 8 of the terms of reference of hearing officers in certain competition proceedings,[21] which held that these 'should be framed as to safeguard the right to be heard throughout the whole procedure'.

Accordingly, it would be wrong to assess the right of a party with sufficient interest to be heard on the basis of the nature of the party's contribution to the procedure. To do so would ignore the existence of a right of its own that a party with sufficient interest has to be heard, provided that it demonstrates that its interests may be affected by a Commission Decision.

Indeed, this requirement would effectively render it harder for parties to intervene in the administrative proceedings prior to a Commission Decision being taken, than to intervene before the European Courts where a Commission Decision is contested.

Further, it appears to run counter to the Commission stated efforts to encourage cartel victims to seek redress before national courts. In short, such a restriction of third party participation shifts the balance strongly towards the protection of public enforcement, to the detriment of private enforcement efforts.

27.8 BALANCING ACT

There is thus scope for the inclusion of the proposed compensation system within Commission proceedings without undermining or disrupting the effectiveness of public enforcement efforts in this area.

Furthermore, to dismiss the proposal on the basis that it has the potential to influence the investigation process seems excessively protective of the public enforcement system. It seems that a more balanced solution might be found by ensuring that the timing of any discussions on compensation is

---

[20] The Hearing Officer's Guidance Paper is included on the webpage linking through to antitrust legislation under the section Best practices (applicable provisionally). See http://ec.europa.eu/competition/antitrust/legislation/legislation.html.

[21] Commission Decision of 23 May 2001 on the terms of reference of hearing officers in certain competition proceedings, OJ L162/21.

subsequent to the substantive investigative process, in which case such a potentially adverse impact on the investigation would be minimal or non-existent.

It is submitted that, were any discussions on compensation to take place following the oral hearing, any influence or disruption of the investigative process, if any, would be minimal and in turn be outweighed by the positive effects of ensuring effective compensation for the victims of the anticompetitive behaviour.

This is because after the oral hearing, barring exceptional circumstances, no further investigatory actions by the Commission take place. The file and the investigation are, in principle, complete. Therefore, the likelihood of adversely influencing or disrupting the Commission proceedings is minimal. The evidence supporting the case is final, including any evidence relevant to the quantification of the damages suffered by the victims of the competition law infraction. In addition, if the injured parties have been granted access to a non-confidential version of the statement of objections as complainants, or as interested third parties (see section 27.6 above, Third Party Influence in Public Enforcement), they will have received most of the information relevant for the establishment of the damage: detailed description of the products, geographic scope of the infringement, identity of the parties, period of infringement for each party, etc.).

From the moment of the oral hearing until the quantification of the fine(s) in the final Commission Decision, several months will elapse: typically between three to six months or even longer. Both infractors and victims have a limited window of opportunity within which to reach an agreement for compensation of the damages suffered. Critically, as this agreement would be reached prior to the establishment of the fine(s) by the Commission, the voluntary compensation to the victims could easily be taken into account by the Commission and lead to a reduction in the level of the fine(s). The attainment of a settlement between offenders and injured parties could be facilitated if the parties agree to submit to an independent arbitration or mediation system.[22]

[22] See Wills, *supra*, pp. 1–26, at p. 21: 'Such a policy could help the victims of the antitrust violation to obtain compensation at a lower cost, without undermining deterrence and without using significant public enforcement resources'.

The day the long-awaited Directive on damages[23] and the promised Guidelines on methods for the quantification of damages[24] are adopted, infringing parties, victims, arbitrators/mediators, and the Commission will have a clear framework within which to implement the Jacques Bourgeois proposal.

27.9 CONCLUSION

It is settled case law that Articles 101 and 102 TFEU produce direct effects in relations between individuals and create rights for the individuals concerned that the national courts must safeguard,[25] as well as obligations that national courts must enforce.

The numerous hurdles facing 'private enforcement' or damages actions in the EU mean that, to date, this form of enforcement remains rare. In this context, proposals such as the Jacques Bourgeois proposal are both necessary and welcome in that they seek to render a right, that in theory is agreed to be essential, a practical reality for those seeking to enforce it.

That this might raise legitimate concerns as to its effect on public enforcement proceedings is understandable, but this cannot be a blanket justification for failing to improve the current system.

---

23 Speech by Commissioner Almunia, Valladolid, 15 October 2010 (Speech/10/554): 'Once we have agreed on the principles, I intend to present to the Commission a specific proposal on antitrust damages actions, hopefully in the second half of 2011. The initiative will set common standards and minimum requirements for national systems of antitrust damages actions to ensure that rights are a reality for all.'

24 White Paper on Damages actions for breach of the EC antitrust rules. Brussels, 2 April 2008 (COM(2008)165 final (p. 7): 'To facilitate the calculation of damages, the Commission therefore intends to draw up a framework with pragmatic, non-binding guidance for quantification of damages in antitrust cases, e.g. by means of approximate methods of calculation or simplified rules on estimating the loss.'

25 Judgment of 20 September 2001, *Courage and Crehan* (C-453/99 [2001] ECR I-6297), para. 23 and case law cited therein.

28. When the judge prosecutes, power prevails over law*

Catherine Smits and Denis Waelbroeck**

As is well-known, the right to a fair trial as enshrined in the European Convention for the Protection of Human Rights and Fundamental Freedoms (ECHR) implies that charges shall be determined by an independent and impartial tribunal at first instance, following a hearing of the parties that is public and held before the persons actually adjudicating the case. In the absence of this, at the very least, in the few cases where the European Court of Human Rights (ECtHR) accepts that sanctions be imposed by administrative authorities (generally minor offences), a court should exercise full jurisdictional review over the decision taken by the authority.

The case has already repeatedly been made that EU competition law proceedings under Articles 101 and 102 TFEU do not satisfy these requirements.[1] This is so in particular as investigational, prosecutorial, decisional, and policy-making powers are centralized in the hands of the European Commission. Moreover EU Courts exercise only 'marginal' or 'light touch' judicial review over Commission decisions in this area. Despite the Commission's reluctance to engage in any form of significant reform as regards its current procedures,[2] it is our contention that fundamental reform of EU

* '*Ubi iudicat qui accusat, vis, non lex, valet*', Publilius Syrus, Sentenciae, first century BC.

** The authors are indebted to Donald Slater for his invaluable comments on the text.

1 GCLC, Report of Working Group III, 'Enforcement by the Commission, the Decisional and Enforcement Structure in Antitrust Cases and the Commission's Fining System'; *International Chamber of Commerce*, 'Due process in EU antitrust proceedings', 8 March 2010.

2 See for instance EU Competition Commissioner Joaquín Almunia's recent speech at the European Competition Day: 'I am convinced that our administrative system complies with due process requirements at least at the same level than those based in the judicial principle. Our checks and balances, from transparency to the role of the Hearing Officers, are adequate. But as I said several times in previous

competition proceeding is mandated by the provisions of the ECHR. Moreover, it is our view that more fundamentally the quality of decisions and of justice is dependent on impartial decision-makers and proper judicial review. In particular, the levels of fines imposed on companies in recent years[3] would urge appropriate changes in this regard.

In reply to the above, the claim is sometimes made (mostly from inside of the Commission) that, despite the increase of the levels of antitrust penalties imposed by the Commission in recent years, there is no real need for change in the current enforcement system.[4] This is so – it is claimed – because the ECtHR makes a distinction between cases that belong to the so-called 'hard core' of criminal law, and those that may be of criminal nature – such as competition law but do not require as stringent procedural safeguards. Reference is made in this regard to the following passage from the *Jussila v Finland* judgement:[5]

> While it may be noted that the above-mentioned cases in which an oral hearing was not considered necessary concerned proceedings falling under the civil head of Article 6 § 1 and that the requirements of a fair hearing are the most strict in the sphere of criminal law, the Court would not exclude that in the criminal sphere the nature of the issues to be dealt with before the tribunal or court may not require an oral hearing. Notwithstanding the consideration that a certain gravity attaches to criminal proceedings, which are concerned with the allocation of criminal responsibility and the imposition of a punitive and deterrent sanction, it is self-evident that there are criminal cases which *do not carry any significant degree of stigma. There are clearly 'criminal charges' of differing weight.* What is more, the autonomous interpretation adopted by the Convention institutions of the notion of a 'criminal charge' by applying the Engel criteria have underpinned a *gradual broadening of the criminal head to cases not strictly belonging to the traditional categories of the criminal law*, for example administrative penalties (Öztürk v. Germany), prison disciplinary proceedings (Campbell and Fell v. the United Kingdom, judgment of 28 June 1984, Series A, no. 80), customs law (Salabiaku v. France, judgment of 7 October 1988, Series A no 141-A), *competition law* (Société Stenuit v. France, judgment of 27 February

speeches, every time I will consider that our procedures, and the rights of the parties, can be improved without putting at risk the fulfilment of our own responsibilities, I am ready to introduce such changes' (Brussels, 21 October 2010).

[3] For a recent example, the Commission has fined six LCD panel producers a total of €648,925,000 for price-fixing cartel (IP/10/1685, 8/12/2010).

[4] See e.g. Wils, W.P.J., 'The Increased Level of EU Antitrust Fines, Judicial Review, and the European Convention of Human Rights', *World Competition*, Vol. 33, No. 1, March 2010.

[5] ECtHR, Judgement of 23 November 2006, *Jussila versus Finland*, para. 43, emphasis added.

> 1992, Series A no. 232-A) and penalties imposed by a court with jurisdiction in financial matters (Guisset v. France, no. 33933/96, ECHR 2000-IX). Tax surcharges differ from the hard core of criminal law; consequently, *the criminal-head guarantees will not necessarily apply with their full stringency* (see Bendenoun and Janosevic, § 46 and § 81 respectively, where it was found compatible with Article 6 § 1 for criminal penalties to be imposed, in the first instance, by an administrative or non-judicial body: *a contrario*, Findlay v. the United Kingdom, cited *supra*).

The argument is not that competition law is not 'criminal law' within the meaning of Article 6 ECHR, a fact that is hard to deny, and that follows indeed from the above passage (as well as from *inter alia* paragraph 46 of the judgement in *Bendenoun*[6] and paragraph 81 in judgement in *Janosevic*).[7] The reasoning is rather that:

- competition law does not belong to the 'traditional' categories of criminal law; and therefore
- competition law is not 'hardcore' criminal law; and therefore
- the guarantees provided for by the ECHR do not 'necessarily' apply to antitrust procedure 'with their full stringency'; and therefore
- these guarantees 'need not apply at all'; and therefore
- the guarantees provided that '*need not apply*' are among others:
  - the right to have such 'non-hardcore' antitrust proceedings tried at first instance by a non-independent body;
  - the right to have an oral hearing by the decision-maker;
  - the right to have full judicial review of the decision by such a body.

This reasoning contains a number of basic and fundamental flaws. The purpose of this short chapter is to highlight the main ones.

First, whilst it is true that the ECtHR refers in the above quote to a recent extension of the concept of criminal law to cases 'not belonging to the traditional categories of the criminal law' this does not imply that none of these 'new categories' fall into 'hardcore' criminal law category, nor that none of these requires the panoply of guarantees generally required in criminal law proceedings. It is clear that it is not only offences established a long time ago that deserve a procedure guaranteeing respect for the more stringent requirements of Article 6. The seriousness of an offence is in no way related to its novelty or not (and indeed, even if it were, there are strong

6 ECtHR, Judgement of 24 February 1994, *Bendenoun*, para. 46.
7 ECtHR, Judgement of 23 July 2002, *Janosevic*, para. 81.

grounds for arguing that competition laws are very old).[8] As a result, it is mistaken to assume that because it does not fall within the traditional categories of criminal law, it cannot be considered as 'hardcore' criminal law.

Second, there is no attempt to analyze the conditions under which an offence can be categorized as 'hardcore' and whether they are met in the case of antitrust proceedings. In the *Jussila* case, the ECtHR recognizes the existence of 'criminal charges of differing weight' with the 'degree of stigma' carried by the offence being a key element for categorization as hardcore criminal law. In the *Jussila* case, no specific stigma was found to be attached to a tax rectification resulting from the applicant's incomplete VAT declarations. Antitrust fines, on the other hand, are not comparable to a simple tax rectification. The process of imposing fines involves an assessment of evidence and complex evaluations that are highly disputed and results in decisions often widely commented on in the media. In particular, during the mandate of EU Commissioner Neelie Kroes, the levels of cartel fines have soared, the rhetorical emphasis on deterrence has increased and references to criminal offences of theft etc. have become systematic in the speeches of the EU Commissioner in the name of its so-called 'zero-tolerance' approach towards cartels.[9] Further evidence of the stigma attaching to antitrust offences can be found in the nature and seriousness of their consequences. Penalties are so massive and receive so much publicity that the stigma attached to them for both the businesses and persons concerned is significant. Other repercussions for companies, their directors and other employees are just as significant and again confirm the extremely serious nature of antitrust offences, justifying their categorization as hardcore criminal law. Natural persons involved in antitrust infringements in practice generally suffer serious negative personal and professional consequences. Often, persons involved will lose their job and will have difficulties being recruited anywhere else. The huge fines imposed can have very severe consequences for the companies concerned, in some cases even forcing

---

[8] Examples of laws against anticompetitive conduct date back at least to the Roman Empire (see e.g. *Lex Julia de Annona*, dating from 50 BC, combatting the practice of discrupting supply ships).

[9] For examples, Neelie Kroes' speech of 8 October 2009 referring to cartels as 'adapting like viruses to fight our attempts to kill them off' (speech/09/454); Neelie Kroes' statement of 7 October 2009 referring to rebates of dominant companies as a 'rip-off by the self-appointed "Gentlemen". The Commission will not hesitate to increase fines for repeat offenders until they have learned the lesson that cartels do not pay' (IP/09/1432) or speech of 11 November 2009: 'I have no time for arguments that our fines are too high. Tell that to the businesses and consumers who still suffer at the hands of cartels' (speech/09/521).

them to close down or reduce their activities with very negative consequences for employees and shareholders alike.[10]

The defenders of the existing procedural regime will perhaps retort that the above analysis is not rigorous enough and thus does not provide 'proof' that antitrust law is hardcore. To this objection, we would anticipate the following reply:

- it is not up to those invoking the standard procedural guarantees of Article 6 ECHR that are under an obligation to justify their application. Rather it is up to the defenders of the existing regime to justify a derogation from these fundamental rules;
- in invoking *Jussila,* defenders of the existing regime do not enter into any analysis *at all* of the stigma attaching to antitrust offences. It is simply assumed that they are not 'hardcore'. The serious difficulties attaching to such assumptions are discussed above;
- it seems paradoxical, to say the least, for the Commission to underline the seriousness of antitrust offences and the parallels with theft etc. and then argue that they are not that serious after all;
- some of the most compelling evidence of the stigma attaching to antitrust offences concerns the career prospects of the individuals involved in such conduct. It is clearly not appropriate to discuss details of these here. Nonetheless, the contempt with which such consequences are treated (where they are not ignored entirely) can only be deplored.[11]

Third, the rule is that the ECHR requirements fully apply to criminal charges. Exceptions to the safeguards provided by Article 6 ECHR are essentially for criminal cases involving 'minor offences' and must be construed narrowly. Derogating from the general principle is only permitted in

---

[10] See e.g. the *Pre-insulated Pipes Cartel* case where numbers two and three in the market (*Løgstør Rør and Tarco*) were forced out of the market as a result of the fines and of the ensuing damages actions. See also the *TACA* case where – were it not for the annulment of the fine by the ECJ – the company DSR Senator Lines would have been driven out of the market.

[11] See e.g. Advocate General Ruiz-Jarabo Colomer in Case C-338/00-P, *Volkswagen* [2003] ECR I-9189, '[competition law is designed] to protect the community of individuals which constitutes society and is composed of groups of consumers against powerful corporations with significant resources. To accord such offenders the same procedural safeguards as those accorded to the most needy individuals, *apart from being a mockery*, would entail, essentially, a lower degree of protection, in this case economic protection, for the individual as the main victim of anti-competitive conduct', at para. 66 (emphasis added).

exceptional circumstances. Here we find another serious error in the reasoning set out above. *Jussila* states that there are some offences that are not hardcore and that among those offences there are *some* offences to which the guarantees of Article 6 ECHR need not necessarily apply with their full stringency. *Jussila* emphatically does not state that in the case of *all* non-hardcore offences there is an automatic justification for not applying those guarantees with their full stringency. In the particular circumstances of the *Jussila* case, the ECtHR concluded that the offence in question was not only hardcore, but also minor, involving quite simple issues (a relatively straightforward and mathematical tax rectification). Note that none of this applies to the extremely complex nature of antitrust proceedings, where swingeing fines are imposed and other seriously negative consequences often follow.

Fourth, once it is established that an offence is not 'hardcore' and is of the type that justifies a relaxation of some of the Article 6 ECHR procedural guarantees, it must still be established which guarantees will not apply. Again it must be emphasized that derogating from the general principle is only permitted in exceptional circumstances where, for example, the systematic holding of hearings could be an obstacle to the flexibility and efficiency required in a tax rectification or a social security case.[12] In the *Jussila* case, the ECtHR thus found that the requirements of due process did not necessitate an oral hearing, in the particular circumstances of the case. This was based on a series of important factors, including (1) the reasons for requesting a hearing concerned in large part the validity of the tax assessment, which as such fell outside the scope of Article 6, (2) the information provided by the applicant himself formed a sufficient factual basis for the consideration of the case, which could be dealt with more efficiently in writing, (3) no issues of credibility arose in the proceedings that required oral presentation of evidence or cross-examination of witnesses, (4) issues of fact and law could be adequately addressed in, and decided on the basis of, written submissions, (5) the applicant was not denied the possibility of requesting an oral hearing, although it was for the courts to decide whether a hearing was necessary (and the Court considered the point and reasoned its refusal), and (6) the sum of money at stake was minor. All these factors contrast starkly with (1) the complexity of antitrust proceedings, (2) the huge sums of money at stake, (3) the absolute refusal to accord the procedural guarantees of trial at first instance by an impartial body or full judicial review, and (4) the impossibility of palliating the absence of these procedural guarantees through other means.

---

[12] ECtHR, Judgement of 23 November 2006, *Jussila v Finland*, para. 42.

Fifth, there is clearly a significant difference between, on the one hand, dispensing with an oral hearing in case of a minor offence, for particular reasons of flexibility and efficiency and, on the other, dispensing with a series of 'more fundamental' procedural rights, namely the right to an independent hearing at first instance, the right to have the hearing attended by the decision-maker, the right to have the case decided by an independent judge and not the prosecutor, and the right to full judicial review of any decision. In this regard, the critical nature of these aspects of the procedure cannot be emphasized enough. Indeed, they go to the heart of the independent and impartial nature of the finding of criminal liability. This can be contrasted with the oral hearing, which regardless of its importance, does not ultimately affect the identity, nature and impartiality of the decision-maker. This is not to downplay the crucial nature of the oral hearing, which is of course key. However, the issue here is whether one can legitimately argue that cases such as *Jussila,* which recognize a limited possibility to relax specific elements of procedural guarantees, can be read by analogy to justify a total dispensation from fundamental aspects of the procedure. We would argue strongly that they cannot. In this regard, the possibility mentioned in *Jussila* that in some cases written arguments may be an adequate and indeed more efficient way of presenting evidence must be underlined. In other words, the reasoning in *Jussila* is *not* that the procedural guarantees are suppressed but replaced/adequately covered by alternative mechanisms.

Sixth, one variation on the reasoning set out above is that antitrust proceedings may not be heard at first instance by an independent tribunal, but that (1) this less stringent application of Article 6 ECHR is justified, and (2) the review conducted by the European Court of Justice is adequate (i.e. the right to a fair and impartial hearing by an independent tribunal is not suppressed but replaced by an alternative mechanisms, namely judicial review of the decision). We have explained above the multiple reasons why point (1) is wrong. Concerning point (2), the ECtRH case law still requires subsequent full jurisdictional review by an independent tribunal. Having 'full jurisdiction' within the meaning of the ECHR entails that the judicial body must have 'the power to quash in all respects, on questions of fact and law, the decision of the body below'.[13] In other words, the court or the tribunal must proceed with a *de novo* review of all facts and evidence considered by the Commission. In their current case law, EU Courts refrain however from substituting their own appraisal to that of the Commission (they may *a fortiori* not replace the decision by a new one). In particular, the

[13] ECtHR, Judgement of 23 October 1995, *Schmautzer v Austria*, para. 36.

courts do not control so-called 'complex economic appraisals' made by the Commission, and limit themselves to verifying whether the relevant rules on procedure and on the statement of reasons have been complied with, whether the facts have been accurately stated and whether there has been any 'manifest' error of appraisal or misuse of powers.[14] Such standard of scrutiny is hardly reconcilable with the ECtHR case law that makes it clear that judges are entitled to reconsider the administrative decisions, whether of fact or of law.[15] The key question for liability should not be whether the Commission is manifestly wrong but whether the company infringed a clear and unequivocal legal rule.[16]

Finally, even where the EU Courts have unequivocally unlimited jurisdiction, i.e. with regard to fines imposed by the Commission, they often do not use their unlimited jurisdiction to set themselves the amount of the fine on the basis of their own assessment independently of the methodology used by the Commission. More generally, they restrain themselves to verifying whether the Commission has complied with general principles of law and has correctly applied its own Guidelines on the methodology for setting the amount of fines. In doing so, they tend to apply again a 'manifest error' of assessment test and afford thereby the Commission a very high

---

[14] Case 42/84, *Remia and Others v Commission* [1985] ECR 2545, para. 34; Joined Cases 142/84 and 156/84, *BAT and Reynolds v Commission* [1987] ECR 4487, para. 62; and Case C-194/99 P, *Thyssen Stahl v Commission* [2003] ECR I-10821, para. 78.

[15] See Waelbroeck, D. and Slater, D., 'Marginal Review by the European Court of Justice in Competition Cases and its Compatibility with Fundamental Rights', to be published by Global Competition Law Center, 2011.

[16] For example, in *Microsoft* case, the Court concludes that the Commission's findings to the effect that Microsoft's refusal limits technical development to the prejudice of consumers within the meaning of Article 102 TFUE 'are not manifestly incorrect', Case T-201/04, *Microsoft Corp.* [2007] ECR II-3601, para. 665; in *Wanadoo* case, the Court finds that 'even though WIN were to prove that the method which it advocates is appropriate in some respects, this would be insufficient to prove that the method used by the Commission in the present case is unlawful. It is for the applicant to prove that unlawfulness. However, the foregoing assessment has shown that the Commission did not commit a manifest error of assessment in choosing that method', Case T-340/03, *Wanadoo* [2007] ECR II-107, para. 153; in *Deutsche Telekom* case, Deutsche Telekom submitted in appeal that the Commission should not have applied the margin squeeze test and that the judgment of the General Court was based on a vicious circle as the General Court had applied the test chosen by the Commission itself (the margin squeeze test) to determine matters which had to be covered by an examination of the Deutsche Telekom's charges, Case 280/08, *Deutsche Telekom*, 2010, not yet published, para. 149.

level of discretion.[17] It is difficult to reconcile the expansion of self-imposed limitations on the degree of scrutiny exercised by the EU Courts over Commission decisions, as a consequence of the spreading use of the manifest error of assessment test, with the unlimited jurisdiction given to the EU Courts even with respect to fines with Article 6 ECHR.

On the basis of the above, we can only conclude that:

- ECtHR case law (*Jussila* included) shows that competition law is 'criminal' within the meaning of Article 6 ECHR and indeed in light of the level of fines imposed by the Commission in recent years and the considerable stigma attached to competition law infringements, 'hardcore' criminal law.
- Article 6 ECHR requires that sanctions be imposed, at first instance, by an independent and impartial tribunal. The European Commission as administrative body combining investigator, prosecutorial, decisional, and policy-making functions, does not fulfil the condition of being an 'independent and impartial tribunal'.
- The only exception concerns minor offences (e.g. road traffic) and does not apply to competition law.
- Even if such exception were to apply, *quod non*, the ECHR requires subsequent full jurisdictional review of the administrative authority's decision. This requirement is difficult to reconcile with the current expansion of the manifest error of assessment test in EU case law and the self-imposed restraints on the degree of scrutiny exercised by the EU Courts over Commission's decisions.

[17] In accordance with settled case law, the Commission has a particularly wide discretion as regards the choice of factors to be taken into account for the purposes of determining the amount of fines, such as, *inter alia*, the particular circumstances of the case, its context and the dissuasive effect of fines, without the need to refer to a binding or exhaustive list of the criteria which must be taken into account (see, *inter alia*, the order in Case C-137/95 P, *SPO and Others v Commission* [1996] ECR I-1611, para. 54, and Case C-219/95 P, *Ferriere Nord* v *Commission* [1997] ECR I-4411, para. 33).

29. Shaping or administrating the law? Reflections on the European Courts' decision-making practice in the field of competition law*

Frank Montag**

29.1 INTRODUCTION

When I was invited by the editors to make a contribution to this *liber amicorum* for Jacques Bourgeois, I did not hesitate one second to agree. I have known Jacques for more than two decades. For me he has always been a most admired example of encyclopaedic knowledge of European competition and trade law combined with the sound judgement of a seasoned practitioner both as a European official and later in private practice – and he has a great sense of humour. My brief reflections concern issues that, I believe, have been close to Jacques Bourgeois's heart, namely the role of the European courts in developing the law and reviewing the decisions of the European Commission.

I will make two main propositions. The first is to remove existing legal uncertainties in European competition law: courageous courts, which take a lead in actively exercising the discretion they have been granted, are needed. The second is that the Commission's decisions must be subject to full and unfettered judicial scrutiny, a demand that will be at the centre of the discussions below.

* This contribution is based on a discussion statement by the author at the 4th Luxembourg Expert Forum on the Development of Union Law, 6 and 7 September 2010.

** The author thanks his colleagues Joanna Goyder, Daniel Colgan and Anselm Rodenhausen for their input and the translation of the German original into English.

29.2 MANOEUVRING ROOM OF THE COURTS

In legal literature, the term 'manoeuvring room' (in German '*Gestaltungsspielraum*') usually refers to the freedom of action of the executive or legislative branches of government and the control exercised over them by the courts. It is, however, also possible to use the term 'manoeuvring room' to denote legal areas in relation to which the use of discretion is possible or indeed required. The present chapter will analyze the margin of discretion exercised over such areas by the courts. Several areas will be identified that require active development by the European courts. To this end, the focus will not so much be on dogmatic questions, such as the function of decisive courts as a source of law. Rather, the emphasis will be on the importance of this issue for the practitioner.

From a practitioner's perspective, the need for a judiciary that fully exercises its margin of discretion can be readily explained: companies have a legitimate interest in having existing ambiguities in the field of competition law removed by the European courts. Besides the general value of legal certainty, legal questions may have an enormous economic significance for parties entangled in competition proceedings. For companies that are not (yet) involved in competition proceedings, legal uncertainties result in a lack of predictability. Thus, companies have a legitimate interest that the European courts do not seek to avoid fundamental open questions in competition law, but rather that they recognize and decide such questions in an unambiguous manner. This is all the more the case in relation to previously undefined legal terms requiring an economic evaluation. Recent court decisions provide both positive and negative examples of court approaches to such issues.

29.2.1 Scope of Article 101(1) TFEU

A positive example of how the courts actively live up to their role is provided by the discussion on the rationale for the restrictions contained in competition law – that is, whether Article 101(1) TFEU is aimed at protecting consumers or competitors or competition as such.

The growing emphasis in recent years on the use of a 'more economic approach' seemed to suggest that the competition policy of the Commission was increasingly focused on consumer interests.[1] This led to the idea that the Commission might require consumer harm as a prerequisite for a

---

[1] Cf. Commission's Guidelines on Vertical Restraints, C 291, 13 October 2000, p. 1, paras. 102 *et seq*.

finding of a violation of Article 101 or Article 102 TFEU. Since EU competition law has – historically – not been limited to this purpose, this recent development resulted in legal uncertainty for both the legal profession and the companies concerned.

In *T-Mobile*[2] and *GlaxoSmithKline*,[3] the Court of Justice of the European Union (ECJ) stated that, under Article 101 TFEU,[4] it is not required to prove that an agreement deprives consumers of certain benefits in order to establish anticompetitive effects. Therefore, individual competitors as well as the structure of the market (and, hence, competition as such) are protected:[5]

> With respect to the Court of First Instance's statement that, while it is accepted that an agreement intended to limit parallel trade must in principle be considered to have as its object the restriction of competition, that applies in so far as it may be presumed to deprive final consumers of the advantages of effective competition in terms of supply or price, the Court notes that neither the wording of Article [101(1) TFEU] nor the case-law lend support to such a position.
> First of all, there is nothing in that provision to indicate that only those agreements which deprive consumers of certain advantages may have an anticompetitive object. Secondly, it must be borne in mind that the Court has held that, like other competition rules laid down in the Treaty, Article [101 TFEU] aims to protect not only the interests of competitors or of consumers, but also the structure of the market and, in so doing, competition as such. Consequently, for a finding that an agreement has an anti-competitive object, it is not necessary that final consumers be deprived of the advantages of effective competition in terms of supply or price [...]

Without attempting to assess the overall merits of this judgment, it can be observed that the explicit clarification by the ECJ in *T-Mobile* and *GlaxoSmithKline* provides a welcome example of how the courts may actively exercise their margin of discretion.

29.2.2 Relationship between Article 101(1) and (3) TFEU

A negative example is, however, the reluctance of the courts to deal with the issue of the relationship between Article 101(1) and 101(3) TFEU.

---

2 Case C-8/08, *T-Mobile Netherlands BV and Others v Raad van bestuur van de Nederlandse Mededingingsautoriteit* [2009] ECR I-4529.

3 Joined Cases C-501/06 P, C-513/06 P, C-515/06 P and C-519/06, *GlaxoSmithKline Services v Commission* [2009] ECR I-9291.

4 In the interests of consistency, reference will be made to Articles 101 and 102 TFEU even where judgments refer to Articles 81 and 82 EC.

5 Joined Cases C-501/06 P, *GlaxoSmithKline, supra,* paras. 62–3.

Ever since *Remia/Nutricia*,[6] the question whether European competition law is subject to a 'rule of reason' has been extensively discussed. In other words, can positive effects of an agreement already be considered at the level of Article 101(1) TFEU, or only as grounds for individual exemption under Article 101(3) TFEU?

In 2001, the General Court (EGC) ruled in *Métropole Télévision*[7] on the statutes of the European Broadcasting Union (EBU) and, in particular, whether the EBU statutes could be used to prevent the broadcaster M6 from participating in direct sports transmissions in the framework of Eurovision. The ECJ held that, in as far as they had not been expressly exempted under Article 101(3), restrictions in the EBU statutes could not be justified under Article 101(1).[8] This decision has been considered as an outright rejection of a 'rule of reason' approach in European competition law.[9]

However, the ECJ decided only a year later in *Wouters* that the prohibition of mixed partnerships between lawyers and accountants in a regulation of the Bar of the Netherlands, while constituting a restriction of competition, was justifiable under Article 101(1). This was because the restriction could reasonably be considered to be necessary in order to ensure the proper practice of the legal profession.[10]

Similarly, the ECJ ruled in 2006 in *Meca-Medina*,[11] that the doping control practices of the International Olympic Committee and the International Swimming Federation constituted restrictions of competition but were nonetheless permissible in as far as they were necessary to ensure the proper functioning of sporting contests. Ensuring fair contests between athletes was held to constitute a legitimate, justifying purpose.[12]

Both in *Wouters* and in *Meca-Medina*, the ECJ took into account legitimate interests at the level of Article 101(1) TFEU. De facto, this practice can be seen as an application of a 'rule of reason'; a fact that the

---

6 Case 42/84, *Remia BV and Others v Commission*, 1985, ECR 2545.

7 Case T-206/99, *Métropole Télévision v Commission* [2001] ECR II-1057.

8 Case T-206/99, *Métropole Télévision,* para. 51 *et seq.*

9 See also González-Díaz, E., in U. Loewenheim, K. Meessen, and A. Riesenkampff (eds), *Kartellrecht*, Munich, Beck, 2nd edn, 2009, Art. 81 EC para. 136; and Aicher, J., Schuhmacher, F., Stockenhuber, P., and Schroeder, D., in E. Grabitz and M. Hilf (eds), *Das Recht der Europäischen Union*, Munich, Beck, 40th edn, 2009, Art. 81 EC, para. 20.

10 Case C-309/99, *Wouters and Others v Algemene Raad van de Nederlandse Orde van Advocaten* [2002] ECR I-1577.

11 Case C-519/04 P, *Meca-Medina and Majcen v Commission* [2006] ECR I-6991.

12 Case C-519/04 P, *Meca-Medina, supra*, para. 45.

ECJ did not, however, expressly explain. The decisions of the EGC and the ECJ are thus contradictory. While the legal literature has sought to reconcile these cases, the discussion is ongoing.[13]

As a consequence, the legal profession and the companies involved face significant legal uncertainty as to the extent to which positive effects can be considered in the assessment of a restrictive agreement. The legal dispute over the existence of a 'rule of reason' has, at least since the ruling in *Wouters*, been in the spotlight.[14] The *Meca-Medina* judgment that was handed down five years later therefore represents a missed opportunity finally to decide the fundamental question as to the existence in principle of a 'rule of reason'.

29.3 MARGIN OF DISCRETION OF THE COMMISSION ('LIGHT JUDICIAL REVIEW')

In the legal context, the term 'manoeuvring room' often denotes a scope for a margin of appreciation or discretion granted to decision-makers. It is directly related to the question whether decisions of an administrative institution may be reviewed in full by the courts, or whether certain assessments shall – in view of the expertise of the administrative institution – only be subjected to a limited judicial review. This question as to the level of scrutiny of the judicial review is also pertinent in relation to decisions by the Commission.

Already some time ago, the debate arose whether the standard of review exercised by the European courts, the so-called 'light judicial review', remained appropriate in competition cases, given the very far reaching consequences of the Commission's decisions. Lawyers (Ian Forrester),[15]

---

[13] See, *inter alia*, Ackermann, T., *Art. 85 Abs. 1 EGV und die Rule of Reason*, Cologne, Heymanns, 1997, pp. 190 and 207 *et seq.*; also Emmerich, V., in U. Immenga and E.-J. Mestmäcker (eds), *Wettbewerbsrecht: Kommentar zum Europäischen Kartellrecht*, Munich, Beck, 4th edn, 2007, Art. 81(1) EC, para. 248, and further references.

[14] Cf. Bailey, D., 'Scope of judicial review under Article 81 EC', *Common Market Law Review*, Vol. 41, 2004, p. 1328; see also Vesterdorf, B., 'Standard of proof in merger cases: Reflections in the light of recent case law of the Community Courts', *European Competition Journal*, Vol. 1, 2005, p. 3.

[15] See Forrester, I., 'A bush in need of pruning: The luxuriant growth of light judicial review', in C.-D. Ehlermann and M. Marquis (eds), *European Competition Law Annual 2009: Evaluation of Evidence and its Judicial Review in Competition Cases*, Oxford, Hart Publishing, forthcoming 2011.

active judges (Nicholas Forwood[16] and Hubert Legal[17]) as well as judges-turned-lawyers (Bo Vesterdorf)[18] were involved in the discussion. The starting point of the debate about the standard of review is the notion that decisions of the Commission, imposing fines that can reach billions of euros or prohibiting mergers of major economic importance, are not subject to an extensive judicial review of the findings as to facts and the economic conclusions drawn. The debate has been fuelled by the fact that, in 2009, the EU Charter of Fundamental Rights acquired full legal force, and also by the expected accession of the European Union to the European Convention on Human Rights (ECHR).

In the following, the standard of review applied by the courts will be analyzed and, subsequently, the concerns from a practitioner's perspective will be put forward. Finally, support will be lent to the distinction between 'difficult' and 'complex' appraisals, as proposed by Nicholas Forwood.

29.3.1 Standards of Review in Decisional Practice

In its judgment in *Remia/Nutricia*, the ECJ proclaimed a limited standard of review where the Commission has to 'appraise complex economic matters' – in that case concerning the assessment of a contractual non-compete clause.[19] The ECJ held:[20]

> Although as a general rule the Court undertakes a comprehensive review of the question whether or not the conditions for the application of Article [101(1)] are met, it is clear that in determining the permissible duration of a non-competition clause incorporated in an agreement for the transfer of an undertaking the Commission has to appraise complex economic matters. The Court must therefore limit its review of such an appraisal to verifying whether the relevant procedural rules have been complied with, whether the statement of the reasons for the decision is adequate, whether the facts have been accurately stated and whether there has been any manifest error of appraisal or a misuse of powers.

---

16 Cf. Forwood, N., 'The Commission's more economic approach – Implications for the role of the EU Courts, the treatment of economic evidence and the scope of judicial review', in *European Competition Law Annual 2009*, Oxford, Hart Publishing, forthcoming 2011.

17 Cf. Legal, H., 'Standards of proof and standards of judicial review in EU competition law', in B. Hawk (ed.), *International Antitrust Law & Policy: Fordham Corporate Law 2005*, Oxford, Juris Publishing, 2006, p. 114 *et seq*.

18 See Vesterdorf, B., 'The Court of Justice and unlimited jurisdiction: What does it mean in practice?', *Antitrust Chronicle*, Vol. 9, No. 2, 2009.

19 Case 42/84, *Remia, supra*.

20 Case 42/84, *Remia, supra*, para. 34.

This standard of review, which has become known as 'light judicial review', has been applied by the European courts both in cases under Article 101 and under Article 102 TFEU.

In the *Microsoft* case, the EGC extended the scope of this limited standard of review from 'complex economic appraisals' to 'complex technical appraisals'.[21] Even prior to the EGC's *Microsoft* judgment, the ECJ had considered in a similar vein the complex assessments in the medico-pharmacological field.[22] Referring to that ECJ decision, the EGC noted in *Microsoft*:[23]

> Likewise, in so far as the Commission's decision is the result of complex technical appraisals, those appraisals are in principle subject to only limited review by the Court, which means that the Community Courts cannot substitute their own assessment of matters of fact for the Commission's.'

Moreover, in *Wieland-Werke*, the EGC applied the limited standard of review even to the calculation of fines.[24] It did not review the calculation of the fine in full, but assessed only whether the Commission had adhered to the calculation method set out in its 'Guidelines on the method of setting fines'. In stark contrast to the unfettered jurisdiction for judicial review granted by Article 31 of Regulation 1/2003, the EGC held:[25]

> The self-limitation on the Commission's discretion arising from the adoption of the Guidelines is not incompatible with the Commission's maintaining a substantial margin of discretion. The Guidelines display flexibility in a number of ways, enabling the Commission to exercise its discretion in accordance with the provisions of Regulation No. 17, as interpreted by the Court of Justice (Dansk Rørindustri, para. 267). Moreover, in areas such as determination of the amount of a fine imposed pursuant to Article 15(2) of Regulation No. 17, where the Commission has a discretion, for example, as regards the amount of increase for the purposes of deterrence, review of the legality of those assessments is limited

---

21 Cf. Case T-201/04, *Microsoft v Commission* [2007] ECR II-3601.

22 Case C-459/00 P(R), *Commission v Laboratoires pharmaceutiques Trenker* [2001] ECR I-2823, para. 82 *et seq*., and also Case C-120/97, *Upjohn Ltd v The Licensing Authority established by the Medicines Act 1968 and Others* [1999] ECR I-223, para. 34; cf. Case T-179/00, *A. Menarini–Industrie Farmaceutiche Riunite Srl v Commission* [2002] ECR II-2879, para. 44 *et seq*.; and Case T-13/99, *Pfizer Animal Health v Council* [2002] ECR II-3305, para. 323.

23 Case T-201/04, *Microsoft, supra,* para. 88.

24 Case T-116/04, *Wieland-Werke v Commission* [2009] ECR II-1087.

25 Case T-116/04, *Wieland-Werke, supra*, paras. 31–2, referring to Joined Cases C-189/02 P, C-202/02 P, C-205/02 P to C-208/02 P and C-213/02 P, *Dansk Rørindustri and Others v Commission* [2005] ECR I-5425.

to determining the absence of manifest error of assessment (see, to that effect, Case T-241/01 Scandinavian Airlines System v Commission [2005] ECR II-2917, para. 79).

The decisional practice relating to European merger control, however, stands in contrast to the above described practice in Article 101 and Article 102 cases. It is widely recognized that the Commission enjoys a certain margin of discretion under Article 2 EUMR in relation to the assessment of mergers.[26] Nonetheless, the courts have at times conducted very rigorous appraisals in merger cases.[27] In *Tetra Laval*, the ECJ shaped the scope of the limited standard of review in a manner that allows even complex assessments to be reviewed in relation to procedure, and the requirements for the provision of reasoning, as well as in relation to findings of fact and manifest errors of assessment:[28]

> Whilst the Court recognises that the Commission has a margin of discretion with regard to economic matters that does not mean that the Community Courts must refrain from reviewing the Commission's interpretation of information of an economic nature. Not only must the Community Courts, inter alia, establish whether the evidence relied on is factually accurate, reliable and consistent but also whether that evidence contains all the information which must be taken into account in order to assess a complex situation and whether it is capable of substantiating the conclusions drawn from it.

Hence, the European courts apply two different levels of review. The extensive level of review represents the default standard. However, in as far as 'complex' economic appraisals or, more recently, technical appraisals or fine calculations, are concerned, only a limited review will be conducted.

29.3.2 A Practitioner's Concerns

The limitation of judicial review of Commission decisions in the field of competition law raises numerous concerns from the practitioner's perspective. These concerns are of a constitutional, economic and practical nature.

---

[26] Cf. Schmidt, C.R., *Die 'Entwicklung des technischen und wirtschaftlichen Fortschritts': Der Konflikt Wettbewerbspolitik – Industriepolitik in der Europäischen Fusionskontrolle*, Nomos, Nomos, 1992, p. 175 *et seq.*; also Immenga, U. and Körber, T., in U. Immenga and E.J. Mestmäcker (eds), *supra*, FKVO (EG) 139/2004 Art. 2, para. 352; see also Opinion of Advocate General Kokott in Case C-413/06, *Bertelsmann and Sony v Impala* [2008] ECR I-4951.

[27] See Case T-342/99, *Airtours v Commission* [2002] ECR II-2585; Case T-310/01, *Schneider Electric v Commission* [2002] ECR II-4071; cf. also Case C-413/06, *Impala*; and Case C-12/03, *Commission v Tetra Laval* [2005] ECR I-987.

[28] Case C-12/03, *Tetra Laval, supra*, para. 39.

It must be noted from the outset that an investigation by the Commission involves the same authority conducting the investigation, evaluating the facts and (potentially) imposing severe fines. Constitutional considerations alone dictate that such far-reaching decisions should be subject to full judicial review.

In particular, the extension of the limited standard of review to *technically* complex appraisals lacks any justification. There is no apparent reason why the assessment of technical issues should be limited to the realm of the Commission alone. The theoretical justification for a limited standard of review, if such a standard can at all be considered justifiable, is based on the premise that the Commission possesses, thanks to the relevant experience of its personnel, superior economic expertise. This reasoning, however, cannot be maintained as far as technical issues are concerned. It is not apparent why the Commission's economists and lawyers necessarily have more expertise in technically complex issues than a judge.

A comparison with the activities of the courts in the member states also supports calls for an extensive standard of review. Every day, the courts of the member states assess difficult issues in fields such as criminal law, tax law or medical law without hiding behind a limited standard of review. Instead, even complex issues are adjudicated upon, using, where appropriate, the support of independent experts. In Germany, for example, a limited standard of review is – in view of the guarantee of access to the courts under Article 19(4) of the German constitutional law – very exceptional and is restricted to a few isolated cases, such as review of (university) exams. It is not apparent why the standard of review of the European courts should be lower than that in the member states. In fact, the standard of review should be expected to increase in line with the importance of the case at hand. Likewise, how can the companies concerned be expected to understand that purely domestic disputes before national courts of the member states are subject to extensive judicial review whereas, in disputes with the Commission involving complex appraisals (that often have a far greater economic impact than purely national procedures), a limited standard of review applies?

Furthermore, the expected accession of the European Union to the ECHR points towards the need for an unrestricted standard of review. Article 6 of the ECHR requires that administrative decisions imposing criminal sanctions be subject to full review by a court of law.[29]

In addition to these partially academic concerns, practitioners encounter a significant practical issue: the delineation of economically complex and

---

[29] Cf. *Schmautzer v Austria* [1996] 21 EHRR 511.

non-complex issues is far from being clear-cut. The decisional practice discussed above shows that fundamentally different situations have been classified by the courts as economically complex. Even for an experienced lawyer, it may in individual cases be challenging to predict whether the court will review the Commission's appraisal in full. This is all the more of a problem for the companies concerned, for whom it is even less predictable whether proceedings have any chance of success or whether the crucial question is exempt from judicial review from the outset. This legal uncertainty, coupled with the significant related litigation risk, is irreconcilable with the importance of European competition law.

At the end of the day, there is no practical reason why the courts should be prevented from fulfilling their responsibilities in competition cases. In particular, the courts have at their disposal the necessary procedural tools to investigate and adjudicate even difficult cases. This is exemplified by numerous decisions in which the relevant courts have conducted extensive factual investigations, such as *Woodpulp*[30] in the field of cartel proceedings or the above-cited judgments in merger control cases.[31]

29.3.3 Distinguishing between 'Difficult' and 'Complex' Subject-Matters

It cannot be denied that particular issues may arise in the field of competition law that do not lend themselves to an unequivocal answer by economists. These are, for example, questions of economics that are highly controversial or even borderline cases that may have several differing solutions that are equally defensible from an economic perspective. It appears sensible to reserve the final decision to the Commission in these exceptional cases. The difficulty lies, however, in distinguishing such particular cases from all other cases and circumstances. In the absence of a uniform method, the area outside of the scope of judicial control can be expected to expand. This risk has materialized on several occasions when the limited standard of review has been applied to technically complex assessments and the calculation of fines.

A welcome starting point to solving this problem was provided by Nicholas Forwood, judge at the EGC, who proposed a distinction between

---

[30] Joined Cases C-89/85, C-104/85, C-114/85, C-116/85, C-117/85 and C-125/85 to C-129/85, *Ahlström Osakeyhtiö and Others v Commission* (*Wood Pulp II*) [1993] ECR I-1037.

[31] Case T-342/99, *Airtours*; Case T-310/01, *Schneider Electric*; as well as Case C-413/06, *Impala*; and Case C-12/03, *Tetra Laval*.

'difficult' economic subject-matters and 'complex' economic subject-matters.[32] Forwood warns that the level of complexity of a case or line of argumentation (economical or technical) should not be confused with the existence of a complex economic assessment. Only the latter should be subject to a limited standard of review.[33]

'Difficult' according to Forwood are those subject-matters that require the application of economic theories; which sometimes includes a comprehensive examination of economic arguments or an extensive investigation of the evidence. The mere fact that such an appraisal could prove challenging for the courts does not render the appraisal 'complex'.[34]

Issues should only be regarded as 'complex' if the application of the relevant economic theories does not yield a single correct answer, but rather several answers appear to be economically justifiable. Only for 'complex' issues in this sense should the Commission be granted a margin of appreciation and the judicial review be conducted in accordance with a limited standard of review.

The practical application of this approach would result in the courts not immediately assigning a situation that at first blush presents itself to the practitioner as economically challenging, to a limited standard of review. Rather, as a first step, the courts should obtain independent economic expert advice, even if this would make the handling of the case more difficult for the court. Only when, following such expert advice, the case qualifies as 'complex', that is economic expertise cannot provide an unequivocal answer, should the Commission be granted a margin of appreciation.

This approach would be most welcome from a practitioner's point of view, since it would provide a method for preventing growth of the control vacuum in competition law. Further, the distinction between 'complex' and 'difficult' appraisals achieves this goal without compromising the existing doctrine and terminology of the courts. This is because the Commission retains its margin of appreciation in 'complex' economic appraisals – so that this approach would not be in conflict with previous decisions of the courts. Rather, the approach would assist in delineating the boundaries of the Commission's margin of appreciation as precisely as possible. According to *Forwood*, this distinction is to a certain extent also reflected in the existing decisional practice – albeit not by reference to the terms 'complex' and 'difficult'. At least during its first decades, the ECJ used the term

---

[32] Forwood, *supra*.

[33] Forwood, *supra*, p. 13.

[34] Forwood, *supra*, p. 10.

'complexity' when referring to the nature of the assessment to be conducted and not in connection with evidential or technical difficulties.[35]

In this context, it can be observed that the underlying rationale for Forwood's distinction between 'complex' and 'difficult' assessments is far from being novel. It can be found in the differentiation between, on the one hand, the margin of appreciation a legal provision confers upon an authority and, on the other hand, the standard of proof in establishing the facts that an authority is subject to independently of the margin of appreciation conferred by the legal provision. This distinction can readily be found in the practice of the European courts.[36] *Josef Azizi*, another EGC judge, has noted in relation to state aid procedures that, in assessing complex economic situations, two different factors should be distinguished: first, the selection of the economic theory that underpins the assessment, and second, the evidential process.[37] *Azizi* points out that this distinction is expressed in the judgments of the EGC and the ECJ. He also stresses that, in the assessment of complex issues, compliance with the procedural framework is crucial.[38] It could be concluded from this that the European courts are sufficiently aware of the problem and that the distinction proposed by Forwood would not provide any additional value.

This is, however, not the case. On the one hand, it should be noted that *Azizi*'s comments concern state aid legislation. This field is characterized by the balancing of the Commission's margin of appreciation concerning economic questions with the political independence of member states in economic assessments.[39] Therefore, there is a greater awareness in state aid matters of a politico-economic sphere that is not to be confused with questions of evidential argumentation. In competition proceedings, this awareness does not appear to be equally well developed; as evidenced by the EGC's recent expansion of the use of a margin of appreciation to the field of technically complex assessments in the *Microsoft* case. Hence, initiatives such as *Forwood's* proposal, that can serve as a guideline to the courts when delineating the boundaries of the limited review standard in competition proceedings, remain very relevant.

---

[35] Forwood, *supra*, p. 13.

[36] However, the dogmatic classification and meaning of the terms '*Ermessen*' (discretion) and '*Beurteilungsspielraum*' (margin of appreciation) appear to remain outstanding – in contrast to the position under German administrative law.

[37] Azizi, J., 'The Tension between Member States' autonomy and Commission control in State aid matters: Selected aspects', in H. Kanninen, N. Korjus, and A. Rosas (eds), *EU Competition Law in Context: Essays in Honour of Virpi Tiili*, Oxford, Hart Publishing, 2009, p. 307 *et seq*.

[38] Azizi, *supra*, p. 311.

[39] Cf. Azizi, *supra*, pp. 313 and 320.

In addition, the distinction between 'complex' and 'difficult' assessments could provide guidance not only to judges, but also to the companies concerned. In particular, this approach would lead to more legal certainty since companies, assisted by their legal counsel, may well be in a position to ascertain if it is only the evidence that is difficult, or if their case does indeed involve an economically 'complex' problem. Although the distinction between 'complex' and 'difficult' situations may not be a panacea, it nevertheless represents a workable approach to address the above concerns raised by recent decisional practice.

Index